FrontPage® 2003 All-in-One Desk Reference For Dummies®

Cheat Sheet

General FrontPage Shortcut Keys

To Do This	Press
Display the Folder List	Alt+F1
Refresh the view	F5
Preview a Web site using Internet Explorer 6	F12
Select everything on the current page	Ctrl+A
Copy data from the screen	Ctrl+C
Find text on the current page	Ctrl+F
Go to a particular place on the page	Ctrl+G
Replace text on the current page	Ctrl+H
Check out a document for editing	Ctrl+J
Check in a document from editing	Ctrl+Shift+J
Insert a hyperlink	Ctrl+K
Open a file	Ctrl+O
Print a file	Ctrl+P
Display the Quick Tag Editor	Ctrl+Q
Save a file	Ctrl+S
Paste data to the screen	Ctrl+V
Cut data from the screen	Ctrl+X
Redo an action	Ctrl+Y
Undo an action	Ctrl+Z
Display the Task Pane	Ctrl+F1

Working with Code View

To Do This	Press
Increase the code indent	Tab
Decrease the code indent	Shift+Tab
Insert a comment	Ctrl+/
Toggle a bookmark	Ctrl+F2
Go to the next bookmark	F2
Go to the previous bookmark	Shift+F2

Useful VBA Shortcut Keys

To Do This	Press
Open the VBA editor	Alt+F11
Display a list of macros	Alt+F8
Perform an emergency stop of a running program	Ctrl+Break
Display the Immediate window	Ctrl+G
List the quick information for the selected element	Ctrl+I
List the properties and methods for an object	Ctrl+J
Display the Project Explorer	Ctrl+R
List the parameter information for the selected element	Ctrl+Shift+I
List the constants associated with an enumeration	Ctrl+Shift+J
Move to the next Code or UserForm window	Ctrl+Tab
Get help on any selected item	F1
Display the Object Browser window	F2
Display the Properties window	F4
Start the program	F5
Display the Code window after selecting a form or control	F7
Add a breakpoint	F9
Display the form that corresponds to the active Code window	Shift+F7
Add a quick watch for the highlighted text	Shift+F9

For Dummies: Bestselling Book Series for Beginners

FrontPage® 2003 All-in-One Desk Reference For Dummies®

Cheat Sheet

Activities You Can Perform from the Task Pane

To Do This	Select
View the scripts associated with a particular Web-page element	Behaviors
Format the information within a layout	Cell Formatting
Add media to your Web page, organize media for use with your Web site, search through media for ideas on constructing a new Web site	Clip Art
See the information currently found on the Clipboard, paste information from the Clipboard onto the current document	Clipboard
View and use data sources available to SharePoint team members	Data Source Catalog
Obtain information about the details of a particular SharePoint data source	Data View Details
Locate a SharePoint data source based on a particular need	Find a Data Source
Open a Web site, reopen a previously opened Web site, open a Web page, reopen a previously opened Web page, copy or create a new Web page or Web site	Getting Started
Get help on FrontPage features, discover VBA features, contact Microsoft, or discover what's new in FrontPage	Help
Organize the content of a Web page using layers	Layers
Organize an existing Web page using tables	Layout Tables and Cells
Create a new blank Web page, use a Web page or template to create a new Web page, create a new blank Web site, define a Web site based on a Web package or SharePoint team Site, view or use the most recently selected templates	New
Locate any information about either FrontPage or VBA	Search
Change the aesthetic appeal of a Web site and unify the design of the Web pages it contains	Theme

Copyright © 2005 Wiley Publishing, Inc. All rights reserved.

Item 7531-7.

For more information about Wiley Publishing, call 1-800-762-2974.

For Dummies: Bestselling Book Series for Beginners

FrontPage® 2003
ALL-IN-ONE DESK REFERENCE
FOR
DUMMIES®

FrontPage® 2003
ALL-IN-ONE DESK REFERENCE

FOR

DUMMIES®

by John Paul Mueller

WILEY
Wiley Publishing, Inc.

FrontPage® 2003 All-in-One Desk Reference For Dummies®

Published by
Wiley Publishing, Inc.
111 River Street
Hoboken, NJ 07030-5774
www.wiley.com

About the Author

John Paul Mueller is a freelance author and technical editor. He has writing in his blood, having produced 64 books and over 300 articles to date. The topics range from networking to artificial intelligence and from database management to heads down programming. Some of his current books include several C# developer guides, an accessible programming guide, a book on .NET security, and books on both Amazon Web Services and Google Web Services. His technical editing skills have helped over 35 authors refine the content of their manuscripts. John has provided technical editing services to both *Data Based Advisor* and *Coast Compute* magazines. He's also contributed articles to magazines including *InformIT*, *SQL Server Professional*, *Visual C++ Developer*, *Hard Core Visual Basic*, *asp.netPRO*, and *Visual Basic Developer*. He's currently the editor of the .NET electronic newsletter for Pinnacle Publishing (`http://www.freeenewsletters.com/`).

When John isn't working at the computer, you can find him in his workshop. He's an avid woodworker and candlemaker. On any given afternoon you can find him working at a lathe or putting the finishing touches on a bookcase. One of his newest craft projects is glycerin soapmaking, which comes in pretty handy for gift baskets. You can reach John on the Internet at `JMueller@mwt.net`. John is also setting up a Web site at: `http://www.mwt.net/~jmueller/`, feel free to take a look and make suggestions on how he can improve it. One of his current projects is creating book FAQ sheets that should help you find the book information you need much faster.

Dedication

This book is dedicated to Jif, the latest addition to our family and a new guardian of the apples.

Acknowledgments

Thanks to my wife, Rebecca, for working with me to get this book completed. I really don't know what I would have done without her help in researching and compiling some of the information that appears in this book. She also did a fine job of proofreading my rough draft and page-proofing the final result.

David Clark deserves thanks for his technical edit of this book. He greatly added to the accuracy and depth of the material you see here. I really appreciated the time he devoted to working with the various FrontPage elements, especially the accessibility issues. David also provided a number of insights as I discussed the book with him over e-mail during the writing process.

Eva Beattie contributed significantly to the book by reading and commenting on every chapter. She helped me develop a better understanding of the uses for FrontPage, and provided input on how best to approach specific problems. Bill Salkin also provided invaluable assistance with some of the chapters. He helped me understand some of the business and training goals better from an Information Technology (IT) perspective. I would also like to thank the other people who read specific sections of the book and provided their expertise in just those areas. Several people commented on areas such as accessibility and the usefulness of specific techniques in the office environment.

Matt Wagner, my agent, deserves credit for helping me get the contract in the first place, and taking care of all the details that most authors don't really consider. I always appreciate his help. It's good to know that someone wants to help.

Finally, I would like to thank Terri Varveris, Christopher Morris, Barry Childs-Helton, and the rest of the production staff at Wiley for their assistance in bringing this book to print. It's always nice to work with such a great group of professionals.

Publisher's Acknowledgments

We're proud of this book; please send us your comments through our online registration form located at www.dummies.com/register/.

Some of the people who helped bring this book to market include the following:

Acquisitions, Editorial, and Media Development

Project Editor: Christopher Morris

Acquisitions Editor: Terri Varveris

Senior Copy Editor: Barry Childs-Helton

Technical Editor: David Clark

Editorial Manager: Kevin Kirschner

Permissions Editor: Laura Moss

Media Development Supervisor: Richard Graves

Editorial Assistant: Amanda Foxworth

Cartoons: Rich Tennant, www.the5thwave.com

Production

Project Coordinator: Courtney MacIntyre

Layout and Graphics: Andrea Dahl, Lauren Goddard, Denny Hager, Joyce Haughey, Stephanie D. Jumper, Michael Kruzil, Lynsey Osborn, Jacque Roth, Julie Trippetti

Proofreaders: Laura Albert, John Greenough, Betty Kish, Brian H. Walls

Indexer: Richard T. Evans

Publishing and Editorial for Technology Dummies

    Richard Swadley, Vice President and Executive Group Publisher

    Andy Cummings, Vice President and Publisher

    Mary Bednarek, Executive Acquisitions Director

    Mary C. Corder, Editorial Director

Publishing for Consumer Dummies

    Diane Graves Steele, Vice President and Publisher

    Joyce Pepple, Acquisitions Director

Composition Services

    Gerry Fahey, Vice President of Production Services

    Debbie Stailey, Director of Composition Services

Contents at a Glance

Table of Contents

Introduction

*F*rontPage 2003 All-in-One Desk Reference For Dummies is your gateway to everything FrontPage. Through this book, you discover everything that FrontPage can do. From basic HTM pages to complex pages with Cascading Style Sheets (CSS), this book covers it all. The latest version of FrontPage includes better database connectivity, access to a lot of great new themes, and better ways to organize your information on-screen. In fact, this book even helps you discover methods you can use to create your own themes and organizational aids, so you don't have to do things the Microsoft way.

FrontPage is an exciting way to create great-looking Web sites. However, it's even better than you might think. It would be easy to say that FrontPage creates and manages Web pages, but it does so much more. Sure, I'll show you around the FrontPage way of doing things, but then I get into scripting and working with VBA as a way to improve productivity. You'll see that FrontPage works with PHP (an open-source, server-side scripting language), and you can even use it to work directly with Web services. As I said — and this book shows why — FrontPage is really the tool of choice for many Web sites!

Because Web sites are very serious undertakings, this book won't just tell you about all the great features that FrontPage provides. You'll also discover new techniques that make your work more efficient, help you create secure Web sites, and ensure that everyone who visits can appreciate your efforts. Accessibility issues are always important — and you'll see them discussed in some detail throughout the book.

FrontPage 2003 All-in-One Desk Reference For Dummies is a reference book. You don't have to read it in any particular order, and you can skip anything that you don't find interesting. Readers who really don't want to use VBA to enhance FrontPage don't have to read that section — skip to another section that shows (for example) the new security techniques that FrontPage helps you implement.

Conventions Used in This Book

I always try to show you the fastest way to accomplish any task. In many cases, this means using a menu command such as Tools➪Macro➪Visual Basic Editor.

I'm assuming you've worked with Windows long enough to know how the keyboard and mouse work. You should also know how to use menus and other basic Windows features.

Whenever possible, I use shortcut keys to help you access a command faster. For example, you can open a new file by pressing Ctrl+O.

This book also uses special type to emphasize some information. You'll always see entries you need to type in **bold**. All code, Web site URLs, folder names, and on-screen messages appear in `monofont` type. Whenever I define a new word, you'll see that word in *italics*.

When a chapter begins, I assume you're in FrontPage working with your example Web site (unless I've specified otherwise). All the commands in that chapter are for FrontPage until I specifically move the discussion to another application. I also specifically tell you when it's time to move back to FrontPage.

What You Should Read

As with many reference books, it's easy to get a bit overwhelmed if you don't already know much about FrontPage. Anyone who hasn't used FrontPage before or worked with a Web site should read the first three books in this volume to get a handle on what FrontPage provides. After you complete the first three books, feel free to move on to other interesting topics.

Intermediate readers can probably browse Book I or perhaps skip it completely and refer to it as needed. Book II also presents basic principles, but you'll want to at least scan it so you can see any unique features that FrontPage provides that you didn't know about. However, by Book III, you should find a lot of useful FrontPage-specific information that will make your job a lot easier.

Expert readers will likely want to check some of the unique topics in the book first. For example, some people are under the impression that FrontPage doesn't provide much in the way of XML support. They might be surprised at how much you can do with XML in FrontPage. Of course, for truly unique topics, take a look at Book IX: For example, discovering that you can build pages using ASP or PHP with equal ease in FrontPage is a great way to begin extending this product to do more than ever before.

What You Don't Have to Read

Most of the chapters contain some advanced material that interests only some readers. If you happen to see a specialized topic (say, writing information to the Windows Registry) that doesn't connect to your situation, feel free to skip it. The specialized topics usually reside in sidebars that are easy to spot.

You can also skip any material marked with a Technical Stuff icon. This material is helpful, but you don't have to know it to use FrontPage. I include this material because I find it helpful in my development efforts and hope you will too.

Don't assume that you have to read any of the more complex topics to use FrontPage efficiently. I know many people who have never written a line of VBA code, never added scripting to their Web pages, or never delved into the mysterious world of FrontPage extensions — and they have perfectly usable Web sites. In fact, simple is often better because you save time and effort in maintenance and there are fewer compatibility issues to confront. The idea here is straightforward: Do what works.

Foolish Assumptions

You might find it difficult to believe that I have assumed anything about you — after all, I haven't even met you yet! — but I have made a few assumptions. Although most assumptions are indeed foolish, these assumptions provide a starting point for the book.

I'm assuming you've worked with Windows long enough to know how the keyboard and mouse work. You should also know how to use menus and other basic Windows features. Some portions of the book work with Web pages, Visual Studio .NET, and XML; you need to know at least a little about these technologies to use those sections. You don't have to be an expert in any of these areas, but more knowledge is better.

You don't need to know anything about FrontPage to use this book. I purposely include sections that describe FrontPage in detail so you can use this book at any skill level.

How This Book Is Organized

This is a book of books. In fact, there are nine books in this single book. Each book contains chapters related to that book's topic, just as you would find in a separate book anywhere. The book topics run from basic to advanced; each one's title cues you as to whether or not you need to read that book. (For example, an advanced FrontPage developer probably won't spend much time in Book II because it describes how to create basic pages.) Of course, a little review for the old hands — or a look ahead for the newcomers — can't hurt. Feel free to explore.

This book also contains a wealth of source code. You can find the source code for this book on this book's companion Web site at

www.dummies.com/go/frontpage2003

Book 1: Essential Concepts

This book helps you understand FrontPage from a usage perspective. Spend time here when you want to kick the tires so to speak and see what FrontPage can do. By the time you complete the three chapters in this book, you'll have had experience with many of the menu commands and features of FrontPage. In fact, you'll have created your first Web page.

Book II: Basic Pages

Many developers become overwhelmed in the course of building a Web site because they haven't been exposed to all the possible ways to create Web pages. This book shows a multitude of page types. You probably won't use them all — and won't need more than one technique for most Web sites. However, it's always a good idea to have a wealth of tools at your disposal; you never know when one of those tools will help you create just the right presentation on a particular Web page. This book is all about design options.

Book III: Webs

Check this book for management techniques. FrontPage helps you save time by helping you manage your Web site efficiently. You have more than one view of each Web site you can use to see it from different angles. Various reports help you recognize and diagnose problems before anyone else even sees them. The goal is to provide you with the tools you need to keep all the pages on your Web site updated and usable — without tearing your hair out in frustration over checking every page individually.

Book IV: Advanced Design

Many Web sites today are extremely flexible and dynamic. The information changes as new information becomes available. Technologies such as Cascading Style Sheets (CSS) help users have things their way. Sure, the information is the same, but the use of a different CSS page can make a big difference in how the user sees it. CSS is an essential accessibility aid. Advanced design means adding Office objects directly into the Web pages — and choosing Smart Tags that help users work with data in more than one way. In addition, every book on advanced design should include security — always a hot topic, and even hotter today. By the time you complete this book, you know how to create some terrific-looking, secure Web sites with plenty of pizzazz.

Book V: Databases

FrontPage provides good database support. You can access most database types using a number of technologies — including Open Database Connectivity (ODBC). This book shows how to work with three kinds of databases: Excel, Access, and SQL Server. The principles you discover here help you work with any database you encounter as you build your Web site.

Creating a connection isn't the end of working with databases — it's only the beginning. The various chapters also describe presentation. The examples demonstrate various kinds of presentation, including the use of pivot tables to combine and analyze data in new ways.

Book VI: XML and XSLT

The eXtensible Markup Language (XML) is a great technology because it lets people store information as text without losing the formatting and content associated with the information. In fact, many people view XML as the best way for businesses to exchange information and to present certain kinds of information (such as magazine articles) on Web sites.

XML isn't all that readable, however — so that's where eXtensible Style Language Transformation (XSLT) comes into play. This technology takes the XML you provide and transforms it into a legible Web page. In fact, you can use a number of XSLT files to create different views of the same data. Although this book isn't a complete XML or XSLT reference, it does demonstrate how you can use both technologies effectively in FrontPage.

Book VII: Scripting

Scripting lets you work with user input and perform other tasks on a Web page. For example, many of the special effects you see on Web sites — such as data fields that change when you hover the mouse pointer over them — rely on scripting. This book demonstrates how you can use scripting in FrontPage to create special effects, work with user data, save and restore user settings, and modify the Web-page interface to meet specific user needs.

Book VIII: VBA Programming

Visual Basic for Applications (VBA) isn't specific to FrontPage. In fact, many applications use this language to provide scripting support. Because this book is all about enhancing FrontPage so it can do more for you, faster, and with less effort on your part, VBA can play a part in that enhancement. You don't use VBA on a Web page but rather within FrontPage to put the fun back into Web-page development.

Book IX: Advanced Programming

This book is truly for the advanced reader. It discusses four topics of special interest. The first is using FrontPage to work with Active Server Pages (ASP). The client-side scripting described in Book VII goes only so far in meeting user and business needs. Sometimes you need server-side scripting to provide better database support and a higher level of security — or simply to ensure that your users have full access to your Web site, even when client-side scripting isn't an option.

For those who have to work with platforms other than Microsoft Windows, it's possible to create PHP Hypertext Processor (PHP) scripts with FrontPage. Like ASP, PHP is a server-side scripting solution; unlike ASP, it works on a lot of platforms — and won't cost you a cent to install. FrontPage provides only minimal support for PHP, so this server-side scripting technique isn't for everyone.

The big news of the day is Web services even though some people feel the promise of Web services hasn't yet been met. This book demonstrates how to work with two public Web services that already exist — Amazon Web Services and Google Web Services — and tells you where to find others. The promise of Web services is still emerging; it's one of the best-kept secrets in computing today.

The final chapter in this book answers the question of what to do when VBA can't meet a specific FrontPage-extension need. This chapter demonstrates a technique for using Visual Studio .NET to build extensions to the FrontPage environment. By using this technique, you can move well beyond simple additions to FrontPage — you can create an entirely new interface.

On the accompanying Web site

This book contains a lot of code and you might not want to type it. Fortunately, you can find the source code for this book on the Dummies.com site at `www.dummies.com/go/frontpage2003`. The source code is organized by book and chapter; I always tell you about the example files in the text. The best way to work with a chapter is to download all the source code for it at once and work with it through the chapter.

Icons Used in This Book

Tips are nice because they help you save time or perform some task without a lot of extra work. The tips in this book are timesaving techniques or pointers to resources that can help you get maximum benefit from FrontPage.

I don't want to sound like an angry parent or some kind of maniac, but you should avoid doing anything marked with a Warning icon. Otherwise, you could find that your program melts down and takes your data with it.

Whenever you see this icon, think *advanced tip or technique*. You might find these tidbits of useful information just too boring for words — or they could contain the solution you need to get a Web site up and running. Skip these bits of information whenever you like. They'll be there if you need them later.

If you don't get anything else out of a particular chapter or section, remember the material marked by this icon. This material usually contains an essential process or bit of material that you must know to create great Web sites or use FrontPage efficiently.

Where to Go from Here

It's time to start your FrontPage adventure! I recommend that anyone who has only a passing knowledge of FrontPage go right to Book I, Chapter 1. This chapter contains essential, get-started information that you need to use FrontPage.

Anyone who already knows FrontPage might want to skip to one of the chapters in Book III. The examples are more complex than those in the previous books, and you'll still get to see some more of what FrontPage can do before you get into the detailed examples in the books that follow.

Book I

Essential Concepts

The 5th Wave   By Rich Tennant

J & R HYPNOSIS CLINIC
Overcome Technophobia
Contact our Web site
WWW.JRHYPNO.COM

"You know, it dawned on me last night why we aren't getting any hits on our Web site."

Contents at a Glance

Chapter 1: Introducing FrontPage 2003

You can develop Web sites using nothing more than a plain text editor. For many years, that's all some people used. The reason that FrontPage and other products like it are so popular is that they save time and effort. FrontPage 2003 saves time by providing hints about the special information used to create a Web page. It also helps you organize your Web pages so they make sense and even provides reports on Web page usage. In fact, I'll go so far as to say that FrontPage makes creating Web pages fun.

Before you can create the next great Web site, however, it's important to discover just what FrontPage can do. Some people think that creating a Web page is hard because of all the special tags and formatting required. FrontPage removes the need to remember all these special tags. You still have to know what task the tag performs, but FrontPage helps you get past weird tags and into the information you want to present. Consequently, FrontPage is a tool that reduces work and lets you become more creative.

Understanding FrontPage

FrontPage is a part of Microsoft Office, even though it's sold separately. As shown in Figure 1-1, FrontPage shares the look and functionality of other Office 2003 products. In addition, FrontPage also supports many of the new features that you'll find in other Office 2003 products such as the ability to work directly with XML files. You can also write special extensions for FrontPage using products such as Visual Studio .NET. All the new interface features are also present, such as the new help system that makes it easier to find precisely what you want. It's not important to understand all the features that FrontPage provides right now; this section simply provides a quick overview of what FrontPage can do.

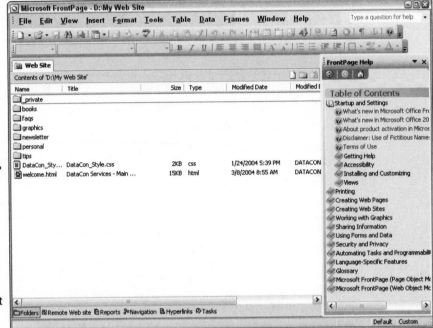

Figure 1-1:
Rely on
the new
FrontPage
2003
features
to make
Web page
development
easier.

Even with all these new additions, FrontPage is still a design tool for Web pages. Yes, you can use it to write content, much as you would use a word processor. However, the goal is to organize the content so you can present it to other people in a way that makes communication easy. FrontPage isn't just about presenting information; it's about making that information easy to understand.

You'll also use FrontPage to manage your Web site. Management means everything from moving content from your local system to a Web server to ensuring the graphic images you create are updated properly. FrontPage makes it easy to see how your Web site is arranged and how each page plays a role in communicating the information you want to provide. For example, the Navigational view shown in Figure 1-2 shows how your pages are arranged. In this case, the home page (the one with the house icon) appears at the top. A folder named Newsletter (shown with a navigational bar icon) holds a single Web page. To get to this Web page, the user would click a link on the home page.

FrontPage includes a number of other management views. These views are often linked to still other views so you can drill down into your Web site and see precisely how the various pages interact. For example, when you click an entry in the Navigational view, you can click the Hyperlink view and see all the links on that page. Figure 1-3 shows the list of hyperlinks for the home page in Figure 1-2. Clicking any of these hyperlinks shows you that page.

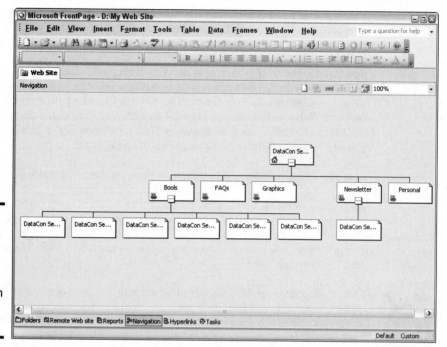

Figure 1-2:
Use
FrontPage
views to
see the
organization
of your
Web site.

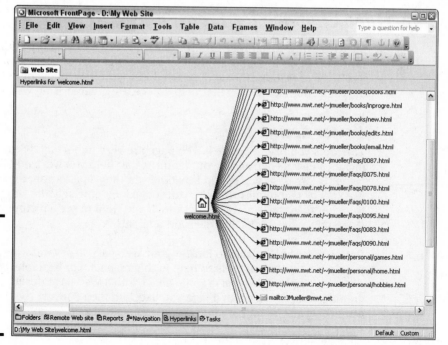

Figure 1-3:
Use
interrelated
views to
see your
Web site
in depth.

When you get past the communication and management needs for a Web site, you must consider the maintenance requirements. A Web site ages — sometimes the owner doesn't realize that a feature that worked yesterday no longer works today. For example, your favorite Web site might move. If you have a link to this Web site on your Web page, that link won't work anymore and the Web site's users will complain. FrontPage includes tools that help you maintain your Web site. You can ask FrontPage to check all the links on your Web site to ensure they still work. FrontPage can also perform other maintenance tasks, such as ensuring that your Web site meets accessibility requirements and optimizing pages so they load fast.

Sometimes FrontPage can't perform a task for you automatically. In that case, you can add the task to a list of tasks that FrontPage manages for you. As you accomplish tasks, they come off the list. If you keep your Web-site tasks separate from other task lists you maintain, it's easier to stay focused on your Web site when you maintain it. Fortunately, even when you do need to perform a task manually, you can create a macro to make the task easier and faster to perform.

FrontPage may appear complex. If you break the product features into small pieces, however, you find that you can create a Web site right away, updating it later as you discover more FrontPage features. It's important to concentrate on the main goal for using FrontPage— communicating with other people.

Important Changes for FrontPage 2003

Microsoft tries to improve FrontPage with every new version. FrontPage 2003 is no exception to that rule; some of the changes are so significant that it's worth a closer look at what they can do for you. The following sections focus on a selection of features that help you create great-looking Web sites fast.

Better design tools

The tools you use to create a Web page are very important. FrontPage 2003 includes new design and layout features that help you work quickly. The new layout is larger, so you spend less time scrolling. In addition, the layout tools use special techniques to make your page look precisely the way you want it to rather than the way HTML dictates. If you want to see a picture on the right side of the page, that's where FrontPage puts it.

Design means being able to look at your Web page in several ways. FrontPage provides a number of tools to help in this respect. For example, you can use *image tracing* to convert a graphic image into a Web-page design. You use a graphics tool to create an image you like, and then convert that image into something a browser can understand. You can also *layer* your Web page's elements so you can peel them back later and concentrate on just the elements you're working with at the moment.

FrontPage also gives you plenty of layout help in the form of *themes* — structures you can use when you lay out the information you want to present. Using themes, you can easily create a series of Web pages that all have the same look, which adds continuity to your Web site. The user ends up looking at the content rather than at some extra or misplaced element on the page.

Sometimes an important change appears in a small package. The new FrontPage editor is an example, and it's much smarter than the one in previous versions. It includes new features such as Smart Search and Replace. Imagine for a moment that you've made the same mistake on just about every page on your Web site. Instead of replacing the text by hand, you can make the change once and let the smart-search-and-replace feature make the change in every other location.

The editor has other types of improvements too. For example, you can get FrontPage to intelligently edit any kind of text file. (*Intelligent editing* means that FrontPage highlights keywords and provides other forms of help such as IntelliSense — a technology that interprets what you type and suggests what to type next.) For example, you can load an XML or script file and edit it without using another editor. The IntelliSense feature even helps you make changes to many text files so you don't have to remember arcane coding syntax.

The same editor can optimize your HTML, so it loads faster and presents fewer compatibility problems. FrontPage can do some optimization automatically — for example, it can remove unnecessary white space, empty tags, and even empty styles from the page. In some cases, you can also use FrontPage to remove or change other features. The basic requirement is that you must define the feature as a specific kind of HTML tag.

Improved user support

Nothing's worse than going to a Web site and finding that the designer had a huge monitor with great resolution. The only problem — you don't have the designer's setup, so you can't see the site very well. FrontPage helps you get around this problem by showing you (as designer) what the user's browser sees, at multiple resolutions. The result is that you can detect potential problems with your Web page design before the user has to deal with them.

FrontPage also provides accessibility support, including support for the U.S. government's Section 508 requirements. Accessibility support makes it possible for anyone with special needs to access your site. For example, someone who has vision problems can rely on nonvisual aids to interpret and understand your site. By making your site accessible, you open the door to sharing information with a much broader range of users.

Updated graphics

One of the more interesting additions to FrontPage is the capability to use Macromedia Flash. This means your Web page can include movies, animations, and other glittering effects. FrontPage helps you create a pleasing Macromedia Flash presentation by making it easy to change features such as the repeat rate for graphics or how long an animation will *loop* (replay itself).

FrontPage has improved graphics handling overall. For example, you can now define which editor to use for a particular kind of graphic. (The integration between FrontPage and the selected editor is better, although not necessarily seamless.) FrontPage also helps you understand how it works with a particular graphic file type when you import it into the environment. This support helps you make better decisions on how images are presented and saved.

Enhanced coding support

Not every Web page requires code. In fact, it's better to *avoid* using code unless you actually need it; code usually adds to the complexity of the Web page and can reduce compatibility. However, when you do need to use code, FrontPage makes it a lot easier to create good code that runs with a range of browsers. In fact, many new coding features come in the form of "canned" code that Microsoft has created for you. For example, you can use the new server Behaviors feature to improve the interactivity of your site. A *behavior* can make the Web page perform a task, such as changing a specified graphic when the user passes a mouse pointer over it. The coding support also includes code snippets and smart buttons that you don't have to program.

Some coding support comes in the form of editor aids. For example, FrontPage now includes IntelliSense support. IntelliSense watches what you type, guesses what you'll type next, and provides help with that particular input. In many cases, you can ask IntelliSense to complete the input for you so you don't have to type the entire line. The result is that you get the text typed faster and more accurately. You'll also find a number of other helpful features such as line numbers, preset indentation, and automatic tag completion.

Front Page actually supports several levels of coding. Don't worry too much about committing these levels to memory or being able to rattle off precisely what they do. The first level is the code you can add to a Web page to make it work better. A script can help users make decisions on what kind of information to send back to you or can make the page friendlier. The second level is special code you can use to make Web-page content change automatically. The Web page could be connected to your database or another source of information. The code would change the content to reflect new information you add to these sources. The third level of code is macros you can create to make FrontPage easier to use. A *macro* is a small program created by storing the keystrokes you use to perform a task. FrontPage plays the recording to perform the task automatically for you. The fourth level of code encompasses special extensions you create for FrontPage. The extensions could do anything from adding a new feature to FrontPage to making it easier to add special features to your Web site.

Better data handling

It's important to present data quickly and clearly in today's Web environment. Users no longer tolerate old or inflexible data displays. With this in mind, FrontPage makes it easy to present data from a number of sources. For example, you can present data from any data source that conforms to Object Linking and Embedding-DataBase (OLE-DB) requirements, which includes products such as SQL Server and Access. You can also create OLE-DB data sources from products such as Excel, use any type of XML file (including URLs that return XML as output), or use Windows SharePoint Services data.

Another new feature is the Web Part. Imagine setting up a master view that manipulates details on-screen. For example, the user could select a particular geographical region and see all the details change to match that region. The addition of this feature means you can now set up a Web page to behave dynamically according to a specific set of rules — for example, you can add new behaviors that depend on the options a user selects.

Finally, FrontPage 2003 makes it possible to create specific data views. The underlying data is the same; only the presentation changes. You can already perform this task using standards-based technologies such as eXtensible Stylesheet Language Transformations (XSLT), but FrontPage makes it easier to create the required views. The presentation of data is essential — it defines your ability to communicate with the users of your site in a meaningful way.

Easier Web content publication

Previous versions of FrontPage often made it difficult to move the Web pages you created from your hard drive to the Web site. In addition, these earlier versions depended on functionality provided by Internet Information Server (IIS). FrontPage 2003 corrects this problem, at least to an extent. You do get better performance if you use IIS, but now you have the option of using other remote sites.

Remote site support is especially important for people who use hosted sites where you might not have much control over the server. To address this issue, FrontPage supports standard File Transfer Protocol (FTP) and Web-based Distributed Authoring and Versioning (WebDAV) uploads.

Users familiar with WebDAV know it provides *file locking* — groups of people can collaboratively edit content without overwriting each other's work. FrontPage also provides support for Macromedia Dreamweaver LCK (locking) files. This means you can work in a mixed environment with Macromedia Dreamweaver users.

Essential Web-Page Concepts

Before you get started creating Web pages, consider a few essential concepts:

✦ Keeping your Web site focused

✦ Organizing your Web site for maximum efficiency

✦ Keeping the design simple but effective

The following sections provide helpful hints you can use to make your Web site work better from the start.

Maintaining a focus

It's easy to get sidetracked by all the glittering displays and fancy graphics of many Web sites. After you look at enough Web sites, it's even easy to forget the real purpose behind a Web page.

The most important concept about Web pages is that they let you exchange information with other people. In simple terms, a Web page is all about communication — your communication. When a Web page fails to communicate, then it has failed to accomplish the most basic task it can perform.

FrontPage can solve many of the difficult technical issues for you. When you decide that you want to highlight certain words in red (for example), FrontPage provides the tools needed to perform that task. However, FrontPage isn't creative — you're the creative element. It's important to separate creativity — the need to communicate — from the tool that helps you present the information. Some people think FrontPage will solve their communication problems, but it can't. It helps you solve the technical issues, but it's still up to you to present the information. Of course, presenting the information — saying something important — is the easy part of the task for most people.

Using organization effectively

One essential issue to think about is the communication factor behind Web development. When you create a Web page, consider what message that page is presenting — which means organizing the Web page to ensure it works well. FrontPage makes it easy to create a design you can control closely, deciding on the page for each message and then looking at all the messages your Web site presents. That's one reason to use the Navigational view shown in Figure 1-2.

Organization isn't a matter of just keeping your ideas focused. Every Web page you design should have a single focus — one idea you want it to present. Careful organization also makes it easier to create large Web sites that are easy to maintain. FrontPage helps you organize your ideas by using a combination of folders and individual Web pages. It also helps you maintain all the support elements for the Web page (such as graphics and sounds) that you want to use.

Keeping it simple

Many Web sites are so complex that they become hard to use. You can avoid hiding the message you want to present by keeping your design and its operation simple. For example, don't use graphics unless they serve a purpose. Of course, you can decorate your pages by making graphics part of the message. Some Web sites add too many graphics that detract from the message the page is supposed to present (and make it slow to load).

Keep scripts and other gizmos to a minimum — many users have shut off support for them because of the security problems on the Internet. It doesn't pay to have a fancy Web page that no one can view because the message is hidden by the gizmos. The best page is one that everyone can use, no matter which browser they choose.

Chapter 2: Getting Started

In This Chapter

✔ Using the Integrated Development Environment (IDE)

✔ Locating help

✔ Modifying the work environment

✔ Working faster with keyboard shortcuts

*B*efore you can begin creating Web pages, you need to explore the FrontPage interface. The tools that FrontPage provides are easily accessible; you just need to figure out where they are. Sometimes it's interesting just to click something to see what happens, but it's better to see how things work in a logical order. In the first part of this chapter, you explore the FrontPage interface — the Integrated Development Environment (IDE).

The people at Microsoft make assumptions about you when they configure FrontPage during installation. Some of these assumptions are probably correct, but even Microsoft can't guess everything about you. It's important to discover how to change your working environment. The first step is to look through the help provided with FrontPage to see what's possible. You can make some changes immediately. For example, using keyboard shortcuts greatly reduces the time to accomplish a task. You can also customize your toolbars to make them friendlier. After all, this copy of FrontPage is yours, so you need to make it work your way.

Using the IDE

The IDE is the part of FrontPage that you see. Whenever you start FrontPage, you'll see one or more windows that contain information about your Web site and the FrontPage environment. The combination of all these windows is the FrontPage IDE. You probably won't need to use all these windows immediately — you might never need some of them — but you can access the ones you do need by clicking their tabs at the bottom of the IDE. These tabs include

✦ Folders

✦ Remote Web site

✦ Reports

✦ Navigation

✦ Hyperlinks

✦ Tasks

The following sections describe these various windows and tell you what they can do for you.

Working with folders

FrontPage has two folder views that you can use. These folder views have about the same purpose as the two windows you see when you use Windows Explorer. The Folder List, shown in Figure 2-1, acts the same as the left pane in Windows Explorer. You use the Folder List to select a folder you want to view in Folders view (on the right side of the page). The Folder List can also show individual files.

You don't have to keep both of these views visible. To remove the Folder List from view, click the Close box in the upper-right corner of the window. Use the View⇨Folder List command to display the Folder List window again. The Folders view is always accessible using the tabs at the bottom of the window. You can also use the View⇨Folders command to display it.

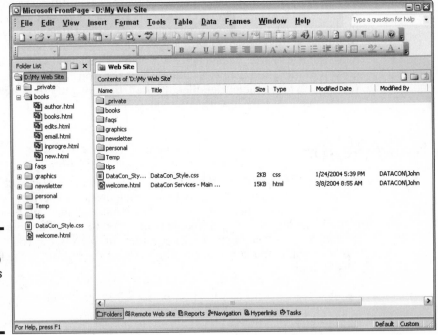

Figure 2-1:
Use the two folder views to make it easier to locate files.

The two folder views let you open documents, create new documents, delete documents you don't need anymore, and rearrange your Web site. FrontPage provides other methods for performing these tasks as well, but this is the method that many people find most comfortable. You can display a list of the actions you can perform in either of the folder views, using one of two methods:

✦ **Right-click any clean area.** FrontPage displays a context menu (similar to the one in Figure 2-2), listing actions you can choose.

✦ **Right-click any object in either folder view.** A context menu appears and shows you what you can do with (or to) the object.

Go ahead; it's a lot of fun!

Figure 2-2:
Right-click various objects to see what you can do.

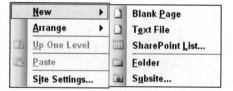

Viewing documents

Seeing your documents listed in one of the folder views is a good start but doesn't allow you to do anything with them. To view a document in FrontPage, double-click its entry in one of the folder views. FrontPage opens the document, using a text view or a special view (depending on the file type and the settings you made to the application). Figure 2-3 shows a typical specialty view for working with HTML pages.

Look at the top of the Web page shown in Figure 2-3. The welcome.html tab is the current document. Whenever you open a document, FrontPage adds a tab for it so you can access it easily. To get back to the folder view you saw earlier, click Web Site.

In some cases, you won't want to take the time to look for a file in one of the folder views — or you might need to open a file that isn't in one of the folders. To open a file without using the folder view, use the File⇨Open command or click the Open button on the Standard toolbar. Select the file you want to open in the Open File dialog box and then click Open. You can also double-click the file in Windows Explorer in most cases. As long as the file is associated with FrontPage, you can open it in Windows Explorer.

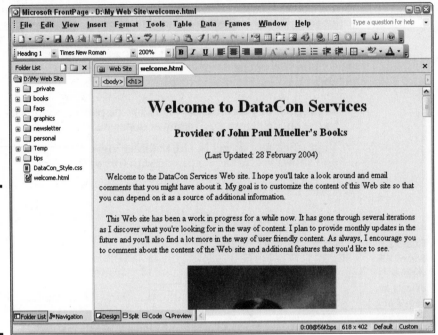

Figure 2-3:
Use special
FrontPage
views like
this one
to edit
documents
whenever
possible.

The best way to determine how FrontPage will react to a specific file type is to check the file type's settings in the Options dialog box. Use the Tools⇨ Options command to open this dialog box. Select the Configure Editors tab to see the list of options shown in Figure 2-4.

Figure 2-4:
Change how
FrontPage
reacts to
documents
using the
Configure
Editors tab.

Figure 2-4 shows that FrontPage can open HTML files using the special viewer shown in Figure 2-3. This setting shown is the default — the one FrontPage uses if you don't make a specific choice. FrontPage can also open the HTML file as text or use an external editor (Notepad, in this case). You can use this dialog box to add new file extensions, new editors, change the order of the editors in the FrontPage list of preferences, or remove options you don't need.

To open a document using one of the FrontPage alternatives, right-click it in one of the folder views. Select the Open With command from the context menu, and you'll see a list of options for opening the file as shown in Figure 2-5. Notice that the first three options match the options that you saw in Figure 2-4. Windows provides the remaining two options as registry settings for those applications.

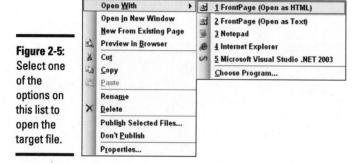

Figure 2-5: Select one of the options on this list to open the target file.

Using the Remote Web Site view

The Remote Web Site view shows how your local copies of a Web site's files compare with the published versions of those files on a private or public Web site. You use this view to move files that you've worked on locally to a remote site. This view also makes it possible to download files that appear on the remote site to your local machine. Figure 2-6 shows a typical example of a Remote Web Site view (don't worry about its details right now).

You can use the Remote Web Site view to transfer and update files. In general, you click specific arrows in the view:

✦ **To move a file from your local machine to the Web site:** Select the file in the Local Web Site pane (normally on the left side of the display) and click the right arrow between the two panes.

✦ **To move a file from the Web site to your local machine:** Click the file in the Remote Web Site pane (usually on the right side of the display) and then click the left arrow.

✦ **To update the oldest file:** Select the newest of the two files and click the double arrow.

✦ **To update the entire site:** Select one of the Publish All Changed Pages options and then click Publish Web Site.

It's also possible to use this view to rename and delete files as well as arrange the files in various ways. For example, you could arrange the files by status so that you can easily see which files you need to update. To perform any of these tasks, right-click in the appropriate window and choose one of the options shown in Figure 2-7. When you want to delete or rename a file, you must right-click that file.

Publish from local site

Publish from remote site

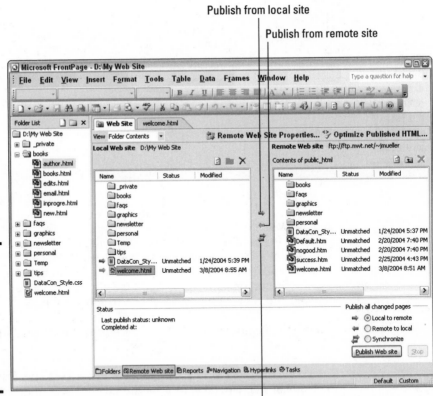

Figure 2-6: Use the Remote Web Site View to synchronize local and remote sites.

Synchronize selected files

Book I
Chapter 2

Getting Started

Figure 2-7:
Rearrange,
delete, or
rename files
as needed
using the
context
menu
options.

Using the Reports view

The Reports view contains information about your Web site in report format.
The first report you see is the Site Summary shown in Figure 2-8. The Site
Summary provides statistics about your Web site, such as the number of
pictures your site contains or how many broken hyperlinks you need to fix
to make the site usable.

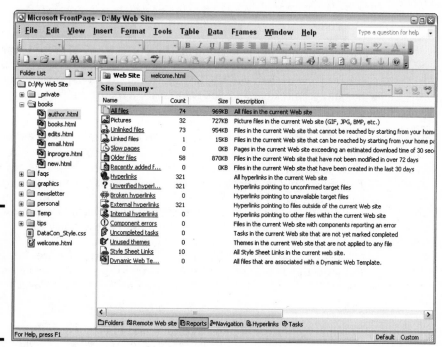

Figure 2-8:
Discover
interesting
facts about
your Web
site using
the Reports
view.

Many entries on the Site Summary have links you can use to see other, more detailed reports. For example, click All Files and you'll see a complete list of all the files on your Web site. The listing includes important information such as the last time you updated the information in the file. This view also contains any comments you made about the file. This view is helpful when you want to locate files that require work.

After you click one of the links on the Site Summary, however, you'll find that there isn't any obvious way to get back to it. To go to one of the other reports — including the Site Summary — click the report title in the upper-left corner of the window. You'll see a list of reports grouped by type, as shown in Figure 2-9.

Figure 2-9:
Select
one of the
reports
using the
title menu.

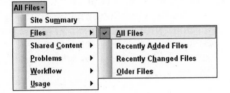

The title menu contains a total of 32 reports. Many of these reports also appear on the Site Summary, but not all of them, so always look through the title menu when you need a report that doesn't appear on the Site Summary. For example, if you want to see a report on theme usage, choose Shared Content➪Themes from the title menu.

Not all reports are useful for every Web site. Some reports, such as those on the Usage menu, require that you use a FrontPage-friendly server application such as Internet Information Server (IIS). This server has special support for FrontPage built into it. Consequently, you can use FrontPage to build a Web site on a hosted server (one over which you have no control), but you can't use FrontPage to obtain usage reports in this environment unless the host is using IIS and allows you to access the FrontPage extensions.

No matter what kind of Web site you use, some reports are very useful. For example, the Slow Pages report helps you locate performance problems on your site. To access this report, choose Problems➪Slow Pages from the title menu.

Another useful report is the Review Status report. It's important to review Web pages periodically to ensure they are updated and display data in the way you expect. The Review Status report helps you keep track of which pages have received reviews lately. You can access the Review Status report by choosing Workflow➪Review Status from the title menu.

Sometimes two FrontPage reports look as if they should deliver similar information, but each report has a different purpose. For example, you might think the Older Files report would tell you which files contain old content. However, this report simply tells you which files haven't changed for a given time. A page that has received a change recently can still contain old content. Even though older content can still be valuable, the Older Files report does help you locate files that might require additional review and support. You can access the Older Files report by selecting Files➪Older Files from the title menu.

Navigating through your site

Creating a picture of your site layout is important because a graphical representation can help you locate problems quickly. For example, a page might contain too many destinations. To help people find what they need, you can consolidate some of those destinations on other pages. The Navigation view is important because it's the first step in understanding the layout of your Web site. To fully appreciate this view, you'll normally want to get rid of some on-screen clutter (such as the Folder List). Figure 2-10 shows a typical example of the Navigation view.

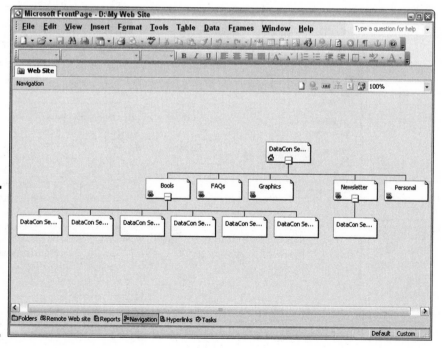

Figure 2-10:
Use a graphic view of your site to see problems such as too many destinations.

You can perform many of the same tasks with the Navigation view that you can with either of the folder views. For example, you can create new documents, delete documents you don't need, and open documents for editing.

Discovering links

The first task every Web site performs is to present information. The second task is to provide links to other sites with related information. The reason the Internet works as well as it does is that many pages have connections to other pages. You can start at one location and end up in an entirely different location on the Internet as you read information. For this reason, it's important to know about the links on your Web site so you can define the message the links present to other people. The links you present add to the message that the content on your Web site provides. Figure 2-11 shows a typical view of Web site links.

To display links for a particular page, locate that page on the Navigation tab shown in Figure 2-10 and click Hyperlinks. The view in Figure 2-11 shows what you'll typically see. The page you selected is on the left side of the display. The linked pages appear to the right, ordered as they appear on the page.

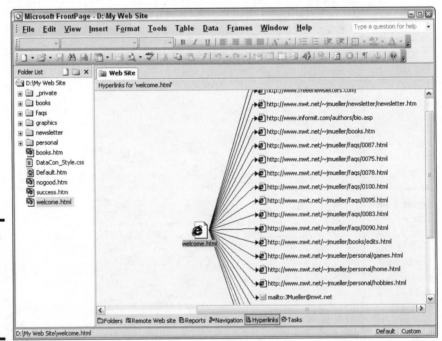

Figure 2-11:
Use links to
add to the
information
your
Web site
presents.

Figure 2-11 shows two kinds of hyperlinks. Every type of hyperlink uses a different icon so you can identify it easily. In this case, most of the hyperlinks are for other Web pages. Near the bottom of the screenshot you see a `mailto` hyperlink that lets someone send e-mail immediately to the person whose address appears in the hyperlink.

Whenever you select a hyperlink, the arrow pointing to that hyperlink changes color. This feature helps you accurately select hyperlinks on a crowded display. The following sections describe other tasks you can perform with this view.

Displaying additional information

The initial display shows limited information. To add to the information you see, right-click any blank area of the window. You see the context menu shown in Figure 2-12. Select the Show Page Titles option when you want to see the page title rather than the filename in the Hyperlinks view. Select Hyperlinks to Pictures to see the picture hyperlinks as well as those used to access other Web sites. Even though the icon is the same for both page and picture hyperlinks because it's the same kind of hyperlink, FrontPage uses a different arrow color for picture hyperlinks. Select the Repeated Hyperlinks option to display hyperlinks that appear more than once on the page — FrontPage normally displays just the first occurrence of a link.

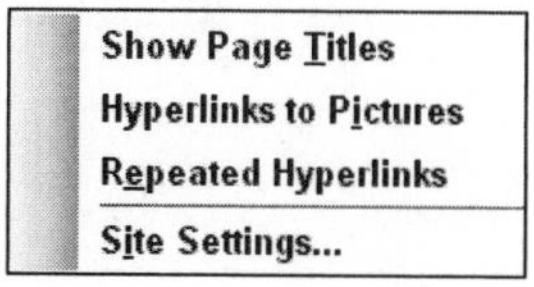

Figure 2-12:
Add information as needed to the Hyperlinks view.

Show Page Titles
Hyperlinks to Pictures
Repeated Hyperlinks
Site Settings...

Selecting a hyperlink view

The normal display shows the page you selected as the center of the hyperlink universe. You change this view by right-clicking one of the links and selecting Move to Center from the context menu. Doing so changes the view (as shown in Figure 2-13).

Now the display shows all pages associated with this link, including the original link. The new page appears on the right side of the display; all the parent links appear on the left side of the display. This technique works best for child pages that appear on more than one page — a typical example of which is a *stylesheet* (a special file that defines the formatting for a Web page). The list shows Web pages that reference the stylesheet. You can select a different parent page from the list by right-clicking and choosing Move to Center from the context menu.

Verifying a hyperlink

Another special task you can perform with this view is to *verify* hyperlinks (that is, check for broken links left because a page moved or doesn't exist anymore). To verify a hyperlink, right-click the hyperlink and choose Verify Hyperlink from the context menu. FrontPage displays an error message if the hyperlink doesn't exist. (No special success message appears for valid hyperlinks — the FrontPage presentation doesn't change in any way.)

Opening documents and hyperlinks

As with most other FrontPage views, you can open documents shown in this view by double-clicking them. Unlike other views, however, you can also open hyperlinks by double-clicking them. The page appears in FrontPage as a standard Web page. You can view the code and see how the page appears on screen. This technique works even on pages you didn't create that are simply linked to your Web page.

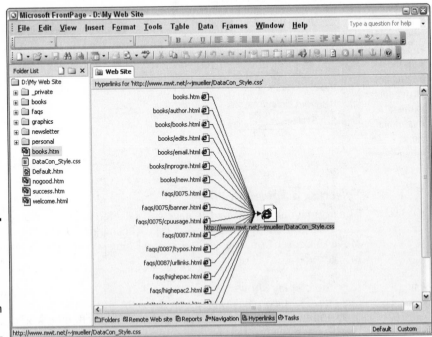

Figure 2-13: Display all of the links for a child page by centering on that page.

As a handy learning aid, you can open pages that you've linked to in order to see how another developer creates special effects or handles user input. Opening the link in FrontPage allows you to see the code with the special highlighting that FrontPage provides. The highlighted text makes it easier to understand the code that someone else wrote.

Setting document properties

The Hyperlinks view offers information not found in the other views. It helps you see a fuller view of a particular page by showing the connections it has to other documents. Describing documents and placing them into a particular workgroup is important. The documentation process tells you how a page fits within the Web site as a whole. To set the properties of a page based on the Hyperlink view, right-click the page and select Properties from the context menu. You see the Properties dialog box shown in Figure 2-14.

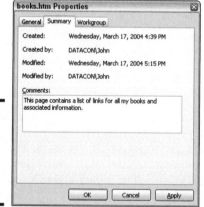

Figure 2-14:
Document a page using the Properties dialog box.

The three tabs in this dialog box let you set the page title, write a summary, and select workgroups. The title is the content of the `<title>` tag that you place in the document. The summary is FrontPage-specific and doesn't appear anywhere within the Web page. You can write notes to yourself about the page and tell why you created it.

The Workgroup tab shown in Figure 2-15 is special. Use this tab to assign a page to a particular workgroup in your organization. Optionally you can assign a specific person to manage the page and define a status for it.

Copying documents

You can quickly start a new page, in some cases, by copying an existing page. The various views help you decide whether an existing page will fulfill a new task. The Hyperlinks view is especially handy because it helps you see the information a page contains in context of the pages it references. You create a copy of a page in this view by right-clicking a page and selecting New from Existing Page on the context menu. FrontPage opens a new document based on the existing document. The new document doesn't become permanent until you save it to your project.

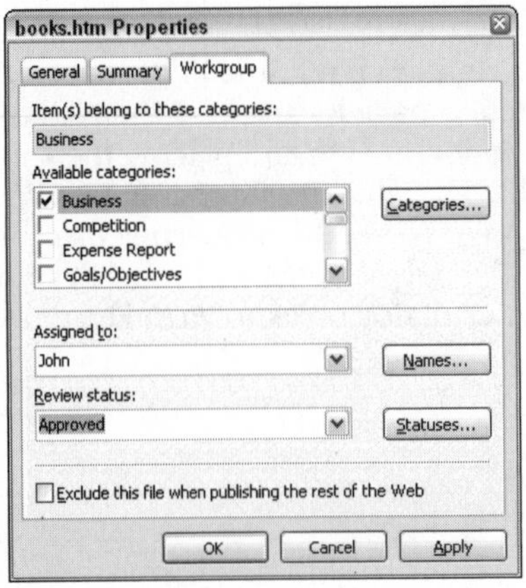

Figure 2-15: Define a status for a page in a workgroup.

Creating a task list

Managing tasks for your Web site is vital — otherwise you might forget to add a change or create new content. A developer is normally very busy; it's worth your while to prioritize tasks to ensure you get the most important tasks completed quickly — and FrontPage can help. It provides a task manager you can use to keep your Web-site-development tasks separate from the other tasks you perform. Figure 2-16 shows a typical Task view.

You can sort the tasks in a number of ways — for example, by status so you know immediately which tasks aren't complete. To sort the tasks, right-click an open area of the window and select one of the Arrange menu options shown in Figure 2-17.

To add a new task, right-click an open area of the window and select Add Task from the context menu. FrontPage displays the New Task dialog box shown in Figure 2-18. Always provide a Task Name field entry; nameless tasks get lost. Make sure the name is descriptive so you can determine what to do quickly. Assign the task a priority (so you can decide which tasks to perform fast); you don't always have to provide a description if you write a complete task name. The Description field should include amplifying information, such as where to find resources to perform the task.

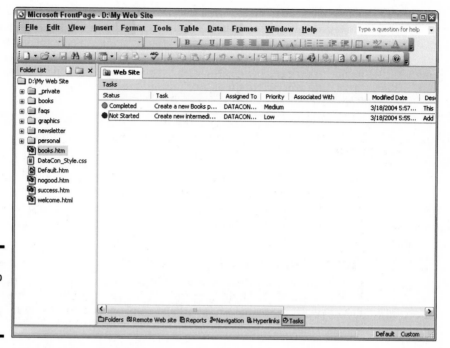

Figure 2-16:
Use tasks to
keep your
Web site
updated.

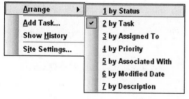

Figure 2-17:
Sort your
task list to
locate items
quickly.

Figure 2-18:
Create
descriptive
tasks so
you quickly
remember
what to do.

Sometimes you need to edit a task to include additional details or change the task name so it's clearer. To edit a task, right-click the task entry and select Edit Task from the context menu. Likewise, when you complete a task, right-click the task entry and select Mark Complete from the context menu. FrontPage changes the icon from red to green. You can see completed tasks until you delete them by checking the Show History option shown in Figure 2-17.

Getting Help

FrontPage provides several forms of help — all of which demonstrate methods for performing tasks or answering questions about FrontPage and associated products. The following sections describe various kinds of user-level help that FrontPage provides.

Accessing general help topics

In most cases, FrontPage doesn't provide context-sensitive or dialog-box-level help. To access help, press F1 or choose the Help⇨Microsoft Office FrontPage Help command. FrontPage displays help in the Task Pane on the right side of the display, as shown in Figure 2-19.

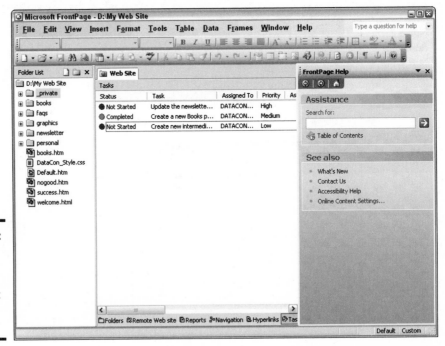

Figure 2-19: Look for help in the Task Pane on the right side of the display.

This initial help page provides several methods of accessing the special help you need. Here's how each method works:

✦ **Type one or more search words in the Search For field and click Start Searching (the green arrow).** Front Page displays a list of topics that match your search criteria. Click the link that matches the help topic you want to find. FrontPage displays the help topic on-screen in a separate window. This technique is best when you know the help topic you want or can choose from a relatively small list of help options. Figure 2-20 shows a typical example of a specific help topic.

✦ **Click Table of Contents in the Task Pane.** FrontPage displays a hierarchical list of help topics in the Task Pane, from which you select a subject. FrontPage displays the topics associated with that subject. Continue selecting topics until you reach the specific topic. FrontPage displays a full-page view of the help topic (like the one in Figure 2-20) when you find the topic you want. This search technique is best when you don't know precisely what you're looking for and want to browse the help topics.

✦ **Select one of the See Also options.** These options also appear on many of the help topic pages. The See Also options help you locate related content after you find a main help topic.

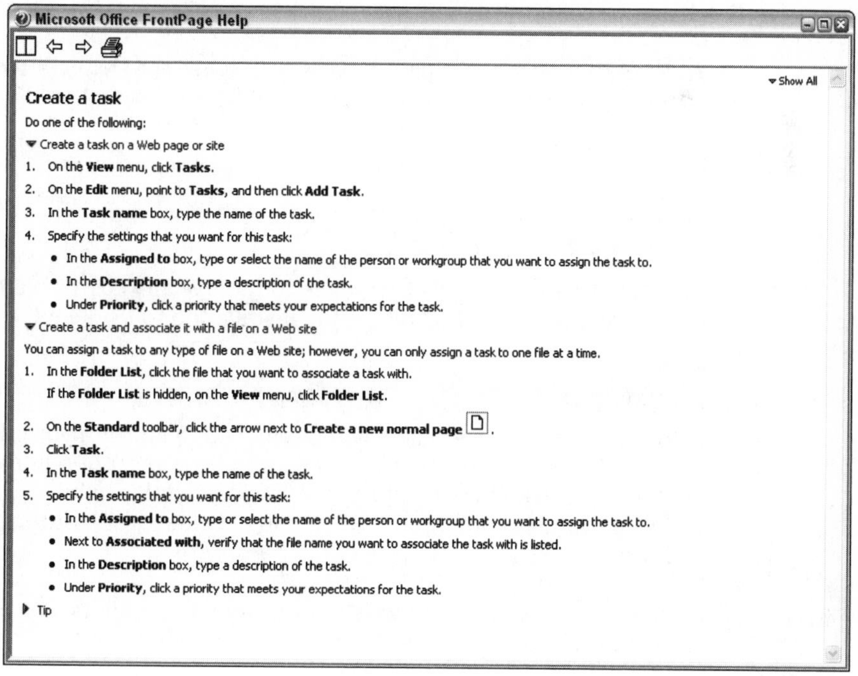

Figure 2-20:
Click Show
All to see all
of the help
topics on a
help page.

Microsoft Office FrontPage Help

Create a task

Do one of the following:

▼ Create a task on a Web page or site

1. On the **View** menu, click **Tasks**.
2. On the **Edit** menu, point to **Tasks**, and then click **Add Task**.
3. In the **Task name** box, type the name of the task.
4. Specify the settings that you want for this task:
   - In the **Assigned to** box, type or select the name of the person or workgroup that you want to assign the task to.
   - In the **Description** box, type a description of the task.
   - Under **Priority**, click a priority that meets your expectations for the task.

▼ Create a task and associate it with a file on a Web site

You can assign a task to any type of file on a Web site; however, you can only assign a task to one file at a time.

1. In the **Folder List**, click the file that you want to associate a task with.
   If the **Folder List** is hidden, on the **View** menu, click **Folder List**.
2. On the **Standard** toolbar, click the arrow next to **Create a new normal page**.
3. Click **Task**.
4. In the **Task name** box, type the name of the task.
5. Specify the settings that you want for this task:
   - In the **Assigned to** box, type or select the name of the person or workgroup that you want to assign the task to.
   - Next to **Associated with**, verify that the file name you want to associate the task with is listed.
   - In the **Description** box, type a description of the task.
   - Under **Priority**, click a priority that meets your expectations for the task.

▶ Tip

Obtaining updates

Microsoft constantly provides bug fixes, patches, and other updates
for FrontPage. To ensure you have the latest updates, choose the Help⇨
Check for Updates command. FrontPage checks for updates online and
helps you install them. Sometimes this command won't work if you don't
have the correct features installed on your system. You can also check
for Office updates at

```
http://office.microsoft.com/officeupdate/default.aspx
```

Repairing an installation

No human creation, software included, is perfect; a FrontPage installation
can fail in a number of ways. The three most common types of failure are

+ The FrontPage installation fails to work.

+ Problems show up in the way various features work.

+ You make changes to FrontPage settings that don't work as you intended.

In many cases, you can reverse problems by selecting a special command. For
example, when you make color choice changes, you can click Reset Colors
to return FrontPage to its default color settings. However, sometimes these
choices aren't available or won't work because other errors have occurred.

To reverse changes or repair problems, you use the Help⇨Detect and Repair
command, which displays the Detect and Repair dialog box. This dialog box
contains two options. Select one of them and click Start to begin the repair
process:

+ One option tells FrontPage to restore all of its shortcuts as it repairs the
  installation.

+ The other option tells FrontPage to remove any custom settings you
  might have made and return the installation to its default setup.

Determining your FrontPage version

Before you update FrontPage, you often need to know the precise version
you're using. That way you can ensure you have recent updates installed.
In addition, the Microsoft support staff will need this number to help you
with any problems you report when you use newsgroup or telephone
support.

Product names aren't the same thing as version numbers. For example,
FrontPage 2003 is a name — it's not a specific version number.

To obtain the specific version number, choose the Help⇨About command. You see the About Microsoft Office FrontPage dialog box. Look at the top-most line of text in the dialog box. This line contains the product name and the actual version number in parentheses. The version number consists of three parts, separated by periods. Reading left to right, these are the major version number, the minor version number, and the build number.

You can obtain even more information by clicking System Information. FrontPage displays the System Information application, which polls your system for the information and then displays it on-screen. You can view various categories of information and provide them to Microsoft support or as input for peer support on a newsgroup.

Customizing Toolbars

The toolbars that FrontPage provides meet the needs of most people in a general way. Many people who use the toolbars consistently find that they could provide some additional features or might require rearrangement for optimal use. Fortunately, FrontPage makes it quite easy to change the tool-bars to meet your specific needs. You can even create new toolbars that Microsoft didn't think to include.

To make any change to a toolbar, right-click the toolbar area and choose Customize from the context menu. FrontPage displays the Customize dialog box (shown in Figure 2-21). This dialog box helps you perform the tasks described in the following sections.

Figure 2-21:
Customize the FrontPage toolbar to make it easier to perform tasks.

Creating a new toolbar

Creating custom toolbars is an efficient way to hold any special commands you want to use. It also comes in handy when you want to create a custom layout. Using a custom toolbar maintains the default toolbars in their default state so other users don't get confused.

To add a new toolbar, select the Toolbars tab in the Customize dialog box. Click New and you'll see a New Toolbar dialog box. Type the name of the new toolbar and click OK. FrontPage displays the new toolbar. Customize the new toolbar by choosing specific commands. For example, you might want to create a custom toolbar for any macros you create or group commands that you use a lot onto a single toolbar.

Changing an existing toolbar

An existing toolbar might not have all the commands you want — or you might have a new toolbar that you want to customize. In both cases, you need to add or remove commands. To change a toolbar, select the Commands tab of the Customize dialog box. You'll see a list of commands that FrontPage supports, including any custom macros that your organization may have created (as shown in Figure 2-22).

Figure 2-22: Select commands from the list that FrontPage provides.

Locate the command you want to add to the toolbar and drag it to the toolbar. The same technique works with menus. Some commands appear as icons; others as word buttons, depending on the way Microsoft created the command. You can modify the command settings to change its appearance on the toolbar or menu. These changes don't affect the command itself, just the instance of the command on the toolbar or menu.

To modify a single button on a toolbar or an entry on a menu, right-click the button or entry. You see a context menu like the one shown in Figure 2-23. Use the Reset option to change the button or entry to its default configuration. The Name field contains the text that appears in the menu entry or toolbar button. Add an ampersand in front of the letter that you want to underline (use as an accelerator). The menu also lets you add an image to commands that might not have one. Use the Begin a Group option to create a vertical line on toolbars and a horizontal line on menus.

Figure 2-23:
Modify
buttons to
make them
fit your
needs.

One of the most important selections appears near the bottom of the list. The Default Style setting option displays the button using the settings that Microsoft chose when designing FrontPage. The other three settings choose an image, text, or both text and image for the menu entry or toolbar button.

Modifying the toolbar options

Some toolbar and menu options affect FrontPage as a whole. These options appear on the Options tab of the Customize dialog box, as shown in Figure 2-24. For example, you can tell FrontPage to display the standard toolbar (the one that includes the File Open button) and the formatting toolbar on two lines. This configuration helps when you have a small display or you want to see all the options in a larger format.

One new feature that I dislike about Office is the default setting that hides the menus. I like to see the whole menu whenever I open it because I don't use the same features every day. When Office hides the menu, I forget some of the options that are there and end up making more work for myself. The Options tab helps by letting me tell FrontPage to always show full menus.

Figure 2-24:
Set global options as needed to make the toolbars and menus easy to see.

You might have noticed that the standard toolbar icons are very small, making them hard to see when your eyes are tired. Use the Large Icons option to make the icons bigger so you don't suffer as much eyestrain. This feature is also handy when you want to create a presentation or teach others to use FrontPage.

ScreenTips provide helpful information on the purpose of a button on a toolbar, so it's usually a good idea to activate them using the Show ScreenTips on Toolbars option. If you find constant pop-up text annoying, you can just as easily turn off this feature. It's also possible to show the shortcut key for a particular command as part of the ScreenTip.

Using keyboard shortcuts

Some people like to keep their hands on the keyboard rather than make extensive use of a mouse. Moving your hands from the keyboard to the mouse takes time — some people are fluent enough at typing that they prefer to use keyboard shortcuts rather than click their way to the menu commands. Most FrontPage menu commands have keyboard shortcuts associated with them. The keyboard combination appears to the right of the command when you look at the menu. (For example, to open an existing document, you press Ctrl+O.) Unfortunately, it's not easy to modify existing keyboard shortcuts or add new ones.

Chapter 3: Creating Your First Web Page

In This Chapter

✔ Creating a well-designed Web site

✔ Changing the properties of a page

✔ Defining text elements

✔ Defining hyperlinks

✔ Checking your work for errors

✔ Determining the page download time

Creating a Web page is pretty exciting. You mix equal parts knowledge, art, communication, and fun to create something unique. The first time you put a Web page together and see it in your browser is the best. It doesn't have to be a perfect page — the point of creating your first page is understanding how your tools work and what you can do with them. (Besides, there's that fun aspect to consider.)

After you get past the initial excitement of seeing a few words and images in a browser, you want to add other features. The most common feature is the hyperlink, which lets Web page users access content related to the information on your Web page. Eventually, you want to add lists to make it easier to find pieces of information. To ensure that you don't make your page too large, you can check to see how long it takes to download the page. After all, not everyone has a high-speed connection.

FrontPage also makes it easy to view your Web page in various ways. Each view has its own uses:

✦ **Design:** This view lets you drag items from a toolbox and drop them on the page so you can see the results of a change quickly.

✦ **Code:** When you need a little better control over the appearance of an item, use this view to fine-tune the code that controls the look of your page.

✦ **Split:** When the Code view isn't enough — and you really need to see the changes as you make them — use this view.

✦ **Preview:** Use this view when you want to see how the page appears in the browser — to see what your visitor sees.

You can download the sample page that appears in this chapter from the book's companion Web site. Please refer to this book's Introduction for instructions on accessing the site.

Understanding Good Web Page Design

As with all the best Web pages, yours should contain everything a user needs to understand your message. Part of the communication process is in the words you type, but part of it's also subliminal. For example, the layout you use is important because a good layout helps people find information quickly. A glitzy layout makes your Web page look commercial, but it can also hide some of the information you want people to see. Commercial Web sites use glitz to impress and excite the people who visit. A simple layout may look home-grown, but it also makes people feel comfortable with your page and helps them find information quickly. The layout you choose depends on how you want people to feel about your site.

Try to present a focused message on your Web page. When you think of other messages you'd like to present, write them down and use other Web pages to discuss them. Connect all these pages so you start with general messages and work your way into specific information. The idea is to set a goal for each Web page, write it down, and then remain focused on that goal as you build the page.

As part of your Web page design, consider people who have special needs. The addition of pop-up text to describe part of your page in more detail might not seem like much, but screen-reader applications for the blind use that same text to describe your page to someone unable to see it. Likewise, careful use of color helps someone who has color blindness.

Good design also means playing with your page. Don't settle for the first design you create. Keep the fun factor in play by trying different fonts, color combinations, and other features. You use properties — specialized HTML words — to control the appearance of your Web page.

Defining Page Properties

Before you can add content to a Web page, you need to create that Web page and assign properties to it. These properties describe the Web page to the browser so it knows how to display the page on-screen. To add a new Web page to FrontPage, right-click in any clear area of the Folders view and choose New⇨Blank Page from the context menu. When the file defines the first Web page in a Web site, FrontPage names it Default.htm, but you can rename the file if desired.

The reason you want to retain Default.htm when working with Internet Information Server (IIS) is that the Web server looks for this name when directing users to your site. When a user types just the path as the URL, IIS loads this page as the default page. Other Web servers use other names for the default page. (For example, Apache normally uses index.html.) Check with the Webmaster to ensure that you're using the correct filename.

Understanding a new Web page

When you create a new Web page, you actually create a series of text entries called *tags*. The browser doesn't display the tag; instead, it uses the tag to interpret what to display on the Web page. The tag itself is special text that begins with an angle bracket, <, contains a keyword such as html, and ends with an angle bracket >. Most tags come in pairs — an opening and a closing tag. The closing tag includes a slash before the keyword. When FrontPage creates the Web Page for you, it uses tags as shown in the code in Listing 3-1.

Listing 3-1: A New Web Page

```
<html>

<head>
<meta http-equiv="Content-Type" content="text/html;
      charset=windows-1252">
<title>New Page 1</title>
</head>

<body>

</body>

</html>
```

The <html> tag pair shows the beginning and the ending of the document. The browser ignores any text that appears outside this area. The <html> tag tells the browser this is a Web page and not some other kind of document.

The <head> tag pair appears within the <html> tag pair but before anything else. This tag pair contains special instructions for the browser. You see the effects of the tags in this section of the document, but you don't see the actual text.

FrontPage automatically adds two tags to the <head> area. The first is a <meta> tag. You'll see many kinds of <meta> tags; this one tells the browser that the document contains both text and HTML (tags) that use the windows-1252 character set. Don't worry about setting this tag manually; you can change it by using special FrontPage features.

The <title> tag also appears in the <head> area. This tag tells the browser what title to display in the title bar. Any descriptive text you type between the <title> and </title> tags then appears in the browser's title bar when it displays the page.

The <body> tag pair defines the beginning and end of the content of the Web page. This is the information you do see when you load the page into your browser. The <body> area can contain text and tags. The tags define the appearance of the text or provide some other form of user-related functionality, such as telling the browser what to do when a user clicks a button on your Web page.

Assigning standard properties

After you add the new Web page, right-click its entry in the Folders view and select Properties from the context menu. You see the Properties dialog box, as shown in Figure 3-1.

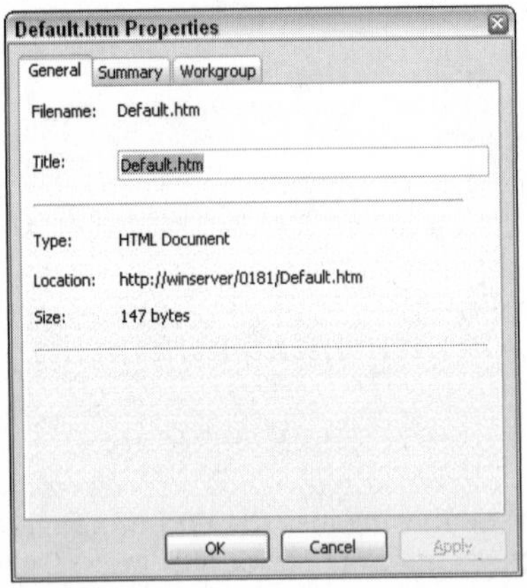

Figure 3-1:
Add
properties
to your Web
page before
you open it.

As a minimum, type a title for your Web page using the Title field on the General tab. Any title is fine as long as it's descriptive. For example, My Home Page is descriptive, yet it isn't complex.

You can also type a summary, a description, of the Web page on the Summary tab. Use specific terms to describe the Web page. An example of such a summary would look like this:

```
This is the home page for my Web site. It provides links to
all the detailed information I want to provide.
```

The idea is to describe the Web page so you remember why you created it and can focus on the purpose for that Web page.

Finally, when more than one person has to be able to work on the Web page, you should associate the Web page with a workgroup, using the options on the Workgroup tab, as shown in Figure 3-2.

Figure 3-2:
Use the Workgroup tab to assign this page to any co-creators.

The term *workgroup* is a bit of a mistake because it limits what people think about doing with this tab. For example, the Available Categories field on the Workgroup tab can categorize the Web page any way you want, not just as workgroup areas. For example, you can categorize the Web page by type so you know which pages have a lot of graphics and which have a lot of links. Select a category by checking its entry in the list. You can assign more than one category to a Web page, which allows you to keep better track of precisely how the Web page is used by letting you look at it in more than one way. To add new categories, follow these steps:

1. **Click the Categories button.**

2. **Type a name in the New Category field of the Master Category List dialog box, and then click Add.**

3. **Click OK to close the Master Category List dialog box.**

Initially, the Assigned To field won't have any name. To add a new name, follow these steps:

1. **Click the Names button.**

   The Usernames Master List dialog box opens.

2. **Type a name in the New Username field of the Usernames Master List dialog box.**

3. **Click Add.**

4. **Click OK to close the Usernames Master List dialog box.**

5. **Select a name from the Assigned to drop-down list to assign the new page to someone you work with.**

The Review Status field reflects the current state of the Web page. Options such as Code Review tell you where the Web page is in the development process. You add new status types to the list by following these steps:

1. **Click the Statuses button.**

   The Review Status Master List dialog box opens.

2. **Type the new status in the New Review Status field of the Review Status Master List dialog box.**

3. **Click OK to close the Review Status Master List dialog box.**

Click OK when you finish configuring the Web page to close the Properties dialog box.

Assigning page-specific properties

After you assign general properties, you need to open the Web page so you can assign specific properties. When you double-click the new Web page in the Folders view, FrontPage displays it for you. Normally, FrontPage opens the Web page in Design view. However, if FrontPage opens the page to another view, click Design at the bottom of the window to access the Design view. To start assigning page-specific properties, right-click the page and then select Page Properties from the context menu. You see a Page Properties dialog box, as shown in Figure 3-3.

Notice that FrontPage fills in the Title field for you based on your previous entries. Unlike the summary you created earlier for your own use, the Page description field contains a summary of the page for users who want to visit your site. Make the summary inviting and tell the user what the page contains.

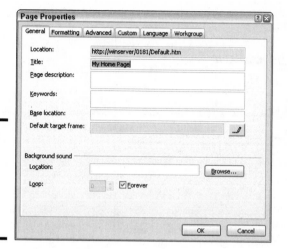

Figure 3-3:
Add page-
specific
properties
to define
the page
for users.

The Keywords field contains words that describe the page to search engines. These words define the keywords that others may type into the search engine to locate your Web page, so the choice of keywords is very important. (Search engines do use other criteria for finding your page, such as the page's content, but keywords are very important.)

When you type the keywords, use specific terms. For example, if you have a hobby, don't use `hobby` as a keyword. Focus instead on the activity, such as ceramics or poetry. Use single words. The search engine won't see *writing poetry* as a single term — it will see two separate ideas.

Filling out the Page description and Keywords fields is another part of the design process. Adding this information should help you focus on the message that this Web page delivers. Make sure you focus on the Web page and not your Web site as a whole. Each Web page should stand on its own as well as direct people to other locations on your Web site.

Many of the settings you make during this setup phase of the Web page affect a special kind of entry called a *meta tag*. A meta tag appears in the heading of the Web page; you don't normally see it as output. In most cases, the meta tag affects the Web page appearance overall, provides documentation for other developers, or provides information to search engines. You add special meta tags on the Custom tab shown in Figure 3-4.

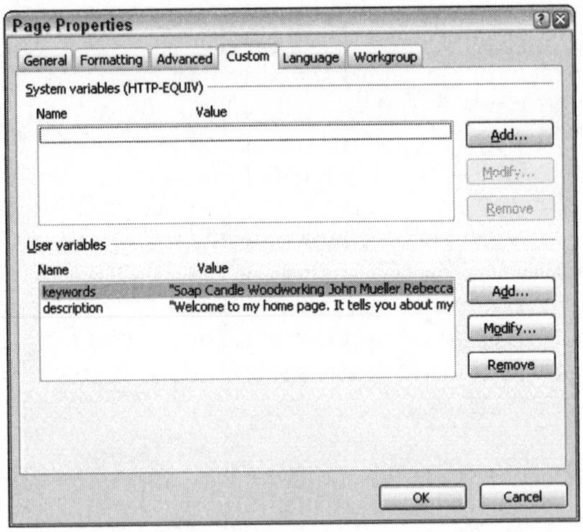

Figure 3-4:
Use meta
tags to
document
your Web
page.

Notice that Figure 3-4 shows two meta tags defined in other areas of this chapter. Developers use many kinds of meta tags, but here are two that you should consider adding to all your Web pages:

✦ **The** author **meta tag:** This one identifies who created the page — it's for documentation.

✦ **The** title **meta tag:** This one acts as input made available to search engines. The search engine uses this information to provide a descriptive title for your page when people look for pages like yours.

You'll discover other meta tags as the book progresses. To add a new meta tag, follow these steps:

1. **Click the Add button in the User Variables section.**

You see a User Meta Variable dialog box.

2. **Type the name of the meta tag, such as** author **or** title**, in the Name field.**

3. **Type the value of the meta tag in the Value field.**

4. **Click OK to complete the meta tag.**

The final page-specific property you should always set appears on the Language tab of the Page Properties dialog box. Most Web pages use a specific language as the basis for the content they contain. To ensure that search engines can mark your page appropriately, select a language in the Mark Current Document As field. Search engines such as Google can even use this information to offer translations to users who want to view your Web page in another language.

Defining standard special effects

Some people like to add background sound to their Web pages. The sound plays while someone views the site. To add a sound to a Web page, select the General tab of the Page Properties dialog box shown in Figure 3-3. The Background Sound area contains several fields that define the sound for your Web site. The Location field tells the browser where to locate the sound you want to play. The Loop field defines how many times the sound plays (or whether it plays forever). Avoid using sounds when you think someone will visit your Web site from a busy environment or one where quiet is essential (such as an office). Limit the number of times the sound plays to avoid annoying people who might otherwise like your site but don't like the particular sound you chose.

Adding special formatting to your page can make it look more professional and easier to use in some cases. These options appear on the Formatting tab shown in Figure 3-5.

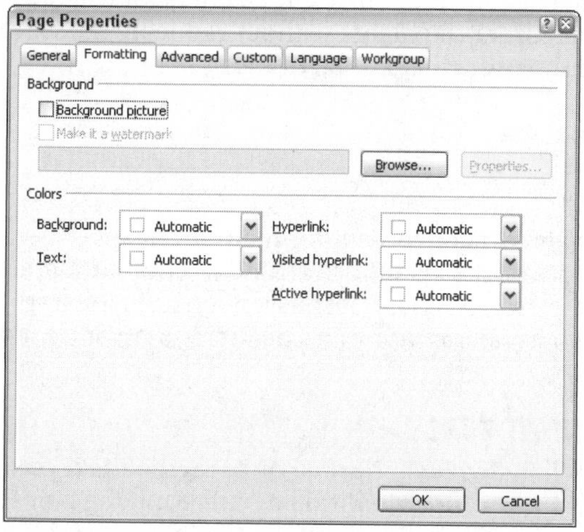

Figure 3-5:
Add special
formatting
to dress up
a page.

The type of formatting you choose depends on what you're using it for. Here are the general types available on the tab:

✦ **Background image:** Check Background picture and add a URL for the image to make it appear on the Web page. Select Make it a Watermark if you want the background image to appear light as a subtle addition to the page that won't interfere with the text. Avoid using background images that make the text hard to read. Images with muted colors and low contrast tend to make the best background images.

✦ **Coloration:** The Background and Text color selections change the background and foreground colors of the information you present. The Hyperlink selection changes the color of the hyperlinks the user hasn't seen yet, and the Visited Hyperlink selection defines the color of the hyperlinks the user has seen. The Active Hyperlink selection is used only when the user's mouse hovers over the hyperlink. Avoid setting background and foreground colors that would cause problems for someone who is colorblind. The wrong settings can actually make your page nearly invisible to people who have this problem. Avoid changing the hyperlink colors at all unless you want to create a highly stylized Web site.

✦ **Advanced settings:** These special settings in the Margins area help you set the viewing area for your document. Margins on a Web page work much like the margins in a word-processed document — you set the left, right, top, and bottom margins to help meet specific needs (legibility, efficient use of screen space, and so on).

Use these settings carefully. Some users will want to change the size of the text on the page so they can see it easily. Adding margins tends to make your text harder to enlarge without reducing the viewing area to a point where the user can't see anything.

Working with Text

Text defines the main form of content for many Web pages. Because text is relatively easy to add, it's also the first kind of content that many people create. Not all text is created equal. Just as a book has paragraphs and headers, Web pages also use paragraphs and headers to organize ideas.

Defining normal text

What's normal? Well, it depends. Normal or paragraph text comes in several forms. The simplest form appears within a paragraph tag pair that looks like this: `<p>Some text</p>`. FrontPage automatically adds these tags for you, but it's important to know the tags are there. The beginning paragraph tag, `<p>`, and the ending paragraph tag, `</p>` tell the browser where the paragraph starts and finishes.

To start another paragraph, simply press Enter. In the background, FrontPage creates another tag pair to hold a paragraph. Any text you type appears within the tag pair automatically.

You add colors and other features to the text by highlighting the words you want to change and selecting the text formatting features you want to use. For example, you can change the text font, color, and style by highlighting the words you want to change and selecting the changes from the Formatting toolbar.

As you define the content of your Web page, you might decide to change one or more elements. The easiest way to do so is to place the cursor within the text element you want to change and select the tag you want to modify from the Quick Tag Selector at the top of the Design window. Figure 3-6 shows a typical example of how this feature works.

Notice the hierarchy shown in the Quick Tag Selector. It begins with the `<body>` tag that contains all the content displayed on-screen, moves on to the `<p>` that contains the entire paragraph, and finally goes to the `<font>` tag that defines the formatting of a particular word. To change the characteristics of the selected tag, choose Tag Properties from the context menu.

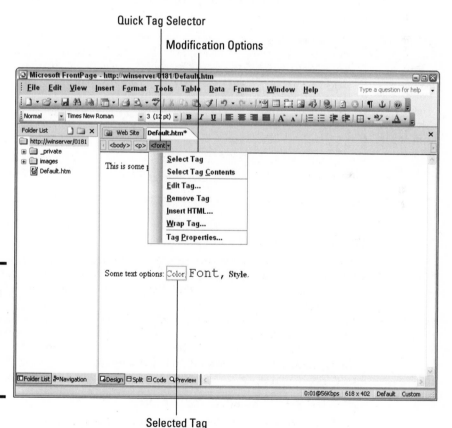

Figure 3-6:
Select tags using the Quick Tag Selector at the top of the design window.

The properties dialog box varies by the kind of tag you select. For example, if you select Tag Properties for a `<font>` tag, you'll see the Font dialog box shown in Figure 3-7. This dialog box helps you change everything about the font, including its size and color. You can also choose special effects, such as strikethrough, overline, and underline.

To change the characteristics of your font, you don't have to write any code by hand. Selecting options in the Properties dialog box changes the settings and the code for that particular tag.

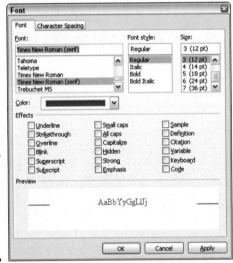

Figure 3-7:
Change the font settings to meet specific needs.

Adding headings

Headings work just like regular text in some respects. The only difference is that you use the heading tags in place of the paragraph tag. A heading tag consists of the letter h, followed by the heading level as a number, so a first level heading uses the `<h1>` tag.

To add a heading to your page, start with a blank line. Select one of the heading levels from the Style list on the Formatting toolbar. FrontPage automatically changes the paragraph tag to a heading tag.

Defining terms and acronyms

FrontPage doesn't define every tag you need, but it does provide a method for adding tags. When you add special terms to the content of your Web page, you want to define those terms so other people don't get frustrated reading the information you provide. Three of the most important tags you can add to FrontPage are those that allow acronyms (`<acronym>`), abbreviations (`<abbr>`), and definitions (`<dfn>`).

To add a new tag, follow these steps:

1. **Place the cursor where you want the content to go.**

2. **Select the Insert HTML option from the Quick Tag Selector context menu.**

You see a Quick Tag Editor dialog box.

3. **Type the tag that you want to add.**

For example, when you want to add an abbreviation such as CPU to your Web page, you type

```
<abbr title="Central Processing Unit">CPU</abbr>
```

4. **Press Enter.**

FrontPage adds the tag to your page.

Now any user who passes the mouse cursor over the abbreviation *CPU* on your Web page sees the definition you provided as pop-up text. All three tags use the same format.

The beginning `<abbr>` tag contains a special entry named `title`, which is an attribute or an argument depending on whom you talk to. The `title` argument defines the abbreviation. The term is between the beginning and ending `<abbr>` tags. Finally, the `</abbr>` tag tells the browser that the abbreviation has ended.

Not every browser understands every tag. When a browser sees a tag it doesn't understand, it ignores the tag and displays the content. Almost every browser understands the `<acronym>` and `<dfn>` tags, but only a few understand the `<abbr>` tag. To ensure that everyone can see the abbreviations you define, use the `<acronym>` tag even if what you're showing isn't (strictly speaking) an acronym.

Working with Hyperlinks

Hyperlinks are sets of instructions that create connections between Web pages on your Web site — as well as with pages on other sites. A hyperlink uses the special `<a>` tag to create a connection between pages or even different areas on the same page. For example, you can create a navigation bar at the top of your page that quickly takes users to the area they want.

To work with all browsers, a hyperlink must include the protocol you want to use, the name of the computer that contains the information, the path to the information on that computer, and finally the name of the file. For example, in the hyperlink `http://www.mysite.com/myfolder/myfile.htm`, the protocol is `http` (HyperText Transport Protocol), the name of the computer is `www.mysite.com`, the path is `myfolder`, and the filename is `myfile.htm`.

Setting the base location

Browsers locate hyperlinks using a URL you provide. Typing a complete URL every time you access something on the same Web page can get annoying after a while, so browsers recognize a special configuration setting called the base location. When a browser sees an incomplete URL in a hyperlink, it adds the base location to the URL to make the hyperlink complete. For example, if the base location is `http://www.mysite.com/` and the URL in the hyperlink is `mypage.htm`, then the complete URL is `http://www.mysite.com/mypage.htm`.

Customarily, you set only one base location per page; most developers use the current Web site and folder as the base location. That way, creating a hyperlink for the current site is a matter of simply typing the filename — the browser fills in the rest of the URL. To set a base location for a page, right-click the page and select Page Properties from the context menu. You see the Page Properties dialog box shown in Figure 3-3. Type the partial URL in the Base Location field and then click OK — presto, new link.

Pointing to the same page

The first kind of hyperlink that many developers create is one that points to a different location on the same page. To create this kind of hyperlink, you need to make two entries. The first entry is the *anchor* — the location you want the user to end up at when they click the hyperlink. FrontPage calls this kind of hyperlink a *bookmark*.

To add the bookmark, follow these steps:

1. Highlight the text you want to use as an anchor.

2. Choose the Insert⇨Bookmark command.

You'll see a Bookmark dialog box.

3. Type the name you want to use for the anchor and click OK.

The second step is to add the hyperlink. Here's how:

4. Go to another area in the same document and select the text you want to use for the hyperlink.

5. **Choose the Insert⇨Hyperlink command.**

   You see the Insert Hyperlink dialog box shown in Figure 3-8.

6. **Select the Place in this Document option.**

7. **Highlight the bookmark you want to use and click OK.**

   FrontPage creates the hyperlink for you.

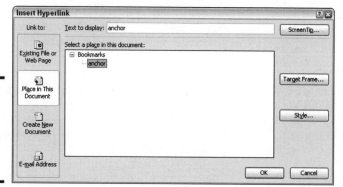

Figure 3-8:
Select the
bookmark
you want to
use for the
hyperlink.

Pointing to different pages

FrontPage provides a number of ways to create a link to a second page. The easiest method for creating links to pages on your Web site is to drag the page from the Folder List and drop it on the page. FrontPage automatically creates a hyperlink for you.

A second technique is as follows:

1. **Go to the site you want to link to using your browser.**

2. **Highlight a word describing the location you want to link to and choose the Insert⇨Hyperlink command.**

3. **Select the Existing File or Web Page and Browsed Pages options.**

   You see the Insert Hyperlink dialog box shown in Figure 3-9.

4. **Select the link you want to add from the list and click OK.**

   This technique ensures you add the correct hyperlink the first time.

Other options for creating hyperlinks include adding links to documents you've opened recently or you can create a new document. When you know the URL you want to add and don't want to browse to it first, you can type it into the Address field and add it directly.

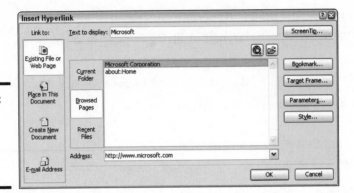

Figure 3-9:
Use your
browser
to locate
existing
pages.

A special kind of hyperlink lets people who visit your site send you e-mail. To add this kind of hyperlink, start by selecting text you want to use for the hyperlink. Open the Insert Hyperlink dialog box and select the E-mail Address option. Type your e-mail address in the E-mail Address field and a topic of discussion in the Subject field.

Always provide a topic of discussion when you place an e-mail hyperlink on your Web site. Including a topic of discussion offers two advantages:

✦ It helps you discover what other sites the user visited.

✦ It means you won't receive mystery e-mails that lack a subject. You can tell right away when a message is one of yours.

Describing your links

A hyperlink should include a few simple words to tell advanced users where the link goes. Users with a little less experience might require additional information. You can use the `title` attribute to define the hyperlink better.

To add the `title` attribute to an existing link, place the cursor within the hyperlink on-screen and select the Edit Tag option from the Quick Tag Selector. You see a Quick Tag Editor dialog box. Add the `title` attribute like this: `<a href="#anchor" title="This link takes you to the anchor location on this page.">`. A user who hovers a mouse pointer over the link immediately sees your explanatory text.

Working with Lists

Lists help you organize short pieces of information. Web pages support two kinds of lists: numbered and bulleted. You use numbered lists to lay out procedures (say, how to make toast or juggle beanbags) or to rank information (such as a top-ten list of odd movies, from least to most odd). Use bulleted lists for short pieces of unranked information, such as a list of links to your favorite Web sites or reasons why you like to go to the mall.

To add a numbered list to a page, start a new blank line. Click Numbering on the Formatting toolbar.

Likewise, to add a bulleted list, start a new blank line and click Bullets on the Formatting toolbar. Figure 3-10 shows the location of the Numbering and Bullets buttons as well as typical examples of each list type.

Lists use two sets of tags to define the presentation. The `<ol>` tag pair defines a numbered list, and the `<ul>` tag pair defines a bulleted list. Within the list are the individual list elements, each defined with the `<li>` tag pair.

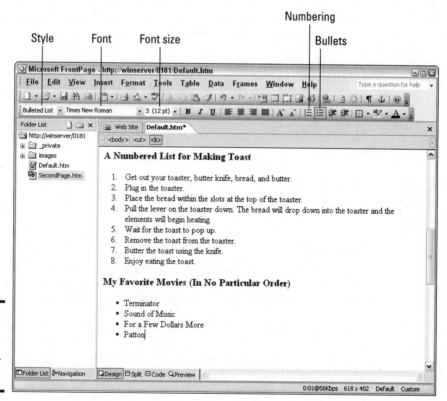

Figure 3-10:
Use lists to make your page easier to read.

Viewing the Results

The Design view works well for many, if not most, tasks that simple Web pages carry out. You never need to look at any other view if you plan to create pages that have simple text and few pictures. Other views are helpful when you need to create complex pages or want to see the effects of your changes without opening a browser. You select a particular view by clicking the options at the bottom of the design window in FrontPage.

Using Design view

Design view helps you create new text and graphic elements on a Web page. You also use it to create various tags using the techniques described in this chapter. FrontPage does most of the work for you in the background, so you don't need to know a lot about the tags, just that they exist. This view is perfect for creating the initial page. When you want to start adding complex features such as scripts, you need to work with either the Code view or the Split view. Use the Preview view when you want to see what the page looks like without starting a browser to view it.

Using Split view

The Split view divides the screen to show both the Design view and the Code view (as shown in Figure 3-11). You use this view to watch the effects of a change you make in the code appear immediately in Design view. To use this view, you must know the tags that Web pages rely on to display and format information.

One of the most interesting uses of this view is to see how FrontPage creates code for you. Observing the code creation process helps you discover new tags.

Using Code view

The Code view shows you the code without any graphic presentation. You use this view when you want to work exclusively with code. For example, you use this view to write scripts or add special attributes to existing tags.

FrontPage includes a number of helpful features for the Code view. The most important feature is IntelliSense. Figure 3-12 shows how IntelliSense looks when you modify a tag. The list of things you can do with an ⟨h1⟩ tag appears immediately when you press the spacebar. In this case, you can tell the browser to align the text differently, give it a particular style, or add pop-up text, among other things.

Book I
Chapter 3

Creating Your
First Web Page

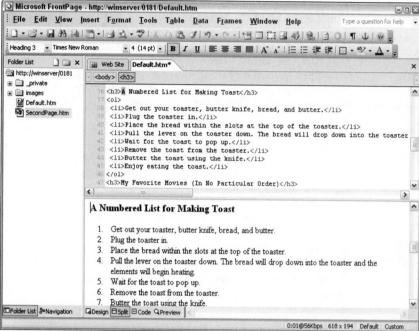

Figure 3-11:
Use the Split view to see your Web page as code and graphic elements.

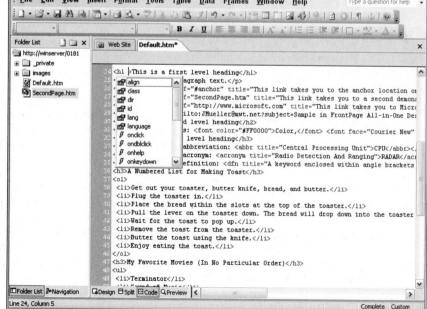

Figure 3-12:
Expect help writing code from IntelliSense when you work on Web pages.

Using Preview view

It's easy to confuse the Design view and the Preview view at first because they look the same in many cases. The Design view does show you graphic elements, but doesn't always present them in the same way that a user would see them. The Preview view shows the page as it appears to an Internet Explorer user. When you want to see the page as it looks in other browsers, such as Mozilla or Opera, you need to view the page using that browser.

The Preview view also displays special elements you create for a Web page. For example, you must use the Preview view to see definitions you create for entries on the page. The Preview view also shows how pictures actually appear on the Web page and helps you check the help text you provide for hyperlinks.

You also use the Preview view to size the content of a page. Select one of the page size options available on the View⇨Page Size menu to see how the page will look to someone with a browser that uses that size display. In some cases, you find that you need to move elements around or make some elements smaller so users can see the page as you intended.

Timing the page download

Some Web pages become so large that you can get a cup of coffee and read *War and Peace* while you wait for them to download. Unfortunately, most users won't wait very long for a page to download. They'll click Stop on their browser to see whatever they can immediately. Most developers assume that most users have enough patience to wait a mere ten seconds or less for the page to download. Sometimes that's true, but if the page isn't interesting enough without all the bells and whistles, the user will leave for another site.

To ensure you keep your audience captivated so they don't vote with their virtual feet and jump to another site, you need to know how much time it takes to download your page. FrontPage makes this easy by telling you the download time when you're in Design or Split view. The Estimated Time to Download indicator in the status bar tells you how many seconds the page requires to download at a given speed.

The default download speed is a high-speed modem running at 56 Kbps. Nearly everyone in the United States has a modem that runs at this speed. When you expect a lot of visitors from other countries, you might have to time the download at 28.8 Kbps to ensure it doesn't take too long. In other cases, you might want to use a higher download speed. A game Web site can usually assume the user has a new machine with a high-speed Internet connection, so using a higher download speed is fine.

Book II

Basic Pages

"What I'm looking for are dynamic Web applications and content, not Web innuendoes and intent."

Contents at a Glance

Chapter 1: Designing Pages with Controls

In This Chapter

✔ Understanding when to use controls

✔ Using labels with standard or read-only textbox controls

✔ Adding inputs to an application

✔ Specifying decorative on-screen elements

✔ Creating applications with banners

*A*s you work with Web pages, you discover many kinds of controls. The controls in this chapter are all simple user-interface elements — they all help the user understand and interact with your application in some way. You rely on user-interface controls all the time in FrontPage (and other applications) — toolbars, on-screen buttons to click, and such — so you already know what a control looks like (and implies) from a user perspective.

Developing a great Web page means, in this case, using FrontPage controls well. You use such controls as labels, inputs, and decorative elements to create a complete experience for the user — and they allow the communication to be two-way. Even so, you don't always have to create an application when you use these controls. Sometimes they serve as a means of organizing your Web-page data — and that is the focus of this chapter.

Using Controls Efficiently

Placing a control on-screen is easy. Using the control *efficiently* is a little more difficult because the part you see isn't the whole picture. To perform useful work, controls include a number of "unseen" features that you must configure for maximum efficiency. For example, a *textbox* control (the rectangular box that receives input in most applications) has a size attribute that defines the length of the textbox on-screen. Likewise, controls have *events* (things that a user can do) associated with them; for example, a pushbutton control has a click event associated with it. Differences in attributes make controls useful in their specific ways, but they also mean you must define the effect of a control before the user can interact with it.

Working with properties

When you look at a Web control in the Code view, you see a tag with some attributes associated with it. The control uses its attributes in specific ways; most developers call these *properties*. A property defines some aspect of the control. For example, the property can affect the appearance of the control (such as its size or color), or how it reacts to user input (such as when a user assigns a name to the control).

Although FrontPage provides access to most properties from Design view, the only way to see all properties available for a particular control is to view them in Split or Code view. When working with controls, the Split view is actually better; you see the graphic and code representation at the same time. The effects of a property change are immediately visible.

Understanding events

Events always happen as the result of some action on the part of the user, the operating system, or the browser. When a user clicks a pushbutton, an event occurs. The browser registers the user's action and tells your Web page about it. You can choose to do something about the event, or you can ignore it. The event still happens, but if you want your Web page to do something about the event before anything happens in response, you have to tell it so. That's where the IntelliSense feature of FrontPage comes in handy.

IntelliSense makes it easy to differentiate between control properties and events. Figure 1-1 shows a label control and a partial list of the properties and events associated with it. Note that properties use an icon that differs from the one used by events.

Adding comments

As Web pages become more complex, developers find it hard to remember what exact purpose a control serves, or why a particular control appears in a certain position. *Comments* — notes that serve as internal documentation — provide reminders to the developer and describe how the Web page works (handy for other developers). To create a comment, choose Code view and type `<!--`, then type the comment, and finally `-->` to end the comment. Here's a typical comment:

```
<!-- This comment was inserted from Code view. -->
```

Comments you enter manually into Code view normally won't appear in Design view. If you want the comment to appear in Design view, you must tell FrontPage to make it visible by adding special information to the comment. This comment appears in Design, Code, and Split views, but not in Preview view because the browser won't display the comment.

```
<!--webbot
    bot="PurpleText"
    PREVIEW="This comment was inserted from Code view." -->
```

The first line tells FrontPage to use a `webbot`, a special kind of control. The second line tells what kind of `webbot` to use. The code uses the `PurpleText` `webbot`, in this case. The reason it's called a `PurpleText` `webbot` is that the comment text actually appears in purple when you see it in Design view. The third line contains the comment. FrontPage displays this text in all three views.

A comment can say anything you want, but the best comments provide detailed information. For example, saying that a particular control is a pushbutton isn't helpful — anyone viewing the code can see that. On the other hand, a comment that says a pushbutton `displays a little red light on the form` is more helpful because that information might not be apparent from the code.

Use the Insert⇨Comment command to insert a comment from Design view. When you see the Comment window, type the comment and click OK to add it to the Web page. A comment added in Design view using the Comment window automatically uses the `PurpleText` `webbot` so you can see it in all three views.

**Book II
Chapter 1**

**Designing Pages
with Controls**

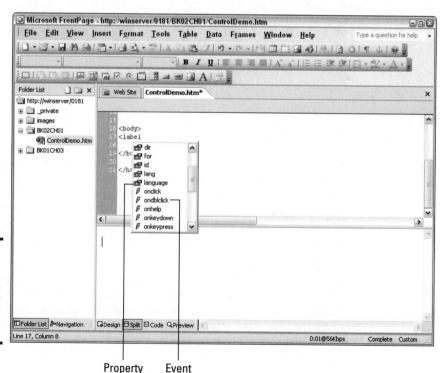

Figure 1-1:
Add
properties
to your Web
page before
you open it.

Property   Event

Using Labels

A *label* is a piece of text that contains output information or identifies the purpose of another control. Labels are normally short — you shouldn't use them as a replacement for paragraph text. For example, `Your Name` is good content for a label associated with a textbox used to type your name. The label is associated with the textbox, so the two work as a team to help users understand what to do.

One example of output information is the result you get back from a calculation. Some developers avoid using labels for output because the developer can make textboxes read-only (so the user can't type anything in them). Here's an example of a simple label.

```
<label>This is a label </label>
```

This is a standalone label that isn't associated with any other control on-screen. The `<label>` tag appears as a pair with the text that you want to appear in the label between the tags. When you create a standalone label, you should also add the `title` attribute to provide additional information to the user without affecting the control (for example, without making the textbox read-only). The label contains the output information, and can change, but the title tells what the information means to the user (so it doesn't change). For example, if you add a `title` attribute for the standalone label given here, it looks like this:

```
title="This is an example of a standalone label"
```

Working with Inputs

Input controls receive data from the user. For example, a textbox receives text input. The user could type a name or other piece of information that can't be described in some other way. All input controls rely on the `<input>` tag. Unlike other tags, you must define which kind of `<input>` tag you want to use, so this tag always includes the `type` attribute. For example, you define a textbox using the `<input type="textbox">` tag.

Using textboxes

You use *textbox* controls as on-screen places to hold a single line of text, generally as a means of getting input from a user: The user types a value (such as a name) in the textbox. However, you can also make textboxes read-only by using the `readonly` attribute. The user can't type any information into a read-only text box, but it's useful for sending information *to* users in a form that they can easily copy and paste into other documents.

A simple textbox includes just the `<input type="textbox">` tag. A textbox this simple, however, is usually inadequate for two reasons:

✦ It doesn't tell the user how to use it.

✦ You can't easily get information from it.

A more complete textbox is needed for most applications. One that fills the bill includes the elements shown here:

```
<p><label for="MyText">
    <span style="TEXT-DECORATION: underline">
    A</span>ssociated Label</label>
  <br/>
  <input type="text"
         name="MyText"
         id="MyTe[DMC1]xt"
         size="20"
         maxlength="25"
         tabindex="1"
         value="Simple Text"
         title="This is an example of a simple textbox."
         accesskey="A"></p>
```

**Book II
Chapter 1**

**Designing Pages
with Controls**

This code snippet shows some typical features of a no-frills textbox. Here are some ways to ensure that your textbox gets the job done:

✦ Always associate a label with the textbox so the user knows what the information in the textbox represents.

✦ Use the `for` attribute and the name of the textbox to make the association.

✦ Type a short value for the label that represents the content of the textbox.

This label uses a new tag called a `<span>` to underline the first letter of the label text. The `style` attribute tells how to decorate the text. The example adds an underline for the first letter of the label to tell the user which Alt key combination to press to access the textbox. To make this feature work properly, you must also define an `accesskey` attribute for the textbox. Figure 1-2 shows how the `<span>` affects Web-page output in the Preview view.

In addition to the required tag elements, the textbox should include a `name` attribute for identification. The user doesn't see this attribute, but the browser uses `name` to send information that the user types to you; you also need it when you create scripts that involve the textbox.

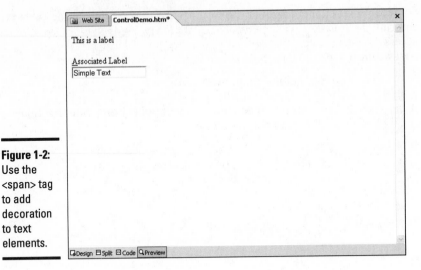

Figure 1-2:
Use the
<span> tag
to add
decoration
to text
elements.

The `size` attribute determines the number of characters the user sees on-screen. This attribute doesn't control the number of characters the user can type, so someone can send as many characters as they want to you. When you want to control the amount of text the user types into the textbox, use the `maxlength` attribute. Setting a maximum input length can help you avoid a few of the security problems that Web-site developers face, while ensuring that you get just the amount of information you want.

Many users rely on the Tab key to move from field to field on a Web site. Normally a browser uses the order in which items appear in the Web-page code to determine the *tab order* — the order by which the user selects inputs using the Tab key. Use the `tabindex` attribute to change the normal tab order.

Always assign a value to the textbox if possible so the user has some idea of what to type. The `value` attribute defines the text the user sees in the textbox. You also use the `value` attribute to discover the content of a textbox in a script and the browser uses the `value` attribute to send information to you after a user fills out a form.

The label associated with a form suggests what you need as input. When you add a `title` attribute to a textbox, the textbox produces a pop-up with additional information when a user hovers the mouse over it. In addition, users with special needs require the `title` attribute content; that way they understand what information you want them to provide. For example, screen readers use this attribute to describe the textbox to a blind user.

Sometimes you need a textbox that displays password characters (such as asterisks) rather than the actual text a user types. To display password characters on-screen, set the `type` attribute to `password`, rather than `text`. The password textbox acts like a standard textbox in all other ways.

Using pushbuttons

Pushbutton controls let the user signal a need of some kind. The need could be as simple as resetting the form so the user can fill out the information from scratch. The `<input>` tag as shown here is basic to a pushbutton control:

```
<p><input type="submit"
          name="Submit"
          title="Send the data. Alt+S"
          accesskey="S">
   <input type="reset"
          name="Reset"
          title="Reset the data. Alt+R"
          accesskey="R">
   <input type=button
          name="ClickMe"
          value="Click Me"
          title="This button isn't functional. Alt+C"
          accesskey="C"></p>
```

**Book II
Chapter 1**

**Designing Pages
with Controls**

User needs are diverse, so pushbuttons have to be versatile. In fact, Web pages support three kinds of pushbuttons, all of which rely on the `<input>` tag:

✦ **The** `submit` **pushbutton sends data on a Web page to the server.** Notice that you don't define a `value` attribute because this button has a default caption. This pushbutton also has a default action, so it's functional even if you don't assign a script to it.

✦ **The** `reset` **pushbutton returns the contents of a form to its default state.** Doing so allows a user to start from scratch easily after making a series of mistakes. As with the `submit` button, you don't have to provide a `value` attribute and this pushbutton has a default action.

✦ **The generic pushbutton doesn't have a default action.** You use this one for any task that the `submit` and `reset` pushbuttons can't fulfill. This type of pushbutton doesn't have a caption, so you must provide a `value` attribute to add text to it.

Notice that none of these pushbuttons has a label associated with it because the text appears directly on the pushbutton face. Although there isn't any recognized convention for assigning access keys to pushbuttons, I normally use the first letter of the pushbutton caption. Because you can't underline a letter in the pushbutton caption, you should include any access-key combination in the pop-up text defined by the `title` attribute.

Using checkboxes

You use *checkbox* controls to define the answer to a yes or no, on or off, or some other Boolean question. Checkboxes are easier to fill out than textboxes because the user doesn't have to figure out what input to provide. In addition, checkboxes are safer from a security perspective because the user can't send a virus as input to your question. To make the purpose of a checkbox clear, you must provide an associated label as shown here.

```
<p><label for="MyCheckbox">
    <span style="TEXT-DECORATION: underline">
    M</span>y Checkbox</label>
  <input type="checkbox"
        name="MyCheckbox"
        id="MyCheckbox"
        title="This is a typical checkbox."
        accesskey="M"
        checked></p>
```

A checkbox requires very little configuration. You provide checkbox for the type attribute, along with a name, title, and accesskey — the same attributes every other control uses. The unique attribute is checked. Add this to the checkbox when you want it to appear checked by default.

Using option buttons

Option buttons (also called *radio buttons*) are controls that provide all the security and ease-of-use benefits of checkboxes, but also allow a wider variety of responses. You define one option button for each possible input. The user selects between the options; only one option is selected at any given time, and only the selected option runs. You must provide one associated label for each option button, as shown here.

```
<p><label for="Option1">Option
    <span style="TEXT-DECORATION: underline">
    1</span></label>
  <input type="radio"
        id="Option1"
        name="OptionSet"
        value="Option 1"
        title="The first option"
        accesskey="1"
        checked><br/>
  <label for="Option2">Option
    <span style="TEXT-DECORATION: underline">
    2</span></label>
  <input type="radio"
        id="Option2"
        name="OptionSet"
```

```
value="Option 2"
title="The second option"
accesskey="2"></p>
```

The `for` attribute of a label is normally the same as the `name` attribute of the associated control. In this case, the `for` attribute is the same as the `id` attribute of the control because the `name` attribute is used to associate the option buttons in a group. Two option buttons are in this group; you can select either of them, but not both. When you want to create more than one option button group on a Web page, you must use a different name for each group.

The `value` attribute doesn't appear on the display, but the browser does use it to send data selections. You can also access this information with a script. You must assign a different `value` attribute to every option button in a group; doing so ensures that you know which option button the user selected.

Creating Decorative Elements

It's helpful to add decorative elements to a Web page to further divide information into groups. A simple break or horizontal rule can signify the end of one kind of data and the beginning of a new type of data. You can also add a time and date to a page to track your last edit. Finally, you can use special characters to create special effects or present information in other languages.

Inserting a break

Web pages use breaks to finish one line of information and start on another line. Unlike a `<p>` tag, the `<br/>` (break) tag doesn't add an extra space. You can use the break tag to create groups of information, such as a series of option buttons. A `<br/>` tag normally appears as a single tag, and doesn't include any formatting (although you can include formatting if you want). Here's a mix of paragraphs and breaks:

```
<p>Start of text<br/>text after a break</p>
<p>Another line<br/>with a break.</p>
```

When you view this text on-screen, you don't see either the `<p>` or the `<br>` tags, but you see their effect. Figure 1-3 shows the results of the previous code. Notice how the Split view shows you the precise location of the break in both the Design and the Code windows.

Using the horizontal rule

A *horizontal rule* is simply a line that extends across the screen. You use this visual effect to separate various kinds of data. For example, you can separate heading levels with a horizontal rule or provide a horizontal rule between groups of data. This is one of the few decorative tags you can present alone or with special attributes. Here's an example of a horizontal rule:

```
<hr align="center"
    noshade
    size="3"
    width="60%">
```

The `align` attribute tells where to place the horizontal rule. You choose left, center, or right placement. The default places the horizontal rule on the left side of the Web page.

Most browsers present a horizontal rule using the same 3D shading used for other on-screen elements. You can tell the browser to present the horizontal rule as a flat line by using the `noshade` attribute.

The default settings for a horizontal rule presents a thin, one-pixel line, across the entire Web page. You adjust these settings using the `size` and `width` attributes. The `size` attribute affects the thickness of the line; the `width` attribute affects the amount of space used for the horizontal rule on the Web page. You normally express the `width` attribute as a percentage; that way the horizontal rule maintains a specific presentation when the user resizes the page.

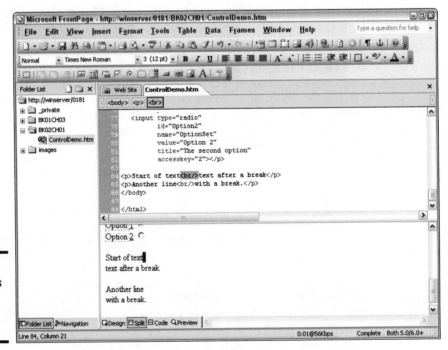

Figure 1-3:
Use breaks
to move
data to the
next line.

Adding the date and time

Users often want to know the date you last updated your Web site. It's not always easy to remember to change the date, so you can ask FrontPage to perform this task for you. FrontPage uses a `webbot` to perform this task, as shown here.

```
<!--webbot bot="Timestamp"
           S-Type="EDITED"
           S-Format="%d %B %Y %I:%M %p" -->
```

The `bot` attribute defines the kind of `webbot` — a `Timestamp`. The `S-Type` attribute tells what kind of timestamp to create. The `EDITED` type defines the timestamp as one where you manually updated the page. You can also choose to show automatic updates. Finally, the `S-Format` attribute defines how the date and time appear. Fortunately, you don't have to remember all of the odd formatting strings. To insert the date and time on your Web page, choose Insert⇨Date and Time. You see the Date and Time dialog box shown in Figure 1-4.

**Book II
Chapter 1**

**Designing Pages
with Controls**

Figure 1-4:
Add the
date and
time to
show your
last update.

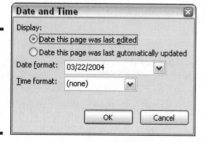

The Display options tell when to update the timestamp, whether during a manual or an automatic update. Use the Date Format and Time Format options to choose a format for that part of the timestamp. You can also choose to leave out the time or date.

Defining special characters

You might not need special characters very often, but most developers need them at some point. A special character could be a copyright symbol, a drawing character, or a special language symbol. Developers currently use two different techniques to create special characters. FrontPage supports the first method directly by supplying the special characters — but you have to type the second method yourself. Here are the two types of special character entries:

```
<font face="Times New Roman">(c)</font> Copyright, first method
&#169; Copyright, second method
```

The problem with the first method is that it assumes the users have the font you selected installed on their machines. When you choose a common font, chances are good that a user will have the required font, but some users are going to see something other than the intended symbol. To add a special symbol using this technique, choose Insert⇨Symbol. When you see the Symbol dialog box shown in Figure 1-5, select the character you want to use and then click Insert. FrontPage adds the symbol for you. Click Close to close the Symbol dialog box.

Figure 1-5:
Insert
special
symbols by
carefully
selecting a
common
font.

The second technique is the official standards-recognized approach, but using this technique requires more effort on your part. The International Standards Organization (ISO) 8859-1 chart at `http://home.online.no/~pethesse/charcodes.html` contains most of the symbols you need. Locate the symbol you want to add in the chart and type the special symbol number. For example, you type `&#169` to display a copyright symbol.

Adding Banners

A *banner* is text that can include a decorative element. It acts as a heading or title for your Web page. You can add a banner to your Web site in a number of ways. The easiest method is to create a level-1 header (`<h1>` tag) and type some text between the beginning and end of the tag. Many Web sites use this approach because it's easy and guaranteed to work with all browsers — the problem is that it isn't very automatic. You must type a new banner for every page you create.

A second approach is to create a standard graphic that appears on every page. This method relieves you of having to come up with a new banner for every page — and it tends to tie together all the Web pages on a site. However, if you choose to change the graphic, you must change it on every page individually.

FrontPage has a way around these issues. You add yet another in a series of webbot tags to your code to make the header changes automatic. Here's an example of a webbot tag for a text banner.

```
<!--webbot bot="Navigation"
          S-Type="banner"
          S-Orientation="horizontal"
          S-Rendering="text" -->
```

The bot attribute specifies a Navigation webbot. The S-Type attribute specifies this is a banner, while the S-Orientation attribute tells you that the banner appears horizontally and the S-Rendering attribute tells you this is a text banner. What the webbot doesn't tell you is where the text for the banner comes from. FrontPage creates this text automatically when you place the page within the navigational structure of a Web site. The text is the <title> tag, which means that all pages automatically get the right banner.

To use this technique, choose Insert⇨Page Banner. You see the Page Banner Properties dialog box. Then select either the Picture or Text option and click OK. FrontPage adds the webbot into your Web page at the point you select.

Book II
Chapter 1

**Designing Pages
with Controls**

Chapter 2: Working with Forms

In This Chapter

✔ Designing a form

✔ Adding inputs to a form

✔ Creating an application to send data

✔ Creating accessible forms

*M*ost people have used a paper form at one time or another. A form on a Web page performs essentially the same task as any other form you use. The online form gathers all the controls that represent various kinds of information and defines where the information will go once the user completes the form. Unlike paper forms with printed submission instructions, the form on a Web site provides explicit destination details and performs the submission automatically — which means Web page forms are a little less error-prone than the paper variety.

Creating a Simple Form

A form is simply a method of grouping controls, but it does require a special tag. Whether you code a form by hand or use design view, all forms rely on the <form> tag to hold everything together. The easiest way to add a form tag to your application is to choose Insert⇨Form⇨Form. FrontPage automatically creates a form with a Submit and a Reset push-button, which is all you need to use the examples in this chapter.

Displaying the Form toolbar

Normally, to display a toolbar, you just right-click the toolbar area and choose one of the toolbars from the list. Microsoft includes all the common toolbars you need in this list, but the Form toolbar doesn't appear in the list. Working with forms, however, is made easier by using controls on the Form toolbar. To make this toolbar appear on screen, follow these steps:

1. **Select Insert⇨Form.**

   You see a list of form controls, at the top of which is a series of dots.

2. **Hover the mouse pointer over the dots.**

   A message appears: Drag to make this menu float.

3. Drag the menu to the Design area.

The Form toolbar appears. Figure 2-1 shows this toolbar and explains the purpose of each control.

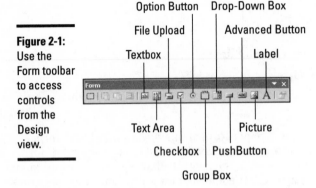

Figure 2-1:
Use the Form toolbar to access controls from the Design view.

Adding and configuring input controls

Typing the code to create an <input> tag by hand isn't a lot of fun. Fortunately, FrontPage provides the controls on the Form toolbar to make things easier. This section discusses a textbox, but you can use the same techniques to add and configure any other control.

Unless you want the textbox to perform a special task, you can usually rely on the features provided in Design view to add the textbox to the form. To create a textbox input control in Design view, follow these steps:

1. Add a new line to your form or placing the cursor next to an existing control.

For details on adding a new line, see Book 2, Chapter 1.

2. Click Textbox on the Form toolbar.

FrontPage creates a new textbox with the default settings. In many cases, you'll want to change these settings (for example, by setting the textbox to a specific size or ensuring that the user can type in only a certain number of characters).

3. Select the newly created textbox in Design view.

Doing so begins the process of configuring the new textbox control.

4. Choose Tag Properties from the <Input> tag entry on the Quick Tag Selector.

The Text Box Properties dialog box appears, as shown in Figure 2-2.

Text Box Properties

Name: MyTextbox

Initial value: Some Special Text

Width in characters: 25   Tab order:

Password field: ○ Yes   ⊙ No

[Style...] [Validate...]   [OK]   [Cancel]

Figure 2-2:
Configure
the textbox
so it meets
your needs.

5. **In the Text Box Properties dialog box, type a name for the textbox in the Name field and provide a default value in the Initial Value field.**

   For more about why naming a textbox is important, see Book 2, Chapter 1.

6. **Change the size of the textbox to match the number of characters you expect most people to type by changing the Size field.**

   Notice that you can change the type of ⟨input⟩ tag to password by setting the Password Field option to Yes. Also, you can optionally set the Tab Order field to control the tabbing order of the form. The Submit button Tab Order field is normally set to 0 so it's the first selected control. The textbox works at this point, but it isn't complete.

7. **Click Validate.**

   The Text Box Validation dialog box appears, as shown in Figure 2-3. The most important validation feature shown in this dialog box is Data Length, which you configure in the next step.

8. **Check Required and type a maximum character count in Max Length.**

   This particular change is also the most browser-friendly change you can make. The other changes in the Text Box Validation dialog box might not work with all browsers, but you should try them with your setup to see whether they will.

You might have noticed that there aren't any settings in the dialog boxes shown in Figure 2-2 or 2-3 for the accesskey or title attributes. Why? Simple — the Design view doesn't include these settings.

The easiest way to add these settings in Design view is to select Edit Tag from the ⟨Input⟩ tag entry on the Quick Tag Selector. When you see the Quick Tag Editor, type the accesskey and title settings into the editor and then press Enter. You'll also need to perform this step on any controls (such as the Submit and Reset buttons) that FrontPage creates for you automatically.

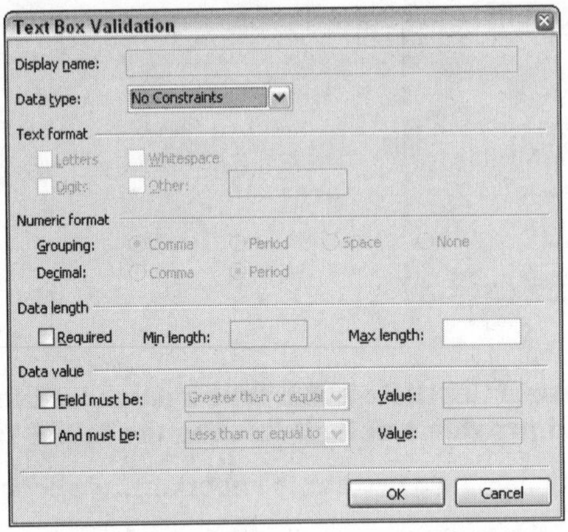

Figure 2-3:
Improve the
security of
your Web
page by
including
validation.

Associating the input control with a label

It's essential to create labels to identify controls that need them. You also want to associate the label with the control. Fortunately, FrontPage makes this task very easy in Design view.

Begin by placing the cursor on the left side of the control (such as a textbox) that you want to identify and type the label text. Highlight the label text and the associated control. Click Label on the Form toolbar and FrontPage creates the label for you. It also automatically associates the label with the control you highlighted.

To ensure that the user knows which access key to use, highlight the letter in the label and click Underline on the Formatting toolbar. Unfortunately, FrontPage still relies on the ⟨u⟩ (underline) tag to perform this task.

Changing <u>s to <span>s

Using the ⟨span⟩ tag makes it easier to add multiple effects to text and enhances accessibility as well. You can easily change the ⟨u⟩ tag to the more flexible ⟨span⟩ tag by selecting Edit Tag from the ⟨u⟩ entry on the Quick Tag Selector. Type **<span>** in place of the ⟨u⟩ in the Quick Tag Editor dialog box. Press Enter. The ⟨u⟩ entry on the Quick Tag Selector changes to a ⟨span⟩ entry.

To underline the letter again, select Tag Properties from the new ⟨span⟩ entry on the Quick Tag Selector. You see the Modify Style dialog box. Choose Format➪Font. You see a Font dialog box. Select Underline and click OK twice. The letter is now underlined using a ⟨span⟩ tag.

Working with Alternative Inputs

You create most simple inputs for a Web page using the `<input>` tag. However, these aren't the only inputs available. Web pages can also use a number of alternative input types including drop-down boxes and text areas. These inputs don't rely on the `<input>` tag.

Creating a drop-down list

The drop-down list is one replacement for option buttons. The biggest benefit of using a drop-down list control is that it requires less screen space; you can use it where space is at a premium. Its biggest disadvantage is that (more often than not) the user can't see all options at one time.

Basic configuration of a drop-down list

To add a drop-down list to your form, create an empty space or place the cursor where you want the drop-down list to appear. Then follow these steps to make some basic configurations:

1. **Click Drop-Down List on the Form toolbar.**

   Although FrontPage creates a blank drop-down list for you at this point, this control has absolutely no functionality unless you configure it.

2. **Start configuring the drop-down list by selecting the control on screen and choosing Tag Properties from the `<select>` tag entry on the Quick Tag Selector.**

   You see a Drop-Down List Properties dialog box similar to the one shown in Figure 2-4 (this one is already filled out).

Figure 2-4:
Configure a
drop-down
list by
adding a
name and
options.

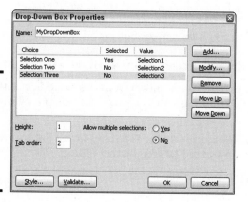

3. **Add a name to the drop-down list so you can access it easily from any scripts you create or use.**

Adding a name also makes it easier to see any selections the user makes when the browser sends data. Two more tasks complete this step:

- Determine whether you want to allow multiple selections.

- Provide a Tab Order value if you want to control tabbing.

4. **Type a value into the Height field to specify how many options the user can see without using this drop-down list.**

Use a value of 1 to create a drop-down list box and a number that matches the number of options you provide for a standard list box.

5. **Click Add to start adding options to the drop-down list box.**

You see the Add Choice dialog box.

6. **Type the text you want the user to see in the Choice field.**

This field can contain spaces if necessary.

7. **If the selection contains multiple words, click Specify Value and type a single word value in the Specify Value field.**

8. **Specify whether this option first appears on-screen as selected.**

You do so by setting the Initial State to Selected or Not Selected. After you've made your choice, click OK.

Make sure that at least one value in the list appears on-screen as selected when the box appears.

Beyond basic configuration of a drop-down list

You change the options for a drop-down list by using the other pushbuttons in the Drop-Down List Properties dialog box. Use the following procedure to perform an advanced drop-down list configuration.

1. **Use the Modify button to change features of the selected option.**

The Remove button deletes an option from the list. Select either Move Up or Move Down when you need to change the position of the selection option in the list.

2. **Change the validation options for the drop-down list by clicking Validate in the Drop-Down List Properties dialog box.**

Doing so makes your form more secure.

3. Check Data Required and type a friendly error message in the Display Name field.

Choosing this option ensures that the user must select one of the items in the list before the browser accepts the form.

Two finishing touches complete your drop-down list. First, make sure you set the `title` and `accesskey` attributes to ensure the user gets all the information needed to use your control. Second, associate a label with the control to identify its purpose.

Defining a text area

Sometimes a textbox doesn't provide enough room to display output or accept some types of input. For example, if you want a user to describe a specific problem, you use a *text area* to ensure that the user has enough space to write. A text area always has at least two lines — and can extend across the entire Web page if necessary. You can add a scrollbar to make it easy to look at text that doesn't fit within the viewing area. To add a text area to your form, follow these steps:

1. Place the cursor on a new line and click Text Area on the Form toolbar.

FrontPage adds the control to the form.

2. Select the Text Properties from the `<textarea>` tag on the Quick Tag Selector.

You see a TextArea Box Properties dialog box.

3. Configure the text area by adding a name to the Name field and some text to the Initial Value field.

4. Size the text area by defining values for the Width in Characters and Number of Lines fields.

5. Be sure to add the usual `title` and `accesskey` values by editing the tag code.

Although it might sound like you should use a text area instead of a textbox for every need, the text area is a lot harder to secure. You should define the maximum length of the field if possible, but making this change isn't always possible. To add a maximum length, click Validate in the TextArea Box Properties dialog box. You see the Text Box Validation dialog box. Check Required and type the maximum number of characters in the Max Length field.

Sending Data

Generally, you want the user to send data to you when you create a form. A form has several configuration settings that determine how the browser sends the data and where the information is sent. FrontPage provides a default form setup that works well for testing, but you need to create a specific setup before you use the form on a *production site* (a site that people are actually using for business).

Understanding the default form settings

The `<form>` tag can appear by itself, but some additional information is required to make the form useful. Here's the default FrontPage `<form>` tag.

```
<form method="POST" action="--WEBBOT-SELF--">
<!--webbot bot="SaveResults"
          U-File="0181/_private/form_results.csv"
          S-Format="TEXT/CSV"
          S-Label-Fields="TRUE" -->
```

This form uses the `POST` method, which means that none of the data appears as part of the URL in the Address field of the browser. A developer can also choose the destination of the data using the `action` attribute. In this case, the `action` attribute relies on a `webbot` to define the remote location. The `bot` attribute defines this as a `SaveResults` webbot.

The `U-File` attribute determines the location of the data on your system. In this case, the data is going to a special folder on the host machine and is named `form_results.csv`. The server saves the data in a Comma-Separated Value (CSV) file.

 You can read this (or any) CSV file with a text editor, but it's easier to work with when you open it in an application designed to read such files. Excel is a good application to use for the task, but you can also import the file into most database applications, including Access and SQL Server.

The `S-Label-Fields` attribute tells the server to save the field names at the top of the list so Excel (or a database manager) knows what field names to use. It pays to include the field values to make it easier to troubleshoot a form that you create.

You must open the example form in a browser to test it — with the result that the Preview view in FrontPage will fail. When you test the example form, try changing all three of the entries. Click Reset and you'll notice the entries automatically change back to their default values. When you click Submit, you see a confirmation appear on-screen. You didn't create this confirmation, it's supplied as part of FrontPage. Open the CSV file and you'll see the values sent from the form.

Sending data to e-mail the FrontPage way

If you have a hosted Web page, one where you don't have access to the server, you might think it's impossible to use forms. Not true: You can use forms on a hosted site. Simply send the output to your e-mail address. To change a FrontPage form to use e-mail as the output destination, choose Tag Properties from the `<form>` tag on the Quick Tag Selector. You see the Form Properties dialog box shown in Figure 2-5.

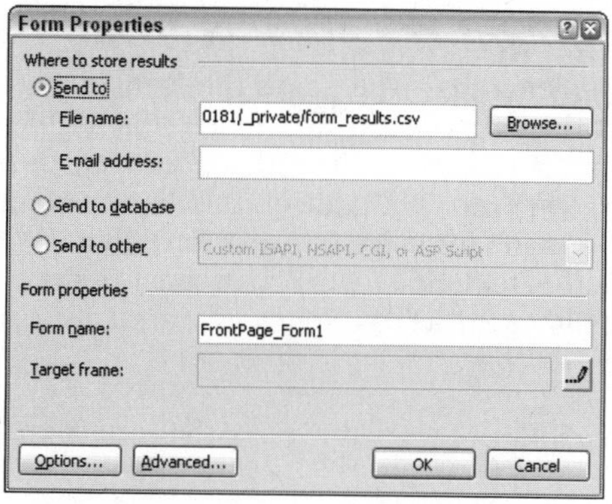

Figure 2-5: Change the destination of a form as needed.

To set this form up for e-mail delivery, follow these steps:

1. **Clear the File Name field and type your e-mail address in the E-mail Address field.**

2. **Type a name in the Form Name field.**

   This entry is important because it appears as part of the e-mail message in most cases.

3. **After you complete the basic setup, click Options.**

   You see the Saving Results dialog box.

4. **Select the E-mail Results tab.**

5. **Select a format for the e-mail.**

   For example, you can send the data as text or as an HTML page. The XML option is best if you plan to put the data into a database or spreadsheet and the application supports XML. Otherwise, you can use one of the text database options.

6. **Type a subject in the E-mail Message Header field or choose the Form Field Name option.**

   The latter option places the name that you typed in the Form Name field earlier into the subject of the e-mail message.

7. Provide a value for the Reply-To Line field.

In most cases, the default option of using the Form Field Name is fine.

8. Click OK twice.

FrontPage sets the form up to use e-mail with a `webbot`.

You'll find this example in the `SendEmail.htm` file of the source code on this book's companion Web site.

Sending data to e-mail the standard way

Unfortunately, FrontPage-generated Web pages that send a message using e-mail might not work with every hosted site. When this problem occurs, you can easily transform the page to use standardized transmission techniques. The `SendEmail2.htm` file (available on this book's companion Web site — refer to the Introduction for more information) contains the code for this technique. To make this technique work, you must remove the form-related `webbot` entries. Change the FrontPage-generated code so it looks like this:

```
<form action="mailto:JMueller@mwt.net?subject=Sample Email"
      method="post"
      name="EmailResponseForm"
      enctype="text/plain">
```

The `action` attribute points to my e-mail address and it includes a subject of Sample Email. The method the form uses is still `POST`, rather than `GET`. The name of the form is `EmailResponseForm`. The `enctype` attribute is very important because this technique only works well as text. You can try other encoding methods, but they don't work as well.

When you click Submit, your browser warns you that it's sending the form using e-mail. After you click OK, the browser displays the recipient of the message and the message subject. Finally, it sends the form as an e-mail message. The recipient receives the data in fieldname and value pairs; a script can easily convert these into usable information.

Sending data to a server

Sending a form to a file or e-mail address means that you must work with it in some way. FrontPage also makes it possible to send the data directly to a location on your server that's designed to store the data automatically. The two choices, in this case, are using a database for storage or letting the output from the current page act as input to a script. FrontPage even includes special handlers for discussion and registration forms. All such methods do something automatically with the data.

To use the database object, select Send to Database in the Form Properties dialog box. Click Options. You see the Options for Saving Results to Database dialog box. In most cases, you need to create a new database to hold the data from this form, so click Create Database. When FrontPage finds a copy of SQL Server, it automatically sets up all the required tables for you and tells you about their location. Once you set up a database, click Update Database to add any modifications you make to the form to the database automatically.

You have three options when working with scripts: a custom page written in languages such as Active Server Pages (ASP), the discussion handler, and the registration handler. When working with a script, click Options and you see the Options for Custom Form Handler dialog box. Type a custom action string in the Action field, a posting method in the Method field, and the technique used to transfer the data in the Encoding Type field.

When working with discussion or registration forms, you must provide some configuration information by clicking Options. You provide a name and location for the discussion in the Options for Discussion Form Handler dialog box. You provide a Web server name, username, and password when working with the Options for Registration Form Handler dialog box.

Deciding whether to GET or POST data

As mentioned earlier, using the POST method ensures that none of the data submitted with a form appears as part of the URL in the Address field of the browser. In many cases, it doesn't matter whether you use the GET or POST method for a form. Both techniques send data to the server. Any server-side coding must know what to expect from the form, so the techniques aren't interchangeable, but the results are the same.

Many developers prefer the POST method because the browser's Address field remains clean and it's less likely that the user will modify the contents of the data sent to the server. Unfortunately, the POST technique really doesn't keep the data much safer — a determined cracker can still access it. The POST technique is best used on sites where you want to maintain some level of data hiding.

Some Web sites actually encourage use of the GET method because they want users to maintain the list of values they sent to the server. For example, search pages often rely on the values stored as part of a URL to return the user to the same place without having the fill out the search form again. In fact, some users rely on this behavior to modify the URL to obtain more precise results — or even create a list of URLs on a custom Web page.

Making Forms Accessible

It's relatively easy to make a form accessible when you create the controls by hand because you can see the `title` attribute needed to display pop-up text. You can easily see where to place an underline to make the label text associated with a control match the `accesskey` attribute of that control. When you make the `accesskey` value equal to (say) the letter A, then you must underline an A in the label text as well.

As you might imagine, using the Design view makes creating a Web page faster and easier. You don't have to worry about the functional control code for the most part, but these accessibility elements are easy to forget when you don't see the code that FrontPage produces. One way to overcome this problem is to work in Split view.

When you see that FrontPage doesn't provide access to a feature you need to code for the Web page, you can add it manually using the Code window displayed in Split view. This technique is actually best — and easiest — because you get the benefit of automated design, yet retain control over the final code. Unfortunately, using Split view means you don't see as much of the Design window and might not get the full view of your Web page while you're working out its details.

Fortunately, FrontPage offers some automation for accessibility issues. Choose Tools➪Accessibility and you see the Accessibility dialog box. Click Check and you see the results as shown in Figure 2-6. Note that Figure 2-6 shows the dialog box after running the test — the action items in your dialog box could differ.

Figure 2-6:
Test your Web page for accessibility before making it public.

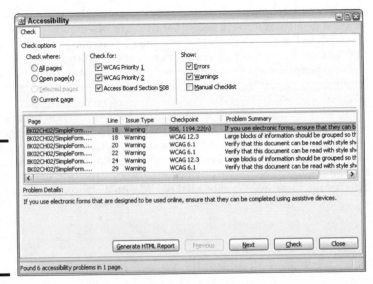

Using the default setup, the example page (`SampleForm.htm`) generates six accessibility errors. Create a checklist for yourself by clicking Generate HTML Report to make finding the problems easier. The report for the example page appears in `AccessibilityReport.htm`. You should consider this test the minimum you can do to ensure your page is accessible. Real-world testing with users is better.

Make sure you test the page with accessibility devices and software whenever possible. Microsoft supplies accessibility software as part of the Windows Accessibility Options. Turn the screen reader on as you check the page. Close your eyes so you have to hear the words, rather than view them as part of the complete environment. Ask yourself whether you can understand the page based on what the screen reader provided — many Web pages can't pass this simple test.

**Book II
Chapter 2**

Working with Forms

Chapter 3: Working with Tables

In This Chapter

✔ Creating a table

✔ Creating a table caption

✔ Designing accessible tables

✔ Working with layout tables and cells

*W*hen you present data to other people, you want to make it as easy as possible for them to understand it. Many kinds of data work best in tabular form. Placing such data in paragraphs hides the information; using a list makes the presentation look messy (you end up adding highlighting and other elements to differentiate the data types). A table separates the data elements and makes them easy to use. The rows and columns make the data look neat and easy to understand.

Web-page tables fulfill the same purpose as tables you create on a piece of paper. The advantage to a Web page table is that you can move things around as you build your presentation, without having to erase. When a column no longer fulfills a purpose, you can remove it. Sometimes you might want to rearrange the information so that someone visiting your Web page sees the most important information first. Old data is easy to remove — simply delete the row.

Using tables also makes it easier to move information from a local database to your Web site. Your database manager also uses rows and columns to store information, so tables allow you to create an exact representation. In fact, some Database Management Systems (DBMSs) actually include features to output data as HTML tables — which makes them easy to incorporate directly into your Web site without adding much code.

Defining a Table

Tables consist of rows and columns. The columns define the kinds of data you want to present. For example, if you want to display a table of associates, you could create a series of columns that include the person's name, address, affiliation, and anything else you feel is important. Database developers recognize table columns as *fields*. The rows contain individual instances of all the data defined by the columns. In the table-of-associates example, you could create a single row for each associate in your list. Database developers recognize table rows as *records*.

The first step in defining a table is to decide what kind of information it contains so you can describe the columns to FrontPage. When working with a database, you already know the column names — they are the same as the fields in the database.

Tables you develop from scratch should include one column for each kind of data you want to present. Place each data element in a separate column so it's easy to see. For example, don't place the entire address of an associate in one column; include separate columns for address, city, state, and ZIP code. You might even provide more than one address column in case an associate has more address information than you can fit into one line.

After you decide what your table will look like, click Insert Table on the Standard toolbar. You see a grid as shown in Figure 3-1. Select the number of cells that you want your table to include. Don't worry if you can't select enough cells at first — it's easy to resize the table later. You normally want to create two rows for your table. The first row contains the headers, while the second row contains the first record. (The data rows increase as you add information to the table.) Click the last cell in the selection. FrontPage creates a new table at the current cursor position.

Figure 3-1:
Select the
number of
rows and
columns
you want in
the initial
table.

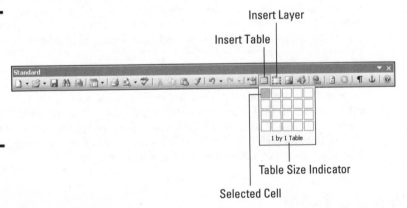

Setting the table properties

After you create a table, you want to set the table properties so the table works well with your data. To set the table properties, right-click the table and choose Table Properties from the context menu. You see the Table Properties dialog box shown in Figure 3-2.

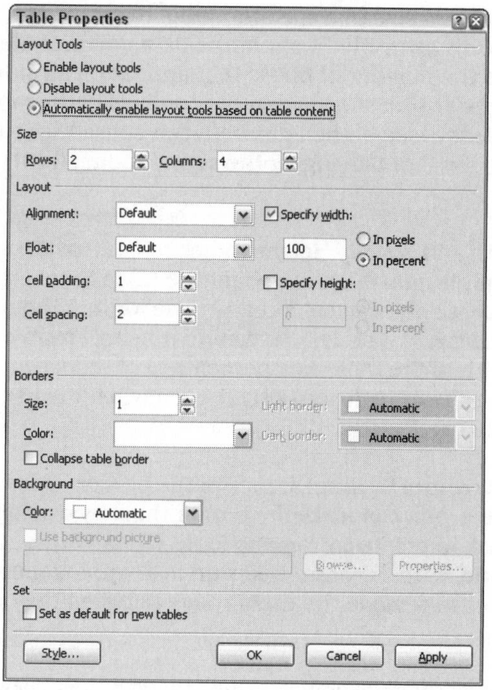

Book II
Chapter 3

Working with Tables

Figure 3-2:
Set the table
properties
to match
your data
needs.

These settings apply to the table as a whole, not to the individual cells. The Layout Tools options refer to a special kind of table setup discussed in the "Using Layout Tables and Cells" section of this chapter. You use these tools to modify some table properties using Design view, rather than with the settings in the Table Properties dialog box or hand coding.

Use the Size options to modify the number of rows and columns in your table. As your data grows, so does the table.

The Layout options are a little hard to understand until you work with them for a while. When FrontPage creates your table, it encloses the table in a ⟨div⟩ tag. The ⟨div⟩ tag lets you group things together so the entire table is a unit. The Alignment field controls where items in the ⟨div⟩ tag appear. When you set this value to Left, all the elements appear on the left side of the display.

Within the ⟨div⟩ tag is a ⟨table⟩ tag that defines the actual table. The ⟨table⟩ tag encloses all of the table elements. The Float field controls the alignment of the table. When you set this value to Default, the alignment of the table is the same as the alignment of the other elements in the ⟨div⟩ tag, which is controlled by the Alignment field. Setting this field to any other value controls the alignment of the table independently of the other ⟨div⟩ tag elements.

Unless you set the column size to a specific value, the table automatically sizes the individual cells as needed to hold the data you provide. The Cell Padding field defines the number of pixels that appear on all sides of a data entry so it doesn't appear squashed within the confines of the table. The Cell Spacing field controls the size of the lines between cells. A larger number produces a larger grid without changing the actual room allowed around each data value.

Use the Specify Width and Specify Height values to control the actual size of the table. For example, you might not want the table to take up the entire width of the Web page, so you can set a certain size for it. Although it's uncommon to control the height of a table, you can do it using FrontPage. The best idea is to set the width of the table as a percentage of the viewing area. Using this technique ensures your page looks right even when the user has a relatively small viewing area.

The Borders options control the appearance of the border — the line around the outside of the table. You can make the border thick by changing the size. Make the border thick to create a dramatic look. When you set the Color property to Automatic, a thick border takes on a 3D appearance. Check Collapse Table Border to remove the extra space between the border and the table grid.

When your Web page is up and running, it has to work seamlessly with the users' browsers or the table won't display properly. Some Border and Background options work only if you set browser compatibility to work with Internet Explorer only. For example, you can't set the Dark Border and Light Border properties if you don't have the compatibility set for Internet Explorer 5.0. To change browser compatibility, follow these steps:

1. **Choose Tools⇨Browser Compatibility.**

You see the Browser Compatibility dialog box.

2. **Click Change.**

You see the Page Options dialog box.

3. **Set the Browsers field to Microsoft Internet Explorer Only.**

4. **Select 4.0 Browsers and Later in the Browser Versions field.**

5. **Click OK to close the Page Options dialog box.**

6. **Click Close to close the Browser Compatibility dialog box.**

The Background options affect the area behind the text. You can set a background color or add an image. When using an image, make sure the image is light enough that it won't affect the user's ability to see the text. FrontPage doesn't provide the watermark feature in this case, so the user sees precisely what the picture contains.

Setting the cell properties

Tables also have properties for rows, and individual cells. You set all these properties using the cell properties that FrontPage provides. To select an entire row or a column, move the cursor near the border until the shape changes to an arrow and click. FrontPage selects the entire row or column. You can also drag the mouse along the row or column to select it.

The first change you always make to a table is to add column headings. Select the first row, right-click the table, and choose Cell Properties from the context menu. When you see the Cell Properties dialog box shown in Figure 3-3, check the Header Cell option. Click OK to close the dialog box. FrontPage creates a column header row.

**Book II
Chapter 3**

Working with Tables

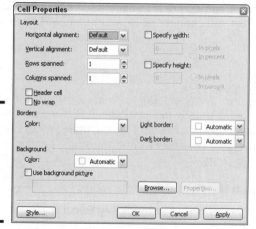

Figure 3-3:
Create a column header row by setting the cell properties.

The header row differs from the data row by the tag used for the individual cells. A row begins with the `<tr>` tag. A header row uses the `<th>` tag for each cell within the row, while a data row uses the `<td>` tag.

Positioning data within the cells is important to the appearance of the table — not the content — so (in most cases) you can use the default alignment options so the text appears as it would in a book. Remember, however, that tables don't have to contain just text. Developers place links, pictures, and other elements in those cells. Sometimes these data elements do require special alignment that you control by using the Horizontal Alignment and Vertical Alignment fields. For example, pictures normally look best when centered in the cell.

Web browsers assume that you want to space the cells in a table evenly, unless a particular column has a significant amount of data to display. In some cases, you want to ensure that a column receives a specific amount of space, as when, for example, the column contains long words that you don't want to appear on more than one line. Use the Specify Height and Specific Width options to control cell spacing.

Generally, how you specify column height and width should fit the type(s) of item you want to use. You have two methods available:

✦ Use a specific number for items that require only a certain amount of space (such as graphics that can't shrink or grow).

✦ Use percentages for items that should receive a larger percentage of the space (for example, columns containing a lot of text).

As with the table options, you can specify border and background settings for an individual cell. Most of the special effects, such as the use of individual light and dark border colors, are Internet Explorer specific, which means they aren't active unless you change the browser compatibility settings.

Adding a Caption

Many developers use the `<caption>` tag to create a caption for a table; you can still add this tag manually in FrontPage. A better and easier approach, however, is to create a heading for the table within the `<div>` tag that Microsoft provides. To create a caption using a header and the `<div>` tag, follow these steps:

1. **Place the cursor on the right side of the table.**

You see just the `<div>` tag on the Quick Tag Selector.

2. **Choose one of the heading levels from the Style list on the Format toolbar.**

Most developers find that a heading level 3 or 4 works well as a table caption. FrontPage now creates a header for the table. The alignment of the header depends on the layout settings you use for the table.

3. **Type the table caption.**

Making Tables Accessible

Tables require a little extra work to make them accessible to a broad range of people. Most of the required additions appear within the `<table>` tag. To make the essential changes, place the cursor anywhere within the table and choose Edit Tag from the `<table>` tag entry on the Quick Tag Selector. You see the Quick Tag Editor.

The example table used for the discussion in previous sections already contains a number of attributes within the `<table>` tag. To these attributes, you need to add a `summary` and a `title` attribute. The `summary` attribute describes the content of the table. (Screen readers provide this information to users who can't see your table.) Make the `summary` attribute relatively short, but descriptive.

The `title` attribute provides additional information in the form of a pop-up that everyone can use. Make this attribute descriptive enough to answer the questions that most users are likely to have about *why the table is important,* rather than what's in it.

Using Layout Tables and Cells

Creating Web pages that display items in order in a straight line gets your message across. This simple structure is very easy to maintain and you don't have to worry as much about accessibility issues. However, sometimes you want to add a special layout to a Web page to help organize the information in an aesthetically pleasing way. You might have groups of information about one focused topic that you want to present, or you might want to provide navigational aids in a separate section of the page. Some developers like to use graphics to convey part of their message and want to see the graphics mixed with the text.

No matter what reason you have for displaying information in a form other than the usual straightforward layout, FrontPage makes the task easier with Layout Tables and Cells. You use this feature to create cells that hold bits and pieces of information, and organize the layout of a particular page around a table made up of those cells. Some Web pages you see online use this feature to good effect.

Using this feature also reduces the accessibility of your Web page. When you choose to use this technique, you also choose to keep some people from using your Web page, which is why you want to avoid using it unless necessary.

Adding the layout

Always add the layout to your Web page as the first element after you define the Web page properties. It's very hard to add a layout to a Web page after you have data in place. In addition, adding the layout before you add content means you can plan the content format better and get the full benefits of using a layout.

The Layout Tables and Cells feature simplifies adding a layout to your Web page. Just follow these steps:

1. Choose Table⇨Layout Tables and Cells.

You see the Layout Tables and Cells Task Pane shown in Figure 3-4. (Normally the Task Pane appears on the right side of the display — the screen shot shows the Layout Tables and Cells Task Pane floating free so you can see it better.)

2. Examine the standard layouts.

When you hover the mouse pointer over each standard layout at the bottom of the Task Pane, FrontPage tells you about the layout's elements:

- The first entry in the table tells FrontPage not to use any layout at all.

- The second entry is a full-page layout, which appears not to have any features.

- The third entry consists of a corner for a logo, the header, the left side for links, and the body area. (Many Web pages use layouts based on this setting, as does the example given here. You can choose any layout that works with your data.)

3. Click the layout that suits your purpose.

FrontPage adds the layout to your current Web page. Figure 3-5 shows the example layout, which includes four major measurements (two rows and two columns); you see four sizing labels.

4. Click a sizing label.

A context menu appears. You get two options for changing the size of the row or column:

- You can set the row or column so it automatically stretches to accommodate the content you add.

- You can add a column-spacer image that imposes a fixed width on the column.

To display the sizing labels whenever you need them, click the `<table>` tag on the Quick Tag Selector.

Modifying the layout settings

Before you begin adding data to the new layout, set up the layout to accept the data correctly. You need to tweak these settings as you work on the Web page design, but getting the basic setup in place helps you standardize your pages so they all have a similar appearance.

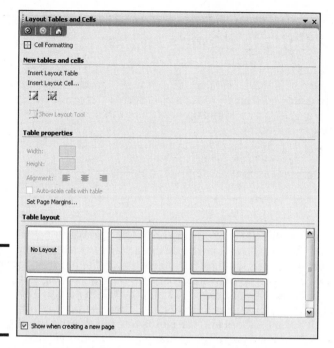

Figure 3-4:
Select a
layout for
your Web
page.

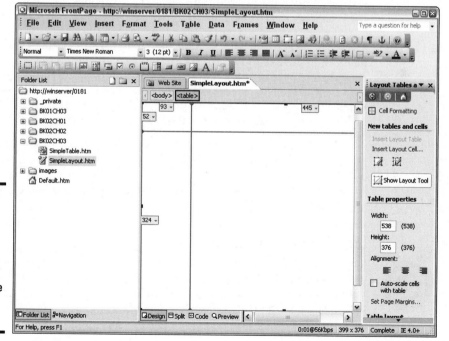

Figure 3-5:
Use the
layout
features to
customize
the
appearance
on your
Web page.

Adding the column spacer image

The column spacer image (essentially a transparent picture) is a special file that FrontPage adds for you. It ensures that the spacing you specify for a particular page element stays that size, even when the user resizes the browser window. Previous editions of FrontPage don't include this feature — the Web page author actually had to create a transparent image

by hand and place it on the page. The problem is significant enough that you can find Web pages such as the one at FrontLook.com (`www.frontlook.com/newsletters/tip 3-9.asp`) that explain how to create a column spacer image for previous versions of FrontPage.

Begin by setting the page size using the Height and Width fields in the Layout Tables and Cells window. (I normally use a standard-size display area based on a screen 800 pixels wide by 600 pixels high.) The browser takes up some of this space, so you have to size your Web page accordingly. In general, this means setting the Height field to 423 and the Width field to 774 to accommodate a standard Internet Explorer display. These settings assume the user displays all three toolbars and the status bar, but doesn't use the Explorer Bar. It also assumes the user has a standard-size font installed. The default FrontPage settings assume the user has one of the standard Explorer Bars installed, which is the major difference between my suggested settings and the FrontPage default settings.

The example actually uses smaller Height and Width settings to accommodate the 18 pixel margins. To ensure the page fits on one screen, you must account for the size of the margins, borders, and other features you add to your page (assuming seeing everything in one screen matters). Consequently, the example works with a width of 738 (774 – 18 pixels for the left border – 18 pixels for the right border) and a height of 387 (423 – 18 pixels for the top border – 18 pixels for the bottom border).

The next step is to set the margins for your Web page. Adding a margin makes it easier for the user to see the content and ensures that none of the content flows off the ends of the viewing area. To modify the margins, click Set Page Margins in the Layout Tables and Cells window. You see the Page Properties dialog box shown in Figure 3-6.

Notice that all these measurements are in pixels — it's more accurate than any other measurement you can use when you're using a computer to lay out a page. A good rule to use for converting pixels to inches is to define 1 inch of screen space as 72 pixels. So, when you want to set a ½-inch margin, set the number of pixels to 36. Although you can't create precise, universal measurements on a Web page — in part because pixel size can vary from one user's monitor to the next — this measurement is close enough to cover most cases. The example uses ¼-inch margins, so I set the border fields to 18 pixels.

After you set the page size and margins, you set the column and rows sizes. For the layout used in the example, you normally want to set the corner size first because it normally contains a company logo or other form of identification. The other areas take up the remaining space.

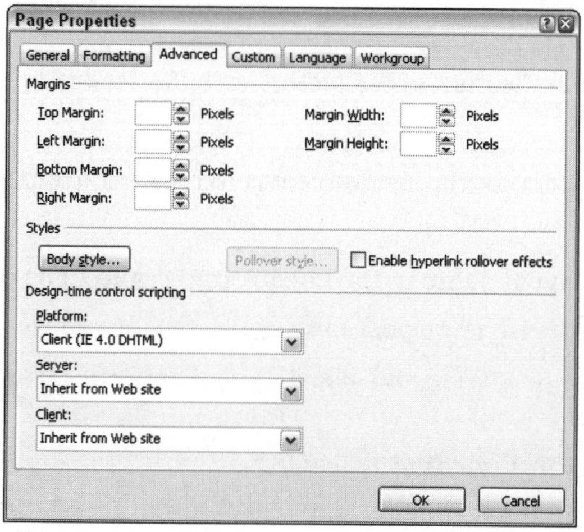

Book II
Chapter 3

Working with Tables

Figure 3-6:
Set page margins to help users see your Web page content.

To set the size of the corner, follow these steps:

1. **Choose Set Column Width from the sizing label marked 93 in Figure 3-5.**

   You see the Column Properties dialog box.

2. **Type the width of your logo into the Column Width field and click OK.**

3. **Next, select Set Row Height from the sizing label marked 52 in Figure 3-5.**

   You see the Row Properties dialog box.

4. **Type the height of the logo into the Row Height field and click OK.**

To ensure that you don't waste the remaining space, make sure you set the size of the remaining column and row to take up the rest of the space. For example, when you set aside a 72-pixel-by-72 pixel logo area on a 774 by 423 pixel page, you need to set the remaining column to use 702 pixels (774 – 72) and the remaining row to use 351 pixels (423 – 72). When you use a more complicated layout, you'll need to set the column and row sizes for other cells within the layout.

Creating new cells

The basic four-cell layout (refer to Figure 3-5) provides space for a logo in the upper left corner, a heading of some sort at the top, links on the left side, and the content you want to provide (body area). You might want to provide additional layout for a picture or other content on your Web site, which means adding cells to the existing layout.

The example discussed in this section adds a picture square in the upper-left corner of the body area. Unfortunately, that would mean the layout has a rectangular area cut out of the square cell that makes up the body area. To wrap content around the cut-out area, you need to create to more cells. The first such cell appears to the right of the picture cell; the second appears below both of those cells.

The easiest way to approach this problem is to create the upper and lower areas first:

1. **Click Insert Layout Table in the Layout Tables and Cells window.**

   FrontPage creates a new layout table consisting of a single cell.

2. **Right-click the new table and select Table Properties from the context menu.**

   You see the Table Properties dialog box.

3. **Set the Row property to 2 (for upper and lower areas), the Specify Width field to match the current body area width, and the Specify Height field to match the current body area height.**

4. **Click OK.**

   FrontPage creates the new upper and lower areas. You should size the two new areas to match the picture height and the remaining content area.

Now create the right and left areas of the upper section:

1. **Place the cursor in the upper section and Click Insert Layout Table in the Layout Tables and Cells window.**

   FrontPage adds another single-cell layout table.

2. **Right-click the new layout table and select Table Properties.**

   You see the Table Properties dialog box.

3. **This time set the Columns field to 2, the Width field to 720, and the Height field to the picture height.**

4. **Size the first column to accept the picture and the second column to take up the remaining content area.**

Figure 3-7 shows a typical view of all the example page's features, with the various sections labeled.

Adding a header and footer

A header provides content at the top of a cell, while a footer provides content at the bottom of a cell. The header and footer aren't the same as a Page Banner. A Page Banner is a `webbot` that appears within a specific cell in your Web page and is based on the title of the page. You must make the page part of the navigation for the Web site to make the Page Banner work. A header and footer accept whatever text you type.

To add a header, footer, or both to a cell, follow these steps:

1. **Select the cell and choose Cell Formatting in the Layout Tables and Cells window.**

The Task Pane switches to the Cell Formatting window.

2. **Click Cell Header and Footer.**

The window changes to show the header and footer for this cell.

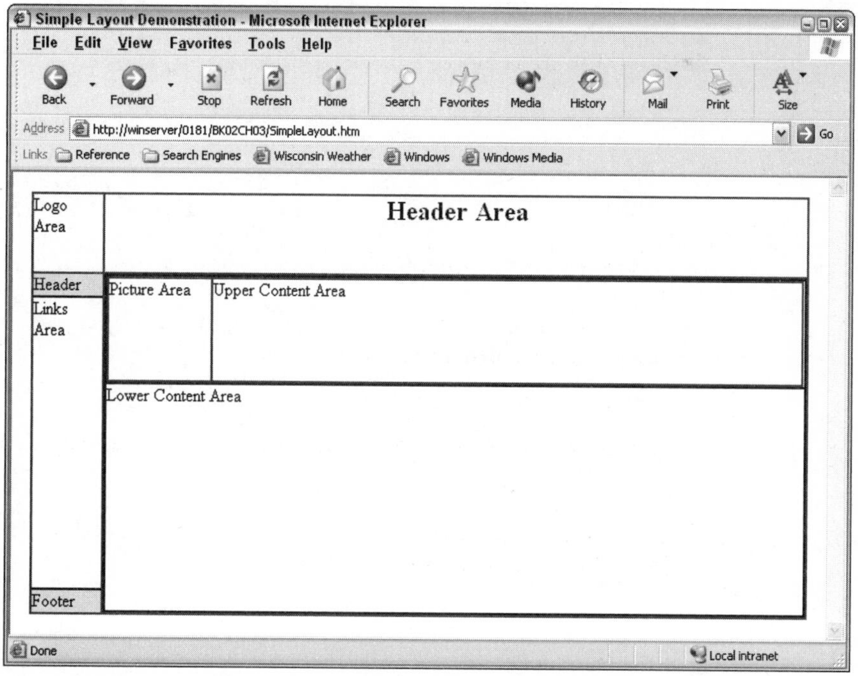

Book II
Chapter 3

Working with
Tables

Figure 3-7:
Creating a complex setup is relatively easy.

3. **Check Show Header or Show Footer as needed.**

   You see the header or footer added to the cell.

4. **Set the new header or footer Background Color, Border Width, and Border Color options as needed.**

5. **Type the header or footer in the new areas that FrontPage created.**

   Figure 3-7 shows a header and footer added to the links area of the page.

Chapter 4: Working with Frames

In This Chapter

✔ Using frames effectively

✔ Designing with frames

✔ Changing a frame layout

✔ Designing with inline frames

✔ Developing frames with accessibility in mind

*F*rames are one of the oldest Web technologies for organizing informa-tion on-screen. They work because the idea behind them is very simple. A main page acts as a container or frameset for a number of child pages or frames. The main page controls the organization of each frame and each child controls the content for an area of the display. Visually, you can't really differentiate frames from other forms of page organization, but the actual code for a frame is simpler than using techniques such as tables.

Developers often find frames far more convenient to use than other methods; for example, frames are easier to create and modify than tables. FrontPage pro-vides special features that makes using frames a drag-and-drop experience — seldom do you need to resort to writing a lot of code by hand. In short, frames make it easy to create great-looking Web pages in a very short time and main-tain those pages with relative ease, especially with the features that FrontPage provides.

However, not everyone is happy about using frames. Many public Web sites have stopped using frames because they present some user challenges (for example, they can confuse screen readers and cause script errors). Although frames are probably acceptable for a corporate Web site, avoid using them on a public site unless you take precautions to make them user-friendly.

Reasons to Use Frames

The main reason to use frames is to organize data using a technique that is more flexible and less error-prone than complex techniques such as tables. A series of frames can present information in a way that makes each element completely independent of every other element. For example, when the con-tent you provide in a frame is too large, the frame automatically creates a scrollbar so you can move around and see everything the developer provides.

Because frames are an older technology, most browsers support them. Unlike some organizational techniques, they don't tend to present you with weird results. Each frame stays put within the frameset; you don't need to tweak the content to fit as you would if you were using tables.

FrontPage makes frames easy to use by providing templates — structures you can use to display the data consistently. Normally, you don't even have to worry about creating the frame-specific code (even though it's wise to know about the tags used to create frames so you can make small modifications and repairs as needed). All you really need are the FrontPageWeb pages — standard pages without extra coding — used to house the content of the frameset.

Creating a Web Page with Frames

You must create two types of pages when working with frames. The type of page you create depends on what you want your Web page to do:

✦ One page type uses the `<frameset>` tag as a container for individual frames. Each frame relies on a `<frame>` tag to reference the Web page that contains the content you want to appear in that location.

✦ The other page type is a standard Web page. All it contains is, well, the *content* you want to display within the frame.

Defining the main page

Always create the main page — the one with the frameset — first; all other design decisions rely on your frameset selections. To create a main page, follow these steps:

1. **Use File⇨New to display the New window in the Task Pane.**

2. **Click More Page Templates in the New Page section of the New window.**

You see the Page Templates dialog box.

3. **Click Frames Pages.**

You see a list of frame-page templates, as shown in Figure 4-1. This is a list of *main pages* with framesets, not the content pages you create later.

4. **Select the template you want to use and click OK to create the page. (The example uses the Banner and Contents template.)**

FrontPage creates the new page for you. Figure 4-2 shows how the new template appears.

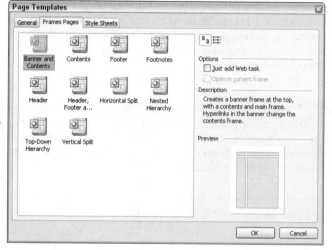

Figure 4-1:
Select a template that reflects the organization you want to use.

Book II
Chapter 4

Working with
Frames

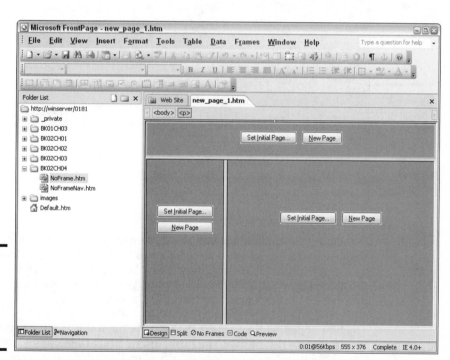

Figure 4-2:
Add new pages to the frames in the template.

Before you go any further, save the new page. Set the page properties and perform any required initial configuration. Special configuration items appear on the Frames tab of the Page Properties dialog box (which you access by right-clicking the page and selecting Page Properties from the context menu).

Set the Frame Spacing property to the number of pixels you want to separate individual frames. (Generally, you can use a value of 96 pixels for each inch of screen space; although, this value isn't necessarily accurate on every machine.) Clear the Show Borders check box if you don't want users to see borders between frames.

Customizing frame properties

The template you use makes certain assumptions about the design of your Web page. For example, Microsoft had to define a generic frame size. You might find that these settings don't meet your needs. In addition, you should define some frame properties to ensure users can completely enjoy your efforts. To customize the frame settings, right-click the frame you want to modify and choose Frame Properties from the context menu. You see the Frame Properties dialog box shown in Figure 4-3.

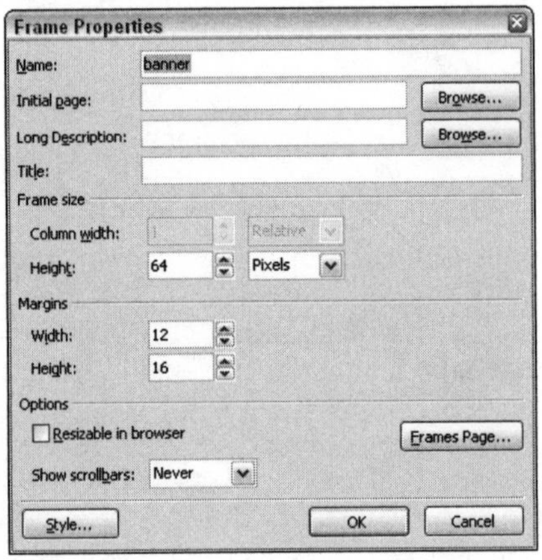

Figure 4-3:
Change
the frame
properties
to meet
specific
needs.

Depending on which frame you select, some features might not be available because they have no effect on the frame's functionality. (Unavailable features appear grayed out in the resulting dialog box.) For example, when you select the banner frame in a three-frame setup, it doesn't provide a Column Width property setting because the frame fills the entire column.

The first adjustment you make is to ensure the frame is large enough to accommodate the content you provide by setting the Column Width and Height fields in the Frame Size area. Setting the values to a percentage ensures the page scales well when viewed in a smaller browser. However, using a precise number of pixels ensures critical content won't get squeezed in an area that's too small. Use the Width and Height fields in the Margins area to control the spacing of the field content. These settings are always expressed in pixels.

As a minimum, you should provide a description of the frame in the Title field so users of assistive technology know what purpose the frame serves. When a short description doesn't provide enough information, make sure you create a description on a separate (simple, non-frame) Web page and place the URL in the Long Description field.

Some browsers support resizable frames. When you check Resizable in Browser, the user normally has a chance to resize the frame as needed to see content. To ensure that the user can see content even if the resizing feature doesn't work, make sure you select either If Needed or Always in the Show Scrollbars field. The only time you don't want to select this option is when the size of the content is fixed (for example, when you display a logo).

Adding pages to the frameset

After you perform the initial configuration steps, you can begin adding pages to the frames that this main page provides. You must create new pages for these frames unless you have the required content already defined. To use existing content, click Set Initial Page in Design view.

One important difference between the Design view and the Preview view for frames is that Preview view doesn't allow access to any of the buttons.

When FrontPage displays an Insert Hyperlink dialog box, select the existing Web page you want to use and click OK. You see the page added to the selected frame.

To create a new page for the frame, click New Page. FrontPage displays a new page directly in the selected frame of the main page. You might find this confusing at first, but the technique works very well because you see the page as it appears in the frame, rather than as an individual entity (where design can become difficult). To save this new page so you can configure it before you add content, click Save. FrontPage displays a special Save As dialog box, as shown in Figure 4-4.

This dialog box has several special features that are worth noting. Here is a summary of the most important features:

+ When the Base Location property, located on the General tab of the Page Properties dialog box, is configured correctly, FrontPage knows exactly where to save the new frame page.

+ The picture on the right side of the dialog box shows which frame you're saving. When you save multiple frames, the picture shows the current page.

+ FrontPage displays the Save As dialog box once for each new page you save. Use the picture to ensure that you save the correct elements and have given them the right names.

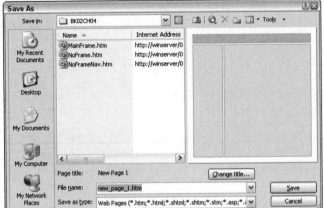

Figure 4-4:
Save and
configure
frame pages
as you
create them.

Configuring a frame page is a little different from configuring other Web pages. The following steps show why:

1. **Set the file properties as usual (right-click the file in the Folder List and select Properties).**

2. **Configure the Web page by right-clicking its frame in the main page, and then select Page Properties.**

You see the same Page Properties dialog box as you normally see when configuring a Web page with one important change — the Default Target Frame property now contains `Contents` as its value (FrontPage sets this value for you automatically).

3. **Finish configuring the Page Properties dialog box as you normally do.**

Add any new pages to your main page by using this same technique.

The size of a frame can vary in response to the browser settings that a user selects. The frameset automatically resizes the frames unless you specify a particular size — and you should do so. Although users often expect a content frame to include scrollbars when the browser uses a small page size, scrollbars don't work well in some areas (such as the banner for the page). Sometimes the user expects a vertical scrollbar but not a horizontal scrollbar (or vice versa); for example, when the user views a list of links, a vertical scrollbar is quite acceptable. Test the page using various browsers' sizes to ensure that your frame usage meets user expectations.

Using the No Frames view

Not every browser supports frames and even those that do usually provide some means of turning off frame support. The reasons vary, but it usually comes down to a matter of a user's personal choice or need. The `<noframes>` tag offers a way to address this problem by presenting a non-framed page to view your Web site. You can see the content of the `<noframes>` tag in the No Frames view. (The No Frames view tab appears between the Split and Code view tabs at the bottom of the window when you work with a Web page that relies on frames.) Unfortunately, the Microsoft-provided response — This page uses frames, but your browser doesn't support them. — has all the tact and pizzazz of a slap in the face; the user can't even view the content on your site.

Depending on what you want to do, you can use the No Frames view to create alternatives to the frames that you normally provide. The easiest solution is to create a new presentation that includes a header, a simple message, and a list of the links to the frames normally found on your site. In this presentation, you should provide an explanation of what each link provides. To add the links to the page, drag the file entry from the Folder List and drop it where you want the link to appear. Figure 4-5 shows one approach to this problem.

Book II
Chapter 4

Working with Frames

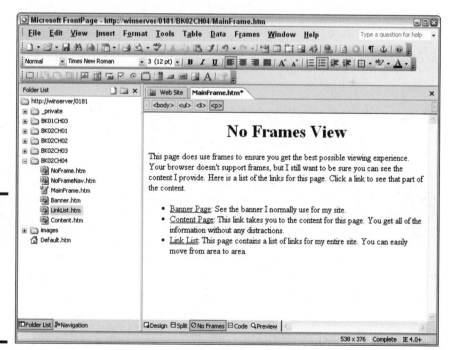

Figure 4-5:
Create a friendly and useful view for browsers that don't support frames.

Another approach to the problem of not having frames is to create a no-frames version of the content page — and then use a script to redirect users to that area. This approach has the advantage of letting you add a special, no-frames hyperlink to the content page that directs a user to the frameless version of the content. The only problem is that not everyone turns on scripting support — which means you must structure the page so it also provides a link that the user can click.

To use the dual page approach, follow these steps:

1. **Right-click the current content page and select Copy from the context menu.**

2. **Right-click the folder in which the content page appears and select Paste from the context menu.**

FrontPage creates a copy of the page.

3. **Rename the file so it reflects the no frame content.**

Now you can add a link to that page on the original content page and also use it in the <noframe> tag area. Follow these steps every time you change the content page to ensure that your no-frames page content remains synchronized with the original content page.

Organizing Frames

The Page Templates dialog box contains a number of setups (refer to Figure 4-1). Most developers find a setup they like or at least one that contains most of what they need. Fortunately, you can customize the frame setup to meet specific needs. For example, you might want a separate frame for a logo or an area to use for notices. In some cases, a frame might outgrow its original use and you see a need to split it so you can redefine two separate uses for the content.

Normally you want to modify the organization of a page *before* you add frame content. Modifying a frame after adding content can prove difficult because the original content can end up in the wrong location. Normally hand-coding techniques resolve errors of this sort: You move the reference from one <frame> tag to another to correct the problem.

Adding and splitting frames

You always have at least one frame on a frames page. During the design phase, you might decide that you need additional frames, or that some frames are wrongly placed. Adding a new frame is a matter of choosing a frame to split to obtain the additional space.

For example, you might decide that you want separate areas for a banner and a logo on a page. Splitting an existing banner frame would achieve your goal. To add a new frame or split an existing frame, follow these steps:

1. **Select the host frame.**

2. **Use Frame⇨Split Frame to display the Split Frame dialog box.**

3. **Choose the Split Into Columns (vertical split) or Split Into Rows (horizontal split) option and click OK.**

   FrontPage splits the frame.

Deleting frames

When you see a frame you no longer need, you can delete it. To perform this task, select the frame you want to remove and choose Frame⇨Delete. FrontPage removes the frame you selected.

Remember that frames provides structure, not content. When you accidentally delete a frame you need, you don't have to worry that the content is also gone; the content resides in a separate file. To return the frame to its former state, choose a frame to split and then configure the new frame to display the existing Web page.

Combining actions

Sometimes you can't accomplish a goal without combining delete and split actions unless you want to code the changes by hand. For example, you might want to add a navigation frame between the banner frame and the content frame of a three frame setup. To perform this task, you must first delete the existing links or content frame, split the remaining frame horizontally, and then split the lower frame vertically. Figure 4-6 shows a unique page setup based on a series of combined actions.

After you create a complex page design that you intend to use for your Web site, save the frame's place but don't place any actual frames within it. Instead, use this blank frame page as a template to create the other pages on your site. To perform this task, follow these steps:

1. **Choose File⇨New.**

   The New window appears in the Task Pane.

2. **Choose From Existing Page in the New Page area.**

   FrontPage displays a New from Existing Page dialog box.

3. **Specify a location for the new frame-page template file.**

   FrontPage copies that file as a new frame page you can fill out.

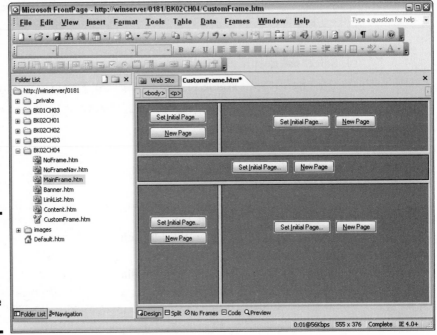

Figure 4-6:
Combine
splits and
deletes to
create
unique page
setups.

Using an Inline Frame

Inline frames (or IFrames) are different from standard frames. Avoid confusing frames and IFrames because they use different tags and accomplish different purposes. The IFrame relies on the `<iframe>` tag to perform its work. An IFrame lets you include content from another Web page or other resource such as a graphic in the current page. The included content is "inline" with (in other words, part of) the existing content on the page so all the content appears as a single entity even though the content exists on multiple pages. The current page doesn't act as a frameset — it usually includes content of its own.

It's best to avoid using IFrames whenever possible because it isn't standardized and many browsers don't support it. A browser that supports standard frames doesn't necessarily provide support for IFrames. You can achieve effects similar to the `<iframe>` tag by using the `<object>` tag. See the "Using the `<object>` tag" section for details.

Despite compatibility concerns, you may find that your Web site has an appropriate use for IFrames. If so, you can define an IFrame page by following these steps:

1. **Create a new blank page by right-clicking the host folder in the Folder List and choosing New➪Blank Page from the context menu.**

   FrontPage creates the new blank page.

2. **Define file and page properties as you normally would.**

3. **Add an IFrame to the page by choosing Insert➪Inline Frame.**

   FrontPage displays an IFrame on the page.

4. **Use a combination of IFrames to create pages that are similar to those you create using standard frames.**

   Figure 4-7 shows an example of a typical three-pane view.

Configuring an IFrame is similar to configuring a standard frame, but there are differences. To configure an existing IFrame, follow these steps:

1. **Right-click an existing IFrame and select Inline Frame Properties from the context menu.**

   You see the Inline Frame Properties dialog box shown in Figure 4-8.

2. **As a minimum, provide the IFrame's name, purpose, and location.**

   Type a descriptive name for the IFrame in the Name field, a description of the page purpose in the Title field, and the location of the file in the Alternate Text field.

**Book II
Chapter 4**

**Working with
Frames**

Figure 4-7:
You can design page layouts with the IFrame that mimic standard frame setups.

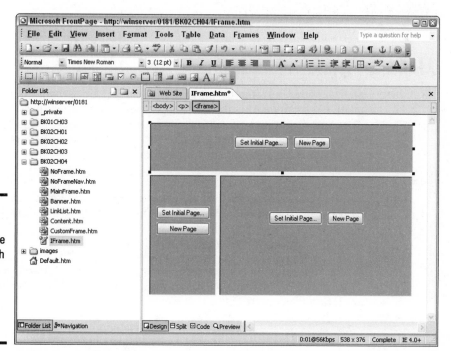

When a user accesses an IFrame page with a browser that lacks the proper support, the page displays the content of the Alternate Text field, which is the same content provided for standard frames. In this case, the difference is that you can't really provide a nice display because of the way the IFrame works. You can provide the location of the content by adding text like this to the Alternate Text field:

```
View the <a href="Banner.htm">Banner</a> separately.
```

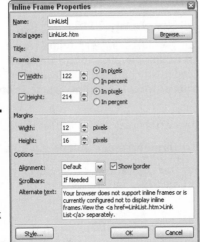

Figure 4-8: Configure the IFrame to ensure that your users know how to work with it.

Making Frames Accessible

You use frames to organize information, but a great presentation isn't worth much if you can't get people to visit your site. Many users hate frames because they won't work with their browser or because a frame organization presents too much information at once. The use of multiple pages within a single host page creates a host of problems — even for people who don't normally use accessibility aids — such as these:

✦ You generally have to use scripting to provide the Back button functionality found in most browsers — using multiple pages breaks the normal Back button functionality.

✦ Frames are less compatible with older browsers than are tables.

✦ It's impossible to get the current state (settings and condition) of a frameset because the multiple pages change the state — this means any scripts you create that use the current state of the frame will break.

- ✦ Opening a new frame in a browser can disorient or at least annoy users.

- ✦ Placing content designed for a single page in multiple individual frames makes it difficult (even impossible) for accessibility devices and software such as screen readers to work properly when they access your page.

It pays to check for browser compatibility issues as you work with various technologies on your Web site. Because browsers are constantly changing, you need a good resource that is updated often. The Webmonkey reference chart at `http://hotwired.lycos.com/webmonkey/reference/browser_chart/index.html` provides a good resource that is updated often.

Understanding the standard frame fixes

Fortunately, you can make frames friendlier to everyone by making a few simple changes. The most important change is to provide a `title` attribute for every frame so someone using a screen reader can identify the frame and use it properly.

Another way to make frames friendlier is to provide alternative, frame-free content. Use the `<noframes>` tag to define a location for an alternative page like this:

```
<noframes>
   <A href="NoFrames.htm" title="Content without frames">
      View just the content of the page without frames.
   </A>
</noframes >
```

This technique lets someone view a properly designed content page without using frames. Now, a good basic design for a page contains the essential elements — including content, disclosures, notices, and any company-specific information — in the page itself, not in the other frames. Those contain nonessential (but nice-to-have) information such as links, special notes, tips, a table of contents, or anything else that isn't directly related to the essential content. Keeping the non-frame design synchronized with the framed setup is easy because both use the same content frame.

Use the `alt` and `longdesc` attributes to describe each of the frames so the user can discover their purpose and arrangement with other frames. The `alt` attribute is short and provides a self-contained description for simple frames. To add this attribute, provide a description such as the following:

```
alt="This frame contains a series of links to other locations
      with helpful information. It appears on the lower left
      side of the frameset."
```

The `longdesc` attribute points to a separate page with a detailed description of complex pages. To add this attribute, create a Web page with the description, and then point to it like this: `longdesc="Description.htm"`.

You could also provide a table of contents of frames in a `<noframes>` tag. A user with a browser that doesn't support frames will see the list of individual links, making it possible to select the individual frames within a frameset. Although this arrangement isn't as visually appealing as using frames, the user still gains access to all of the information and you don't have to maintain two sets of pages.

Avoiding frame display issues

Graphics can present special problems in frames because FrontPage lets you place the graphic directly in the frame, which can cause accessibility tools to malfunction and can increase compatibility problems with some browsers. The frame ends up with code like this:

```
<frame name="MyPicture" src="MyPicture.gif" title="This is a
    picture of the author.">.
```

Instead, always create a Web page for the image and then use the Web page as the frame source like this:

```
<frame name="MyPicture" src="MyPicture.htm" title="This is a
    picture of the author.">.
```

This approach lets you describe the image so users who can't see it can still understand what the graphic represents.

It might be tempting to create a no-frames version of a Web page that uses pop-up windows. The original window would contain the content and the pop-ups would contain the extra information. Resist the temptation; a screen reader won't know that the page has changed in response to a pop-up, and the user will receive confusing information. In addition, the use of pop-ups makes it hard for the user to know which window to access.

Using the <object> tag

A number of non-frame choices exist. One of these easiest solutions is to use an `<object>` tag to hold the information. The `<object>` tag has several advantages. You can make the page look just like it has frames, but you can also move the `<object>` tag around and create other presentations. Here is a typical example of an `<object>` tag alternative that you can see in the `NoFrame.htm` file on this book's companion Web site.

```
<p>
   <object data="NoFrameNav.htm" width="200" height="200">
      Go to the <A href="NoFrameNav.htm"
      title="Other page content you might want to view.">
         other content for this page.
      </A>
   </object>
</p>
```

To use the `<object>` tag, follow these general steps:

1. **Create the frames as you normally would and provide them as part of the** `data` **attribute.**

2. **Create one** `<object>` **tag for each frame.**

3. **Size the frames using the** `width` **and** `height` **attributes.**

   Make sure you include these two attributes or you won't see the frame content. Figure 4-9 shows the output of this example.

You can discover other techniques for accessible frame usage at `http://webaim.org/techniques/frames/`.

**Book II
Chapter 4**

**Working with
Frames**

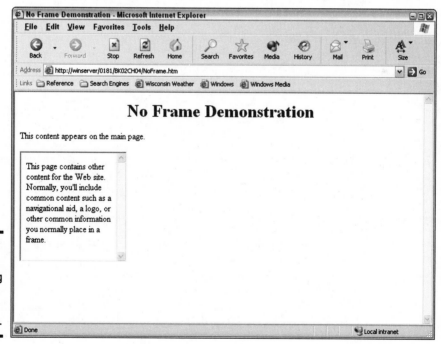

Figure 4-9:
Use an
<object> tag
to create a
frame-like
appearance.

Chapter 5: Designing with Templates

In This Chapter

✔ Using templates effectively

✔ Using templates to create Web pages

✔ Getting more templates

✔ Creating templates from existing Web pages

✔ Using templates to create Web sites

A template is a blueprint or pattern for designing Web pages. You use a template to create pages that have the specific characteristics it holds. The template provides structure, not content, in most cases. Using a template saves time because you don't have to recreate a design from scratch. For example, if you create a generic search page, you can use that search page to put its characteristics everywhere you need them on your Web site. The specifics of the search page may change to meet specific needs, but the structure — the template — remains the same.

FrontPage provides two kinds of templates. One helps you design Web pages; the other helps you design entire Web sites. Even though these templates are somewhat generic in design, they can help you get started quickly. After you create specific designs, you can rely on those designs as templates for future projects. The idea is to build the pieces of your Web site so you can reuse as much of the design, code, and generic content as possible.

Templates aren't the same as themes. It's easy to confuse the two if you don't consider how FrontPage uses them. A template creates an actual site or page; a *theme* adds decorative elements to an existing page. Themes are the second step in many Web page designs — templates are the first step in the process.

Reasons to Use a Template

The biggest reason to use templates is to save time. Starting with a blank page every time you create a new Web page is going to waste time. To bring your projects in on time and within budget, you need to grab every potential aid that results in real time savings. Templates provide a real time saving and generally don't have any negative features that would tend to reduce their potential benefit. Here are some of the best reasons to use them:

✦ **Templates ensure consistency.** No one memorizes every piece of code they create. Creating a template is like leaving yourself a note so you don't have to remember what you did the last time — everything is written down so you can replicate a design easily. Consistency is especially important as the number of users increase because any inconsistencies increase training and support costs. Most companies do everything they can to reduce both.

✦ **Group projects benefit from templates because everyone starts with the same design for their pages.** The more precise a template becomes, the less one page varies from another and the less time you spend reworking pages so they conform to whatever standard your company sets.

✦ **Looking at new templates can generate ideas for your Web site.** An idea that you used earlier (or that someone else created and you downloaded) can lead to better Web sites. You can apply the idea for its intended purpose or use it in a new application. Making tweaks to existing templates is often more efficient than building the new idea from scratch.

✦ **Sharing ideas can help both the group and the individual.** Some people develop templates and upload them for others to use freely; others charge for the privilege of using an existing template. Both are examples of sharing ideas between individuals who have no other connection. In the Microsoft Office community, sharing templates can help everyone become more efficient — and helps keep a great idea from getting lost because only one person knows about it.

Designing with the Page Templates

The template you use most often is the page template. In fact, every example in the book to this point relies on a page template. The Normal Page template isn't much to look at because it's a blank page, but it's a template — the default template that many developers start using during their initial FrontPage programming sessions.

As developers move on to more advanced programming techniques, they also use the other templates that FrontPage has to offer. FrontPage provides several types of templates:

✦ **Templates that use frame technology to build Web pages.** The resulting pages can provide content outright or make use of other pages to provide content. Book II, Chapter 4 describes their use.

✦ **Web-page templates that use no frames.** These are for situations in which frames would hamper the effectiveness of the Web page. (See Book II, Chapter 4.)

✦ **Style-sheet templates.** A *style sheet* helps you create better Web pages by placing the formatting information in a separate, generally accessible area. The Web page uses the style sheet for formatting; the developer uses it to hold just the content.

Using the general pages

When you right-click a folder and choose New⇨Blank Page, FrontPage automatically creates a page based on the Normal Page template. You use a blank page when you begin a generic Web site or when the templates won't do the job. As the Web site grows, you begin using template pages to create a unified look so users know they're still on your site because the look and feel make the whole site feel like the same place.

Defining new pages using templates

Not every page has to start as a blank page, even when you create a new Web site. FrontPage provides a number of starter pages for general use. For example, you don't have to create a guest-book page from scratch — FrontPage provides one for you. To see the general templates that FrontPage provides, use File⇨New to display the New window in the Task Pane. Click More Page Templates and FrontPage displays the Page Templates dialog box shown in Figure 5-1.

Book II Chapter 5

Designing with Templates

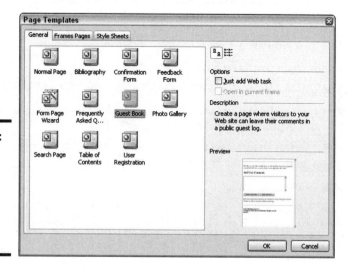

Figure 5-1: Choose a template that provides the basic service you need.

Displaying templates

In this dialog box, you don't have to display the templates as icons. Some people find it difficult to read the template name information when using the icon display. Click List in the Page Templates dialog box to change the presentation to a list display. This display is the same as a list display in Windows Explorer — the icons appear along the left edge of the list and the text flows out to the right from the icons. This display makes long template names easier to read. Click Large Icons to display the icons again.

FrontPage includes templates for many common uses such as registration forms and tables of contents. You see the basic appearance of the template in the Preview area of the dialog box. The Description area tells you about the intended purpose of the template. Sometimes, you can change a template from its intended purpose to a new purpose by carefully editing some entries. Even though Microsoft says a template is for a specific purpose, you can use it for practically anything you want — try various modifications (read on for some suggestions). Have fun making your Web site perfect while reducing the time you spend doing mundane chores by changing the templates to meet your needs.

Adding a new page as a Web task

You also see two options on the General tab of the Page Templates dialog box: Just Add Web Task and Open in Current Frame. To add a new page as a new Web task in the Task List, follow these steps:

1. **Click Just Add Web Task and then click OK.**

   FrontPage displays the Save As dialog box.

2. **Type a name for the new Web page in the File Name field.**

3. **After typing the name, add a title to the Web page by clicking Change Title and typing the title in the Page Title field.**

   Adding a title ensures you can easily identify the Web page in Task view when you look at your FrontPage Task List later.

4. **Click Save.**

   FrontPage saves the new Web page to disk, closes it, and adds it as a task to the Task List — reminding you to complete the page later (that's the task).

Now, when you want to return to the Web page, you can access it through the Task List. To start the task, follow these steps:

1. **Double-click its entry in the Task List.**

You see the Task Details dialog box shown in Figure 5-2.

2. **Click Start Task.**

The page you created earlier opens.

3. **Make any changes you want and then click Save.**

FrontPage reminds you that this page appears on your Task List and asks whether you want to mark the task as complete.

4. **Click Yes or No to answer the question, or Cancel to do some more editing.**

If you click Yes, FrontPage marks the task completed. If you click No, FrontPage saves your changes but keeps the page listed as a task. You can access the page again through the Task List.

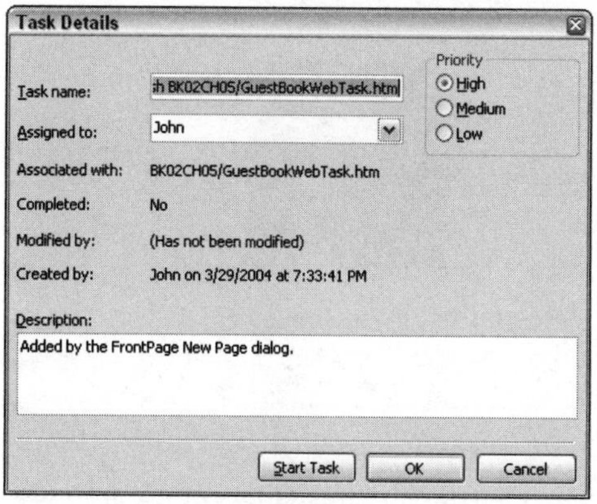

Figure 5-2:
Open the
Task Details
dialog box
when you
want to start
a task.

Task Details	
Task name:	sh BK02CH05/GuestBookWebTask.html
Assigned to:	John
	Priority
	⊙ High
	○ Medium
	○ Low
Associated with:	BK02CH05/GuestBookWebTask.htm
Completed:	No
Modified by:	(Has not been modified)
Created by:	John on 3/29/2004 at 7:33:41 PM
Description:	
Added by the FrontPage New Page dialog.	

Start Task   OK   Cancel

Adding a new page to an existing frame

The second option on the General tab of the Page Templates dialog box is Open in Current Frame. Check this option when you want to add a page to the currently selected frame. When you click OK in the Page Templates dialog box, the page appears within the frame, rather than as an independent page.

Working with embedded template files

Some templates also create additional files. For example, when you choose the Photo Gallery template, FrontPage includes some sample images. You choose whether to save these images so you can see them on-screen, replace them with new images of your choosing, or simply delete them so you can add images to display later on.

You should save the images the first time you create a Photo Gallery template page because it shows how to place pictures when you edit the resulting page.

FrontPage asks where you want to store any extra files when you save the page by displaying the Save Embedded Files dialog box shown in Figure 5-3. This dialog box shows what the picture looks like in the Picture Preview area. You can use the dialog box to change the names of any embedded files, and choose whether FrontPage saves a new copy of the file or uses the existing copy.

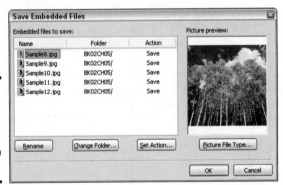

Figure 5-3:
Save any embedded files for the current Web page.

When selecting a storage location for these files, make sure you place the files in a location that's consistent with the rest of your Web-site design. Some developers place all the graphics for a site in a special Images folder, while others store the graphics in the same folder as the Web page. Using a centralized location makes it easier to update the pictures and lets you use one copy of the image for every page that needs it. Storing the pictures with the Web page makes it easier to locate all the files that go with a certain Web page when you need to edit it.

Another feature of the Save Embedded Files dialog box appears when you click the Picture File Type button. The Picture File Type dialog box displays the current type of embedded image. You use this dialog box to convert the picture to another file type to gain certain advantages such as color depth or download speed. For example, selecting the JPEG type lets you decrease the quality of the image — with an associated reduction in file size — making the file faster to download.

Using the frames pages

Developers use frames within Web pages to help organize information. The Frames Pages tab of the Page Templates dialog box contains a list of standard frame setups, as shown in Figure 5-4. (For more on frames, see Book II, Chapter 4.)

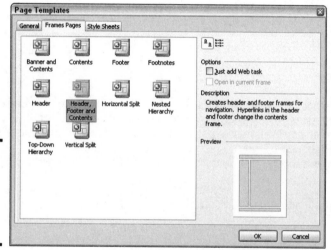

Figure 5-4:
Use frames to organize information on a Web page.

The Preview and Description areas tell you about the selected frames page. The Preview area shows how the page looks, while the description provides some ideas of how to use the frames page. A frames page provides organization, not content, so the ideas in the Description area are really just suggestions.

You might think that the Open in Current Frame option is useful only when working with Web pages. It's possible to use this option in the Frames Pages tab too. Use this feature to create complex layouts based on two or more of the simple layouts that Microsoft provides. Some layouts are especially useful as beginning frames. For example, it would be difficult to use the Banner and Contents layout within another frame, but the Horizontal Split layout works fine as an addition to an existing frame.

Always begin your layout with the complex main frames page. You can then add more frames pages as needed to complete a design.

The frame-within-a-frame layout technique is definitely different from splitting a frame. When you split a frame, the changes reside within a single Web page (see the `SplitFrame.htm` file in the source code for this chapter for details). The code that does the job looks like this:

```
<frameset rows="64,*">
 <frame name="banner" scrolling="no" noresize
        target="contents">
 <frameset cols="150,*">
  <frame name="contents" target="main">
  <frameset rows="*,49%">
   <frame name="main">
   <frame name="main1">
  </frameset>
 </frameset>
</frameset>
```

Notice that the code FrontPage creates doesn't include any reference to an external page. When you use the frame-within-a-frame technique, you actually create *two* Web pages, each with its own layout information. The first is the initial main frames page, the second is the fames page you added to the existing frames page. The code for this method looks like this:

```
<frameset rows="64,*">
 <frame name="banner" scrolling="no" noresize
        target="contents">
 <frameset cols="150,*">
  <frame name="contents" target="main">
  <frame name="main" src="HorizontalSplit.htm">
 </frameset>
</frameset>
```

The code for the main frames page is actually easier to understand in the second case, but notice that it references another file, `HorizontalSplit.htm`, which contains the additional layout information. The visual effect is the same in both cases. To see how this technique works from a coding and visual perspective, see the `FrameWithinAFrame.htm` file in the source code for this chapter.

The advantage of using this second technique is that you control each element of the layout as a separate Web page. You can display subordinate Web pages either individually or in the frames-within-frames collection. The disadvantage of using this technique is that you have more files to manage, which often results in errors. If you modify the wrong file, changes that you thought you made might not appear on-screen.

Correcting the table formatting in default templates

While working with the default templates, I noticed a problem. The table formatting doesn't appear to work correctly. Changing the target browser to another browser type doesn't appear to fix the problem in this case. This problem doesn't affect the operation of the stylesheet as a whole, so you don't have to make any changes if you don't want to. However, to see the colors of the table border as Microsoft intended, you must modify the style sheet code, as shown in bold.

```
table
{
    table-border-color-light:
    rgb(255,102,153);
    table-border-color-dark:
    rgb(102,51,153);
    border-left-color:
    rgb(255,102,153);
    border-top-color:
    rgb(255,102,153);
    border-right-color:
    rgb(102,51,153);
    border-bottom-color:
    rgb(102,51,153);
}
td
{
    border-left-color:
    rgb(102,51,153);
```

```
    border-top-color:
    rgb(102,51,153);
    border-right-color:
    rgb(255,102,153);
    border-bottom-color:
    rgb(255,102,153);
}
th
{
    border-left-color:
    rgb(102,51,153);
    border-top-color:
    rgb(102,51,153);
    border-right-color:
    rgb(255,102,153);
    border-bottom-color:
    rgb(255,102,153);
}
```

The problem is this: The `table-border-color-light` style is supposed to mimic the Light Border color setting found in the Table Properties dialog box. Likewise, the `table-border-color-dark` style is supposed to mimic the Dark Border color setting. Neither of these styles works as intended. To create the 3D look created with the Light Border and Dark Border properties, you must define the border colors manually as shown. The `SweetsDemo.css` file on the companion Web site already has this change in place so you can see how it affects the presentation.

Using the style sheets

Style sheets don't actually contain any content — they define the formatting of the content of a Web page. By separating the content of a Web page from the formatting, you make it possible for a user to display the Web page with any formatting that meets a specific need. For example, the user might require a larger font to make the page readable or a different color setup to see the page details. A Web page can achieve different looks for the same content by using a different style sheet.

Creating an initial style sheet can require more time than creating the content for the first Web page when you want to achieve a particular look. Using the style sheet templates on the Style Sheets tab of the Page Templates dialog box (as shown in Figure 5-5) can reduce development time.

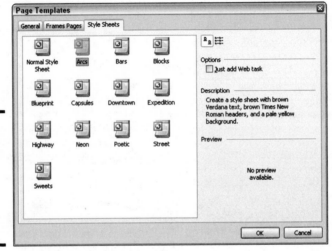

Figure 5-5: Use CSS to separate content from formatting on your Web page.

One of the first problems you see when you select a style sheet is that the Preview area is blank. Because a style sheet contains only formatting and no content, FrontPage can't display anything without creating a Web page to display the information. Unfortunately, this is an issue that Microsoft chose not to address.

The example code on the companion Web site includes the StyleSheetCheck.htm file, along with a series of Cascading Style Sheet (CSS) files that are unmodified versions of the Microsoft templates. Use the following procedure to see how the various templates work:

1. Choose Format⇨Style Sheet Links.

You see the Link Style Sheet dialog box.

2. Select the current style sheet and click Remove.

FrontPage removes the existing style sheet.

3. Click Add.

You see the Select Style Sheet dialog box.

4. **Select the source-code folder, BK02CH05, in the Look In field.**

   You see a selection of CSS files. Each file shows the name of the template, followed by the word `Demo`; when you want to see the Arcs template that appears in Figure 5-5, select the `ArcsDemo.css` file.

5. **Double-click the style sheet you want to use.**

   The style sheet's name appears in the Link Style Sheet dialog box.

6. **Click OK.**

   FrontPage changes the formatting of the sample Web page to match the style sheet you selected.

Obtaining Additional Templates

The templates that you get with a default FrontPage installation are a good starting point. These templates answer some basic needs that most developers have. You can further increase the productivity gains that templates provide by downloading specialty templates from online sources. Getting specialized templates reduces development time by reducing the number of changes you have to make.

At first, I was going to concentrate strictly on Microsoft supplied templates in this section — that was before I started seeing the wealth of templates online. Many developers provide templates you can use within FrontPage. The best place to get high-quality templates from someone you know is still Microsoft. You can download them at

`http://office.microsoft.com/templates/default.aspx?CTT=98`

Not every template on this site is for FrontPage, however. Drill down through the list of template categories to locate a template of the type you need. The icon next to a template tells you which Office application can use it.

The Microsoft template Web site also includes other essential links. For example, you can make suggestions for new templates. You'll also find links for the Office newsletter and other helpful sources of information.

The next best place to look for templates is on Microsoft's Office Marketplace at

`http://office.microsoft.com/marketplace/default.aspx?CTT=98`

The companies that appear on this site are reliable and have a business relationship with Microsoft, so you can be reasonably sure the products they produce are of high quality and reliable. To locate templates, click the Template link in the Creating Documents portion of the page.

After you exhaust the Microsoft resources, you can begin looking at sites that specialize in templates. For example, FrontPage Template World (`www.fpworld.com/`) has templates for just about any need. If you don't see what you want, they'll build a custom template for you. Another good place to look is Classy Themes (`www.classythemes.com/`). This site also provides services for Webmasters who want to serve client needs without investing a lot of time creating templates and themes. The only problem with sites such as these is that you end up paying a small fee for every template you download.

Using an Existing Page as a Template

No matter how hard you search online, you still create some pages by hand. A few of these pages are so unique that you don't gain any advantage by creating a template from them. Only when you can use the same basic design more than once should you consider creating a template from it. Most companies have a basic design they use for all Web pages, so that's where you can start creating your custom templates.

Defining a page as a template

When you create a page that you want to use as a template, you should concentrate more on the page layout than on the content. The idea is to replicate the features that are common to all pages of that type. If you plan to include some common content, it should appear in the template, but leave out any unique content. For example, a company logo will likely appear on every page, so you should include it with the template — but a page title is unique, so leave that out.

Designing templates points out the need to plan your Web site. A plan doesn't necessarily describe content in detail, but it should contain enough information to identify any common elements. Creating a mockup of several sample pages helps. Grouping the pages according to type is also helpful. All these discovery mechanisms help you create better templates. A good template saves time by letting you concentrate on unique content for the pages you create.

Using the template page locally

After you design a template page, you should test it locally to ensure it works as planned. It's unlikely that you'll see any actual errors. The purpose of local testing is to ensure that you add all common content — but no unique material — to your template. To ensure that your template works as planned, use it to design several pages for your Web site. Make notes as you create the pages of anything you feel is common enough that you should include it in the template.

To test a template locally, follow these steps:

1. **Use File⇨New to display the New window in the Task Pane.**

2. **Click From Existing Page.**

FrontPage displays the New From Existing Page dialog box.

3. **Locate the page you want to test as a template and click Create New.**

FrontPage creates a new page based on the template.

The new page will look and act like a new page that you create using any other template — the only difference is that the template is from a local source.

For the purposes of an example, I modified a copy of the SplitFrame.htm file, SplitFrame2.htm. The file now includes a banner at the top and uses the Table of Contents template page on the left side. Try this design out and you'll see it always includes the added pages and graphics in the new page.

Adding the template to FrontPage

After you create a template and test it locally, you want to make it accessible to others as a standard entry on the Page Templates dialog box. To perform this task, you need to create a few additional files and set up a folder in a specific location on your hard drive (or the hard drive used for templates in your workgroup). The standard location for page templates on a local system is \Program Files\Microsoft Office\Templates\1033\ PAGES11. Open this folder in Windows Explorer and you see a list of familiar names — the same names that appear on the General tab of the Page Templates dialog box.

To define your own entry, create a new folder in the PAGES11 folder (this name will vary when you use older versions of FrontPage) by right-clicking the right pane in Windows Explorer and choosing New⇨Folder from the context menu. The folder name begins with the name you want to use for the template, followed by a period, followed by the tem (template) extension. For example, to create a template called MyTemplate, you create a folder named MyTemplate.tem. The name of the folder has to match the name of the main Web page. (The example uses SplitFrame2.tem.)

Copy all the files required to create the template into this folder. For the SplitFrame2.htm file, you also need the SplitFrameBanner.htm, SplitFrameContents.htm, and the MyBanner.jpg files because all these files appear as part of the template.

At this point, you need a picture of the template. Even though Microsoft doesn't include this feature, trying to use the templates without a preview image is difficult at best. Open the template in your browser and use a screen capture program to create the picture. The picture appears in the Preview area of the Page Templates dialog box after you save it to the template folder. You need a graphics application that can produce a Device-Independent Bitmap (DIB) file. A number of graphics applications, such as PaintShop Pro (`www.jasc.com/`), can take screenshots of your template, reduce the size of the image to 110 pixels wide by 124 high, and save it as a DIB file. The name of the DIB file is very important — it must match the name of the main Web page in the template, which means the example file is named `SplitFrame2.DIB`.

The final piece needed to create a permanent template is an INF (information) file. This file tells FrontPage what to display as a template name and provides a description of the template that appears in the Description section of the Page Templates dialog box. As with everything else, the name of this file must match the name of the main Web page. Here are the contents of the `SplitFrame2.inf` file.

```
[info]
_LCID=1033
_version=11.0.4819.0
title=Split Frame with Banner and Contents
description=This page contains the company banner, a table of
    contents, and two areas for content.
```

The `[info]` entry identifies the kind of information in this section of the file. Some INF files contain multiple sections, but this one contains only one.

The `_LCID` entry identifies the language reference number (locale) for this template, which identifies the language. If you're not sure what number to use, just set this value to match other templates in your copy of FrontPage. The number 1033 is for the United States. Many Web sites — such as the International LCID (Locale Identifier) Code Chart at `http://krafft.com/scripts/deluxe-calendar/lcid_chart.htm` — provide a list of LCIDs you can use when you want to create a template in a language other than the one your copy of FrontPage supports.

The `_version` number entry doesn't affect the appearance of the template or change how FrontPage interacts with it. The number used with the example is for FrontPage 2003. Normally, I use the same version number as the other templates in the version of FrontPage that I used to create the template for documentation purposes. However, you can use any version numbering scheme that suits your needs.

The title and description entries contain the title used to display the template in the Page Templates dialog box. The title appears with the template icon; the description appears in the Description area of the dialog box.

After you create the new template, test it. The procedure looks like this:

1. **Close FrontPage (if you have it open) and then reopen FrontPage.**

2. **Select File⇨New to display the New window in the Task Pane.**

3. **Click More Page Templates and you see the Page Templates dialog box.**

4. **Select your new template.**

Figure 5-6 shows the example template. Notice that all entries correctly identify the template. When you select this template, it creates a framed page with a banner and contents section.

**Book II
Chapter 5**

Designing with Templates

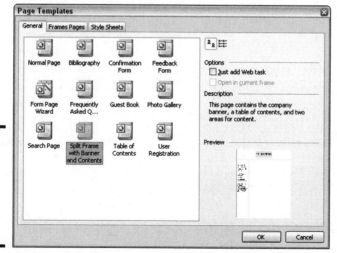

Figure 5-6:
Create and test new templates as needed for your Web site.

Using Web Site Templates

Depending on how you use FrontPage, the Web site templates can prove useful for a number of needs. Even a small company can often make use of multiple Web sites — one to provide a public interface and another used by one or more groups of employees. A temporary Web site can act as a focus point for a project where some people are working off site. Generally, though, you use Web-site templates less often than any other part of FrontPage (unless you develop Web sites professionally).

Defining a new site

To create a Web site using a template, use File⇨New to display the New window in the Task Pane. Click More Web Site Templates. You see the Web Site Templates dialog box shown in Figure 5-7.

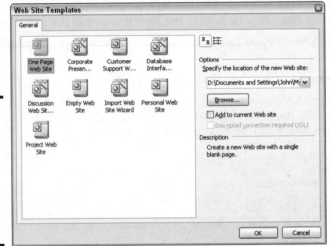

Figure 5-7: Use Web site templates to create permanent or temporary Web sites.

Select a template and you see a description of it in the Description area. The description tells you the purpose of this Web-site template. Unlike those of Web-page templates, the descriptions are usually very accurate; you won't have a lot of room for making changes unless you're using a generic template such as One Page Web Site or Empty Web Site.

Choosing site within a site or separate site

You can place the new Web site within an existing Web site by clicking Add to Current Web Site. You access this new site by using the current site as a starting point. The only problem with this approach is that there's no separation between the initial site and the new site. When you create a new Web site this way, the content from both sites mingles; it's hard to remove the new site later.

A better option is to create a new *subsite* that uses the current site as a starting point. To use this technique, follow these steps:

1. **Type the URL for the current site in the Specify the Location of the New Web Site field.**

2. **Add one or more levels of folders to hold the subsite.**

3. Click OK.

FrontPage creates the site in the new location. The site contains any Web pages defined by the template, along with other support files.

This way of creating a separate site makes the Web server view it as a new location or as a Web application. This means you can place restrictions on this subsite that differ from those placed on other subsites in the same main Web site. It's also a lot easier to clean up the subsite when you finish using it, so this is the best option for temporary Web sites you want to use for collaboration or other purposes.

FrontPage also treats subsites as separate *applications*. You can open the subsite as a unique project and work with the files as if there weren't any other files to consider. Everything is separate from the main site; managing the project is much easier.

Using secure communication

When a Web server provides the required support for Encrypted Connection Required (SSL) capabilities, FrontPage enables them as an option. Check this option when you want to create a secure connection with the user. The user must access the site using HyperText Transport Protocol Secure (HTTPS), rather than normal HTTP.

The advantage of a secure site is that others can't monitor your communication to hunt for information they shouldn't have. You use this option when you want to obtain personal or sensitive information from the user. The disadvantage of this technique is that it's much slower than using nonsecure communication. The user waits longer, which means there's a better chance the user will get tired of waiting and move to another location.

Book II
Chapter 5

Designing with
Templates

Chapter 6: Working with FrontPage Themes

In This Chapter

✔ Creating unique Web pages with themes

✔ Designing Web pages with FrontPage themes

✔ Designing Web pages using custom themes

A *theme* defines a consistent appearance for the content of a Web page. Unlike a template, it doesn't define the structure or layout of the Web page — but it doesn't define the content either. You use a theme to determine the color scheme of the page and any background images. Themes act as a unifying influence over the Web site, providing visual (and sometimes aural) cues that define the look and feel of your Web site for the user. A theme in FrontPage has the same purpose as themes you use in Windows.

FrontPage provides a number of themes you can use to create standard looks on your Web site. These themes lack the pizzazz of a theme you create for your own use, but they're quick to implement and provide an aesthetically pleasing appearance. You can also create and store themes that you devise. In most cases, you start by experimenting with a Web page in FrontPage to develop the theme, and then store the theme for use with other Web pages.

Using themes can make the Web experience better for some visitors to your site, but not everyone can use them. Make sure you use a theme that doesn't distract from the message you want to present and also addresses the needs of all users. For example, a user with color blindness might not be able to see your site if you use the wrong colors. Using themes can also interfere with accessibility hardware and software, which means you lose potential visitors because they can't access your site.

Defining a Unique Look with Themes

A theme can improve the appearance of your Web site by adding a unifying look to the display. A theme can work with the message you want to present, giving the viewer a focused emotional impact or producing subtle changes in the way a viewer sees the Web page. For example, using pastels in a Web-page design produces a muted overall feeling; using primary colors such as red and blue produce a more energetic atmosphere. Consequently, the theme you choose has to work with the message you want to present.

Normally, combining a theme with a layout helps ensure that every page has the same basic structure. Combining a theme and layout with the message you present gives the site a consistent emotional impact, while making it easy to use and understand. The best way to experiment with themes is to select one of the page templates that FrontPage provides and then change the theme to see how it affects the page. Figure 6-1 shows a combination of the Guest Book template with the Bars theme.

Themes also work well with layouts. When you combine a layout and a theme, the entire page uses that theme. The use of tables to hold the various data items doesn't affect the theme appearance. For example, Figure 6-2 shows a combination of the Centered Header and Centered Body layout and the Modular theme when displayed in Preview view. (Note that the figure also includes content so you can judge the effect of the theme.) The advantage of this technique is that you define the page content. It's relatively easy to turn a layout, theme, and standard content into a template that you can use for all your Web pages.

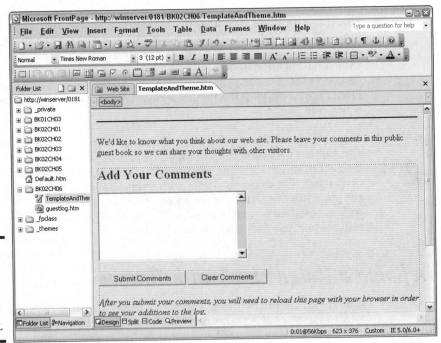

Figure 6-1:
Combine layout and themes to produce a unique look.

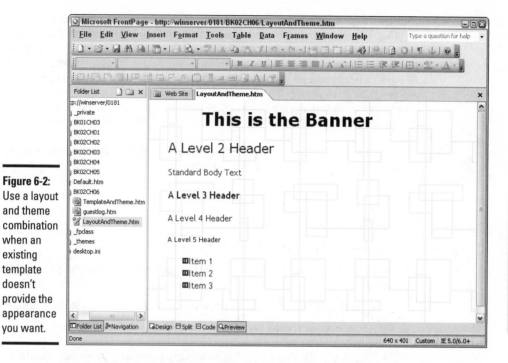

**Book II
Chapter 6**

**Working with
FrontPage Themes**

Figure 6-2:
Use a layout
and theme
combination
when an
existing
template
doesn't
provide the
appearance
you want.

It's a lot harder to use a theme with frames because the frame layout relies
on individual pages. To present a unified look, you must apply the theme to
every page presented in the frames page.

The lack of good theme support is another reason to avoid using frames
when you can.

Using the Standard Themes

Microsoft provides a wealth of themes you can use to customize your Web
pages. When you don't find a theme you like, you can also obtain themes
from third parties (some of which charge a fee for the privilege of using their
theme). Unless you're a professional artist with Web-design experience, it
probably pays to use these predefined themes to get an aesthetically pleasing result. Even when you choose to create a custom theme, looking at these
other offerings can provide ideas to use in your own design.

Adding a theme to a Web page

Before you add a theme to an existing page, it pays to look at what the theme
has to offer. The only way to accomplish this task is to create a test page

that contains a series of design elements that let you see what the theme has to offer. You want to use a test page that's small enough to see in the Design and Preview views, but offers a sampling of the design elements you use on a production page (although not necessarily the order in which you use them). Always concentrate on the design elements you actually use, and ignore the elements you won't use. The `SimpleTheme.htm` page provided with the source code on this book's companion Web site provides a list of standard elements you can try.

You must add the `SimpleTheme.htm` page to your navigational structure to see the effect of the theme on the banner.

To add a theme to your Web page, follow these steps:

1. **Choose Format⇨Theme.**

You see the Theme window in the Task Pane.

2. **Scroll through the Select a Theme list and click the theme you want to use.**

FrontPage changes the appearance of the Web page to match the theme.

3. **Customize your theme by using one of these three options:**

- Use the Vivid Colors option to modify the colors used for standard styles of content such as headers and links.

- Use the Active Graphics options to intensify the colors of bullets, banners, and other foreground images.

- Use the Background Picture option to add a background picture to the display.

The various combinations create eight versions of the same theme, so a single theme is more flexible than it first appears. Theme changes aren't automatic — you must apply them to every page that uses the theme on your Web site. Whenever you change one option, you must reapply the theme to a page by clicking the theme entry in the Select a Theme window to see the effect of the change.

Look at the small picture provided with each theme in the Theme window. The picture elements change to show the effect of a particular option. The top line in the figure is the banner, followed by interactive buttons, headers, regular text, navigational bar, regular hyperlink, and followed hyperlink. Figure 6-3 shows a typical theme with all options enabled.

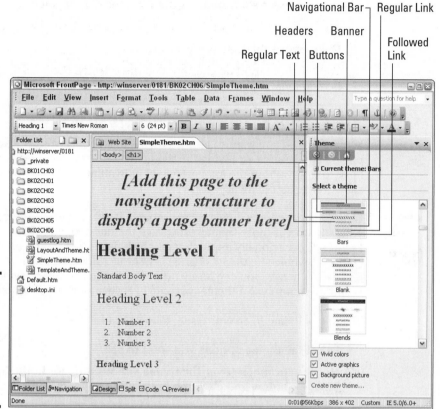

Book II
Chapter 6

Working with
FrontPage Themes

Figure 6-3:
Select a
theme and
customize it
to present a
particular
view of your
content.

Applying a theme to selected files

After you decide on a particular theme and set of customizations, you
want to apply it to one or more other pages on your site to provide a unified
look. FrontPage doesn't force you to open each file individually to apply the
theme — you can apply the theme to a group of files. To apply a theme to a
group of files, follow these steps:

1. **Select the files you want to change in the Folder List.**

2. **Select the options you want to use with the theme.**

3. **Hover your mouse over the theme entry in the Select a Theme window
and click the button that appears on the right side of the theme entry.**

You see a context menu.

4. **Select Apply to Selected Page(s) from the context menu.**

   The display flashes; for a moment, nothing seems to happen.

5. **Open one of the files you changed.**

   You see that FrontPage has applied the selected theme, using the specified options.

Applying a theme to a whole Web site

In many cases, you want to apply a theme to an entire Web site so it has a unified appearance. Applying the theme to the whole site means you don't have to worry about the appearance of individual pages — they all use the same theme automatically.

Exercise care when you use this approach; it affects every Web page on your site except those that already have themes applied (older versions of FrontPage occasionally apply themes to all pages, regardless of current status). A whole-site theme change is nonreversible. Although, after you make this change, you can apply other themes to the site or even tell FrontPage not to use a theme, you can't retrieve earlier customizations.

To apply a theme to an entire site, follow these steps:

1. **Select the theme options you want to use.**

2. **Hover your mouse over the theme you want to use in the Select a Theme window and click the button that appears to the right of the theme.**

   You see a context menu.

3. **Select Apply as Default Theme from the context menu.**

   FrontPage displays a warning about applying the theme.

4. **Click Yes only if and when you're sure you want to apply the theme.**

   The display flashes; the themes for any open pages change when FrontPage is finished applying the new theme. FrontPage doesn't display a special message to tell you when the conversion is complete.

Applying the theme can require quite a bit of time when you have a large Web site. Make sure you wait long enough for the change to occur.

Creating Your Own Theme

The themes provided with FrontPage are nice, but might not meet the specific content needs for your Web page. Fortunately, you can further customize a theme to meet special needs in FrontPage.

To get a theme ready to customize, follow these steps:

1. **Hover your mouse pointer over a theme entry.**

2. **Click the button that appears on the right side of the entry.**

   You see a context menu.

3. **Select Customize from the list.**

   You see the Customize Theme dialog box shown in Figure 6-4.

The Preview area shows what the theme looks like. It provides a standard Web page. However, this Web page is designed to show all the theme features and might not be very representative of how you actually use the theme on your Web page. Even so, the Preview area provides enough information to start customizing a theme.

Notice the Save button is disabled in Figure 6-4. You can save modified themes only under a different name. FrontPage-supplied themes are marked as read-only; you can use them, but can't modify them. When you save a theme with changes under a different name, FrontPage enables the Save button.

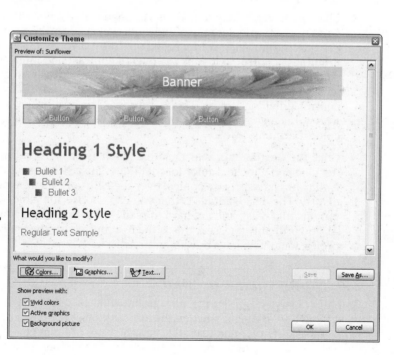

Figure 6-4: Perform special theme customization as needed.

FrontPage provides the means to modify themes in the three ways that matter most: color, text, and graphics. You can start with a blank theme and create something completely different from what Microsoft provides, or you can rely on Microsoft's themes as a starting point and make specific changes.

Modifying theme colors

The theme colors define everything from the appearance of the headings to the shade of the background. To change the colors, click Colors and you see the Customize Theme dialog box shown in Figure 6-5.

FrontPage provides three methods of changing color. Each has its own advantages:

✦ **Choose one of the existing color schemes.** The advantage of using this method is that the colors are already set up to harmonize well together. You don't need to worry whether the colors will work together and not present a conflicting message on-screen. The disadvantage is that the number of choices are limited to those that Microsoft offers. This is the best option for users who want a somewhat custom look, but don't want to spend a lot of time putting it together.

✦ **Click the Color Wheel tab.** You see a page with a color wheel. Move the pointer to a particular area of the color wheel. FrontPage automatically chooses harmonizing colors based on the area you choose. Use the Brightness control to modify the overall contrast and intensity of the colors. The advantage to this method is that you obtain an almost infinite variety of base color choices. The disadvantage is that you can't control individual colors. This is, however, the best option for someone who wants a completely custom look but also wants to ensure that the colors harmonize well.

✦ **Click the Custom tab.** Select an item (such as Background) from the Item list and choose a color for that item. The advantage of this method is that you have precise control over the color of every element of the display. The disadvantage is that you can choose some hideous color options that clash and are hard to read — and FrontPage won't stop you. As you probably guessed, this is the best option for the trained eye of a professional Web-page developer or artist.

Modifying theme graphics

Graphics of any type (pictures, background images, or other graphic elements) have a very big impact on the appearance of the page. Unlike the subtle effects of color and text style, graphics are prominent — even small changes show up, and the user is going to see them. Consequently, you need to select new art with care to ensure the page has a well-defined appearance. To change a graphic, click Graphics. You see the Customize Theme dialog box shown in Figure 6-6.

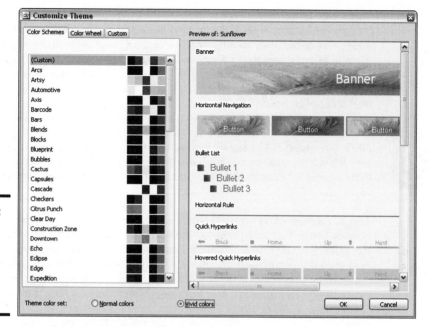

Figure 6-5:
Select colors for every aspect of the Web page.

**Book II
Chapter 6**

Working with FrontPage Themes

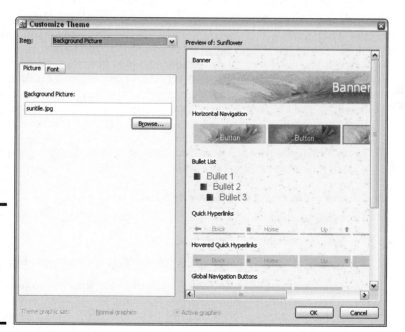

Figure 6-6:
Select colors for every aspect of the Web page.

FrontPage relies on a number of Joint Photographic Experts Group (JPEG) images for its graphics. You can also use Graphics Interchange Format (GIF) images for graphics you supply in a theme. (Missing from the FrontPage arsenal are newer graphics formats, such as Portable Network Graphics (PNG), which offer more functionality than either JPEG or GIF.) Both file formats have advantages when used with specific kinds of images or to perform specialized tasks.

The best rule to follow when you want to improve the speed of your Web site's download is to use GIF format when you want to display simple images and JPEG for complex images. One of the best discussions of graphics formats to use for specific circumstances appears on the Web Page Design site at http://coe.sdsu.edu/eet/Articles/wpdgifjpg/start.htm.

The advantage of using JPEG (or JPG) images is that you can create a high-quality image that compresses well with complex images. You can choose the quality of the image, balancing how well the picture compresses against how nice it looks on-screen. Unfortunately, the compression can come with a loss of detail — the more you compress the image, the more the loss of detail becomes apparent. You also lose a little detail every time you save a JPEG image. A JPEG offers higher color resolution than the 256 colors provided by GIF, so you can provide subtle shading effects.

The GIF format is *lossless* — you don't lose any information when you save the image to disk. This format, however, uses interlaced display, which makes the image appear (at first) in a rough, jagged form that at least loads quickly. The resolution of the image improves from that point as the browser loads more details from the Web site. Consequently, this format is especially good when you expect to support large numbers of users with dial-up connections. The GIF format also offers animation effects — you see them all the time on Web sites.

Every FrontPage theme requires multiple graphics. Assigning a new image to a graphic is a pretty quick process:

1. **Select the feature from the Item list.**

2. **Click Browse.**

   You see an Open File dialog box.

3. **Locate the image you want to use for that feature and click Open.**

   FrontPage modifies the specified item to use the new graphic element.

Many graphic elements also include separate Normal Graphics and Active Graphics settings. To select a different graphic for each setting, choose either Normal Graphic or Active Graphic. Select the graphic for that setting. Repeat the change for each other setting. Now, when you change from normal to active graphics, the theme looks different because it uses a different image.

Some graphics elements, such as the Banner, also have a text element. You can modify this portion of the graphic element by clicking Font. When the options on this tab are enabled, the selected item has a text element. Figure 6-7 shows the font changes you can make.

Each element has a different font associated with it, so you need to select the element you want to change, such as Banner, from the Item list before you make a change. To change the font for the selected element, begin by choosing a typeface from the Font list. Select the style, size, horizontal, and vertical alignment that you want for that element. Try various settings to see what looks best on a mockup Web page.

Figure 6-7:
Define
the font
character-
istic for
images that
have text
components.

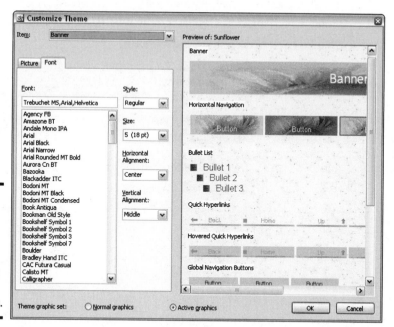

Modifying theme text

The *theme text* is content that appears as text, formatted separately from the graphics. For example, the banner is a graphic element; as such it isn't affected by general theme-text settings. A paragraph, on the other hand, is general, non-graphic text; theme-text settings affect it.

Setting theme text

Setting the theme text is a pretty straightforward way to customize a theme. To do so, follow these steps:

1. **Click Text in the Customize Theme dialog box.**

   You see the Customize Theme dialog box shown in Figure 6-8.

2. **In the Item list, select the text element you want to change.**

   The Preview pane shows the text elements you can choose.

3. **Select a typeface from the Font list.**

   FrontPage changes the typeface used for that text element on-screen.

4. **Change each text element individually.**

   This approach is necessary if (for example) you want to use the same font for all elements in a theme.

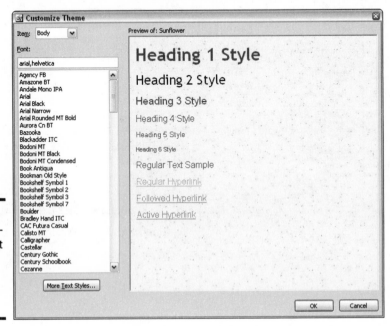

Figure 6-8: Modify non-graphic text as needed to present content clearly.

Modifying the theme-text font

Changing the typeface can have a major impact on the appearance of a particular theme — but you can add other enhancements to make the theme look even better. To create unusual font effects, follow these steps:

1. Click More Font Styles to display the Style dialog box shown in Figure 6-9.

The Style dialog box contains every style associated with this theme or the layout you choose. You see a lot of nonstandard styles when the List field is set to User-defined Styles. The standard HTML tags appear when you select HTML Tags in the List field. Make sure you start with the correct selection in the List field to find the style you want to modify.

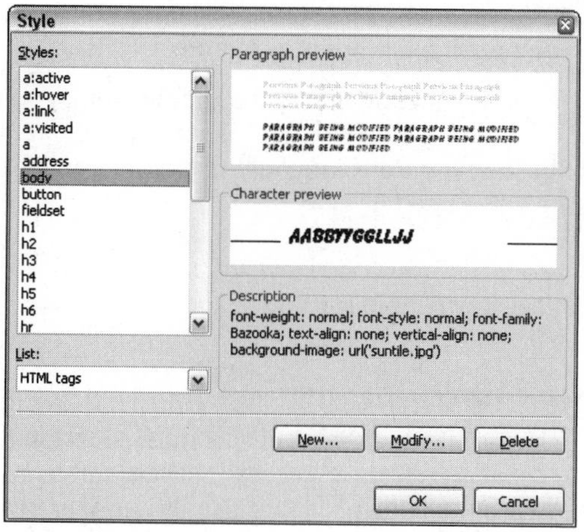

Figure 6-9:
Modify non-graphic text as needed to present content clearly.

2. Select a style.

The Paragraph Preview and Character Preview areas change to match the formatting provided by that style. Use these displays to determine what changes you want to make and to see how changes you make affect the style as a whole.

If you don't see a style you want to modify, click New to create one. Use Delete to remove any styles that you don't want any longer.

3. Click Modify when you want to make changes to the style.

You see a Modify Style dialog box.

4. **Click Format to see a list of changes you can make.**

These include the font (how the text appears), paragraph (line spacing and indentation), border (lines around the text), numbering (includes both bullets and numbers), and position (how other text interacts with this style).

Saving the new theme

After you make a few changes to your new theme, you want to save it to disk to ensure no changes are lost should an error occur with your system. To save a new theme to disk, follow these steps:

1. **Click Save As in the Customize Theme dialog box (refer to Figure 6-4).**

FrontPage displays a Save Theme dialog box.

2. **Type a descriptive name for your new theme.**

You might want to use a specially formatted name when you plan to create multiple themes for a single Web site. For example, you might want to use a name such as MyCompanyContentsPage to ensure you can find the theme quickly when you need it.

3. **Click OK.**

FrontPage saves the new theme for you.

Sharing a theme with others

The new theme you created doesn't exist in the same location as other FrontPage themes — other users can't access it. Microsoft assumes that any themes you create are for your personal use. When you work in a group, however, other people need to use your themes or the Web site won't have a consistent look.

To share a theme with others, you must first locate it on the hard drive. The themes you create are stored with all the other documents you create in the following folder on your hard drive:

```
\Documents and Settings\<Your User Name>\Application Data\
    Microsoft\Themes\
```

Each theme appears as a separate subfolder in the Themes folder and will have the name you assigned to it. When you want everyone on the same machine to use your theme, copy the theme folder to the following location:

```
\Program Files\Common Files\Microsoft Shared\THEMES11
```

You can also move the theme to individual `\Documents and Settings` folders when you want to share with just one or two people.

This folder contains a minimum of three files: an ELM file, a PNG file, and an INF file. Each has a distinctive purpose:

✦ The ELM file contains a description of your theme.

✦ The PNG file contains eight pictures of how your theme looks with eight different setting combinations a user can make in the Select a Theme window of the Task Pane.

✦ The INF file contains the settings for your theme.

These FrontPage-supplied files work fine for the most part, but you do need to make a few small changes to the INF file before you can share the theme. Open this file using any text editor (such as Notepad). Here is a modified version of the standard text that FrontPage provides:

```
[info]
readonly=true
codepage=65001
version=1.00
format=2
title=My Sample Theme
refcount=0

[titles]
1033=My Sample Theme
```

Begin by changing the `readonly` entry to `true`. The default setting of `false` lets anyone make changes to the theme or delete it. Changing this setting to `true` ensures that someone can't delete or modify the theme from within FrontPage.

The second change is to add any entries needed to the `[titles]` section to support other languages. The default setting consists of a language identifier or LCID (1033 in this case) and the name of the theme in that language. When you want to support other languages, you must provide an LCID for that language and a descriptive name. For example, if you want to provide support for Spanish (from Spain) you would add an entry like this to the `[titles]` section (note that this translation might not be precise):

```
1034=Mi Tema De Muestra
```

Removing themes you don't want

At some point, you'll have a number of themes on your system that didn't quite make the grade. Yes, they're nice themes (potentially, anyway), but you've created better themes since you started and don't really need those old ones anymore. To remove a theme you don't want, follow these steps:

1. **Hover the mouse pointer over the theme in the Select a Theme window of the Task Pane.**

2. **Click the button that appears to the right of the theme.**

   You see a context menu.

3. **Select Delete from the list.**

   Note that you can delete themes you create. However, you cannot delete the themes provided with FrontPage.

Book III

Webs

Contents at a Glance

Chapter 1: Working with an Existing Web Site

In This Chapter

✔ Getting ready to import the site

✔ Creating a new Web from an existing site

✔ Describing the site properties

✔ Providing site views

Web is the FrontPage term for an entire site. A simple Web is one in which there's a single Web site. However, a Web can include a main site and a number of subsites. Each subsite is accessible as a separate Web site and has its own characteristics. Think of a Web as the root of the tree that defines your Web site, with leaves describing each destination Web page. In FrontPage, the effect of a Web (that is, of a Web site) is to provide organization and added functionality.

You can open a Web site and modify it without ever converting it to a Front-Page Web. FrontPage still provides standard editing features for pages and you can perform various configuration tasks. However, when you convert a site to a Web, you gain the advantage of referencing the site as an entity. That means you can import and export the site *as a package*. Before you can convert an existing site to a Web, however, you need to clean it up. And after you import it, you must perform some initial setup and maintenance tasks.

A Web can make use of features that a standard site doesn't have, so you perform some FrontPage-specific tasks with the new Web. These tasks include defining the new Web properties and configuring it to use the special views and reports that FrontPage provides. When you complete the task, FrontPage can help you manage your Web site in ways that weren't possible before.

Cleaning Up Before You Import the Site

Your current Web site probably works fine. You know where everything's stored and you know why you organized the pages in a certain way. The problem is that you haven't documented your setup and your technique for managing the site has changed as your knowledge increased. Even though your site works fine, you still need to perform some cleanup before you import it into FrontPage. The goal of this cleanup process is to make it easier to manage the site after it is in FrontPage.

Most Web sites have a few "dead" pages, which are pages that you could access at one time but are no longer accessible. Perhaps the page contains information that you're saving for later use, much as someone stuffs an old chair in the attic, hoping to use it again someday. FrontPage views all pages on your site as usable and connected; you need to remove any dead pages. You can even archive them in another location for future use. The point is to clean them out of the site you want to import.

Another problem area is the use of folders instead of Web pages for organizational needs. When you create a navigational view of your site, FrontPage looks at the direct connections between pages — it doesn't see the actual folders you create. A page with 30 hyperlinks has 30 connections — even if those connections are to different folders on your Web site. Yes, you can cure this trouble after you import the site into FrontPage, but it's a lot easier to clean it up *before* you import the site.

It's also time to fix any known errors you have on your site, such as links that no longer connect to any location. Links are one area where FrontPage can help, but fixing known errors before you import the Web site saves time later. FrontPage can't help you fix other common errors (for example, broken scripts), but this transitional time is a perfect opportunity to perform all those consistency changes you plan to make as well.

A few Web sites I've seen have links to other areas of the same site that don't reside in the current folder. Make sure your entire site appears within the same main folder on your system or your server. Don't assume FrontPage can find the redirected folder that provides access to your database pages because it probably won't.

The cleanup phase is also the time you gather any information you need about your Web site. For example, if you use a hosted site, you want to know precisely how to upload pages to the site so you can set up a remote Web site in FrontPage. You also want to check your Web pages for any special functionality they require. For example, a page that contains special plug-in support will probably require additional import editing to ensure you see it properly in FrontPage.

Developers who plan to use the remote Web-site feature of FrontPage should also check the local and remote files. Yes, FrontPage will help you synchronize the two sets of files, but FrontPage can create duplicates of files when a local name differs from a remote name. A little work cleaning up such files now can prevent a lot of confusion later when you try to make your local files work with the files on the remote site. (FrontPage can also directly manipulate files on the remote site, but this isn't the best option when using a hosted site — because the hosted site may view it as a security breach, you might find that FrontPage works unreliably (crashes), or the connection might be terminated by the hosted site. For more on the remote Web site feature, see Book I, Chapter 2, and Book III, Chapter 2.

In FrontPage, using two sets of files, local and a remote copies, has some significant advantages; you might want to consider creating a local copy if you don't have one now. Having a local copy makes a connection to the remote site unnecessary when you make changes. You could edit Web pages on your laptop from any location and upload the changes you make later, when a connection becomes available. A local copy also makes it easier to make major changes to a Web site without disrupting the people using the older version. You can test changes locally before you make them part of your production Web site. For this reason and many others, consider creating a local copy of your Web site as one of your cleanup tasks.

Importing the Site

Importing your site into FrontPage isn't too difficult when you perform the proper cleanup. The important starting tasks include creating the Web, performing some setup tasks, and making sure that the hyperlinks work. It's also important to establish a connection with the remote Web site so you can synchronize your local and remote files.

Creating the Web

Creating a Web begins when you choose the storage location for your files. It's important to differentiate the storage location from the usage location when you edit your files locally. The local storage area is the one you want to use when working with a hosted site. You edit the files locally and then upload them to the remote location so everyone can see your work. Follow these steps:

1. **When you know where the storage location is, choose the File➪Open Site command.**

You see the Open Site dialog box.

2. **If you're working with local files, click My Computer. Locate the folder that contains the files you want to use as a local Web and press Open.**

or

If you're working with a remote site, click My Network Places. Type the URL of the remote site in the Site Name field and click Open.

In both cases, FrontPage opens the site for you. You see the files and folders that make up your Web site.

3. **Right-click the main folder for your site and choose Convert to Web from the context menu.**

FrontPage displays a dialog box that warns that this change can affect your links and even break some of them. This change can also affect any changes you made with FrontPage earlier. For example, any themes you applied to Web pages could become lost. In general, you have to per- form some updates after you create a new Web.

4. **Click Yes.**

FrontPage converts the Web site to a Web.

The biggest change you notice immediately is the addition of a _private folder that FrontPage uses to store some settings. Because you haven't added any settings, the _private folder is empty. You also notice the folder icon has changed into a Web icon.

Deleting a Web

Anyone can make a mistake. When you find that you set up your Web in the wrong location, don't try to fix the error by using a program other than FrontPage. Fixing the error outside FrontPage means that FrontPage will retain the erroneous site indefinitely. (Even uninstalling and reinstalling FrontPage doesn't appear to help with this particular problem.)

Always remove Webs that you don't need from within FrontPage to keep your FrontPage setup clean. To remove a Web you no longer need or one that you created by mistake, follow these steps:

1. **Close the erroneous site by selecting the File⇨Close Site command.**

2. **Select the File⇨Open Site command.**

3. **Choose a location that's one step above the Web location.**

For example, if you have your Web on D:\MySite, open D:\ as the new site. Click Open. You see a list of folders and files.

4. **Right-click the folder that contains the Web and choose Convert to Folder from the context menu.**

FrontPage warns that some theme information is going to be broken. In addition, people who don't have access to the parent site will lose access to the information on this Web. All settings you created for the Web are also lost.

5. **Click Yes.**

FrontPage removes the Web.

Performing the initial setup

After you create a Web, you configure it for use. The first step in this process is to create the required comments and other information about the individual pages in the Web. This is also the time you create new statuses and categories for the Web site. Even though your Web site has operated for a long time without this information, adding it will help manage the Web site and make it more efficient.

To perform the configuration, follow these steps:

1. **Right click each file in turn and choose Properties from the context menu.**

You see the Properties dialog box for that page.

2. **Select the Summary tab and type a summary.**

Describe the task this page performs in a sentence or two.

3. **Select the Workgroup tab and assign the page to a category (often a workgroup), a person within that workgroup, and give the page a status.**

When necessary, create new categories, add new names, and define new status levels for your Web site. You perform these tasks one page at a time when creating a new Web. When working with an existing site that you import into FrontPage, you perform this configuration task on all pages at once.

 The initial setup gives you another opportunity to check individual pages within the Web site. When you discover a page that you can't summarize or that no one maintains, you need to consider whether that page is still an active part of your Web site. Although configuring all the pages before you proceed with the next step might seem inefficient, it's far from a waste of time; it's really important to the setup process.

Part of your initial setup is to check the page properties as well. These settings should already appear in the Web site, but it pays to verify they're consistent and truly reflect the current page. To check the page properties, open the page. Right-click the page and choose Page Properties from the context menu. You see the Page Properties dialog box. Verify that the entries on each tab are correct and consistent with your policies for the Web site.

Setting the home page

The final step in the initial setup is to define a home page. FrontPage uses this entry as a starting point for many reports and views. For example, the Navigation view uses the home page as a starting point. To create the home page, right-click the page you want to use and choose Set as Home Page from the context menu.

**Book III
Chapter 1**

**Working with an
Existing Web Site**

It's at this point something strange could happen. If you named your default Web page anything other than what FrontPage thinks you should have named it, FrontPage will rename it for you. FrontPage depends on its knowledge of the server to choose a name for you. When your Web runs on IIS, FrontPage commonly uses `Default.htm` as the default name. Likewise, when running on a UNIX server, FrontPage normally defaults to `Index.htm`. Only when you work on a local hard drive — without any server connection — does FrontPage leave your home-page name alone.

You can prevent this renaming on IIS (and possibly other Web servers) when you have access to the server. Here's how:

1. **Select the Internet Information Services console entry found in the Administrative Tools folder of the Control Panel.**

You see the Internet Information Services console.

2. **Right-click the server entry for the server that hosts your Web and choose Properties.**

You see the Server Properties dialog box.

3. **Select WWW Service on the Internet Information Services tab and click Edit.**

You see the WWW Service Master Properties dialog box. This dialog box contains settings that affect the entire Web site, and it's the settings that FrontPage depends on to make the file renaming decision.

4. **Select the Documents tab.**

5. **Click Add in the Enable Default Document section.**

You see the Add Default Document dialog box.

6. **Type the name of the default document you want to use in the Default Document Name field.**

7. **Click OK.**

You see the new default document added to the list.

8. **Click OK twice.**

You have added a new default document to the server setup, but FrontPage won't know about it.

9. **Close and then reopen FrontPage.**

10. **Set the home page.**

FrontPage will likely to rename it for you despite the server change. However, now you can rename the document to its original name, and it will remain a home page because it appears as one of the default document names that the server supports.

Configuring the FrontPage Server Extensions

Use the FrontPage Server Extensions when you want full FrontPage inter-action with the server and support for special features such as e-mail. A new Web often requires server configuration when you choose to use the FrontPage Server Extensions. The FrontPage Server Extensions are Internet Information Server (IIS)-specific, so you don't need to check this feature on a hosted Web site where you can't access the server. FrontPage relies on the FrontPage Server Extensions to provide services such as using e-mail as a destination for user feedback and to provide page management.

To change the FrontPage Server Extension settings, follow these steps:

1. **Open the Internet Information Services console located in the Administrative Tools folder of the Control Panel.**

   If you don't see such a folder, you can't administer the server and will need to request changes through your network administrator.

   The Internet Information Services console contains a single Microsoft Management Console (MMC) snap-in named Internet Information Service. Within this snap-in is a list of computers you can access.

   If you don't see the computer that contains the Web displayed, try this:

   a. **Right-click Internet Information Services and choose Connect from the context menu.**

   You see the Connect to Computer dialog box.

   b. **Type the name of the computer that contains the Web you want to change in the Computer Name field and click Connect.**

   The Internet Information Services snap-in displays the new computer.

2. **Locate the folder that contains the Web you created.**

3. **Right-click the folder and choose Properties from the context menu.**

   You see a Web site Properties dialog box.

4. **Click Server Extensions and you see a dialog box similar to the one shown in Figure 1-1. (The title bar and a few other minor features differ from site to site.)**

To enable FrontPage to work with the Web server, you must check the Enable Authoring check box. Clear this setting when authoring is complete, the server is ready for production, or you don't want any accidental changes.

Book III
Chapter 1

Working with an
Existing Web Site

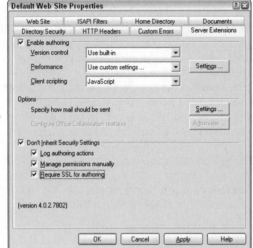

Figure 1-1:
Configure
the
FrontPage
Server
Extensions
to meet your
needs.

When working in a group, make sure you select some form of version control to ensure changes are recorded. FrontPage comes with built-in version control, and you can purchase third party version control packages for large groups. A small setup with one or two developers probably doesn't need version control as much (although it's still recommended).

The Performance field defines how FrontPage interacts with the Web server and how the Web server allocates memory and other resources for the Web. The default settings tune the Web for less than 100 pages, between 100 and 1,000 pages, and over 1,000 pages. You can use one of these settings or create custom settings to match your server and Web configuration. To use a custom setup, click the Settings button in the Performance area. You see the Performance dialog box. These settings control the number of in-memory documents, including support and image files you can use. The default image file setting is very small. Change this setting when you have a lot of images to display. You also find settings for the search index and the maximum size of any single document. Set these values as appropriate for your Web. For example, a research site will definitely need a larger search index than the 1MB the default setup provides.

The Client Scripting field defines the default scripting language for the Web. You can set this value differently than IIS as a whole or other Webs that FrontPage manages. The default setting is JavaScript. You can also choose VBScript.

The Specify How Mail Should Be Sent setting is especially important when you want to use e-mail for communication. FrontPage doesn't make any assumptions, so this setting isn't configured. Each Web on your Web server can have different contact information. To configure e-mail, follow these steps:

1. **Click the Settings button in the Options area.**

2. **Type the e-mail address of the person who manages the Web in the Web Server's Mail Address field.**

3. **Type the e-mail address of the support person (the one who handles problems for this Web) in the Contact Address field.**

4. **Add the Simple Mail Transfer Protocol (SMTP) server address in the SMTP Mail Server field.**

5. **Finally, select values for the Mail Encoding (the way the mail is formatted) and Character Set fields if necessary.**

Normally, the default values work fine — the only time you should change these settings is when you have your server configured for one language and you need to use another for this Web.

Check the Don't Inherit Security Settings check box when you want to use special settings for FrontPage developers. Normally, FrontPage inherits the default settings for the site. When you use the Don't Inherit Security Settings option, you must set the permissions for each folder individually by right-clicking it and choosing Properties to display the Properties dialog box, which contains the various security options. In general, you won't have to set special settings when your Web site is secure. However, you want to select all three check box options for public Web sites to ensure you get the added security required. The logging feature is especially important because it can help you discover unwanted intrusions. (The location of the log depends on your custom Web site setup. For more on security, see Book IV, Chapter 7.)

Verifying site hyperlinks

At this point, the Web is ready for initial use. However, you have moved pages around, deleted those you don't need, and performed a number of other tasks that could cause broken links. Whenever you think you might have broken links on a Web, it's time to verify them. In many cases, FrontPage can help you locate and fix the broken links. In other cases, FrontPage can locate the links, but you must fix them yourself.

The first step is to see what FrontPage can do to address this problem. Choose the Tools⇨Recalculate Hyperlinks command. FrontPage displays a message box telling you what tasks this command performs. Click Yes. FrontPage begins checking and repairing hyperlinks. After a few minutes, you see the display blink — FrontPage has completed the task but doesn't display a message saying so.

Now that the links that FrontPage can fix are checked, you need to look for broken links it can't fix. Click Reports on the bottom of the Web Site tab. You see a list of standard FrontPage reports. Click Broken Hyperlinks. FrontPage offers to verify the hyperlinks on the Web site. Click Yes. FrontPage begins looking for broken hyperlinks.

As shown in Figure 1-2, you can see the status of hyperlinks as FrontPage checks them. Unverified hyperlinks have Unknown next to them; the hyperlink that FrontPage is currently checking has Verifying next to it; good hyperlinks have OK next to them; and broken hyperlinks have Broken next to them. The status bar shows the percentage of hyperlinks checked. This check takes much longer than the hyperlink recalculation. Plan on waiting for at least 15 to 20 minutes for a moderately sized Web (around 75 pages) with a fast connection. When the process completes, the status bar tells you how many links are broken.

Sort the hyperlinks by clicking the Status column. The broken hyperlinks appear at the top of the list. To fix a broken hyperlink, right-click its entry and choose Edit Hyperlink from the context menu. You see an Edit Hyperlink dialog box. Type the new hyperlink in the Replace Hyperlink With field. You can choose to replace the hyperlink in all affected pages by selecting the Change in All Pages option. Click Replace. FrontPage makes the required changes.

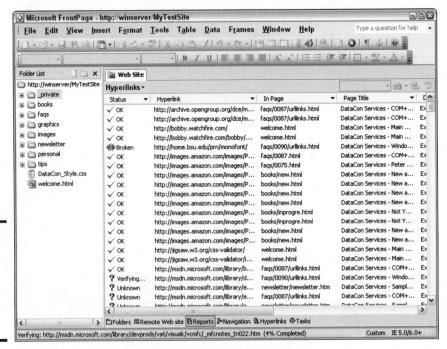

Figure 1-2:
Verify links on your Web site to ensure they aren't broken.

Sometimes you don't have a substitute hyperlink for the affected page. When this occurs, click Edit Page in the Edit Hyperlink dialog box. FrontPage displays the affected page. Remove the hyperlink and repair any affected text or graphics as needed. After you edit the affected page, the Status column will contain Edited with a question mark. You'll need to perform the broken link check again to ensure all links work.

Defining Site Properties

A Web has special properties that define how it interacts with FrontPage. For example, you can reduce potential coding problems in a workgroup setting by ensuring everyone checks out documents for editing and back in when the editing session is complete. The special features can help you perform tasks more quickly and with fewer errors. To begin setting the site properties, choose the Tools⇨Site Settings command. You see the Site Settings dialog box shown in Figure 1-3.

**Book III
Chapter 1**

**Working with an
Existing Web Site**

Figure 1-3:
Change the
site settings
to enable
special
FrontPage
features.

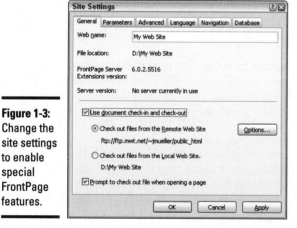

The General tab contains the name of the Web, the name and version of the server, and determines whether FrontPage users have to check documents in and out. The options on this tab reflect your Web setup — the remote options are available only when you have a local and remote set of files. Choose the location where you'll edit the files, not the location where the files will go when you publish them.

If you're working with a remote location, click the Options button. You see the Remote Check Out Options dialog box. Type the name of the person performing the edits in the Check Out Name field. Check Include My FTP Login Name when more than one person could use the same editing name or you check in using more than one identity. Always include the optional Check

Out Email Address field entry so others can contact you when you fail to check a document in after editing it. Otherwise, other people who want to edit the document will have to wait until they can contact you in some other way (usually not nicely).

Creating Required Views

FrontPage relies on views to help you see the structure of your Web site. The three important views for starting a new Web based on an existing Web site are the Navigation, Hyperlinks, and Tasks views. Generally, you want to create these views in order because each view builds upon the other. For example, you must have a Navigation view to use the Hyperlinks view. Even though you can create tasks before you build anything else, the Navigation and Hyperlinks views provide needed input.

Defining a navigational view

The Navigation view shows the structure of your Web site — how various pages connect and the resources they require. Creating a home page places the first entry in the Navigation view. The home page acts as the base of the tree that describes your Web site.

Not everything has to connect to the tree, but most items do. All Web pages for your site should connect to the tree — make sure you figure out why a page doesn't connect. Graphics should always connect to a page unless they're a generic graphic such as a logo or picture that appears on more than one page. Any Cascading Style Sheet (CSS) files will probably appear separately from the rest of the Web site because they affect every page.

To add a new page to the Navigation view, drag it from the Folder List and place it where it should appear in the hierarchy. You see a line link from the home page to each top-level page as you add it. Drop the page when it connects to the correct page in the hierarchy. Support files, such as graphics, appear with the name of the file and a red circle with a slash through it to show they're support files and not Web pages.

It doesn't take long, even with a complex Web site, to build a Navigation view of your site using this technique. What you see when you get done might horrify you. I know I was quite surprised when I finished the Navigation view the first time. Figure 1-4 shows a typical example of what many people see the first time. The home page really is working overtime to connect all the pieces in this Web site.

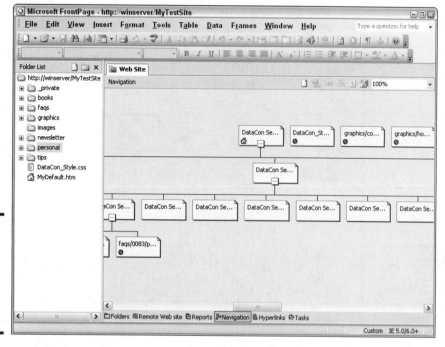

**Book III
Chapter 1**

Working with an
Existing Web Site

Figure 1-4:
Creating a
Navigation
view dem-
onstrates
problems in
your layout.

At this point, FrontPage can help you design a more effective layout. If you relied on folders to provide the only structure for your Web site in the past, the Navigation view quickly shows the problem this layout strategy can create. From a user perspective, a page with too many links and too little organization presents a problem in finding information quickly. Reorganizing your Web site to provide a better layout is a good first step in using FrontPage effectively.

Figure 1-4 demonstrates another problem. The default Navigation view can't show the entire Web site at once. This problem will still exist even after a Web reorganization. To see the entire Web at one time, select Size to Fit in the Zoom field of the Navigation view. In most cases, you can't read the text for each page when you do this, but hovering the mouse over a block shows its title. After you locate a particular area of the Web site, you can zoom to that section to see the details.

In a few cases, it also helps you switch from a landscape to a portrait presentation by clicking Portrait/Landscape in the Navigation view. Figure 1-5 shows how this presentation differs for the example Web site from the typical landscape view.

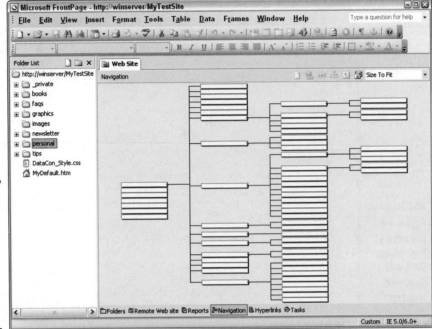

Figure 1-5:
Use the
portrait
orientation
to gain a
different
perspective
of your
Web.

To fix a site with organizational problems, you might need to create buffer pages. Simply create a blank page as you normally would and add the links to child pages — those that physically appear in a single folder on the Web site. After the buffer page is complete, create a link from the main or other parent page to this new buffer page. These pages essentially replace the folders as organizational aids from the user perspective. You still rely on folders for physical page organization, but now the site is also easier to use because the links are organized.

Defining hyperlinks

After you create a basic organization that works using the Navigation view, use the Hyperlinks view to refine the layout. This view helps you look at the links between pages from two perspectives: default and linked page. The default perspective shows the actual links. This view often reflects the physical layout of your site by showing which links are related and where they fall within the directory structure as shown in Figure 1-6.

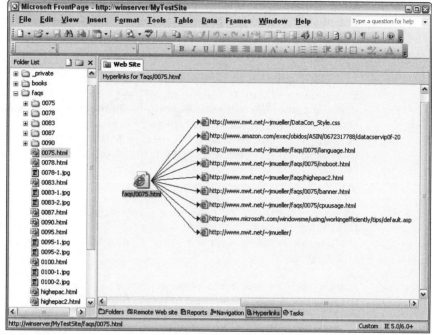

Figure 1-6:
Check the
physical
layout of
links on your
site first.

**Book III
Chapter 1**

**Working with an
Existing Web Site**

Unfortunately, FrontPage shows the links in the order in which they appear
on the page, so you often need to look through the list several times to see
problems in the links. In addition, FrontPage assumes you don't want to see
repeated links, but that's one problem you should look for at this stage of your
Web development. Fortunately, you can show repeated links by right-clicking
the design area and choosing Repeated Hyperlinks from the context menu.

Generally, a well designed Web page doesn't have repeated links. When a site
includes repeated links, you must provide a means of bypassing them to
maintain accessibility.

To check your entire Web, you must go page-by-page and view the results in
the Hyperlinks view. The page you select in the Navigation view is the one
that appears in the center of the Hyperlinks view. You can also move from
area to area by right-clicking a link of interest and choosing Move to Center
from the context menu. Moving a linked page to center displays the linked
page perspective. This technique doesn't guarantee that you'll visit every
page on the Web, however, so you shouldn't rely on it as an accurate means
of checking your site for errors.

Note that the standard view doesn't show graphics links. In many cases, you won't need to check the graphics links immediately because you've already verified that the link is valid using the Broken Hyperlinks report. You can display graphics links by right-clicking the design area and choosing Hyperlinks to Pictures when necessary.

Sometimes, you want to see the actual page title in Hyperlinks view, rather than the partial URL shown in Figure 1-6. Right-click the design area and choose Show Page Titles to see the page title in place of the URL. In many cases, this is a great way to verify each page has a properly constructed title that meets any guidelines set by your organization.

Creating initial update tasks

As you work with the Web you create, you begin to compile a list of the tasks it needs from time to time — everything from fixing broken links to much-needed organization. For many developers, this list soon becomes unmanageable.

FrontPage provides a Tasks view where you can create a list of updates to perform on your site. You want to create tasks in such a way that you can easily sort them by priority. It's also better to create a task that you can accomplish during one editing session, rather than a gruesome project guaranteed to last a week or more. Dividing tasks into small pieces so you can easily manage them gives you a sense of accomplishment and makes the project seem easier.

Consider the task of fixing broken links. Some links are essential because users rely on them all the time. Pages that users visit frequently should receive a higher priority than pages that users visit less often. Broken links that have an update should exist in a different category than those you can't fix with a simple replacement.

I use special naming for tasks to make them easier to sort. For example, all link-related tasks begin with the word `Links`; all organizational issues begin with the word `Organization`. Using a keyword in this way can make title-sorting a lot more efficient, as shown in Figure 1-7. Make sure you use the same keywords consistently to ensure sorting actually provides a benefit.

To create a new task, right-click the Tasks view and choose Add Task from the context menu. You can also choose the Edit⇨Tasks⇨Add Task command. You see the New Task dialog box shown in Figure 1-8.

Begin by typing a title for the task. Make the title descriptive but short. The Tasks view contains a limited amount of space for displaying the title, so you need to exercise care in choosing a title. After you type the title, assign the task to someone. When you work on a site alone, the person doing the work is always going to be you.

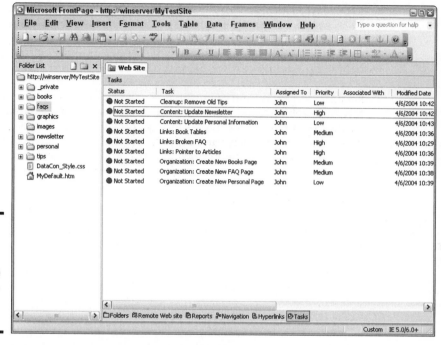

Figure 1-7:
Sort tasks
in various
ways to see
how best to
accomplish
your work.

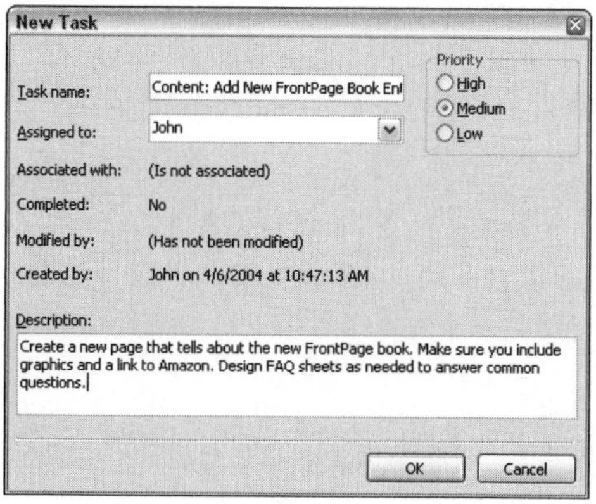

Figure 1-8:
Provide a
descriptive,
but short,
title for the
new task.

Assign a priority to the task next. If you're tempted to give *everything* a
high priority, you're not alone — but doing so would defeat the purpose
of using priorities. In practical terms, there's always a range: A few items are
high-priority; a few more are probably low-priority, with some tasks falling
into the medium range. I often base priority on the amount of time I have.
All high-priority items get accomplished because I specifically set time aside

to do them. The medium priority items are likely to get accomplished, but because there isn't a specific time set aside for them, I might not accomplish them all. All low-priority items are accomplished only when I have extra time. They eventually get accomplished during slow periods but might end up waiting a month or more before I have time.

Finally, write a description for the task. Add all the information you can possibly think of to ensure you have everything needed to accomplish the task quickly. For example, if I'm working with broken links, I include the specific links and where they appear on my site (easier than trying to find them in the Broken Links report). In short, use the information from the various reports to create tasks so you don't have to create the report again.

Chapter 2: Creating a New Web

Many people see the need for an application like FrontPage after creating a basic Web site using Word or even a simple text editor. These tools provide a good starting point but don't offer the features that FrontPage provides for creating Web sites quickly. Consequently, the first experience many users have with FrontPage is updating and fixing an existing Web site. Of course, you won't always have an existing Web site to use with FrontPage. In some cases, you create a new Web site based on a specific need.

Creating a new *Web* (the FrontPage term for Web site) from scratch is easier than working with an existing Web site for a number of reasons — the most important of which is that you don't have to rework anything you've already created. You can create the Web without any preconceived ideas of how the pages should fit together, so you get a better design from the outset.

One decision you make at the outset with a new Web site is where to store the data. Some developers like to use a remote connection for all activity because it lets them update everything immediately. In addition, the technique can work better with groups. Other developers like to store the data locally and publish it to the remote site. This technique has the advantage of letting you test everything before you make it public.

To make development easier, FrontPage also includes a number of templates you can use. These templates make the process easier by creating a Web site that conforms to good design principles at the outset. The templates provide structure, and you provide the content to go with the structure.

Understanding Webs

Webs always provide structure for your Web site. However, when you create a new site, a Web also provides a starting point in the design process. You begin with the Web, add major design features such as themes, move on to the home page, and then begin structuring the site as a whole. The Web provides the starting point you need to create a well-designed Web site that's feature rich from the very start.

The term *Web* normally refers to the starting point for an entire site. You create a Web from a folder on your server. In some cases, a Web becomes so complex that you want to split it into pieces. Each piece acts like a room in a house. Even though the room is part of the house, you tend to focus on just the features in the room while there. The two ways to split a Web are to create other Webs (Webs within Webs) or create subsites. Using subsites is helpful because FrontPage can help you create special looks.

Creating a new Web

Before you create a new Web, one that doesn't rely on an existing Web site, you need a folder. You can create a local folder using Windows Explorer or FrontPage. It's also possible to create a folder on a remote Web site using FrontPage.

Don't use the highest-level (root) folder of either a local drive or a Web site as the location for a Web — always create a folder for the Web. Using this technique helps you maintain security and makes it easier to remove the Web should you need to get rid of it at some point.

Creating a local Web

A local Web is one that resides on your hard drive. You can do almost everything with a local Web that you can do with a remote Web. The main difference is that people can't see the information on a local Web because there isn't a Web server to send them the information. Use the following steps to create a local Web:

1. **Select the File⇨Open Site command.**

You see the Open Site dialog box.

2. **Select My Computer.**

You see a list of all the local drives and networked drives you can access.

3. **Double-click a drive entry.**

You see the folders for that drive, as shown in Figure 2-1.

4. **Click Create New Folder.**

You see the New Folder dialog box.

5. **Type a name for your new Web (the example uses MyLocalWeb) and click OK.**

FrontPage automatically displays the new folder.

6. **Click Open.**

FrontPage displays an Add FrontPage Information to the Folder dialog box telling you what changes FrontPage will make to open this folder as a site.

7. Click Yes.

FrontPage opens the new folder as a local Web. It adds at least two folders: _private and images.

The Web has special entries and a unique icon so you can easily recognize it. To see this icon, right click the folder and choose Properties. Select the Customize tab and you see the specialized icon as shown in Figure 2-2.

Create New Folder

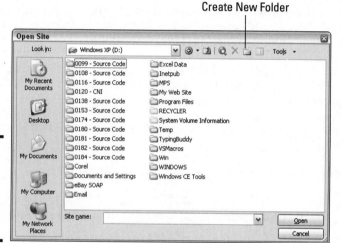

Figure 2-1:
Select a
location for
the new
Web on a
local drive.

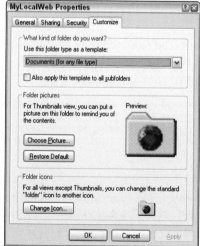

Figure 2-2:
Change the
appearance
of the Web
icon to meet
specific
needs.

After you create a local Web, you can start by selecting a theme and other layout information for it. Add a home page and then start adding other content pages as needed. You can't perform some steps, such as setting security for the Web, because there isn't a local server. You'll also find that server-side activities, such as server-side scripting, aren't available. Even so, using a local Web can save significant time because you can set everything up before you upload it to public view.

Creating a Web on a server

A remote Web provides everything needed to create a site. The precise level of control you obtain depends on the kind of server you use. Using Internet Information Server (IIS) provides you with additional configuration options as well as functionality. However, you can just as easily use other server types, such as Apache, and still see webbots and other FrontPage features in action. Make sure you install FrontPage extensions on such machines to get the full benefits they can provide.

To create a new folder on a remote Web server using FrontPage, follow these steps:

1. **Open the Web site by choosing File⇨Open Site.**

You see the Open Site dialog box.

2. **Type the Uniform Resource Locator (URL) for the site and click Open.**

FrontPage displays the remote site. Now you need to create the folder.

3. **Right-click the entry (usually the Web site URL folder) that will hold the new Web and choose New⇨Folder from the context menu.**

You see a new folder.

4. **Type a name for the folder (the example uses MyRemoteWeb) — this is the name of your new Web, so name it carefully.**

The new folder is just a folder until you make it a Web.

5. **Right-click the new folder and choose Convert to Web from the context menu.**

FrontPage displays a message telling you what it needs to do to make this folder a Web.

6. **Click Yes.**

FrontPage creates the new Web. The Web folder uses a different icon than other folders in the list. In addition, you can't see the contents of a Web folder from within the current view.

To open the new Web, double-click its entry in FrontPage. You see a new copy of FrontPage open that contains the new Web. The Web contains at least two folders: _private and images. At this point, you can begin designing your site.

Creating a new subsite

A subsite provides a separation from the current Web. You create a new element based on a template, rather than by creating an empty folder. (See the difference by looking at the MyRemoteWeb and NewWebSubsite folders in the source code for this book, available on the companion Web site.) To create a new subsite on an existing Web, follow these steps:

1. **Right click a folder in the Folder List (including the URL folder) and choose New⇨Subsite from the context menu.**

   You see the Web Site Templates dialog box shown in Figure 2-3.

Wizard Template icon

Standard Template icon   Includes Web site name

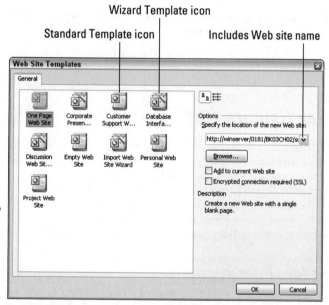

Figure 2-3:
Choose a
template for
your new
subsite.

2. **Begin by selecting one of the templates listed.**

   • All templates except the One Page Web Site option provide pages designed for specific purposes. See the "Selecting a Web Template" section later in this chapter for more information on the various templates.

   • You can choose the One Page Web Site option when you don't need any prebuilt infrastructure for the new subsite.

Don't check the Add to Current Web Site option when you want to create a subsite. Checking this option will add the content of the template to the current Web site rather than place the information in a separate location. The information is added according to the template specifications beginning at the root of the current Web site, so checking this option can cause problems when you have already created pages with the same name. FrontPage warns you before it overwrites the files, but it's still too easy to replace information you want for the current Web when you check the Add to Current Web Site option.

FrontPage provides the unimaginative name subsite for the new site as part of the Specify the Location of the New Web Site field.

3. **Replace the word** subsite **with the name you want to use for the new subsite.**

4. **Click Browse to choose a different location if the one you selected won't work.**

5. **To add security to the subsite, check the Encrypted Connection Required (SSL) check box.**

Secure Sockets Layer (SSL) is a standardized secure communication technology.

Using Local or Remote Connections

FrontPage supports both local and remote connections with equal ease. The standard assumption is that you create pages locally and upload them to a remote site or you modify the pages directly on the remote site depending on your needs. Some people also use FrontPage only for local connections. Before you can do too much with a Web, you must decide how you plan to use it, where the information must appear for other people to access it, and how to create connectivity between local and remote sites when necessary.

Using local connections

It's easy to assume that you always need a remote connection for FrontPage, even when you use a local Web to create content. All templates and other configuration items provided with FrontPage tend to enforce this idea. Many people use FrontPage to create local collections of data, some use FrontPage to create networked data sources, and still others create Web sites for intranets that are never shared outside the company. All of these uses can rely on a local connection that you modify directly and never upload anywhere.

Examples of local data collections include help files. Many Microsoft help files are now collections of Web pages displayed in a special kind of browser rather than standard Windows help documents built into an application as a feature. You can create specialized help documents for applications you create or simply define local collections of data in an easy to read format. Many open-source and third-party document sets are now just collections of Web pages. You download a series of Web pages and view them with a browser like Internet Explorer. It's even possible to create shortcuts for such documents so you access them from the Start Menu just as you would any other help file.

Another use of local Web pages is as a filing system. Instead of constantly telling people where to find a piece of data on the company network, you can create Web pages that contain hyperlinks to the required information. A hyperlink, especially one used for local resources, need not point to a Web page — it can point to any kind of information. Again, you could place a shortcut in the Start Menu to open the starting page for such an information resource in any browser. A second choice would be to create a company Web site that doesn't have any outside connection that you could use to hold the document index.

A company Web site is also a valuable resource you can maintain with FrontPage. In this case, you can send files directly to the network folder that contains the Web site files. Obviously, you can also use the local to remote connection that you would use for a remote Web site as well, but it's not necessary in this situation. The company Web site can hold anything from a standard Web site with company data to a document directory to a list of procedures. The Web site could contain listings of company standards or help users print out standard company forms (or download the PDF equivalent).

The point is that you shouldn't assume that FrontPage is only for Web sites and only for remote communication. FrontPage helps you work with all kinds of data in a number of ways. Anything that you can reference or display on screen can become a FrontPage project.

Selecting a remote Web site connection type

When you want to send data from a local source to a remote Web site, you need to create a connection between the two, which requires you to select a connection type. For example, many hosted sites require that you use a File Transfer Protocol (FTP) setup. A company intranet could use a simple network connection. Sometimes a remote site will support specialized communications such as a FrontPage or SharePoint Services connection. A few Web sites support Web-based Distributed Authoring and Versioning (WebDAV). Make sure you find out which connection your Web server supports before you begin creating a remote connection.

To start the connection process, open the local site in FrontPage. Choose the Remote Web Site tab. Unless you created a connection earlier, this tab is blank. Click Remote Web Site Properties. You see the Remote Web Site Properties dialog box shown in Figure 2-4.

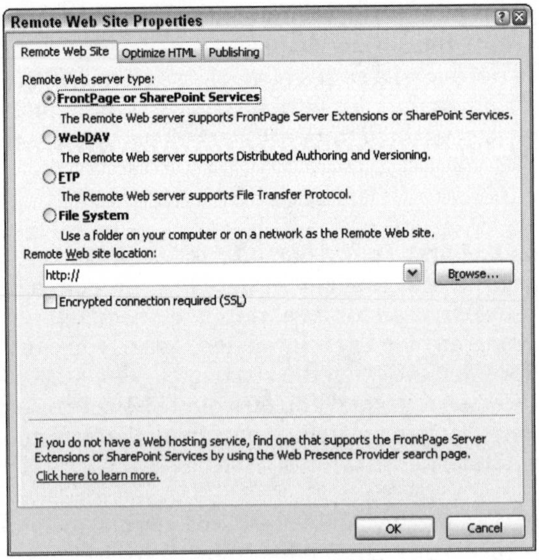

Figure 2-4:
Select a
remote
connection
type.

The setup for each connection differs slightly. Each is explained in the following list:

✦ The FrontPage or SharePoint Services option relies on a Web server that has FrontPage extensions installed and that is FrontPage compatible. With this option, you provide a HyperText Transport Protocol (HTTP) URL for the server. FrontPage also allows secure communication through SSL.

✦ The WebDAV option requires a server that has WebDAV support, which might be more common than you think. WebDAV is a standard-based open connectivity option that you can find on servers of all types. Discover more about WebDAV at http://www.webdav.org/. With this option, you provide a HyperText Transport Protocol (HTTP) URL for the server. FrontPage also allows secure communication through SSL.

✦ The FTP option uses a standard connection that most servers support. This is a good option because FTP is generally faster than other technologies. The problem with FTP is that it isn't very secure and you don't get as much feedback from it as you do with newer technologies. To use an FTP connection, you need to provide an FTP URL and provide starting directory on the FTP site. FrontPage also offers use of Passive FTP — a technology where the server uses a different port every time you communicate with it. Using a different port each time enhances security by making it harder for someone to listen to your conversation, but it's not that much of an advantage.

✦ The File System option relies on a network drive as a remote communication point. You don't have to use a mapped drive to work with this option.

FrontPage can also use Universal Naming Convention (UNC) paths such as \\MyServer\MyDrive\MyFolder to create the connection.

After you choose a connection method and provide connection information for it, click OK. FrontPage creates a connection between the local drive and the remote site. When FrontPage can't create the requested connection, it displays an error message and gives you a chance to choose another connection type. For example, you can't use WebDAV to access a Web server that has FrontPage Extensions or SharePoint Services installed. After you create a successful connection, FrontPage displays the Remote Web Site window shown in Figure 2-5.

Synchronizing a local Web site copy

When you create content locally and upload it to a Web, you need to perform a synchronization process. This process generally moves content from the local site to the remote site. It can also move content from the remote site to the local site when necessary. For example, you might want to download survey forms that users have filled out since the last update of the site. The process of moving files is *publishing*. In effect, when you write the content you want others to see locally and put it up on your Web site, you've published it.

Book III
Chapter 2

Creating a New Web

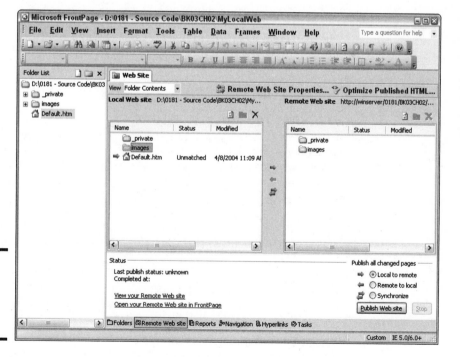

Figure 2-5:
Use this display to transfer files.

To synchronize your Web site, select the Remote Web Site tab. You see the window shown in Figure 2-5. Notice the window contains two panes. The pane on the left is the local drive; the pane on the right is the remote Web site. The local drive has a file not found on the remote Web site, so FrontPage marks it as unmatched. Notes such as this one are your cue that you need to synchronize content (assuming the content is approved).

Begin the synchronization process by selecting a direction using one of the arrow buttons between the two panes. Choose Local to Remote when you want to send content from your local drive to the remote Web site. Choose Remote to Local when you want to download new information from the remote Web site. Choose the Synchronize option when you want to transfer data in both directions. Click the Publish Web Site button. FrontPage performs the requested transfers. You can see the results of a transfer by clicking View Your Published Log File. FrontPage displays a list of actions that it performed using a standard Web page.

Sometimes you don't want to publish every change file on your site. When this situation occurs, highlight the files you want to transfer, and then click the directional arrow between the two sites that matches the action you want to perform.

To verify changes made to the remote Web site, click View Your Remote Web Site. FrontPage opens the default page on the site. You'll need to click the links of the pages that have changed to see them. It's also possible to open the remote Web site in FrontPage so you can see the changes directly. Click Open Your Remote Web Site in FrontPage to see the remote Web site as a whole. Check individual pages by double-clicking them in the Folder List or Folders view.

Optimizing uploaded content

Your local copy of a Web page contains a lot of information you need but others don't. For example, you add comments to the local copy to ensure you remember why you formatted text in a certain way. By and large, other people don't need to know this information, so removing the comment makes sense when you publish the material.

Web pages don't just contain comments though. When you add a time or date stamp to a Web page, FrontPage creates a webbot to show where the time or date stamp appears. Even though there isn't anything secret about a webbot, it does increase the size of the page, which means it requires more time to download.

A good Web page developer also includes *whitespace* in the page code to make it easier to edit. The whitespace actually makes the document bigger, so removing it when you're done editing the code decreases download time.

Even though these changes might seem small, they do add up. You can usually shave a few seconds off the download time for even a simple page by deflating the document before you publish it.

The problem is that you still need the comments to produce good Web pages, so editing your current document isn't a good idea. Fortunately, FrontPage can automatically perform these optimizations for you. To add optimizations to the publishing process, click Optimize Published HTML. You see the Optimize HTML tab of the Remote Web Site Properties dialog box shown in Figure 2-6.

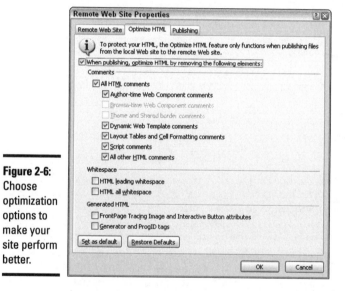

Figure 2-6: Choose optimization options to make your site perform better.

Select optimizations based on how you want your Web page to look online. The example saves space and keeps comments private by removing all HTML comments regardless of how they are created. The page retains its ease of reading (for people who use View➪Source in Internet Explorer to look at your code) by keeping the whitespace intact. The example doesn't use a theme, nor does it have any browse-time webbots included, so these options are disabled.

You can verify that an optimization took place in several ways. One way is to open the remote site and compare the size of the file with the local file size. The local file should be larger. This method lets you compare download times as well so you can actually see the performance gain. The second technique is to click View Your Publish Log File. The log contains special entries for any optimizations FrontPage performs on your behalf.

Setting publishing guidelines

FrontPage provides settings that help control the publication of new content on a Web site. To view these settings, click Remote Web Site Properties and choose the Publishing tab. You see the Remote Web Site Properties dialog box shown in Figure 2-7.

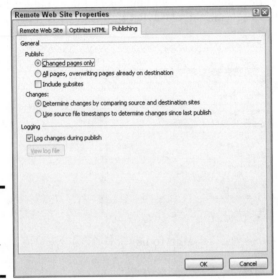

Figure 2-7:
Define a
publishing
strategy for
your site.

The default settings send only changed pages to the remote Web site and performs a comparison of the files to determine the direction of publication. The default settings also create a log during publication, but these setting changes don't include subsites. You use the All Pages, Overwriting Pages Already on Destination option when you suspect that an outsider might have changed the page content — or when you want to refresh the content of your site so the pages on your system match those online.

Normally, you don't want to update subsites automatically. The reason is that subsites are separate Webs so you should treat them as such. This option can save time and effort when you're the only one making updates and you want to publish all new content at once. It's also good to use this feature when you're setting up a new server (the server doesn't have any of the data loaded) or you want to refresh all content for every Web you maintain.

Select the User Source File Timestamp to Determine Changes Since Last Publish option when data always flows from the local site to the remote site. Using this option saves time because FrontPage doesn't have to request information from the remote site when you use it. In fact, considering most hosted pages won't allow your Web pages to create data on the server, this is a better option to choose for hosted sites.

There isn't a good reason to clear the Log Changes During Publish option because this feature helps you track changes to your Web. It shows precisely what changes FrontPage made on your behalf so you can verify the changes are correct. Without the log, you don't have any way of checking these changes except manually by verifying one Web page at a time. The only benefit you obtain from clearing this option is to save a little disk space (a few thousand bytes) and to reduce the time for uploading the files (a few milliseconds).

Selecting a Web Template

Web templates save you time by creating a setup based on standardized instructions. The template Web sites include consistent features that you can use to your advantage. All you need to do is add the custom content and any unique pages — the template has already defined the standard pages and their associated content for you. FrontPage supplies two template types: those that rely on standard page setups and those that use a wizard to create unique setups.

Don't assume that you always need to use a template. The templates provide a quick method of starting a Web site, but they certainly don't fulfill every need. When FrontPage or a third-party provider offers a template that meets your needs, you can save a great deal of time by using it. Using the wrong template, however, can actually *increase* the time required to create the Web site. In short, templates are simply a tool — not a fix for every problem.

Using standard Web templates

A standard template doesn't do anything special. You select the template you want to use in the Web Site Templates dialog box shown in Figure 2-3. Choose a name for the site, and then click OK. FrontPage copies *static* (unchanging) pages from the template folder to the Web site you defined. It sets the site up as a Web and that's it. This type of template works well because it's simple and easy to understand.

Using wizard Web templates

Sometimes you can't easily define a Web site based on the content of a few static Web pages. FrontPage also provides wizard templates. These templates use a special icon as shown in Figure 2-3. The advantage of a wizard template is that you can describe custom settings. The template produces content that better meets your needs. The disadvantage of using wizard templates is that they ask questions and less qualified uses have trouble answering. For example, try the Corporate Presence Wizard template. The following steps lead you through the use of a wizard Web template:

1. **Click Next to get past the welcome message.**

   The wizard asks which pages you want to include in the new Web site. Instead of getting all the pages the template has to offer, you can choose which pages to include. For example, you might not want to provide a What's New page on your site.

2. **Check the page options you want to use and click Next.**

   The wizard asks which topics you want to discuss on the home page. This page helps you customize the standard content for the Web site. When using a standard template, you receive all the content the author thinks you want, which means you might have to delete some items before you can begin working on unique content.

3. **Check the topics you want to discuss and click Next.**

   The page you see depends on which optional pages you selected. When you choose the What's New page, the wizard asks what content you'd like to present on that page. Likewise, when setting the content for the Products/Services page, the wizard will ask how many products and services you plan to discuss. The wizard continues through each page you selected until you describe content for each page. Finally, the wizard asks what should appear at the top of each page. These common content items appear on every page of the new Web site.

4. **Choose the items you want to appear on every page of the Web site and click Next.**

   The wizard asks whether you'd like to add a special symbol to show which pages are under construction.

5. **Select Yes or No, and then click Next.**

   The wizard asks you to provide your company's information, including address. The wizard includes several of these dialog boxes.

6. **Type your company name, address, and other identifying information. Click Next after each dialog.**

   You see the final dialog box where the wizard offers to create a task list of items you must complete.

7. **Check the Show Tasks View After Web Site is Updated option if you want the wizard to provide this service for you. Click Finish.**

   FrontPage creates the Web site for you.

Defining your own Web template

As you create new Web sites and hone your development skills, you begin building projects and combinations of Web pages that could prove useful as the starting point for new projects. Fortunately, you can create your own Web site templates and have them appear in the Web Site Templates dialog box shown in Figure 2-3. All of these templates appear in the following folder, in the drive that contains your FrontPage installation:

```
\Program Files\Microsoft Office\Templates\1033\WEBS11\
```

Creating an INF file

The first step in creating a new Web template is to gather all the files you want to use for that template. Make sure you include all unique Web pages and the support files they require. In other words, you need to set up a Web site with all the required layouts and support features but without the unique content a Web site will have. Don't create a directory structure for the template — place all the files into a single folder. The idea is to create as many of these pieces as possible, without creating work for yourself by generated content that you'll have to change. After you complete this folder, copy it to the `\Program Files\Microsoft Office\Templates\1033\WEBS11\` folder of your hard drive. Give the folder a name that ends with a TEM extension, such as `MyTemplate.tem`.

A Web site template can have a number of support files other than those required by the Web site itself. The most important file is the INF file. A simple template requires a simple INF file. Here's an example of an INF for a simple Web site.

```
[info]
_LCID=1033
_version=11.0.4819.0
title=Simple Web Site
description=Define a new simple Web site.
theme=NONE
```

The `[info]` section marker is just one of several markers you can see inside a Web site template information file. This section describes the template and every template has it. The `_LCID` entry identifies the locale or language for this particular template. The number `1033` indicates that this is a United States English template. The `title` entry provides a short description of the template. It appears directly beneath the template's icon. The `description` entry provides more details about the template. This information appears in the Description section of the Web Site Templates dialog box. Finally, the `theme` entry should reflect any theme you have attached to the template. You must include this entry with a value of `NONE` if your template doesn't use a theme.

Adding a file list

Most Web site templates include a file structure of some type. This information is lost when you place all the files in a single folder. To define a directory structure for a template, you include the [FileList] section. This section appears after the [info] section. Here's a typical example of a [FileList] section.

```
[FileList]
Default.htm=
SubPage1.htm=SubDir1/SubPage1.htm
SubPage2.htm=SubDir2/SubPage2.htm
```

To use this section properly, you need to list every page and resource your template uses, including graphics files. When a file appears in the main (root) folder of the Web, you list with an equals sign and nothing afterward as shown for Default.htm. A file that appears in another location includes that location after the equals sign, as shown for SubPage1.htm and SubPage2.htm. In this case, the template creates two subdirectories with a single file in each one. (You can see the full example in the SiteWithDirectory.tem folder of the source code for this chapter.)

Adding a project.map file

There's one final piece to the puzzle for most standard templates. Some FrontPage features rely on the appearance of a page in the Navigation view to work. For example, you can't create a banner without placing the page in the Navigation view. The table of contents and other webbot features won't work either. The way you place pages in the Navigation view automatically is by adding a structure=project.map entry to the [info] section of the template. You then create a project.map file that lists the pages that should appear in the Navigation view. Here's an example of a project.map file.

```
1,SubPage1.htm,1st Test Page,1000
2,SubPage2.htm,2nd Test Page,1000
3,SubPage3.htm,3rd Test Page,1,1
4,SubPage4.htm,4th Test Page,2,1
5,SubPage5.htm,5th Test Page,1,2
6,SubPage6.htm,6th Test Page,1,3
7,NoWhere.htm,Contents,0
```

The coding process consists of four columns:

1. The first column is a sequential number for this navigational item.

2. The second column contains the filename of the Web page.

The Web page must exist in the root Web site folder or FrontPage ignores it. This issue is the reason why you see so many FrontPage templates with all their pages stuffed into the root folder rather than sorted into subdirectories.

3. The third column contains the name of the page as it appears in the Navigation view.

This name also affects some webbots, such as the `banner` webbot. The name you type is the name you see in the banner.

4. The fourth column contains one of several number patterns. You see three kinds of numbers when working with this column in FrontPage:

- A value of 1000 places the page directly beneath the home page in the hierarchy. Consequently, `SubPage1.htm` and `SubPage2.htm` are directly beneath the home page.

- A two-number combination falls between one of these parent pages. A value of 1,1 would indicate the first parent page, `SubPage1.htm`, and the first item beneath that page. The 1,2 and 1,3 entries also fall beneath the `SubPage1.htm` entry. A value of 2,1 places the page beneath the second parent or `SubPage2.htm`.

- When you see a page with a 0, it appears at the same level as the home page. Figure 2-8 shows the Navigation view produced by this `project.map` file.

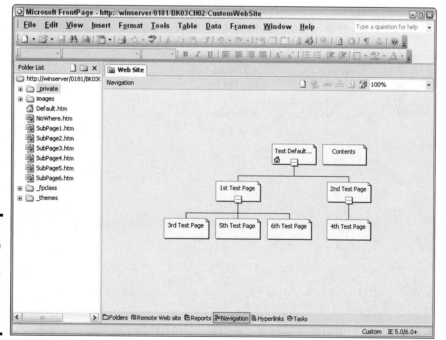

Figure 2-8: Create up to three levels of hierarchy with a project.map file.

Book III Chapter 2

Creating a New Web

Chapter 3: Using FrontPage Views

*T*he Web is the basis for many FrontPage features and the presentations provided by views permit you to work with Webs efficiently. Admittedly, you can use other products to get many of the features that FrontPage provides. Sure, the webbots are a convenient way to perform certain tasks and the support for themes creates nice-looking pages, but other products manage to get the same results by other methods. However, FrontPage provides a number of unique views that help you see your Web site in interesting ways.

These views help you create better Web sites by showing where changes are needed or where you can improve a presentation. The statistics FrontPage provides through its views help you understand which strategies work and which don't. Interactions between views create new forms of presentation that can help you see new ways of working with content. In short, knowing how to use FrontPage views makes you more efficient and enhances the Web sites you design and maintain.

Understanding Views

A FrontPage *view* is both a structure and a filter — a way of looking at the Web site as presented from a unique and consistent perspective. The Web site is the same as before, but how you see it changes. The view you use defines and selects the information you get from FrontPage. Consequently, use the view that is correct for the task you want to perform. For example, when you want to see the Web site as a whole, it might be tempting to use the Folders view, but the Navigation view is actually better. The Navigation view presents the Web site as the user would see it — moving from one page to the next — while the Folders view simply displays a list of files you can change.

Views also require interpretation. A view can show you information about your Web site, but only you can act on the information the view provides. When FrontPage tells you (for example) that something's wrong, it doesn't always correctly identify the source of the error. Suppose a particular page isn't getting very many hits, and FrontPage tells you there's a problem with this page. If the content on the page is esoteric enough that only a few people really care about it, then the low hit rate is expected. FrontPage doesn't know that.

Now, some developers would see a page with a low hit rate and immediately assume a problem with the content — or that the page isn't advertised properly. The problem (if it exists) could just as easily be a lack of accessibility features or an errant script that causes errors in some users' browsers.

The view can tell you that the page might have a problem, but it's still up to you to identify, locate, and fix the problem; the view is a great tool, but it's just a tool. As with any other tool, you can get the most value from a FrontPage view when you apply a few handy principles:

+ **Know what the tool can do and (more important) what it can't do.** I always find that part the most exciting; discovering new uses for a view is a kind of adventure.

+ **Decide how to interpret the results you receive from the view.** Sometimes that means deciding that although the view has provided you with correct information, it indicates only that everything is normal and there really isn't a problem.

+ **Create connections between views.** One view can feed the information provided by another so you wind up with a tool that does more than either could do alone. The most pronounced use of combined views is the Navigation view and the Hyperlinks view, but many other combinations exist.

Using the Page View

The Page view is what you see when you open a file; it's where you perform many page-specific tasks using the standard tools. But this view also interacts with other views, including a special version of the Navigation view. Beyond that, the Microsoft Office Clipboard provides another means of interacting not only with other views but also other applications such as Internet Explorer, from Page view: You can transfer data seamlessly.

You also use the Page view to design the elements that appear in every other FrontPage view. Creating (for example) your own frame and table layouts can save time and effort and meet your specific needs. You can also create capabilities that FrontPage doesn't have —for example, if you'd rather not hassle with the limitations of standard frames, you can create special frame layouts that rely on the `<OBJECT>` tag instead.

Interacting with the Navigation view

Whenever you open a new Web page, FrontPage adds another tab to the left pane (the Navigation Pane). The Navigation Pane and the Folders List share screen space: You can select one or the other. You always see a landscape view of the pages on your Web site when you use the Navigation Pane, as shown in Figure 3-1.

The Navigation Pane lets you move links for pages from the navigational organization of your Web site rather than the physical organization shown in the Folders List. To move a link, just drag it from the Navigation Pane and drop it where you want it to be on the current Web page.

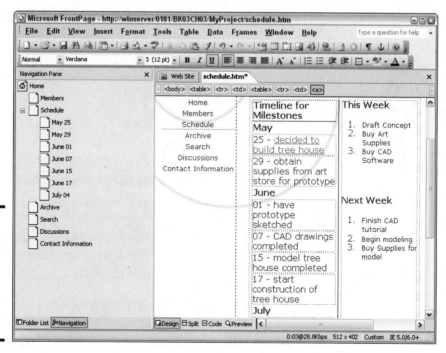

Figure 3-1:
Use the
special
Navigation
Pane view
to add links
to a Web
page.

**Book III
Chapter 3**

**Using FrontPage
Views**

The link FrontPage creates assumes you want to use the name of the page as it appears in the Navigation Pane. It also assumes you want to place the link on a separate line. To place the link on the same line as the current text, follow these steps:

1. **Place the cursor at the beginning of the link and press Backspace.**

Alternatively, you can choose the Remove Tag option from the drop-down list box of the <p> tag from the Quick Tag Selector.

2. **Edit the tag text.**

This isn't quite as easy as getting rid of the extra space because of the way that FrontPage inserts the new link. You have two options, one of them risky:

- You can highlight the text and start typing the new information, but often this act erases the link.

- To ensure that you keep the link, place the cursor on the link and select Tag Properties for the <a> tag in the Quick Tag Selector. When you see Edit Hyperlink dialog box, type your text in the Text to Display field and then click OK.

FrontPage changes the text in the link.

After you place all the links you need on-screen, it helps to check them for errors. Here's the most efficient method:

1. **Press and hold Ctrl, and then click a link.**

FrontPage opens the Web page that the hyperlink indicates. If you don't see the Web page you expected, then there's an error in the hyperlink.

2. **If necessary, fix the hyperlink using one of these methods:**

- Delete the incorrect link and drag the correct one to the Web page from either the Folder List or Navigation Pane

- Select Edit Tag from the drop-down list for the <a> tag in the Quick Tag Selector. You see the Quick Tag Editor. Type the correct URL after the href attribute and then click OK.

Adding data with the Office Clipboard

Every time you press Copy on the toolbar or use the Edit⇨Copy command, the Office Clipboard collects the information. The Office Clipboard doesn't collect this information forever, it only collects it during the current session (the time you remain logged on to your computer). In addition, when the Office Clipboard gets too full, it automatically removes old content. The Office Clipboard, despite its name, isn't just for Office products — it collects information you copy from other applications, too.

Office Clipboard is an exceptionally useful FrontPage tool. You can use it to create pages quickly by copying what the Office Clipboard holds and then pasting it wherever needed on the current Web page. To view the Office Clipboard (and edit what's on it if necessary), choose the Edit➪Office Clipboard command. Figure 3-2 shows some typical information you might see on the Office Clipboard.

You can also use special key combinations to place data on the Office Clipboard. For example, highlight a URL in the Address field of Internet Explorer and press Ctrl+C. You see the URL added to the Office Clipboard. Any application that can use the Clipboard can send information to FrontPage using this technique. In fact, many dialog boxes that don't look like they provide any Clipboard support will let you select text and press Ctrl+C to copy the information to the Office Clipboard.

Book III
Chapter 3

Using FrontPage
Views

Excel spreadsheet

E-mail message

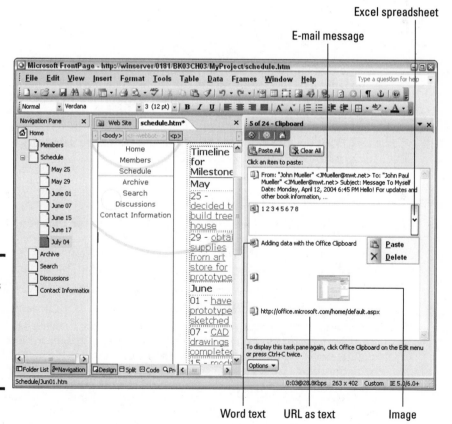

Figure 3-2:
Place items on the Office Clipboard for use in your Web pages.

Word text   URL as text   Image

FrontPage also has to be able to accept the data to use it. Generally, you won't run into a problem unless the data is esoteric and you wouldn't normally use it with FrontPage. You can easily copy everything from spreadsheets to standard text to FrontPage using the Office Clipboard. It's even possible to copy items that you might not ordinarily consider, such as e-mail messages.

After you place the data on the Office Clipboard, you can use it within a Web page. Place the cursor where you want the item to appear. Click the item entry you want to paste within Office Clipboard. FrontPage places the information in the position you selected on the current Web page. You can also use the context menu shown in Figure 3-2 to paste the item on-screen.

Figure 3-2 shows another important context menu entry. When you no longer need an item, you can delete it from the Office Clipboard by selecting the Delete option of the context menu. The context menu entry affects just the selected entry. To delete all of the items in the Office Clipboard (to save system memory or simply to ensure no one else can use the items for security reasons), click Clear All.

Note that FrontPage treats any URL you copy onto the Office Clipboard as text, not as a URL. Copying the URL as text can have advantages when you want to display the URL and not create a hyperlink. To create a hyperlink, perform these steps:

1. **Visit the site you want to add to the Web page using any browser with a history feature.**

2. **In FrontPage, choose Insert➪Hyperlink.**

   You see the Insert Hyperlink dialog box.

3. **Select the Browsed Pages option and locate the URL you visited.**

4. **Highlight the URL and click OK.**

   FrontPage adds the URL to the Web page.

Using the Grid and Ruler

Sometimes Web pages require accurate positioning to ensure that the data appears correctly on-screen. The idea is to create spaces for positioning the data, not to define specific font sizes or other display elements that could hinder others from viewing your Web page. The Grid and Ruler features help you create precise positioning. The Grid is a network of lines that appear in Design view but not in Preview view. The Ruler appears in two places, across the top and along the left side of the image. Use the View➪Ruler and Grid➪Show Ruler command to display the Ruler and the View➪Ruler and Grid➪Show Grid to display the Grid. Figure 3-3 shows a typical Design view with the Grid and Ruler added.

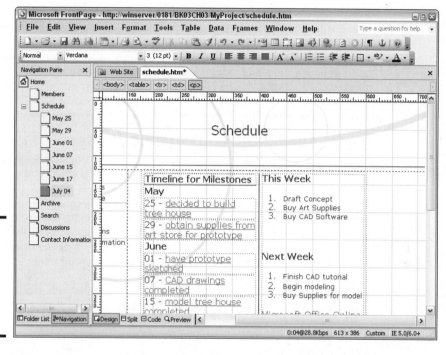

**Book III
Chapter 3**

**Using FrontPage
Views**

Figure 3-3:
Create precise layouts using the Grid and Ruler.

FrontPage actually supports two kinds of grids: the Display Grid (the one you see in Figure 3-3) and the Snapping Grid. The Snapping Grid causes items you place on a Web page to automatically align within precise increments. The Snapping Grid helps reduce the work required to create a perfect presentation by causing on-screen elements to align automatically but also makes it impossible to move items small distances other than the interval you set for the Snapping Grid. To turn the Snapping Grid on, right-click the Ruler and choose Snap to Grid from the context menu. Clear the context menu item to turn the feature back off.

Figure 3-3 shows the default settings for the Grid and Ruler, which rely on pixels as a unit of measure. Although using pixels as a unit of measurement can help you keep the size limitations of the browser you're targeting in mind, most people don't think in pixels. To make the measurements a little easier to use, you can select other units including inches, centimeters, and points (½ inch). To change the settings, right-click the Ruler and choose Configure from the context menu. You see the Page Options dialog box.

The Ruler and Grid are designed to work together, so you set the unit of measure the same for both items using the Ruler and Grid Units field. After you select a unit of measure, you can select Display Grid and Snapping Grid intervals using the Spacing field for each Grid. The value is in the unit of measure you select. When you choose 50 and the unit of measure is pixels, the grid uses a 50 pixel interval or spacing.

The Display Grid has additional features. You can choose a line type: solid (the default), dashes, or dots. FrontPage also lets you choose a color for the Display Grid. It often helps to choose a bright contrasting color so you can see the Display Grid easily and position elements accurately.

Creating your own accessible frames

Frames generally cause problems for most people because they rely on technology that some browsers don't support, and even when you do get browser support, the page isn't accessible. The use of frames makes it difficult for many people to move around the Web site and causes a number of other problems. Fortunately, there's a good alternative in the form of the `<OBJECT>` tag. With this tag, you can create layouts that simulate frames but without some of the drawbacks. The only problem is that FrontPage doesn't offer support for `<OBJECT>` tag frame substitutes, so create your own.

The example begins with a specialized Web page that relies on the `<OBJECT>` tag in place of frames. The appearance is the same as a page with frames but with fewer problems. Figure 3-4 shows that the layout is similar to the Banner and Contents frame layout that FrontPage provides.

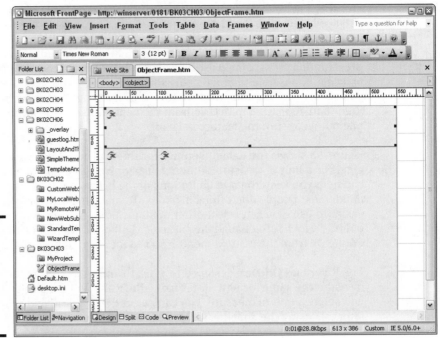

Figure 3-4: Design substitutes for frames using the `<OBJECT>` tag.

Notice that the 0 on the ruler in Figure 3-4 is centered on the upper-left corner of the banner frame. The 0 is called the origin, and you can set the origin on an object on a page to make it easier to measure the position and size of other objects in relation to the selected object. To set the origin, select the object you want to use. Right-click the ruler and choose Set Origin from Selection from the context menu. You can select any item on the page as the origin. Return the origin to its original setting by right-clicking the ruler and choosing Reset Origin from the context menu.

The template in Figure 3-4 is a standard Web page that has blanks for the pages you want to insert within the frame area. You generally need to create this code by hand because the Design view doesn't offer much support for the <OBJECT> tag. Listing 3-1 shows the code that creates the frame appearance shown in Figure 3-4.

Listing 3-1:   Creating a Frames Template with <Object> Tags

```
<body>
    <!--"The banner frame." -->
    <object data="" width="550" height="75">
        <A href=""
           title="Other page content you might want to view.">
           Other Content
        </A>
    </object><br/>

    <!--"The links frame." -->
    <object data="" width="100" height="300">
        <A href=""
           title="Other page content you might want to view.">
           Other Content
        </A>
    </object>

    <!--"The main content area." -->
    <object data="" width="450" height="300">
        <A href=""
           title="Other page content you might want to view.">
           Other Content
        </A>
    </object>
</body>
```

In each case, the <OBJECT> tag includes all of the components needed to support the page — it just doesn't contain any content. The width and height attributes define the size of each area on the page. Remember to include a hyperlink within each <OBJECT> tag to support users who have browsers that don't work with the <OBJECT> tag. Even when a browser doesn't support the <OBJECT> tag, using the <OBJECT> tag makes the page more accessible than using frames.

After you create the template, create a folder with a name that has the TEM extension, such as `ObjectFrame.tem`, to hold the template. You also need to create an INF file for the template that has precisely the same name as the template, such as `ObjectFrame.INF`. The INF file contains the following entries:

```
[info]
_LCID=1033
_version=11.0.4628.0
title=Object Tag Frame Simulation
description=Creates a frame-like appearance that includes a
            banner, links, and content frame.
noframesURL=
layout=
    [R(75,300)F("banner",[C(100,450)F("links","content")])]
```

The `_LCID` entry identifies the language for the template. Use the `_version` entry to define the template version. Normally, you want to use the same version number as all other templates for the version of FrontPage that you use to create the template. The `title` entry contains text that appears with the frame template icon on the Frames Pages tab of the Page Templates dialog box. The `description` property content appears in the Description area of the Page Templates dialog box. The `noframesURL` entry defines the location of the no frames content. Don't add this entry for a template based on the `<OBJECT>` tag. Finally, that odd bit of code for the `layout` entry describes the layout of this frame.

The easiest way to look at the `layout` entry is to break apart the design you create. Imagine you're creating the frames by using the Frames⇨Split Frame command. The `R(75,300)` entry describes the first split, which is horizontal when you look at the layout in Figure 3-4. The code in Listing 3-1 tells you that this split is 75 pixels for the banner frame and 300 pixels for the remaining two frames. The `F("banner"` entry tells you that this first split is the banner frame.

The `[C(100,450)` entry describes the second split. This split is vertical, not horizontal, so you use a C rather than an R. The left pane is 100 pixels wide in the code, and the right is 450 pixels, so these are the numbers you use in the code. Finally, the `F("links","content")` entry defines the left pane as the links pane and the right pane as contents.

After you finish these two files (the template and the INF file), you place the entire folder in the `\Program Files\Microsoft Office\Templates\1033\FRAMES11` folder of your machine. The template appears on the Frames Pages tab of the Page Templates dialog box.

Creating your own layouts

Layouts are very convenient, and they don't suffer some of the problems that frames do. Most browsers can use layouts easily, and the accessibility problems of using a well-defined layout aren't quite as significant as using frames (although, the problems do exist). FrontPage provides a number of common layouts, but you might find that you want to use a custom layout for the Web pages on your site. In addition, you can predefine some elements that a standard layout doesn't, such as the author of the document or other preferences. The layout could even include predefined elements such as your company logo.

Creating a layout is similar to creating a new frames page. You begin by designing the layout you want to use, but carefully avoid adding any content that isn't common to all layouts. Figure 3-5 shows a layout you could create to hold a company logo, a banner, a list of links, a new content section at the top, and an existing content section at the bottom.

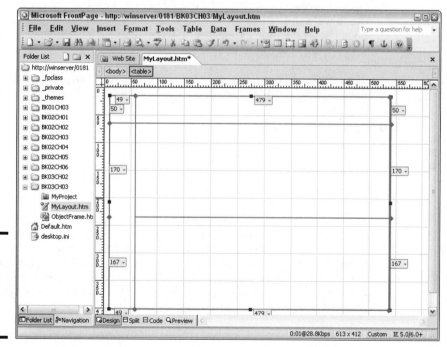

Figure 3-5:
Creating a layout that includes new content.

Book III
Chapter 3

Using FrontPage Views

After you have a new layout designed, create a folder to hold it. This folder must have the name of an existing layout. You could create a folder with a unique name, but FrontPage won't recognize it as a layout without adding entries to the registry. Given that it's unlikely that you use every layout Microsoft provides, replacing an existing layout is far easier.

Look in the `\Program Files\Microsoft Office\Templates\1033\` `Layouts11` folder for an existing layout you don't use and would like to replace. Rename the existing folder to something like `OLD_ CHLB_T` so that you can easily retrieve this layout if you need it later. Give the new folder and the new layout you created the existing folder name. The example replaces the CHLB_T layout, so the folder has the `CHLB_T` name and the layout file has `CHLB.HTM` as a name.

The Layout Tables and Cells window of the Task Pane contains a Table Layout area that shows pictures of the various layouts you can use. To create a picture for this area, you must get a screenshot of your layout in BMP (Windows bitmap) format. (Alternatively, you can also draw the layout by hand.) Set the layout border to 2 or 3 to get the best screenshot. The picture must be 58 pixels wide and 76 pixels high. You name it with the same name as the template but with a BMP extension, so the example uses a filename of `CHLB.BMP`. Add the BMP file to the folder.

The last piece is an INF file. The new INF file must have the same name as the template and BMP file, so the example uses `CHLB.INF`. Here's an example INF file.

```
[info]
_LCID=1033
_version=11.0.4628.0
title=Corner, Header, Left, New Area, and Body
rtitle=Corner, Header, Left, New Area, and Body
```

The INF file begins with the usual entries including the `[info]` section heading, the local (`_LCID`) entry, and the version information (`_version`). The `title` entry contains the text you see when you hover the mouse over the layout picture in the Layout Tables and Cells window. Some layouts have companion layouts. The `rtitle` entry identifies the companion layout of the current layout. Use the same text for the `title` and `rtitle` entries when there isn't any companion layout.

Using the Folders View

The Folders view is a more complete version of the information located in the Folder List. It includes additional information such as the date the file was last modified and any comments you associated with the file. In addition, the

Folders view shows who is assigned to maintain the file, the file size, and its type. The Folders view and the Folder List can interact to let you move files from one area of the Web site to another. You use Folders view to perform tasks such as creating new files and copying existing files.

Sorting files

The Folder List always displays the file according to filename, which makes files easy to find when you need to create a link in a Web page or add a file to the Task view. However, you don't always want to see the files in name order. In some cases, you might want to see the largest or the oldest file. The Folders view lets you sort files by any of the criteria it supports

One of the sort criteria includes the Comments field. You can use the Comments field of the Summary tab of the file Properties dialog box to provide specialized information about the file to make it easier to sort into unique categories. For example, you could assign a file a priority and sort them using this unique requirement. The Comments field can contain any information you want. The important thing to consider is that FrontPage sorts this field alphabetically, so choose the first words in the Comment field carefully and consistently to assure good sorting results.

Publishing files

One task that Folders view can perform easily is publishing individual files. After you finish a particularly important edit, you might want to publish the file immediately. Before you can publish files, you must set up a remote connection. To publish one or more files, begin by highlighting the files. Right-click any of the highlighted files and choose Publish Selected Files from the context menu. You see a Confirm Copy dialog box. FrontPage automatically removes the dialog box when the copy process is complete.

The Folders view can also make it possible for you to exclude files from publication. Perhaps you have only started an edit on the file and don't want to publish it until the edit is complete. To exclude files from publication, begin by highlighting the files. Right-click any of the selected files and choose Don't Publish from the context menu. FrontPage marks the highlighted files with a special icon to show that it won't publish them during the next publishing cycle.

After you finish editing the files, you must mark them as ready for publication. Highlight the affected files and choose Don't Publish from the context menu. FrontPage changes the icon back to the standard icon for that file.

**Book III
Chapter 3**

Using FrontPage Views

Using the Reports View

The Reports view contains a number of specialized views of your Web site, everything from broken links to the number of hits a particular Web page receives. Most of these reports provide specialized uses that you already know about or will discover as you perform specific tasks.

The intention of the Reports view is to help you see your Web site in different ways so you can manage it better. Unfortunately, you can't change the reports that Microsoft provides or add new ones. Even so, you gain access to a wealth of knowledge about your Web site and the server it runs on.

Ensuring the reports work as intended

Before you can collect some of the information that FrontPage 2003 can deliver about your Web site, configure your server correctly. Currently, only Windows XP provides full FrontPage 2002 Server Extension support out of the box.

To add FrontPage 2002 Extensions support to Windows 2000 Server or Windows 2000 Professional, you must download it from Microsoft's Web site and install it on the machine. The file you download is an executable — simply double-click it and follow the instructions. (You shouldn't have to provide any information.) These extensions run on any Internet Information Server (IIS) 4.0 or above setup. They may also run on other servers. See the download site at `http://www.microsoft.com/downloads/details.aspx?displaylang=en&FamilyID=5CC0A845-1884-4A16-A8CB-25D2F0815FA3` for more information.

After you download and install the server extensions, follow these steps:

1. **Open the Internet Information Services console located in the Administrative Tools folder of the Control Panel.**

2. **Right-click the Default Web Site entry and choose Properties from the context menu.**

   You see the Default Web Site Properties dialog box.

3. **Select the new Server Extensions 2002 tab, which was added by the installation program.**

4. **Click Settings.**

   Interestingly enough, IIS opens a Web page that contains the settings information as shown in Figure 3-6.

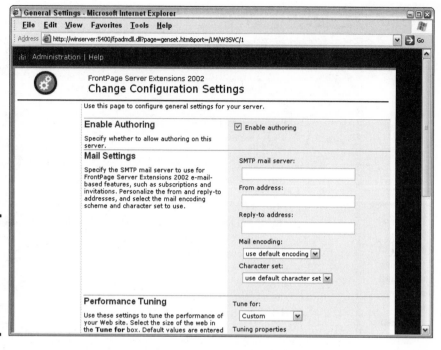

Figure 3-6:
Define the
settings
for the
FrontPage
2002 Server
Extensions.

**Book III
Chapter 3**

**Using FrontPage
Views**

The first page you see is a Change Configuration Settings page.

5. **Set the entries as you normally would for using FrontPage Extensions —
   this part of the process hasn't changed.**

6. **Click Submit.**

   You see the Virtual Server Administration page.

7. **Click the Upgrade Virtual Server with FrontPage Server Extensions
   2002 link.**

   You see the Upgrade Virtual Server with FrontPage Server Extensions
   2002 page.

8. **Make sure the administrator name is correct and click Submit.**

   You see the Server Administration page again. However, now it tells you
   that the Default Web Site can use FrontPage Server Extensions 2002.

   You still haven't set the server to provide usage details, but the server
   does have the required support.

9. **Click the Set Installation Defaults link.**

   You see Usage Details settings shown in Figure 3-7.

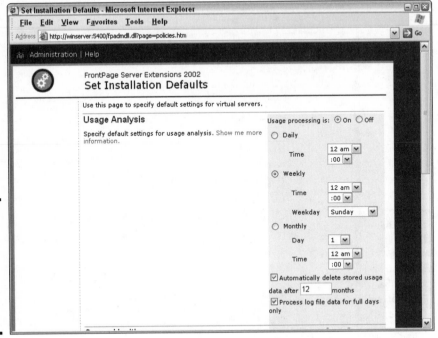

Figure 3-7:
Set the
interval for
collecting
usage and
server
health
information.

10. **Make sure the Usage Processing Is field is set to On. Another setting controls the server health report. Set both areas to collect data at the interval you require.**

For example, if you want to generate reports each week on Friday, it's probably best to collect the data on that day shortly before you get into work so the statistics are as fresh as possible.

Configuring the reports

Microsoft configures the reports to provide the best results for the average Web site. Your above average Web site probably requires configuration to ensure the reports actually reflect what you need. For example, you might not want to consider a Web page "old" when it reaches 30 days — perhaps the data is already too old at 15 days.

To configure reports to properly reflect your Web site strategy, follow these steps:

1. **Choose Tools⇨Options.**

You see the Options dialog box.

2. Select the Reports View tab.

This dialog box lets you choose how FrontPage calculates the reports and sorts resources into various areas.

3. Configure the age of documents on your site.

The "Recent" Documents Are Less Than field defines what you consider a new document. A document might be new for just a few days on a Web site with rapidly changing information but might be new for weeks or months on a Web site that sports historical information. Likewise, describe an old document by changing the "Older" Files Are More Than field. This value is always greater than the "Recent" Documents Are Less Than field, and it should include a time interval for files that aren't new but aren't old either.

4. Configure the page speed.

The page speed is a very important statistic because the next site is always a click away. If your site takes too long to download, users are going to go somewhere else. The problem is that you might have a high speed connection and a great developer machine, so estimating a long download is difficult. You set up reports that tell you when a page takes too long to download by changing the "Show Pages" Take at Least and the Assume Connection Speed Of fields. Most developers use a "Show Pages" Take at Least time of 10 seconds or less. Shorter times are usually better because most users won't wait long. A site that sells merchandise requires a very fast download speed even when the user has an older modem connection of 28.8 Kbps. A gaming Web site can probably assume the user has a fast modem speed 56 Kbps as a minimum, and it probably isn't too much to assume even faster speeds.

5. Configure the usage reports.

The usage reports show a specific number of months. The FrontPage selected average of 12 months works fine for many sites. However, you might want to change this interval when your site works with data that changes particularly fast or slow or needs more historical content than the standard setting provides.

Using the Tasks View

The Tasks view helps you keep track of tasks you must perform on your Web site. Keeping the tasks in one location makes it easier for you to track each Web site you manage as an individual entity. In addition, using Tasks view helps coordinate the efforts of a team.

You know how to manually add tasks to the Tasks view, and you also know that some FrontPage tasks automatically add entries to the Tasks view. For example, when you create a new Web page, you can create it as a task rather than an actual page. The problem with manually added tasks is that they aren't associated with any of the FrontPage resources. In other words, you have to provide enough detail to know which files to open. On the other hand, even though FrontPage created tasks are associated with a file, you don't have any control over how these tasks are created.

Fortunately, by using the Folder List you can create a combination of a manual entry and one that's associated with a particular resource. The file can contain anything associated with your Web site, including graphics. Simply drag the file from the Folder List to the Tasks view, and you see a New Task dialog box. Enter the usual information, including a task title, priority, and description. Click OK to add the task to Tasks view.

When you want to perform the task, right-click the entry and choose Start Task from the context menu. When FrontPage provides support for the file, you see it opened in FrontPage. Otherwise, FrontPage will open an external program to perform the task.

Normally, after you edit a file, FrontPage asks whether the task is complete. If so, you can click Yes in the dialog box, and FrontPage automatically marks the task as complete in Tasks view. When you use an external program to modify the file, FrontPage doesn't know that you've edited the file, so you need to manually manage the Tasks view.

Chapter 4: Creating Navigational Views

In This Chapter

✔ Using the Navigation view

✔ Adding navigational bars

✔ Creating new pages

✔ Organizing the navigational view

✔ Modifying the site settings

Getting from one place to another, whether it's from your home to a vacation spot or from one site to another on the Internet, often requires a map. As long as you know where you're going (and sometimes the map tells you that, too), you can discover ways to get somewhere else. The FrontPage Navigation view is more than a hierarchical display of the pages on your Web site; it also provides a map you can use to move from one page to another without actually opening the pages. A well-designed Navigation view can help you locate Web pages that require change quickly — and help you understand the flow of information on your site.

One especially handy feature the view provides is a *navigation bar* — an on-screen collection of settings you use to create automatic links between pages, based on their position in the Navigation view. (An upcoming section of this chapter shows you how to create one.) The first several things you need to know about the Navigation view are these:

✦ **Sometimes it's quicker to create a page directly in Navigation view before you link it.** That way, you get a clear look at how it fits into the logical or mapped scheme of your Web site.

✦ **The view is versatile, but what it does is up to you.** Take a little time to develop techniques for organizing the Navigation view so it works as intended with your particular Web site.

✦ **Always make the correct page and site settings part of your Navigation view setup.** Not every setting affects the Navigation view; some settings are essential for creating a well-designed custom view of your Web site and its linkages.

Understanding the Benefits of the Navigation View

Some people would decide the Navigation view provides a means for organizing their sites — and stop there. Yes, the Navigation view does provide this feature, but if you've used it at all, you already know it does a lot more. In fact, FrontPage makes great and extensive use of the Navigation view, so a little time spent here pays big dividends in improved Web site functionality and reduced development time.

Many FrontPage features won't work unless you create a Navigation view. For example, the Page Banner feature doesn't work unless you add the page to the Navigation view. The name of the page as it appears in Navigation view is the name that you see in the Page Banner. Because FrontPage relies on webbots to perform certain tasks, you need to provide the webbots with the information they need by building a good Navigation view.

Every navigational feature also requires a complete Navigation view setup. FrontPage supports various types of links to make your Web site easy to get around:

+ **Back and Next links:** These allow forward or backward navigation.

+ **Automatic page links:** These you base on specific criteria (for example, you can decide whether to include a link that goes automatically to the home page).

+ **Custom links:** These are configurable; you decide precisely what the navigational aid should look like.

You can also choose features, such as the Table of Contents component, that provide a view of your site that's similar to the table of contents in a book. The idea is to make it very fast for users to locate information on your site based on category.

Layout is an essential part of the Navigation view but not just from an organizational perspective. You use Navigation view to establish the user's ease of movement from page to page. Changing one item in the layout can make a significant change in how the user sees navigation on a particular page. FrontPage bases its control of movement on the Navigation view rather than on the physical layout of your site.

The settings you make for the Navigation view also affect the way various Web elements interact. For example, you don't have to use the terms *forward* or *back* for movement between pages — you could use *next* and *previous* instead. FrontPage provides settings that modify these values, so you can use any terms that make sense to the Web site user.

Creating a New Navigation Bar

FrontPage has a navigation bar for every occasion. Don't confuse a navigation bar with the Navigation view — the navigation bar is a control for moving between pages, but the Navigation view shows the connections between pages. You use one or more of them to give the user a way to move from one location to another on your site. For example, the navigation bar across the top of the page might let the user move between top-level Web pages such as the home page, general information about your company, how to contact various people, and a link to a search engine or a site map. Along the side of the page you can include a different type of navigation bar that lets the user drill down into the data that the current page supports. These scenarios represent just two of many navigation needs.

You always select a navigation bar using the same technique. The following steps get you started.

1. **Place the cursor where you want the navigation bar to appear on the page; then choose Insert⇨Navigation.**

   You see the Insert Web Component dialog box shown in Figure 4-1.

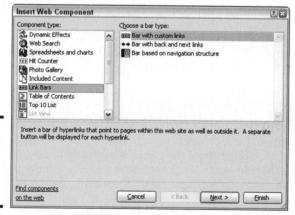

Figure 4-1: Choose one of the navigation bar types.

Book III
Chapter 4

Creating Navigational Views

2. **Select one of the navigation bars in the list. Click Next.**

   FrontPage asks you to select a bar style, as shown in Figure 4-2. The bar styles include both graphic and text types. The text types are more accessible and easier to use; the graphic styles have more visual appeal.

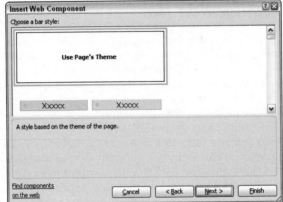

Figure 4-2:
Select a bar
style that
matches
your current
page
design.

3. **Select a bar style and click Next.**

   FrontPage asks you to choose an orientation for the navigation bar. Main selections normally appear across the top of the display; subordinate links (which access content or other Web pages) appear along the side.

4. **Choose an orientation and click Finish.**

   FrontPage asks you questions specific to the navigation bar you selected.

At this point, you need to provide navigation bar specific information. Of course, the secret is to know which navigation bar to use, which is the topic of the sections that follow.

Adding Back and Next links

The Back and Next links assume that you want the user to follow a specific order. For example, the user might need to follow a procedure or fill out multiple pages of forms. The order of the pages is normally important, so you want the user to see them in order. You could even use this form of navigation link to display a book online. Each link could represent a chapter or a portion of a chapter. You use the Bar with Back and Next Links option located in the Link Bars component type to produce this kind of navigation bar.

This navigation bar assumes that you create a beginning point that also acts as a top-level page. A navigation bar controls movement from one leaf (content) page to the next.

After you get past the initial configuration described in the introduction to this section, you see a Create New Link Bar dialog box. From there, follow these steps to create this navigation bar:

1. **Type a name that describes the sequence of pages you want to create.**

For example, you might type Supply Request Form when you create a series of pages for a complex request form.

2. **Click OK after you type the name.**

You see a Link Bar Properties dialog box that has everything blanked out.

3. **Add the current page to the navigation bar to ensure it's part of the navigation scheme and also appears as the first page on the list.**

4. **Click Add Link.**

You see the Add Link to Bar dialog box.

5. **Locate the Web page in the hierarchical folder list and then click OK.**

You see the Web page URL added to the Links list. Figure 4-3 shows a Link Bar Properties dialog box with several links included.

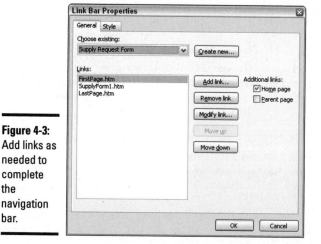

Figure 4-3:
Add links as needed to complete the navigation bar.

6. **Add Additional Links options, if necessary.**

To provide movement to upper levels of the Web site, you normally select one or both Additional Links options. The Home Page option always takes the user to the very beginning of the Web site. Use the Parent Page option to let the user move up one level (to the parent of the current page).

7. **Click OK.**

For whatever reason, FrontPage normally displays an error message stating, "[Edit the properties of this link bar to either rebuild it or choose a different link bar that already exists in this web.]" on the Web page at this point. Don't worry — the links will work.

Creating a single page back and next link navigation bar is sort of like listening to the sound of one hand clapping. You can do it, but it doesn't accomplish very much. To add more pages to the list, simply design the page, and then add the Bar with Back and Next Links navigation bar to it. The steps are about the same. However, this time FrontPage takes you directly to the Link Bar Properties dialog box where you click Add Link again to add the new page. In many cases, you won't want to select either of the Additional Links options for middle pages (just beginning and end pages) to ensure the user completes the series. Continue adding Web pages until you add all the pages in the series.

Let's say you don't want to spend the rest of your life adding these navigation bars one at a time. It's possible to create a template or a special layout that includes the navigation bar, or even simply to copy and paste the navigation bar to another page. The only problem is that you haven't created any linkage between the new page and the navigation bar. To add the required linkage, right-click the navigation bar entry and choose Link Bar Properties from the context menu. You see the Link Bar Properties dialog box. Click Add Link to add the new Web page to the list.

Creating linkage to the home page

Depending on how you set up the navigation for your site, you end up with one or more isolated islands that are inaccessible from the home page. For that matter, you might not have any navigation in place on the home page because you created all of the topics you want to discuss first.

Creating linkage from the home page to all of the isolated islands you've developed is a two-step process. First, you need to create a navigation bar for the home page if you haven't done so already. Second, you use the Navigation view to connect the various islands to your home page.

To add the navigation bar, select the Bar Based on Navigation Structure option of the Link Bars component type. You can use other suitable navigation bars such as the For This Web Site option of the Table of Contents component type, but the Bar Based on Navigation Structure is the most common type. After you select the usual options, you see a Link Bar Properties dialog box similar to the one shown in Figure 4-4.

The figure on the left side shows how a particular selection works. In this case, FrontPage supplies links for any child pages, including navigation bars, that appear directly under the home page in the hierarchy. Some of the options aren't quite as comprehensive. For example, when you choose the Global Level option, FrontPage selects only Web pages that appear at that level, not navigation bars.

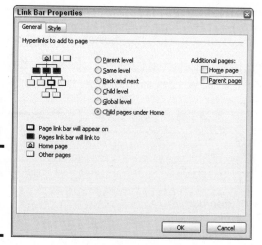

Book III
Chapter 4

Creating
Navigational Views

Figure 4-4:
Choose the
level you
want to use
for linking.

Developers normally add two bars to the home page. The first shows all of the top-level or global pages for the Web site. This is a horizontal navigation bar that appears at the top of the page. The second shows the content below the current page. It appears as a vertical navigation bar along the right or left side of the page (with left being the most common placement).

After you add the navigation bars, you want to create some linkage for them. To perform this task, select the Web Site tab and then the Navigation view. You see that the home page is sitting by itself. To the right of the home page is a navigation bar and below this all the pages that you added to it. Connect the navigation bar to the home page by dragging the navigation bar under it. FrontPage shows a line between the two elements, as shown in Figure 4-5. You perform the same organizational task for every navigation bar you design.

Developing automatic page links

Some navigation bars, such as the Bar with Back and Next Links style, require some configuration on your part to use. Other navigation bars are a lot less work. You drop them in place, and they display any new or existing links automatically, depending on how you set the link up. The most common automatic link is the Bar Based on Navigation Structure option of the Link Bars component type.

Using this navigation structure lets you move elements around without breaking anything because the links shown on the page depend on where the page appears in the hierarchy. The down side of this method is that it's not as automatic as using a navigation method that relies on a navigation bar. You use the Navigation view to initially place the page and maintain its position afterward.

Home or other top-level page

Navigation bar

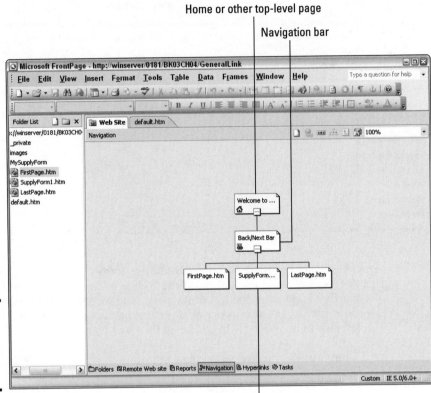

Figure 4-5:
Choose the
level you
want to use
for linking.

Leaf (content) pages

Understanding the navigation types

The automatic links permit you to work at a number of levels as shown in Figure 4-4. The Global Level and Child Pages Under Home options only work with the home page. You can add them to any other page, but the effect isn't dynamic — you always end up at the top level.

Use the Parent Level setting to create a list of previous destinations for a leaf or content Web Page. Using these links lets a user go up one level without having to go all the way back to the home page in a Web site that has multiple navigation levels.

Use the Same Level option when you want to move between pages at the same hierarchical level. The pages must have the same parent. You won't see links for pages that have a different parent. By using a combination of the Same Level option with the Parent Page and Home Page options checked, you can create a very efficient means for moving around a specific area of a Web site.

The Back and Next option has the same effect as using the Bar with Back and Next Links option located in the Link Bars component type but without the navigation bar. This means the pages aren't added automatically — you add them using the Navigation view. However, it also means you can create multiple levels of back and next pages. The navigation bar limits you to a single level.

The Child Level option lets you display links for the children of the current Web page. These links let users drill down to the next level of the Web site.

Modifying the link bar style

You might decide that you really don't like the current setup for your page. It might be better to display the links vertically, or you might want to use a different style of link. In addition, the initial setup doesn't allow you to specify the kind of links you receive. FrontPage assumes you want to use the standard link style. Fortunately, you can change the settings by right-clicking the link bar entry and choosing Link Bar Properties from the context menu. Select the Style tab, and you see a number of configuration options as shown in Figure 4-6.

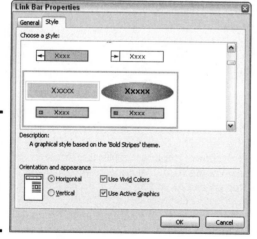

Figure 4-6: Use these settings to modify the appearance of the links on a page.

The Choose a Style area shows all of the styles you can use to display links. The entries on the left are the standard setup, and the entries on the right show what you can get when select the Use Vivid Colors and Use Active Graphics options.

The Description tells you what this style is based on. Read the description carefully to ensure the style you select matches or at least coordinates with the theme you select for a Web page. You can always ensure the style will match the page theme by selecting the Use Page's Theme style.

The Horizontal and Vertical options affect the placement of the link bar on the Web page. Select the Use Vivid Colors option when you want the links to appear in bright colors. Checking the Use Active Graphics option displays an artistic view of the links rather than the flatter view provided by the standard option.

Working with a Custom Link Bar

Sometimes you don't want a series of calculated or automatic links — you want to define specific links and keep track of them wherever they might appear on your Web site. A custom link bar, one created using the Bar with Custom Links option in the Link Bars component, can accommodate links to other pages. The pages don't have to appear in any specific order or in any specific place.

After you create the basic bar, you see the Link Bar Properties dialog box shown in Figure 4-3. This dialog box might not contain any navigation bars, or it could contain navigation bars that you created earlier. To create a unique set of links, you need to create a new navigation bar by clicking Create. FrontPage displays a Create New Link Bar dialog box. Type a name for this navigation bar and click OK.

The interesting part of this type of navigation is the navigation bar doesn't appear attached to the rest of the hierarchy. The page you create links the navigation bar to the home page. The link is within the page.

One problem that occurs, in this case, is that the navigation bar uses link information for the title rather than the actual page title. This technique gives you links that include " ../MySupplyForm/SupplyForm1.htm". To overcome this problem, you rename the links in Navigation view by right-clicking the page and choosing Rename from the context menu. Type a readable name into the entry and press Enter.

Another way to rename links is to click Modify Link in the Link Bar Properties dialog box. You see the Modify Link dialog box. Type a new name for the link in the Text to Display field and click OK.

Using the Table of Contents component

The Table of Contents component can create two kinds of output. The first style uses the current Web site as the basis for entries. The second style creates a table of contents based on the category that you assigned to the page.

Using the Web site style

Unlike other navigational aids, you don't need to provide a bar style or orientation when working with the Table of Contents component. Simply select the table of content types and click Finish. You see the Table of Contents Properties dialog box shown in Figure 4-7.

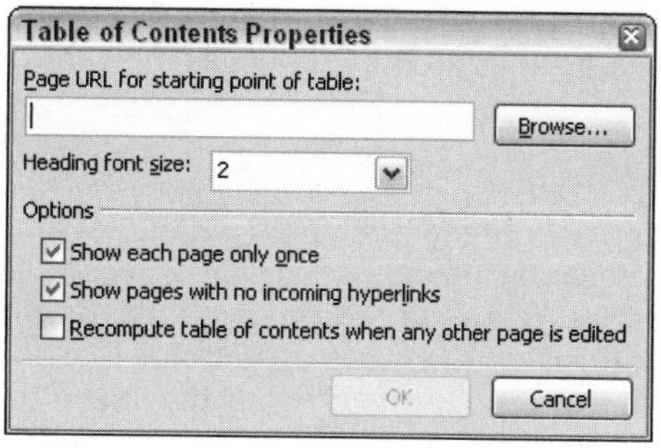

Figure 4-7:
Define the starting point and characteristics of the table of contents.

When working with a table of contents, you must define a starting point for the entries. In many cases, you'll use the home page as the starting point, especially when you want to display the entire Web site. However, you can start at any point on the Web site. The table of contents will start at that point in the hierarchy and move to lower levels. You must also define the size type you want to use for the entries. The default setting normally works fine.

The three options on the Table of Contents Properties dialog box are important because they affect how the page looks and works. If you want your site to have a book-like table of contents, then you need to clear the Show Each Page Only Once option. FrontPage selects this option by default because many developers only want a list of links — eliminating duplicate entries makes the list easier for others to use.

Clear the Show Page with No Incoming Hyperlinks option when you want the user to see only links to pages that appear as children of the current page. You might not want to create a table of contents that contains every page on your site. Another way to eliminate a page from the table of contents is to right-click its entry in Navigation view and choose Included in Link Bars. The page will change color (normally gray) to show it's no longer selected.

The Recompute Table of Contents When Any Other Page is Edited option is useful when you expect a lot of changes to your site and want to be sure they all appear in the table of contents. The down-side of using this feature is that it uses computing cycles that you could use for some other purpose.

Your system could literally slow down for every page change that you save to disk. When you work on a remote site, the slow down becomes even more noticeable. The performance impact is the reason Microsoft probably turns this feature off by default.

After you finish the table of contents, click OK. You see the table of contents added to the Web page. Like any other navigation tool, you can edit your choices after you create the table of contents. Right-click the table of contents entry and choose Table of Contents Properties from the context menu.

Using the categories style

The Based on Page Category option of the Table of Contents component lets you create a table of contents based on the workgroup assigned to manage a page or status of that page. You don't have to support all workgroups or every possible status. The goal of this table of contents is to make it easier for other members of your team to locate the files they need to work on.

This table of contents doesn't require that you choose a bar style or orientation. Simply select it and click Finish in the Insert Web Component dialog box. You see the Categories Properties dialog box shown in Figure 4-8.

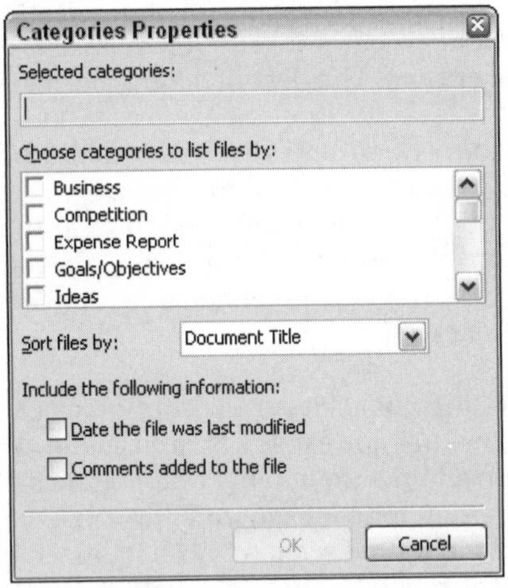

Figure 4-8:
Choose the categories you want to appear in the table of contents.

Begin by selecting the categories you want to see in the table of contents. As you select categories, they appear in the Selected Categories field at the top of the dialog box.

You can perform a few extra tricks with this table of contents. For example, you can sort it by the document title or the date the document was last edited. The table of contents can also contain the date the file was last edited and any comments attached to the file, in addition to the normal document title.

When you finish selecting the document options, click OK. FrontPage adds the table of contents to the Web page.

Defining a top-ten list

The top-ten list relies on statistics to create a list of links for people to visit. For example, you can create a top-ten list of the pages people visited most often on your site. You can also display external sites. There's a top-ten list for domains that make referrals to your site. Theoretically, you could combine a number of these lists to create a utility page that can monitor your Web site. To create a top-ten list, follow these steps:

1. **Choose Insert⇨Web Component.**

The Insert Web Component dialog box opens.

2. **Select one of the usage lists supported by the Top 10 List component.**

FrontPage asks you to select a top-ten list style. The top-ten list styles include options based on a particular need, such as the search strings users enter most often or the browsers that most users have.

3. **Click Finish.**

You don't need to provide style or orientation information. FrontPage displays the Top 10 List Properties dialog box shown in Figure 4-9.

Click OK to display the default top-ten list.

Figure 4-9:
Select a presentation style for your top-ten list.

You can modify the list title and style if you want. For example, when you use the top-ten list for statistical displays, you'll also want to check the Include Date Usage Processing Was Last Run option. This option shows whether the data is fresh and whether you need to verify the server settings to ensure the usage processing is run often enough.

Using the Visual InterDev Navigation Bar Component

To use this particular navigation bar, you must have Visual InterDev (the Microsoft visual environment for software development) installed on your server. Otherwise, a needed capability is missing, and FrontPage waits for you to install it before it allows this navigation bar (which acts as a component of Visual InterDev) to work. Using this component without having Visual InterDev installed displays a placeholder,], on the Web page:

```
[FrontPage vinavbar Component]
```

You also see the following error message when you open the Page Properties dialog box:

```
(1) Cannot open DLL "fp5Avnb.dll"(The specified procedure
    could not be found.)
```

The odd thing is that the required DLL is already installed. It came aboard with FrontPage, in the following folder:

```
\Program Files\Common Files\Microsoft Shared\Web Server
    Extensions\50\bots\vinavbar
```

It's just sitting there, regardless of whether you've installed Visual InterDev.

The Visual InterDev Navigation Bar component has all the same features as the Link Bars component. The advantage of using this component is that you gain a little extra control over the interface settings; a single dialog box sets up every kind of navigation bar it supports, and some developers feel it works faster.

To use this component, select the Visual InterDev Navigation Bar entry in the Additional Components component type in the Insert Web Component dialog box. Click Finish. You see the Visual InterDev Navigation Bar Component Properties dialog box shown in Figure 4-10.

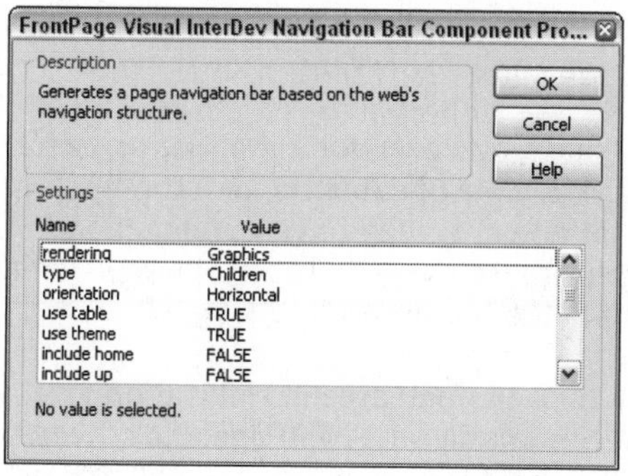

Figure 4-10:
Choose
setup
options
for the
navigation
bar you
want to
create.

Some of the terms used in Visual InterDev are (as you might expect) very developer-oriented, but most of them match up to similar settings in the Link Bars component of FrontPage. You do, however, have some additional options. For example, you can choose text, graphics, or HTML *rendering* (the method of displaying the information). Graphics give you the artistic rendering supported by the active graphics and vivid colors that the Link Bars component provides as options. The Visual InterDev navigation bar supports a number of navigational features, as well as various ways to refine the look of your page — for example, these:

✦ You can also use the navigation bar to create a banner.

✦ You can select the kind of output you want to create by specifying the Type setting.

✦ When selecting output, you can choose to place the information in a table; FrontPage will set it up for you automatically, in response to your settings.

✦ You can impose a consistent look by applying the current FrontPage theme.

One place where the Visual InterDev navigation bar doesn't provide the same capability as the Link Bars component is that it lacks support for other themes. When you want to use a theme with the navigational component, you're limited to the one that the current page uses and can't mix themes for special effects.

Adding New (Top-Level) Pages

When you add a new page to the Navigation view, it's subordinate to no other pages on your site. Thus every page you create in Navigation view is known as a *top-level page* — which FrontPage normally displays in a special color that sets it apart from the leaf pages. To avoid confusing the user, normally you use top-level pages only for organizational needs.

Top-level pages are also handy, however, for a number of useful (but optional) pages — say, a search page, a table of contents, or a top-ten list. The idea is to create a global page that doesn't really have a connection to anything else. The user will want to access these pages from anywhere in your Web site, so you place them at the top of the hierarchy.

To add a new page, right-click an open area in Navigation view and choose New⇨Top Page from the context menu. FrontPage adds the new page at the top of the display. Notice that this page isn't connected to anything, but you can drag it anywhere you need it. Talk about convenient — the page won't even exist on the hard drive until you open it to edit it.

Organizing the Navigation View

You can base the navigation for your Web site on the entries you make in a Web page, or you can design the navigation within Navigation view first and then add the appropriate components. This second technique relies on the Custom Link Bar rather than add the Custom Link Bar to a Web page and design the site using the pages. Instead, you add the Custom Link Bar to the Navigation view. That's it. This technique lets you see the design as you create it; you can organize material that might not be easy to place in a specific order.

The technique that uses Navigation view relies on a series of top-level or *node pages* and *leaf pages*. The leaf pages contain the content you want the user to see; the node pages identify the places you want to put the content. The top-level pages contain Custom Link Bars to organize the information. When you find a page in the wrong place, you move it to the node that it does belong to. The connections between pages are completely fluid.

The first page you create, the home page, is always a top-level page. You attach a Custom Link Bar to it, and then add other top-level pages and leaf pages as needed to create the structure. The resulting layout lets users move from area to area with ease, yet lets you maintain control over which pages they see and at what time.

Adding a Custom Link Bar

You add Custom Link Bars as needed to separate the data elements. The example uses the form of a book. Depending on the book, you use a Custom Link Bar for the front matter and each of the chapters. Remember, though, that you get only one level of detail below the Custom Link Bar, so you might have to use a different structure for complex books.

The idea is to create a navigational structure where the leaf nodes are sections or individual pages in the book. The steps to add a Custom Link Bar look like this:

1. **Right-click a clear area in Navigation view.**

A context menu appears.

2. **Choose New⇨Custom Link Bar from the context menu or click the New Custom Link Bar button on the toolbar.**

FrontPage displays a new Custom Link Bar at the top of the Navigation view.

3. **Drag the Custom Link Bar where you need it.**

4. **Right-click the new Custom Link Bar.**

A context menu appears.

5. **Choose Rename from the context menu.**

FrontPage makes it possible to edit the title.

6. **Give the Custom Link Bar a name that describes its organizational function and press Enter.**

FrontPage changes the name of the Custom Link Bar.

A top-level page can have as many Custom Link Bars as needed. Each link bar separates groups of pages. For example, if you want to separate each section of a book or online manual, you can use a Custom Link Bar to do it. The absolute separation of content helps readers know when they've completed a section.

You don't have to write a book to use a Custom Link Bar to separate data into useful segments. A Custom Link Bar can separate all kinds of data. For example, you could use one Custom Link Bar for each series of pages used to create a form. The Custom Link Bar helps your users know they've completed all the pages of the form.

Defining new top-level page

The "Adding New Pages" section describes how to add new top-level pages. This name is somewhat misleading. You can use a top-level page for any purpose. Drag it under a Custom Link Bar, and it changes color to indicate use as a leaf page.

You can use this flexibility to your advantage. Create the complete structure of your Web site, move things around, and organize pages using Custom Link Bars — all before you've actually created a single page. Figure 4-11 shows an example of the complex layouts you can create using this technique.

Book III
Chapter 4

Creating
Navigational Views

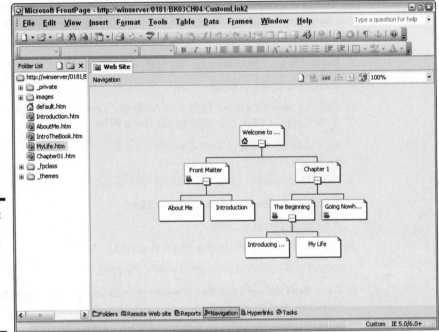

Figure 4-11: If you want to to create specialized layouts, organize the page directly.

Changing the Site Settings

FrontPage provides site settings that determine the text a user sees by default when working with navigational elements. For example, the button that takes the user to the home page says *Home* on it. (You might want to use different text on some other Web pages.)

To change the default button text, follow these steps:

1. **Right-click anywhere in the Navigation view.**

A context menu appears.

2. **Choose Site Settings from the context menu.**

FrontPage displays the Site Settings dialog box.

3. **Select the Navigation Tab.**

You see four fields: Home Page, Parent Page, Previous Page, and Next Page.

4. **Type the text that you want to use for each of these button types.**

5. **Click OK.**

FrontPage automatically changes the captions for all buttons on your Web site. (Make sure you click Refresh so your browser downloads the new version of the page from the Web site.)

Chapter 5: Using FrontPage Reports Efficiently

In This Chapter

✔ Considering the ways to use the Reports view

✔ Making the best use of the Site Summary

✔ Creating reports about files

✔ Monitoring shared content via reports

✔ Fixing problems with the help of reports

✔ Managing workflow with (you guessed it) reports

✔ Setting up reports to monitor site usage

FrontPage provides a wealth of reports as part of the Reports view. These reports help you monitor, manage, and fix your Web site. For example, when importing a Web site into FrontPage, you know to use the Broken Hyperlinks report to check for broken links on the site.

Good reports are valuable to everyone. Even if you're creating a site for your personal use on a hosted Web site, the FrontPage reporting feature helps you review your site, check it for errors, and ensure it's performing as expected. For example, you might want to verify that all files on your site have links — that they aren't simply sitting on the server without any way for the user to access them. The Unlinked Files report helps you obtain this information.

In the end, reports are essential because they help you understand your Web site better. As you get a clearer picture of the practical needs of the Web site and the people who visit it, you can fine-tune your content and presentation. This process ensures that your Web site grows as more people come to realize its value. All this comes from using reports efficiently.

Understanding the Reports

FrontPage groups reports into a number of functional areas. Each area includes a summary report and a number of detail reports. Here's a list of reports you can find in FrontPage, and their main uses in maintaining your Web site:

✦ **Site Summary:** This is a list of the most common reports. When you don't see the report you want, be sure to check the report categories; you'll probably find one to fit the needs of your site.

✦ **Files:** These reports help you monitor the status of files on your site by checking which files you changed recently, which files are old (and probably require update), and which files you recently added.

✦ **Shared Content:** These reports show which files or resources are used by more than one Web page. For example, you can check the status of themes and style sheets on your Web site. You can also check for dynamic Web site and shared border use.

✦ **Problems:** These reports help identify trouble on your Web site when you may not otherwise know it exists. They help you locate broken links, unlinked files (those the user can't access), slow pages, and component errors.

✦ **Workflow:** These reports are designed for managing group work activities. They tell you the review status, category, and publication status of all Web pages. You can also monitor Web-page assignments and determine who has a page checked out for editing.

✦ **Usage:** These reports tell you how visitors are using your Web site. You can monitor the overall status of the Web site on a daily, weekly, or monthly basis. It's also easy to check which browser and operating systems your users have so you can tune your pages to meet their needs.

Accessing the reports

To access a particular report, click the drop-down list box in the upper-left corner of Reports view, as shown in Figure 5-1. Click the report and FrontPage shows it to you. Reports you can't access are grayed out.

You might see a few reports in this chapter that don't appear in your copy of FrontPage — or you'll find them disabled. Although many FrontPage reports are available no matter which Web server you use (because they rely on the local project), a few are not — unless you configure your server to use FrontPage Extensions. That normally means using Microsoft Internet Information Server (IIS), a separate server application. For example, you can't create a workflow report without the FrontPage Server Extensions installed. In some cases, you have to go even further and ensure you have FrontPage Extensions 2002 (the most current version) installed on the organization's server. In such cases, you won't get any usage information about your Web site unless you make this configuration change.

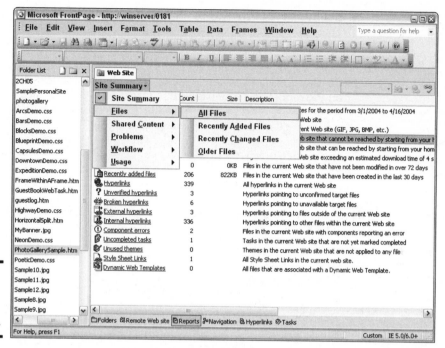

Figure 5-1:
Choose the report you want to see.

Modifying the report content

You can't choose the content or the presentation of the report, but you can choose the way FrontPage collects data for the report. To change the default report settings, choose Tools➪Options. Select the Reports View tab. You see the Options dialog box shown in Figure 5-2.

Each of these settings affects more than one report. The following settings are typical examples:

✦ **File Ages:** Changing this setting affects all reports on the Files menu. For example, setting the recent files setting higher means that FrontPage considers a file as new for a long timeframe and means a file won't appear on a report for editing as often.

✦ **Connection Speed:** This setting changes the way FrontPage views the page from a user perspective; it's a way of accommodating FrontPage to a variety of possible connection speeds. The report that is most affected by this setting is the Slow Pages report on the Problems menu; you set it one way if most of your users connect via DSL, another way for dial-up. However, this setting also changes how FrontPage creates some statistical reports.

✦ **Number of Months Shown:** This setting affects the density of a report. When you create reports that use graphs, you want to see the data points easily. A setting that's too high here can have a negative impact on your ability to interpret the report.

✦ **Display Gridlines When Viewing Reports:** This setting displays a grid on the report. In some cases, this makes the report easier to read by reducing the need to interpret where data intersects with a specific value. You can also compare data with greater ease. Using gridlines can also obscure precise data points (when a data point is near the grid line) and reduce how well a user can see the display of trends. The gridline can actually cause the viewer to see the data in segments rather than as a continuous whole.

These aren't the only settings at your disposal — these are just the global settings. You also have individual settings that the other sections of this chapter discuss as part of the individual reports.

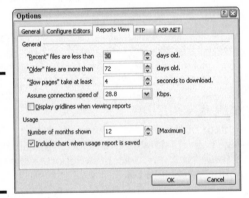

Figure 5-2:
Select the report options for the reports you want to create.

Printing a report

You might have noticed that FrontPage disables all print options when you view a report. It's impossible to print any of the reports directly, which seems a little counterintuitive given the need to share reports with other people. FrontPage doesn't offer a means to print the report, but you can copy it. To copy the report, right-click anywhere in the report and choose Copy Report from the context menu, which places a copy of the report on the Clipboard.

The easiest way to print the report or make it generally available for some-one to see is to create a new Web page and copy the report to it. Simply place the cursor where you want the report to appear and click Paste. You can see example reports in the source code for this chapter, which is available on the Wiley Web site. Interestingly enough, the only report you can't copy and paste is the Site Summary. This is an odd restriction because the Site Summary contains a few statistics you can't get elsewhere. After the report is pasted into a Web page, you can print it from inside FrontPage or use any other technique you normally use for printing Web pages.

Fortunately, you don't have to stop with the simple printing offered by FrontPage. Paste the report into Excel, and you suddenly have the means to use the data as you would in any database. Charting the data is relatively easy, too. Paste the report into Word, and you can format the data to meet any word-processing need. You can also use the same data in products such as Microsoft Publisher. It's also easy to send the report to other people by pasting it into an e-mail message. Pasting the report also works in most applications that support some type of text formating (unfortunately, not Notepad). Do not use Wordpad because it adds control characters!

Verifying hyperlinks

The Reports view includes a toolbar with four entries you can use anytime FrontPage activates them as shown in Figure 5-3. The only button that's always active is Verify Hyperlinks. (Other sections in this chapter discuss report specific options on the toolbar shown in Figure 5-3.) Click Verify Hyperlinks when you want to check the status of hyperlinks on your Web site.

Instead of immediately verifying all hyperlinks on your site, clicking Verify Hyperlinks gives you choices: It displays the Verify Hyperlinks dialog box. You choose to verify all hyperlinks or just the broken ones, and then click Start. FrontPage performs the check and returns you to the Hyperlinks report.

When you highlight one or more hyperlinks in the Hyperlinks report, you can also choose to verify just the link you've highlighted. The Verify Selected Hyperlink(s) option is available only when you highlight one or more entries in the Hyperlinks report.

The Verify Hyperlinks dialog box also contains an option for continuing a disrupted verification cycle. Choose Resume Verification and click Start to resume the verification cycle. This option is active only when you stop a verification cycle before it completes its job.

Book III
Chapter 5

Using FrontPage Reports Efficiently

Verify Hyperlinks (Always Active)

Edit Hyperlink (Active with Hyperlinks report)

Chart Type (Active with Usage reports)

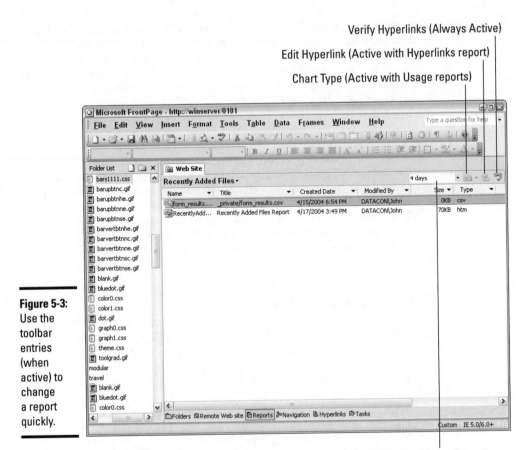

Figure 5-3:
Use the
toolbar
entries
(when
active) to
change
a report
quickly.

Report Setting (Active with Files, Slow Pages, Categories, Visiting Users, Operating
Systems, Browsers, Referring Domains, Referring URLs, Search Strings reports)

Using the Site Summary

The Site Summary report is the best way to get a quick overview of your
Web site. It contains statistical information such as the number of graphics
files your Web site has. You can also learn the amount of space consumed by
your Web site as a whole and by specific file types such as slow pages.

The number of statistics you see depends on the configuration of your Web
site and the capabilities of the Web server. For example, you won't see usage
statistic reports if your server doesn't support them. In some cases, you
must perform a task before the data provided by the Site Summary is valid.

For example, the broken links entry isn't valid until you validate the links. All the report tells you when you create a new Web site is that FrontPage hasn't found any broken links.

Most entries have a link associated with them so you can discover more about that topic. For example, click Style Sheet Links and you see the Style Sheet Links report. This report tells you which files have style sheets associated with them — and which style sheets those are.

A few of the entries don't have links. For example, FrontPage doesn't provide details statistics about the pictures on your site — all you can find out is how many pictures (graphics files) you have. The only way to see specific information about the graphics files is to choose the All Files report and sort the information by type. The All Files report tells you the location of the file, its size, the date it was last modified, and how many hits it has received (when you have usage data available). You can also discover who is responsible for the file and see any comments associated with the file.

Working with Files

Keeping track of your files is essential to the life of your Web site. Not only do you want to ensure that the files are up-to-date and connected to other files on your Web site, but you also want to ensure that you know precisely what task each file performs. In general, that means adding comments to the files and assigning them to someone to maintain. The Files menu contains four report options, which allow you to keep track of your files:

**Book III
Chapter 5**

**Using FrontPage
Reports Efficiently**

✦ All Files

✦ Recently Added Files

✦ Recently Changed Files

✦ Older Files

These reports are discussed in the next section.

Using the various Files reports

When working with a new Web site, you want to use the All Files report to look for files that you haven't documented in some way. Sometimes, this means opening the file to see what it contains. Make sure you understand what task a file performs before you let it onto your Web site; there's a difference between thoroughness and clutter. Of course, you don't want to eliminate essential files either, so it's important to track down each file.

The All Files report demonstrates a failing with FrontPage. As you design Web pages, FrontPage adds files for you. Some of these files support themes on your site, and others support layouts and other needs. The problem is that you can end up with a lot of clutter on your Web site as you experiment with different settings because FrontPage doesn't remove old files. Fortunately, you can decipher the purpose of many files by looking at their location. For example, the _themes/Bars/ folder contains the files needed by the Bars theme. When you decide you don't want to use this theme, you can remove the associated folder.

Use the Recently Added Files report to see which files require additional documentation and finishing content touches. This report can also alert you to recent configuration changes made by other workgroup members. For example, suppose a new entry in the _themes/ folder tells you that someone changed a theme. Interestingly enough, you can also use this report to see suspicious changes quickly. When you see a new file that no one in your workgroup added, someone outside the group added it — and finding out why — quickly — is a good idea.

Most developers use the Recently Changed Files report to see which older files have updates. This is the list to check when you want to verify and approve changes to the Web site before uploading them to the Web server. You can also use this report to reduce publication time. Simply select all files in this list, right-click the highlighted area, and choose Publish Selected Files from the context menu. This report also provides a means of detecting unauthorized or suspicious changes. You should know why each file was changed and who performed the work.

The Older Files report points out files that might require update. Generally, when a file hasn't received an update for a long time, the content becomes outdated, and users lose interest. You keep a Web site interesting by updating older files as needed.

Of course, not every older file is outdated. Sometimes an older file contains a table of useful-but-static information, such as a list of connector types for an electronics Web site. To see the content of an older file quickly, right-click the file and choose Preview in Browser from the context menu. FrontPage opens the file in a browser. FrontPage normally tries to open all files using the browser, but when the browser sees it can't work with the file, it then opens the file using the appropriate helper application. For example, if you try to open an Excel file, the browser starts a copy of Excel so you can see the file.

Another use for the Older Files report is to verify updates. Sometimes a publication cycle will fail with just one or two files. Perhaps someone has them checked out for editing. This report can alert you to those failures so you can fix them quickly.

Controlling the report settings

Except for the All Files report, the reports on the Files menu include a special Report Setting field on the Web Site toolbar that you can use to adjust the timeframe for the report. In this field, you can choose the number of days that FrontPage should use when creating the report. The Recently Added Files and Recently Changed Files reports share the same setting. This adjustment means you can tailor the output of these two reports without having to open the Options dialog box to make the change.

Working with Shared Content

Shared content is resources required by more than one Web page. The FrontPage reports tell you about four kinds of shared content:

✦ Dynamic Web pages

✦ Borders

✦ Cascading Style Sheets (CSS)

✦ Themes

Each of these resources has a separate report so that you can track them as needed. The reports contain one or two columns of specialized information. In all other respects, the reports look and act like the All Files report.

A dynamic Web template controls some of the content in a page that uses it. The dynamic Web template includes editable regions the developer can edit and fixed regions the developer can't edit. You attach a dynamic Web template to an existing Web page to create a consistent look across an entire Web site. The template could include features such as a theme, company logo, generic page content, and other Web page features. The associated Dynamic Web Templates report shows which dynamic Web template a Web page relies on for content.

Shared borders let you create a setup where every page has the same border information, but the central content is different. The shared borders can include anything you'd normally provide on a Web page. The difference is that this information appears on the border of the affected pages. For example, a border element might be a page heading, or you could create a standard list of links. The Shared Borders report shows which Web pages use the Shared Borders feature. In addition, it tells which borders are in use (top, right, left, or bottom). For example, you might want to ensure that all pages use the top border so they all have the same banner information but that only top-level pages have the left border, which contains the global links for the Web site.

Developers use Cascading Style Sheets (CSS) to create a standard method of formatting a Web page, such as the typeface and colors used for text. The formatting includes every tag-related feature you want to define. For example, you create an ⟨a⟩ tag entry when you want all pages to have the same hyperlink formatting. A Web site can use multiple CSS files to provide custom formatting for various sections. The Style Sheet Links report tells you which CSS files are assigned to each page. (For more about CSS, see Book IV, Chapter 1.)

Themes also affect the appearance of each page through predefined setups. In this case, FrontPage relies on a set of custom files, which are based on the appearance of an existing Web page. The report shows which theme each Web page on your site uses. In addition, the report tells you how the theme is configured using separate columns for vivid colors, active graphics, and background picture settings.

Fixing Problems

Some FrontPage reports help you locate and fix problems. You could possibly use the reports for other purposes, but Web site maintenance is their main function. The Problems menu doesn't contain an overview report, but you can see reports about various troublesome conditions not long after they emerge:

✦ Unlinked files

✦ Slow pages

✦ Broken hyperlinks

✦ Component errors

These are discussed more fully in the next few sections.

Taking care of unlinked files

The Unlinked Files report helps you locate files that aren't accessible by the user — at least not directly. Not every unlinked file is a candidate for removal. For example, you might have theme files that appear unlinked but are actually used by one or more of the Web pages. The best way to use this report is to sort it by the Links To column. Place all the entries with 0 at the top to make them easy to find. Look for entries in the Links From column that have a value of 0. When both columns are 0, the file doesn't have any links, and it might be isolated. After you discover the file isn't used for any purpose, remove it from your Web site.

Bringing slow pages up to speed

The Slow Pages report is affected by two settings: download speed and download time. You use the Report Setting field on the toolbar (see Figure 5-3) to change the number of seconds that the user requires to download the page. Set the download speed using the Assume Connection Speed Of field on the Reports View tab of the Options dialog box (refer to Figure 5-2). Using a setting of 10 seconds ensures most people will wait to see your site. Higher settings could mean that some users will leave your site in frustration. Lower settings generally make it hard for you to provide all the content you want. The idea is to discover which pages will cause problems by making the user wait too long. You should consider redesigning or streamlining pages that appear on the Slow Pages report. In some cases, you might have to divide the page into two in order to meet the download time expectations of people who visit your site.

Tracking the missing link (s)

The Hyperlinks report tells the status of each hyperlink on your Web site. The focus of this report are the broken hyperlinks. When FrontPage can't verify a hyperlink, you have three options:

✦ Repair the broken link.

✦ Find an alternative link that provides the same information.

✦ Remove the hyperlink from your site.

To see the link, highlight its entry and click Edit Hyperlink on the toolbar. Many hyperlinks fail because a Web site moves or changes the organization of their content. In some cases, you might see a lot of broken links. When this problem occurs, make sure you also check your connection to the Internet to ensure FrontPage has the connection required to verify the link.

Fixing component errors

Component errors have a number of sources. You might not have the correct component installed on your system, the component might not be installed correctly, or the Web page can have a configuration error. No matter the source of the error, the Component Errors report tells you about it. The problem is that the error messages can be somewhat obscure or simply misleading. All FrontPage provides is the error message that the component creates. You can narrow the problem down, sometimes, by viewing the Web page. Make sure you understand how the component works before you begin troubleshooting.

**Book III
Chapter 5**

**Using FrontPage
Reports Efficiently**

Designing Workflow

The Workflow menu contains a number of reports — all of which help you manage your Web site, especially when working in a team environment. These reports help you discover the status of your Web pages as described here.

✦ **Review Status:** This report describes where the document is in the editing process. Developers can use terms such as *just started* or *manager review* to indicate the status of the Web page. You can change this setting using the Review Status field on the Workgroup tab of the Web page Properties dialog box.

✦ **Assigned To:** This report tells who is currently working on the document. No one else should check the document out to work on it. You can change this setting using the Assigned To field on the Workgroup tab of the Web page Properties dialog box.

✦ **Categories:** This report tells which category the page belongs in. FrontPage provides default categories such as expense report and in process. You can also create custom categories as needed. You can change this setting using the Available Categories field on the Workgroup tab of the Web page Properties dialog box. The Report Setting field on the toolbar selects which category you see in the report (or you can choose to see all categories).

✦ **Publish Status:** This report contains a Publish column that defines whether FrontPage is publishing the page with other pages on the Web site during an update. You change this setting by right-clicking the file entry and choosing Don't Publish from the context menu. The Review Status column of the report helps you to decide whether to publish the file or not.

✦ **Checkout Status:** This report tells who has checked out a particular file and when they checked it out. FrontPage includes a document management system that helps members of a team manage the files on a Web site. This report is part of that management system.

Most of these reports provide simple information about the Web page. However, the Checkout Status report requires special interpretation and a special setup. The following sections describe this report in more detail.

Using the Checkout Status report

The Checkout Status report contains a list of files, the title, the file type, and the folder where the file is located. The special information in this report is the file version number, which tells you how often the file has received edits.

When someone checks out the file, his name appears in the Checked Out By column. The Locked Date column shows when the person checked out the file.

Files can remain locked between FrontPage sessions. As long as a user has a lock on a file, no one else can check it out to modify it. Closing a file isn't sufficient to check it in — you must right-click the file and choose Check In from the context menu to perform this task. Files you've checked out appear in most reports, the Folder List, and the Folders view with a check mark next to them.

When you make an error editing a file, you can easily reverse all the changes to that file when using the FrontPage checkout feature. Instead of checking the file in after you make the edits, right-click the file entry and choose Undo Check Out. FrontPage returns the file to its previous condition. You can't use this option after checking the file in because the edits become permanent at that point.

Special setup for the Checkout Status report

Even if you have FrontPage Server Extensions installed, you can't access the Checkout Status report unless you also require the user to check files in and out of the server. To set FrontPage to require the user to check documents in and out, choose Tools⇨Site Settings. You see the Site Settings dialog box shown in Figure 5-4. Then you can check the Use Document Check-in and Check-out options, and your setup is in progress.

Figure 5-4:
Set
FrontPage
to use
document
check-in
and check-
out.

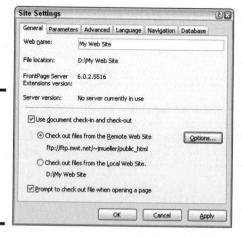

When you set up FrontPage for a remote connection using the settings on the Remote Web Site view, you see two options for checking documents in and out:

✦ **Remote connection:** Choose this option when everyone uploads changes directly from their local hard drives to the remote site.

✦ **Local connection:** Select this option when everyone uses a local data store for changes before sending them to the Web server.

Selecting the remote option enables the Options button. Here's how you use it:

1. **Click Options to set the name you want to use to check-out the documents.**

   You see the Remote Check Out Options dialog box.

2. **Type the name you want to use in the Check Out Name field.**

   You may optionally provide the FTP login name and an e-mail address as part of the document check-out.

3. **Click OK to close the Remote Check Out Options dialog box.**

   The Prompt to Check Out File When Opening a Page option shown in the Site Settings dialog box is a good safety feature to select. Choosing this option helps ensure developers on your team check documents in and out properly.

4. **After you finish selecting any document check-in and check-out options, click OK.**

   Now you can use the Checkout Status report.

Developing Usage Statistics

FrontPage provides usage statistics for your Web site based on a daily, weekly, or monthly schedule. When a report doesn't provide a specific time interval, FrontPage generally collects the data on a monthly basis for the number of months specified by the Number of Months Shown field on the Reports View tab of the Options dialog box.

Using the Usage reports

The Usage Statistics menu begins with a Usage Summary report. Unlike most reports that FrontPage provides, you can't copy this report to the Clipboard and paste it into another document for printing. The Usage Summary contains an overview of the statistics for your Web site and links to detail reports where you can find additional information. The amount of information you find in this report depends on your server configuration.

The Daily Summary, Weekly Summary, and Monthly Summary reports tell how many hits your Web site has had, the number of individual visitors, and the number of bytes downloaded. These summaries don't include any details — they just provide a quick overview so you can track the daily usage of your site. You use these reports to follow general trends. For example, you can determine whether more people are visiting your site on average and see whether there are dips and peaks in your site's popularity.

The Daily Page Hits, Weekly Page Hits, and Monthly Page Hits reports provide detailed Web-page statistics. You use these reports to discover which Web pages your visitors like best. In addition, these reports help you determine which Web pages require updates to maintain their popularity — and which you should consider removing or changing because they aren't popular.

The Visiting User report is useless unless you require visitors to log onto your Web server. Otherwise, visitors view your site anonymously. This report displays lists of people who visit your site.

The Operating Systems and Browsers reports tell you about visitors to your site even when you don't require them to log in. Use these reports to tailor your content to meet visitor needs. For example, when you see the majority of your visitors use Windows 2000, you can make a few assumptions about their setup and equipment. Likewise, the browser information tells you how to format Web pages to ensure maximum compatibility.

The Referring Domains and Referring URLs reports tell you how users get to your Web site from other places on the Internet. You can use these reports to determine the effectiveness of advertising or other means of selling your site. It also helps you determine the effectiveness of keywords used by search engines to help visitors find your site.

Displaying reports in graphic form

FrontPage displays the initial Usage reports in tables. Reading row upon row of statistics is helpful when you need specific bits of information but isn't particularly helpful when you're looking for trends. Graphics are better for displaying Web site trends.

To display the reports in graphic format, select a chart type from the drop-down list on the toolbar shown in Figure 5-3. Click the button to display the chart. Figure 5-5 shows typical results.

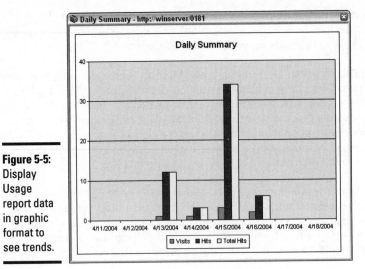

Figure 5-5:
Display
Usage
report data
in graphic
format to
see trends.

To place this information in a written report, right-click the chart and select Copy from the context menu. See the UsageReport.htm file provided with the source code for this chapter on the Wiley Web site for an example of how you can combine the graphic and tabular data on a single Web page.

Book IV

Advanced Design

The 5th Wave   By Rich Tennant

"Look into my Web site, Ms. Carruthers. Look deep into its rotating, nicely animated spiral, spinning, spinning, pulling you in, deeper... deeper..."

Contents at a Glance

Chapter 1: Using Cascading Style Sheets

Cascading Style Sheets (CSS) might sound like something very complex — perhaps even a little fancy — but it's a technology that makes your online life easier, and your Web site a lot easier to use. Users can even customize the appearance of your Web page under certain circumstances. Overall, CSS is one of the best things you can do for your Web site — everyone wins. The secret of CSS is that this technology separates the content of a Web page from the formatting. It's actually a very simple idea — makes you wonder why someone didn't think of it sooner.

The Microsoft people thought CSS so important that they included special features in FrontPage to make using CSS even easier. For example, you have access to a special Style toolbar that lets you add CSS code to your Web page in Design view, rather than coding it separately. In addition, FrontPage provides a number of CSS templates for you to use, or you can create your own.

The best part of CSS is that it makes your Web page accessible. Sure, you might think that red lettering on a green background during the Christmas season is a surefire way to attract attention — but in many cases, people with color blindness won't be able to see your site. Some people need large letters; others don't want any special formatting because they use a screen reader (they can't see the formatting even when it's present).

Some Web sites have seen so many benefits from using CSS that they share the wealth: They offer users some settings to change the appearance of their pages. By providing five or six CSS files with the Web site, the owner is saying that everyone should have the view he or she likes best and that makes everyone happy.

Understanding Cascading Style Sheets

CSS is easy to understand in both concept and implementation. With CSS, your Web page actually consists of two files, each with distinct contents and purpose:

✦ **The HyperText Markup Language (HTML) file:** This is the same file you've used since your first Web page; all it contains is content. The HTML file still contains tags and meta information, but you don't place any formatting in this file at all — not even centering the header tags.

✦ **The CSS file:** This file contains only formatting information. You don't include any content, not even common elements, in a CSS file. Every entry in the CSS file affects a tag directly or it creates a new style that isn't associated with a tag.

For example, you can provide formatting that you want to use with <H1> tags in general, but you can also override that formatting by providing a special style. One CSS file can provide formatting for many HTML files — perhaps all of the HTML files on your Web site. Here's an example of a very simple CSS file that includes a tag style and a custom style.

```
H1
{
    font-size: 200%;
    color: black;
    text-align: center;
}
.highlight-i
{
    font-weight: bold;
    color: red;
    font-style: italic;
}
```

The H1 entry refers to the <H1> tag. The curly braces { } define the beginning and end of the formatting information. Within the curly braces, you see a font-size: entry that tells the browser how big to make the font, a color:

entry that tells what color to make the text, and a `text-align:` entry that tells how to position the text on-screen.

The `.highlight-i` entry is a special style that isn't associated with any tag. You can apply this style anywhere that you need to use italic type — it doesn't matter where the text appears. This style is cumulative with tag-specific formatting you define. When you apply this style to the `<H1>` tag, the browser adds some new formatting, but doesn't change any existing formatting unless you specifically tell the browser to change the formatting. In this case, the `font-weight:` entry tells the browser how to present the font (`bold` in this case) and the `font-style:` entry tells the browser to make the font italic. Notice that both the `H1` and the `.highlight-i` entries have a `color:` entry. When you apply the `highlight-i` style, it overrides the standard `<H1>` tag color (`black`) and makes it red.

One of the biggest advantages that CSS offers the developer is that it's a way to create centralized formatting for your Web site. For example, when you decide the background color of the page should change to pale blue from pale yellow, you only make the change in one place — the CSS file. A single change affects all the Web pages on your Web site — at least all the Web pages that are linked to that CSS file.

FrontPage supports two types of CSS: external and embedded. The embedded version makes the CSS part of the HTML file, so it doesn't rely on a separate CSS page. A Web page that relies on embedded CSS doesn't share the formatting even though the actual page is created in the same way. (See the "Defining an embedded style sheet" section later in this chapter for more information on this technique.) To create a CSS page that everyone can use on all the Web pages on your site, however, you need an external CSS file. This technique is exceptionally flexible and provides the full benefits that CSS can offer, so it's a major focus of this chapter.

To ensure that you can use CSS with FrontPage, you need to adjust the authoring settings for your Web site. You can do it in two steps:

1. **Choose the Tools⇨Page Options command and select the Authoring tab.**

   You see the Page Options dialog box shown in Figure 1-1.

2. **Check the CSS 1.0 (Formatting) and the CSS 2.0 (Positioning) options, and then click OK.**

   FrontPage is set up to use CSS.

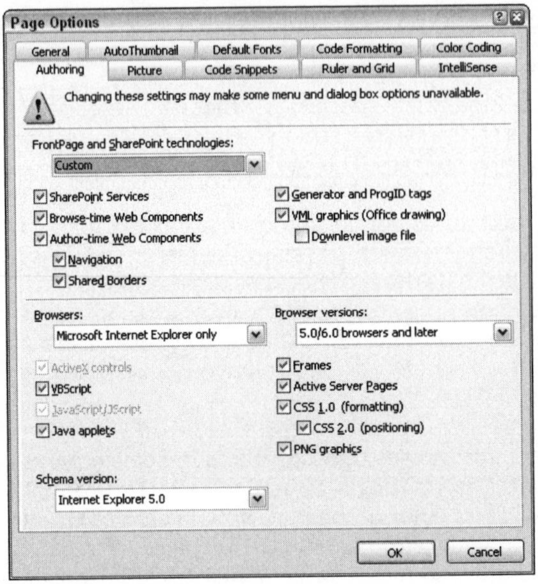

Figure 1-1:
Configure
FrontPage
to support
CSS.

Creating a Simple CSS Page

FrontPage fully supports CSS. You have a choice of predefined CSS styles or you can create a custom style. The predefined styles match the themes that FrontPage supports, so you can create a theme appearance without actually using a theme. After you create a CSS page, you can share it with other people. The following sections tell you how to work with CSS pages. A special section tells how you can augment the predefined CSS styles so they provide more information to people who want to use them.

Using the predefined styles

Each of the predefined styles that FrontPage provides can give your Web page a consistent look. You can modify these styles as needed to provide specialized formatting required for personal or company needs. The FrontPage-predefined CSS pages don't actually exist on your site until after you add them. The following steps help you select a predefined style:

1. **Select the File⇨New command.**

You see the New window in the Task Page.

2. **Click More Page Templates. Choose the Style Sheets tab.**

You see the Page Templates dialog box shown in Figure 1-2. The Normal Style Sheet is blank, so you don't want to choose it unless you want to define your own style or you want to create a special style for people who don't want to see any formatting. Each of the predefined styles includes a description that tells you about color and font choices.

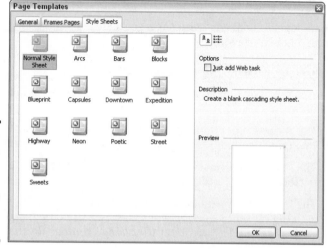

Figure 1-2:
Select one
of the
predefined
styles to use
on your
Web site.

3. **Highlight one of the predefined styles. Click OK.**

   FrontPage displays the new style sheet.

4. **Save the new page to your Web site.**

   FrontPage displays the new CSS page in the Folders List.

After you save the file, you'll want to change its properties. Right-click the entry in the Folder List and choose Properties. You see the file Properties dialog box. As with HTML files, the Title field appears on the General tab and the Comments field on the Summary tab.

When adding this file to a group project, you also want to define the work-group settings located on the Workgroup tab.

Defining your own style

You might decide that none of the styles that FrontPage provides suit your needs, which means you need to create your own style. To create your own style, start by creating a blank CSS page using the technique described in the "Using the predefined styles" section earlier in this chapter. The only difference is that (in this case) you select the Normal Style Sheet.

Working with standard tags

At this point, you're facing a blank style sheet that has all the appeal of a snowstorm in May. Before you do anything, you need to decide which styles you want to create. In many cases, it pays to create all the HTML entries first so you can create user-defined styles only as needed.

For the moment, sticking to basics is a good idea. To add a new style to the CSS page, follow these steps:

1. **Choose the Format⇨Style command.**

You see the Style dialog box (shown in Figure 1-3), with the following features:

- The Styles list contains the common HTML tags that you use. For example, it contains the h1 entry, which corresponds to the <H1> tag.

- The Paragraph Preview and Character Preview tags show how the tag looks now.

- The Description pane tells you which actions you can perform with the current selection when the style uses the default settings. Otherwise, it tells you about the special settings for that selection.

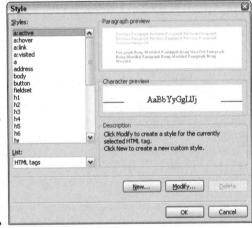

Figure 1-3: Define styles for your custom CSS page as needed.

2. **To modify existing HTML tags, highlight the tag and click Modify.**

You see the Modify Style dialog box, which tells you which tag you're working with, provides a style type, previews the style, and shows a description of the style.

HTML tags normally don't include a description unless you make changes to the default settings. In this case, the Description field contains a list of changes you made.

3. Click Format.

You see a list of formatting options, as shown in Figure 1-4.

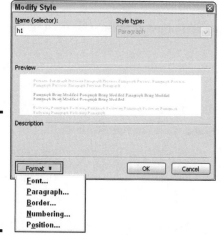

Figure 1-4: Determine which formatting options you want to change.

4. Modify your tags as needed.

Let's say you want to modify the font for the <H1> tag so it appears in blue. You select the Font entry (from the list in Figure 1-4), and when the Font dialog box appears, select Blue in the Color field. FrontPage then changes the color in the field.

5. Click OK three times.

Your formatting modifications are now specified in the file; the CSS page now contains this simple code (in this case, reflecting a color change to blue):

```
h1              { color: #0000FF }
```

As you add more entries to the CSS file, FrontPage automatically adds new text to the CSS page. You don't need to worry about typing any code. FrontPage adds the appropriate code for any changes you make.

Unfortunately, the code can become hard to read after a while unless you format the entries at some point — say, when you make manual changes to them. Manual changes don't affect FrontPage's ability to add changes automatically in response to your formatting selections.

Book IV Chapter 1

Using Cascading Style Sheets

Working with custom styles

After you define all settings for the default tags, you might decide that you need to add some custom styles. For example, you might add an italic style for some text in a paragraph or an underline style to underline the selection letter of a field in a form. Special styles should address needs that standard tags can't — conditions that can't be handled in other ways.

To create a custom style, follow these steps:

1. **Select the User-Defined Style option in the List field of the Style dialog box shown in Figure 1-3.**

   You see a list of styles you've modified — even standard tags.

2. **Click New.**

   You see the New Style dialog box.

3. **Name the style by adding a name in the Name field.**

   When naming the style, make sure you use something unique, but also easy to read. For example, you might name a style for italic characters on your Web page as `char_italic`.

4. **Choose a style type.**

   When you want to modify the appearance of individual characters in a paragraph, select the Character option in the Style Type field.

5. **Finally, create the formatting for this new style and click OK.**

   FrontPage automatically precedes paragraph styles with a period and character styles with the word `span` and a period. So the `char_italic` style would actually appear as `span.char_italic` in the CSS page.

Making a style available to others

After you create a new style, you can make it available for other people to use. The easiest way to do this is to place the CSS file in a central location on your Web server, and then request that everyone link their Web pages to it. Of course, this method assumes that everyone is working on the same Web site and has access to all the required folders.

You can also add a new style sheet to FrontPage. The steps that do so look like this:

1. **Create a new folder in the Program Files folder of your hard drive.**

   The path to the new file should be

   `\Program Files\Microsoft Office\Templates\1033\CSS11`

The new folder should have the same name as your template, with a TEM (for *template*) extension. The name of the example CSS file is `UniqueStyle.css`, so the name of the template folder is `UniqueStyle.tem`.

2. Inside the new folder, create a Device-Independent Bitmap (DIB) of your style.

This is the file that people consult to see what it looks like. The best way to perform this task is to create an example Web page that includes the best features of your style, create a screenshot of the example, size the image so it's 110 by 124 pixels, and then save the screenshot as a DIB file in the template folder. (Many graphics applications such as PaintShop Pro can resize images and create DIB files.)

3. Create an INF file that describes your stylesheet.

The INF file used for the example contains the following code:

```
[info]
_LCID=1033
_version=11.0.4628.0
title=My Unique Style Sheet
description=Creates a stylesheet that includes six levels of
heading styles, a yellow background, an underline and
strikethrough style, and a special announcements style.
```

The `[info]` header is part of the INF file — it simply shows where the information begins. The `_LCID` entry defines the locale (`language`) used for this style sheet. Use the `_version` entry to define a version for this style sheet. It's normally a good idea to use the version of FrontPage you used to create the style sheet. You see the `title` entry under the icon for the style sheet in the Page Templates dialog box. The `description` entry appears in the Description field of the Page Templates dialog box when you select this style.

Correcting the predefined styles

You might have noticed that the predefined styles — except Normal — don't include a preview in the Page Templates dialog box. The lack of a preview makes it difficult to select a style because the template names aren't descriptive and it's hard to visualize what the styles look like based on the description. Microsoft didn't provide DIB files with the style sheet templates, so FrontPage has nothing to display.

Correcting this problem can be time-consuming, but it's definitely worth the effort when you plan to use more than one style in the Web sites you create. You can correct the problem by following three general steps:

1. Create an example Web page that exemplifies the best features of the style sheet.

2. Create a DIB file based on a screenshot of that example Web page.

3. Place copies of the DIB files in each of the template folders located in the following folder:

```
\Program Files\Microsoft Office\Templates\1033\CSS11
```

Voilà — you now have previews that help you choose a new style sheet easily.

Linking CSS to a Web Page

You have a shiny new CSS page to use with your next Web project. Before the CSS page will do anything, you need to link it to the Web page. Unfortunately, you can't do this until after you create the Web page. The linking process is something you do as part of the Web page configuration. The following sections describe two kinds of CSS usage. The first is using standard external style sheets. The second is using embedded style sheets.

Using external style sheets

The only way to use a style sheet you create as a separate file is to create an external link to it. To add a style sheet to any Web page, follow these steps:

1. Select the Format⇨Style Sheet Links command.

You see the Link Style Sheet dialog box, as shown in Figure 1-5. This dialog box shows any style sheets you have linked to your Web page. In this case, there aren't any.

Figure 1-5:
Add a style sheet link to the current Web page.

2. Click Add.

You see the Select Style Sheet dialog box.

3. Locate the style sheet you want to use and click OK.

FrontPage adds the style sheet to the Link Style Sheet dialog box.

4. Click OK.

You normally see the effects of the style sheet on your Web page. In some cases, the changes the style sheet makes won't show up unless you have some text or other content on the page.

FrontPage uses standard means to add the style-sheet link to your Web page. Look in Code view in the header area and you'll notice a new tag that looks like this:

```
<link rel="stylesheet"
    type="text/css"
    href="PredefinedStyle.css">
```

Each of these lines has a distinct function:

✦ The `<link>` tag creates a link between your Web page and the external CSS page.

✦ The `rel` attribute tells you that this file is a style sheet.

✦ The `type` attribute tells you that the file contains a combination of text and CSS entries.

✦ Finally, the `href` attribute defines the name and location of the CSS page.

Defining an embedded style sheet

Some developers use embedded CSS to ensure the formatting remains linked to the page. The main benefit to this approach is that you don't need two files to use CSS on your Web page. For some developers, the use of a single page for everything does make it easier to learn CSS. Using embedded CSS makes it easier to see how everything fits together. So this method is effective for understanding how CSS works.

The disadvantages of this approach are numerous — so numerous that I really hope you don't use embedded CSS. Whatever apparent advantage that technique might seem to offer, the developer actually loses. That's because one of the benefits of CSS is *centralized management of formatting*. Embedding wipes out the advantage; now you have to change the formatting in every page. In effect, CSS has been made no better than using HTML to specify formatting. The user loses out, as well: There's no way to change the formatting because it's linked directly to the page. Instead of creating an environment in which everyone can see content as they prefer, everyone still ends up using the same formatting.

**Book IV
Chapter 1**

**Using Cascading
Style Sheets**

To embed CSS directly in an HTML document, select the Format➪Style command. You see the Style dialog box shown in Figure 1-3. Create a style for an HTML tag or a user-defined style just as you would for an external style sheet. (For more on this, see the previous section, "Using external style sheets.") The only difference is that the styles appear as part of the HTML document, rather than an external document. All the styles appear within the `<style>` tag, as shown here.

```
<style>
<!--
h1          { color: #0000FF;
              font-variant: small-caps;
              text-indent:-10 }

-->
</style>
```

Notice the construction of this tag. When a browser doesn't understand the `<style>` tag, it just ignores it. However, the browser won't ignore the style definition because it isn't a tag. To keep browsers that don't understand styles from reading the style information and getting confused, FrontPage automatically identifies that information as a comment.

The `<H1>` tag formatting is straightforward. The `color` attribute shows that this tag is blue. The font itself is in small caps, which means lowercase letters are capitalized and shown in a smaller sized font. Finally, the `text-indent` attribute is –10. This means the header is actually outdented. Here, because I wanted most of the text indented on the first line, the `<body>` tag contains an indent. For additional details on the embedded formatting for this Web page, see the `EmbeddedCSS.htm` file supplied with the source code for this chapter on the Wiley Web site.

Using the Style Toolbar

FrontPage automatically displays the Style toolbar when you perform certain tasks, such as linking a Web page to a CSS page. You can also display the Style toolbar by right-clicking the toolbar area and choosing Style from the context menu. In both cases, you see the Style toolbar shown in Figure 1-6.

The Style toolbar works with the Style field of the Formatting toolbar. Both let you add a formatting style to your Web page. The Style toolbar works with actual tags, while the Style field works with individual characters or paragraphs. Always use the Style field when you want to assign formatting to characters using a character style. The Style toolbar is more convenient for changing the style after you assign it.

Figure 1-6:
Use the
Style toolbar
to work with
custom
styles.

Formatting Style Selection

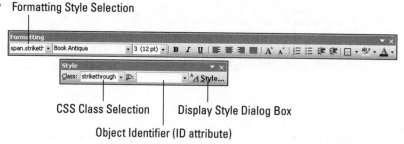

CSS Class Selection   Display Style Dialog Box

Object Identifier (ID attribute)

To assign a character style to a range of text, highlight the text and select the character style that you want from the Style field. All character styles that you create using FrontPage begin with the word span for a good reason. The formatting creates a `<span>` tag, as shown here:

```
<span class="strikethrough">strikethrough</span>
```

This tag includes the `class` attribute, which assigns the strikethrough style to the text between the `<span>` and `</span>` tags. Every time you assign formatting to a group of characters using FrontPage, you see the `<span>` tag and associated `class` attribute.

When you view this text in the Style toolbar, you see just the class name in the CSS Class field. You can change the style by choosing a different option in the CSS Class field drop-down list. The reason you want to use this feature is that the CSS Class field contains only custom styles, so you have fewer styles to look through to locate the style you need.

The Style toolbar also contains an Object Identifier field. This field modifies the `id` attribute of the tag you're working with. Most tags don't include an `id` attribute by default, so typing a value in the Object Identifier field creates an `id` attribute like this one:

```
<span class="strikethrough"
      id="Strikethrough1">strikethrough</span>
```

Providing a meaningful `id` attribute for each of your formatting entries makes it easier to locate them later. It's best to use the name of the style followed by a sequential number because every `id` must be unique. When you want to locate all the entries that use that style, select the Edit⇨Find command. You see the Find and Replace dialog box. Type the name of the style in the Find What field and click Find Next. FrontPage will take you to each entry that uses a style in turn. This technique helps you locate text that uses a particular style quickly so you can make changes as needed.

**Book IV
Chapter 1**

**Using Cascading
Style Sheets**

Because paragraphs already have a tag associated with them, you can simply place the cursor in the paragraph and choose a style from the CSS Class field. Using this technique enforces the idea that the paragraph won't use the standard formatting — that the formatting is unique in some way. As with character formatting, FrontPage assigns the style to the tag using the `class` attribute, like this:

```
<p class="announcement_header">This is an Announcement</p>
```

You can assign special formatting to any tag by using the `class` attribute. For example, you can create special headers. When a tag doesn't have a `class` attribute associated with it, it relies on the standard formatting you provide or the default formatting used by the entire Web page.

Designing Efficient Styles

One of the problems with many style sheets is that the developer decided to define every possible formatting element of the style, whether it made sense or not. Solving this problem is the reason you want to define all your tags first, and then consider the special styles. You should also work from the top of the Web page down to the details. For example, define the overall appearance of the page first by selecting styles for the `<BODY>` tag. When all page elements use the same font, define it as part of the `<BODY>` tag rather than as part of the individual elements.

Every time you make a selection at a top level that affects a lot of tags, you reduce the number of lower-level tag changes. The reason you want to avoid making more changes than necessary is to ensure that your CSS page works efficiently. The browser requires less time to make one change than to make twenty or thirty changes. The time you save might seem small when you're working on a local machine, but it can make a visible difference in the download speed of the page when you're using a dial-up connection.

A top-down design translates into other benefits. It's relatively easy to create a messy CSS page that no one can follow, much less want to use. By organizing your development efforts, however, you can keep your CSS entries in order, too — which makes them easier to find. Place exceptions to rules at the end of the CSS file so other people can understand the normal layout of the Web page *first* and see the exceptions as needed.

Sometimes developers create a CSS page that's almost completely composed of exceptions. When this occurs, consider whether the original design was well thought out, and consider redoing it. Sometimes you can make a few top-level changes that make lower-level exceptions unnecessary.

In some cases, you might find that odd effects crop up or certain pages don't work well when you add too many exceptions. For example, using italics to identify special terms is one thing — adding an odd character as a special effect is quite another. Exceptions to the rule should make your Web page easier to read and use. When an exception doesn't help the Web page user, consider eliminating it.

Using CSS for Accessibility Needs

Using CSS makes your Web pages more accessible. When you provide multiple styles that users can choose from, you ensure that the user can see your Web page completely. Make sure you include styles with large fonts and at least one without any special formatting at all. These special CSS files make it possible for someone with special needs to use your Web page.

Many modern browsers make your job easier by including accessibility features, some of which rely on CSS. When you create a Web page that uses CSS, you give the user a chance to substitute his or her own style sheet, one that is completely designed for his or her specific needs. For example, Internet Explorer 6 provides this setting. To see the difference for yourself, add a custom style sheet (use any style sheet you want) by using the following steps:

1. **Choose the Tools⇨Internet Options command.**

You see the Internet Options dialog box.

2. **Select the General tab. Click Accessibility.**

You see the Accessibility dialog box.

3. **Check Format Documents Using My Style Sheet. Type the name of your style sheet in the Style Sheet field or click Browse to locate the file on your hard drive. Click OK.**

Internet Explorer changes the formatting of the page to match the style sheet you selected.

4. **Click OK to close the Internet Options dialog box.**

Internet Explorer makes the changes permanent (until you decide to change the style sheet again).

Chapter 2: Working with Clip Art

In This Chapter

✔ **Creating your own drawings**

✔ **Using layers to organize content**

✔ **Placing images on a Web page**

✔ **Working with the Clip Art Organizer**

✔ **Describing your images**

✔ **Defining an image map**

✔ **Getting pictures from other places**

*F*or many people, the visual experience of working with graphics puts the fun into Web-page development. Adding graphic content opens new methods of communication. Drawing images or using clip art adds pizzazz your Web page would otherwise lack. In fact, some people would go so far as to say that graphics are the best part of developing a Web page because you can be creative in so many ways.

FrontPage provides a wealth of methods for working with graphics of various types. You decide how the image appears on-screen and can provide your own images whenever needed. Of course, you also have access to the wealth of predrawn images included with FrontPage (and from other online sources). It's also possible to use special techniques to position the graphics on-screen. Adding accessibility information to graphics ensures that everyone can enjoy them. In addition, you can create graphics that perform actions. Click in a certain location on the image and you go to another place on the Web site.

Using the Drawing and Drawing Canvas Toolbars

Most of the drawings and pictures you see on Web sites appear in separate files. The developer creates a link between the graphic image and the Web page, using the `<img>` tag. A number of new technologies are appearing on the scene, however, and FrontPage includes support for one of them called *Vector Markup Language* (VML). You really don't need to know how this language works to use it. In fact, when you look at the number of entries even a simple VML drawing creates, you understand why you want to make changes using Design view, rather than fussing with it by hand.

This technology has a lot of advantages. It's fast and easy to use. In addition, it helps you create Web page graphics very quickly and modify them directly on the page. Despite all the advantages of using VML, it's relatively new, so not every browser supports this technology. Web site visitors who have older-technology browsers won't be able to see your drawings. It's worth weighing the convenience this technology provides against the needs of the people who want to visit your site. Also, this technology can cause problems with accessibility aids, so it might not be the best solution if you need to support visitors with special needs. For example, someone who has special visual needs won't be able to see your drawing. A user who can't see your drawing will need a text description to participate on your site, making the description exceptionally important.

Adding VML support

Before you can begin drawing directly on the Web page, VML support must first be enabled. Here's the drill:

1. **Select the Tools⇨Page Options command.**

You see the Page Options dialog box.

2. **Select the Authoring tab and check the VML Graphics option.**

To ensure maximum compatibility, make sure you choose Both Internet Explorer and Navigator in the Browser field and 4.0 Browsers and Later in the Browser Versions field.

3. **Click OK.**

Creating a canvas

In FrontPage, a *canvas* is a designated drawing surface. You don't always have to create a canvas for a drawing, but using one can making working with complex images a little easier. The canvas acts as a means of grouping all the image elements together. You can also create a background for the canvas and give it a border — effectively creating a frame for your drawing.

To create a new canvas, select the Insert⇨Picture⇨New Drawing command. You see a new canvas added to the Web page, as shown in Figure 2-1. Change the size of the canvas by using any of the eight sizing paddles, as shown in the figure. The hashed outer block lets you move the canvas around on the Web page.

Use the options on the Drawing Canvas toolbar to modify the canvas and, optionally, any drawing elements it contains. FrontPage doesn't display the Drawing Canvas toolbar by default — right-click the toolbar and choose Drawing Canvas to display it.

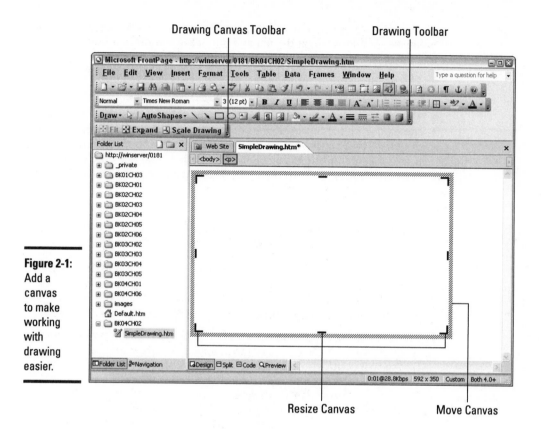

Figure 2-1:
Add a
canvas
to make
working
with
drawing
easier.

Configuring the canvas

Before you create a drawing, define some of the canvas elements. Right-click
the canvas and choose Format Drawing Canvas from the context menu. You
see the Format Drawing Canvas dialog box shown in Figure 2-2.

The dialog box contains several tabs, some of which won't be active (depending on your settings). The tabs of interest include these:

✦ The Colors and Lines tab lets you add a background color and border to
  the drawing canvas.

✦ The Transparency slide lets you set the opacity of the canvas. A value of
  0 makes the canvas opaque, so you can't see anything behind it. Set the
  value higher to gradually let the user see items behind the canvas until
  the canvas becomes almost completely invisible.

✦ The Style setting is a little deceiving at first — it shows a series of solid lines — but look down the list and you'll see options for creating effects such as ridges for the border of the canvas.

✦ The Dashed setting adjusts the line used to create the border of the canvas — it can be solid, dotted, or a pattern.

✦ The Size tab shows the height and width of the canvas. You can also set the *scaling* factor of the canvas — a process that shrinks or grows the drawing as you move the canvas borders. To enable this option, click Scale Drawing on the Drawing Canvas toolbar. The Lock Aspect Ratio option tells FrontPage to maintain the drawing proportions as you scale it using the canvas.

✦ The Layout tab defines how text and other resources surround the canvas. You can tell FrontPage not to use any wrapping at all, or the text can wrap on the right or left side of the canvas. This tab also contains positioning information — where the canvas appears on the page relative to other elements. You can choose between no positioning (the canvas appears wherever you place it on-screen), absolute (the canvas appears in a specific location even if you place it somewhere else), and relative (the canvas appears in a position relative to the other elements on-screen).

✦ The Site tab is exceptionally important. Always provide a description of the image on the canvas. Users with special needs require this information to work with your Web page. All users can use this information when the picture is missing or if it doesn't download (the user might have pressed Stop on the browser). Finally, search engines rely on this information to help people find pictures on your Web site. The "Describing an Image" section provides more details on this particular tab and it's purpose.

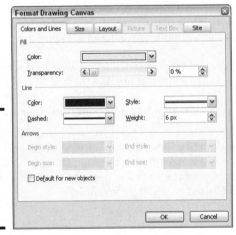

Figure 2-2:
Select configuration options for the drawing canvas.

Adding a drawing

The Drawing toolbar contains a wealth of drawing tools you can use —
everything from simple lines to boxes to complex shapes. You can create
3D effects with many of the shapes. The AutoShapes menu on the Drawing
toolbar is the place to go if you have a basic shape in mind but lack drawing skills to create something complex. The results you obtain using the
AutoShapes menu options can be quite interesting and professional-looking.
For example, the banner in Figure 2-3 consists of a canvas, a Horizontal
Scroll (found in the Stars and Banners collection), and a little text.
Everything else is configuration.

You don't have to use a canvas with your drawing. The canvas provides a
way to group a series of elements together. When a drawing consists of no
more than a single element, no canvas is needed.

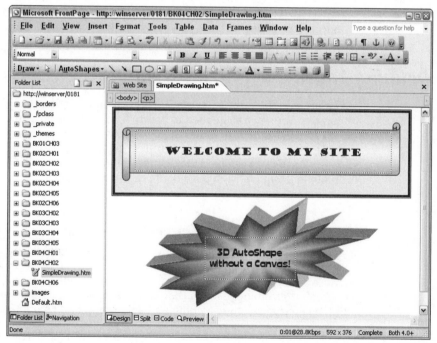

Figure 2-3:
Create great
results with
just a little
effort using
AutoShapes.

**Book IV
Chapter 2**

Working with
Clip Art

For a single-element drawing, you can use an AutoShape. Configuring an AutoShape without a canvas is similar to configuring a canvas:

1. **Right-click the AutoShape you want to use.**

A context menu appears.

2. **Choose Format Text Box from the context menu.**

You see the Format AutoShape dialog box which contains the same tabs as the Format Drawing Canvas dialog box shown in Figure 2-2. The important new addition is the Text Box tab that lets you set the internal margins for the text box in the AutoShape.

3. **Change the margins to help the AutoShape work better with various shading, 3D, and text effects.**

Figure 2-3 shows one of many possible Explosion 2 (located in the Stars and Banners group) setups you can create. See the `SimpleDrawing.htm` file located in the source code for this chapter on the Wiley Web site for additional ideas.

Defining Layers for Organization

Layers provide the means to create groups of information that you can move around the Web page as needed to create a certain effect. A layer relies on the `<div>` tag, a standard that many browsers recognize, to perform its work. The layer can have certain features, such as a border and internal color, but its main purpose is to organize information and allow you more flexibility in designing Web page content. The following sections describe layers in more detail.

Understanding why layers are useful

Layers are useful because they use a common tag to enable you to create very specific Web designs. You can move items around as needed, limit the extent to which users can view them, and even change their shape. The idea is to create a grouping of items that you can move and manipulate as a single item. The group can share a common background and characteristics.

A layer can contain anything you can place on a Web page. For example, when you want to create text you can move anywhere on the page, place a standard heading or paragraph in a layer. The text appears just as it always has, so if a browser doesn't understand layers, the user still sees the information you provide. The only difference is that the user sees the text as a standard Web page would display it, rather than with any extra positioning you provide. Here's an example of the code for a layer:

```
<div style="position: absolute;
    top: 19px; left: 10px;
    width: 147px; height: 36px; z-index: 1" id="Heading">
  <h1>This is the Heading</h1>
</div>
```

The tags and attributes in the example break down this way:

✦ The `<div>` tag pair identifies the beginning and end of the layer.

✦ The `style` attribute tells you that this `<div>` sets the absolute position of an item on the Web page.

✦ The `top` and `left` attributes set the upper-left corner of the layer, and the `width` and `height` determine the size of the layer.

✦ The `z-index` attribute determines the order in which the browser displays this element. Layers with high `z-index` numbers appear in front of those that have lower numbers because the browser draws lower-numbered layers first.

✦ The `id` attribute is a special identifier for the layer.

Look at the next line:

```
<h1>This is the Heading</h1>
```

This is a standard header tag. A header tag normally appears before the content that it applies to, so the next line would contain content. The important issue to remember is that some browsers don't know how to interpret the `<div>` tag, so you need to maintain the standard order of items in the Web page so these browsers display the Web page in an appealing way (items in the correct order and with proper headers). The Web page that can't interpret `<div>` tags won't have all the pizzazz of one that uses layers, but the user can still read it.

Creating a new layer

Adding a new layer to a Web page is a two-stage process. It involves creating the page and then applying the formatting — both before you add any content to the page. The process looks like this:

1. **Click Insert Layer on the Standard toolbar or select the Insert⇨Layer command.**

FrontPage displays a new layer that you can size and position as needed to hold the content you want to create.

2. **Prepare to configure the layer by right-clicking it and choosing Layer Properties from the context menu.**

   You see the Layers window of the Task Pane, as shown in Figure 2-4. This window displays all layers you have defined, along with their Z-index values and current identifiers.

3. **Change the new layer's default identifier.**

   FrontPage assigns a value of Layer1 (where 1 is the next number in sequence) to the layer, which isn't helpful. Right-click the layer entry and choose Modify ID from the context menu. When FrontPage changes the ID column into an edit box, type the new identifier and press Enter. You can change the visibility and Z-index of the layer by using the same technique.

4. **Format the layer's positioning.**

   To do so, right-click the layer entry and choose Positioning from the context menu. You see the Positioning dialog box, which offers different ways to position and wrap data outside the current level. This dialog box also helps you fine-tune the position and size of the layer. Finally, you can use this dialog box to change the Z-index of the layer. (For more about positioning, see the upcoming section.)

5. **Format the layer's border and shading.**

   Change the border and shading (background color) by right-clicking the layer entry and choosing Borders and Shading from the context menu. You see the Borders and Shading dialog box, which contains two tabs: one for Borders, one for Shading.

   - Use the Borders tab to choose a border color, width, and style. The styles include solid and dashed borders, along with special effects such as a ridged border. This tab also lets you adjust the padding or margins inside the layer so the text doesn't touch the edge (making it hard to read). The Preview area shows what the borders look like as you make changes.

   - Use the entries on the Shading tab to adjust the background and foreground (text) colors.

   You can also assign a picture to the background. The Preview area shows the results of any changes you make.

Using the Positioning toolbar

The Positioning toolbar can help you fine-tune the size and position of a number of layers quickly. FrontPage doesn't display this toolbar automatically; to display it, right-click the toolbar area and choose Positioning from the context menu. You see the Positioning toolbar shown in Figure 2-5.

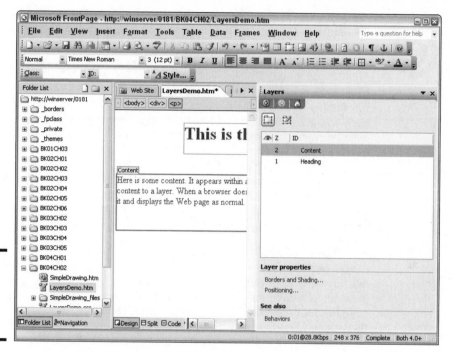

Figure 2-4:
Configure the layer before you use it.

Figure 2-5:
Modify the position and size of an existing layer or create a new one.

The main feature of this toolbar is its series of entries that let you change the size and position of a layer: You can define all four sides directly, use just one corner to position the layer, or change the layer's height and width. Although FrontPage defaults to using the upper-left corner, you can use any corner as a starting point for a measurement. You also don't have to use the default unit of measure (pixels) to adjust the layer settings. It's perfectly acceptable to use percentages, inches, centimeters, or any other unit of measure that a Web page normally uses.

Use percentages whenever possible for positioning. A percentage helps you maintain the appearance of a Web page even when the user resizes the window. For example, when a header takes up 50% of the page, setting the Left field to 25% centers the header on-screen.

It's easy to use the Positioning toolbar to create a layout from existing material. Simply highlight the material you want to see within the layout, and then click Absolute Positioning. FrontPage creates a new layout. The only difference between this layout and any other layout you create is that it doesn't have an identifier. Provide an identifier for the layout before you save it.

Use the Move Backward and Bring Forward buttons to change the Z-index of a layer. Layers with high numbers appear in front of those that have lower numbers because the browser draws lowered numbered layers first.

Using CSS with layers

Layers perform a very useful task in positioning your data on-screen, but formatting each layer on a Web page individually could become time-consuming. In addition, individually formatting all those layers makes the resulting Web page hard for other people to use. Layering can increase load time (because there is more code to download) and can interfere with accessibility devices. Unfortunately, FrontPage doesn't provide a quick method of creating a style for your layer.

The best way to create and format layers quickly is to use Cascading Style Sheets (CSS). To perform this task, create a layer and format it the way you want. Then select the Code view and copy the <div> tag formatting information to a new style in a CSS page. Remove the formatting from the original <div> tag and assign it the style you just created using the class attribute.

You can also create the CSS style using the Style dialog box entries. However, using this method saves time because you see the layer as it actually appears as you define the various entries. Moving the style information to a CSS page afterward is fast and easy.

Adding Images to a Web Page

You can add images to a Web page in a number of ways. The easiest method is to drag the image from the Folder List and drop it where you want the image to appear on-screen. This action produces an <img> tag that describes the image within the Web page. Here's a typical example of an <img> tag:

```
<img border="0" src="home.gif"
     width="52" height="46"></p>
```

The most important attribute is `src` because it points to the image you want to use. The `border` attribute defines the width of the border placed around the image. The `width` and `height` attributes show the finished size of the image. Always include these attributes because they tell the user what size image to expect after the browser downloads it. The user can rely on this information to time the download or choose to click Stop after the text appears on screen. Sizing the image also reduces text movement as the page loads.

Another technique to use is to copy the image from a graphics application and then paste it onto the Web page. When you use this technique, FrontPage asks you to provide a storage location for the image on the Web server (or on a local storage device when you're working on a local intranet). You can also use the Clip Art window of the Task Pane — and many of the options on the Insert Picture menu — to add an image to the current Web page. The "Using the Clip Art Organizer" section of this chapter describes some of these other options.

Using Clip Art

Clip art is one of the better ways to add images to your Web page when you're short on time or don't want to create your own images. FrontPage comes with a library of generic clip art images that you can easily modify to meet specific needs. In addition, you'll find a lot of clip art for sale as part of professional packages or available on the Internet. Using clip art helps you create great-looking Web pages quickly and with little effort.

Finding clip art to use with FrontPage

Before you can use clip art on your Web page, you have to find it on your hard drive. FrontPage makes this easy. If you're working with AutoShapes, you can get the most common entries from the drop-down list box of the Drawing toolbar. To locate popular clip art, use the Insert➪Picture➪Clip Art command to display the Clip Art window in the Task Pane, as shown in Figure 2-6.

To search for a piece of clip art, type a keyword into the Search For field. Use single words whenever possible to make the search easier.

Avoid using plurals as keywords. Doing so ensures that you find a piece of art whose filename uses the singular version of the keyword (say, *computer* as opposed to *computers*).

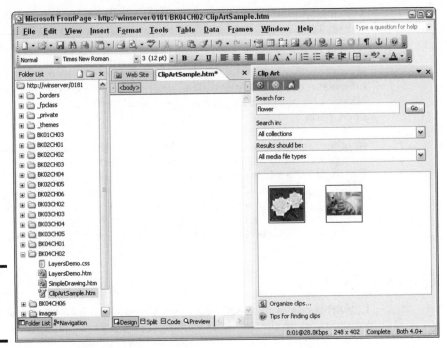

Figure 2-6:
Search for
the clip art
you need.

You can narrow the search by selecting the collection you want to search (for example, the Office Clip Art Collections separate clip art into categories such as animals, buildings, and concepts) and the kind of media you want to use. Which medium you use depends on the kind of clip art best suited to your purpose — and on the presentation you want to create on the Web page. For example, pictures generally use the Joint Photographic Experts Group (JPEG) format because it provides excellent color — and you can make complex images fit into relatively small files. Simple art often relies on the Graphic Interchange Format (GIF) or Portable Network Graphic (PNG) format. These formats allow the quick display of simple images (such as logos or line art) that are easy to compress quickly to very small sizes.

After you define the clip art you need, click Go. FrontPage searches through the clip art to locate the images you specify and displays a thumbnail of them in the results window. You see a button when you hover the mouse over the image. Click this button and you see a list of tasks you can perform with the image, including pasting it on the current Web page.

One of the options on the menu is Find Similar Style. Select this option and FrontPage will locate images with similar features, topics, or drawing style. This search option is helpful when you want to find images with a similar appearance, but isn't particularly helpful if you need additional images with the same *subject,* such as images that contain flowers or cats.

Viewing image properties

Before you paste the image onto your Web page, you should look at its properties to ensure that it fits your needs. Here's how:

1. Select Preview/Properties from the image context menu.

You see the Preview/Properties dialog box shown in Figure 2-7. This window tells you the size and resolution of the image, as well as the image type, and the application used to open or edit the image.

2. If possible, change the keyword or caption to meet your needs.

When you're working with the art that FrontPage supplies, you can't change the keywords or the caption. You do, however, have a couple of ways to get around this problem:

- You can change the caption and keyword for any clip art you add to the clip-art library from some other source.

- You can copy the image to your own personal clip art library using the Copy to Collection option on the image context menu (refer to Figure 2-7), selecting or creating a folder in the Copy to Collection dialog box, and clicking OK. FrontPage copies the art to your personal collection. Now, when you view the image properties, you can add or remove keywords and add a caption.

The caption appears in both the Preview Properties dialog box and on-screen when you hover the mouse pointer over the image in the Clip Art window of the Task Pane.

Figure 2-7:
Verify the image you select meets your needs.

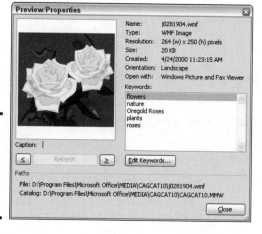

Using the Clip Art Organizer

The Clip Art Organizer lets you work with images directly. You can add, remove, document, and view images stored on your machine. To access the Clip Art Organizer and use it to put your clip art in order, follow these steps:

1. **Click Organize Clips in the Clip Art window of the Task Panel.**

   You see the Add Clips to Organizer dialog box.

2. **Specify when the Organizer should scan your hard drive for images to add.**

   If you want the Clip Art Organizer to do an automatic scan immediately, click Now; click Later if now isn't the time for the scan. If you click Now, follow the rest of these steps.

3. **Click Options.**

   Clip Art Organizer displays the Auto Import Settings dialog box.

4. **Select the folders you want the Clip Art Organizer to check.**

   This introductory scan happens only once. Afterward, you can set up the Clip Art Organizer for automatic scans by selecting File⇨Add Clips to Organizer⇨Automatically.

After the Clip Art Organizer performs any updates, it displays the window shown in Figure 2-8. The left pane contains a list of categories you can use to organize the information. The right pane shows a list of images in the selected collection. When you hover the mouse pointer over an image, you see a button to click that displays the context menu shown in Figure 2-8.

The Clip Art Organizer lets you perform the same tasks as the Clip Art window of the Task Pane in FrontPage. You can use it to manage not only images but also entire collections of images. The following steps show how:

1. **Right-click the collection you want to organize.**

   A context menu appears.

2. **Choose Collection Properties from the context menu.**

   You see the Collection Properties dialog box. The main feature of this dialog box is the capability you use in the next step.

3. **Associate the collection with a specific directory on your hard drive.**

   When you have a specific location in which to store new images, you can let the Clip Art Organizer perform automatic updates from just that folder, adding images to any collection you specify.

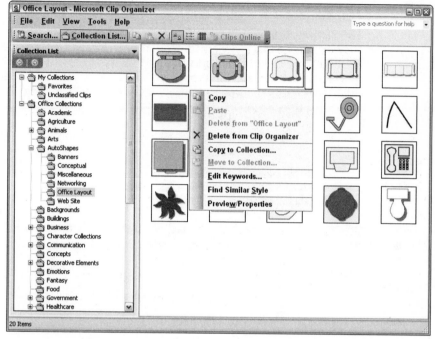

Book IV
Chapter 2

Figure 2-8:
View,
organize,
categorize,
and
document
your clip art.

You can also send the selected image to someone using e-mail. That process looks like this:

1. **Select File⇨Send to Mail Recipient (As Attachment).**

   The Clip Art Organizer displays a new e-mail message with the image attached.

2. **Make sure the subject of the message is the same as the Caption property for the image.**

3. **Provide a recipient and any description needed, and then click Send.**

   Your e-mail program sends the file.

One maintenance task to perform regularly is to compress your collection files. Otherwise they can become quite large as you add and remove files. To perform this task, select the Tools⇨Compact command. A Compact dialog box appears on-screen and automatically disappears when the compression is complete.

Working with
Clip Art

Using the Pictures toolbar

The Pictures toolbar shown in Figure 2-9 provides a host of tools that make it easy to manage images of any type on a Web page. To display this toolbar, right-click the toolbar area and choose Pictures from the context menu. The tools let you rotate and flip the image, as well as adjust both contrast and brightness to obtain better picture quality. You can also crop the image to select just the portion of interest.

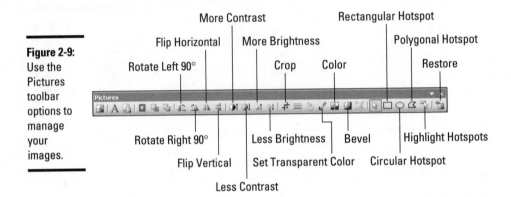

Figure 2-9: Use the Pictures toolbar options to manage your images.

Some image types, such as GIF, include a *transparency color* that lets the background show through. This effect lets you create icons that look as they would in a desktop application. Use the Set Transparent Color tool to set the transparent color used on a particular Web page.

Use the Color menu selections to change the colors of an image in specific ways. For example, you can change a color image to shades of gray using the Grayscale option. The Washout option is especially effective in making the graphic appear old or faded and lets you modify the image for use as a background.

The Bevel tool adds a 3D bevel around the edge of the image. The effect makes the picture stand out from the background. This particular effect uses part of the image, so make sure that the area around the edge of the image is fairly simple, showing fewer (or nonessential) details.

Describing an Image

It's important to provide a written description of the images you display on a Web site. Doing so may seem redundant, but several good reasons exist:

✦ Viewers with special needs require these descriptions when they use accessibility aids.

✦ Some visitors to your Web site may click Stop on the browser before the image download completes. The description gives them some idea of what the material they didn't download looks like.

✦ Search engines use this information, basing referrals to your Web site on descriptions of the images it contains.

To anticipate these situations by describing the images on your Web site, follow these steps:

1. **Right-click the image and choose Picture Properties from the context menu.**

You see the Picture Properties dialog box.

2. **Select the General tab.**

Here you can specify how long a description to include.

3. **Choose the description field that fits the complexity of your image.**

The two fields correspond to the standard HTML attributes `alt` and `longdesc`, as follows:

• **Text:** Use this field if the image is less complex. Its corresponding attribute (`alt`) has a *text* value that appears as a small pop-up label when a user hovers the mouse pointer over the image on-screen.

• **Long Description:** Use this field if the image has to be described in some detail. It uses the `longdesc` attribute, which points to a Web page that contains a complete text description of the image.

The process is pretty straightforward. Unfortunately, two limitations also apply here:

✦ Using images to describe other images doesn't work.

✦ Many browsers, including Internet Explorer, fail to implement the `longdesc` attribute correctly, so the user can't get to your description unless you provide a little help. The best practice is to provide a short description using the `alt` attribute, and then specify the `longdesc` attribute, and finally add a special [D] (for description) link. The code that does the job looks like this:

```
<img border="0" src="j0281904.gif"
     longdesc="RoseIsARose.htm"
     alt="This picture contains two yellow roses.">
<a title="A complete description of the rose picture."
   href="RoseIsARose.htm">[D]</a>
```

**Book IV
Chapter 2**

**Working with
Clip Art**

Creating an Image Map

An *image map* is an on-screen drawing that contains *hotspots* — places the user can click that work as links, directing the user to another location on your Web site or the Internet. Image maps are among the more colorful ways of creating links to other places. Most developers reserve them for global or top-level links. Hotspots have to be well defined on-screen; they depend on text or on distinct, self-contained graphic elements in the image you use.

To create an image map, follow these steps:

1. **Select an image.**

You can't use the VML images that FrontPage can produce — image maps always rely on actual graphics that reside in a file such as a JPEG or GIF.

2. **After you place the image on-screen, choose one of the hotspot tools on the Picture toolbar shown in Figure 2-9.**

3. **Draw a square, circle, or polygon around the hotspot area — the part of the image that defines where you want the user to click to go to a particular Web site.**

FrontPage opens the Insert Hyperlink dialog box.

4. **Choose the location you want the user to go to.**

5. **Click Screen Tip to see the Set Hyperlink Screen Tip dialog box.**

6. **Type the description you want the user to see.**

7. **Click OK twice.**

FrontPage creates the screen tip.

Repeat this process for every hotspot you want to create on the image map.

The image map relies on a series of specialized tags and attributes to create its effect. Here's an example of code that creates an image map; you can see it as part of the ImageMap.htm file in the source code for this chapter on the Wiley Web site:

```
<map name="FPMap0">
    <area alt="See the Clip Art Sample Web page."
        href="ClipArtSample.htm"
        shape="rect"
        coords="31, 40, 126, 84">
</map>
<img border="0"
    src="ImageMap.gif" width="442" height="103"
    usemap="#FPMap0">
```

The image map is encapsulated within the <map> tag, which must have a name attribute. Within the <map> tag is one or more <area> tags that define the hotspots for the image map. The <area> tag attributes include the description text, a pointer to the new Web page, the shape of the hotspot, and the coordinates of the hotspot within the image.

Immediately after the <map> tag is an <img> tag. This tag is normal in all ways except for the addition of a usemap attribute, which points to the image map this image should use.

Using Images from Other Sources

You can use images from a number of other sources. Any clip art that you create for other purposes can appear on a Web page. In some cases, you must convert the clip art to one of the commonly supported image formats found on the Internet, but you can still make use of the image. It's also possible to use photo CDs — the images are already in JPEG format in most cases.

Know your (copy)rights

One of the most important issues is ensuring the image isn't copyrighted by someone. When you want to display a famous logo, a picture of someone famous, or art that you received from another Web site, you need to ensure you have permission to use it. Normally, this means writing to the owner(s) of the image and getting their permission in writing — unless permission is granted on the Web site or within the software package where you found the image. Even when you buy an application that includes clip art, you can't assume you can display that image on your Web site unless the owner gives you permission to use it. Image libraries are almost always marked for personal, non-commercial use, and you need permission to display that image in public.

Another way to locate free clip art is to use an Internet search service such as Google. For example, try the following link:

http://www.google.com/search?as_q=Free+Clip+Art

Here you can discover all the sites that provide free clip art. Exercise care, however, when downloading clip art from free sites. Make sure the site is reputable (asking about it on Microsoft's FrontPage newsgroup is a good start) and that you aren't getting "more" than just the clip art (for example, a hidden virus or spyware program). Many of the reputable sites, such as Free Clip Art (http://www.free-clip-art.com/), allow free downloads for personal and educational uses, but you must join a download service to use the images for commercial uses.

Book IV
Chapter 2

Working with Clip Art

Chapter 3: Adding Multimedia and Components

In This Chapter

✔ Using multimedia effectively

✔ Adding animated GIFs to a Web page

✔ Creating pages with audio files

✔ Creating pages with video files

✔ Using Web components

✔ Designing with Macromedia Flash

Sometimes you want glitz, excitement, and noise to surround your Web site. The Las Vegas appeal of glittering images is just too hard for some developers to resist. In some cases, such an approach really can help your Web site attract more attention, but misuse of these techniques can be detrimental. (Imagine what would happen if every business Web site used multimedia — the resulting cacophony would drive the Internet out of offices everywhere because no one could get any work done.)

Fortunately, you can use measured approaches to multimedia. The animated GIF has been around for a long time, and you still see new effects produced by these simple files all the time. Careful use of audio and video — with requisite controls for turning the multimedia off — can produce good effects, but you have to use them carefully. FrontPage also provides a number of components with multimedia effects that you can add to a Web page when warranted.

By the time you add Macromedia Flash presentations, however, you're into full-fledged multimedia — and you need to consider whether your audience really needs all the bells and whistles. When such a presentation is appropriate, you can create sights and sounds that will impress most people, and get your message across in a new way while you're at it.

Understanding Multimedia Use Issues

Most people equate multimedia with some combination of moving pictures (animation) and sound. Movies are a prime example of the form of multimedia that many people consider standard. Theoretically, however, multimedia is any form of presentation in which someone is using more than one sense to receive your message — say, combine a tactile approach with something visual, or sound with smell (science fiction, anyone?). Until someone comes up with the smell-o-computer, though, you're probably stuck with more common forms of presentation.

The main reason multimedia is so attractive to most people is that it helps get the message across — usually better than a single form of communication (such as words) can do. Combining multiple senses helps the viewer better remember what your Web site has to say, making multimedia a very effective way to communicate with others.

Some ideas are actually easier to communicate using multimedia techniques. A 3D image of a home is better than a flat picture because the viewer can see more of the house. When you combine that image with movement, the viewer can rotate the house and see it from all angles, making the decision to buy that much easier. Scientific and engineering disciplines of all types have long known the value of seeing a multimedia presentation of a new design; sometimes tables of bland numbers and facts just don't get the job done.

Even if you aren't trying to sell something or you don't want to present the next picture of the DNA double helix, you can still use multimedia. A few trendy developers have created presentations showing their children and pets in multimedia form. The results say a lot more than pictures alone can. The viewer can see the whole story.

But every technology has a downside. Before you get too excited about multimedia, consider some of its limitations and the problems it can cause:

+ **Older browsers don't work well with multimedia.** They don't understand the commands and the host system probably doesn't have the required software installed even if the browser were able to comprehend the Web page. The problem can be so significant that viewers might see nothing more than a blank page and wonder why you wasted their time.

+ **Web pages that use multimedia don't work well with a dial-up connection.** Even when the user has a new machine with great software, on a dial-up connection the multimedia presentation comes across in slow motion with lots of skips. Sometimes it might be better if the user hadn't seen anything at all because the results of some failed multimedia presentations are truly disturbing. (The message doesn't get across, the user's machine appears to lock up, or other problems appear that disrupt the user's experience with your site.)

✦ **Using multimedia in an office environment can bother everyone in the area and disrupt productivity.** Sometimes the message becomes so inviting that bosses start to ban your site from their office screens. Then you've actually lost an audience because your presentation is too good.

✦ **Multimedia assumes that the viewer has all the required senses — which leaves out a lot of people with special needs.** You can overcome some multimedia problems by adding accessibility cues — for example, adding closed captioning to online movie presentations so those with special hearing needs can still understand the presentation. Unfortunately, these additions can become expensive to produce, and need sufficient bandwidth to present. Consider whether the value of the presentation exceeds the cost of producing it.

Animated GIFs, the Easiest Multimedia

The animated Graphics Interchange Format (GIF) file is the oldest form of animation on the Internet; you've probably seen animated GIFs on more than one Web site. All those little cartoon characters, twirling banners, and exploding stars are probably animated GIFs.

It often helps to look at other people's animated GIFs as you create your own; their ideas might suggest new approaches for yours. A few quick steps in Internet Explorer can verify that an image on a Web page is an animated GIF:

1. **From Internet Explorer, right-click the image.**

A context menu appears.

2. **Choose Properties from the context menu.**

You see the location and name of the image on the host system — any image that has a file extension of GIF and has an animated effect is an animated GIF.

3. **To save the image to your hard drive for better viewing, right-click the image and choose Save Picture As from the context menu.**

You see a Save Picture dialog box.

4. **Choose a location to which you want to save the image, and then click Save to save the entire animation.**

An animated GIF contains a series of still images that the browser plays back (like a flip book) at a speed determined by the developer. You can also add special effects to GIFs and optimize them for size and playing speed.

One advantage of GIF animation is that most browsers support it. Tools for creating animated GIFs are readily available — often for little or no cost. Consequently, this is the form of animation that most developers experiment with first.

FrontPage supports animated GIF files, but it doesn't provide the tools required to create an animated GIF. To create an animated GIF, you need a drawing program to create the individual frames of the animation program and a program to put them together into a single file.

One of the better products available on the market for creating animated GIF files is the GIF Construction Set from Alchemy Mindworks, available at

`www.mindworkshop.com/alchemy/gifcon.html`

This product is shareware, so you can try it before you buy it. Figure 3-1 shows a typical editing session with this product. Unfortunately, space won't allow a complete step-by-step demonstration of the product, but the example GIF in the `\Animated GIF` folder of the source code for this chapter found on the Wiley Web site provides all the files you need to give the application a good test drive.

Note the series of frames on the left side of the display. When your animation is completed, the browser displays these frames one at a time, flip-book-style, so the picture appears to be moving. Before you get to that point, however, you have to add the frames — like this:

1. **Choose Edit⇨Insert Block⇨Image.**

2. **Double-click an image.**

You see the Edit Image dialog box shown on the right side of Figure 3-1.

3. **Specify a display time for each frame in your animation.**

In Figure 3-1, for example, the Control Block field is checked and the Delay field is set to 1.

Placing an animated GIF on a Web page is like using any other image file. You can copy and paste the file, drag and drop it from the Folder List, or add it using the Clip Art window of the Task Pane. When you place the GIF on the Web page, FrontPage creates an `<img>` tag similar to this one:

```
<img border="0"
    src="AnimatedTime.gif" width="90" height="90"
    alt="This is an animated GIF of a clock.">
```

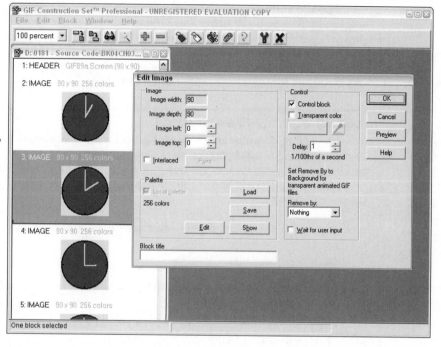

Figure 3-1:
With the GIF
Construc-
tion Set you
can create
a series of
frames and
tell the
browser
how to
display
them.

The use of an <img> tag points to the success of the animated GIF. Even when a browser doesn't provide the required support (which is rare), the use of this standard tag lets the user see the first frame of the animated GIF, so the Web page doesn't look bare. Consequently, always make the first frame of your animated GIF something that can stand alone so the user sees something useful even when the animation isn't available.

Adding Audio

People use audio files for a number of purposes. Some simply like to have background music playing while someone views their site. Other developers use sound as an additional means of communicating content. You'll find sound used as part of a presentation on some sites. No matter how you use sound, it does offer an additional way to communicate with — or distract — other people. The important thing to consider is that you should provide audio content (as opposed to background music) as text so people who can't listen to the content can read it.

You can add audio to your Web page in several ways: by adding automatic background sounds, by providing a hyperlink that plays a sound, or by offering the user a button to control the sound. The first question you have to ask is whether someone sitting in a cubicle in a corporate building somewhere is likely to access your Web site. If the answer is yes, then you don't want to set the audio for your site to play automatically.

Using background sounds

You can add audio to your Web page and get a range of results — from the really annoying (music plays over and over until the user takes a hammer to the speakers) to the less annoying (a momentary fanfare accompanies a splash screen). Here is one of the easiest ways to add a background sound to your Web page:

1. **Right-click the page and choose Page Properties from the context menu.**

You see the Page Properties dialog box.

2. **Click Browse in the Background Sound section to locate a file you want to play.**

FrontPage assumes that you want to play this sound over and over again, which is unbelievably annoying.

3. **Clear the Forever option and choose a number between 1 and 3 in the Loop field.**

4. **Click OK.**

Using this technique creates a `<bgsound>` tag like the one shown here:

```
<bgsound src="tada.wav" loop="1">
```

The `src` attribute tells the browser where to locate the sound. The `loop` attribute tells how many times to play the sound. Use this technique only when you know the Web site viewer can play sounds because the sound will play at least once.

A sudden sound from the PC speakers in an office or other quiet environment can disrupt the work going on — and it isn't wise to assume that your users are listening through headphones.

Using a hyperlink

A better way to add audio to your Web page is to make it optional so the viewer has a choice. Many people turn off background sounds by using options their browsers provide. Giving your users a choice might be the only way to ensure that anyone actually hears the audio you provide.

You find the Play Sounds in Web Pages option in the Multimedia section on the Advanced tab of the Internet options dialog box for Internet Explorer 6. This technique is the best option to use when your audio provides content; the viewer can play the audio as often as necessary to get the message. Provide a text version of the audio so office users and people in other quiet locations don't miss the content you're providing. The easiest way to play sound using this technique is to add a hyperlink like this.

```
<a title="This sound file makes the Tada sound."
   href="tada.wav">Play a Sound File</a>
```

In this case, the `title` attribute provides enough description that someone can decide whether to play the sound. The `href` attribute points to a sound file. When a user clicks Play a Sound File, the browser opens a helper utility such as the Windows Media Player to output the sound.

Using an interactive button

Another way to add audio to your page is to attach it to an interactive button. Choose Insert⇨Interactive Button to display the Interactive Buttons dialog box shown in Figure 3-2.

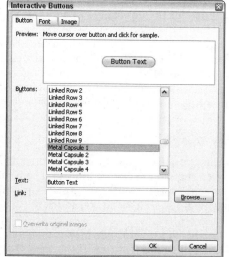

Figure 3-2:
Add a sound to an interactive button to give the page a little pizzazz.

When you have the dialog box on-screen, here's how you do this technique:

1. **Select one of the button styles from the Buttons list.**

2. **Type a caption for the button in the Text field.**

3. **Use the Browse button to locate the audio file you want to play.**

4. **Click OK.**

FrontPage creates the button for you.

To add descriptive text to the button, highlight the button and select the Split view. When you see an `<img>` tag highlighted in the code portion of the window, locate the `alt` attribute and change its text to describe the sound that the button plays.

This technique relies on the use of scripts. Many people have disabled scripts in their browsers because of threats posed by viruses and malicious Web sites. Consequently, even though this technique does produce a better-looking page, it won't work with every browser. Of the three techniques described here — background sound, hyperlink, and interactive button — the hyperlink is the most reliable means of providing audio for the users of your Web page.

Adding Video

If your Web site has a good use for the equivalent of a movie, video presentations offer the advantages of moving pictures and sounds. Using Windows Movie Maker, you can create movies from a variety of sources — including still images, captured video, and video files located on your hard drive. With just a little work, you can create all kinds of interesting visual effects, add titles, and end up with a professional presentation. The only problem with video on the Internet is that the files can become immense in a hurry.

Creating a smaller video

Depending on the application you use, most video-creation software provides settings you can use to reduce the size of the video so it matches the capabilities of the user's machine and connection (smaller pictures run more seamlessly). Unfortunately, Windows Movie Maker hides these solutions.

When you save a movie locally, Windows Movie Maker assumes you want the best possible resolution and sound features. Sometimes that assumption is stupid; before you know it, a very simple slide presentation can consume 3GB or more of disk space. Here's one way to avoid the waste when it comes time to save your Windows Movie Maker movie:

1. **Click File⇨Save Movie File to access the Save Movie Wizard.**

2. **When you get to the Movie Setting page of the Save Movie Wizard, click Show More Choices.**

A list of possible levels of resolution appears.

3. **Select the Other Choices option.**

Buried near the bottom of the list are the Internet options you should choose if you want to conserve your hard-drive space. Figure 3-3 shows some options you should consider, including a selection for users with dial-up connections.

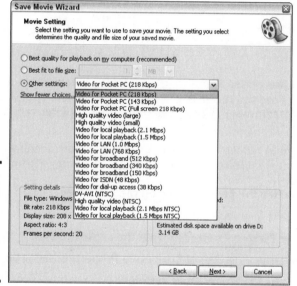

Figure 3-3:
Select video options that are appropriate for Internet users.

 If your Web site is to support just one copy of the file, always choose the option that serves the *slowest* connection you want to support. Choose multiple download rates only when you have space to support them — and remember that you must also provide the user with the same range of rates to choose from. Don't try to detect the user's connection speed; any technique you use is going to be error-prone. Letting the user choose is the most practical approach — after all, the user might not want to use up all available bandwidth to watch your movie.

Adding video as a picture

As with audio, you can set up your video to run when the user loads the page. Unless the user is expecting this reaction, however, you can be sure that some — perhaps most — people are going to complain, especially if the video is long. Not only does your 3GB movie require considerable time to download, but it consumes that much space on the user's machine. That's right: Internet Explorer downloads the whole file onto the user's machine and keeps it there until it's automatically deleted or the user manually erases it. Suddenly the user's 30GB hard drive has shrunk. (By default, Internet Explorer uses 10% of the entire hard drive to store Web content.)

When you do let the users know about the size of the file in advance — and you're sure they're expecting the monster file about to hit their hard drives (and don't mind) — you can go on with the show in one of two ways:

✦ Choose Insert⇨Picture⇨Video command to add the video to your Web page.

Note that this option isn't always available — you must set the Authoring tab of the Page Options dialog box to allow complete FrontPage functionality and the browser must be set for Internet Explorer versions 5.0 and above.

✦ If you have to reduce the chances of someone downloading a video they really don't want to see, you can configure the entry a little differently:

1. **Right-click the picture entry on the Web page.**

   A context menu appears.

2. **Choose Picture Properties from the context menu.**

   You see the Video tab of the Picture Properties dialog box.

3. **Select the On Mouse Over option.**

   Now the user will have to hover the mouse pointer over the image to start the video — which is still a decision the user can make about downloading the file.

This second technique relies on the ⟨img⟩ tag with some special attributes added. Here are entries for both types of video:

```
<img border="0" dynsrc="TimeFlies.wmv" start="fileopen">
<img border="0" dynsrc="TimeFlies.wmv" start="mouseover">
```

This ⟨img⟩ tag includes two new attributes. The first is the dynsrc attribute, which replaces the src attribute for a standard ⟨img⟩ tag — dynsrc tells the name and location of the video file. The second new attribute is start, which defines how the browser should start the video.

Using an <object> tag

It's possible to use an <object> tag to display a video file. In this case, you're using a special kind of program called an *ActiveX control* — a proprietary script that works only on Windows machines. The technique shown in this section works with most versions of Windows other than XP because it relies on an older version of Windows Media Player. You can also use the newer version found in Windows XP when you need added capability.

To add an ActiveX control to your Web page, follow these steps:

1. **Choose the Insert⇨Web Component command.**

You see the Insert Web Component dialog box.

2. **Select the Advanced Controls option in the Component Type list and ActiveX Control in the Choose a Control list.**

3. **Click Next.**

After a few moments, you see a list of controls like the one shown in Figure 3-4.

4. **Select the ActiveMovieControl Object shown highlighted in Figure 3-4.**

5. **Click Finish.**

FrontPage adds an <object> tag for the control to the Web page.

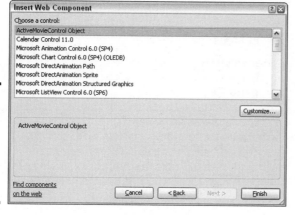

Figure 3-4: Choose the ActiveX control you want to add to the Web page.

Here's the essential code for the <object> tag used for this example (the actual tag contains more code):

```
<object width="200" height="225"
        classid="CLSID:05589FA1-C356-11CE-BF01-00AA0055595A"
        id="Control1>
   <param name="filename" value="TimeFlies.avi">
</object>
```

The width and height attributes control the size of the window. The classid is a special number that identifies an object on your machine when you run Windows. This number tells Windows which object to load and determines what kind of object Windows creates.

When you want to use the newer version of the Windows Media Player on Windows XP machines, use the following classid value:

```
CLSID:22D6F312-B0F6-11D0-94AB-0080C74C7E95
```

The <param> tag defines a special property for the Windows Media Player object — the name and location of the file you want to play. Windows Media Player has many other properties you can define, but this is the only required property.

Each property you want to define appears as part of a <param> tag. After you define the initial <object> tag, look at Design view and you see the object. Right-click the object and choose ActiveX Control Properties. FrontPage displays the Option dialog box shown in Figure 3-5.

Figure 3-5:
Set any required special options for the Windows Media Player object.

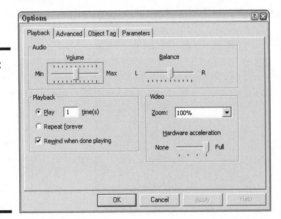

The advantage of this technique is that you have control over every aspect of the video playback. In addition, the user gains access to controls the other methods don't even support. (Figure 3-5 shows some of these controls.) The user can also right-click the control on-screen and make other changes depending on how you set up the video playback. Using the `<object>` tag method is the most versatile approach when you can guarantee the user has Windows installed.

One other issue with this approach is that you have to use Audio Video Interleaved (AVI) files, not Windows Media Video (WMV) files. Unfortunately, current versions of Microsoft's products don't produce anything but WMV files, so you need a converter such as Fx Video Converter to create the AVI file. You can download this product at the following location:

`www.brothersoft.com/Fx_Video_Converter_Download_20561.html`

The vendor markets this product as shareware; you can try it before you buy it.

Other video options

You have two other options for displaying a standard video on-screen. They are similar to options used to include audio:

✦ **You can create a hyperlink.** This technique is similar to the one for audio (in the "Using a hyperlink" section of the chapter). Its advantage is that anyone can use the result; you don't have to worry about browser compatibility. The only issue is whether the user has the player required for your particular video format. In addition, the user can play the video as many times as needed and you can provide multiple links for various connection speeds.

✦ **You can use an interactive button.** The advantage of this technique is that it provides choice and a nice presentation; you can select buttons to match your current theme. To use this technique, follow the steps for an audio file in the "Using an interactive button" section of the chapter.

Working with Web Components

FrontPage provides a number of Web components that you can use to enhance the appearance of your Web page. You've already seen the benefits of one of these components — the interactive button. It's also possible to

**Book IV
Chapter 3**

**Adding Multimedia
and Components**

add marquees, maps, and other features to your Web page to provide additional benefits to the user. However, as with most multimedia, you have to carefully weigh the benefits of the feature against the compatibility and accessibility problems it can cause.

Using standard page components

The standard page components add effects you've seen on a number of sites. For example, FrontPage provides a marquee component that scrolls text across the screen, a hit counter that records the number of visitors, and a search component that helps people locate information on the current site.

Scrolling text with the marquee component

The marquee component displays whatever text you want to see, using special effects such as scrolling. The marquee normally appears at the top of the page and provides some form of advertising for it. However, nothing stops you from placing this component in other areas of the page.

To use the marquee component, follow these steps:

1. **Display the Insert Web Component dialog box using the Insert⇨Web Component command.**

2. **Select Dynamic Effects and then choose Marquee.**

3. **Click Finish.**

   You see the Marquee Properties dialog box.

4. **Type the text you want to see in the Text field.**

5. **If you like, choose special effects for displaying the text.**

   For example, you can choose a display speed by modifying the Amount field or change the time between display cycles using the Delay field.

6. **Click OK.**

   FrontPage creates the marquee.

You can't see the marquee in Design view. To get a better feel for how this component works, view it in Preview view. The marquee component actually relies on the `<marquee>` tag. When a browser doesn't support this tag, the user sees the text you provided without the special effects. Consequently, this component doesn't have any accessibility or compatibility limitations that would prevent a user from viewing your site.

Finding resources with the Web search component

The Web search component makes it possible for the user to locate information on your site quickly. To use this component, follow these steps:

1. **Select Insert➪Web Component.**

You see the Insert Web Component dialog box.

2. **Select the Web Search and then the Current Web entries.**

3. **Click finish.**

You see the Search Form Properties dialog box.

4. **Configure the Search.**

The Search Form Properties dialog box contains a list of prompts the search will use. Change these as needed for your Web site. The Search Results tab has more interesting settings. You use these settings to control the appearance of the results. For example, you can choose to display the score (the closeness of the match), the file date and time, and the file size as part of the results. FrontPage doesn't add these items by default.

5. **After you choose the settings you want to use, click OK.**

At this point, FrontPage creates the search entry on the Web page. This is another webbot, so you won't see a lot of code within the page you create. The webbot includes both client and server elements, so it won't work on a Web server that lacks FrontPage extensions. Here's a typical entry for this component:

```
<!--webbot bot="Search" S-Index="All"
         S-Fields="TimeStamp,DocumentK,Weight"
         S-Text="Search for:" I-Size="20"
         S-Submit="Start Search" S-Clear="Reset"
         S-TimestampFormat="%m/%d/%Y" TAG="BODY" -->
```

The functions of the entry's attributes break down like this:

✦ The `bot` attribute shows that this is a Search webbot.

✦ The `S-Index` attribute tells you that this webbot will search everything.

✦ The `S-Fields` attribute defines the output, which includes a timestamp, the document name, document size, and the score the document received in matching the search terms (higher is better).

✦ The `S-Text` attribute defines the text used to request a keyword.

Book IV Chapter 3

Adding Multimedia and Components

✦ The I-Size attribute defines the width of the input field.

✦ The S-Submit and S-Clear attributes define the button captions.

✦ The S-Timestamp attribute defines the format of the time output.

Keeping track of visitors

The *hit counter* is a visual display of the number of visitors who have seen your site. None of the hit counters I've ever tried are accurate, but they're fun to watch. The FrontPage hit counter tells you the (approximate) number of visits to your Web page — but remember, if the same visitor comes back to the Web page 50 times in a day, the hit counter will show 50 hits. Consider the hit counter as a way to get a rough idea of how many people are viewing the page, but don't count on it for hard statistics.

To use the hit counter, follow these steps:

1. **Select the Insert⇨Web Component command.**

You see the Insert Web Component dialog box.

2. **Choose the Hit Counter entry in the Component Type list.**

You see a number of hit counter types in the Choose a Counter Style list.

3. **Select one of the counter styles and click Finish.**

You see the Hit Counter Properties dialog box. The dialog box shows you the hit counter styles again.

At the bottom of the Hit Counter Properties dialog box you see two options. The Reset Counter To option defines the number that FrontPage uses to reset the counter after you configure the page. Generally, you want to use the default value when you create a new page, but will want to set this option to the last number of visitors when you update a page. The Fixed Number of Digits option keeps the size of the hit counter within a certain range. When the hit counter reaches the specified number of digits, it automatically resets to 0. Unless your page is short on space, you want to keep this option cleared.

This is a *server-side* webbot component; it depends on the server's capabilities, and won't work on a Web server that lacks FrontPage extensions. Here's a typical hit-counter entry.

```
<!--webbot bot="HitCounter" i-image="0" I-ResetValue="0"
          B-Reset="FALSE" I-Digits="0" U-Custom -->
```

The bot attribute identifies this webbot as a hit counter. The i-image attribute defines which of the presentations you chose. For example, the hit counter with yellow letters and a black background is i-image 0. The I-ResetValue and B-Reset attributes determine whether the counter is reset and what value it is reset to. The I-Digits attribute defaults to 0 when you want the counter to keep growing. Assigning it a value other than 0 puts that many digits on-screen. Finally, the U-Custom attribute has an entry only when you use a custom picture for your hit counter.

Using included-content components

Included-content components provide information about a specific aspect of the Web page. To see the whole list of included-content components, use the Insert⇨Web Component command to display the Insert Web Component dialog box and choose the Included Content entry from the Component Type list. The components in the list offer various capabilities, including these:

✦ **Substitution:** You can use this component to display the Web page's author, its last date of modification, who performed the modification, and the page URL.

✦ **Page:** This component displays the content from another page. You can use this feature to create generic content and then display it on the pages that require it without using frames or other methods that have accessibility and compatibility problems. FrontPage actually substitutes the content for the Page webbot. Interestingly enough, when you view the page, you see nothing but the webbot comment and the actual code from the other page. When you need to replace the page content based on a schedule, such as day of the week, use the page based on schedule included-content component. In addition to the Web page, you also provide the time and date the Web page should include this content.

✦ **Schedule:** This component lets you display a picture based on the time and date. You can choose to include an alternative picture that Web server displays at other times.

You already use one form of included content on many pages — the page banner — which is the same page banner you get when you use the Insert⇨ Page Banner command. As with every other kind of included content, this one relies on a webbot to perform its work.

Using MSN and MSNBC components

The MSN and MSNBC components help you include the functionality provided by these online resources on your Web page. For example, you can create a search of the Web using MSN. It's also possible to display the latest headlines. All these resources appear as part of the MSN Mapping Components, MSN

Components, and MSNBC Components you access from the Insert Web Component dialog box using the Insert⇨Web Component command. You can see all these components demonstrated in the MSN_MSNBC.htm file provided as part of the source code for this chapter on the Wiley Web site.

When you're working with the MSN Mapping Components, you have a choice between inserting a map or simply creating a link to it. The insertion option is the best choice when you want to show someone how to get somewhere (say, to your business or home) and don't mind a longer download. The linking option is the best choice when you need to provide instructions for a number of destinations and download time is a factor. In both cases, you need to provide either a precise address or a place name. When you provide a place name of a popular location, such as Wal-Mart, make sure you include a city name as part of the destination (Wal-Mart Milwaukee). After you find a location, click Next and you see a map of the location you want. Then just click Finish to add it to your Web page.

Use the Stock Quote component listed as part of the MSN Components to display the latest information on stocks you own. Likewise, use the Search the Web with MSN component to find resources on the Internet. In both cases, you just select the component and click Finish in the Insert Web Component dialog box. Both components create a search interface where you enter a stock symbol or keywords.

Most of the MSNBC components don't actually display any information on your screen; instead, they provide pointers to the information the user needs. The only component that requires any input is the Weather Forecast from MSNBC — and all it needs is a ZIP code or city name. It's also the only component that displays any information — a quick overview of the weather for the location of choice.

Working with Macromedia Flash

Unlike older versions of the product, FrontPage 2003 provides special support for Macromedia Flash files. You can create presentations with Macromedia Flash and insert them directly into your Web pages using the Insert⇨Picture⇨Movie in Flash Format command. You see the Select File dialog box. Choose the movie you want to present on your Web site and click Insert. FrontPage creates a square where the Macromedia Flash movie plays.

Macromedia Flash relies on a relatively complex <object> tag to do its work. The user must have the appropriate software installed before the movie will play. Here's a typical example of a Macromedia Flash <object> tag entry.

```
<object classid="clsid:D27CDB6E-AE6D-11CF-96B8-444553540000"
        id="obj1" codebase="Download Location"
        border="0" width="160" height="160">
  <param name="movie" value="shell.swf">
  <param name="quality" value="High">
  <embed src="shell.swf"
         pluginspage="Download Location"
         type="application/x-shockwave-flash" name="obj1"
         width="160" height="160">
</object>
```

The <object> tag begins with all the usual entries, including the classid, which is a unique number that identifies the movie player. The codebase points to a location on the Macromedia site where the browser automatically looks for the component, downloads it, and installs it as needed (provided the user doesn't object and the machine's security settings permit the download).

This object has two parameters. The first is the name and location of the movie. The second defines the quality of the presentation. A lower presentation value requires fewer resources on the user's machine — and that can reduce the download time.

The <embed> tag further describes the movie and its requirements. The src attribute should match the movie parameter information. A browser relies on the type attribute to determine which object to use to play the embedded resource. Finally, the pluginspage attribute tells where to download browser plug-in support for this embedded resource (the movie).

Chapter 4: Inserting Office Objects

In This Chapter

✓ Adding Word objects

✓ Getting down to business with Excel data views

✓ Developing reports with Access

Although you can use various FrontPage Web components to add content, you don't have to create every piece of information on your Web page that way. You can work directly with applications such as Microsoft Office. Using Office products to create the content saves time — if you need (for example) spreadsheet data and you use Excel, you're already using the correct tool to accomplish the task. Using FrontPage to create some of the graphs and reports you need is possible, but sometimes other applications can produce the same information faster and a lot better.

This chapter specifically discusses how you can use Office applications with FrontPage — which has some special capabilities to make that easier. Nothing stops you, however, from creating something in a non-Microsoft application and using it on your Web site. The important task is to discover which techniques work with your particular application.

Of course, getting the data onto a Web page doesn't necessarily mean the user can see it. You also need to consider compatibility, usability, and accessibility as you create a bridge between your favorite application and FrontPage. For example, why use tabular data if the user really needs a chart or graph? The goal is to communicate your ideas as well as possible.

Working with Word Objects

Microsoft Word can create effective data presentations that border on desktop-publishing quality. Word documents can have all the required formatting and fonts — along with embedded objects such as graphics — and you can control the appearance of various document elements. Of course, not all this formatting can transfer directly to a Web page, but you can use a number of Word techniques to create a document that looks like a natural part of the Web site.

Copying and pasting information

It might seem like an odd way to do things, but you can simply copy and paste information from Word into your FrontPage document. When you copy and paste the document, FrontPage does more than simply place a text entry in the page. It can also create an embedded Cascading Style Sheet (CSS) that defines the formatting for the document.

Use this technique as early as possible in the Web-page design process. When FrontPage has an element with the same tag name as the text you want to paste from Word, it won't create that embedded CSS element. For example, if you copy a paragraph from Word that's formatted as Heading 1, you'll notice that FrontPage uses the ⟨H1⟩ tag for it. If the existing Web page already has an ⟨H1⟩ tag, FrontPage tends to ignore the Heading 1 formatting you applied to the paragraph you're bringing in from Word; you don't get a complete transfer. Listing 4-1, a typical example of Word data pasted into a newly created Web page, shows what you get instead.

Listing 4-1: Pasting a Word Document

```
<html>
    <head>
        <style>
            <!--
            h3
                {margin-top:12.0pt;
                margin-right:0in;
                margin-bottom:3.0pt;
                margin-left:0in;
                page-break-after:avoid;
                text-autospace:none;
                font-size:13.0pt;
                font-family:Arial}
            p.MsoNormal
                {mso-style-parent:"";
                margin-top:0in;
                margin-right:0in;
                margin-bottom:12.0pt;
                margin-left:0in;
                text-autospace:none;
                font-size:12.0pt;
                font-family:Arial;
                }
            p.CodeList
                {margin-bottom:.0001pt;
                text-autospace:none;
                font-size:10.0pt;
                font-family:"Courier New";
                margin-left:0in; margin-right:0in;
```

```
        margin-top:0in}
      -->
    </style>
  </head>
  <body>
    <h3>Example of a Pasted Document</h3>
    <p class="MsoNormal">The heading and text...</p>
    <p class="CodeList">Here is some text...</p>
  </body>
</html>
```

Except for the <html>, <head>, and <body> tags, FrontPage created all the entries in Listing 4-1 as part of the paste operation. Of course, I pasted the document immediately after creating the Web page. If you try this process after creating a few Web page elements, you find the FrontPage doesn't do nearly as well at transferring the style information from Word even though the text is still there.

You should make one change to the automatic entries. Notice the h3 style in Listing 4-1 doesn't have a qualifier — a special Word addition that makes the text unique such as the p.MsoNormal style. The lack of a qualifier means that every <H3> tag you add will use the Word formatting even if that's not what you want. Changing the FrontPage-supplied h3 style means making two changes. First, change the h3 style entry to something like h3.MsoHeading3 to associate it with word. Second, change the heading entry to match like this.

```
<h3 class="MsoHeading3">Example of a Pasted Document</h3>
```

Using this technique means that your Web content stays separate from your Word content. You could choose to use the same styles, but it's better to have the flexibility that separate styles provide.

If a direct paste won't accomplish what you want, choose the Edit➪Paste Special command to display the Convert Text dialog box shown in Figure 4-1.

Figure 4-1: Choose a technique for pasting text into FrontPage.

The Convert Text dialog box contains options for pasting the text in other ways. The default setting is to use formatted paragraphs. You can also paste the text as a single formatted paragraph, as unformatted paragraphs with line breaks, as one giant unformatted paragraph, or without any conversion at all.

Pasting text as an unconverted paragraph creates straight text without any special characters or formatting, so the results tend to be the least appealing — you could get the same results by typing the text straight into FrontPage, so the only reason to use this option is to save the typing time.

Relying on hyperlinks

Hyperlinks might seem an old technology, but they're extremely reliable and compatible — no problem making a hyperlink accessible. In fact, the only limitation on the use of a hyperlink to access a Word document is that the other party might not own Word. When you can be sure that your users have Word installed on their systems, consider using a hyperlink to display the data (instead of placing the data directly in FrontPage).

One important consideration when you use this technique is to ensure that the user has a way back to the Web page. You can accomplish this task by including a hyperlink in the Word document. Use the Insert⇨Hyperlink command to add the hyperlink to the document. The effect you get by using this technique is a cross between an Internet Explorer page and a Word editing session, as shown in Figure 4-2.

You can make the Word document look more like a Web page if you save it with Web Layout View selected (use either the Web Layout View button in the lower-left corner or choose the View⇨Web Layout command). A good alternative is to save the document in Print Layout View. Both views let the user see the document in an output view. The user can still choose to use another view because all the Word menus (except Window) are available.

Make sure you save the document with a password, set the file for read-only mode, or disable Web publishing on your Web server when you don't want the user to make changes to the document. It's easy to set up the document for editing when you install some Internet Information Server (IIS) features such as Web Publishing or some types of Microsoft software (such as SharePoint Services).

Users who want to modify your document can generally make a local copy by using the File⇨Save As command. The password-protection technique is, however, the only method available to protect the document from changes — local as well as remote. To set a password on a Word document, follow these steps:

1. Choose Tools⇨Options.

You see the Options dialog box.

2. Select the Security tab.

3. Type a password in the Password to Modify field and click OK.

Utilities exist that can break the Word password system. In practice, the password technique only deters the casual user — not someone who's really determined to modify your document.

Creating a direct document conversion

Another good solution for displaying your Word document on a Web site is direct conversion. Why edit your Word document in FrontPage? Well, Word is great for adding formatting features and dressing up the Web page, but FrontPage offers a host of Web-editing features that Word doesn't support — such as banners, themes, and Web-page management. Consequently, you can put the content together in Word, dress up the text, and then use FrontPage to add the finishing touches.

Depending on the version of Word you own, you have several good options. You can save the document as an HTM file, which allows you to edit it in Word. Most versions of Word also support conversion to an HTML format, which means you can add changes in FrontPage. Finally, you can save the document in XML format if you're using Word 2003.

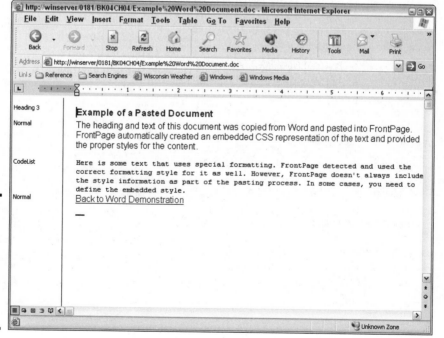

Figure 4-2:
View Word documents directly in Internet Explorer by using a hyperlink.

The default XML file relies on the Word Markup Language (WordML), which makes it hard to edit in FrontPage. However, the document does retain all the data, formatting, and other features you normally associate with Word. You access all these options by using the File⇨Save as Web Page command in Office 2003.

The HTML format is the one you should use for modifying the file in FrontPage. However, when you try to open the file, it automatically opens in Word, not in FrontPage, even when you try to open it in the Folder List. This happens because of a special entry that Word adds to the HTM file. To open the file in FrontPage, right-click the file and choose Open With⇨FrontPage (Open as HTML) from the context menu. FrontPage opens the document. To let FrontPage open the document the next time, make any change to the document and save it.

Adding viewer links to your Web page

At least some of the users visiting your site won't have access to one or more of the Office products. Fortunately, such users don't have to own Office products (such as Word) to view the documents you create; a free viewer is available online. To help your users get hold of it, you can give your Web page a link to the download area for Microsoft Office Viewers at

```
http://www.microsoft.com/
    office/000/viewers.asp
```

The user can download the appropriate viewer from the site to see the content you provide. The site includes links for Word, PowerPoint, Excel, Access, and Visio.

You might think there's a problem with some of the viewers. For example, the Word viewer seems to support only Word 97 and 2000. That's only because the DOC file format hasn't had a major change in years; this older viewer can open your Word 2003 files just fine. Some formatting features have a slightly different appearance, but the user can see the document just fine. The Access viewer does support

the newer Access 2003 files — a good thing because the newer files aren't backward-compatible.

Although the standard Web site provides viewers that work in most situations, you also want to look for viewers at the Microsoft Download Center at the following location:

```
http://www.microsoft.com/
    downloads/search.aspx?
    categoryid=9
```

For example, this site has a link for a special PowerPoint 2003 viewer, which you can download at

```
http://www.microsoft.com/
    downloads/details.aspx?
    FamilyID=428d5727-43ab-
    4f24-90b7-a94784af71a4
```

When you use newer versions of Office products, always look for the newest viewers you can find. The idea is to ensure that your users can see your content as easily as possible.

You also need to consider some of the artifacts that Word adds to the HTML document. Word creates the HTML document with the idea that you'll edit in Word. The problem is the document contains a wealth of information that shouldn't appear on a public Web site. All the information that appears within the document Properties dialog box also appears in the HTML document, as shown in Figure 4-3. A cracker could use this information to conduct an attack on your company using *social engineering* techniques (asking users, usually deceptively, for information such as their passwords).

The `ExampleWordDocument.htm` file provided with the source code for this chapter on the Wiley Web site shows just how much information anyone can find on the Web page. (Use Code view to look at the document.) The information also includes any custom properties you attach to the document — and could include information such as department heads' names and telephone numbers. All these artifacts can cause problems for your company by revealing information no outsiders should know.

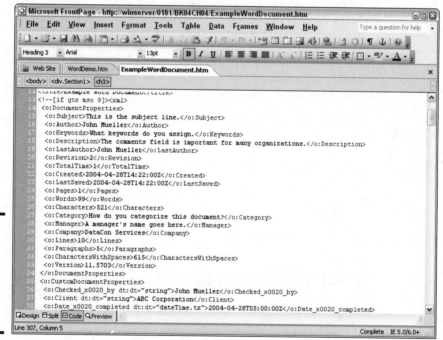

Figure 4-3: Creating an HTML file with Word leaves artifacts in place.

Developing Data Views with Excel

Excel is the application that has the most potential for Web development, in many respects, because you can use it to perform data analysis and create charts for users to see. Sure, the formatting capabilities of Word and the data storage features of Access are assets, but Excel is the visual aid that really shines. This is the one place where Microsoft added a lot of functionality to FrontPage to provide the required support.

Copying Excel data

In many cases, you can create the data you want in Excel and simply copy and paste it into your Web page. When working with a worksheet, FrontPage creates a new table to hold the data. Charts and graphs rely on images that FrontPage creates on the fly. Generally, what you see in Excel is what FrontPage reproduces on-screen.

The only problem with the copy-and-paste approach is that FrontPage doesn't always do a very good job creating the worksheet data as a table. Unlike Word data, the Excel data doesn't rely on CSS — so you end up with entry after entry of formatting information. Every cell has separate formatting information, making it nearly impossible for anyone to view the data when they can't use the formatting you selected. One way around this problem is to create your own stylesheet and edit the table entries to match.

One of the new features of FrontPage 2003 that make it easier to work with Excel charts you paste is the Picture Actions icon shown in Figure 4-4. This icon appears in the upper-left or lower-right corner of the chart after you paste it into the Web page (or after you modify the picture settings to match the size of your Web page). Click the icon and you see a context menu containing several options, one of which is Resample Picture to Match Size. You can resample the image to clean up problems such as jagged fonts and image attributes. This new feature makes it easy to create great-looking charts that actually fit on the Web page.

Using the Web components

You have additional options at your disposal when you install the Web Components feature of Microsoft Office. These options appear as part of the Office Shared Features support when using Office 2003. Use these options to create interactive pages for Access and Excel. (Unfortunately, there isn't any support for other Office products such as Word.) Install these options before you try to use the FrontPage Web components discussed in this section.

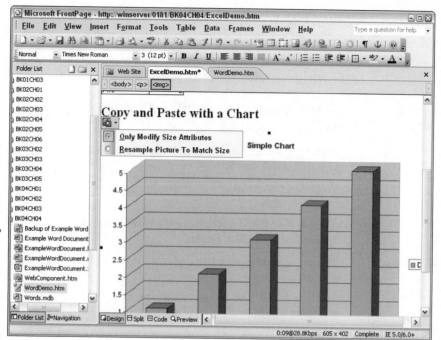

Figure 4-4:
Resample
a chart to
provide
a better
appearance.

Excel users have three special components available for creating connections to FrontPage. To access these components, choose the Insert➪Web Component command. You see the Insert Web Component dialog box. All three of these components appear as part of the Spreadsheets and Charts component, as shown in Figure 4-5. Only the Office Spreadsheet and Office Chart control are directly usable in FrontPage; the Office PivotTable option requires database support.

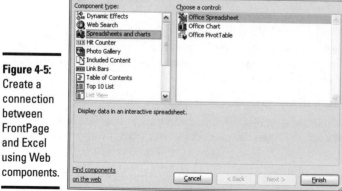

Figure 4-5:
Create a
connection
between
FrontPage
and Excel
using Web
components.

**Book IV
Chapter 4**

**Inserting Office
Objects**

Creating a spreadsheet for your Web page

The components described in this section also rely on complex connections. The easiest way to create a spreadsheet from existing data is to save it in Excel as XML data. To save the data in XML format and add the spreadsheet to the Web page, follow these steps:

1. **Choose the File➪Save As Web Page command.**

   You see the Save As dialog box.

2. **Select the XML Spreadsheet (*.xml) option in the Save as Type field and then click Save.**

   Excel creates the output file, ready to add as a spreadsheet to the current Web page.

3. **Choose the Office Spreadsheet control from the Insert Web Component dialog box and click Finish.**

   You see a blank spreadsheet appear on-screen, ready to contain any data you add.

4. **Right-click the new spreadsheet and choose ActiveX Control Properties from context menu.**

   You see the ActiveX Control Properties dialog box.

5. **Select the Import tag and type the location and name of the XML file in the URL field.**

   You can tell the Web page to automatically update its information by checking Refresh Data from URL at Runtime.

6. **Click Import to import the data and then click OK to complete the modifications.**

   You see the spreadsheet data in the spreadsheet object.

You can almost immediately see some unique advantages to this method of creating a spreadsheet link on your Web page, as shown in Figure 4-6:

   ✦ It's easy to add new information — just type it in.

   ✦ You can sort the existing fields by selecting a column and clicking Sort Ascending or Sort Descending. You just click AutoFilter when you want to see a subset of the values.

   ✦ You can refresh the display by clicking Refresh All.

   ✦ When you finish making changes, you can export the data by clicking Export to Microsoft Office Excel. Excel opens with the spreadsheet loaded.

✦ To access other possible operations, you just click Commands and Options to display the Commands and Options dialog box. Here you can (for example) format the cells and modify the method the spreadsheet uses to perform calculations.

Of course, it isn't possible to get this much functionality without paying a price. In this case, the Office Spreadsheet control relies on an `<object>` tag of such complexity that you should use Design View to modify its features. The feature also runs into problems if you're working with older versions of Office, so you can count on using this technique only for users who have Excel 2003 installed.

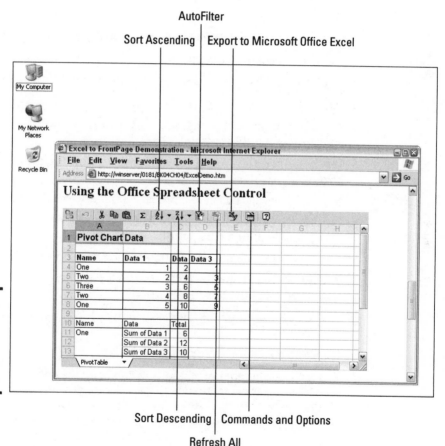

Figure 4-6: Using a Web component has distinct advantages.

**Book IV
Chapter 4**

Inserting Office Objects

Creating a chart

You might have noticed that Excel won't export chart data as XML, so it might seem that you can't use the Office Chart control to display a chart on-screen. Because the charts you create in Excel are based on the data you define, it's possible to use the XML data to re-create your chart on a Web page using the Office Chart control. The important task to perform before you try to use the Office Chart control is to create a spreadsheet using the Office Spreadsheet control.

Sometimes you don't want to display a spreadsheet — all you want is the chart showing on-screen. You still need the spreadsheet to create the chart, but you can make the spreadsheet invisible to the viewer. Here's how to get this result:

1. **Right-click the spreadsheet and choose ActiveX Control Properties.**

   FrontPage displays the ActiveX Control Properties dialog box.

2. **Select the Object Tag tab and set the Height and Width properties to 0.**

3. **Click OK.**

   Although nothing will change in Design view, Preview view shows the spreadsheet has disappeared.

4. **Verify this result by using your browser to view the chart on the Web page.**

   Now you have an "invisible" spreadsheet to use as a data source.

5. **Choose the Office Chart control from the Insert Web Component dialog box and then click Finish.**

   You see the Commands and Options dialog box shown in Figure 4-7.

6. **Choose the Data from the Following Web Page Item and select a source from the list box.**

   The source should be the Web page for which you've created the "invisible" spreadsheet.

7. **Click Ranges.**

   You can use a number of methods to configure the spreadsheet information, but the easiest method is to copy the ranges of cells that you used for the existing chart. Make sure you copy just those ranges and not the page-name information. For example, if your series value in Excel is

   ```
   ='Simple Chart Data'!$B$4:$B$8
   ```

   you can get the same range via the Office Chart control if you type **$B$4:$B$8.**

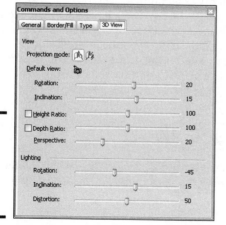

Figure 4-7:
Define a
data source
and data
range for
your chart
or graph.

After you describe what data to use, you need to define how to use it. Click the Type tab and you see a list of chart and graph types. Choose one of the options and click the Close box. FrontPage displays the new chart or graph on-screen.

The Office Chart control is a little confusing to use because it has two different dialog boxes with different tabs and options that use the same name. In addition, you must select the control for editing so it has a hashed border before you can access the dialog boxes. Here's how: With the control selected for editing, right-click and choose Data from the context menu to change the data source information. Right-click the control and select Commands and Options from the context menu when you want to change the configuration of the control — how it displays the data. You see another version of the Commands and Options dialog box, as shown in Figure 4-8.

Figure 4-8:
Choose
display
options for
your chart
or graph.

**Book IV
Chapter 4**

**Inserting Office
Objects**

Unfortunately, neither of the Commands and Options dialog boxes lets you change the `<object>` tag information. You can, however, modify the `<object>` tag indirectly, by changing ActiveX control properties — and it takes only a few steps:

1. Right-click the control when it isn't selected for editing.

You can tell this is the case because there's no hashing around the border. After you select the control, a context menu appears.

2. Choose ActiveX Control Properties from the context menu.

You see the ActiveX Control Properties dialog box. Figure 4-8, for example, shows one of the more interesting configuration options for a chart or graph — using a 3-D chart or graph to change the view with sliders. In this case, you see the effects of changes you make immediately. You can also choose a perspective view or an orthographic view of the chart. When you have the chart the way you like it, FrontPage changes what's in the `<object>` tag to reflect your choices.

If you get the chart or graph too far out of balance to use, click Default and FrontPage changes the settings to their original values.

3. Click other areas of the chart and repeat this process to change other tags.

The tabs change in the Commands and Options dialog boxes to match the configuration needs of each element. For example, when you click the Series axis, you see tabs for changing the format (the font, in this case), the line used to mark the axis, the positioning of the axis ticks, and the axis scale. The General tab contains a Select field where you can choose which chart element you want to modify.

Other techniques

Excel provides a number of other techniques that offer access to spreadsheet information. For example, you can use a hyperlink (as described in the "Relying on hyperlinks" section of the chapter). You can also use direct document translation (as described in the "Creating a direct document conversion" section of the chapter). In addition, third-party vendors make a wealth of products to help FrontPage access your Excel data. You aren't limited to a particular method of displaying your data on-screen.

Creating Report Views with Access

Ironically, Access is one of the least *accessible* Office applications because exercising good control over a database normally means writing application code. You still have a number of ways to work with Access, though. In many cases, you can gain the information you need for a Web site by exercising options you use with other Office products, moving the data to another Office product first, or employing a few unique methods.

Dragging and dropping — or not

By far, the easiest way to create a view of an Access database is to drag a database element (such as a query) from the Access database to the Web page in FrontPage and drop it there. This method always produces a table that contains all the results that the element produces. For example, a query produces a table containing all the information that it normally returns. Likewise, if you select an entire database, you see the whole database on the Web page.

This technique doesn't work especially well with reports. Sometimes you get a report — but more often than not, all you get is an error message. Here's the most reliable way to get reports onto your Web page:

1. **Highlight the report in Access.**

2. **Choose the command appropriate to your source application:**

- **For Word:** Choose Tools➪Office Links➪Publish It with Microsoft Office Word.

- **For Excel:** Choose Tools➪Office Links➪Analyze It with Microsoft Office Excel.

In either case, you can use the techniques in the other sections of this chapter to work with the resulting data.

Copying and pasting

The copy-and-paste technique works slightly differently with Access from the way it does with other Office products: You select entire rows of data. When you want all the rows in a table, simply select the rows you want and copy them. Paste the data into FrontPage and you see a tabular result similar to the one you see when you use the drag-and-drop technique. The difference is that you see *only* the rows you selected.

Create queries when you want just a subset of the data or you want to see the output from multiple tables. Using queries lets you select just the columns you want to see on the Web site. In some cases, it pays to create a temporary query to get the precise results you want. Remember that you can select only rows, so each row has to contain just the data you want to see on the Web page. Editing the information in FrontPage is difficult, to say the least.

It's also possible to copy a single record from a form. Select the entire record and click Copy in Access. Unfortunately, the data isn't formatted as it appears in Access — it appears as a table. The table contains the same elements as the form data, so this technique is useful when you want to display the data provided by a form. In this case, however, you may want to select Edit⇨Paste Special and choose one of the unformatted options. Doing so enables you to get just the data.

Chapter 5: Using Smart Tag Plug-ins

In This Chapter

✔ Developing Web pages with Smart Tags

✔ Adding Smart Tags to a Web page

✔ Preventing use of Smart Tags on your site

✔ Getting other Smart Tags

Smart Tags, a feature that appears in newer Office products, associate an action with a particular piece of information. In some cases, the Smart Tag automates a task, but in others it helps transform the data or lets you perform interesting tasks with the data, such as looking the information up online. For example, you could type a stock symbol into a document. In most cases, the Office product recognizes the stock symbol, associates a Smart Tag with it, and lets you look up information about the stock symbol online.

For example, when you add a picture to a Web page and then resize it, FrontPage displays a Picture Actions Smart Tag that lets you resample the image from the original source to create an image with a better appearance. Resampling removes the jagged edges that resizing can produce. More important, the Picture Actions Smart Tag associates the resampling action with the data, which gives it an intelligence of sorts because you can interact with the data in a different way.

Don't confuse Smart Tags with HTML tags. Smart Tags appear in all Office 2003 applications, even those that have nothing to do with Web design. Even though Smart Tags and HTML tags are both called *tags,* the functionality and purpose of each tag is completely different.

Understanding the Smart Tag Plug-ins

FrontPage directly supports only two Smart Tags, even though you can install the full set of Office Smart Tags. The first is the Picture Actions Smart Tag used for graphics. The second is the Paste Options Smart Tag shown in Figure 5-1. This Smart Tag lets you choose a method for pasting text from another application into your Web page. Sometimes you want the formatting used by the other application, or want to format the information using a CSS file you've created.

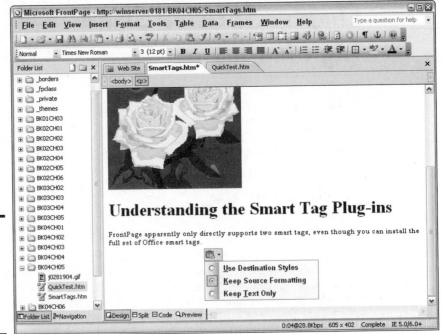

Figure 5-1:
Determine
how you
want to
paste the
text into
FrontPage.

After you get past these two automatic Smart Tags, FrontPage needs a little extra information from you before it can use Smart Tags in your Web pages — configuration, confirmation of required features, that sort of thing. You won't actually see the effect of the Smart Tags in Design view — and sometimes even Preview view balks at working with them — but the Smart Tags do show up in your browser.

Some Smart Tags only work when you have the required Office features installed. For example, the Date Smart Tag appears only when you have Schedule Plus installed (this option appears as part of the Microsoft Office Outlook installation). Otherwise Word still inserts the tag, but you don't see it. Smart Tags also need the Smart Tag Plugins feature installed (choose Office Tools➪Smart Tag Plugins to access it) before your Web page can make use of them.

Seeing Smart Tags on Your Web Page

By itself, FrontPage doesn't provide support for adding Smart Tags to your Web page; you have to add them specifically to the coding. In fact, you can't even see Smart Tags in Design view because of the way you add them. However, you can see the effect of Smart Tags in Preview view and in your browser. If you know that your users will have the correct support installed on their systems, then adding Smart Tags to your Web page makes sense because they can extend the functionality of your Web page considerably. You can find the examples in this section in the `SmartTags.htm` file supplied on this book's companion Web site as part of the source code for this chapter.

Creating the Smart Tag Web-page entries

Using any type of Smart Tag requires special entries in the coding of your Web page. Most of these entries appear within the `<head>` tag, rather than the `<body>` tag, which is why you can't see them in Design view. Four types of entry are necessary:

✦ Namespaces

✦ Smart Tag descriptions

✦ Designation of the processing object

✦ Styles

The following subsections describe each type of entry.

Setting up the namespace entry

The first set of entries actually appears in the `<head>` tag like this:

```
<html xmlns:o="urn:schemas-microsoft-com:office:office"
      xmlns:st1="urn:schemas-microsoft-com:office:smarttags"
      xmlns:st2="urn:schemas:contacts">
```

These entries define three *namespaces*. Namespaces are identifiers for a resource you want to use. The parts of a namespace entry perform the following functions:

✦ The first namespace (which begins with `xmlns:o`) is reserved for Microsoft Office.

✦ The second is a general namespace for Smart Tags (note the `st`).

✦ The third namespace is a special entry for contact information.

✦ Within the second and third namespaces, the Uniform Resource Name (`urn`) portion tells the browser that this is identification information.

✦ The remainder of the namespace is a declaration of the identifier, which are *schemas* (organized listings of data) in this case. A schema defines how the data is put together.

Describing the Smart Tags

With the namespaces established, the next step is to describe the Smart Tags you want to use. Every Smart Tag requires at least one entry; the descriptions tell the Browser how to react to each Smart Tag entry. Here are descriptions for all the Smart Tags that Microsoft Office supports natively:

```
<o:SmartTagType
    namespaceuri="urn:schemas-microsoft-com:office:smarttags"
    name="stockticker"/>
<o:SmartTagType
    namespaceuri="urn:schemas-microsoft-com:office:smarttags"
    name="PersonName"/>
<o:SmartTagType
    namespaceuri="urn:schemas:contacts" name="Sn"/>
<o:SmartTagType
    namespaceuri="urn:schemas:contacts" name="GivenName"/>
<o:SmartTagType
    namespaceuri="urn:schemas-microsoft-com:office:smarttags"
    name="Street"/>
<o:SmartTagType
    namespaceuri="urn:schemas-microsoft-com:office:smarttags"
    name="address"/>
<o:SmartTagType
    namespaceuri="urn:schemas-microsoft-com:office:smarttags"
    name="place"/>
<o:SmartTagType
    namespaceuri="urn:schemas-microsoft-com:office:smarttags"
    name="City"/>
<o:SmartTagType
    namespaceuri="urn:schemas-microsoft-com:office:smarttags"
    name="State"/>
<o:SmartTagType
    namespaceuri="urn:schemas-microsoft-com:office:smarttags"
    name="PostalCode"/>
<o:SmartTagType
    namespaceuri="urn:schemas-microsoft-com:office:smarttags"
    name="time"/>
<o:SmartTagType
    namespaceuri="urn:schemas-microsoft-com:office:smarttags"
    name="date"/>
<o:SmartTagType
    namespaceuri="urn:schemas-microsoft-com:office:smarttags"
    name="phone"/>
```

Each entry in the list includes three items:

✦ **Identifier.** This first item tells the browser that this is an entry for a Smart Tag, based on the Microsoft Office namespace. The `o:` preceding each entry ties it to the Microsoft Office declaration in the `<head>` tag.

+ **Location for the definition for this Smart Tag.** This entry uses a URN, just as the entries in the `<head>` tag do.

+ **Human-readable name for the Smart Tag.**

The `SmartTagType` entries are based on information the vendor provides, the content of an XML file where the Smart Tag file is stored, or on a Registry entry. All Microsoft Office Smart Tag files appear in the following folder on your machine:

```
\Program Files\Common Files\Microsoft Shared\Smart Tag
```

The Registry entries for the Smart Tags appear in another directory:

```
HKEY_CURRENT_USER\Software\Microsoft\Office\Common\Smart
    Tag\Recognizers
```

Identifying the processing object

A special object processes all this information for Internet Explorer. You must add the following `<object>` tag within the `<head>` tag immediately after the Smart Tag declarations to identify that object and activate Smart Tag processing on a Web Page.

```
<object classid="clsid:38481807-CA0E-42D2-BF39-B33AF135CC4D"
        id=IETag></object>
```

Notice that the `<object>` tag doesn't include any parameters or arguments. You can't interact with this object in any way. The `id` value you assign (in this case, `IETag`) is important because you use it to identify the object to the browser.

Adding styles to content via Smart Tags

The final generic step is to add some styles to identify the actual content for the Smart Tags to the browser. This is one situation in which embedded styles are essential. In addition, this is one of the few cases in which a style doesn't affect the appearance of the content — the style affects the behavior of the content. Here are the two styles that work with Smart Tags.

```
<style>
    st1\:*{behavior:url(#IETag) }
    st2\:*{behavior:url(#IETag) }
</style>
```

Notice the two styles point to a behavior URL that has the same identifier as the object: `IETag`. The style behavior URL and the object identifier must match or the Web page won't work.

Don't expect a Smart Tag you use on a Web page to have the full functionality that it has in a Microsoft Office document. The Smart Tag knows it's being used in a Web environment — so it limits context-menu choices to only those that are appropriate for a Web venue. Even so, Smart Tags can reduce the work a user has to perform to accomplish tasks, so they can help improve the user's experience of your Web site.

Using the Stocks and Funds Smart Tag plug-in

The Stocks and Funds Smart Tag detects a symbol that stands for stocks, and then provides the user with access to (and information about) that symbol. To get it to work, however, you provide a special tag in addition to all the generic entries needed to support Smart Tags. The special tag looks like this:

```
<st1:stockticker w:st="on">MSFT</st1:stockticker>
```

When placed in the `stockticker` tags, the stock symbol `MSFT` acts as input for the Smart Tag. When you hover the mouse pointer over the purple line that appears under the stock symbol, you see an `i` in a circle and a square, as shown in Figure 5-2. Click the `i` and you see a context menu.

This example shows some of the power of Smart Tags on your Web page. The entry appears as text, and yet the user can do three things with it — get a stock quote, obtain a company report, or get the latest news about the company in question.

Figure 5-2:
Use Smart
Tags to
provide
the user
with data
manipulation
options.

Using the Name Smart Tag plug-in

The Name Smart Tag is affected by the Microsoft Office options you have installed. It can do everything from help you set up an appointment with the person to creating e-mail or addressing an envelope. Here's the code you add to create a Name Smart Tag entry:

```
<st1:PersonName w:st="on">
    <st2:GivenName w:st="on">George</st2:GivenName>
    <st2:Sn w:st="on">Smith</st2:Sn>
</st1:PersonName>
```

The problem with the Name Smart Tag is that it's affected by the number of Microsoft Office features you have installed. I purposely limited the installation on the test machine to see how few options a user could end up with — and Figure 5-3 shows the results of the test.

When you reduce the number of Microsoft Office features on your machine, the Name Smart Tag becomes almost useless.

Figure 5-3:
Decide in advance how much Smart Tag functionality the user receives.

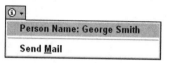

Even though this Smart Tag doesn't turn off completely (as some do when you don't have the proper Microsoft Office support installed), you could easily replace the Smart Tag with a simple link — and a wider range of users would actually be able to use it. A good practical developer's rule is to work with the Web page using the same conditions your users will; Smart Tags are an especially apt illustration. It's easy to create a Web page that doesn't offer much functionality; the question is, *How much is enough?*

Using the Address and Places Smart Tag plug-in

One of my favorite Smart Tags is the Address and Places Smart Tag. You can use this Smart Tag to provide the very practical assistance of driving instructions and a map as the user needs them, as shown in Figure 5-4. The interesting part about this Smart Tag is that you get at least this minimal support without having any Microsoft Office features installed (except FrontPage).

**Book IV
Chapter 5**

**Using Smart Tag
Plug-ins**

Figure 5-4:
Some Smart Tags are useful even without Microsoft Office support.

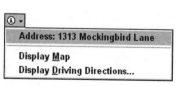

The code for creating an Address and Places Smart Tag is a little more complex. Here's the code you normally need:

```
<h3>An Address</h3>
<p>
    <st1:Street w:st="on">
        <st1:address w:st="on">
            1313 Mockingbird Lane
        </st1:address>
    </st1:Street>
</p>
<h3>A Place</h3>
<p>
    <st1:place w:st="on">
        <st1:City w:st="on">Indianapolis</st1:City>,
        <st1:State w:st="on">IN</st1:State>
        <st1:PostalCode w:st="on">46290</st1:PostalCode>
    </st1:place>
</p>
```

Notice that you need both a `<Street>` and an `<address>` tag to create an address. Likewise, to describe a place, you need a number of tags — including the `<place>` tag. The remaining elements describe a particular city, state, and postal zone. These tags are dual so you can create lists of related entries. A `<Street>` tag (for example) can contain multiple `<address>` tags.

Using the Time and Date Smart Tag plug-in

The Time and Date Smart Tags won't work unless you have the correct Microsoft Office features installed — most notably, the Schedule Plus plug-in. The tags let you set up meetings or perform other tasks based on the time or date you enter. Here's the code that creates a Time Smart Tag.

```
<st1:time Hour="12" Minute="22" w:st="on">12:22 pm</st1:time>
```

Notice that this tag includes special attributes: `Hour` and `Minute`. Because time-display formats can vary from place to place, be sure to give your Smart Tag a time value that your users can easily recognize. The Date Smart Tag works about the same as the Time Smart Tag, as shown here:

```
<st1:date Month="4" Day="29" Year="2004" w:st="on">
    29 April 2004
</st1:date>
```

As with the Time Smart Tag, you must provide an absolute date using the `Month`, `Day`, and `Year` attributes. The actual order of the attributes is unimportant as long as you provide all three entries.

Using the Telephone Smart Tag plug-in

The Telephone Smart Tag is one of those that won't work unless you have certain Microsoft Office features installed. Generally, installing Schedule Plus is enough to activate this tag. There aren't any other special requirements for this tag, as shown here:

```
<st1:phone w:st="on">(317)572-3201</st1:phone>
```

Disabling Smart Tags on Your Site

Some people don't like Smart Tags and what they represent. They don't want their site content to appear as part of a Smart Tag and have no desire to share their information using Smart Tag technology. It's true that Smart Tags have a lot to offer, but developers can also abuse them by overusing them or by creating virus-infected Smart Tags on the Web sites from which they receive data. Fortunately, it's relatively easy to prevent someone from using the content on your site as part of a Smart Tag solution. All you have to do is include the following meta tag at the beginning of every Web page.

```
<meta name="MSSmartTagsPreventParsing" content="TRUE">
```

The `name` attribute defines the kind of information this meta tag contains — a request that Smart Tags not parse the page. The `content` attribute defines all content as off limits. Adding this meta tag doesn't have any effect on the Smart Tags you add to your Web page.

The purpose of this tag is to disable any Smart Tag support added to a browser. A browser with Smart Tag support could visit your site and automatically add your Smart Tags to keywords. The addition wouldn't affect your site, but it would affect how the user sees the site from a usage perspective — and that's what a lot of people are concerned about.

Getting More Smart Tags

A number of third-party vendors provide additional Smart Tags. You can view — and sometimes download — these Smart Tags at

```
http://office.microsoft.com/marketplace/PortalProviderPreview
    .aspx?AssetID=EY010504821033
```

Microsoft also produces some special Smart Tags (such as the euro-conversion Smart Tag, handy for international transactions) that you find at

```
www.microsoft.com/downloads/details.aspx?FamilyID=5879FD92-
6119-4B59-9A62-A7164AC67F40&displaylang=EN
```

But Microsoft isn't the only source. Here are some great places to get more Smart Tags:

✦ ActiveDocs (www.activedocs.com/?from=msomp) helps you create your own custom Smart Tags for classes of information you want tracked. This means you can create additional Smart Tags that FrontPage recognizes automatically or that you can add to a Web page as needed to provide support to the end user.

✦ DataPortal (www.nereosoft.net/ms/dataportal.asp) helps you create Smart Tags for managing your database applications. For example, you could create a Smart Tag in which all the user needs to do to interact with a database is type the database name. The keyword triggers a response that helps the user get database connectivity without having to know anything about the connection itself. The emphasis is on the data.

✦ LexisNexis (http://support.lexisnexis.com/lndownload/) provides a Smart Tag for developers who work with the legal community. For example, the Case Name Smart Tag can search for a case name, legal reviews, and verdict information based on a case keyword typed by the user. Another place to look for Smart Tags for the legal profession is WestCiteLink (www.westlaw.com/citelink).

✦ ProWrite (www.nereosoft.net/ms/) has a Smart Tag that lets you print Avery labels from contact information. You can use this feature to let someone print a label for your company from a Web page when mail contact is required for a transaction. For that matter, you can use the same technique to create labels for items you want to deliver to a customer, basing the transaction on Web-site form data.

✦ WorldLingo (www.worldlingo.com/microsoft/smart_tag.html) provides Smart Tags that help you translate text. You can also obtain quotes for translating large documents, uncover business practices in other countries, and get country-specific data.

These are just a few of the Smart Tags you can obtain. News sites such as MSNBC and travel sites such as Expedia also provide Smart Tags that help you perform tasks with their services. The idea is to provide the Smart Tags that users of your Web site can use best.

Chapter 6: Creating Dynamic Web Sites

In This Chapter

✔ Using dynamic content

✔ Creating shared borders

✔ Developing Active Server Pages

✔ Creating a simple dynamic page

✔ Designing Web pages with the Dynamic Web Template Toolbar

*M*any of the Web sites you see on the Internet are *static* — the content won't change unless someone specifically changes it. When the Web-page developer gets busy, the content can stay static for a very long time. No surprise that the Internet is filled with static content gone bad. In many cases, the information, the links, everything about the Web site is too old — out of date, nonfunctional, an online ghost town. Creating a dynamic Web site can partially solve this problem. Obviously, content has to come from somewhere, but the techniques shown in this chapter make it a lot easier to keep your Web site up to date and fresh.

Fortunately, FrontPage provides special features for making your dynamic Web site work. You still have to do a little more work than you would for a static Web site, but not nearly as much as it takes to create a dynamic Web site by hand.

Part of the appeal of dynamic Web sites comes from *shared borders* — a feature that gives several Web pages the same border: A new link placed on the left side of one page automatically appears on all other pages, which means all pages get the same update. You use this technique to create changing content for all your pages at once. Even a small change like this can make a big difference to users because they know you maintain your site.

Microsoft has created a number of strategies for creating dynamic content. One of those strategies is to rely on a scripting language known as Active Server Pages (ASP) to create the Web page. For a completed ASP page, some content remains the same, but other content changes in response to a particular, specified need. FrontPage 2003 can now create ASP directly, which means you don't have to rely on that old text editor anymore.

Changing Content and Knowing Why

The need for change varies by Web site, but all Web sites experience change, or no one visits them. People expect you to add new content as your Web site grows — at the very least, to move things around and present a few new ideas. For a business, however, change is essential. No one wants to see last week's sales figures — only today's figures are important for the majority of your viewers. Sometimes a Web site that's behind the times can even cause problems. Imagine that you have last year's prices for your products listed on the Web site. Anyone buying from the Web site would expect to pay last year's prices.

Unfortunately, trying to find the time to update your Web site can be difficult. That's why you need to plan and manage the changes you make to your Web site — and have some of them appear automatically as the result of other activities you perform. The idea is to get the software to do as much of the work as possible for you. The software can't do all the work, but you might be surprised at how much work a properly designed site can do.

Updates are important, but so is performing the update correctly. FrontPage gives you four kinds of possible updates:

✦ **Manual:** You perform all required updates without using software. However, you can still save by using cut-and-paste techniques to incorporate standardized features. Using themes and other layout aids also reduces time. Changing content is accommodated by making configuration modifications in Design view in many cases.

✦ **Automatic file updates:** FrontPage performs updates as part of a predefined configuration requirement. For example, using shared borders ensures that common content automatically appears within files when the developer opens the file for an update.

✦ **Template updates:** The developer creates a template that acts as a repository for common data. Creating a custom FrontPage template, as described in Book II, Chapter 5, can save considerable time when you have a lot of common data on each Web page. FrontPage displays the common data and associated fields for new content when the developer creates a new page. In addition, any template changes appear when the developer reopens the file for an edit.

✦ **Script generation:** An application creates input based on client, server, database, or environmental needs. The script can create the entire page, as in the case of Active Server Pages (ASP), and then reside on the server to generate responses (webbots), or reside on the client to perform local processing (JavaScript).

Combining one or more of these techniques lets you update your Web site quickly. The techniques you choose depend on the resources you have, the expectations and capabilities of clients, and the configuration of your Web server. A hosted site has the greatest limitations, especially when the site doesn't have FrontPage Extensions installed. However, even with a hosted site, you have access to client-side webbots, templates, themes, and technologies such as shared borders.

Companies that run their own Web sites and have the required support have almost unlimited resources for making changes to their Web sites. Many FrontPage techniques rely on server-side webbots that require you have FrontPage Extensions installed. Some FrontPage 2003 features require that you have SharePoint Services installed. The added integration (such as access to company databases) provided by SharePoint Services is new for FrontPage 2003.

Using Shared Borders

The FrontPage Shared Borders feature is a series of special HTML pages to be shared by all pages on a particular Web site. You can use any or all the borders that appear at the top, left, right, and bottom of the page, as shown in Figure 6-1.

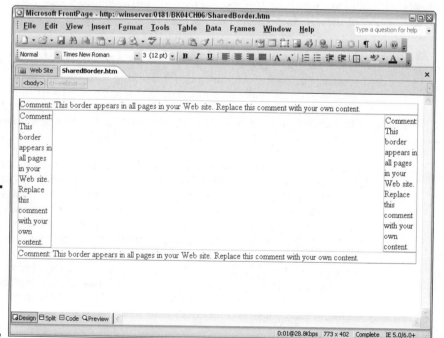

Figure 6-1: Use Shared Borders to display common content on the fringes of a Web page.

Understanding how Shared Borders work

The Shared Borders feature doesn't work the same as other techniques for displaying shared content. When you view a page with shared borders in FrontPage, all you see is the code for the page because the border code is stored in the _borders folder. There aren't any entries for tables or frames, as in older techniques. The only modification is a <meta> tag in the header, like this one:

```
<meta name="Microsoft Border" content="tlrb">
```

The name attribute tells you that this is a special — and shared — border feature that is handled by the server. The content attribute tells you that this page has *top*, *left*, *right*, and *bottom* (tlrb) borders. This codeless feature makes shared borders different from other shared content strategies.

Unfortunately, the actual output still relies on a table. If you look at the page on your Web site with a text editor, you'll see the tables and content you provided because FrontPage adds them to the file as you save it. To see the table code, display the page in your browser, right-click the page, and choose View Source from the context menu. The browser opens, using a text editor such as Notepad to display the page's source code.

The way FrontPage implements this particular feature means you must open the file and save it if you want to see how your changes to the shared border files actually look. Tests show that the changes aren't completely automatic, but they are faster than making the changes by hand.

Attaching a Shared Border to specific Web pages

FrontPage provides two methods for working with shared borders — you can attach them to all pages on your Web site or only to specific pages. It's also possible to combine these methods. For example, you might decide that you want all pages to have the same shared border as a title but only some pages to have a right, left, or bottom shared border.

Shared borders present shared content, but the content need not be the same for every page. For example, you can insert a banner onto a shared border. What appears on the banner depends on the current page's position within the navigational structure of the Web site. Consequently, the shared border is the same for every page because every page contains a banner — but the content of the banner changes to match the specific page.

You can use other components to achieve the same effect. For example, if you insert a table of contents into the right border, then every page that has the right border selected will contain a table of contents — but the table of contents will change to meet the needs of the selected page.

Even with shared borders, the content of the page need not be static.

Of course, the real benefit of shared pages is that the changes you make in just one location affect all the pages on your Web site that use shared borders. Consequently, you can change the dynamic content of the shared border, and every Web page is doubly affected — first by the shared border change, and second by the dynamic content you add.

Creating a Shared Border

Shared borders can appear on any page, but they work best on pages that have no other layout elements (such as tables or frames). To create a shared border, follow these steps:

1. **Choose Format⊏>Shared Borders.**

You see the Shared Borders dialog box shown in Figure 6-2.

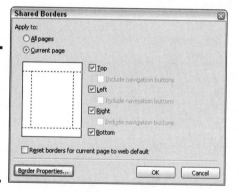

Figure 6-2:
Choose the shared borders you want for all pages or just for this page.

2. **In the Shared Borders dialog box, choose Apply To.**

Here's where you select the scope of the change you want to make. You have two available options, each with its quirks:

• **All Pages:** This setting changes every page on your Web site. When you choose this option, FrontPage enables the Include Navigation Buttons for the Top, Right, and Left options — and the only way you can opt to include navigation buttons is to choose the corresponding shared border. (For the All Pages option, the default setting uses no shared borders.)

Include only navigation buttons on a shared border. Otherwise you see the same navigation aids in every location. In practice, it's better to insert the navigation buttons as separate components rather than insert them here.

- **Current Page:** This affects only the current page. When you select Current Page, FrontPage offers to let you Reset Borders for Current Page to Web Default. If you put a check mark next to that option, FrontPage resets the border options to the defaults that you set using the All Pages option. (This option defaults to not using any shared borders.)

Make sure you set Apply To option correctly or you'll make changes that could cause problems for your Web site later. These changes are independent of each other, so make just one kind of change at a time. When you want to change the settings for all pages, make the changes and then click OK. Don't make changes for all pages and *then* tweak the current page unless you click OK between those operations.

3. **Set the properties of each shared border by clicking Border Properties.**

   You see the Border Properties dialog box shown in Figure 6-3. Select the border you want to configure using the Border drop-down list box. Select a background color using the Color option. Choose a background image using the Picture option. (You can choose both of those options if you want.)

Figure 6-3: Configure the shared borders before you use them.

4. **After you configure the shared borders, click OK.**

   You see the shared borders added to the current page.

When you select options for all pages, FrontPage also changes all pages, a process that goes on in the background. Depending on the size of your Web site, you might see the background hourglass icon for quite some time — the bigger the site, the longer the time. It's usually best to let FrontPage complete this task before you move on to other tasks even though you can begin editing the current page.

At this point, you can change the content of the shared borders. Remember that any change you make to the shared borders of the current page affects the shared borders of every other page on the Web site. Consequently, you don't want to include page specific information in your changes.

Viewing the _borders Folder

Modifying the content of a shared border is easy enough using any of the pages you create using a shared border, but it's actually easier when you open the pages individually. You find the shared border pages: `bottom.htm`, `left.htm`, `right.htm`, and `top.htm` in the `\_borders` folder located directly under the `root` folder for your Web site, as shown in Figure 6-4.

FrontPage automatically provides some features on these Web pages for you — for example, a title — but as a rule, don't change the page properties for these pages. The user will never see them directly anyway — and changing some properties (but not others) can have unexpected results. To modify one of the shared borders, double-click the entry as usual.

Notice that the `\_borders` folder can also have other entries. In this case, the Web site includes `guestlog.htm`. This page contains entries from the guest log page for the Web site. The title includes a pointer to the location of the guest log so you can find it easily.

Oddly, the default FrontPage setup doesn't allow you to access this folder using a browser. You can access individual pages within the folder as long as you know the name of the page, but you can't view the folder itself, even if your default settings allow directory browsing.

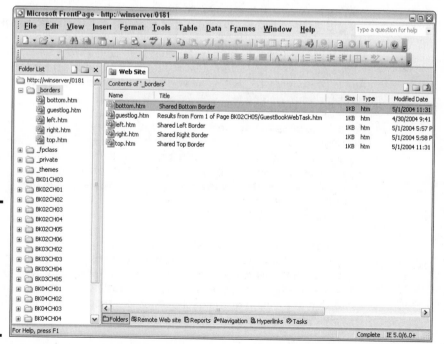

Figure 6-4: Locate the border files in the _borders folder of your Web site.

Normally, my test server has Directory Browsing enabled on the Home Directory tab of the Properties dialog box for the test folders. You access this setting by using the Internet Information Services console found in the Administrative Tools folder of the Control Panel. Enabling directory browsing makes it easier to locate files that a user wouldn't normally need to access — in particular, so you can see how they react in your test browser. The view of the file you see in FrontPage isn't always the one that your users' browsers will show, so it's important to test any changes you make at several levels.

Using Active Server Pages in FrontPage

ASP (Active Server Pages) is one of the easier ways to create dynamic content for your Web site. ASP relies on server-side scripts to present information to the viewer when you use Internet Information Server (IIS) or any other Web server that supports ASP. Microsoft tried a number of other approaches to creating dynamic content for a Web site, such as Internet Server Application Programming Interface (ISAPI), but these efforts failed because they were too difficult to use and maintain. The biggest benefit of using ASP is that it's relatively simple to use, and you can make changes without restarting the Web server.

Advantages of the ASP scripting approach

ASP isn't just a scripting language. It actually relies on a combination of scripting and straight HTML coding. In this respect, ASP is similar to open-source languages such as PHP Hypertext Processor (PHP). Anything that isn't going to change can use the same HTML that you have always used, so you can start simply with ASP and not worry too much about a huge learning curve. ASP is pretty easy to pick up as you go along, whenever you need new features for your Web page.

For a lot of people, any mention of scripting brings visions of hours spent in frustration trying to get complex code working. ASP can become complex, but you really can perform a lot of tasks in it without writing a lot of code. In many cases, simplicity is better than creating something complex because it's easier to maintain. For example, you can create a page that does nothing more than simple value replacements based on content you have stored on your Web server.

True, some scripts that start simple don't scale up well to larger projects, but you can create complex designs with ASP, some of which can start simple and then evolve. The time you spend working with ASP today won't become a losing proposition later. You can add new features to your Web site as needed to meet changing user needs. As a result of this flexibility, many complex Web sites rely on ASP as their means of displaying content on-screen.

ASP also has a relatively long history (at least when you consider how fast most computer techniques come and go). As more people use ASP, Microsoft makes additional features available. The product has matured; you face fewer of the problems that come with raw new technology (such as mysterious unexplained bugs or difficulty getting your applications working). And then there's compatibility with other Microsoft technology; many developers prefer using ASP because it integrates so well with IIS.

The essential strategy is to use only the features you need with a project so you can build your knowledge of ASP slowly, as you have time to work with it.

Every copy of IIS comes with ASP support built in; in effect, you always get ASP with your copy of Windows. The availability of ASP support means you can build an ASP application on your Web server and use it on any other IIS Web server. Sometimes you need to make small tweaks when you use specific object names (such as the name of the server), but there's one other great advantage: ASP is free, and you don't have to install anything to get it.

Creating a simple ASP page

This chapter won't tell you everything there is to know about ASP. The main focus of this chapter is to show you can use ASP with FrontPage. *ASP.NET For Dummies* by Bill Hatfield (Wiley) provides a full explanation of all the ASP.NET nuances. The example is relatively simple so that everyone can use it without knowing a lot about ASP. The example does show some ASP features though so you can see that FrontPage is a true ASP development environment.

Creating the file

Working with ASP in FrontPage isn't as straightforward as it could be in some respects. The problem is that FrontPage assumes every Web page you create has an HTM extension — ASP requires use of the ASP extension. To create other kinds of files, you must change the extension. Here's how:

1. **Right-click the folder you want to use in the Folder List.**

A context menu appears.

2. **Choose New⇨Blank Page from the context menu.**

You see a new blank page created in the Folder List with the name highlighted so you can rename it.

3. **Type the name of the page with an ASP extension rather than an HTM extension.**

FrontPage creates a new ASP page. The new ASP page has a different icon than a standard HTM page, so you can readily identify it. The SimpleASP.ASP file included with the source code for this chapter on the Wiley Web site shows how this type of page appears in FrontPage.

Book IV
Chapter 6

Creating Dynamic Web Sites

This is a situation where creating your own templates really pays off. (See Book II, Chapter 5, for details.) You can create a blank ASP page that includes the basic information these pages require. It's also possible to create ASP pages with some content already defined. Be sure to include a preview of the page as it appears to the end user rather than the script view you see when working with the page.

Designing the page

Design the ASP page as you would any HTML page. You can create blanks on the page that ASP automatically fills in for you (using script to do so). The page can also accept input and modify the data that the user provides. As you design your Web page, think about the data you want to see displayed on the page rather than the technique used to display it.

Make sure you provide a means to read content as well as write it back out to the page. Normally, you use a form and form controls to gain access to the information the user provides. However, you can easily use other techniques to interact with the user. When you want to display information — rather than obtain information from the user — you can rely on paragraph tags.

An ASP script can also interact with objects, so you can use standard FrontPage objects or create objects using the ⟨object⟩ tag. Use this alternative carefully because it adds complexity to the Web page design and the scripting you need to perform. This option also provides a lot of flexibility, and you can perform tasks, such as create interactive video, that simply isn't possible using any other technique.

Adding script elements

After you design your page, you make it dynamic by adding script elements to it. A script element need not be complex or hard to understand. All you need is the right keywords. Microsoft provides a complete reference of ASP keywords at

`http://msdn.microsoft.com/library/en-us/iissdk/iis/iis_web_pages.asp`

Some of the most common keywords include those that request information from the client or the server. Here's an example of a server request.

```
<% Response.Write(Request.ServerVariables("SERVER_NAME"))%>
```

Every ASP script appears within the ⟨% %⟩ characters. This script tells the server to write some information to the client. You use the `Response.Write()` script command to write anything that ASP can write to the client. The information this code writes is a server variable — the server name. Use the `Request.ServerVariables()` command to discover information about the server. To discover all the keywords your server understands, ask for each keyword in turn, like this:

```
<% for each Value in Request.ServerVariables %>
    <% if not Request.ServerVariables(Value) = "" then %>
        <p>
            <%= Value %>
            : 
            <%= Request.ServerVariables(Value) %>
        </p>
    <% end if %>
<% next %>
```

This code tells IIS that you want to look at each value provided with the `Request.ServerVariables` collection. A collection is a set of information that you can access using the server. The next statement tells IIS to ignore any server variable that is blank. This line is necessary because when someone accesses your Web page in anonymous mode, many of the possible server variables are blank.

The variable `Value` has received a server variable name as part of the `<% for each Value in Request.ServerVariables %>` statement. The code can send this value as part of the response using the `<%= Value %>` statement. The equal sign in this statement takes the place of the `Response.Write()` script command. Notice how the code uses a special character, the nonbreaking space (` `) to provide a space between the value name and the actual value. The code also uses `Value` as input to the `Request.ServerVariables()` script command, which prints out the value contained in that server variable.

Notice that the `<% if %>` statement ends with an `<% end if %>` statement, and the `<% for each %>` statement ends with a `<% next %>` statement. You always tells ASP where a statement begins and ends so ASP knows when to start and stop a series of commands. Figure 6-5 shows an example of some typical server variable values.

Some of this information is pretty interesting. For example, the `REMOTE_ADDR` server variable tells you the client address so you can keep track of which client is requesting information. The `PATH_TRANSLATED` server variable shows the actual path to this script on my server. Sometimes you need to know this information so you can access files on the server's hard drive. Move down the list and you can get a look at some information about the server. The `SERVER_SOFTWARE` server variable tells you which operating system and Web server the server is running so you can address any compatibility needs.

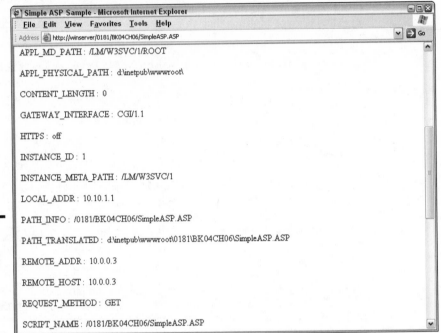

Figure 6-5:
Discover
information
about your
Web site
using ASP
scripts.

A script doesn't necessarily output information. It can interact with the user in other ways. For example, depending on what the user types into a form, you could redirect the client to another Web site or another location on your Web site. Here's an example that shows a combination of a form and an ASP script that redirects the user to another location:

```
<h2>Form and Response Processing</h2>
<form method="GET" name="SendMeTo" action="SimpleASP.ASP">
    <p>
        <label for="MyGoTo">Go To URL: </label>
        <input type="text" name="GoTo" size="40"
                value="http://www.mwt.net/~jmueller/"
                id="MyGoTo"
                title="Type the URL of a Web site.">
    </p>
    <p>
        <input type="submit" value="Submit" name="B1">
        <input type="reset" value="Reset" name="B2">
    </p>
</form>

<%
    if not Request.QueryString("GoTo") = "" then
```

```
      Response.Redirect(Request.QueryString("GoTo"))
   end if
%>
```

The form contains a label, a textbox, and two buttons. When the user types a URL into the textbox and clicks Submit, the page sends the information back to the server as part of the query string. You see this kind of interaction take place all the time on the Internet.

The difference is the script. The script begins by checking the query string for a value named `GoTo`. Notice this is the name of the textbox. Using the `Request.QueryString()` function, the code retrieves this value. If it's blank, then this is either the first time the page is displayed, or the user didn't type anything in the textbox. When the user does supply a URL, the code uses the `Response.Redirect()` function to redirect the user to the new location. It's a simple, but very helpful script that you see used all the time on the Internet.

This section can't describe all the features ASP provides. (You can see a few additional features in the `SimpleASP.ASP` file included with the source code for this Chapter on the Wiley Web site.) The important point is that you don't have to rely exclusively on HTML pages to create your Web site when working with FrontPage — you have a number of other useful options.

Understanding the ASP issues

Even though it works well, FrontPage isn't the perfect environment for creating ASP pages. You do receive some advantages over some environments you might have used in the past. For example, FrontPage properly color-codes the ASP script code so you can easily see it. If you don't get this functionality, choose the Tools⇨Page Options command. You see the Page Options dialog box. There you simply choose the Authoring tab, check the Active Server Pages option, and click OK. Presto — full access to ASP functionality in FrontPage.

FrontPage 2003 also provides full database-integration features for ASP and ASP.NET developer. You create the connection using one of the wizards available in the Insert⇨Database menu. The wizard writes the code for you, but the resulting code still suffers from the same limitations as code that a human programmer would write:

✦ **Because ASP is a server-side script, you lose some advantages that FrontPage 2003 normally provides, such as IntelliSense.** You can still write the script and it still appears in the correct format, but the IntelliSense feature doesn't work because FrontPage doesn't know what to do with the script code you create.

✦ **You lose use of the Preview view.** The HTML elements appear in Preview view but not the results of any ASP code you create. Consequently, you can't use Preview view to test the output of your page — you must use a browser and possibly more than one browser depending on your client requirements.

Developing Simple Dynamic Pages

One of the best additions to FrontPage 2003 is Dynamic Web Templates — a replacement for the Shared Borders technology used in older versions of FrontPage. (You can still use the technology in newer versions of FrontPage, but this technology will produce better results when you need to support changing content.) Dynamic Web Templates, or DWT files, provide a special means of creating content where some information changes based on the template and other information changes based on the individual page. You begin by creating the DWT file, which is a special form of HTML page. Some areas of the HTML page are editable; others aren't. For example, you might include a company logo or list of standard links. Using this technique lets you change all the common areas of a Web page by making a single change. It also reduces the chance that someone using the Dynamic Web Template will change a common area.

Creating a Dynamic Web Template

You won't find a menu option or any other FrontPage feature for creating a Dynamic Web Template. Microsoft suggests you create a standard HTML file, then use the File➪Save As command to save it as a Dynamic Web Template. This technique leaves an extra file on your hard drive, so it's not the best method to use. For a method that doesn't leave any extra files lying around, follow these steps:

1. **Right-click the folder where you want the Dynamic Web Template to appear.**

   A context menu appears.

2. **Choose New➪Blank Page from the context menu.**

3. **Name the file and add a DWT extension to it rather than the normal HTM extension.**

4. **Add all the normal properties to the DWT file, including a title and summary.**

   Don't add a base location for the page because you don't know where the attached page will appear on the Web site. This is one of the items you have to fill out for each individual page.

5. Add examples of all the content you want to see on the page.

When working with common content, make sure the entries are in final form. For example, any logo or common links should contain the real information you want to see on the Web site. On the other hand, provide blank or example entries for content that appears on individual pages. You could type instructions (or some indicator as simple as `The Header`) on the page. The idea is to provide the Dynamic Web Template user some idea of what content to provide.

Providing editable regions

After you finish creating the Web page, you define editable regions for the user. An editable region is an area where the Dynamic Web Template user can make changes. When a page lacks editable regions, the user can't make any changes.

It may seem that a page without editable regions is pretty much useless because the user can't make any changes to it. However, a page without editable regions is useful for certain kinds of information. For example, you might need to provide licensing or other terms as part of a subsite. You can't really point to a central location for the page when a subsite is supposed to remain independent, so using a Dynamic Web Template provides a means to create standardized terms on all subsites. In addition, a single change in the template also affects the subsites, so licensing terms don't get outdated.

To create an editable region, follow these steps:

1. Highlight the area you want the user to edit on your Dynamic Web Template.

2. Right-click the DWT page and choose Manage Editable Regions from the context menu.

You see the Editable Regions dialog box shown in Figure 6-6.

3. Type a name for the region you highlighted and click Add.

4. Click Close.

You see the editable region added to the Design view. The editable region appears as a box around the text with the name of the editable region displayed near the top-left corner. Figure 6-7 shows a typical example of editable regions. The selected editable region appears highlighted — other editable regions appear on-screen but are grayed out.

**Book IV
Chapter 6**

**Creating Dynamic
Web Sites**

Figure 6-6:
Create editable regions so the user can make changes.

From a coding perspective, editable regions appear as special comments. Here's a typical example of an editable region.

```
<!-- #BeginEditable "BookTitle" -->
    the book
<!-- #EndEditable -->
```

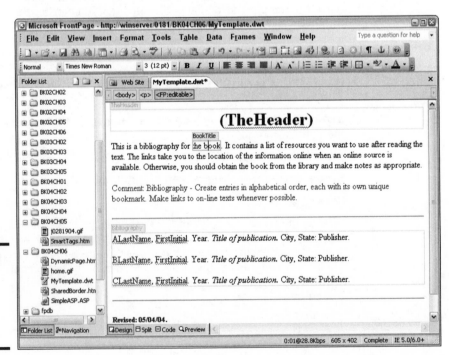

Figure 6-7:
View editable regions in Design view.

The #BeginEditable comment starts the editable region. It always includes the name of the editable region as part of the comment. The #EndEditable comment completes the editable region. You always end the current editable region before starting a new one.

The Editable Regions dialog box also provides options for renaming, removing, and going to editable regions. To use it to rename an editable region, follow these steps:

1. **Right-click an existing editable region.**

A context menu appears.

2. **Select Manage Editable Regions from the context menu.**

You see the Editable Regions dialog box.

3. **Create, remove, or go to an editable region:**

- **To create a New region:** Type a new name for the editable region and click Rename. Note that the Rename button replaces the Add button shown in Figure 6-6.

- **To remove an editable region:** Select it in the Other Regions on this Page list of the Editable Regions dialog box and click Remove.

- **To go to an editable region:** Select its entry in the Other Regions on this Page list and click Go To.

4. **Make sure you add editable regions in Code view as well.**

For example, you want the user to change both the keywords and description for the Web page in most cases. When you don't add editable regions for these entries, FrontPage refuses to let the user change them.

FrontPage automatically adds the doctitle editable region to ensure that the user can at least change the document title, but you must add entries for every other change you want to make. Here are typical editable regions for the keywords and description.

```
<!-- #BeginEditable "Keywords" -->
<meta name="keywords" content="Dynamic Web Template">
<!-- #EndEditable -->
<!-- #BeginEditable "Description" -->
<meta name="description"
      content="This template file contains settings used to
               control the appearance of another Web page.">
<!-- #EndEditable -->
```

You must add these entries manually because you make them in Code view and there isn't any way to add them elsewhere. The Editable Regions dialog box won't highlight the Add button in this case. Make sure you assign unique names to these editable regions. In addition, FrontPage doesn't catch changes to the heading, so you need to manually update your pages in this area when you don't make changes in other areas.

Adding a Dynamic Web Template to an existing page

You can create a page based on a Dynamic Web Template in several ways. The first technique is also the easiest. Right-click the DWT file in the Folders List and choose New from Dynamic Web Template from the context menu. FrontPage creates a new Web page based on the Dynamic Web Template. It automatically opens the file so you can make required changes and perform any required editing. Remember to change the page properties as needed to ensure you document the Web page and its purpose.

Another way to add a Dynamic Web Template is to create a new Web page as usual, and then follow these steps:

1. **Choose Format⇨Dynamic Web Template⇨Attach Dynamic Web Template.**

   You see the Attach Dynamic Web Template dialog box.

2. **Locate the Dynamic Web Template you want to use and then click Open.**

   FrontPage automatically adds all required information to your existing Web page. You see a dialog box confirming the change.

3. **Click Close.**

Performing updates

You perform updates to pages attached to Dynamic Web Templates in a number of ways. The most common technique is to perform the update when you save the page. After you make changes to the DWT file and click Save to save it, FrontPage detects any pages attached to the DWT file. When it detects attached pages, FrontPage displays a dialog box asking whether you want to update the page. Click Yes to perform the update. You can also choose the Format⇨Dynamic Web Template⇨Update Attached Pages command to update the pages as needed.

When you open a page that relies on the Dynamic Web Template, use the Format⇨Dynamic Web Template⇨Update Selected Page command to update it. Normally, you don't want to use this approach because it's better to perform updates on all pages at one time. Using this technique leaves some pages without updates and could cause problems on your Web site. The command is useful as a double check to ensure a change was made and has taken effect.

Heading off trouble with the Dynamic Web Template

When you add a Dynamic Web Template to an existing page, FrontPage overwrites any content that doesn't appear in an editable area. For example, you might set the `author` meta tag to `George Smith` in the original page, like this:

```
<meta name="author"
     content="George Smith">
```

After you add the template, the author name could change to `Amy Cook` when the `author` meta tag doesn't appear as an editable region in the Dynamic Web Template. These subtle changes are often difficult to detect and can cause problems when you build part of the page content before applying the Dynamic Web Template. The easiest way to cure this problem is to apply the Dynamic Web Template as early in the Web page development process as possible.

One change that FrontPage makes to the Code view of Web page that use Dynamic Web Templates is the addition of highlighted code. (The background color is normally yellow.) This code doesn't appear in an editable region in the template. You can change the code, but doing so isn't a good idea because the next update to the template will overwrite your changes. When you make a change in one of these areas, FrontPage displays a Dynamic Web Template Alert dialog box. You can choose to lose the edits you made or keep them. The dialog box warns these changes will disappear during the next update unless you detach the page from the Dynamic Web Template. Select the Detach from Dynamic Web Template option to keep the changes you make permanent.

Using the Dynamic Web Template Toolbar

FrontPage provides the Dynamic Web Template toolbar to make working with DWT files easier. This toolbar doesn't appear by default. To display it, right-click the toolbar area and choose Dynamic Web Template. FrontPage displays the toolbar, as shown in Figure 6-8.

Figure 6-8:
Use this toolbar to manage your Dynamic Web Template.

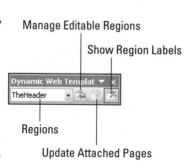

Manage Editable Regions

Show Region Labels

Regions

Update Attached Pages

The Dynamic Web Template toolbar contains only four entries by default. Here's a description of the purpose of each entry.

✦ **Regions:** Contains a list of editable regions on the Dynamic Web Template. Select one of the entries, and FrontPage takes you to that editable region. You can use this feature to locate editable regions quickly so you can edit them. The list won't include any special editable regions, such as those that appear in the document header.

✦ **Manage Editable Regions:** Displays the Editable Regions dialog box. This dialog box lets you add, remove, rename, and locate all the editable regions in your Dynamic Web Template.

✦ **Update Attached Pages:** Lets you update the attached pages without using the menu option.

✦ **Show Region Labels:** Shows or hides the region labels displayed for the editable regions. You normally want to display the labels to make it easier to find an editable region of interest. Hide the labels when you want to verify the layout and ensure it meets specific needs.

Chapter 7: Developing with Security in Mind

In This Chapter

- ✔ Defining security requirements
- ✔ Developing a security plan
- ✔ Securing Web page inputs
- ✔ Tracking security problems

Security is one of the few computer issues that everyone has heard about — the other evening, it made the evening news. It's an issue that many people discuss because there's a lot at stake: The data you create and the information you store are at risk without good security. Even your personal identification could be at risk — identity theft has become more than just a trivial problem encountered by a few people. At the very least, you need to consider what happens when a cracker steals your server and uses it to attack someone else. The blame will rest on you because you're easy to find.

You see a number of confusing terms on the Internet about computer experts who either cause or fix security problems. The correct term in the industry for someone who causes security problems is *cracker*. Crackers usually break into systems to look for data, install special nefarious applications, or perform other misdeeds. A *hacker* (the white-hat variety, at least) is someone who fixes security problems or at least finds their cause. In many cases, hackers work for security companies and locate potential security holes before crackers do. Many hackers who identify themselves openly as such love to work with computers at a low level to help people — and struggle to overcome the stigma created by those who cause problems.

FrontPage provides a number of methods you can use to improve the security of your Web page. In fact, you can thwart the efforts of casual crackers quite easily — but as a cracker's experience improves, the fortifications you set up using FrontPage won't be enough to keep the cracker out. You use monitoring and the services of white-hat hackers to keep advanced crackers at bay. By building security tiers for your system, you can prevent — or quickly detect — most security problems.

Considering the Security Issues

Security isn't just about creating robust applications or restricting user activity. *Great* security relies on a number of techniques. The fundamental word to use with security is *active*. Passive security — building fortifications against outside invaders — simply doesn't work. Any fortification you build is easily overcome by smart crackers. The active developer is the one who wins the day.

Monitoring cracker activities

Knowing your enemies is an important part of keeping them at bay. It's easy to say that you should check your system for signs of cracker activity; it's quite difficult to know where to look. Unless you check every file on your system every day against a known good standard, you can't even be sure that your hard drive is safe, much less the data loaded from the hard drive into system memory. The basics, however, you can implement right away:

✦ **Study up.** The best way to start monitoring cracker activities is to track the exploits crackers are using through trade-press articles. Because cracker exploits are big news, you can monitor them through the major news magazines online such as *eWeek* (http://eletters.eweek.com/), *InfoWorld* (www.infoworld.com/), and *ComputerWorld* (www.computer world.com/). Your local newspaper isn't a good source of information because it normally doesn't track all the current cracker exploits — and only lightly covers those it does.

✦ **Be actively aware of your Web site.** Make sure you visit the site to see how it works. Administrators often get so wrapped up in producing new content that they don't visit the site they create and are unaware of problems with it until a user notifies them. Changes in performance, unexpected content, modified URLs, hidden content, and other problems are all clues that someone has gotten past your security.

✦ **Look at the logs of your system.** When you notice unusual activity by one or more parties, you should suspect potential cracker activity. Someone visiting a Web page with fairly static content is a sign of activity other than simple viewing, especially when that Web page provides data fields or other interaction. A cracker entering a script within the data fields of a form and then submitting it is a common way of gaining access to the server.

✦ **Keep track of the user accounts on your server.** A cracker often begins working with a server by using a current user account, but many crackers use such an account as a steppingstone for creating their own accounts. In many cases, the cracker doesn't create just one account, but several — with varying levels of access — to ensure continued access should you discover one account.

Sometimes your best bet is to employ the services of a good-guy hacker to test your site security. Security firms that employ hackers to test security from the outside can usually tell you which techniques a cracker is likely to employ to gain access to your site. This isn't a one-time check. Sealing the cracks in your security that hackers and crackers know about today won't prevent new security cracks from appearing tomorrow.

Crackers sometimes use odd methods of gaining access to your system. More than one cracker has appeared within the offices of a company as a janitor in order to look for passwords conveniently posted near monitors or in other common places on a desk. Dumpster-diving is another common technique. The piece of paper you throw away today could provide a cracker with access to your system tomorrow — a technique that also works with home users. The cracker commonly looks for a bill from the Web-hosting company for services rendered. The bill commonly contains account information the cracker needs to gain access to your system.

Some people also assume that some passwords are secure. The fact is that once a cracker has an account name, guessing the password isn't all that difficult. Even if you have mangled passwords that contain letters, numbers, and special characters — such as Az2@jiL^)99 — a cracker can use any of a number of special applications to figure the password out. Your only practical defense is to change your password regularly (at least once a month). This technique costs the cracker time discovering your new password.

Checking for viruses

Every Web server should have at least one virus-checking application to monitor the system for infestations. Of course, the virus checker doesn't have much value if you don't keep it updated with new virus signatures; in this area, too, good security is an ongoing process. In addition, you should ensure that the virus checker is set up to monitor the Web server and associated files, as well as the other parts of the server. Keeping the Web server separated from the company network or adding multiple layers of firewalls also helps.

Assuming you've already performed all the usual checks, it helps that you look for the unusual, too. For example, when users complain about system slowdowns, you normally check system performance by using System Monitor (located in the Performance console in the Administrative Tools folder of the Control Panel). When you do detect a performance problem, the next step is to analyze and consider its cause. In some cases, the slowdown is the symptom of a virus at work. A virus, like any other application, uses system resources that you can measure. Changes in available hard-drive space, memory, and processing speed can all indicate the presence of a virus that your virus-checking software hasn't detected.

**Book IV
Chapter 7**

**Developing with
Security in Mind**

Some viruses today are designed to disable virus checking. When you see the virus checker isn't running or doesn't appear to do any useful work, it's time to suspect a virus on your system. Also check for other errors on your Web site. For example, verify that your Web applications all run as expected. Use FrontPage to make the checks easier by running through the files on your Web site quickly.

Considering internal threats

Many organizations consider internal threats a greater problem than anything that occurs outside a company. Part of the problem is the organization most companies use. No one is looking at internal user activities because it's assumed that the threat of job loss is enough to deter most criminal activity. In addition, the internal user already has some level of access to the Web server — you can't block the user completely and expect any progress on the Web site. Finally, most fortifications — including virus checkers and firewalls — point to outside sources of danger. It's actually better to create a wall around every machine in the organization to ensure that a problem on one doesn't spread to others.

You can use FrontPage to monitor internal as well as external threats. For example, FrontPage always shows the last person to edit a file on the system. The Folders view shows this information in the Modified By column. Look for editing patterns. First, look for edits from users who probably shouldn't modify the file in question. Verify they actually made the change and determine why the change was made (when necessary). Second, look at the Modified Date column to determine when the user made the change. A late-night change could indicate the user is overworked, but it could also show changes that could cause problems for your company. Whenever someone begins acting out of character, you need to consider why his or her pattern of working with the Web site has changed.

Make sure you remove accounts for old employees immediately after they leave the company. Ex-employees have a distinct advantage over most crackers because they already have an account (the one you failed to remove) and knowledge of your network layout. Many of the worst security breaches were made by disgruntled ex-employees, not by outsiders who had no knowledge of the company and its procedures.

When you let an employee go, make sure everyone in the company knows about it. The idea is to prevent the ex-employee from gaining access through *social-engineering attacks* — attempts to get remaining employees to reveal sensitive information (including current user names and passwords) by impersonating a network administrator or faking an emergency.

Understanding security fails without monitoring

It's worth repeating: Security isn't a task you perform once or twice and consider done. It's a task you perform continuously — updating and patching software, making sure your virus and firewall protection is up to date, and maintaining protection both internally and externally. Even so, implementing these strategies usually isn't enough.

Only through continuous system monitoring can you hope to achieve a high level of security — and even then you have to prepare for the day when someone gets through your defenses. Nothing you can do will ultimately prevent a determined cracker with the proper resources from breaking through and potentially doing some damage. You can, however, make your security tight enough to discourage the cracker — and you can even detect the cracker early enough to prevent significant damage.

Some developers, after considering all the requirements for good security, throw up their hands and declare it a lost cause. But a secure environment in which to work isn't all there is to good security. Good security also helps reduce a number of other problems:

+ Secure applications are more robust, so they fail less often and are usually easier to use.

+ Developing a secure application also means paying attention to details that could result in improved performance as well.

+ Developing a secure environment means building good applications, updating your system as needed, and monitoring the system for potential problems. All these steps also improve reliability and performance.

Creating a Security Plan

Even if you have a personal Web site that you think no one would ever want to bother, it's important to have some type of security plan in place. The reason for creating a security plan is to ensure you handle security needs consistently and that you have a procedure in place when someone does manage to break into your site. A security plan also provides a means of creating a task list, things you must do to secure the site, so you can track security needs as they become apparent. A good security plan contains the following elements as a minimum:

+ Develop specific security areas such as system patching, virus-checker signature updates, file checking, performance checking, user-account checking, and Web-log verification.

+ Make the security plan organization-specific. Think about the worst things that could happen to your system, such as the release of customer information, and add a security check for that item.

◆ Define who's responsible for particular security areas. Don't assign groups to security; make one person ultimately responsible to ensure that the task is performed.

◆ Implement a contact list that includes local authorities so you don't have to look for the information when a security breach occurs. Define which list members to contact to handle specific kinds of security breach.

◆ Provide a security training schedule and plan. Even if you have a two-person organization, both people should know their roles for maintaining system security.

◆ Create an emergency plan that assigns specific jobs to people in your organization. An emergency plan reduces confusion when an attack does occur and ensures that all requirements are handled.

Even a great security plan is worthless if you don't update it. Plan to review your security plan every time someone on the security team leaves the company. Assign someone to the vacant position immediately — and make the review one of the first tasks for the new employee — to ensure that your security plan continues to work. You should also plan to do regular reviews. Many companies review security annually, but you might want to review your security plan more often when you have a lot of sensitive data to protect.

Checking Inputs

FrontPage provides a number of methods to improve the security of your system. Some of these methods rely on common HTML additions that you should add for other reasons. For example, checking input lengths helps prevent crackers from sending a script to your server. However, it also cues you in to problems the form user might have so that you can offer assistance through a help system. Other techniques help you ensure both the accuracy and security of the data. For example, checking for data input patterns helps ensure the information the user provides is accurate, but it also reduces the chance of a cracker entering the wrong information just to see how the server will react. Only a few techniques are security-specific. Asking a user for name and password — normally done only on secure Web sites — is one of the few exceptions.

Considering the input data length

The easiest defense to implement against crackers is one that many developers fail to use: Define specific input lengths for the data fields on any form you create. By limiting the size of the data input, you limit the things a cracker can do.

For example, it's relatively difficult to create a script that fits within the 14 characters allowed for a typical telephone number (some are longer, depending on where you want to call). Even name and address fields can have specific limits. To ensure maximum compatibility, you can use the HTML approach shown here for a textbox.

```
<input type="text" name="LengthCheck"
       size="20" maxlength="20">
```

The `maxlength` attribute defines the maximum length of this field. Every browser that supports forms also supports and honors this limitation. When you combine this field with a `POST` (rather than a `GET`) submission method, only the most determined cracker can circumvent the length limitation.

Sometimes you don't want the user to submit the form with a blank field, so you define a minimum and maximum field length. The advantage of this approach is better control. The disadvantage is that it's less compatible because it relies on scripting. To use this technique, follow these steps:

1. **Right-click the field and choose Form Field Properties from the context menu.**

   You see the Control Properties dialog box.

2. **Click Validate.**

   You see the Control Validation dialog box shown in Figure 7-1 (this one is text box specific).

3. **Check Required in the Data Length group, type the minimum and maximum field lengths, and click OK twice.**

   FrontPage adds minimum and maximum field length checks.

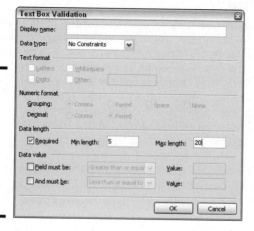

Figure 7-1:
Select text length validation to ensure the user provides required input.

When you view the results of adding the validation to the form, you still see the `maxlength` attribute, so all browsers will check the maximum length. However, the minimum length check relies on a `webbot` as shown here:

```
<!--webbot bot="Validation" B-Value-Required="TRUE"
          I-Minimum-Length="5" I-Maximum-Length="20" -->
```

The Validation `webbot` depends on the `I-Minimum-Length` and `I-Maximum-Length` attributes to define the acceptable input sizes for the field. This is a client-side webbot, so it works even when your Web server doesn't sport FrontPage Extensions. Look in the resulting Web page using a text editor and you see a script that checks for three conditions.

+ **Has the user entered a value?** If not, the check fails and the script displays an error message.

+ **Does the input have the minimum number of characters?** If this check fails, the script displays a different error message.

+ **Is the maximum number of characters exceeded?** If so, the check fails and the script displays yet another error message.

When all three checks succeed, the Web server accepts the form.

Because the validation script performs a second check of the submission data — maximum length — it's even less likely that someone will provide a value that exceeds the maximum length. The first check (the `maxlength` attribute) merely prevents a user from typing any more characters in the field once the maximum length is reached. The second check (the script) actually checks the incoming data to ensure that it doesn't exceed the maximum length. You get two checks instead of one.

Defining data types

In most cases, you can define a maximum length for the input a user will provide and in some cases you can define a minimum length as well. These limits will reduce the chance of getting a virus or a break-in on your Web server, but they aren't always convenient. For example, you might want the user to provide an opinion that could exceed the limits you set. When this problem occurs, you can set a high limit and further reduce the chance of problems by defining a data type. In fact, defining a data type also comes in handy for ensuring the user provides the right kind of data, such as when you need numeric input.

Unfortunately, you can't add any attributes to an HTML tag to check for data type, so you need to use a script. To add a data type checking script to your Web page, follow these steps:

1. **Right-click the control and choose Form Field Properties from the context menu.**

2. **Click Verify.**

You see the control Validation dialog box shown in Figure 7-1.

3. **Choose one of the options from the Data Type field.**

These options include

- **Text:** The user can enter specific kinds of text such as letters, spaces, digits, and special characters. You define the characters the user can input.

- **Integer:** The user can enter only integer values — a whole number without any decimal part.

- **Number:** The user can enter an integer or a real number (one that has a decimal part).

Whenever you set a data type constraint, make sure you include a default value for the field that shows what you expect the user to provide. Include a default value that is the most common value or a default value that you never expect the user to provide. The benefit of the first approach is that you save the user time and effort. However, some users will simply leave the default value even when another value is better. Using the sample you never expect the user to provide makes it possible to check for changes to ensure the user has input a proper value.

Working with text

The Text data type provides the most flexibility in allowing the user to enter information on a Web page. When you select this option, FrontPage changes the control Validation dialog box as shown in Figure 7-2. Notice that the Text Format options are enabled and that the form specifies a maximum field length to ensure the user doesn't input too much data.

The user can type any letter or add a space in this case. However, the user can't type sentences because the field won't allow it. To allow sentences that end with a period, question mark, or exclamation point, you select Other and type these values into the associated field. The user can't type any numbers in this case because they aren't allowed either. Make sure you test out a constraint before you make it active to ensure the user can type needed information without exposing your Web site to bad input.

As another example, you might want to allow the user to input a telephone number. In this case, you select Digits and Other. Type the common additions for telephone numbers, including (,), and -, in the Other field. This technique ensures that the user can type only telephone-like information, but doesn't assure you get a telephone number. A user could simply type

0123456789 and the field would accept it. In short, you can keep the data clean using this technique, but it doesn't ensure that the user provides valid information.

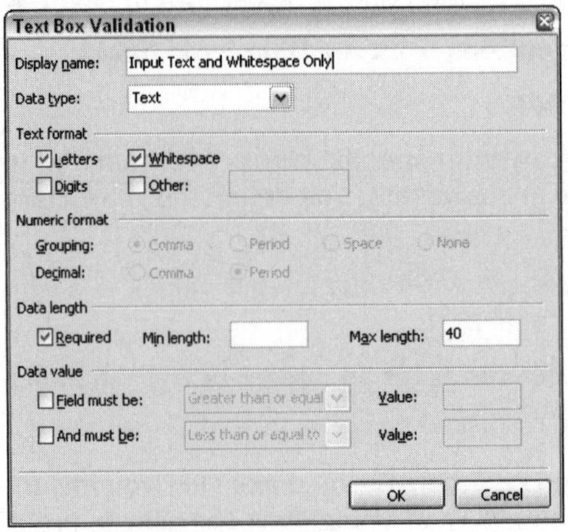

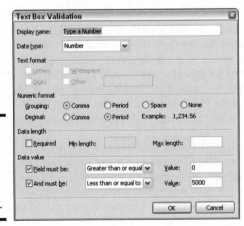

Figure 7-2:
Use the text data type for maximum flexibility.

Working with numbers

Numbers are more flexible than integers because you can enter decimal values such as 1.1. When you select Number as the data type, FrontPage enables the Numeric Format options as shown in Figure 7-3. These options define which characters are allowed in a specific position within the input. Using the current settings, a value of 5,000.0 is acceptable, but 5.000,0 isn't (the Web page would display an error). The special characters are also positional. The user can't type a number such as 50,00.0 because the comma isn't in the right place. The formatting you choose doesn't affect the user's ability to enter the number without formatting — typing 5000.0 is acceptable in all cases.

Figure 7-3:
Define the style of numeric input you can accept.

When working with numbers, you should either set a minimum and maximum field length, or better yet, define the acceptable numeric range. Figure 7-3 also shows how to set the Data Value options. In this case, the field will accept values between 0 and 5,000.

Working with integers

Integers are very restricted when compared to the other data types, but that's what makes them so useful from a security perspective. Use Integer whenever you expect the user to input a value such as 1 and don't want any other kinds of values. For example, you might ask the user how many telephones she owns. No one can own 1.5 telephones, so eliminate this value as a possible response by using the Integer data type.

As with the Number type, FrontPage enables the Grouping options. However, it doesn't enable the Decimal options because the user can't type a decimal with this data type. You also want to provide a valid range of inputs with an Integer to ensure you maintain full control over the input.

Enforcing specific data inputs

The best way to ensure the user provides only the data you want is to limit the responses to those that you expect by using a drop-down list box, checkboxes, or option buttons. All these techniques have one thing in common: They limit the number of choices the user has, as a way of preventing unexpected input. Each of these approaches offers advantages:

✦ Option buttons allow only one choice out of the options provided, so they're very explicit; a cracker would have a hard time passing a script or other unexpected input as part of an option-button field. The option button has a single validation feature; you can require the user to make a choice. However, when you set one of the options as the default option, the user makes a choice automatically, so validation isn't required.

✦ Checkboxes let the user choose one or more choices from a list of selections, so you can get more than one value as input, but only the values you expect. You don't have any validation options with a checkbox because none are needed — the user can't make an invalid selection. Both checkboxes and option buttons let the user see all available choices, so they let the user make a choice quickly. Unfortunately, both options also require considerable room, so they aren't the best options when you need to display a lot of options.

✦ The drop-down list box provides a wealth of options (as shown in Figure 7-4), so you need to set it up carefully. You create two or more options as part of the initial setup. (Theoretically, you can create just one option, but then you should probably use a checkbox instead.)

A drop-down list box can act as an option button or as a checkbox-type selector. Setting Allow Multiple Selections to Yes creates a checkbox-type selector.

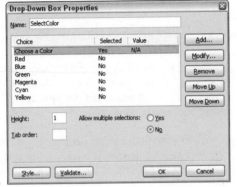

Figure 7-4:
Create various effects using the Drop-Down Box options.

You control two aspects of validation with a drop-down list box. The first is Data Required. This option forces the user to make a choice. The second is Disallow First Choice. Use this option when the first selection is an indicator of what the user should do, rather than an actual option.

Recognizing data patterns

Data patterns reflect the way data is formed. For example, when you see (555) 555-1212, you know that it's a type of telephone number. The pattern defines the kind of data displayed. Of course, people use many other forms of telephone numbers, and not every telephone number is 7 digits long with an optional 3-digit area code. People who live somewhere other than the United States could have any number of digits in the telephone number. The point is that every telephone number has some kind of pattern that you can detect.

FrontPage doesn't have a native capability for data-pattern recognition. However, you can still use data patterns on a Web page without resorting to scripting. The secret is to break down the pattern into something FrontPage can work with and that won't confuse the user.

Creating a data pattern for phone numbers

In the case of a United States telephone number, you can break the problem down into three groups: the area code, the prefix, and the suffix.

To create the data pattern, create three text boxes, each with a specific length. The area code might be optional, so you could set the length to 3 but not specify a minimum length. The *prefix* — the three-digit number that identifies a dialing area — is always required, so you can set the minimum and maximum length to 3. Likewise, the *suffix* (the actual telephone number) is always four digits, so you can give it a maximum *and* minimum length of 4. All three values are digits, so you can choose that text constraint to control the user's input.

Using hidden input to unify the phone number

The only problem with this approach is that you now have three numbers sent to the server as input. At some point, you must combine the individual elements so you can use them as a telephone number. One of the methods you can use to perform this task is to create a hidden input on the page. To create hidden input, follow these steps:

1. **Right-click the page and choose Form Properties.**

2. **Click Advanced and you see the Advanced Form Properties dialog box.**

3. **Click Add.**

    FrontPage asks you for the name of a hidden input.

4. **Type the name in the Name field and a default value in the Value field.**

5. **Click OK.**

    FrontPage adds the hidden input. You won't see this hidden input anywhere except in Code view. (But then, that's the idea.)

After you create the hidden input, add a script to support it. Place this script in the header of the page. It doesn't have to be complicated. Here's a typical example:

```
<script language=javascript>
    function GetTelephone()
    {
        // Update the hidden input so it contains the telephone
        // number.
        MyForm.txtCombinedTelephone.value =
            "(" + MyForm.txtAreaCode.value +
            ")" + MyForm.txtPrefix.value +
            "-" + MyForm.txtSuffix.value;
    }
</script>
```

This script takes the values of the three fields the user can see and adds them to the hidden input. Each of these inputs appears on the `MyForm` form, so that's the first piece of information used to access the input. You supply the name of the input next, followed by the `value` property, which is a means of accessing the value of the input. The code also adds special formatting characters. The resulting output looks like a standard telephone number, `(555)555-1212`.

To get the final form of the input, create a connection between the area code, prefix, and suffix inputs and the script so the hidden input is updated. Here's one of the tags used in the example:

```
<input type="text" name="AreaCode" size="3" id="txtAreaCode"
       value="555" maxlength="3" onchange="GetTelephone()">
```

FrontPage makes all but one of the entries for you automatically. You add the onchange attribute. Whenever the user changes the field, the Web server calls the GetTelephone() script to update the hidden input.

Tracking Security Problems

Assume that someone is going to break your application and overcome all your defenses — because, in the real world, someone almost certainly will. Patching your system does help. Building robust applications really does reduce the chance that someone will find the tiny chink in your application armor. However, the best defense against crackers is monitoring — keeping an eye on your system, knowing how it works, and keeping track of inconsistencies. Careful monitoring helps you locate and deter crackers.

FrontPage can help you achieve this goal. The various reports not only help you monitor the Web site, they also help you create a view of system security. For example, you can check the Recently Added Files report to see which files have been uploaded to the Web site. When you see a new file by George added to the advertising section of the Web site — and you happen to know that George works in accounting — that's a cue that you need to perform additional investigation. In fact, any new or updated file is suspect. Make sure you check the validity of each file.

Another report that provides clues is the Hyperlinks report. Look for unverified hyperlinks. Sometimes a cracker will send users on your site to another location — one with content of dubious value. A hyperlink that you didn't or can't verify always requires checking anyway to ensure the Web page will work as anticipated.

Sometimes a cracker will try to plant software on your system using a modified component. The cracker hopes you won't notice the change; after all, the component is "supposed to" be on the system. Often the modified components display errors that you can detect by using the Component Errors report. When a component suddenly experiences errors after working correctly for a long time, that's a signal to check it as a possible source of infection.

You can use FrontPage to monitor certain kinds of cracker activity, but the protection afforded by FrontPage isn't complete. You also need to choose other monitoring aids. For example, FrontPage doesn't monitor or protect the files on your server's hard drive, so you need to use other applications to perform this task. The idea is that FrontPage provides one more tool in a complete security toolbox. Use an array of tools to cross check areas of your system for possible entry.

But other Windows tools exist, and should be used. For example, when you suspect a user account is compromised, add an audit check to it. The user sees nothing, but the Event Log contains entries that show when the user logs in and out. By monitoring these times and verifying them with your users, you can often detect crackers at work.

Book V

Databases

"Your database is beyond repair, but before I tell you our backup recommendation, let me ask you a question. How many index cards do you think will fit on the walls of your computer room?"

Contents at a Glance

Chapter 1: Creating Interactive Web Pages with Excel

In This Chapter

✔ Working with Excel as a database

✔ Defining a connection to Excel

✔ Using various controls with Excel data

Databases have many things in common. Although freeform databases exist, most databases are organized in some way. The most common organization is the the kind found in relational databases, which relies on records and fields arranged as tables of data. These tables are often related to each other in some way by using common fields. For example, an invoice database could relate an order table and an items table using the customer ID. Using Excel, you can create a specialized kind of database called the flat-file database. A flat-file database is actually less capable than a relational database because it does not allow you to create multiple tables and relate them in some way. For example, a relational database might contain two tables, one for the customer identification and another for customer orders and relate them through a customer ID number. However, flat-file databases are very easy to understand and use for tasks that don't require multiple tables.

As in a relational database, Excel's flat-file databases allow you to create relatively simple tables consisting of *records* (rows) and *fields* (columns). These tables can contain multiple data types and allow you to perform tasks such as sorting the data. Unlike relational databases, however, an Excel flat-file database lacks flexibility. For example, although you can create complex relations between multiple Excel tables, you must provide code to perform the task, rather than rely on Excel to do it for you. True relational databases can create multiple relations between tables automatically.

Excel does stand out in an area that most relational databases don't, however: data analysis. Using Excel, you can not only create tables of data, but also manipulate that data in various ways. You can perform a *what-if analysis* to see what happens when you change one data element in a certain way, solve complex problems with the careful use of formulas, and create different views of the data based on specific input criteria. So, although Excel doesn't offer a perfect database, it does have special features.

FrontPage includes features that help you make the best use of Excel — as both a database and an analysis tool. In fact, Excel provides capabilities that can handle the data that FrontPage generates automatically — for example, compiling the output of forms that users submit on your Web site. Consequently, it's a good idea to know how to combine FrontPage and Excel into a cohesive whole.

Defining Excel as a Database

Most people see Excel as a spreadsheet. It does work best in that capacity. However, Excel also has powerful database capabilities. Microsoft has built more database features into Excel with each version of the product. Early versions of Excel could define a simple kind of database — columns headed with names, and record entries to fill the columns with data — but why stop there? Newer versions of Excel include a wealth of commands for importing, exporting, and manipulating data in various ways. You find all those entries on the Data menu shown in Figure 1-1.

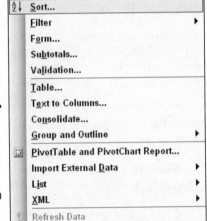

Figure 1-1: Excel 2003 provides a broad range of data-manipulation options.

Understanding Excel database functionality

Database functionality is a measure of what a database management system (DBMS) can do for you. Excel provides a number of standard flat-file database tools. You can sort the data and filter it. Filtering is especially important with long lists of data because it helps you see just the important information and disregard everything else without actually changing the data.

Excel 2003 includes a number of other interesting features, such as the ability to group information, as shown in Figure 1-2. Grouping is a feature you won't find in any database, yet it's consistent with database analysis features that Excel provides. A group can include any set of like data. For example, you could group a list of books by author. You can also outline data. An outline helps you organize data in a top-down fashion so you only see the level of detail you actually need. For example, a sales report could show just the totals, or it could show the information used to create the totals to any level of detail supported by the spreadsheet.

Analysis is the primary feature of using Excel as a database. You can create lists that make it easier to sort and filter the data. Pivot tables make creating special reports easier because you can see the data results as a table. Excel 2003 can export data as eXtensible Markup Language (XML), so you can view it directly within a Web page and modify the data views using techniques such as eXtensible Style Language Transformation (XSLT).

It's also possible to import data for use in a database from a surprising number of sources using Excel 2003. For example, you can head to a Web site, select a table, and import it into your existing worksheet. To import a table from a Web site, select Data➪Import External Data➪New Web Query. Type the URL for the Web site containing the table in the Address field. You see the Web page and associated tables. Select the table and click Import. You can see an example of an imported Web page table on the Web Page Table tab of the `SampleData.xls` file found in the source code for this chapter on the Wiley Web site.

Some Web services, such as the one provided by Amazon.com, even provide enough information so you can make a query and import it into Excel as a database. To try out this Web service feature for yourself, follow these steps:

1. Select Data➪Import External Data➪New Web Query.

You see the New Web Query dialog box.

2. Type this into the Address field and click Go:

```
http://xml.amazon.com/onca/xml3?t=webservices-20&dev-t=Your-Developer-
    Token&AuthorSearch=John%20Mueller&mode=books&type=lite&page=1&f=xml
```

Excel queries Amazon for the data.

3. When you see the document appear in the window, click Import.

You see the Import Data dialog box.

4. Select a location for the data and click OK.

Figure 1-3 shows typical results from this query. You can also see the results on the Amazon Web Services Query tab of the `SampleData.xls` file found in the source code for this chapter on the Wiley Web site. Now that you have the data in Excel, you can easily create a link to it in FrontPage.

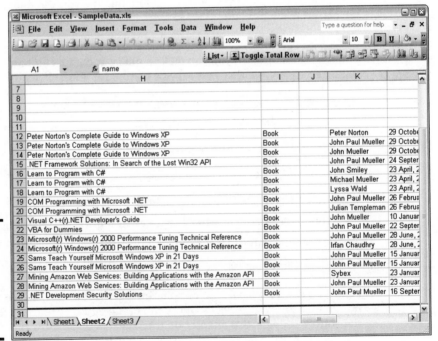

Figure 1-2:
Use groups
and outlines
to organize
Excel data.

Figure 1-3:
Import Web
services
data into
Excel, then
display it in
FrontPage.

The query you created, in this case, includes several variables that are unique to Amazon Web Services. The most important argument, in this case, is AuthorSearch. This entry tells which author to search for. If you really want to work with Amazon Web Services, you should download the required kit from http://www.amazon.com/gp/aws/landing.html/ref=sd_str_as_ws/. My book, *Mining Amazon Web Services* also contains a wealth of information about this topic.

Working with FrontPage data

FrontPage stores data in a Comma Separated Value (CSV) file. The default settings for a FrontPage form place the data a user creates in the _private folder that appears directly below the main folder for your Web site. For example, the output from any forms you create will appear in the _private folder by default in the form_results.csv file. The examples in this chapter use the SecurityCheckOut.csv file provided with the source code for this chapter on the Wiley Web site.

You should use the _private folder to store Web page data for security reasons because this folder isn't accessible to outside parties. A cracker can't come along and use a browser to view the data you receive from other visitors to your site. You change the default output by right-clicking the form and choosing Form Properties from the context menu. You see the Form Properties dialog box shown in Figure 1-4.

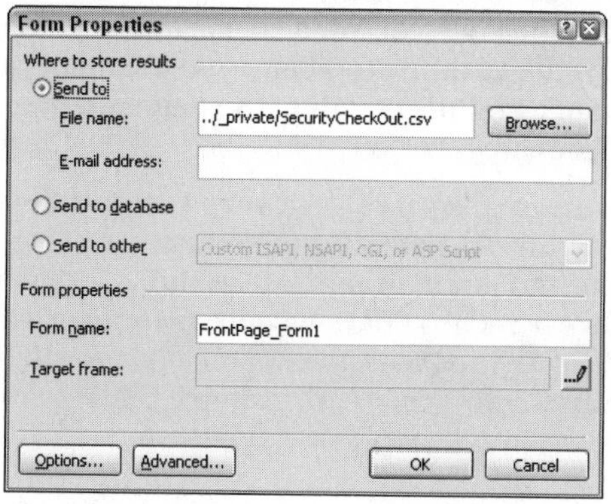

Figure 1-4:
Create a different file for each form on your Web site.

Modify the File Name field to point to a new file. The file always has a CSV extension. You use a separate file for each form on your site so that it's easy to retrieve the data and analyze it. Excel offers great analysis features, but you can use a database such as Access, MySQL, or SQL Server when you want traditional storage capabilities.

Normally, you view the CSV file as text in FrontPage by double-clicking the file. However, FrontPage lacks analysis capability and it's very hard to perform tasks such as sorting the data. A better option is to use Excel to view, edit, and manage the data as needed, even when you eventually display it on a Web page. To open the file in Excel, right-click the file in the Folder List and choose Open With⇨Microsoft Office Excel from the context menu. Excel opens the file and displays it as a table. You can now use any Excel feature to work with the data.

Developing simple tables

You can either create your data in Excel or import data from another application — but Excel won't recognize your data as a table unless you follow some specific rules:

✦ **The first row of data always contains the field names.** The actual data doesn't start until the second row. When you fail to observe this first rule, you find that manipulating the data is much harder and some features won't work.

✦ **You have to provide data entries for every field of every row.** An empty (or *null*) entry can cause problems with some Excel features. If you put a nonentry (such as N/A or 0) in some fields, Excel is at least satisfied that there's something in there, and keeps working.

✦ **The spreadsheet must contain a named range of cells that act as the database.** Make sure you include the field names in the range. To create a named range, select the cells you want to use as the database and click the Name Box field of the Formula toolbar. Type the name you want to use for the named range and press Enter. The named range can't include any spaces or special characters.

✦ **A database table is always "square" — every row has the same number of columns.** You can't create a table that has some optional entries in some fields and not in others. Make sure every field contains just one value and every record contains entries for every field. The `SampleData.xls` file provided with the source code for this chapter on the Wiley Web site shows how to create a simple table on the Simple Table tab.

Creating Links to an Excel Worksheet

You can create links to Excel using a number of techniques. How you go about it depends on the output you expect Excel to provide — and the level of interactivity the user requires. The most straightforward linking mechanism relies on creating a database link. This technique works with a number of Microsoft database products, including Excel, Access, and SQL Server.

Defining a new connection

You must create a new connection at least once while using FrontPage. A new connection can use any Excel file. The following steps describe how to create an Excel link:

1. **Choose the Insert➪Database➪Results command.**

You see the Database Results Wizard dialog box shown in Figure 1-5. FrontPage provides support for both ASP and ASP.NET scripts when working with database connections. Only use the ASP.NET option when you have the .NET Framework installed on the server. Excel only supports two connection modes. You can use an existing database connection or you can create a new database connection.

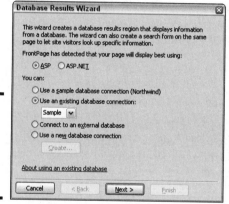

Figure 1-5:
Select a
scripting
type and
connection
mode.

2. **Choose Use a New Database Connection and then click Create.**

FrontPage displays the Database tab of the Site Settings dialog box.

3. **Click Add.**

You see the New Database Connection dialog box shown in Figure 1-6.

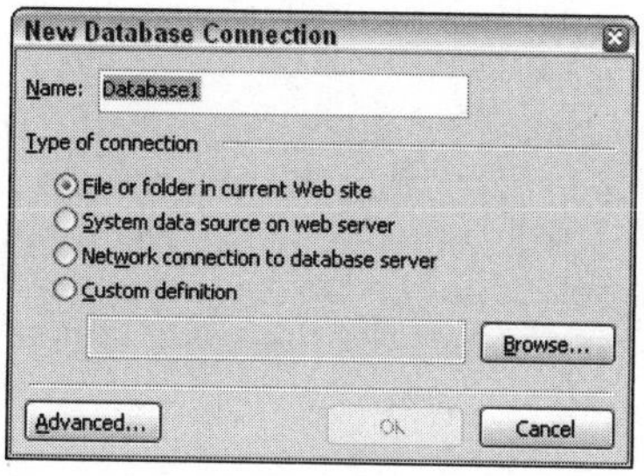

Figure 1-6:
Create a
new
connection
to the Excel
spread-
sheet.

4. Type the connection name in the Name field. Choose File or Folder in Current Web Site. Click Browse.

You see the Database Files in Current Web Site dialog box. FrontPage assumes you want to use an Access database.

5. Change the file view by selecting Microsoft Excel Driver (*.xls) in the File of Type field. Select the file you want to use. Click OK.

FrontPage displays the URL to the Excel spreadsheet in the New Database Connection dialog box. This field appears directly beneath the Custom Definition option in Figure 1-6.

6. Click OK.

FrontPage adds the new connection to the Database tab of the Site Settings dialog box.

You should verify this connection to ensure that it works as anticipated. In some cases, you need to provide a username and password or modify other settings to make the connection work.

7. Click Verify.

FrontPage validates the connection and places a green checkmark next to it.

8. Click OK.

You see the Database Results Wizard dialog box. FrontPage automatically changes the selection to Use an Existing Database Connection and selects the connection you just created.

9. Select Use an Existing Database Connection if FrontPage hasn't already done so. Choose the connection you want to use. Click Next.

FrontPage requests information about the record source you want to use.

10. Select Record Source. Choose a named range from the list of named ranges presented under the Record Source option. Click Next.

FrontPage displays a list of fields for the named range, as shown in Figure 1-7. If you don't see the list of fields or the list is incorrect, stop. Click Cancel.

11. Verify that the named range is correct in your Excel spreadsheet.

To do so, choose Insert➪Database➪Results to display the Database Results Wizard, and start again at Step 9 in this procedure. FrontPage assumes you want to use all fields in the named range. If you don't, then click Edit List to change the fields that FrontPage displays. Click More Options when you want to filter or sort the data as it comes from Excel.

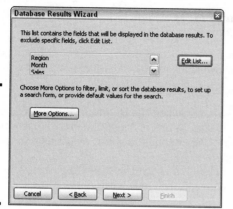

Figure 1-7:
Define the
way you
want to
use the
database
information.

12. **Click Next.**

FrontPage asks how you want to display the data. You can choose from a
table, a list, or a drop-down list. When using a list or drop-down list, you
can select only one field from those chosen from the named range.

13. **Select a presentation format (the example uses the table) and click
Next.**

FrontPage asks how you want to group the records. You can choose to
display all of the records together or split them into group of specific
record numbers. Using the grouping option for larger tables does make
it easier for the user to locate data, but it also splits up the presentation.

14. **Choose a presentation and click Finish.**

FrontPage adds the view to the current Web page. At this point, FrontPage
will tell you to save the file and change the extension to ASP or ASPX (if
you haven't done so already) so the table works as expected.

After you create the new table and save the resulting page with either an ASP
or ASPX extension (depending on whether you used ASP or ASP.NET), you
can view it using a standard browser. The Preview view won't work because
FrontPage doesn't provide ASP support in this view.

Using an existing connection

When you already use an Excel spreadsheet on an existing page, you create a
link to the existing connection, rather than create a new one. Use an existing
connection whenever possible to reduce clutter, improve performance,
decrease memory requirements, and lessen the chance of connecting to an
old spreadsheet. To use an existing connection, choose Insert➪Database➪
Results to display the Database Results Wizard and follow Steps 9 through 14
of the "Defining a new connection" section of the chapter.

Modifying a connection

You can modify the database connection at any time. To start the process, right-click the table entry anywhere and choose Database Results Properties. FrontPage warns you that you'll reenter the Database Results Wizard and will have to make all the same entries you did before.

What actually happens is that you see the Database Results Wizard with all the selections you made earlier in place. All you need to do is follow the same steps as before and make changes to these previous entries.

One of the more common changes you make is when you click More Options after selecting the fields you want to view. You see the More Options dialog box shown in Figure 1-8.

Figure 1-8:
Customize
the output of
the Web
page to
match
specific
criteria.

Customizing the Web page output is what you do to ensure that your user sees just the required information and doesn't have to wait around for nonessential information. Here are five changes you can make:

✦ **Criteria:** Creates a filter for the results. To add a filter, click Criteria. You see the Criteria dialog box. Click Add. Select a field to use for the filter in the Field Name field. Choose an evaluation, such as equals, from the Comparison field. Finally, type the actual criterion in the Value field. The Value field entry must appear in the associated field or provide a comparison value that ASP can make. For example, you could look for all fields with values less than 10.

✦ **Ordering:** Modifies the order in which items are sorted on the page. To make a change, click Ordering. You see the Ordering dialog box. Highlight the first sort field and click Add. (You can add as many fields as needed.) Remove fields by highlighting the field name and clicking Remove. Click Change Sort to alternate between an ascending or descending sort order for a particular field.

✦ **Limit Number of Returned Records:** Determines the maximum number of returned records. No matter how well you define the connection and database query, the result set can be huge. Online connections aren't well suited to downloading huge amounts of data, so you set this field to a reasonable number of records. You don't necessarily want to send all the data to the user — just the most recent data.

✦ **Message to Display if No Records are Returned:** Defines what to display when a query doesn't return any records (although, you should test for this problem). The generic message that FrontPage provides will work, in many cases, but you might want to provide a special message that tells the user what to do about the problem. For example, the message could include the e-mail address of the administrator responsible for providing the data.

✦ **Defaults:** This entry works only when you have SharePoint Services installed on the server. You see the Defaults dialog box which lets you set the entries for a search form. This dialog box also lets you define the entries a user can provide when setting up a table into which the user can enter data.

Viewing Excel Data

FrontPage provides a number of Web components that help you access Excel data directly. You use these components to access and modify data in the Excel spreadsheet. The features that the user sees depend on how the Web component is configured. To access the Web component, follow these steps:

1. **Choose Insert➪Web Component.**

You see the Insert Web Component dialog box.

2. **Choose Spreadsheets and Charts in the Component Type list.**

You see the list of controls shown in Figure 1-9.

3. **Make selections that fit your users' needs.**

When opening a Web page in FrontPage that contains Web components that access a data source such as Excel, you might see a message asking whether it's OK to open the file using your *credentials* (name and password). This feature helps you recognize any unauthorized attempts to access a data source on an untrusted site. You can click Yes for local servers and servers you trust with complete safety. FrontPage normally displays one message for every Web component that relies on a data source. Consequently, you see a minimum of two messages when you have a spreadsheet and chart on the same Web page.

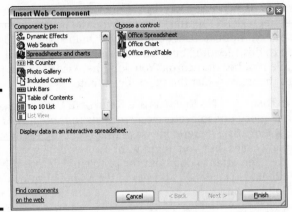

Figure 1-9:
Choose
a Web
component
for
interacting
with Excel.

The advantage of using the display technique in this section is that the user has complete control over the data — at least locally. The user can change spreadsheet data, for example, directly on the Web page. Using this technique, the user can create what-if scenarios and save them to the local machine. Although the user can't change the remote data, the local changes can provide input for meetings or discussions between client and vendor.

Creating an ActiveX control connection

Both the Office Spreadsheet and the Office PivotTable controls rely on database connections you create. It's also possible to create a connection for the Office Chart control. You can interact with the Office Spreadsheet control using other techniques, such as importing the data, but you want to create a database connection to provide full spreadsheet support. The following steps describe how to create a connection for both the Office Spreadsheet and Office PivotTable controls:

1. **Right-click the control and choose ActiveX Control Properties from the context menu.**

You see the ActiveX Control Properties dialog box.

2. **Select the Data Source tab. Click Edit.**

You see the Select Data Source dialog box. When you see the data source you want to use in this dialog box, select it and click Open. Proceed to step 9.

3. **Highlight Connect to New Data Source.odc and click Open.**

You see the Data Connection Wizard dialog box. This wizard lets you connect to a vast array of data sources. For example, you can create a connection to MySQL using an Open Database Connectivity (ODBC) connection when you have the correct drivers installed on your system. For MySQL, use the MyODBC software found at

`http://dev.mysql.com/downloads/connector/odbc/3.51.html`

The default drivers include support for all Office applications, SQL Server, Microsoft Business Services, dBASE, and Oracle.

4. **Select ODBC DSN and click Next.**

   FrontPage displays a list of ODBC drivers and predefined Data Source Names (DSNs). When you see the connection you need defined as a DSN, select the connection and follow the prompts provided by that ODBC driver. Proceed to Step 6.

5. **Select Excel Files and click Next.**

   You see a Select Workbook dialog box. ODBC assumes you want to create a local connection or a connection to a networked drive. However, a Web component requires an Internet connection.

6. **Locate the workbook and click OK.**

   You see the Select Database and Table dialog box shown in Figure 1-10. This dialog box helps you select the content for the Web component. Clear Connect to a Specific Table when you want to display the entire spreadsheet. Otherwise, the list of tables includes entire tabs within the spreadsheet, named ranges, and other special features such as pivot tables.

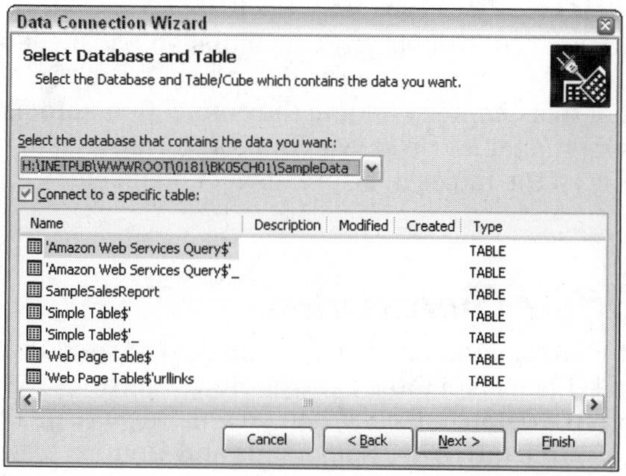

Figure 1-10:
Determine
whether you
want a
single table
or the entire
spread-
sheet.

7. **Select a table or clear Connect to a Specific Table. Click Next.**

   You see the Save Data Connection dialog box.

8. **Type a description in the Description field. Type special terms you can use for searches in the Search Keywords field. Click Finish.**

You see the Select Data Source dialog box.

9. **Choose the connection, unless it's already selected. Click Open.**

When the connection refers to the whole spreadsheet, you see a Select Table dialog box. Select a table and click OK. You see the Data Source tab of the ActiveX Controls dialog box. The Command Text or SQL field content of this dialog box is normally incorrect, so you have to create the correct SQL command.

10. **Type a particular SQL command in the** Command Text **or** SQL **field and then click OK.**

For example, the sample database uses a command of SELECT "SampleSalesReport".* FROM "SampleSalesReport". When you've entered the command, FrontPage displays the data on-screen.

The SQL command portion of the configuration is indispensable. Normally the SQL command is for selecting an entire table or a named range within that table — and the SELECT command specifies what to choose. In the case of the sample, you select the entire named range using "SampleSalesReport".*. You could select specific fields by including just the field name. For example, "SampleSalesReport"."Region" selects just the Region field. The FROM portion of the command tells where to obtain the information. In this case, FrontPage obtains it from the named range, SampleSalesReport.

Using the Office Spreadsheet control

The Office Spreadsheet control displays an actual spreadsheet on the Web page. (You configure it using the process described in the "Creating a connection" section of this chapter.) Adding the connection automatically displays the data from the table you select. You can create as many connections as needed to show all the tables in a spreadsheet. Each entry appears on a separate tab.

Using the Office Chart control

The Office Chart control normally relies on the data located in an Office Spreadsheet or an Office PivotTable control. However, you can create a direct connection to a database too. When you initially create the control, you see the Data Source tab of the Commands and Options dialog box. You can also display this dialog box by right-clicking the control and choosing Data from the context menu. Select the Data from a Database Table or Query option and click Connection. (Use the instructions in the "Creating a connection" section to create a connection to the table and close the Commands and Options dialog box.) The Office Chart control doesn't appear to contain any information, but it does have blanks into which you can drag and drop selected fields.

To add fields to the Office Chart control, right-click the control and choose Field List from the context menu. You see a Chart Field List dialog box, as shown in Figure 1-11. This figure also shows the areas where you drag and drop the fields. Each of these areas appears as a grayed-out square.

Creating the chart isn't difficult, but you have to plan it out. Here's the drill:

1. **Define the X-axis data by selecting a field.**

The example uses the `Region` field to define the X-axis data.

2. **Drag your chosen field from the Chart Field List dialog box to the Office Chart control, and drop it there.**

When you add the field, FrontPage assumes you want to use all possible entries.

3. **For each entry you want, click the arrow next to the entry.**

You see a list of regions. Choose only the regions you want to see on-screen. They will form your X-axis.

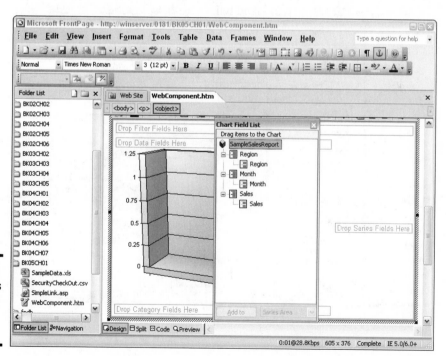

Figure 1-11:
Select fields you want to use for the chart.

4. **Add the Y-axis field.**

Drag the field from the Chart Field List dialog box to the Office Chart control. Again, choose only the entries you want to use.

5. **Add the data to the chart.**

At this point, you should finally see a display of the data.

6. **Adjust the chart type and the two axis selections as needed to create the display you want.**

Figure 1-12 shows typical results, including a list of regions for the current table.

Using the Office PivotTable control

The Office PivotTable control requires that you create a connection to the database before you do anything else. (Use the process described in the "Creating a connection" section to perform this task.) After you have a connection in place, you'll notice that nothing happens — the Office PivotTable control is still blank.

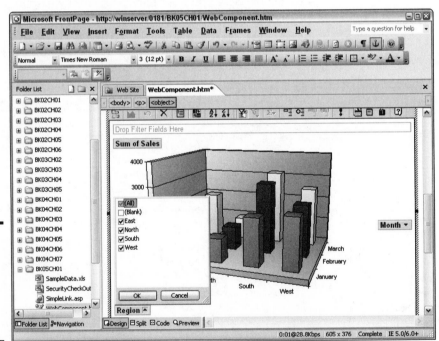

Figure 1-12:
Define
special
effects and
conditions
for your
chart.

To display data within the control, you must adds fields to it. Adding fields to a pivot table is a straightforward process:

1. **Right-click the control and choose Fields from the context menu that appears.**

   You see the PivotTable Field List dialog box.

2. **Drag and drop the fields from the PivotTable Field List dialog box to the Office PivotTable control, as shown in Figure 1-13.**

3. **Close the PivotTable Field List dialog box after you add all required fields.**

   The totals that appear aren't calculated for the table. To add totals to the Office PivotTable control, you must define the type of calculation to perform. The next steps do so.

4. **Right-click any cell that contains data.**

5. **Select Autocalc from the context menu.**

   You see a list of possible calculations for the totals.

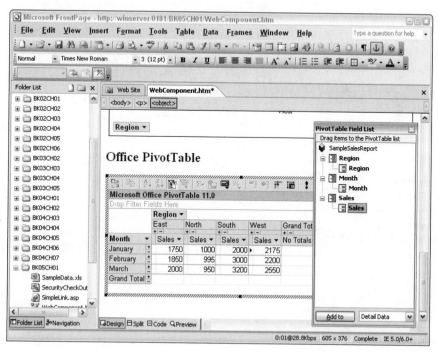

Figure 1-13:
Drag and
drop the
needed
fields on the
pivot table
as needed.

6. **Select one of the Autocalc menu options.**

   The example uses the Sum option. FrontPage calculates the totals, which adds a second line to each of the cells.

7. **To hide the extra information, click the - (minus) sign next to each of the field entries.**

   FrontPage hides the additional information. Figure 1-14 shows typical output for the Office PivotTable control.

8. **Click the arrows next to the Month and Region entries.**

   You see a list of entries for each field. You can choose to display all or just some of the fields on the Web page — making it easier for the user to see the data elements.

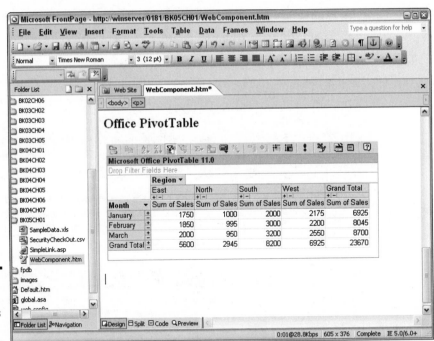

Figure 1-14: PivotTable output looks like this.

Chapter 2: Creating Interactive Web Pages with Access

In This Chapter

✔ Creating links to Access data

✔ Developing simple data views

✔ Working with search forms

✔ Developing views with more than one table

Many Web designers today store page content in databases to ease the process of updating their Web sites. With databases, it's easy to create an application that keeps the database content up to date automatically. Microsoft Access provides most of the relational capabilities that database developers require to create complex applications. It lacks some of the robust features of high-end databases, though, so many developers rely on Access to create local databases that only a few people use. Most developers agree that Access handles 10 users just fine, but you might not get good results when you go beyond that number. Even so, Access is often a perfect solution for a small business or a workgroup within a company.

One of the best parts about using Access is that it's a full-fledged *relational* solution; you don't have to use flat-file techniques (as you would with a spreadsheet). Access can create multiple indexes, multiple table setups, handle queries, and perform data manipulations with scripts.

It's also relatively easy to create reports with Access, which allows you to look at the data in its final form, and makes it unnecessary to modify the final data on the Web page or behind the scenes as part of a server-side script. The same data can act as input for multiple reports — and you can use multiple formats, from simple to complex and from friendly to formal. The idea is to present a view of the data that your user can understand and appreciate.

Developing Links to Access

As with most Database Management Systems (DBMS), you must create a link to the Access database to use it on a Web page. Although Access provides better display capabilities locally than many high end DBMS, you can't use those capabilities in any way on a Web page. (The local display capabilities are provided by design because Microsoft recognizes that some small businesses will use Access directly without any other means of displaying data.)

Choosing between ASP and ASP.NET

Before you can choose a connection type, you need to consider a connection strategy. FrontPage provides ASP and ASP.NET support for Access so you can choose the correct technology for your particular setup. While ASP offers ease of use and compatibility as features, ASP.NET tends to provide better processing speed and greater flexibility.

ASP.NET adds several layers of complexity to your Web site solution. The first layer is the .NET Framework. You download the .NET Framework from the Microsoft site at

```
http://www.microsoft.com/downloads/details.aspx?FamilyID=262d25e3-
    f589-4842-8157-034d1e7cf3a3
```

After you install the .NET Framework, you can run any .NET application, including those created for ASP.NET. This download provides only the .NET Framework, however — not the entire .NET development package.

When you want to develop simple ASP.NET applications, but don't want to buy the entire .NET development package, you can rely on a combination of FrontPage and a free development tool from Microsoft called Web Matrix, available at the following location:

```
http://www.asp.net/webmatrix/default.aspx
```

This tool provides much of what you need to create simple ASP.NET applications. Microsoft originally envisioned Web Matrix as an ASP.NET training tool, but it provides more functionality than many people need.

The second layer of complexity when using ASP.NET is that it can rely on multiple files to accomplish a task. Microsoft chose to separate the presentation of the Web page from the code with ASP.NET. The actual code is compiled — that way you gain a definite speed advantage over ASP. However, if you're a developer who must make changes to the Web page, the use of multiple files complicates matters because you have to look in more than one place to find what you need. The use of multiple files also makes applications harder to distribute and deploy.

When you develop applications for more than one party, ASP.NET isn't necessarily the best choice. Many companies have taken a hands-off approach to anything .NET, so your .NET application might not be very welcome with some companies. In this case, you want the most compatible solution, which is ASP. Every Internet Information Server (IIS) setup and many third party servers can run ASP pages, while ASP.NET requires special handling.

Along with higher processing speed, ASP.NET does provide more functionality. Even with the limited ASP.NET support that FrontPage provides, you can see a definite difference in two areas:

✦ **Presentation of data:** For example, you can make every other line a different color to ensure the user can track a single record entry without problem.

✦ **Usability:** For example, ASP.NET provides a broader range of control types. Even when ASP and ASP.NET have similar controls, the ASP.NET version tends to provide better functionality and performance.

Creating a new connection using the Database Results Wizard

The most common way to create a new connection to Access is to use the Database Results Wizard. You access the wizard by choosing the Insert⇨ Database⇨Results command. The Database Results Wizard dialog box shown in Figure 2-1 has options for creating new or using existing connections to your database. The dialog box also has options that let you choose between ASP and ASP.NET as the language for the Web page. Always provide an ASP file extension when working with ASP.

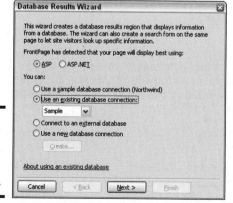

Figure 2-1:
Create a
new or use
an existing
connection.

You must have the .NET Framework installed to use ASP.NET. Download the .NET Framework at

```
http://www.microsoft.com/downloads/details.aspx?FamilyID=262d25e3-
    f589-4842-8157-034d1e7cf3a3
```

This version of the product lets you run any .NET application, including those found on ASP.NET pages. When working with ASP.NET, it's also important to give your Web pages an Active Server Pages eXtended (ASPX) file extension, rather than the ASP file extension used by standard ASP pages.

To begin the process of creating a link, follow these steps:

1. **Choose Use New Database Connection and click Create.**

   You see the Database tab of the Site Properties dialog box. This tab contains a list of the connections you define.

2. **Click Add.**

   You see the New Database Connection dialog box shown in Figure 2-2. It includes three general options for creating a link using Access: direct file, data source, or custom. The Network Connection to Database Server option requires SharePoint Services to use.

3. **After choosing how you want to create a link, type a name for the connection in the Name field.**

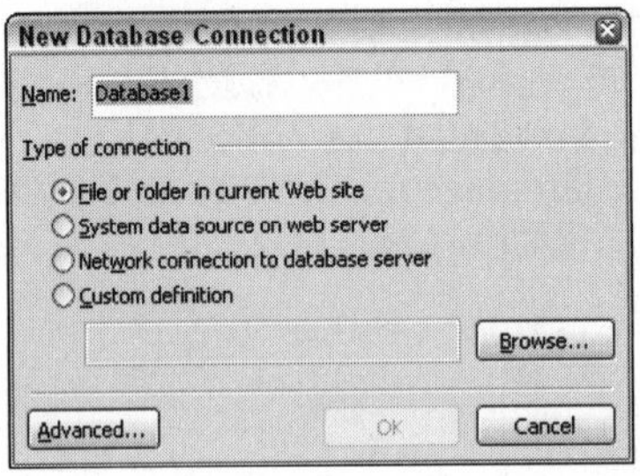

Figure 2-2:
Choose one of the connection types for your Access database.

After you create the new connection, you must select it for use. Use the steps in the "Selecting an existing connection" section (later in this chapter) to select the connection after using one of the following procedures to create the connection.

Defining a file link

The file-link connection works best when the Access database appears within the Web site. You can store the database in the _private folder to keep it safe from prying eyes, but the database must appear somewhere on the Web site to make this connection work properly. The file link is the easiest type to create and maintain. It doesn't require any odd connection arguments, and you don't have to worry about providing details that only a database administrator could love. Here's the drill for creating a file link:

1. **Choose File or Folder in Current Web Site in the New Database Connection dialog box and click Browse.**

You see the Database Files in Current Web Site dialog box.

2. **Locate the file you want to use, highlight it, and click OK.**

FrontPage displays the database connection information in the text box beneath the Custom Definition entry shown in Figure 2-2.

3. **Adjust any advanced settings and click OK.**

FrontPage adds the new connection to the Database tab of the Site Settings dialog box. To ensure that the connection works, you must verify it at this point.

4. **Click Verify.**

When the connection works, FrontPage changes the question-mark icon (next to the connection entry) to a check-mark icon.

5. **Click OK.**

FrontPage displays the Database Results Wizards dialog box. It automatically selects Use an Existing Database Connection and modifies the connection entry to the settings of the new connection you created. Proceed with the instructions in the "Selecting an existing connection" section of the chapter.

Defining a data source link

Use the data source link connection method when you need to create a connection to a database that resides somewhere other than the Web site. The database could even reside on another server. This connection provides enough flexibility that you can define some of the complex criteria used for connections such as timeout values and default passwords. To use this connection type, you must have access to the Data Sources (ODBC) applet in the Administrative Tools folder of the Control Panel (the precise location of this applet varies with the version of Windows you use). Open Database Connectivity (ODBC) is an older, but widely used, Microsoft technology for creating connections to databases of all types. The following steps show how to create a connection using a data source link and starts by using the Data Sources (ODBC) applet to define the connection properties:

1. **Double-click the Data Sources (ODBC) applet in the Administrative Tools folder of the Control Panel.**

You see the ODBC Data Source Administrator dialog box.

2. **Select the System DSN tab, and then click Add.**

You see a Create New Data Source dialog box that lists a number of database drivers. A Data Source Name (DSN) is a label attached to a set of instructions for connecting to a database. The use of a label makes it easy to reference the ODBC instructions.

3. **Highlight the Microsoft Access Driver (*.mdb) entry and click Finish.**

You see the ODBC Microsoft Access Setup dialog box shown in Figure 2-3. Note that every ODBC driver uses a different dialog box. The settings are similar to the one shown in Figure 2-3 but specifically designed to meet the needs of a particular DBMS.

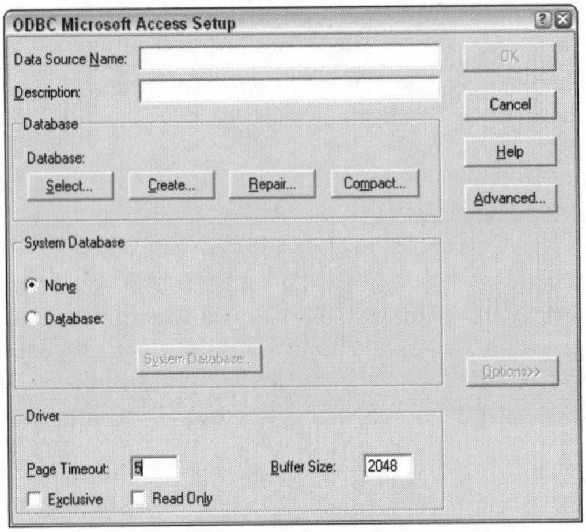

Figure 2-3:
Configure a System DSN connection to access the database.

4. **Type a name for the data source.**

Use a short name that's easy to remember and doesn't contain any spaces or special characters.

5. **Type a description in the description field.**

Make sure you provide enough information that you can identify the connection later.

6. **Click Select.**

You see a Select Database dialog box.

7. **Locate the database you want to use. Click OK.**

The Access ODBC driver adds the database to the Database group. The database connection is usable at this point.

8. **Click OK to add this connection to the ODBC Data Source Administrator (if desired).**

Note, however, that the Access ODBC driver provides a number of other configuration options you might want to try. For example, modifying the Buffer Size field can improve performance when the buffer matches a multiple of the database record size. It's also possible to cure some connection problems by modifying the Page Timeout value. Click Advanced when you want to set connection properties such as login name and password. Microsoft provides more information about the ODBC Data Source Administrator at

`http://msdn.microsoft.com/library/en-us/odbc/htm/dasdkodbcdatasourceadmin.asp`

Use the following steps to create a FrontPage connection for the DSN link:

1. **Choose System Data Source On Web Server in the New Database Connection dialog box. Click Browse.**

   You see the System Data Sources On Web Server dialog box. This dialog box should contain the connection created earlier in this section. Everything FrontPage needs to create the connection appears in the DSN you created.

2. **Choose the DSN you want to use and click OK.**

   FrontPage displays the database connection information in the text box beneath the Custom Definition entry shown in Figure 2-2.

   Don't click Advanced with this type of connection — rely on the information contained in the DSN instead.

3. **Click OK.**

   FrontPage displays the new connection on the Database tab of the Site Properties dialog box.

4. **Click Verify.**

   FrontPage checks the connection to the database. If this connection fails, don't modify the FrontPage settings — check the DSN settings on the server instead.

5. **Click OK.**

   FrontPage displays the Database Results Wizards dialog box. It automatically selects Use an Existing Database Connection and modifies the connection entry to the new connection you created. Proceed with the instructions in the "Selecting an existing connection" section of the chapter.

Creating a custom connection

The custom connection works best when using a Local Area Network (LAN) connection for a company intranet. (When working with local databases, use a file link or data source link.) You use a custom link to define special parameters for the database. In general, a custom connection can help you create specialized setups and use more database types than the standard connections do, but they're also a lot harder to set up. To use this connection type, you must have access to the Data Sources (ODBC) applet in the Administrative Tools folder of the Control Panel. The following steps show how to create a custom connection, using the Data Sources (ODBC) applet to define the connection properties.

1. **Double-click the Data Sources (ODBC) applet in the Administrative Tools folder of the Control Panel.**

You see the ODBC Data Source Administrator dialog box.

2. **Select the File DSN tab. Click Add.**

You see a Create New Data Source dialog box that lists a number of database drivers. A Data Source Name (DSN) is a label attached to a set of instructions for connecting to a database. The use of a label makes it easy to reference the ODBC instructions.

3. **Highlight the Microsoft Access Driver (*.mdb) entry and click Next.**

The Create New Data Source wizard asks you to provide a filename for the data source.

4. **Click Browse. Choose a location for the file DSN, type a name in the File Name field, and click Save.**

The Create New Data Source wizard places the file path and name in the field provided.

5. **Click Next.**

You see a summary of the connection information.

6. **Click Finish.**

You see an ODBC Microsoft Access Setup dialog box that looks similar to the one shown in Figure 2-3. The main difference is that the Data Source Name and Description fields are disabled because you can't provide this information as part of a file DSN.

7. **Click Select.**

You see a Select Database dialog box.

8. **Locate the database you want to use. Click OK.**

The Access ODBC driver adds the database to the Database group.

File DSNs have a lot of advantages over other types of DSNs. They reside in a file, so you can move them to other locations with ease. The contents of the file are simple text, so you can modify a file DSN whenever necessary using a simple text editor such as Notepad. It's also possible to modify the content of a file DSN using a script. For that matter, after you know what the DBMS is looking for, you can conceivably generate a file from scratch using a script. You can see a sample file DSN in the `AccessFileDSN.dsn` file provided with the source code for this chapter on this book's companion Web site.

Now that you have a file DSN to use, it's time to add the connection to FrontPage. The following steps show how:

1. **Copy the file DSN from the** `\Program Files\Common Files\ODBC\` `Data Sources` **folder on your server to a folder within your Web site.**

   You can use the `_private` folder to protect the file from prying eyes when necessary.

2. **Choose Custom Definition in the New Database Connection dialog box, and then click Browse.**

   You see the Connection Files in Current Web Site dialog box. Notice that this dialog box allows you to look only on the current Web site for the DSN file.

3. **Locate the DSN file you want to use and click OK.**

   FrontPage displays the database connection information in the text box beneath the Custom Definition entry shown in Figure 2-2. Don't click Advanced with this type of connection — rely on the information contained in the DSN instead.

4. **Click OK.**

   FrontPage displays the new connection on the Database tab of the Site Properties dialog box.

5. **Click Verify.**

   FrontPage checks the connection to the database. If this connection fails, don't modify the FrontPage settings — check the DSN settings in the DSN file instead.

6. **Click OK.**

   FrontPage displays the Database Results Wizards dialog box. It automatically selects Use an Existing Database Connection and modifies the connection entry to the new connection you created. Proceed with the instructions in the "Selecting an existing connection" section of this chapter.

Adding advanced properties to the connection

Normally, when working with a file connection, you set any advanced properties yourself — that's because the other connection types can incorporate these properties as part of the DSN setup. You can, however, use the advanced properties with any connection. Sometimes, a DSN must maintain a set of properties for existing applications; using advanced connection properties in this situation makes sense as an exception to the rule.

To access the advanced connection properties, click Advanced in the New Database Connection dialog box. You see the Advanced Connection Properties dialog box shown in Figure 2-4. One of the problems of using this technique is instantly shown: The dialog box doesn't contain any parameters you can change, except the common parameters that every database accepts. These common parameters include the username and password, and the connection and command timeout values. The timeout values are especially important. Make sure you set them high enough to ensure that clients aren't disconnected too early (before they get the data they need) — but also short enough so the connection or command doesn't continue to consume system resources.

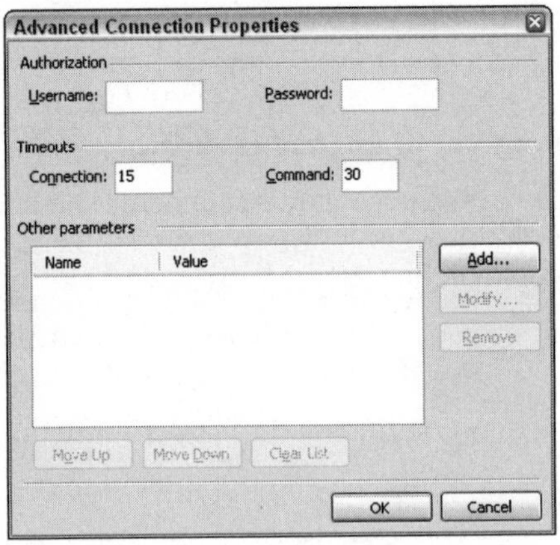

Figure 2-4: Modify the means of connecting to the database through properties.

Fortunately, there are only a few Access parameters that you want to change for a connection. You can find a fairly complete list of ODBC parameters at

```
http://msdn.microsoft.com/library/en-us/odbc/htm/odbcjetaccesssqlconfigdata-
    source.asp
```

Although Microsoft doesn't provide full documentation on this topic, the following list describes a few common parameters you can use to improve connection performance or provide other functionality:

✦ **ExtendedAnsiSql:** Enables extended ANSI SQL support in Access. Set this value to true (1) when you perform complex queries that could benefit from the extended ANSI SQL command set. When performing simple queries, such as a record request, set this value to false (0) to save memory and processing cycles.

✦ **MaxBufferSize:** Defines the size (in KB) of the buffer that Access uses to transfer data — you can use any value divisible by 256. (To improve performance, use large values for a database with big records.) This setting comes at the cost of higher memory usage, however, so you also need to consider system constraints such as available memory.

✦ **MaxScanRows:** Limits the number of rows that Access scans to determine the data type of a column based on its content. This parameter accepts any value between 0 and 16. Using a value of 0 means Access scans all rows, which can take a considerable amount of time. This setting is important only when you want to upload text data; you normally don't set it when using Access for data display.

✦ **PageTimeout:** Limits the time a page stays in the buffer without being used. The setting is in tenths of a second; the default value of 5 is 0.5 seconds. Because Internet connections are slower than those on your network, setting this value higher can often improve performance: A commonly used page isn't loaded and unloaded from the buffer as often, making the server more efficient.

✦ **ReadOnly:** Places the database in a read-only state. Setting this value to true (1) results in better performance on most Web sites because Access can optimize record fetches. In addition, using a read-only connection reduces security risks associated with the connection.

✦ **SafeTransactions:** Creates a safe environment for transferring data between the client and server. Normally you set this value to `false` (0) to reduce the overhead of record fetches when the database is in a read-only state. However, when the client actually uploads data to the server, you want to set this value to `true` (1) to ensure that the data arrives from the client in good condition.

✦ **Threads:** Defines the number of threads Access uses to process requests. Each request requires one thread, so using three threads (the default) means Access can process three requests at a time. Using more threads improves performance — especially when a Web site is used by a number of people, each of whom might make multiple requests. Adding threads uses more memory and additional processing cycles, so balancing system resources with user needs is important.

Tailoring these settings to your system is one clear route to greater efficiency. Here's how to change these parameters:

1. **After you select one or more properties for the connection, in the Advanced Connection Properties dialog box, click Add.**

You see the Add Parameter dialog box.

2. **Type the name of the parameter in the Name field and the value in the Value field.**

   Remember to use 1 for true and 0 for false.

3. **Click OK.**

   FrontPage adds the parameter to the Advanced Connection Properties dialog box.

4. **When you finish adding properties, click OK.**

   FrontPage displays the New Database Connection dialog box.

5. **Continue creating the connection.**

Just in case you're wondering where FrontPage stores all this connection information, look at the Global.asa file in the root folder of the Web site. This is a plain text file you can open in FrontPage. In some cases, you can create a script to read or manipulate the Global.asa file. Make sure you exercise extreme caution if you create such a script; even a small error can cause all the database connections on your Web site to fail.

Selecting an existing connection

When you already use an Access database on an existing page, you create a link to the existing connection, rather than create a new one. Use an existing connection whenever possible to reduce clutter, improve performance, decrease memory requirements, and lessen the chance of connecting to an old spreadsheet. The following steps show how to use an existing connection.

1. **Select Use an Existing Database Connection if FrontPage hasn't already done so. Choose the connection you want to use. Click Next.**

   FrontPage requests information about the record source you want to use. A record source can include an entire table, a query that you've defined, or a custom SQL statement.

2. **Select Record Source (individual tables or predefined queries) or Custom Query (complex queries using multiple tables). You have two possible approaches:**

   • When using Record Source, choose a table from the list of tables presented under the Record Source option.

   • When using a Custom Query, click Edit, type the SQL Statement that you want to use, click Verify to check the accuracy of the query, and click OK to create the query.

3. Click Next.

FrontPage displays a list of fields for the query, as shown in Figure 2-5. FrontPage assumes you want to use all of the fields in the query. You have two options:

- Click Edit List to change the fields FrontPage displays.

- Click More Options when you want to filter or sort the data as it comes from Access.

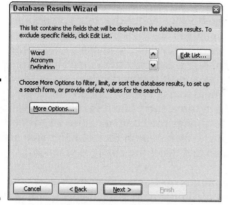

Figure 2-5:
Define the way you want to use the database information.

4. Click Next.

FrontPage asks how you want to display the data. You can choose from a table, a list, or a drop-down list. When using a list or drop-down list, you can select only one field from those chosen from the named range.

5. Select a presentation format (the example uses the table) and click Next.

FrontPage asks how you want to group the records. You can choose to display all of the records together or split them into groups of specific record numbers. Use the grouping option for larger tables to make it easier for the user to locate data, but also splits up the presentation.

6. Choose a record grouping method and click Finish.

FrontPage adds the view to the current Web page. At this point, FrontPage will tell you to save the file and change the extension to ASP or ASPX (if you haven't done so already) so the table works as expected.

Designing Simple Data Views

After you create a connection to the database, you want to create a view of the data. The formats FrontPage provides by default are adequate, but might not reflect the style you want to see on your Web site. (On the other hand, it might be all you need in some cases if you simply want to display the information as a table.) You can perform some simple changes to make the data appear differently or perform major surgery to create a unique presentation. The connection is just a starting point — a way for you to get the data on the page and then do something with it.

FrontPage makes some assumptions about the data you obtain from the database. First, the column names are the same as the field names in the database. The field names work only when you use a single word or you use spaces between words. Many database administrators use underlines between words, however, because it makes the field easier to work with in code. For example, a date field to use the last update for an entry might appear as `Last_Update`. A column entry like this is hardly usable, so the first change you make is to change the column names so they look nicer and work better. Simply place the cursor in the column name area of the table that FrontPage creates and make the changes you want.

Look at the order of the columns on-screen. FrontPage normally places them in the same order they appear in the database. In effect, you have two ways to change the order:

✦ Click Edit List in the Database Results Wizard when you create the connection. The Displayed Fields dialog box lets you move items up or down in the list to change the presentation order.

✦ Use Split view to move the fields around after you create the page. Here's how:

1. **Highlight the header you want to move in the Design view portion and then locate that entry in the Code view.**

2. **Move the entire `<th>` tag to the new position.**

3. **Highlight the data-field entry in Design view and then locate that entry in Code view.**

4. **Move the entire <td> tag to the new position.**

   The `<td>` tag includes a `DatabaseResultColumn` webbot that you move with the `<td>` tag. Exercise care in moving the `<td>` tag to ensure you don't damage the `webbot` entry.

Figure 2-6 shows a table that displays all entries and includes modifications to both column names and column order. This figure also shows the Code view of the webbot entry.

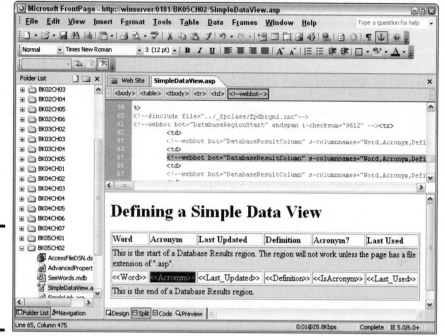

Figure 2-6:
Modify the
column
headings
and order
as needed.

After you get the columns rearranged, you might find that some columns
have special formatting requirements. Before you make any changes to the
cell or column, modify the data format as required. Right-click any of the
webbot entries (third row of the table) and choose Database Column Value
Properties from the context menu. You see the Database Column Value
dialog box shown in Figure 2-7.

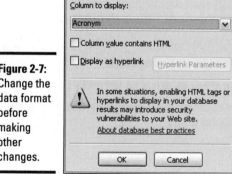

Figure 2-7:
Change the
data format
before
making
other
changes.

The entries help you display the data from your database as HTML. In fact, you can store URLs or other information in the database and use it to create a hyperlink with the table.

When you select Display as Hyperlink, it doesn't necessarily mean the data is a hyperlink. It could simply be data that you want to use to create a hyperlink. The Web page produced by the `SimpleDataView.asp` file of the source code for this chapter on the Wiley Web site is a good example. This sample database contains words, acronyms, and their associated definition.

I've also added a linking mechanism so you can see the same work in both Acronym Finder and Webopedia — two good online sources for words. To make a change of this sort, follow these steps:

1. Check Display as Hyperlink and then click Hyperlink Parameters.

You see the Hyperlink Parameters dialog box shown in Figure 2-8.

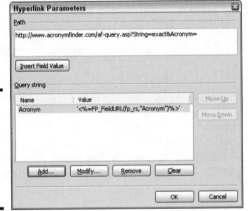

Figure 2-8:
Create hyperlinks from data you provide using a database.

2. Create the acronym by placing the basic URL in the Path field.

The path includes an entry for the acronym.

3. Place the acronym value in the Query String field.

4. Click Add, select the field you want to use, and then click OK.

In some cases, you must make changes to the resulting URL in Code view, but using the editor is a good start.

Creating a Search Form

You might find that you don't know what to expect as a query from the user, so building a specific query isn't possible. In some cases, the database might be too large to display on one Web page and some users will need access to the entire database to perform their work. To provide good access to the database when either of these problems occur, you need a search form.

Begin creating the search form by using the Insert➪Database command and following the steps provided in the "Creating a new connection using the Database Results Wizard" section of the chapter. When you come to the column selection screen shown in Figure 2-5, follow these steps:

1. **Click More Options.**

You see the More Options dialog box.

2. **Click Criteria to display the Criteria dialog box shown in Figure 2-9.**

This dialog box contains the criteria used to choose records from the database. Notice that it includes an option for displaying the criteria as a search form.

Figure 2-9: Define the search criteria for the search form you create.

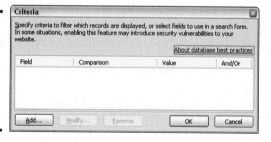

3. **Click Add.**

You see the Add Criteria dialog box.

4. **Choose a field you want to use to create a search in the Field Name field.**

5. **Select an entry from the Comparison field.**

This field controls how the search is performed. When you select Equals as the comparison, the input the user provides must precisely match the information in the database, so this search option usually isn't very useful. A better selection in most cases is Contains. When you select Contains, the search phrase can appear anywhere in the database field, making the user's search a lot easier because the user needs to remember only part of the information.

6. **Select a value name.**

   It normally helps to choose something similar to the field name, but not precisely the same.

7. **Click OK to close the Criteria dialog box.**

   At this point, FrontPage enables the Defaults button.

8. **Click Defaults to define default values for any of the criteria you create.**

   You must combine a default value with a criteria when you use this feature to reduce the number of entries that FrontPage returns from the database without using a search form. When using a search form, the default values are optional.

After you create the connection, FrontPage displays both a table and a search form. The search form labels will have the same name as the variable you created. Make sure you modify the label text as needed to make the purpose of the data entry field clear.

Designing Relational Data Views

Databases seldom rely on a single table to accomplish a task. Normally a database has two or more tables that have a relationship to each other. This fact means you'll probably want to use multiple tables in FrontPage as well.

To create a relational data view in FrontPage, you must begin by creating a query in Access. Because FrontPage allows you to choose only one data source when you create a connection, it's easier and faster to create the query you need within Access and then test it in that environment.

Creating a simple data view

Creating a data view connection using multiple tables in FrontPage is the same as working with a single table. You begin by using the Insert⇨Database command and following the steps provided in the "Creating a new connection using the Database Results Wizard" section of the chapter. The major difference is that you select a query when working with multiple tables, rather than using a single table. When you complete the setup, you end up with a single table that contains the data from however many tables you used to create the query. As far as the user is concerned, all the data came from a single table.

Developing Access views using the PivotTable control

You normally use the PivotTable control with Excel because the amount of data is limited and Excel is normally used to analyze data. However, the PivotTable control also works with Access. In some cases, you can use the PivotTable control to analyze Access data so long as you limit the number of records so the analysis doesn't take the rest of someone's life to perform. Use the following steps to create the PivotTable control with Access data:

1. **Choose the Insert⇨Web Component command.**

   You see the Insert Web Component dialog box.

2. **Select the Spreadsheets and Charts entry in the Component Type list and Office PivotTable in the Choose a Control list. Click Finish.**

   FrontPage creates the PivotTable. At this point, the PivotTable won't contain any data.

3. **Right-click the control and choose ActiveX Control Properties.**

   You see the ActiveX Control Properties dialog box.

4. **Choose the Data Source tab. Select Connection and click Edit.**

   You see the Select Data Source dialog box.

5. **Click New Source.**

   FrontPage starts the Data Connection Wizard.

6. **Select ODBC DSN and click Next.**

   The wizard asks you to select a data connection product or an existing Data Source Name (DSN). When you have Office 2003 installed, you see two entries for Access. Make sure you choose the MS Access Database entry, rather than the MS Access 97 Database entry when present or your connection won't work. Access 97 and Access 2003 use significantly different database engines, so the two connection types aren't compatible. (The example assumes that you're creating a new connection to an Access 2003 database.)

7. **Choose an appropriate data source and click Next.**

   The wizard displays a dialog box in which you can select an existing database.

8. **Select the database and click OK.**

   The wizard asks you to choose a table or query from the database. Avoid choosing entire tables when you can because they contain too much data. In addition, avoid queries that return a large number of records. The PivotTable will fail to perform as expected when you overload it.

9. **Select a table or query from the list and click Next.**

   The wizard asks you to provide a name and description for the connection. You can also provide search terms to make the connection easier to find.

10. **Type a name and description for the connection. Optionally add any search terms you want to use. Click Finish.**

    FrontPage displays a dialog box you use to open the new connection.

11. **Select the connection and click Open. Click OK.**

    FrontPage updates the PivotTable control so you can add fields to it.

12. **Click on the control so you see the hatched lines appear around it.**

    The control is in edit mode.

13. **Right-click the control and choose Field List from the content menu.**

    You see a list of fields you can use to work with the PivotTable control.

14. **Select the fields you want to use and close the PivotTable Field List dialog box.**

    At this point, the control contains data, but no totals.

15. **Right-click within the data area. Select AutoCalc.**

    You see a number of options for calculating a result from the data. Even when the data is text, you should have the option of counting members based on the criteria used to create the PivotTable.

16. **Select one of the options on the AutoCalc menu.**

    FrontPage adds totals based on the calculation you selected.

At this point, the PivotTable is ready to use. One of the important things to remember about using a PivotTable control is that you aren't limited as to what criteria you use. For example, Figure 2-10 shows the output of this example. (In this case, I choose to tally the number of word entries that were modified at a given time, based on whether they had an acronym.)

The goal is to discover something about your data that you didn't know before by analyzing it. Sometimes, a PivotTable won't provide useful information, but in other cases it will. Only by playing with the data in various ways do you discover relationships you didn't know about before.

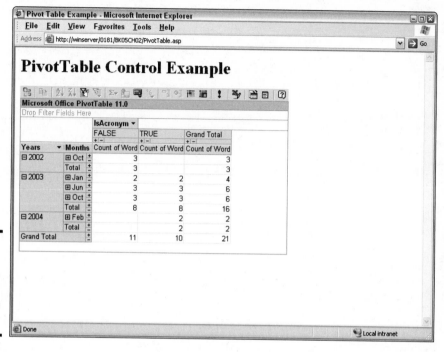

Figure 2-10:
Use the
PivotTable
to calculate
any statistic
you need.

Chapter 3: Developing Applications with SQL Server

In This Chapter

✔ Using SQL Server to full advantage

✔ Creating links to SQL Server data

✔ Developing relational data views

SQL Server is Microsoft's high-end database. It's designed for medium to large sized businesses and stores a lot of data without problems. Compared to database products such as Access and MySQL, you get a lot more in the way of management features with SQL Server and this product also supports a lot of users. Consequently, you probably won't see someone's personal contact list or record collection stored in SQL Server unless it's part of an application designed for company use.

FrontPage also provides more than a modicum of support for SQL Server. In fact, SQL Server is the best-supported database in FrontPage. You can even access the Microsoft test database, Northwind. This database is important because many examples in the Microsoft documentation rely on it. The Northwind database also appears in many books because authors want a database that everyone can use. In fact, you'll use the Northwind database for all the examples in this chapter. Because you'll normally use SQL Server for complex connections, this chapter concentrates on views, rather than on individual tables.

You can perform all the usual database activities with FrontPage. For example, you can create a connection using any of several standard techniques that you would also use with Excel or Access. FrontPage adds other connection methods as well, making SQL Server exceptionally easy to use.

Understanding the SQL Server Advantage

There isn't any doubt that SQL Server works well for large projects. It's designed to let you create databases for immense data stores. In fact, you can create scenarios where a database spans across multiple servers. SQL Server is definitely the right solution for medium-to-large businesses. (Even the cost tends to keep small businesses away.)

The small-business perspective

Fortunately, SQL Server isn't just about immense data stores. If that were all it had to offer, then most businesses wouldn't be very interested in using it. For some situations, SQL Server is the most appropriate selection, no matter what size business you own. For that matter, some types of home-user development projects could benefit from using SQL Server, despite the significant cost.

SQL Server also provides development tools that Access and other smaller database products don't include. For example, you can create a diagram of the data organization you want to create. A pictorial view is often helpful in developing connections between complex data. SQL Server also offers access to stored procedures and better security than products such as Access. You can create user-defined data types when necessary — which means you can handle situations where the standard data types won't meet a specific need.

All these features come into play when you're working with FrontPage. A small business using SQL Server to develop a Web site has better access to the data using a number of techniques that aren't available when working with other DBMS. For example, FrontPage offers additional connection options and helps protect your data better.

Developing secure applications

A number of features that FrontPage provides warn of possible security problems. For example, when you add a search form to your Web page, FrontPage warns that a cracker could possibly use the search form to gain access to the database. This problem is especially significant with less secure databases where you can't control access very well.

Fortunately, FrontPage does provide good security. You can use many of the less secure FrontPage features and still ensure your application remains safe as long as you perform some specific setups. One of the first security updates is to set SQL Server to use Windows security (rather than its own built-in security) to ensure that a user checks in properly before using the Web application — and is properly verified without requiring too many inputs.

You should also limit the length of search inputs, ensure the data is of the correct type, and limit the kinds of data a user can input. For example, when you let the user make a text query, don't allow the user to input special characters.

Finally, you should set up the Web server to provide a secure connection. This step is essential because the Web server will use an anonymous connection otherwise and potentially open your server up to cracker exploits.

If you can't create a secure connection because your Web site is open to the general public, make sure your Web site relies on firewalls and places the various servers in places where crackers can't get to your internal network.

The SQL Server advantage is that you can create a secure environment that is both robust and easy to configure. SQL Server provides settings based on individual accounts, letting you assign rights to the various tables, queries, and reports according to individual needs. In short, SQL Server is the option to use when you require maximum security and maximum flexibility.

Developing Links to SQL Server

Before you can access data within SQL Server, you must create a connection to it. The linking process can occur in a number of ways:

✦ A special link provides access to the Northwind database — a special database used by Microsoft (and by many third parties) for demonstration purposes.

✦ You have access to advanced Microsoft technologies such as Object Linking and Embedding for Databases (OLE-DB). (This connection type isn't available in other environments.)

✦ You have access to all the standard connection technologies, such as Open Database Connectivity (ODBC).

Missing from the SQL Server repertoire is direct file connection. Unlike other DBMSs, SQL Server won't let you create a direct connection to a file — but this lack is actually a safety and security feature. Giving someone access to a file containing data for a large application — one used by hundreds or thousands of people — breaks every security rule for large-database implementation.

Using the Northwind database connection

Some developers would question the purpose and usability of the Northwind database outside of Microsoft examples. The Northwind database is relatively complex, so it makes a good platform to create test applications and for you to perform "proof of concept" modifications to FrontPage. Because this database is well established and is provided with every copy of SQL server, you can create a test application and send it to other developers for comment or analysis. Best of all, the Northwind database provides common data you can use for testing where the results are the same every time and on every platform. Consequently, you should consider the Northwind database for testing, as well as for creating, examples.

To create a connection to the Northwind database, follow these steps:

1. **Choose Insert⇨Database⇨Results.**

   You see the Database Results Wizard dialog box shown in Figure 3-1. Notice the Use a Sample Database Connection (Northwind) option. Select this option only when you have SQL Server installed in a location that FrontPage can access.

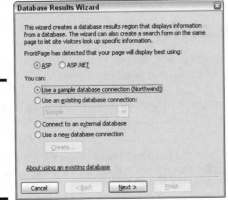

Figure 3-1: Select the Northwind database option for testing purposes.

2. **Choose the Use a Sample Database Connection (Northwind) option and click Next.**

   FrontPage asks which record source you want to use (the example uses Employees). Note that you can interact with the Northwind database as you would any other database on your system. The point is that this database contains test data and you don't have to create a connection to it — FrontPage already knows where to find it. Consequently, you can use a single table, create a special query on the server, or create a custom query within FrontPage. The flexibility that this connection offers lets you test a variety of scenarios.

3. **After you select a query, table, or create a custom query, click Next.**

   FrontPage displays a list of fields associated with the record source you chose. You can modify this list by clicking Edit List. Make sure the fields appear in the order that you want to use them. If you want to select criteria for ordering the data — or to create special features such as search forms — click More Options.

4. **After you define the way you want to use the data fields, click Next.**

   FrontPage asks how you want to display the data. You can choose a simple list, a table, or a drop-down list. It's also possible to configure the various displays. For example, you can choose whether the table includes a border or force the table to take up the entire width of the display.

5. Choose a manner of presentation and click Next.

The final display asks whether you want to display all the data at once or just a few records at a time. Configure the options to match your display requirements. Generally, you want to break long lists into pieces the user can see with greater ease.

6. Click Finish and you see the table displayed on-screen.

Creating a new connection

Before you can create your first database Web page (one that connects to something other than Northwind, that is), you need to create a connection. Unlike some other database choices, you can't access SQL Server through a file connection because of the way SQL Server is set up. You do, however, have a number of options that other database sources don't support.

To create a new connection to SQL Server, use the Database Results Wizard. Here's how:

1. Access the wizard by choosing the Insert⇨Database⇨Results.

The Database Results Wizard dialog box shown in Figure 3-1, appears, offering options for creating new or using existing connections to your database. You can also choose between ASP and ASP.NET as the language for the Web page. To use ASP.NET, you must have the .NET Framework installed — and you can download that at

```
http://www.microsoft.com/downloads/details.aspx?FamilyID=262d25e3-
    f589-4842-8157-034d1e7cf3a3
```

This version of the product lets you run any .NET application, including those found on ASP.NET pages. When working with ASP.NET, be sure to give your Web pages an Active Server Pages eXtended (ASPX) file extension, not the ASP file extension used by standard ASP pages.

2. Create a new link by choosing Use New Database Connection and then clicking Create.

You see the Database tab of the Site Properties dialog box. This tab contains a list of the connections you define.

3. Click Add.

You see the New Database Connection dialog box shown in Figure 3-2. It includes three options for creating a link using SQL Server:

- Data source
- Network
- Custom

These options are discussed in the next few sections.

4. **Whichever option you choose, type a name for the connection in the Name field.**

Figure 3-2:
Choose
one of the
connection
types for
your Access
database.

After you create the new connection, you must select it for use. After using one of the following procedures to create the connection, use the steps in the "Selecting an existing connection" section later in this chapter to select it for use.

Using a data source on the Web server

Creating a connection using a data source on the Web server is a two-part process:

1. You create the connection on the Web server using the Data Sources (ODBC) applet in the Administrative Tools folder of the Control Panel.

2. You access this connection using FrontPage.

The next sections describe these two steps in detail.

Creating the connection on the Web server

Using Open Database Connectivity (ODBC) provides better compatibility with other applications than newer solutions. In addition, ODBC is the option of choice with some Database Management Systems (DBMSs) because this older Microsoft technology works with a wide range of products. However, because it's an older (and slower) connection strategy, you should consider using other techniques — such as a direct network connection — when speed is important. Use the following steps to create the ODBC connection on the Web server:

1. **Double-click the Data Sources (ODBC) applet in the Administrative Tools folder of the Control Panel.**

You see the ODBC Data Source Administrator dialog box.

2. Select the System DSN tab. Click Add.

You see a Create New Data Source dialog box that lists a number of database drivers. A Data Source Name (DSN) is a label attached to a set of instructions for connecting to a database. The use of a label makes it easy to reference the ODBC instructions.

3. Highlight the SQL Server entry and click Finish.

You see the Create a New Data Source to SQL Server dialog box shown in Figure 3-3. Note that every ODBC driver uses a different dialog box, so the dialog box shown here won't match the one used for other DBMS. Each DBMS requires a configuration dialog box selected for its specific needs.

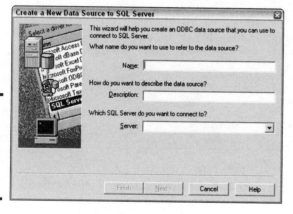

Figure 3-3:
Define a
SQL Server
data source
using this
wizard.

4. Type a name for the data source.

Use a short name that's easy to remember and doesn't contain any space or special characters.

5. Type a description in the description field.

Make sure you provide enough information that you can identify the connection later.

6. Select a server from the Server drop-down list box and then click Next.

The wizard asks what security settings you want to use when connecting to SQL Server.

Generally, the Windows NT authentication is safer, and you should consider using it. However, if you want your Web site to provide secure access to the database without opening the server as well, you can use SQL Server authentication. Doing so ensures that the user inputs the correct information on-screen. Make sure you use an HTTPS (secure) connection when performing this task.

7. Select a connection option and then click Next.

The wizard asks you to select a default database and configuration options for that table, as shown in Figure 3-4. This dialog box normally chooses the master database as the default, and it's easy to miss the required changes. Make sure you select the correct default database as a minimum.

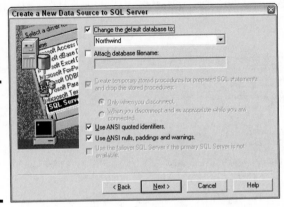

Figure 3-4: Specify the default database and connection options.

8. Check *Change the Default Database to,* select a database from the drop-down list box, and then click Next.

You see settings that change the language used for the SQL Server messages, string encryption, character translation, regional settings, and logging options. None of these settings require changes when you're using the Northwind database (as the example does in Figure 3-4). However, you may need to change them when you're working with real data on your Web site.

String encryption is especially helpful in enhancing the security of your database.

9. Modify any required SQL Server messages, string encryption, character translation, regional settings, and logging options as needed. Click Finish.

You see the ODBC Microsoft SQL Server Setup dialog box, which contains a summary of the settings you defined. This dialog box also lets you test the connection.

10. **Click Test Data Source.**

You see either a success message or an error message. When you see an error message, fix any connection problems and test the connection again.

11. **Click OK twice.**

The ODBC Data Source Administrator adds the new connection to the DSN tab.

Accessing the connection

The database connection is usable at this point. Use the following steps to create a FrontPage connection for the DSN link.

1. **Choose System Data Source On Web Server in the New Database Connection dialog box. Click Browse.**

You see the System Data Sources On Web Server dialog box. This dialog box should contain the connection created earlier in this section. Everything FrontPage needs to create the connection appears in the DSN you created.

2. **Choose the DSN you want to use and click OK.**

FrontPage displays the database connection information in the text box beneath the Custom Definition entry shown in Figure 3-2.

3. **Click OK.**

FrontPage displays the new connection on the Database tab of the Site Properties dialog box.

4. **Click Verify.**

FrontPage checks the connection to the database. If this connection fails, don't modify the FrontPage settings — check the DSN settings on the server instead.

5. **Click OK.**

FrontPage displays the Database Results Wizards dialog box. It automatically selects Use an Existing Database Connection and modifies the connection entry to the new connection you created. Proceed with the instructions in the "Selecting an existing connection" section of the chapter.

Using a network connection

A network connection helps you create a link to your SQL Server database without resorting to an ODBC configuration. The network connection doesn't rely on your having access to the Data Sources (ODBC) applet. All you need is access to the server computer that contains SQL Server — and to the SQL Server application. This connection requires the least amount of work and offers better performance (due to differences in the driver used and other low-level details) in some cases. Use these steps to create such a network connection:

1. **Choose Network Connection to Database Server in the New Database Connection dialog box. Click Browse.**

   You see the Network Database Connection dialog box.

2. **Choose a database driver (either SQL Server or Oracle) and type its name in the Server Name field.**

3. **Type the name of the database in the Database Name field and click OK.**

   FrontPage displays the database connection information in the text box beneath the Custom Definition entry, shown in Figure 3-2 (the example uses Northwind).

4. **Click OK again.**

   FrontPage displays the new connection on the Database tab of the Site Properties dialog box.

5. **Click Verify.**

   FrontPage checks the connection to the database. If this connection fails, don't modify the FrontPage settings — check the DSN settings on the server instead.

6. **Click OK.**

   FrontPage displays the Database Results Wizards dialog box. It automatically selects Use an Existing Database Connection and modifies the connection entry to the new connection you created. Proceed with the instructions in the "Selecting an existing connection" section of the chapter.

Defining a custom connection

Like many other databases, SQL Server can use a file-based DSN connection when the developer needs to create a custom connection that could change at some point in the application setup. The custom connection works best when using a Local Area Network (LAN) connection for a company intranet. In general, a custom connection can help you create specialized setups and use more database types than the standard connections do, but they're also a lot harder to set up.

One potential problem in using a file DSN with SQL Server is that the connection can fail when you attempt to select a query (view) as a record source. Just why the connection fails is something that Microsoft hasn't discussed.

The connection always works with tables, but table connections are nearly useless if you're working with the complex setups that SQL Server manages best. You can normally overcome this problem by creating a custom query that uses the view as input. For example, to perform this task with the Customer and Suppliers by City query, use SELECT * FROM "Customer and Suppliers by City" as the custom query.

To use this connection type, you must have access to the Data Sources (ODBC) applet in the Administrative Tools folder of the Control Panel.

Defining the connection properties

The following steps show how to create a custom connection. They start by using the Data Sources (ODBC) applet to define the connection properties.

1. **Double-click the Data Sources (ODBC) applet in the Administrative Tools folder of the Control Panel.**

   You see the ODBC Data Source Administrator dialog box.

2. **Select the File DSN tab. Click Add.**

   You see a Create New Data Source dialog box that lists a number of database drivers. A Data Source Name (DSN) is a label attached to a set of instructions for connecting to a database. The use of a label makes it easy to reference the ODBC instructions.

3. **Highlight the SQL Server entry and click Next.**

   The Create New Data Source wizard asks you to provide a filename for the data source.

4. **Click Browse. Choose a location for the file DSN, type a name in the File Name field, and click Save.**

   The Create New Data Source wizard places the file path and name in the field provided.

5. **Click Next.**

   You see a summary of the connection information.

6. **Click Finish.**

   You see a Create a New Data Source to SQL Server dialog box that looks similar to the one shown in Figure 3-3. The main difference is that the Data Source Name field is disabled because you can't provide this information as part of a file DSN.

7. **Type a description for the connection in the Description field. Select your server from the Server field. Click Next.**

   The wizard asks what security settings you want to use when connecting to SQL Server.

8. **Select a connection option and then click Next.**

   The wizard asks you to select a default database and configuration options for that table, as shown in Figure 3-4. This dialog box normally chooses the master database as the default; it's easy to miss the required changes. Make sure you select the correct default database as a minimum.

9. **Check *Change the Default Database to,* select a database from the drop-down list box, and click Next.**

   You see settings that change the language used for the SQL Server messages, string encryption, character translation, regional settings, and logging options. (The example uses the Northwind database, as shown in Figure 3-4.)

10. **Modify any required SQL Server messages, string encryption, character translation, regional settings, and logging options as needed. Click Finish.**

    You see the ODBC Microsoft SQL Server Setup dialog box, which contains a summary of the settings you defined. This dialog box also lets you test the connection.

11. **Click Test Data Source.**

    You see a success or error message. When you see an error message, fix any connection problems and test the connection again.

12. **Click OK twice.**

    The ODBC Data Source Administrator adds the new connection to the DSN tab.

Adding the DSN connection

When you have a file DSN set up and ready to use, it's time to add the connection to FrontPage. The following steps show how:

1. **Copy the file DSN from the** \Program Files\Common Files\ODBC\ Data Sources **folder on your server to a folder within your Web site.**

   You can use the _private folder to protect the file from prying eyes when necessary.

2. **Choose Custom Definition in the New Database Connection dialog box. Click Browse.**

You see the Connection Files in Current Web Site dialog box. Notice that this dialog box allows you to look only on the current Web site for the DSN file.

3. **Locate the DSN file you want to use and click OK.**

   FrontPage displays the database connection information in the text box beneath the Custom Definition entry shown in Figure 3-2.

4. **Click OK.**

   FrontPage displays the new connection on the Database tab of the Site Properties dialog box.

5. **Click Verify.**

   FrontPage checks the connection to the database. If this connection fails, don't modify the FrontPage settings — check the DSN settings in the DSN file instead.

6. **Click OK.**

   FrontPage displays the Database Results Wizard dialog box. It then automatically selects Use an Existing Database Connection and modifies the connection entry to the new connection you created. Proceed with the instructions in the "Selecting an existing connection" section of the chapter.

Choosing an external connection

An external connection lets you connect directly to the database without creating a DSN or even a special connection first. Instead of working through several processes to obtain data from SQL Server or Oracle, you go directly to the source in a single process. The advantage of this technique is that it's very fast and easy. The disadvantage is that you don't save the connection information — which means you have to recreate it for every connection. In some respects, this technique is also wasteful of system resources, but the additional disk space required is minimal. The following steps show how to create an external connection:

1. **Choose the Insert⇨Database⇨Results command.**

   You see the Database Results Wizard dialog box shown in Figure 3-1.

2. **Select Connect to an External Database and click Next.**

   FrontPage asks you to supply the database type (Oracle or SQL Server), server name, and database name. You must also supply a username and password when you set the system to use SQL Server security or the server isn't set to require a username and password.

3. **Type the required information and click Next.**

   FrontPage displays list of record sources you can use or you can create a custom query. When creating a custom query, you must type a SQL statement to retrieve data from the server.

4. **Select Record Source (individual tables or predefined queries) or Custom Query (complex queries using multiple tables):**

   • When using Record Source, choose a table or view from the list presented under the Record Source option.

   • When using a Custom Query, click Edit, type the SQL Statement that you want to use, click Verify to check the accuracy of the query, and click OK to create the query.

5. **Click Next.**

   FrontPage displays a list of fields for the table or query, as shown in Figure 3-5. FrontPage assumes you want to use all of the fields in the query. You have two options:

   • Click Edit List to change the fields FrontPage displays.

   • Click More Options when you want to filter or sort the data as it comes from Access.

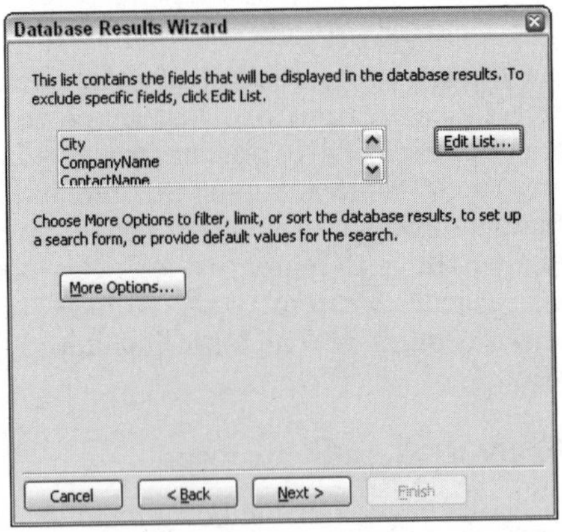

Figure 3-5:
Define the way you want to use the database information.

6. **Click Next.**

   FrontPage asks how you want to display the data. You can choose from a table, a list, or a drop-down list. When using a list or drop-down list, you can select only one field from those chosen from the named range.

7. **Select a presentation format (the example uses the table) and click Next.**

FrontPage asks how you want to group the records. You can choose to display all of the records together or split them into groups of specific record numbers. Use the grouping option for larger tables; doing so makes it easier for the user to locate data, but also splits up the presentation.

8. **Choose a record grouping method and click Finish.**

FrontPage adds the view to the current Web page. At this point, FrontPage will tell you to save the file and change the extension to ASP or ASPX (if you haven't done so already) so the table works as expected.

Selecting an existing connection

SQL Server developers usually create just a few connections and then reuse them in a number of views. Use an existing connection whenever possible to reduce clutter, improve performance, decrease memory requirements, and lessen the chance of connecting to an old database. Even when you create a new view, FrontPage returns you to the Database Results Wizard dialog box with the Use an Existing Database Connection option selected and the new connection displayed in the associated drop-down list box. The following steps show how to use an existing connection.

1. **Select Use an Existing Database Connection if FrontPage hasn't already done so. Choose the connection you want to use. Click Next.**

FrontPage requests information about the record source you want to use. A record source can include an entire table, a query that you've defined, or a custom SQL statement.

2. **Select Record Source or Custom Query. When using Record Source, choose a table or view from the list presented under the Record Source option. When using a Custom Query, click Edit, type the SQL Statement that you want to use, click Verify to check the accuracy of the query, and click OK to create the query. Click Next.**

FrontPage displays a list of fields for the table or query, as shown in Figure 3-5.

3. **Click Next.**

FrontPage asks how you want to display the data. You can choose from a table, a list, or a drop-down list.

4. **Select a presentation format (the example uses the table) and click Next.**

FrontPage asks how you want to group the records. You can choose to display all of the records together or split them into groups of specific record numbers.

5. **Choose a record grouping method and click Finish.**

FrontPage adds the view to the current Web page.

Creating Relational Data Views

SQL Server is an industrial strength database designed to work with large data sets. Developers who use SQL Server seldom rely on a single table to accomplish a task. Normally, a database has two or more tables that have a relationship to each other — so you'll probably want to use multiple tables in FrontPage as well. FrontPage always lists multiple table relations in SQL Server as a view.

To create a relational data view in FrontPage, you must begin by creating a query in SQL Server. These queries appear in the Views folder for the database in Enterprise Manager. You use Query Analyzer to check the view before working with it in FrontPage to ensure you can easily locate the source of any problems.

Correcting a security problem

One problem you might encounter when working with SQL Server is that the database won't display error messages correctly or at all. A typical error message looks like this:

```
The operation failed. If this continues, please contact your server administrator.
```

A number of problems could cause this error to appear, but the most common problem is security. You can fix this problem by using a number of the following techniques (in order of preference):

✦ Set directory security on the Directory Security tab of the directory Properties dialog box in the Internet Information Services console so that anonymous access is disabled.

✦ Create the DSN so that it uses SQL Server security and then supply a default name and password to access the data.

✦ Create an external connection using FrontPage.

✦ Supply a name and password in the Advanced Connection Properties dialog box within FrontPage.

✦ Add the anonymous user account to SQL Server with significant restrictions on the acts the anonymous user can perform.

✦ Create a custom script to make the connection manually.

Developing SQL Server views using the PivotTable control

Unlike Office applications, the analysis tools provided with SQL Server are a little limited unless you buy an add-on product. This limitation is inconsistent with the purpose Microsoft had in mind when designing SQL Server — as a database that handles large amounts of information, which normally requires robust analysis tools.

In some cases, you can use the PivotTable control to analyze SQL Server data so long as you limit the number of records so the analysis doesn't take the rest of someone's life to perform. Use the following steps to create the PivotTable control with SQL Server data:

1. **Choose the Insert⇨Web Component command.**

   You see the Insert Web Component dialog box.

2. **Select the Spreadsheets and Charts entry in the Component Type list and Office PivotTable in the Choose a Control list. Click Finish.**

   FrontPage creates the PivotTable. At this point, the PivotTable won't contain any data.

3. **Right-click the control and choose ActiveX Control Properties.**

   You see the ActiveX Control Properties dialog box.

4. **Choose the Data Source tab. Select Connection and click Edit.**

   You see the Select Data Source dialog box.

5. **Select New SQL Server Connection.odc and click Open.**

   FrontPage starts the Data Connection Wizard. The beginning dialog box lets you choose a server and credential option. The most secure connection method is Use Windows Authentication. However, on a public Web site where users log on anonymously, you might have to rely on the Use the Following User Name and Password option.

6. **Type the server name in the Server Name field and choose a log on credential option. Click Next.**

   You see the Select Database and Table dialog box. This dialog box lists all of the options for connection with SQL Server on the server you choose.

7. **Select a database from the drop-down list (the example uses Northwind).**

   FrontPage populates the Connect to a Specific Table list.

8. **Choose a table (the example uses Summary of Sales by Quarter) and click Next.**

You see the Save Data Connection and Finish dialog box. Use the filename, description, and keyword entries in this dialog box to identify the connection.

9. **Type a filename, description, and key words, and then click Finish.**

FrontPage fills in the Connection and Use Data From fields of the Data Source tab of the ActiveX Control Properties dialog box.

10. **Click OK.**

FrontPage updates the PivotTable control so you can add fields to it.

11. **Click on the control so you see the hatched lines appear around it.**

The control is in edit mode.

12. **Right-click the control and choose Field List from the content menu.**

You see a list of fields you can use to work with the PivotTable control.

13. **Select the fields you want to use and close the Pivot Table Field List dialog box.**

At this point, the control contains data, but no totals.

14. **Right-click within the data area. Select AutoCalc.**

You see a number of options for calculating a result from the data. Even when the data is text, you should have the option of counting members based on the criteria used to create the PivotTable.

15. **Select one of the options on the AutoCalc menu.**

FrontPage adds totals based on the calculation you selected.

At this point, the PivotTable is ready to use. One of the important things to remember about using a PivotTable control is that you aren't limited as to what criteria you use. The goal is to discover something about your data that you didn't know before you analyzed it. Sometimes a PivotTable won't provide that kind of useful information, but in other cases it will. Only by playing with the data in various ways do you discover relationships you didn't know about before.

Book VI

XML and XSLT

Contents at a Glance

Chapter 1: Working with XML

Many applications — even some that have nothing to do with the Internet — use eXtensible Markup Language (XML) as a way to save information. For example, Microsoft Office applications use XML as a means of saving data in an easily transferable format. Visual Studio uses XML to save settings, as do technologies such as ASP.NET. You might be seeing a translated form of XML when you view your favorite magazine or other writing online. In fact, these days it's hard to use a computer at all without running into some use of XML. That's because XML is so flexible and easy to understand.

The easiest way to think of XML is as a specially formatted kind of text that includes both data and tags that define data elements. XML looks like HTML in some respects, but it isn't limited to the tags that someone else decided you should use — you can create your own tags as needed. In addition, XML is better organized than HTML, so it's easier to read and understand. This chapter assumes that you know what XML is and are mainly interested in discovering how to work with it using FrontPage.

FrontPage includes a number of features for working with XML documents. You can view XML documents within FrontPage with highlighting and other clues in place that make working with XML a lot easier than using a text editor or other less capable editor. In addition, FrontPage provides a special XML Toolbar that makes working with XML faster because you don't have to rely on the menu system to perform other tasks. Finally, FrontPage provides import features so you can take XML from any location and use it as part of your Web page.

This chapter doesn't include an exhaustive list of XML features, but it does discuss the most common. When you have questions about current XML usage, always refer to the XML standard. You can find it at

`http://www.w3.org/TR/REC-xml.`

The document that defines the standard can be a little confusing to read, however, so use the annotated version to answer questions about the interpretation of the standard. You can find this version at

`http://www.xml.com/axml/axml.html`

Using XML Effectively

XML is a standard for combining data with context, such as a Word processor does by combining the text you type (data) with formatting (context). The context can include everything from the arrangement of the data to techniques for formatting it. The idea is to preserve the data and the information you use when you're working with the data. Nothing in the XML standard limits the interpretation of XML — the standard leaves the interpretation up to whoever is applying the standard (that is, the implementer). Many other standards define how to interpret XML, but XML itself doesn't define anything but the basic requirements for the document — in particular, the format of the data within the document.

One of the reasons that XML is so popular is that its documents appear in plain text. Every computer can read and understand text. In fact, text is the common format for all computers, even computers too old to perform useful work today. Given enough time, anyone can read and understand an XML document by using a simple text editor such as Notepad. You have other means of reading XML at your disposal, but you don't have to use any special application.

Many applications now produce XML output. By discovering the interpretation of the XML document, you can create your own presentations on a Web site. The presentation doesn't have to precisely match the presentation of the document in the application that creates it. Because XML is freeform, you transform it to meet whatever needs you might have.

You can also create documents of your own. Effective use of XML requires that you define the structure of the content you want to create. A document could include formatting or structure information, or even both. You decide how someone should interpret the content of the XML document. As long as your document follows the XML rules, you won't experience any difficulty in storing the information you need in the way you want. These rules are discussed in the next section.

Using XML in FrontPage

XML doesn't have very many rules to consider — but the few it does have are absolute. When a document you create follows all the rules, applications designed to work with XML see it as *well formed*. A well-formed XML document includes specific features that clue the reader (the application parsing, working with, the content) in on the content of the document and tell it how to display the information.

Working with processing instructions

Every XML document begins with a processing instruction. The processing instruction tells an application designed to work with XML what to do with the document. You must begin the XML document with this processing instruction or the reader won't interpret it correctly. Here's a typical example of this processing instruction:

```
<?xml version="1.0" encoding="utf-8" ?>
```

A processing instruction always appears within a combination of angle brackets and question marks like this: `<? ?>`. This processing instruction defines the document as an XML document. It has two attributes:

Book VI Chapter 1

Working with XML

✦ The `version` attribute identifies the version of XML used for this document. (All XML documents currently use version 1.0, but that could change in the future.)

✦ The `encoding` attribute defines the character set used for the document. In this case, the document uses 8-bit Unicode Transformation Format (UTF-8), which is essentially plain text.

An XML document can have other processing instructions unique to the document — these appear only when needed to change the interpretation of the document. Normally, you won't see these other processing instructions unless a special transformation instruction creates a particular presentation for your document. Then you may see additional special processing instructions in word processed or other complex documents. The only standard processing instruction is the XML header that appears at the beginning of every XML document. Other processing instructions are application and document specific, so you need to consult the documentation provided by the vendor or other party who created the document schema for descriptions of other processing instructions.

Most processing instructions are titled after the application that uses them. For example, the required XML processing instruction refers to all XML applications. When you want to add a special processing instruction for your particular application, name the processing instruction appropriately, so other applications won't misinterpret it. For example, a processing instruction for MyApp might look like this.

```
<?myapp dosomething="different" ?>
```

In this case, the special processing instruction is directed toward MyApp. No other application will do anything with the processing instruction. The dosomething entry defines the special instruction type. The different value tells the application how to do it, or what value to use. Processing instructions are quite powerful — but they're only *useful* when you have an application that will do something with them.

Working with elements

An *element* is a single piece of information within the XML document. It provides a name for the information within the document. The name could define everything from the format of the information to the kind of information contained within the element. An element doesn't even need to contain information — it can simply serve as a means for organizing the information within the document. Here's the simplest form of element you can create.

```
<PersonalData />
```

An element always appears within angle brackets. You must include a beginning and ending bracket for all elements. This element has a name of PersonalData. The element must end with a slash, as shown. This is a special form of element — known as an *empty element* because it doesn't include any data. You can also create elements in tag pairs, as shown here:

```
<Name>John</Name>
```

The angle brackets ⟨ ⟩ define the opening and closing of the element with (respectively) a start tag and end tag. The start tag and end tag have the same name; you can tell them apart because an end tag always includes the slash as shown. You use the first kind of element as an organizational aid or as a means of storing data as attributes. The second kind of element contains data between the start tag and end tag.

Elements can also contain other elements. You might decide to create an address book consisting of person records. (The actual tags you use depend on what you define — XML is completely open to your needs.) Listing 1-1 shows your first XML document.

Listing 1-1:   Simple XML document consisting of elements

```
<?xml version="1.0" encoding="utf-8" ?>
<AddressBook>
    <Person>
        <Name></Name>
        <Address>
            <AddressLine></AddressLine>
            <AddressLine></AddressLine>
        </Address>
        <City></City>
        <State></State>
        <ZIP_Code></ZIP_Code>
        <Telephone></Telephone>
        <PersonalData />
    </Person>
</AddressBook>
```

This XML document is functional. It includes the processing instruction that identifies it as an XML document. The document contains a series of elements that use the required formatting. In fact, the only thing missing from this XML document is some data. It doesn't contain any information. (Details, details.)

Notice that the element name is a single word. When you want to use more than one word for the element name, combine the words together. An element name can't contain a space. Some developers use an underline as a separator between words. For example, Personal_Data is an acceptable element name.

Working with values

Values — data in the form of words or numbers — are the most common form of information added to an XML document. The information you add is always in text form, but can describe anything, including pictures and sounds. For example, you could include a URL to a picture that the application reading the document will retrieve and display on-screen. Generally, all values in the document are data that you want to send; a value always appears within an element. For example, here's an element with a value included:

```
<Name>George Smith</Name>
```

The association of the element with the data tells you about the kind of information provided by the value. You know by looking at the code that George Smith is a name. A value can contain spaces and some other special characters. When you can't produce a special character conveniently, use the same techniques you use in an HTML document. For example, you can create an ellipsis (the three dots used to show the omission of additional content) by adding the `&#8230;` character code. You can find a list of additional character codes at `http://home.online.no/~pethesse/charcodes.html`.

Some special characters that you can produce with the keyboard — for example, an angle bracket — do pose a problem: The application reading the XML document won't know how to interpret the resulting text. For example, `<Equation>5 < 10</Equation>` creates a problem because of the less-than sign that looks too much like a left angle bracket. You have two ways to correct this problem. The first is to replace the less-than sign with the `&#60;` HTML character code. You can also place the information in a special coding construct called a *CDATA* (or *character data section*) like this:

```
<Equation>
    <![CDATA[5 < 10]]>
</Equation>
```

A CDATA section always begins with `<![CDATA[` and ends with `]]>`. You place your data within the square brackets, as shown in the code. Although this second method of handling special characters looks harder to use than HTML character codes, it has distinct advantages.

✦ Helps other people understand that the data contains special characters.

✦ Makes it possible to include longer pieces of text without having to replace every special character individually.

✦ Reduces the chance that a special character will appear in the XML document without conversion.

✦ Many viewers display a CDATA section in a special color, making it easier to locate information with special characters.

Working with attributes

You use *attributes* to describe either an element or the data it contains (or sometimes both). Although an attribute can be considered data of a sort, it's not the essential information in the XML document. For example, you might want to tell the viewer that some text is underlined, so you add a special attribute that says the text is underlined. The attribute is important data, but it isn't the text within the element — the information the viewer is most concerned about seeing.

Attributes always appear as a name and value pair. The name defines the attribute type, while the value defines the attribute status. Here's a typical example of an element that contains both a value and attributes.

```
<Number Location="Home">(555)555-1212</Number>
```

The element name is `Number`, and it contains a telephone number — in this case, the data that the viewer is most interested in seeing. However, the viewer doesn't know what kind of telephone number it is without the `Location` attribute. The `Location` attribute describes where the viewer can call with the associated telephone number — this is the person's home telephone number and not their office telephone number. The value of `Home` shows that this is a home telephone number.

You can use attributes only in start tags and empty elements. An attribute doesn't have to relate to any specific data. For example, you can use one or more attributes to define document settings. The attributes could include anything from the document author to the margin settings used to display the document.

A series of attributes can also define complex data, but this use is less common. As a rule, you can use attributes or elements with equal ease as long as the document's user understands its construction. Here's an example of a position on a chart described with both attributes and elements. First, the attribute version:

```
<Position X="15" Y="20" Z="18" />
```

Notice that this form relies on a single element. Second, the element version:

```
<Position>
    <X>15</X>
    <Y>20</Y>
    <Z>18</Z>
</Position>
```

Both versions of the code say essentially the same thing — the XML points to a position on a chart where the X-axis value is 15, the Y-axis value is 20, and the Z-axis value is 18. The attribute form is more compact, but harder to interpret and less flexible. You couldn't add an attribute to the X-axis, for example, because the X-axis value is already an attribute. The version of the code that uses elements is bulkier — which could pose transmission problems when you have a lot of data — but it's also the form that most people expect.

Adding comments

Comments are notes you make to yourself in the code or provide as documentation for other people. These comments will not appear in the final XML output. The application that processes your XML code ignores any comments you include; the comment isn't treated as data. Comments are essentially nonentities within XML; you can put them nearly anywhere in the document. Here's an example of a comment:

```
<!-- This is a list of my personal names and addresses -->
```

A comment always begins with <!-- and ends with -->. You can place any text you want within the comment. Even additions such as angle brackets that normally cause problems don't cause a problem within a comment.

The only character combination to avoid when you're writing a comment is the series of characters that denote the end of the comment — until, of course, you get to the end.

Understanding the concept of nodes

Look again at Listing 1-1. Notice the <AddressBook> element. The document contains only one such element — and it holds all the other elements in the document. This special element is known as a *root node*. Just as every XML document must begin with an XML processing instruction, an XML document must also have a root node — a container for other elements in the document.

The <Address> element is also special. Notice that it contains a series of <AddressLine> elements. The <Address> element is also called a *parent node*. Like the root node, a parent node doesn't necessarily contain any data, but it does act as a container for other elements that do contain data. In most cases, parent nodes serve to organize data to make it easier to access, but they can serve other purposes, too.

The <AddressLine> elements are *child nodes*. You can view them as children of the <Address> element. In some cases, you also see child nodes referred to as *leaf nodes* when they are the last element in a hierarchy (as is the case for the <AddressLine> elements).

Not every piece of information in even a simple XML document is a node and you need to recognize the difference to interpret the document correctly. Listing 1-2 shows the complete version of the sample XML document found in the First.XML file in the source code for this chapter (on this book's companion Web site).

Listing 1-2: Example XML Showing Standard Features

```
<?xml version="1.0" encoding="utf-8" ?>
<!-- This is a list of my personal names and addresses -->
<AddressBook Version="1.0">
    <!-- Each person record contains the person's name and
         address, as well as one or more telephone numbers. A
```

```
        person record can also include special notes and
other
        personal data. -->
    <Person>
        <Name>George Smith</Name>
        <Address>
            <AddressLine>1234 West Street</AddressLine>
            <AddressLine>Suite 20</AddressLine>
        </Address>
        <City>Somewhere</City>
        <State>WI</State>
        <ZIP_Code>54001</ZIP_Code>
        <Telephone>
            <Number Location="Home">(555)555-1212</Number>
        </Telephone>
        <PersonalData>
            <Note Type="TimeToCall" Hour="PM">
                8:30
            </Note>
            <Note Type="SpouseName">
                Nancy
            </Note>
        </PersonalData>
    </Person>
    <Person>
        <Name>Amy Wright</Name>
        <Address>
            <AddressLine>99 Lear Street</AddressLine>
        </Address>
        <City>Edge</City>
        <State>CA</State>
        <ZIP_Code>99122</ZIP_Code>
        <Telephone>
            <Number Location="Office">(555)555-1234</Number>
            <Number Location="Home">(555)555-9876</Number>
        </Telephone>
        <PersonalData />
    </Person>
</AddressBook>
```

The XML processing instruction isn't a node. In fact, none of the processing instructions you add to a document are nodes because they don't contain viewable data. For this same reason, comments also aren't nodes. Only elements are nodes. Even empty elements are still leaf nodes because they convey the lack of data or null data. The empty set is an important kind of data that tells the viewer the data doesn't exist, rather than you simply didn't add it.

Simple Techniques for Displaying XML

The easiest way to view XML is as plain text — from the command prompt. Several other possibilities also exist:

✦ **Use a text editor:** XML is simple text; any editor that can display text can also display XML. Unfortunately, if the XML document is color-coded to reveal its features, this technique isn't particularly helpful (most text editors won't highlight the XML code using color). Even so, you can usually make small changes — or view short XML documents — with little difficulty if you use a text editor (such as Notepad) for the purpose.

✦ **Use your browser:** Most modern browsers, such as Internet Explorer, provide special features for seeing XML, as shown in Figure 1-1. The advantage of using this technique is that you see the XML using highlighted text. In addition, click any of the minus signs to collapse a section of the XML so you get just an overview of the document. Click a plus sign to expand a collapsed section of the document. This option works anywhere, even on Web sites that don't give you direct access to the document. (Unfortunately, however, you can't edit a document using a browser.)

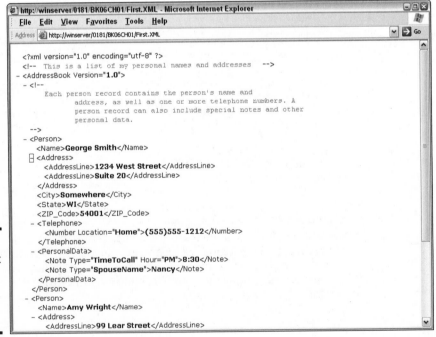

Figure 1-1:
Use Internet
Explorer to
view XML
documents
anywhere.

✦ **Open your XML document directly in FrontPage:** This approach is shown in Figure 1-2. Unlike Internet Explorer, you can't collapse or expand various levels of the document, so you have to page back and forth within the document as you view it. However, the advantage of this technique is that you can edit the document, and FrontPage provides some features for working with XML that you don't get with Internet Explorer, such as verification. See the "Organizing and checking the document" section of this chapter for details.

✦ **Use a third-party editor specifically designed for working with XML:** You can find a number of these products online, but you only really use them when you want to perform complex tasks with XML. FrontPage is perfectly suitable for working with simple XML documents and discovering how you want to work with XML.

If you do want to go the third-party route, you have a range of options. Each has its own attractions and limitations, as the following sections show — starting with the simplest of the XML viewers available.

**Book VI
Chapter 1**

Working with XML

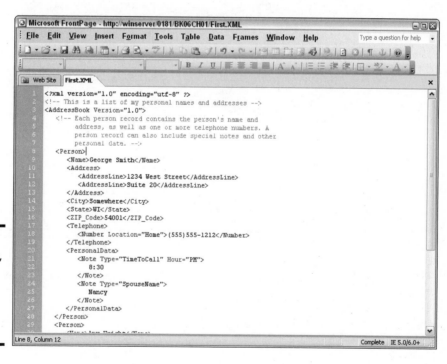

Figure 1-2:
Edit, format, and verify your XML document using FrontPage.

XML Notepad

You might want to start with an older Microsoft product called XML Notepad. Although Microsoft doesn't support this program any longer, you can download it from SnapFiles at

http://www.snapfiles.com/get/xmlnotepad.html

This editor has several advantages over FrontPage as an XML viewer, as shown in Figure 1-3. You can see the nodes in a Windows Explorer-like tree view with the content of the element shown in the right pane. The use of special icons makes using this editor particularly easy even for large documents. You can also expand and collapse the nodes as needed. The only problem with XML Notepad is that it supports only basic XML constructs — you need a better editor when working with complex documents. In addition, XML Notepad doesn't work with XML support files, so you might find it limited as you explore XML in greater depth.

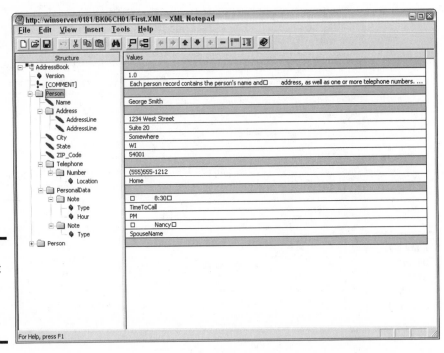

Figure 1-3:
Experiment with XML editors using XML Notepad.

XMLFox

Another good free option is XMLFox (`http://www.xmlfox.com/`). The left side of the XMLFox display is yet another version of the standard tree display — this one sports special symbols and colors. The unique feature of this product is that it uses a tabular view of the XML data, which works pretty well with some types of complex XML files. XMLFox includes some advanced capabilities that support even complex XML documents. The disadvantage of this product is that you must download several Microsoft products to use it including the .NET Framework. One drawback: Download time can become expensive.

XMLwriter 2

Some people prefer not to use a tree view. FrontPage supports XML without using a tree view — and so do other products. One of the better alternatives is XMLwriter 2 (`http://www.xmlwriter.net/`). This is a try-before-you-buy (shareware) product. (I won't say that this product is shareware in the strictest sense because the trial period limits use to 30 days.) Unlike many other XML editors on the market, XMLwriter 2 also uses a Notepad-style document display for editing. This product automatically assumes you want to use color-coding for keywords. You'll also find the use of automation nice. For example, when you type an opening tag, XMLwriter 2 automatically creates a closing tag for you. The IDE also features an XML checker. Simply right-click the document and select Validate XML File from the context menu. Any errors appear in a TODO list at the bottom of the IDE.

XMLSpy

At some point, you might need an XML editor that provides automatic generation of complex data because writing complex XML documents by hand is a time consuming and error prone process. One of the most popular high-end XML editors on the market today is XMLSpy (`http://www.xmlspy.com/`). You can download a limited time evaluation copy of the product from the Altova Web site. After the evaluation period ends, you must either remove XMLSpy from your system or buy a copy. The feature that makes XMLSpy so useful is the extreme automation it provides. In addition, XMLSpy provides support for the full range of XML features, including most of the features for add-on standards and file types. You can use this product to create and manage entire XML projects.

Using the XML View Toolbar

If you're looking at your XML document directly in FrontPage, you're using some direct XML functionality that doesn't rely on a particular server setup.

You can rely on this functionality even when you use a server without Internet Information Server (IIS) or FrontPage Extensions installed. The next few sections discuss FrontPage's XML features in detail.

Creating the document

FrontPage doesn't provide a means for creating an XML file directly. Before you can work with an XML file, you must either create it externally, or create another file type with FrontPage and rename it. The best way to create a new XML file directly in FrontPage is to right-click the folder you want to use for storage and select New➪Text File from the context menu. FrontPage creates the new file. Give the file a name with an XML extension and you're ready to create an XML document. Using the text file option ensures the file is blank when you open it.

After you create the file, you can add properties to it just as you do for any other FrontPage file. Right-click the file and choose Properties from the context menu. These entries appear in Folders view. Unlike HTML files, XML files don't require you to provide properties within the file — you can't use meta tags or other means of identification within an XML file.

It pays to create a page template for XML files when you plan to work with them regularly. Creating an XML page template lets you use the New window of the Task Pane.

Organizing and checking the document

After you create your XML document, it's important to organize it and check it for errors. The XML View toolbar provides two buttons for this task, as shown in Figure 1-4. FrontPage doesn't display this toolbar by default. You display the toolbar by right-clicking in the toolbar area and choose XML View from the context menu.

Figure 1-4:
Manage XML documents using the XML View toolbar.

Formatting the document automatically

The XML View toolbar contains two buttons. Each offers a different approach to formatting your XML document:

✦ **Reformat XML:** Click this button to format the XML tags in a document according to the options you set on the Code Formatting tab of the Page Options dialog box. This feature is especially useful when you obtain the XML document from another source. The XML standard doesn't specify any form of formatting for the XML document, so some automated software leaves any white space out, making the document extremely difficult to read.

✦ **Verify Well-Formed XML:** Click this button when you want to check the document for errors. This check also ensures the nesting of the XML document is correct so a reader can understand the document properly. When the check passes, FrontPage displays a dialog box to tell you the document is well formed and well nested. Otherwise . . .

Dealing with XML errors in FrontPage

Suppose you used the Verify Well-Formed XML button but the document turned out other than well formed or well nested. If that happens, you see an XML Validation dialog box, listing any errors that FrontPage finds. Then you click Go To Error and FrontPage takes you to the location of the error it found in the document.

When you're working with a nesting error, FrontPage takes you to the first location of a mismatch, which might not be the location of the problem end tag. Make sure you look several lines above and below the error to verify there are no errors in the other lines of XML code. Otherwise, you might end up chasing several errors when only one exists in the document. For example, look at the following code.

```
<Note Type="SpouseName">
    Nancy
</PersonalData>
    </Note>
```

FrontPage stops at the `</PersonalData>` end tag as the error. Even though this is the first location of an error, the actual error is on the next line with the `</Note>` end tag. Simply move the `</Note>` end tag up one line to fix the error.

Creating XML Data from Existing Sources

Sometimes you want to work with XML data from other sources. For example, you might want to present an Office document on-screen as XML so that you can create multiple views of the information. Many applications output XML data today because it's such a convenient method of exchanging data with other platforms and other applications. The next few sections discuss working with XML from other sources.

In some cases, application vendors won't actually tell you that their applications output data in XML format — or that bit of information is deeply buried in the documentation and hard to find. For example, many people don't realize that Visual Studio outputs a lot of its data in XML format. Knowing this information can help you create unique data presentations and help build a data store of information from other sources that you could access with common applications such as a browser.

Modifying the document encoding

One problem you could encounter when using data from another application is that the encoding is incompatible with another application or platform. Fortunately, FrontPage makes document encoding easy to change. You can change the document encoding with a few quick steps:

1. **Right-click the XML document and choose Encoding from the context menu.**

You see the Text File Encoding dialog box shown in Figure 1-5.

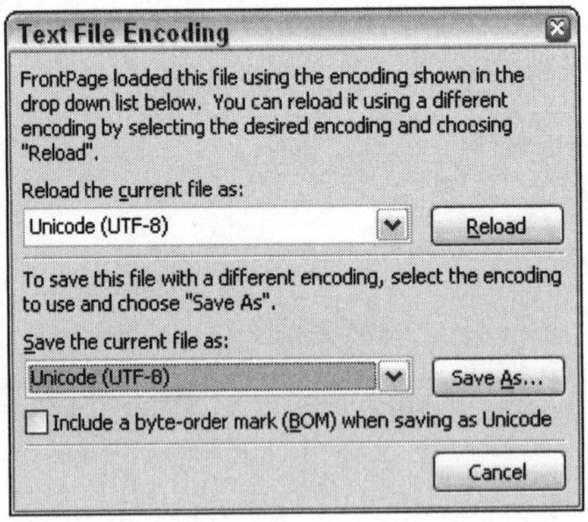

Figure 1-5:
Modify the
encoding for
a document
as need
to view it
in other
applications.

Text File Encoding

FrontPage loaded this file using the encoding shown in the drop down list below. You can reload it using a different encoding by selecting the desired encoding and choosing "Reload".

Reload the current file as:

Unicode (UTF-8) [Reload]

To save this file with a different encoding, select the encoding to use and choose "Save As".

Save the current file as:

Unicode (UTF-8) [Save As...]

☐ Include a byte-order mark (BOM) when saving as Unicode

[Cancel]

2. Choose what to do next from the upper and lower sections of the dialog box.

You have two options you can choose while the dialog box is open:

- Load a document using a specific encoding.

- Save the document with a specific encoding that's different from the original.

Don't attempt to perform both tasks without closing the dialog box first or you'll experience errors.

3. If necessary, change the encoding of the document so it's readable.

The "Now you read it, now you don't" sidebar shows how; refer to Figure 1-6.

Book VI
Chapter 1

Working with XML

Creating XML output with Office 2003

Microsoft has made it pretty plain that Office 2003 sports some fancy new XML features. The problem is most users don't fully understand these features. This section relies on Word, but the process is about the same for other Office 2003 products.

The example in this section exports an outline you create in Word to XML format so you can exchange it with other people. When you want to export your document, you need to decide how to export it to FrontPage. For example, you need to decide whether you want the full Word functionality, or just the formatted data. When you use the XML Document (*.xml) option for saving the document, what you really get is WordML (Word Markup Language), which is a type of XML, but probably not what you expected. You can see such a document in the `MyBookWordML.XML` file provided in the source code for this chapter on this book's companion Web site. The XML document includes everything you add to your Word document, including properties such as the author name.

Creating an XSD file

To save just the data from your Word file, you need to create a document that has XML data in it. A Word document doesn't include any XML data — Word views the data as formatted text. To create the XML data, you must tag the information so Word associates each piece of information in the document with a tag in the XML document. You can use an existing XML document as a source for a schema or you can create a new eXtensible Schema Definition (XSD) file. An XSD file defines the order and presentation of the information in an XML file.

You already know a lot of about XSD files because they rely on XML. An XSD file is merely a description of how you want your XML document to appear. Listing 1-3 shows an XSD file. You can also find this code in the `MySimpleBookDefinition.XSD` file found in the source code for this chapter on this book's companion Web site.

Listing 1-3: XSD File for a Word Outline

```xml
<?xml version="1.0" encoding="utf-8" standalone="yes"?>
<xs:schema xmlns:xs="http://www.w3.org/2001/XMLSchema"
 targetNamespace="http://www.mysite.com"
 xmlns="http://www.mysite.com"
 elementFormDefault="qualified">

<xs:element name="MyBook">
   <xs:complexType mixed="true">
      <xs:sequence>
         <xs:element name="TitleArea" minOccurs="1"
                  maxOccurs="1">
            <xs:complexType mixed="true">
               <xs:sequence>
                  <xs:element name="Title" type="xs:string"
                           minOccurs="1" maxOccurs="1" />
                  <xs:element name="Heading1Area"
                           maxOccurs="unbounded">
                     <xs:complexType mixed="true">
                        <xs:sequence>
                           <xs:element name="Heading1"
                                    type="xs:string"
                                    minOccurs="1"
                                    maxOccurs="1" />
                           <xs:element name="Heading2"
                                    type="xs:string"
                                    minOccurs="0"
                                    maxOccurs="unbounded"
                                    />
                        </xs:sequence>
                     </xs:complexType>
                  </xs:element>
               </xs:sequence>
            </xs:complexType>
         </xs:element>
      </xs:sequence>
   </xs:complexType>
</xs:element>

</xs:schema>
```

The XSD file begins with an XML processing instruction, just like any other XML document. So, even though the file has an XSD extension, it's still just XML in disguise.

The next tag is what makes an XSD file different from a standard XML file, and you'll run into this difference with every other XML variation. The `xs:schema` tag actually contains two elements `xs` (a namespace) and `schema` (a tag name). A *namespace* is a reference to a location that contains rules for working with a particular kind of data. In this case, the rules define how to work with XSD data, but you see namespaces used for many other kinds of XML implementations.

The next part of the tag, `xmlns:xs="http://www.w3.org/2001/XMLSchema"`, is an attribute, just like any other XML attribute. This attribute begins with another special namespace, `xmlns`, which provides a pointer to the namespace for this particular XSD file. The `xs` portion defines where to find a definition for XSD rules. Try it out and you'll discover that the URL really does take you to a Web site that tells you about XSD. You can find additional information about XSD at `http://www.w3.org/TR/2001/PR-xmlschema-0-20010330/primer.html`.

The `targetNamespace` attribute defines which namespace to use to resolve all local definitions. You always set this to the local namespace.

The `xmlns` attribute describes a unique location for this XSD file. You should use a location on your own Web site to ensure the namespace is unique. The URL doesn't have to point anywhere, but you can use a real URL that points to a description of your namespace. Whether you create such a URL or not depends on how the XSD file is used — XSD files for public use should probably have a real URL with a description of this XSD file.

The `elementFormDefault` attribute tells whether locally defined complex data types are namespace qualified. Always set this attribute to qualified. You set it to unqualified in special circumstances that most developers won't need.

After you define all of the required references, you begin creating a definition for an outline. The outline defines a *book*, so the first element type is MyBook. Whenever you describe a document, break it down into pieces beginning with the largest or most complex element and moving down to the smallest or least complex piece. Every piece of the document is called an element and you use the `<xs:element>` tag to describe it. The `name` attribute defines the kind of element.

A page of a book isn't simple — it contains many elements, so it's a complex type. The `<xs:complextType>` tag says that this is a complex type that contains a mix of other types. There are many ways to create complex types, but an outline is really a sequence that begins with the book title, so the XSD file uses the `<xs:sequence>` tag to define the book as a sequence of elements.

The second `xs:element` tag describes the `TitleArea`, which is essentially a container for holding the title and everything that comes after it. A book only has one title, so the `TitleArea` has two attributes that restrict the title area to one and only one occurrence using a combination of the `minOccurs` and `maxOccurs` attributes.

The `TitleArea` is a complex type that consists of another sequence. First, the user has to define a `Title`. This is a simple type. Notice the `type` attribute is a string. The user provides a string that describes the title. The `Title` can appear only once, and then the user has to add headings to describe the content of the outline. So, the second element of the sequence is another complex type, `Heading1Area`.

An outline can contain any number of headings, so the `Heading1Area` element is unbounded. When you set the `maxOccurs` attribute to unbounded, the element can occur any number of times. The `Heading1Area` element is a complex type that must contain at least one `Heading1` element and any number of `Heading2` elements (the next level of the outline). The `Heading1` and `Heading2` elements are simple types that consist of strings. Notice that the `Heading2` element has a `minOccurs` value of 0, which means that you don't have to include a `Heading2` element within the `Heading1Area` element.

Adding the XSD file to Word

After you create an XSD file that describes your document (an outline in this case), you add it to the Word document. You then tag the various document elements and save just the data to an XML file. FrontPage can read this data and you can use it as part of a Web site page. The following steps tell you how to perform these tasks:

1. **Open the document in Word. Select the XML Structure window from the Task Pane.**

   You see the nearly blank XML Structure window with a Templates and Add-Ins link.

2. **Click Templates and Add-ins.**

   You see the XML Schema tab of the Templates and Add-ins dialog box.

3. **Click Add Schema.**

   You see an Add Schema dialog box.

4. Locate the XSD file you created and click Open.

You see a schema settings dialog box.

5. Type a name for the schema in the Alias field and click OK.

Word automatically adds the new schema to the Available XML Schemas list on the XML Schema tab of the Templates and Add-ins dialog box. It also checks this option so the current document uses it.

6. Click OK.

The XML Structure dialog box changes to show the first element type you can add to the document. This is MyBook in the case of the example. The schema will reflect whatever top level (root) element you choose for your document.

7. Click the top level element (MyBook for purposes of the example).

Word asks whether you want to add the element to the whole document.

8. Click Add to Entire Document.

Word tags the entire document with the top level element.

9. Highlight each document area in turn and choose the correct element from the element list.

You see an outline of XML elements similar to the one shown in Figure 1-6 built as you tag elements.

Book VI
Chapter 1

Working with XML

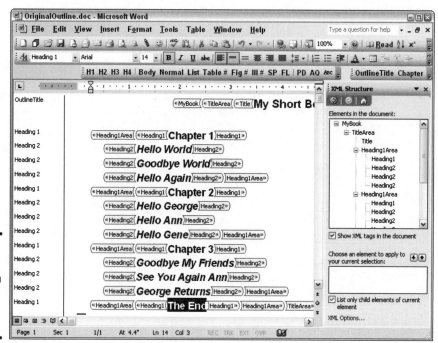

Figure 1-6:
Create an
XML version
of your
outline
using tags.

10. **Choose the File⇨Save As command.**

You see the Save As dialog box.

11. **Select XML Document (*.xml) in the Save As Type field. Check Save Data Only. Click Save.**

Word saves just the XML data.

When you open the document in FrontPage, click Reformat XML in the XML View toolbar. You'll see a properly formatted and nested version of the Word document in XML form. This XML document contains just the data without any other Word information, so you can safely send it to someone else or use it as part of a Web site display.

Chapter 2: Developing an Interpretation with XSLT

In This Chapter

✔ **Working with XSLT**

✔ **Defining an XSLT document**

✔ **Choosing data from an XML document**

✔ **Deciding how to interpret XML data**

✔ **Performing tasks more than one time**

✔ **Creating XML data views using XSLT**

*V*iewing XML by itself is only the beginning. Yes, you can eventually decipher the meaning of even the most complex document, but computers are supposed to make life *easier,* right? XML might make data exchange easier, but it doesn't do much to make the data easier to work with. That's why eXtensible Style Language Transformation (XSLT) is such an important technology. This complex-sounding phrase describes a process that accepts XML as input, transforms it to human-readable form, and styles it for easy reading. In essence, XSLT is a special XML file with its own language. This chapter discusses how XSLT affects XML input.

XSLT can perform translation tasks beyond what it can do with XML. (For example, some developers create a text description of simple applications and use XSLT to write the required code.) In fact, XSLT can transform any text input into any other text input — but it doesn't do anything by itself. You use XSLT to create a particular kind of output based on an input document; XSLT affects that input but doesn't generate any data.

Like any scripting language, XSLT includes features for selecting data, making decisions, and performing tasks multiple times. The chapter describes many of the basic XSLT constructs — enough so you can perform many transformation tasks. When you decide you want to work with some of the more obscure XSLT features, check the reference at

`http://www.zvon.org/xxl/XSLTreference/Output/index.html`

You can also look at the standard at `http://www.w3.org/TR/xslt`.

The FrontPage offers two ways to connect with XSLT. Each uses XML with a different degree of complexity:

✦ You can create single views of an XML data source, just as you would for any Web page.

✦ You can create multiple views of the same data. This capability combines XSLT with XML, and differentiates XSLT from static page-creation techniques. You can present the same data in multiple ways, making XSLT extremely flexible and user-friendly.

Understanding How XSLT Affects XML

XSLT is a means of transforming — rather than creating — data. XSLT output doesn't necessarily even appear on-screen, but it's easy to create XSLT that accepts XML as input and creates standard text as output. Given enough time, you could take XML and convert it directly into a Word document — or even into a database file. The most important thing to remember about XSLT is that it accepts any text input and creates any text output. With the addition of a few specialized techniques, you can even create binary output, such as an application, sound file, or graphics file, if you want.

Given the current widespread use of HTML in Web pages, it follows that the most common current use of XSLT is to transform XML input into an HTML page. It's important to consider the whole process when you view this particular use of XSLT:

First, a user creates Web-page content using any of various applications (including specialized database applications).

The application outputs this content as XML, so there's little chance of getting poorly constructed XML or having gaps in the content.

XSLT accepts this XML as input and outputs an HTML page. Consequently, content changes no longer affect the design of the Web page and vice versa.

Changes are made independently, so you don't see odd effects because someone didn't know the right series of HTML tags to use. Everyone can concentrate on the job they know best.

Creating a Basic XSLT File

FrontPage provides good support for XSLT files. In fact, you'll find that even IntelliSense works well with XSLT files — and that using IntelliSense makes the task of writing XSLT code significantly easier. Like many other file types, FrontPage doesn't provide a direct method for creating XSLT files. To create an XSLT file, right-click the folder where you want the file to appear and select New⇨Text File from the context menu. Give the file name an XSLT extension.

An XSLT file is an odd amalgamation of XML and other elements. In this chapter, you combine XML and HTML to create an XSLT file — and the output can consist of any kind of text (in addition to the XSLT statements). Listing 2-1 shows a typical example of a starting XSLT file for converting an XML document into a Web page.

Listing 2-1:   Defining a Basic XSLT File

**Book VI
Chapter 2**

**Developing an
Interpretation
with XSLT**

```
<?xml version="1.0" encoding="utf-8"?>
<xsl:stylesheet version='1.0'
 xmlns:xsl='http://www.w3.org/1999/XSL/Transform'>
<xsl:output method="html" indent="yes" />
<xsl:template match="/AddressBook">

<HTML>
<HEAD>
   <TITLE>Personal Address List</TITLE>
</HEAD>

<BODY>
<H1>Personal Address List</H1>

</BODY>
</HTML>

</xsl:template>

</xsl:stylesheet>
```

Like every other XML document you create, an XSLT document begins with an XML processing instruction. The `<xsl:stylesheet>` tag defines the entire document as a version-1.0 XSLT file — and provides the URL where you can find instructions for processing such a file.

The `<xsl:output>` tag defines the kind of output this XSLT file creates. The `method` attribute tells you that this XSLT file creates HTML output. The `indent` attribute indicates that the output should contain indentation to make it easier to read.

The first tag that actually handles an incoming XML file is the `<xsl:template>` tag. In this case, the `match` attribute indicates the XSLT file will process all children of the `<AddressBook>` tag, which is the root node of the `First.XML` file used for demonstration purposes. You can find this file in the source code for this chapter on this book's companion Web site. To process the whole XML file, including the root node, you use the `<xsl:template match="/">` tag.

The remainder of this sample contains an essentially empty HTML page. You could easily create a page template using this setup and add it to the New window of the Task Pane.

To view the output of this XSLT file, you must attach it to an XML file. This requires the addition of another processing instruction to the XML file so the browser or other reader knows to use the XSLT file for process. (You can also accomplish this task using a script and other means, but the processing instruction is the fastest and easiest method.) Here's the code you need to add (in bold):

```
<?xml version="1.0" encoding="utf-8" ?>
<?xml-stylesheet type="text/xsl" href="First.XSLT"?>
<AddressBook Version="1.0">
```

The XML-Stylesheet processing instruction must appear after the XML processing instruction, but before the root node. The `type` attribute defines the content of the XSLT file. In this case, the file contains both text and eXtensible Style Language (XSL) content. The `href` attribute tells where to locate the XSLT file. In this case, the file appears in the same folder as the XML file in the `First.XSLT` file.

Selecting Data

Before you can do anything with the XML input provided to your XSLT file, you have to select the data. An element provides a means of selection, and you can read both attributes and values for any given element. The selection strategy relies on the hierarchy of elements from the very beginning of the XML document to the lowest leaf. Think of it in the same way as you do your hard drive because you use the same technique to access the various nodes. Consider this XML segment:

```
<A>
    <B>
        <C />
    </B>
</A>
```

To access the `<C>` node, you refer to it as A/B/C, as you would for a folder on a hard drive. Note that you use a forward slash instead of a backward slash as you would for a hard drive, but the principle is the same.

XSLT complicates matters somewhat by letting you define a starting position using the `<xsl:template>` tag, as shown in Figure 2-1. You set the starting position using the `match` attribute. So, if you create an XSLT document with a tag like this: `<xsl:template match="/A">`, you can select the `<C>` node using `B/C`.

A simple list of nodes without any data doesn't do much but sit there — so Listing 2-2 shows the sample XML document used as input for the examples in this chapter. The listing includes two records that contain nonuniform data so you can see how XSLT reacts in various circumstances. You can also find this file in the First.XML file located in the source code for this chapter on this book's companion Web site.

Listing 2-2:   Input XML Document

```xml
<?xml version="1.0" encoding="utf-8" ?>
<?xml-stylesheet type="text/xsl" href="First.XSLT"?>
<AddressBook Version="1.0">
   <Person>
      <Name>George Smith</Name>
      <Address>
         <AddressLine>1234 West Street</AddressLine>
         <AddressLine>Suite 20</AddressLine>
      </Address>
      <City>Somewhere</City>
      <State>WI</State>
      <ZIP_Code>54001</ZIP_Code>
      <Telephone>
         <Number Location="Home">(555)555-1212</Number>
      </Telephone>
      <PersonalData>
         <Note Type="TimeToCall" Hour="PM">
            8:30
         </Note>
         <Note Type="SpouseName">
            Nancy
         </Note>
      </PersonalData>
   </Person>
   <Person>
      <Name>Amy Wright</Name>
      <Address>
         <AddressLine>99 Lear Street</AddressLine>
      </Address>
      <City>Edge</City>
      <State>CA</State>
      <ZIP_Code>99122</ZIP_Code>
      <Telephone>
         <Number Location="Office">(555)555-1234</Number>
         <Number Location="Home">(555)555-9876</Number>
      </Telephone>
      <PersonalData />
   </Person>
</AddressBook>
```

The file begins with two processing instructions. The first is the standard XML processing instruction and the second is the XML-Stylesheet processing instruction that connects the input file to the XSLT file. (See the "Creating a Basic XSLT File" section earlier in this chapter for more about this second processing instruction.) The root node for this file is `<AddressBook>`, and it contains two child records named `<Person>`. Each `<Person>` node has similar children, each record is also unique and presents special processing challenges (as you find in any input XML file). The code in Listing 2-1 shows that the example begins processing with the `<AddressBook>` node.

Obtaining a value

Selecting a node isn't enough. You must indicate the information you want from the node. The most common data taken from XML documents is the node value. To access the node value, you use the `<xsl:value-of>` element like this:

```
<xsl:value-of select="Person/Name" />
```

In this case, XSLT selects the `<Name>` node and returns the value of this node. Look again at Listing 2-2. The first `<Name>` node contains George Smith, while the second contains Amy Wright. An `<xsl:value-of>` element can only select the first of these two nodes. The "Performing a Task More Than Once" section, later in this chapter, tells how you can use repetition to read each of the nodes in turn.

Obtaining an attribute

Sometimes you need to display attribute values. For example, when the XML input includes several kinds of the same information, you need to differentiate the information in some way. A telephone number might be for home, office, or mobile use, so you need to display that information on-screen. The example in Listing 2-2 differentiates this information using an attribute for the `<Number>` node named `Location`. To display an attribute on-screen, you access the element first, and then use a special symbol to access the attribute, like this:

```
<xsl:value-of select="Person/Telephone/Number/@Location" />
```

You use the same selection method for defining the element location as you do when getting a value. Accessing the attribute means adding the @ (at) symbol in front of the attribute name. This code tells XSLT to access the `Location` attribute in the `<Number>` node and obtain its value. When an element has multiple attributes, you can select each attribute by name. You must use a separate `<xsl:value-of>` element for each selection, as shown here:

```
<xsl:value-of select="Person/PersonalData/Note/@Type" />
<xsl:value-of select="Person/PersonalData/Note/@Hour" />
```

Adding text

You add text using any of several techniques. The first technique is to place it between standard HTML tags or make it part of an HTML tag. Listing 2-1 shows numerous examples of how you can use HTML tags to your advantage within an XSLT document. However, HTML tags aren't always usable because you create complex mixes of XML and HTML data as output. For example, you might want to display a person's name and their telephone number using the data from Listing 2-2. When you want to combine text, HTML, and XML to produce output, you use the `<xsl:text>` tag, as shown here:

```
<p>
<xsl:value-of select="Person/Name" />
<br />
<xsl:value-of select="Person/Telephone/Number/@Location" />
<xsl:text> Telephone Number: </xsl:text>
<xsl:value-of select="Person/Telephone/Number" />
</p>
```

This example combines all three elements to produce the output shown in Figure 2-1. No one looking at this output would know that the information comes from so many sources. Notice how the example uses an opening and closing `<xsl:text>` tag. An important concept to remember when working with XSLT in this way is that you must use character codes for some characters such as the angle brackets.

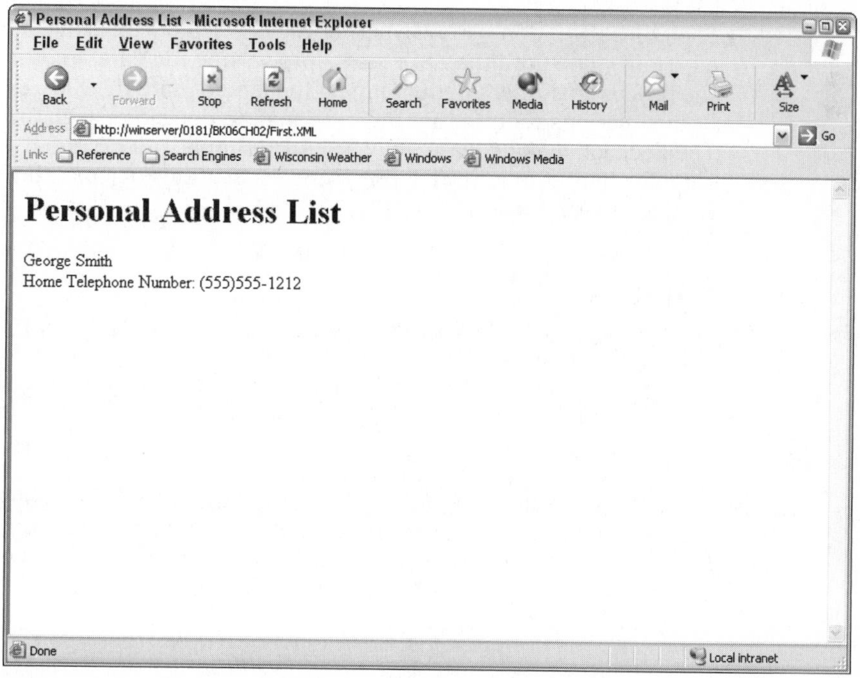

Book VI
Chapter 2

Developing an
Interpretation
with XSLT

Figure 2-1:
Combining HTML, XML, and text produces useful output from XML input.

Using functions

XSLT provides a number of built-in functions. A *function* is a special entry that references code to perform work. For example, you might want to know how long an entry is so that you can process it correctly. To determine an entry's length use the `string-length()` function, as shown here:

```
<xsl:text>The telephone number is </xsl:text>
<xsl:value-of
    select="string-length(Person/Telephone/Number)" />
<xsl:text> digits long.</xsl:text>
```

Using the example XML shown in Listing 2-2, this XSLT code displays a string, "The telephone number is 13 digits long." The `string-length()` function processes the node by counting the number of characters in the value before turning the result over to XSLT, which then displays the function results. Notice how the function appears within the double quotes with the rest of the text for the `select` attribute. Functions always appear with the data as a single entity. You can discover other useful functions at

`http://www.zvon.org/xxl/XSLTreference/Output/xpathFunctionIndex.html`

I also include many useful functions as part of the examples in this chapter.

Making Decisions

Sometimes you don't know whether the data you need is available or has a certain value until the XSLT starts processing the data. In other cases, the processing differs depending on the kind of data the XML contains. Both situations require that the XSLT make a decision based on the input. The decision-making features of XSLT are simple, but essential for creating complex output from XML input. The next sections discuss some of these decision-making features.

Using <xsl:if>

You use the `<xsl:if>` element when the decision is a simple yes or no. For example, you might want to know whether someone has an office telephone number listed in the database. When the entry has an office telephone number, you display one message; otherwise, you display another message.

An `<xsl:if>` element makes a Boolean (yes/no or true/false) decision, so you have to create code that produces a Boolean result. In many cases, this means using both operators and functions. An *operator* is a comparison symbol between two values. (For example, when you want to compare the value of A with B, you use the equal sign like this: `A = B`.) To determine whether a person has an office telephone number on file, you make a comparison with the Location attribute of the <Number> node — like this:

```
<xsl:if test="string(Person/Telephone/Number/@Location)
   != 'Office'">
      <xsl:text>No Office Phone</xsl:text><br />
</xsl:if>
```

The example begins with the <xsl:if> element. It contains only one attribute, test, which defines what information to compare. In this case, the code uses the string() function to convert the Location attribute to a string (a series of characters) and then compares it with the word Office. The code relies on the != (or not equal) operator. When the Location attribute is not equal to Office, then XSLT outputs the text No Office Phone.

Notice how the word Office appears within single quotes. Placing Office within single quotes tells XSLT that this is a value and not something else like an element. Whenever you want to use a value in XSLT, enclose it within single quotes.

**Book VI
Chapter 2**

**Developing an
Interpretation
with XSLT**

Using <xsl:choose>

Sometimes a simple <xsl:if> element won't work because it can only handle yes and no questions. The <xsl:choose> element lets you look for one of several possible answers and handle situations where none of the answers is present in the data. You combine the <xsl:choose> element with the <xsl:when> and <xsl:otherwise> elements to test for specific value or attribute data in an element. The <xsl:otherwise> element doesn't actually test for a value — you use it as a way to do something when none of the <xsl:when> element tests pass. Here's a typical example of an <xsl:choose> element in action:

```
<xsl:choose>
   <xsl:when test="string(Person/PersonalData/Note/@Type) =
   'TimeToCall'">
      <xsl:text>Best Calling Time: </xsl:text>
      <xsl:value-of select="Person/PersonalData/Note" />
      <xsl:value-of select="Person/PersonalData/Note/@Hour"/>
   </xsl:when>
   <xsl:when test="string(Person/PersonalData/Note/@Type) =
   'SpouseName'">
      <xsl:text>Spouse Name: </xsl:text>
      <xsl:value-of select="Person/PersonalData/Note" />
   </xsl:when>
   <xsl:otherwise>
      <xsl:text>Note Type Not Recognized</xsl:text>
   </xsl:otherwise>
</xsl:choose>
```

The code checks notes for specific types. The example data in Listing 2-2 contains two types of notes: `TimeToCall` and `SpouseName`. The first `<xsl:when>` element tests for the `TimeToCall` attribute value. When this value is present, the code displays a message with the best time to call. Notice how this example combines text with both a value and an attribute. The second `<xsl:when>` element tests for the `SpouseName` attribute value and displays an appropriate message when it's present. Finally, the `<xsl:otherwise>` element is chosen when none of the `<xsl:when>` elements are triggered and displays a generic message.

Performing a Task More Than Once

It's common to find multiple copies of some types of XML data in the input — and you'll also have to process multiple records. You usually don't know how many duplicate elements or records you need to process, so having a way to perform the same process over and over is important. Processing in a loop (multiple times) is a common programming task. As with decision-making, XSLT takes a very simple approach to loop processing.

The only loop processing that XSLT provides is the `<xsl:for-each>` element. This loop-processing element keeps performing a given set of tasks as long as there are elements with the appropriate name. When it runs out of duplicate elements, the `<xsl:for-each>` loop automatically exits and XSLT begins with the next statement. Here's an example of the `<xsl:for-each>` element in use:

```
<!-- Process all of the telephone numbers. -->
<xsl:for-each select="Telephone/Number">

    <!-- Display a telephone number and its length. -->
    <xsl:value-of select="@Location" />
    <xsl:text> Telephone Number: </xsl:text>
    <xsl:value-of select="." /><br />
    <xsl:text>The telephone number is </xsl:text>
    <xsl:value-of select="string-length(.)" />
    <xsl:text> digits long.</xsl:text><br />
</xsl:for-each>
```

Look again at Listing 2-2. Notice that the `<Telephone>` element is parent to one or more `<Number>` elements. To process multiple `<Number>` elements, the `<xsl:for-each>` uses the select attribute to choose the `Telephone/Number` element.

The selection process incurs another problem: Now that the `<Number>` element is selected, you must find a way to refer to its value. Normally you would select the `<Number>` element as needed — but it's already selected, so you can't select it again. Here's where you use the . (period) to choose the current element. The example code shows how you use the . to select the current element in a number of situations. You still choose attributes using the @ sign as usual. For example, to display the Location attribute, you select @Location in the code.

Creating a View of XML with XSLT

Knowing about all the XSLT elements is a nice place to start, but putting them together into a *view* is better. The important idea is to create a view that displays the data in a way that benefits the user. You don't have to use every piece of information in the XML file — in fact, you can leave unimportant information out of the view. Listing 2-3 shows a complete XSLT file you can use to display the XML file presented in Listing 2-2.

Listing 2-3:   Defining a Simple View with XSLT

```
<?xml version="1.0" encoding="utf-8"?>
<xsl:stylesheet version='1.0'
 xmlns:xsl='http://www.w3.org/1999/XSL/Transform'>
<xsl:output method="html" indent="yes" />
<xsl:template match="/AddressBook">

<HTML>
<HEAD>
   <TITLE>Personal Address List</TITLE>
</HEAD>

<BODY>
<H1>Personal Address List</H1>

<!-- Process all of the people in a loop. -->
<xsl:for-each select="Person">

   <!-- Display each record in a separate paragraph. -->
   <p>

   <!-- Get the person's name -->
   <xsl:value-of select="Name" />
   <br />

   <!-- Display the address information. -->
   <xsl:text>Address: </xsl:text>
   <xsl:value-of select="Address" /><br />
   <xsl:value-of select="City" />
   <xsl:text>, </xsl:text>
   <xsl:value-of select="State" />
   <xsl:text>     </xsl:text>
```

(continued)

Listing 2-3 *(continued)*

```
<xsl:value-of select="ZIP_Code" /><br />


<!-- Test to see whether the person has an office
     telephone. -->
<xsl:if test="string(Telephone/Number/@Location) !=
 'Office'">
   <xsl:text>No Office Phone</xsl:text><br />
</xsl:if>

<!-- Process all of the telephone numbers. -->
<xsl:for-each select="Telephone/Number">

   <!-- Display a telephone number and its length. -->
   <xsl:value-of select="@Location" />
   <xsl:text> Telephone Number: </xsl:text>
   <xsl:value-of select="." /><br />
   <xsl:text>The telephone number is </xsl:text>
   <xsl:value-of select="string-length(.)" />
   <xsl:text> digits long.</xsl:text><br />
</xsl:for-each>

<!-- Test for certain types of personal data and act on
     it. -->
<xsl:for-each select="PersonalData/Note">
   <xsl:choose>
      <xsl:when test="string(@Type) = 'TimeToCall'">
         <xsl:text>Best Calling Time: </xsl:text>
         <xsl:value-of select="." />
         <xsl:value-of select="@Hour" /><br />
      </xsl:when>
      <xsl:when test="string(@Type) = 'SpouseName'">
         <xsl:text>Spouse Name: </xsl:text>
         <xsl:value-of select="." /><br />
      </xsl:when>
      <xsl:otherwise>
         <xsl:text>Note Type Not Recognized</xsl:text>
      </xsl:otherwise>
   </xsl:choose>
</xsl:for-each>
</p>

<!-- End of person processing. -->
</xsl:for-each>

</BODY>
</HTML>

</xsl:template>

</xsl:stylesheet>
```

This may look like a lot of code, but all these elements appear somewhere in the chapter. No mysteries here. The important idea is to look at each tag individually, comment on what it does, and move on to the next tag. After you look at the information for a while, you begin to understand how everything works together to create a comprehensive view of the data shown in Figure 2-2.

The code begins by creating the HTML document head and body. The heading includes a title, just like the one you might include on any Web page. The code displays a heading for the data — no surprises here.

Processing the data comes next. The <AddressBook> node contains multiple <Person> nodes, each of which contains data you want to see on-screen. The code creates a loop for processing each person individually and places this data within an HTML <p> tag.

Displaying the person's name and address comes first. All you need is a combination <xsl:value-of> and <xsl:text> elements to perform this task. Notice that the code takes a shortcut with the <Address> node. Each <Address> node contains one or more <AddressLine> nodes. You can display all the <AddressLine> nodes at once by using the <Address> node as input to the <xsl:value-of> element. The two <AddressLine> nodes for the first record appear on a single line with a space between them.

**Book VI
Chapter 2**

Developing an
Interpretation
with XSLT

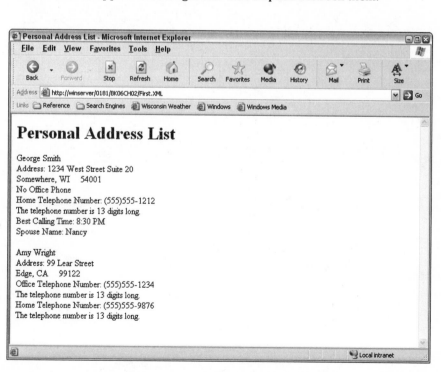

Figure 2-2:
See the XSLT output as a comprehensive view of the XML data.

Processing the telephone numbers comes next. The first task is to check whether the first entry in the database contains an office number. Using this technique assumes that the XML file will always contain the office telephone number first. You can't always make this kind of assumption, but it works in this case. After the code looks for an office telephone number and reports on it, the code processes each of the telephone numbers in turn by displaying the location, telephone number, and number of digits in the telephone number.

The code finishes by processing the notes. Some records don't contain a note, so the <xsl:for-each> element simply moves to the next statement. Whenever a record lacks a feature required to trigger a given response, XSLT simply skips that code, so you should create your XSLT document with this kind of processing in mind.

The code ends by completing the HTML document first and the XSLT document second. Always follow this sequence when you create an XSLT document to ensure it works as anticipated. (For example, when you leave off the </HTML> tag, your browser reports an error instead of displaying the data.)

Chapter 3: Creating Dynamic XML Pages

In This Chapter

✔ Using XML as a data source

✔ Updating an XML data source

✔ Performing XML tasks automatically

*I*nteractive, reactive, ever-changing Web sites that constantly reflect changes in personal, corporate, and viewer needs are somewhat rare today. Although these dynamic Web sites are becoming more common, you're certainly on the bleeding edge of technology when you implement this technique on your own Web site. FrontPage 2003 makes that task easier, especially when you use eXtensible Markup Language (XML) data sources. XML makes working with the data easier.

Using various XML technologies, it's possible to create Web pages that don't exist anywhere but the client's or server's memory. Unlike standard Web pages, these pages don't exist on the machine's hard drive — the server creates them as needed based on the XML data. The same data can appear in multiple forms depending on a user's needs. A huge database that provides more information than the typical user will ever need (or want) can meet the needs of an entire company. Each user probably needs different combinations of data, but no one user will need the entire database — which is why the capability of XML to create unique views is so valuable.

Developing an XML Data Source

XML files contain data you can organize into records for display on-screen. It's unlikely that you'll create such files by hand and will rely instead on application to do the work for you. Consequently, the application you use acts as a database management system (DBMS); the output is the database it provides. Accessing this database requires use of some type of data source. You create a connection to an XML data source so you can display the information on-screen.

Some data-source techniques require the use of scripts. In other cases, you have to create the reference in other ways. For example, you might create an object to display the data on-screen. Such objects can include application interfaces — it's possible, for example, to display XML data within an Excel spreadsheet object on your Web site. You could also create a report out of the same database, using Word. There are many possible techniques — and this section discusses a few of the unique options.

Considering the security issues of XML data

One word of warning about using an XML data source: Remember that XML is text, plain and simple. Anyone who can access the XML data source can read it and possibly modify it. Consequently, you need to protect XML data sources as much as possible and keep sensitive data, such as someone's social security number or credit card information, out of XML files.

Several vendors are currently working on ways to make XML more secure, but the bottom line is that XML can have unexpected and hidden security liabilities. For example, in many cases, all you need to do to view XML data is to right-click the browser display and choose View Source from the context menu.

Amazingly, you see the raw XML, in most cases, rather than the interpreted output presented on-screen. Someone could see the entire content of a data record, rather than the small piece you want them to see. Assuming that the data is hidden because you can't see it when you open the page is one way to create a major security leak.

Always consider the risk of any information you decide to display on a Web page — both hidden and visible data. Sometimes the risk seems minimal, but it really isn't. A contact telephone number, leaving the wrong names in a file, or other forms of "soft" security problems that XML effectively hides from view can cause all kinds of problems. For example, with the right set of names, a cracker can employ a *social-engineering attack* on your network. All the cracker needs to do is find someone at your company who has the right information, drop the name, and use it to gain access. Then even a simple sentence — such as, "Hey, Joe tells me there's a problem with your account, but I need your password to fix it." — can result in a security breach.

Working with Web services

Many people are beginning to look at Web services (a way of using programs that reside on someone else's machine through an Internet connection) as a means of making data available in an easy-to-use format over the Internet. More than a few public Web services are available and you should use them as starting places (examples, as means of testing a client technology, and so on) for creating your own private Web services. The most tested, accessible, and well-known Web services include those from Amazon (http://www.amazon.com/gp/aws/landing.html), Google (http://www.google.com/apis/), and eBay (http://developer.ebay.com/DevProgram/). This section provides a quick overview of how Amazon transmits data using XML, but the same principles apply to other Web services.

One of the first tasks you must perform is to gain access to the XML data. In most cases, you must get a license to work with the vendor data, even when this data appears on a public Web site. For example, you need a developer token (identifier) to use Amazon Web Services. You obtain this token by filling out a form and agreeing to the terms of use for the Web service.

After you get the required token, you can make a request for the information you need. For example, to request information from Amazon, you use a URL similar to this one:

Book VI
Chapter 3

Creating Dynamic
XML Pages

```
http://xml.amazon.com/onca/xml3?t=webservices-20&dev-t=Your-
    Developer-Token&AuthorSearch=John%20Mueller&mode=books&
    type=lite&page=1&f=xml
```

The URL accepts a number of input arguments, just like the arguments you might see after filling out a form on a Web site. Each of these arguments tells Amazon Web Services something about the information you want. For example, the t argument contains your Amazon Associates identifier, so you receive credit for any sales you make, and the dev-t argument contains your developer token. (You can get a closer look at these arguments when you download the developer kit that Amazon provides.)

For this discussion, the two most important arguments are AuthorSearch, which determines what to look for, and f, which determines what format Amazon uses to return the information. This search returns a list of my books in XML format, as shown in Figure 3-1.

The reason I decided to use the Amazon Web Service as an example is that it provides a special feature: You can replace the f argument with a URL for an eXtensible Style Language Transformations (XSLT) file. The URL must point to a publicly accessible file. The rest of the information remains the same, so you can make an XSLT request using a URL such as this one:

```
http://xml.amazon.com/onca/xml3?t=webservices-20&dev-t=Your-
    Developer-
    Token&AuthorSearch=John%20Mueller&mode=books&type=
    lite&page=1&f=http://www.mycompany.com/MyTransform.xsl
```

Even though the information is the same, you receive a Web page in return, rather than the XML you received earlier (as shown in Figure 3-2). Not many Web services provide this feature, but it's a nice addition because you get the benefits of XML data *and* XSLT transformation without having to rely on any code.

Figure 3-1:
All Web services return the data you need in XML format.

Figure 3-2:
Some Web services include integrated transformation services.

Working with local sources

Local sources of XML data can include everything from an Office document to the latest copy of your database. The advantage of local sources is that they're under your control, so you determine when to perform an update. The form of the data is also under your control. You can choose to use pure text for the XML data source, or you can include HTML tags with the data so the information is automatically formatted on-screen. The point is that if you have some data in an XML document, you can create a Web page from that data when you use some type of transformation technology such as XSLT or scripts.

Using built-in XML functionality

Many applications provide the means to create XML output today and some even include the ability to use macros to create all of the required data manipulation, including attaching an XSLT file. For example, you can create a VBA macro in any Office product to save the data on disk — with all required information (the information you need to use the data, the information the host application requires, and so on) in place. All the user needs to do is click a button that you attach to a toolbar (or access the macro via Tools➪Macro➪ Macros).

The example in this section uses a tagged outline that you see in the `OriginalOutline.doc` file found in the source code for this chapter on the companion Web site. The object is to automate the process for outputting this document as it changes so the user doesn't have to remember to perform the task. Listing 3-1 shows such a macro for Word 2003.

Book VI Chapter 3

Creating Dynamic XML Pages

Listing 3-1: Creating XML Output Using Word

```
Public Sub DoXMLSave()
    Dim XMLDoc As DOMDocument50
    Dim XSLTProc As IXMLDOMProcessingInstruction
    Dim NewData As IXMLDOMNode

    ' Make sure to save only the data.
    ThisDocument.XMLSaveDataOnly = True

    ' Save the document.
    ThisDocument.SaveAs _
        ThisDocument.Path + "\Temp.xml", _
        WdSaveFormat.wdFormatXML

    ' Load the resulting document.
    Set XMLDoc = New DOMDocument50
    XMLDoc.Load ThisDocument.Path + "\Temp.xml"
```

(continued)

Listing 3-1 *(continued)*

```
    ' Add the XSLT processing instruction.
    Set XSLTProc = _
        XMLDoc.createProcessingInstruction( _
            "xml-stylesheet", _
            "type='text/xsl' href='MyBookDataOnly.XSL'")
    XMLDoc.InsertBefore XSLTProc, XMLDoc.ChildNodes(1)

    ' Create the new data node.
    Set NewData = XMLDoc.createElement("MyBook")

    ' Add the data nodes from the current entry.
    NewData.appendChild XMLDoc.ChildNodes(2).ChildNodes(0)

    ' Remove the old data node.
    XMLDoc.RemoveChild XMLDoc.ChildNodes(2)

    ' Add the new data node.
    XMLDoc.appendChild NewData

    ' Save the document to disk.
    XMLDoc.Save ThisDocument.Path + "\MyBookDataOnly.xml"

    ' Close the document so the user doesn't reuse it.
    ThisDocument.Close
End Sub
```

This short macro performs three essential tasks: It creates the original XML output, adds XSLT processing instructions, and removes the namespace so the file displays correctly using XSLT. (If you haven't already worked with VBA, Book 8 contains most of the essentials needed to understand this code.)

Before you begin typing code, you need to add the Microsoft XML, v5.0 library that comes with Office 2003 to the project. You can do so in just two steps:

1. **Choose Tools➪References in the Visual Basic Editor.**

The References dialog box appears, as shown in Figure 3-3.

2. **Check the Microsoft XML, v5.0 entry in the list and click OK.**

The code begins by saving the XML document. It sets the XMLSaveDataOnly property to True to ensure that the output doesn't use WordML (or any other Office derivatives).

The output is the same output you could obtain using the File➪Save As command with the XML Document (*.xml) option selected in the Save As Type field of the Save As dialog box. The name of this file is Temp.xml because it isn't in the final format yet. The file lacks a link to the XSLT file — and it also includes the namespace reference you provided as part of the XSD information for tagging the document (see Listing 1-3 in Chapter 1 for details on the XSD file mentioned in this chapter).

All the Office products insist on adding a namespace to the XML output, which makes it extremely difficult to translate the file using XSLT. The only way to get rid of the namespace information in the XML file is to redesign the XSD file so only the first node has any namespace information attached to it and then use the script to remove the namespace from this first node.

To modify the content of this XSD document, the code creates a new XML document, the DOMDocument50 object. This object is a copy of the contents of the XML file, but it resides in memory so you can modify the information easily. The object lets you access the various nodes, attributes, values, and other XML information individually.

Now that the code has a document to work with, it uses the resulting XMLDoc object to create a new processing instruction using the createProcessingInstruction() method. The processing instruction will contain the linkage to the XSLT document. Remember that the first processing instruction in an XML file is the XML processing instruction — the second processing instruction contains the XSLT link. Consequently, the code uses the InsertBefore() method to add the new processing instruction before the data nodes of the XML file.

**Book VI
Chapter 3**

**Creating Dynamic
XML Pages**

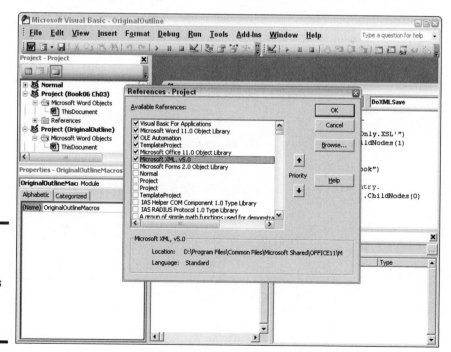

Figure 3-3:
Manage
XML
documents
using the
XML View
toolbar.

The code begins by creating a new <MyBook> node, one that lacks the name-space information that Word automatically adds. The next step is to add all the child nodes from the original <MyBook> node to the new node using the append Child() method. Finally, the code removes the existing <MyBook> node from the document and adds the new <MyBook> node.

After the stored-in-memory version of the XML document is correct, the code saves it to disk using the Save() method. Notice that the code saves it as MyBookDataOnly.xml to avoid conflicts with the open Temp.xml document. The final step is to close Temp.xml to ensure the user doesn't acciden-tally use it for some other task.

Using a script

One problem you might face is that your data source doesn't provide a means of loading and viewing the XML it outputs. Sure, you can output an XML docu-ment, but the document doesn't contain the required XSLT linkage. When this problem occurs, you can create a Web page that relies on JavaScript to per-form the task for you. Book 7 contains a lot of information about using JavaScript if you haven't used it in the past. Listing 3-2 shows a technique for loading an XML document and viewing it using JavaScript.

Listing 3-2: Viewing an XML Document Using JavaScript

```
<html>
<head>
<script lang="JavaScript">
    function OnLoad(XML_File, XSL_File)
    {
        // Create an XML document object and load the data from
        // the XML file into it.
        var XMLData =
            new ActiveXObject("Msxml2.DOMDocument.5.0");
        XMLData.async=false;
        XMLData.load(XML_File);

        // Create an XSLT document and load the transform into
        // it.
        var XSLTData =
            new ActiveXObject("Msxml2.DOMDocument.5.0");
        XSLTData.async = false;
        XSLTData.load(XSL_File);

        // Display the output on-screen.
        document.write(XMLData.transformNode(XSLTData));
    }
</script>
```

```
</head>

<body onload='OnLoad("First.XML", "First.XSLT")'>

</body>

</html>
```

This listing contains everything needed to load and display an XML document. All the developer needs to do is ensure the XML file remains updated to ensure the Web page works as intended. Notice that the Web page doesn't even include any data — just an empty body. The data resides in the XML file and the presentation resides in the XSLT file. The Web page serves as a means of connecting the two.

When a user selects the Web page, the page executes the onload event, which calls the OnLoad() JavaScript function. The OnLoad() function requires two inputs. The first input is the XML file you want to use, while the second input contains the name of the XSLT file. These two inputs will accept any URL the Web page user can access.

The JavaScript code begins by creating a Microsoft XML, v5.0 object. This document holds XML data in memory, so you can change it as needed. Given the nature of the application, most versions of Microsoft XML work fine, so you can change the version number as needed to meet specific needs.

The first task is to load the XML file. Make sure you set the async property to false so the code doesn't try to do anything until after the file is completely loaded. The load() method loads the XML file into memory. Loading the XSLT file into memory is the same process.

Now that the code has both files in memory, it can use the document.write() method to send the results of any operation performed on the XML to the display. The code uses the transformNode() method to transform the XML input file using the XSLT file. The resulting HTML appears on-screen.

Performing XML Updates

An XML data source used to create a dynamic Web page isn't all that helpful if you don't have some means to update it. Generally, you want to create the data and make it immediately available for use by Web site users. Of course, company requirements may dictate that someone sign off on the content before making it public. The idea is to create a rapid exchange of data between the person creating the data and the person viewing the data to ensure the user gets the most current information possible.

Using Office 2003 applications

Office 2003 provides a level of automation and XML support that greatly exceeds the capabilities of previous versions of the product. Using these automation features, it's possible to attach VBA macros to various activities the user performs with an Office 2003 application. One of those activities, for example, is closing a file after editing it. The simple act of exporting the document to an XML file after the edit can provide a means to create a dynamic update for a Web site.

The biggest problem with Office 2003, however, is ensuring the Microsoft extras, such as namespaces, don't prevent the end user from actually seeing the data. In some cases, a perfectly usable XSLT file will fail to perform a required transformation because of one of these little additions. Generally, you should look at both the XSLT file and the source data when looking for errors.

Using databases

Databases provide an extremely flexible means of storing and managing XML data. You can use database information directly as a single source of XML data or you can use the database to store and organize data from other applications. Businesses often combine both functions. For example, you could create a database to store XML versions of Word documents that you want to make available on a Web site.

The benefits of using databases to store and manage XML data are many. For one thing, you don't have myriad XML documents floating around on the hard drive from unknown sources. The very idea of a database is to store data in a form that is easily recognized and accessed. Another benefit of using databases is speed. You can often get the required XML documents faster from the database than you can by searching for them on the local drive.

A problem with databases is that they almost make things too easy. Some data will sit around for a long time before someone updates it or removes it from the system. For this reason, you need to perform data aging (removing old data that isn't current) based on the time that the user originally created the information. Generally, you can perform this task using stored procedures or other scripted mechanisms provided by the database manager.

Automating the Process

Automating XML updates is a key factor in creating dynamic Web sites. The problem with many Web sites isn't the design or the intent of the developer, but the ability of the developer and other contributors to keep the Web site updated. Manual updates do work, but it pays to automate the update process whenever possible. In most cases, this means tying content to the Web page by generating the Web page as requested, rather than maintaining a static copy of the information on the Web site.

Understanding process automation

The primary benefit of automating the update process through scripts, Active Server Pages (ASP), or other means is that the user always gets fresh content. In addition, there's less chance that an update will go unmade as long as the contributors keep the data source updated. Because it's likely the data source is used for other purposes, the chances are smaller that an update won't get made on time.

**Book VI
Chapter 3**

Creating Dynamic
XML Pages

The drawbacks of automation include performance degradation of the server. Whenever you ask the computer to do more, it must allocate processing cycles, memory, and other resources to the task. Dividing your computer's facilities among many resources always results in performance loss. In addition, there's a tendency for people to forget how things work. One day the automation fails to work and no one really knows how the process works any longer. Unless you maintain very good notes and other documentation, an error in the automation can result in loss of data — or at least several days of downtime. Even with good documentation, downtime for an automated process is usually greater than a corresponding manual process.

Scripting updates generally fall into two categories, depending on whether they service the client side or the server side:

✦ **Client-side scripting:** The client issues a request, receives the data in XML format, and processes the data in some way. The advantage of this method is that you see a smaller performance hit on the server. The disadvantage is that you must have a smart client — such as a desktop system, notebook, or Pocket PC.

✦ **Server-side processing:** The server makes a request for the client, processes the information, and sends the resulting Web page to the client. The advantage of this method is that security is improved (the client can't access the full data) and you send less data, which improves network performance. In addition, this method supports all clients — including cellular telephones. The disadvantage is that the server's performance suffers, and the application is far more complex because you have more failure points (including those on the server).

Relying on script updates

The kind of scripting discussed in this section is client-side scripting — the kind you find in an application or a local Web page. When working with a

Web page, the client can have a local copy installed as an application or download a copy from the server. In all cases, the client makes a request, processes it, and displays the result on-screen. Listing 3-3 shows a request that obtains data from Amazon.com. You must have an Amazon developer account to work with Amazon data, but sign-up is relatively easy (see the "Working with Web services" section for details). This code appears in the `AmazonClientScript.HTM` file in the source code for this chapter on this book's companion Web site.

Listing 3-3: Getting XML Data from Amazon

```
function GetData(XslFile)
{
    // Convert the author name to use %20 instead of spaces.
    var AuthName = SubmissionForm.AuthorSearch.value;
    AuthName = ReplaceCharacter(AuthName, ' ', '%20');

    // Build a string that will hold the complete URL.
    var XmlFile = "http://xml.amazon.com/onca/xml3?" +
                  "t=" + SubmissionForm.t.value + "&" +
                  "dev-t=" + SubmissionForm.devt.value + "&" +
                  "AuthorSearch=" + AuthName + "&" +
                  "mode=" + SubmissionForm.mode.value + "&" +
                  "type=" + SubmissionForm.type.value + "&" +
                  "page=" + SubmissionForm.page.value + "&" +
                  "f=" + SubmissionForm.f.value;

    // Create an XML document object and load the data from
    // the Amazon Web Service into it.
    var XMLData = new ActiveXObject("Msxml2.DOMDocument.5.0");
    XMLData.async=false;
    XMLData.load(XmlFile);

    // Create an XSLT document and load the transform into it.
    var XSLTData =
        new ActiveXObject("Msxml2.DOMDocument.5.0");
    XSLTData.async = false;
    XSLTData.load(XslFile);

    // Display the output on-screen.
    document.write(XMLData.transformNode(XSLTData));
}
```

Here's the sequence of the actual events that correspond to this code:

1. The code begins by getting by the author's name from the Web-page form.

2. The code replaces any spaces in the author's name with %20.

Doing so ensures that Amazon receives the entire request (otherwise the server could mistake a space for the end of the request).

3. Your next step is to create a request string so the code has something to work on.

The "Working with Web services" section of this chapter describes how this string works. Essentially, you tell Amazon about yourself and what information you want it to return. The data is in XML format, as shown in Figure 3-1.

4. When the code has a request to use, it creates a local XML document to hold the information.

Be sure to set the `async` property to `false`. (Other examples in this chapter might work if you don't do that — but this one won't.) The code executes the next line of instructions long before the request returns data, so you must set the `async` property to false.

5. The code loads the XML response from Amazon.

6. The code loads a local XSLT file to interpret the data just received.

It uses the same process as it does for the XML file, but loading the information locally is much faster.

7. Finally, the code outputs the resulting HTML file.

It does so via the `document.write()` method, using the results of the `XMLData.transformNode()` method to create the output.

Listing 3-4 shows the XSLT file used for this example. You can also see this code in the `AmazonTransform.XSL` file supplied as part of the source code for this chapter on this book's companion Web site.

Listing 3-4:   Defining an XSLT File for Amazon Data

```
<?xml version="1.0" encoding="UTF-8"?>
<xsl:stylesheet version="1.0"
   xmlns:xsl="http://www.w3.org/1999/XSL/Transform"
   xmlns:fo="http://www.w3.org/1999/XSL/Format">
<xsl:template match="/">
<html>
<head>
   <title>XSLT Transformation Example</title>
</head>
<body>
   <!-- Display a heading. -->
   <h1 align="center">
      Translated Amazon Web Server Results
   </h1>

   <!-- Displays the arguments used for the call. -->
   <table align="center" border="1" width="60%">
```

(continued)

Listing 3-4 *(continued)*

```
    <caption>Search Result Arugments</caption>
    <tbody>
        <tr>
            <th>Name</th>
            <th>Value</th>
        </tr>
        <xsl:for-each select="ProductInfo/Request/Args/Arg">
            <tr>
                <td><xsl:value-of select="@name"/></td>
                <td><xsl:value-of select="@value"/></td>
            </tr>
        </xsl:for-each>
    </tbody>
</table>

<!-- Display the search result values. -->
<table align="center" border="1" width="100%">
    <caption>Books Returned from Query</caption>
    <tbody>
        <tr>
            <th>Book Title</th>
            <th>ISBN</th>
            <th>Release Date</th>
            <th>Publisher</th>
        </tr>
        <xsl:for-each select="ProductInfo/Details">
            <tr>
                <td><xsl:value-of select="ProductName"/></td>
                <td><xsl:value-of select="Asin"/></td>
                <td><xsl:value-of select="ReleaseDate"/></td>
                <td><xsl:value-of select="Manufacturer"/></td>
            </tr>
        </xsl:for-each>
    </tbody>
</table>

</body>
</html>
</xsl:template>
</xsl:stylesheet>
```

This example of an XSLT file is a little more complex than previous examples.
In this case, I wanted to use standard formatting, so I created a reference to
the correct standardized formatting at the following site:

```
http://www.w3.org/1999/XSL/Format
```

You don't have to perform this step unless you want to use standardized formatting.

The code begins by displaying a standard header. In this case, the data in XML is complex enough that multiple displays work better than stuffing everything into a single listing, table, or other display element — so the code creates two tables:

✦ **The first table lists the arguments used to request information from Amazon:** These arguments appear in a series of `ProductInfo/Request/Args/Arg` nodes. Each node contains a pair of attributes, `name` and `value`. The code relies on a `<xsl:for-each>` element to go through the list of arguments and create a single table entry for each pair.

✦ **The second table displays the actual data:** Included are book title, ISBN, release date, and publisher. Unlike the argument data, this information actually appears as a collection of element values. The `ProductInfo/Details` nodes contain a lot of other information, but the example limits the data to what the user needs to see, as shown in Figure 3-2.

Book VI
Chapter 3

Creating Dynamic XML Pages

Using ASP

Microsoft created Active Server Pages (ASP) as a means for defining a Web page with a combination of HTML and script so that a developer could include features like server information as part of the Web page. Working with ASP is like working with any other scripting language. You get many of the same benefits — and problems — as you would if you were working with a scripting language in a browser or local machine. For example, you can make changes to an ASP file and test them immediately — no waiting around to compile the file and get it placed on the server. However, the downside of ASP is that the debugging resources are less available — and you do place your source code on the server, which means anyone with access (including crackers) can see it.

An advantage of using ASP is that you can secure the information you work with better and ASP has access to many of the server resources. The end user sees a Web page that could appear on disk in any format. There isn't any clue that the source data is actually XML or that more data could exist. Listing 3-5 shows a typical ASP example. You can find the complete example in the `ViewXMLData.ASP` file found in the source code for this chapter on this book's companion Web site.

Listing 3-5:   Loading and Displaying XML with ASP

```
<%@LANGUAGE="JavaScript"%>
<%
    // Create an XML document object and load the data from
    // the XML file into it.
    var XMLData = new ActiveXObject("MSXML2.DOMDocument.4.0");
    XMLData.async = false;
    XMLData.load("http://winserver/0181/BK06CH03/Second.XML");

    // Create an XSLT document and load the transform into it.
    var XSLTData =
        new ActiveXObject("MSXML2.DOMDocument.4.0");
    XSLTData.async = false;
    XSLTData.load(
        "http://winserver/0181/BK06CH03/First.XSLT");

    // Display the output on screen.
    Response.Write(XMLData.transformNode(XSLTData));
%>
```

The code is relatively straightforward. It begins by creating an XML document and loading the Second.XML file into it. Make sure you set the async property to false to ensure the document completes loading before the code continues. Notice that unlike a browser version of the JavaScript, you must provide a full URL for the XML file or ASP won't find it.

The second step is to create another XML document to hold the XSLT file. The code uses the load() method to obtain a copy of the XSLT file. Notice Again that you must provide a full URL to the source information.

The final step is to generate the HTML page using the Response. Write() method. To do so, the code relies on the output of the XMLData. transformNode() as a source for the full HTML for the Web page. However, remember that XSLT is very flexible, as is XML. You could generate part of the output within the ASP file and use one or more data transformations to generate the other part.

Book VII

Scripting

The 5th Wave — By Rich Tennant

"Great goulash, Stan. That reminds me, are you still scripting your own Web page?"

Contents at a Glance

Chapter 1: Extending a Page with Scripting

In This Chapter

✔ Using scripts effectively

✔ Developing scripts using the `<Script>` tag

✔ Using page objects and variables

✔ Deciding on a course of action

✔ Using loops to repeat tasks

✔ Working with browsers that don't support scripts

Some people hear the term *script* and instantly think it refers to tasks that only developers perform. However, scripting languages are designed to be simple enough that anyone can automate tasks. Scripting need not be a difficult undertaking — it's simply a way for you to perform tasks faster.

Scripts reside within a special `<Script>` tag in your Web page so the browser knows to treat them appropriately: Browsers that support scripting read them as scripts, and browsers that don't ignore the script code. Most modern browsers include script functionality, but this special tag also provides support for situations where the user turns off scripting support. Finally, the tag offers a way to indicate a special course of action when a browser doesn't support scripts through the use of a `<NoScript>` tag.

Scripting lets you access *page objects* — interactive on-screen features such as the textboxes on a form. Page objects help you obtain access to data, change the information displayed on-screen, and interact with both the user and the browser. In addition to working with objects, your script can use local variables, modify the variable value, and then do something with the result. In some cases, the resulting data requires that your application make a decision. For example, you might perform an action, such as displaying a message box, when a number (perhaps user input) is below a value. Finally, scripting supports *looping,* which helps you perform the same task more than once (especially useful for repetitive procedures).

Understanding How Scripting Can Help

Anyone who can write a simple series of steps for someone to perform can also write a script. Writing a script is like writing a note to a friend that lists steps to perform while you're gone on vacation. You provide the steps required to water the plants, feed the cat, or take in the mail. In some cases, the steps are more complex because the person also needs to turn on the lights and enable the security system in addition to the previous steps. Scripting is simply a series of steps you write for the computer to perform. Often, these steps are the same steps you perform to accomplish the task manually.

Scripting can help you accomplish specific goals. It's important to balance your needs with the needs of the user — and those of the application — so everything works as intended. Here are some goals you can accomplish with scripts (but could also accomplish using other technologies such as CSS):

✦ **Enhance performance:** Exchanging data between a client and server requires passing that information over a slow connection. The interactivity results in a performance loss because of the time required to send and receive the information. Using scripts lets you perform some tasks locally, which reduces the amount of network traffic and enhances overall performance. You can also use scripts to enhance client or server performance by moving more of the processing to the other machine.

✦ **Increase flexibility:** Most static Web pages are inflexible because they can't react to existing conditions or user input. Scripts enhance flexibility by making it possible for pages to react to the environment, the browser, user input, or server setup. The goal is to accomplish a given task with the least amount of work and in the fastest possible time, without any loss of user-interface capabilities.

✦ **Reduce security risks:** You can use scripts to check for certain types of data, environment, browser, or user-security risks. For example, you can use scripts to reduce the risk that someone will successfully send a virus instead of the requested data.

✦ **Create special effects:** Although special effects are essentially eye candy that won't perform any useful work, most developers and users alike still find them fun (or at least interesting). For example, adding a *mouseover* effect (which changes the appearance of a button when the mouse pointer touches it) is interesting, but not necessarily helpful. You can accomplish some of the same goals using unscripted options such as tooltips, but special effects add pizzazz that your page might not otherwise have.

✦ **Handle special user needs:** Users often have special needs that you can handle using scripts. For example, someone who needs a plain page (one without formatting so a screen reader can describe it) could choose a different CSS page using an option on your form. The request would automatically download the new page from your Web site, and a cookie would tell the browser to use the same CSS page during subsequent visits.

Finally, scripting actually adds a new dimension to Web-page design — it helps you provide a better environment for the user and accomplish tasks that manual techniques can't normally handle. Here's a list of special tasks you must accomplish with scripts:

✦ **Automate tasks:** The whole idea behind using scripts is to automate tasks so that you don't have to perform them manually. Task automation is an important time saver and reduces support costs, in many cases, because the automation reduces the number of steps the user has to perform.

✦ **Access special objects:** Many tasks require the use of special objects. For example, when you want to display a chart on-screen, you need access to a special object that displays the chart. Although you don't have to use scripting if you want to display static data using a page object, adding a script lets the user change the object and work with it — and that means you don't have to create multiple static displays to satisfy everyone's needs.

✦ **Transform data:** The raw data a user or server provides normally requires some kind of manipulation. For example, a user might enter a temperature in Fahrenheit and expect to receive the output in Celsius. A server might provide data in XML format that the client has to transform into a Web page using XSLT — scripting can provide a means of combining the two processes.

✦ **Make requests:** Requests come in a number of formats. Some requests don't require scripts, such as a request made using a form. In other cases, you do need to create a script to make a request, such as gaining access to data provided by a Web server using the Simple Object Access Protocol (SOAP). The kind of request you want to make determines the technique used to make it.

✦ **Add user aids:** Some user's aids (such as context-sensitive help) are incredibly difficult to add to a Web page without scripts. In some cases, such as an interactive user guide, you can't really create all of the required user interface elements without scripting. For example, I recently visited a Web site that shows how to install a new component on a machine. The step-by-step instructions are animated so you can see precisely how the parts fit together. You can also ask questions as part of the step. Such user aids would be very difficult to implement without scripts.

Using the <script> Tag

All scripts that reside on a Web page rely on the <script> tag. Like many tags, the <script> tag has two components, the opening and closing tags. You always work with the <script> tag using Code view — even when the script appears in the body area of the Web page, there isn't any visual component to a script so you won't see it in Design view. For this reason, using the Split view usually isn't worthwhile when working with scripts because the Code view provides more screen space for the editor.

Depending on your FrontPage and Internet settings, some scripts might not work properly (or at all) from Preview view. Although you can perform some testing with Preview view, always check your scripts using an actual browser to ensure you see what the user sees.

You can (theoretically) place a script anywhere within the Web page — including outside the <html> tag. However, most developers choose to place scripts within the <body> or <head> tags to ensure that the browser can find the script — and to make it easier for other developers to understand the page functionality. The next two sections discuss the differences between these two placements in detail.

Placing scripts in the body

Scripts that are within the <body> tag normally execute immediately as the page is opened or when the user performs an action. A body script is also normally short and interface-related. None of these conventions are set in stone, however; you can work with any kind of script within the <body> tag.

An example of a script that executes within the body of the Web page is one that displays a message or performs some type of configuration based on the users' browsers. Here's a simple example of a script that displays a message when you load the Web page:

```
<script language="javascript">
    alert("Hello World!");
</script>
```

This script appears within the <script> tag. It uses a special function, alert(), to display a message box on-screen with the text, Hello World!. When the user clicks OK, the message box disappears and the browser displays whatever appears after the script on-screen.

Unfortunately, the script executes only once and without the user's permission or under user control. Whenever possible, you should request user action to execute a script to ensure the user wants to perform that task. You can attach a script to a control on the page by using an event. An event occurs whenever the environment changes or the user performs a specific act such as clicking a button. Here's a script that executes when the user clicks a button on the page.

```
<input type="button"
       id="btnClickMe"
       value="Click Me"
       onclick="alert('You clicked Click Me!')">
```

This script relies on the same `alert()` function to display a dialog box on-screen. The message is different this time. Notice that the script actually appears as part of the `<input>` tag. The `onclick` attribute is an event and you use the equals sign to attach the script to this event. The browser "fires" the `onclick` event every time the user clicks the button.

FrontPage makes it relatively easy to find events for a particular tag. It uses a special icon in IntelliSense so you can detect which entries are events and which are properties. Figure 1-1 shows the `onclick` event entry highlighted. Notice that it uses a lightning bolt as an icon.

Book VII Chapter 1

Extending a Page with Scripting

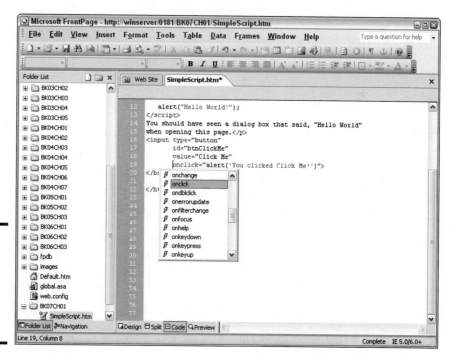

Figure 1-1: Determine which entries are events by looking at the icon.

Placing scripts in the header

Developers normally place complex scripts in the `<head>` tag of the Web page. This standard programming practice makes it easier for other developers to find the script and also reduces the clutter in the `<body>` tag of the Web page. Nothing prevents you from placing complex scripts in other pages in the Web page, but using the current convention means that your script is less likely to cause problems in the future.

Placing a script in the `<head>` tag requires performing a little additional work because it forces you to associate the script with an event and to provide a means of identifying the script. Listing 1-1 shows a Web page that places the script in the header.

Listing 1-1:   Defining a Script in the Header

```
<html>

<head>
<script language="javascript">
    function DisplayMessage(Message)
    {
        alert(Message);
    }
</script>
</head>

<body>
<input type="button"
       id="btnClickMeToo"
       value="Click Me Too"
       onclick="DisplayMessage('You Clicked Me Too!')">
</body>

</html>
```

Notice the script appears in the `<head>` tag and it relies on the usual `<script>` tag as a container. In this case, you use the keyword `function` to define a special piece of code within the `<head>` tag. The identification I've come up with for this function is `DisplayMessage`. The `DisplayMessage()` function accepts a message as an input. It displays a dialog box on-screen with the `alert()` function using the `Message` argument as input.

Having the script in place doesn't accomplish anything; you must tie the script to an event or call it as part of another function. In this case, the Web page has a button defined as part of an `<input>` tag. Notice the use of the onclick attribute to attach the DisplayMessage() function to the button. When a user clicks the Click Me Too button, the browser executes the DisplayMessage() function with the message shown.

You might wonder why I added the Message argument to the DisplayMessage() function when it would have been easier to simply add the message to the script. This addition makes it possible to use the DisplayMessage() function for any number of buttons and any number of messages. Using this technique makes it possible to use the code for another Web page without rewriting it — the DisplayMessage() function has greater flexibility because I added the Message argument.

Understanding Scripting Languages

Developers have created a number of scripting languages — and you're free to use any language you want, as long as your browser supports it (either natively or through an add-on). The two most common scripting languages are Visual Basic Script (VBScript) and JavaScript. Of these two, JavaScript is the most popular language because it has the best support from browsers. In fact, you can consider JavaScript the language of choice simply because it's the most popular and compatible. For these reasons, all scripting examples in this book rely on JavaScript, rather than on a mix of languages. In fact, you can see a list of browsers that support JavaScript at

http://hotwired.lycos.com/webmonkey/reference/browser_chart/
    index.html

Don't confuse JavaScript and Java. Even though the two languages have similar names, they have nothing in common — and equating them will only cause you grief. JavaScript is an open language that is also called European Computer Manufacturers' Association Script (ECMAScript) or JScript (Microsoft's name). Java, on the other hand, is a semi-open language designed and maintained by Sun (http://java.sun.com/). You can find standards for the ECMAScript language at

http://www.ecma-international.org/publications/standards/
    Stnindex.htm

Although the basic implementation of a scripting language remains the same in most browsers, you'll notice some differences between browsers. Browser vendors normally add special features to their scripting-language implementations to make their browsers stand out from the crowd. Even though these additions make each browser special, they can also cause problems by introducing compatibility problems. Don't assume that following the standards ensures success: Many browsers were written before the standards arrived — and some vendors chose to ignore the standards even after they arrived. The best way to ensure that your Web page will work as expected is to test your scripts using as many different browsers as you can.

Because there are so many scripting languages available and FrontPage supports a number of them, you need to define which scripting language you use on your Web page, using the `language` or `lang` attribute as shown here:

```
<script language="javascript">
    alert("Hello World!");
</script>
```

An advantage of using the `language` attribute is that FrontPage provides IntelliSense support for this attribute (as shown in Figure 1-2). Using the `language` attribute reduces typing time and makes it easier to choose a language when you're unfamiliar with the options.

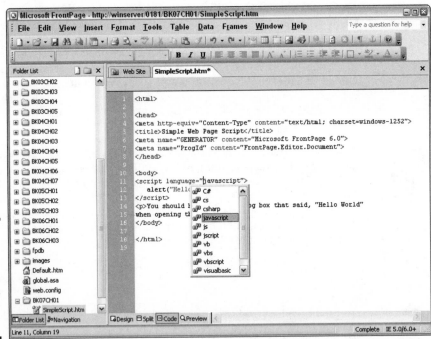

Figure 1-2:
Select the language you want to use from the options presented.

Working with Page Objects

Most scripting languages rely on the concept of objects to make it easier to work with the browser, user, and Web page. Think of an *object* as you would any real-world object. When you see an apple, you recognize a color, shape, whether it's shiny, and so on. You know that you can eat the apple, use it for applesauce, or target it with an arrow (hopefully not on someone's head). The apple automatically produces an odor and will eventually rot, at which point you'll see the skin color change (among other things). You can visualize computer objects using properties, interact with them using methods, and notice automatic changes in them through events.

Although JavaScript objects aren't precisely the same as objects used by other languages, they're close enough that you can read the following sections and understand how objects work in most scripting languages. Understanding how various objects work is essential to writing good scripts.

Using properties

Properties define the characteristics of the object. A pushbutton has a `value` property that defines the text on the button face. This same property defines text for other common controls such as textboxes. Many properties affect the physical appearance of an object. For example, the `bgColor` property defines the background color. A few properties tell you about the condition of the object. The `isDisabled` property tells whether the object is usable — a user sees a disabled object, but can't interact with it (as when an option is grayed out on-screen).

Working with properties means interpreting or changing the state or appearance of the associated object. You read a property to interpret its content and write a value to it to change it. When you make an illegal change, the object raises an error that the browser displays for you. In some cases, a property is read-only or write-only, which means you can only perform that task with the property.

You work with properties through the object hierarchy. The hierarchy begins with a window. Within the window is a document (among other objects, properties, methods, and events). The document contains a number of items, including any forms you create. A form can contain a pushbutton or other control. At each of these levels, you can interact with objects by specifying properties. Here's an example of a script that works with objects at various levels in the object hierarchy.

```
<script language="javascript">
    // Display the browser name and version.
```

```
        alert("You're using:\r\n" +
            window.clientInformation.appName +
            "\r\nVersion: " +
            window.clientInformation.appVersion);

        // Make the background color red.
        window.document.bgColor = "red";

        // Change the button caption.
        window.document.MyForm.btnTest.value = "Hello";
</script>
```

This example works with four objects: `window`, `document`, `MyForm`, and `btnTest`. The `window` object contains a `clientInformation` property, which is actually a complex property because it contains other properties. The example uses the `alert()` function to display the `appName` and `appVersion` properties of the `clientInformation` property.

Notice, also, the use of the special `\r\n` character sequence. This character sequence is called an *escaped character set* because it represents special control characters. The `\r` entry tells the browser to insert a carriage return (a return to the beginning of the line). The `\n` entry tells the browser to add a newline (linefeed) character that advances the cursor to the next line. Together, they display the various pieces of information on separate lines of the dialog box displayed with the `alert()` function (as shown in Figure 1-3).

Objects, Controls, and Components

Some object-related terms might seem confusing at first because some people use them without explaining what they mean. The term *object* refers to any encapsulation of code and data that you work with using properties, methods, and events. When an object has a visual interface and it provides special user interaction functionality, developers call it a *control*. For example, a pushbutton is a control. Some objects work in the background (without visual interfaces) and provide special services — developers call them *components*. A database connection is an example of a component because it lacks a visual interface, yet provides a valuable service to the user.

Some objects cross boundaries, so it's hard to classify them. For example, some developers say an Excel spreadsheet is a control because it provides a visual interface and also interacts with the user. On the other hand, many developers would call it a component because it provides low-level services to the user. Generally, it doesn't matter whether an object is a control or a component — you use the same techniques to interact with both. Whenever you see a confusing mix of object, control, and component references, always remember that every control — and every component — *is* an object. Objects are the technology that you should think about when writing code for your scripts.

Figure 1-3:
Use control
characters
to format
the content
in a dialog
box.

The next entry uses the `document` object. Notice the `document` object appears as part of the `window` object. The code changes the `bgColor` (background color) property to red.

Within the `document` object is a form named `MyForm`. The `MyForm` object contains a pushbutton named `btnTest`. The pushbutton has a `value` property that changes the caption. The code sets this property to `Hello`.

Using methods

Methods define activities you can perform with an object. A window has certain characteristics that allow you to perform specific tasks. For example, the `alert()` function that appears in several listings is actually a method that belongs to the `window` object. The use of *method* and *function* as terms for the same feature can be confusing; here's an example that illustrates both:

```
<script>
    // Using alert as a function.
    alert("This is a function");

    // Using alert as a method.
    window.alert("This is a method.");
</script>
```

The first version of `alert()` is the function form. It appears as a separate entity without any object association. The second version uses the dot syntax associated with objects. This form tells you that `alert()` is a method that is part of the `window` object. Although both forms of `alert()` produce the same result, it's important to consider the source of the functionality.

IntelliSense displays method entries in the list of object elements with a purple cube. When you select a method for your script, IntelliSense also displays the arguments for that method so you know what to type. For example, when you use the `window.alert()` method, IntelliSense tells you that it requires a message as an input argument. *Arguments* define how you want the method to perform a task or what you want it to use as information. In this case, the `window.alert()` method accepts a single input argument that contains the sequence of characters (a string) you want to display on-screen.

Unfortunately, IntelliSense doesn't display output information for a method. Some methods, such as `window.confirm()`, don't work well without this knowledge — after all, the point of using the method is to obtain information from the user. The `window.confirm()` method asks the user to confirm an action before your script performs it. FrontPage doesn't document scripting functions. To discover the output arguments that methods support, use online sources such as Gecko DOM Reference at

```
http://www.mozilla.org/docs/dom/domref/dom_shortIX.html
```

or the JScript Language Tour at

```
http://msdn.microsoft.com/library/en-us/jscript7/html/statement.asp
```

Using events

Events define self-generating activities on the part of the object. Events occur due to internal needs, changes in the environment or application, or activities on the part of the user. When a user clicks a button, the button generates an event. You can choose to ignore the event (the default action) or you can do something about it.

You can track a number of events associated with every control or major object (such as the `<body>` tag) on a Web page. The event you choose depends on what action you want to track. For example, it makes sense to track user clicks when you're working with a button, but you might want to use the `onchange` event when you're working with a textbox: In this case, the focus event is changing the content of the textbox.

Working with events is a two-part process. First, you create a connection between the event and the code that you want to use to handle the event. Second, you create the event handling code. In some cases, you can combine the two steps, as the example in the "Placing scripts in the body" section of the chapter shows. To use the more traditional approach, begin with a call to a method, as shown here:

```
<p><input type="text" id="txtInput"
          value="Change Me!"
          onchange="txtInput_Change()"></p>
<p><input type="button" id="btnTest"
          value="Test" disabled
          onclick="btnTest_Click()"></p>
```

This code shows two `<input>` tags. In the first tag, the `onchange` attribute attaches the `txtInput_Change()` function to the textbox. Whenever a user changes the content of the textbox, the textbox will call the `txtInput_Change()` function to handle the event. Likewise, the button in the second tag has the `btnTest_Click()` function attached to the `onclick` event. Whenever the user clicks the Test button, the button calls the `btnTest_Click()` function.

Notice the names of the functions. You can call the functions anything you like and, in some cases, you won't want to use this naming convention, but combining the control `id` value with the event name is common practice for naming event handlers. Using this technique makes it easier for other people to understand your code and you to make modifications later. (The one time you definitely *don't* want to use this naming convention is when one event handler works with more than one control.)

After you associate an event with a function, you create the code to handle the event. You can use any code needed to interact with the user. Here are the two event handlers for this example — they simply display a dialog box:

```
<script language="javascript">
    function txtInput_Change()
    {
        // Tell the user something changed.
        alert("The test button changed!");
    }
    function btnTest_Click()
    {
        // Register the click event.
        alert("The text box says " + MyForm.txtInput.value);

        // Make a change.
        MyForm.txtInput.value =
            "Type some new text and press Tab!";
    }
</script>
```

Creating Variables

A *variable* is like an empty box — you can place something in it until you need it later. Script variables can contain any kind of data including objects you create. Depending on the script language, you might have to follow certain rules when using variables. Fortunately, using variables with JavaScript is easy because JavaScript has relaxed variable rules. Here's an example of using a variable:

```
<script language="javascript">
    function btnPrompt_Click()
    {
        // Holds the output of the prompt.
        var Output

        // Display a prompt.
        Output = prompt("Type a string:", "Default String");

        // Display the result.
        alert(Output);
    }
</script>
```

You declare a variable using the special `var` keyword. A variable can have any name, but you need to start it with a letter or one of the few special symbols that JavaScript allows. The best principle is to begin all variable names with a letter of the alphabet to avoid problems later.

A variable has the special value of `null` when you first create it. A `null` value means empty — the box doesn't contain anything. You can display a `null` value on-screen and JavaScript won't complain. However, JavaScript will complain if you try to perform a useful task with a `null` value because there isn't any value to work with.

The example assigns the output of the `prompt()` function to `Output`. The `prompt()` function displays a message to the user and provides a default string (when you supply one). The user can type a new string or accept the default. When the user clicks OK, `Output` receives the string from the `prompt()` function. On the other hand, when the user clicks Cancel, JavaScript places a null value in `Output` to show that the user didn't enter any information.

Making Decisions

Sometimes you have to make a decision when you're writing a script. For example, you might want the script to react differently to various kinds of user input. In many cases, you won't know what specific browser functionality or settings to expect, so you have to create a decision-making feature to handle the unknowns in your Web-page application.

JavaScript relies on the `if` statement to make decisions. The decision is based on a Boolean (true or false) value that you enclose in parentheses. When the Boolean value is true, then JavaScript executes the statement that follows. An optional `else` clause lets you choose between two courses of action — one that occurs when an evaluation is `true` and another when it's `false`. Here are examples of both forms of `if` statements:

```
<script>
    // Determine whether the button is enabled. If not,
    // enable it.
    if (window.document.MyForm.btnTest.isDisabled)
        window.document.MyForm.btnTest.disabled = false;

    // The window object has many other interesting functions,
    // such as a form of alert you can use to confirm actions.
    if (window.confirm("Are you sure?"))
    {
        window.alert("You're sure.");
        window.document.MyForm.btnTest.value = "Sure";
    }
    else
    {
        window.alert("You aren't sure.");
        window.document.MyForm.btnTest.value = "Not Sure";
    }
</script>
```

In the first case, the code makes a simple decision — when the button is disabled, enable it. Otherwise the code doesn't need to do anything because the button is already enabled. The `isDisabled` property in this example is special because it provides a Boolean output and it's read-only. Controls often provide these status properties. To change the status of the button, you modify the state of the `disabled` property by setting it to `true` or `false`. (These are Boolean values when used without double quotes.)

The second example requires the `else` clause, in many cases, because the dialog box displayed by the `window.confirm()` method contains two buttons: OK and Cancel (the script engine adds these buttons automatically). The method returns `true` when the user clicks OK or `false` when the user clicks Cancel. Using the `else` clause lets you react to either event.

Notice how the second example uses curly braces { }to enclose multiple statements. When you want a single decision to apply to multiple actions, use curly braces to enclose the actions. Otherwise you can simply follow the decision immediately with the executable statement, as shown in the first example.

**Book VII
Chapter 1**

**Extending a Page
with Scripting**

Performing Repetitive Tasks with Loops

Sometimes you need to perform a task more than one time. For example, you might want to retrieve information from a database. You use the same series of steps to retrieve every record, so it's easier to write the required code once and simply tell the computer to perform the coded steps more than once. Repeating a task multiple times is called *looping*.

Using the for loop

Use a for loop when you know precisely how many times you want to perform a task before the loop begins. A for loop begins by defining three expressions: the beginning value of a counter variable, the value the counter must obtain to end the loop, and the method to use to change the counter variable. Here's an example of the for loop:

```
function btnForLoop_Click()
{
    // Get the number of times to perform the loop.
    var Perform =
        parseInt(prompt("Times to Perform Loop", "5"));

    // Perform the loop the desired number of times.
    for (Counter = 1; Counter <= Perform; Counter++)
    {
        // Display a message box.
        alert("Hello " + Counter + " time.");

        // Change the output text box.
        txtLoopValue.value = Counter;
    }
}
```

The code begins by obtaining the number of times the user wants to perform the loop using the prompt() function. The output of the prompt() function is a string, and you can't easily create a comparison using a string value — numeric values work better. This example uses the parseInt() function to convert the string input from the prompt() function into a number.

When the user types something other than a number, the parseInt() function outputs 0, which means the loop won't execute. This is a safety feature; the user can't type an unusable value or enter a virus and still get the loop to work. The conversion process enhances security by making it impossible to enter anything but a number.

The for loop begins by assigning a value of 1 to the Counter variable. The next step is to compare Counter to Perform. When Counter is less than or equal to Perform, JavaScript executes the code within the curly braces. In this case, the code simply displays a dialog box with the current Counter value and places this value in a textbox. The final step is to increment Counter. The Counter++ statement tells JavaScript to add 1 to the value of Counter, which increments it. The loop begins again with the comparison — JavaScript only performs the assignment step the first time. When Counter is greater than Perform, the loop ends.

Using the while loop

Use a while loop when you aren't sure how many times a loop will execute. A while loop could detect the end of a database, environmental conditions, or an action on the part of the user. A while loop simply checks for a condition. When the condition is met, the while loop ends. Here's an example of the while loop:

```
function btnWhileLoop_Click()
{
   // Create a loop variable.
   var Counter = 1;

   // Get the number of times to perform the loop.
   var Perform =
      parseInt(prompt("Times to Perform Loop", "5"));

   // Perform the loop the desired number of times.
   while (Counter <= Perform)
   {
      // Display a message box.
      alert("Hello " + Counter + " time.");

      // Change the output text box.
      txtLoopValue.value = Counter;

      // Increment the counter.
      Counter++;
   }
}
```

The code begins by creating Counter. In this case, Counter is simply part of a condition, not necessarily a counter variable. The code obtains the number of times the user wants to perform the loop and places this value in Perform.

The while loop begins by checking the loop's condition. When Counter is less than or equal to Perform, JavaScript executes the code contained within the curly braces. In this case, the code displays a dialog box showing the current counter value and updates a textbox on-screen. Because a `while` loop doesn't include a counting mechanism, you must increment the counter as a separate step. Otherwise the loop becomes endless — it keeps executing because the ending condition never occurs.

Using the <noscript> Tag

Scripts aren't always a usable option. Sometimes users turn off scripting support for their browsers because they have had bad experiences with poorly-written scripts (or even viruses) in the past. In addition, many users turn scripting support off because it causes other applications and browser add-ins to malfunction. Consequently, you can't assume that a user has scripting support on a public Web site and need to provide an alternative in the form of a `<noscript>` tag. A browser only displays the content of the `<noscript>` tag when it doesn't have scripting support or scripting support isn't turned on.

When you have access to a Web server, you can usually use a combination of client-side and server-side scripting to provide alternatives for the user. The server-side script lets the user interact with your site, albeit at a greatly reduced speed. Listing 1-2 shows an example of how you can implement this technique using an Active Server Pages (ASP) script on Internet Information Server (IIS). (Note that some nonfocal code was removed in the interest of brevity — see the `DoMath.asp` file in the source code for this chapter on this book's companion Web site for details.)

Listing 1-2: Using a <NoScript> Tag with ASP

```
<%@ Language = "JavaScript" %>
<% Response.Buffer = true %>

<html>
<head>
    <title>Accessible Friendly Script Demonstration</title>
    <script language=javascript>
      function DoAdd()
      {
          var Value1 = parseInt(TheForm.InValue1.value);
          var Value2 = parseInt(TheForm.InValue2.value);
          TheForm.Output.value = Value1 + Value2;
      }
    </script>
</head>
<body>
```

```
<form method=get id=TheForm>
    <H1 align="center">Math Demonstration</H1>
    <INPUT type=text id="InValue1"
        <%if (Request.QueryString("Input1").Count > 0)
        {
            Response.Write("value=")
            Response.Write(Request.QueryString("Input1")(1))
        }
        else
            Response.Write("value=0")%>
        name=Input1>
    <LABEL> Input Value 1</LABEL><br />
    ... The Second Input ...
    <INPUT type=text id="Output"
        <%if ((Request.QueryString("Input1").Count > 0) &&
        (Request.QueryString("Input2").Count > 0))
        {
            var Value1 =
                parseInt(Request.QueryString("Input1")(1));
            var Value2 =
                parseInt(Request.QueryString("Input2")(1));
            var Sum = Value1 + Value2;
            Response.Write("value=");
            Response.Write(Sum);
        }
        else
            Response.Write("value=0")%>
        readonly >
    <LABEL> Output Value</LABEL><br />
    <BUTTON onclick=DoAdd() id=AddNumbers>Add</BUTTON><br />
    <NOSCRIPT>
        <p>
            Your browser doesn't support scripts.
            Use this button instead.
        </p>
        <BUTTON type=submit id=NoScriptAdd>
            No Script Add
        </BUTTON>
    </NOSCRIPT>
</form>
</body>
</html>
```

This page combines a number of scripting and ASP elements to create a cohesive application. The DoAdd() script is JavaScript that the server sends to the client. The client executes this code when it has scripting enabled. The script creates two variables — Value1 and Value2 — adds them together, and places the result in a textbox named Output.

The page also includes some ASP script which always appears between the `<%` and `%>` entries. One of the entries reads the query string from the URL and uses the information to update the values for the `Input1` and `Input2` textboxes. Notice that the ASP script looks very much like the JavaScript discussed in the chapter. It makes a decision based on whether the query string exists. If it doesn't, then the code sets the value of the textbox to 0.

Figure 1-4 shows how the query string appears as part of the Address field in a browser. The `?Input1=1&Input2=2` portion of the URL is the query string. It includes two entries: `Input1` and `Input2`. Notice that these values equal the values of the textboxes. The `Request.QueryString()` method obtains these values from the URL so that you can use them in your code.

The `<button>` tag produces the same result as the `<input type="button">` tag — it's just a little shorter. Some people prefer it because it's a little clearer and more accessible as well. Notice that the `<button>` tag has the `onclick` event attached to the `DoAdd()` function, but this function only works when the user has scripting enabled.

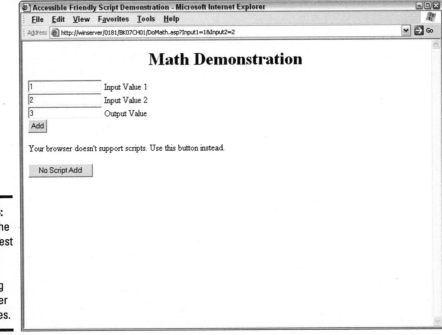

Figure 1-4:
Process the user request locally or remotely depending on browser capabilities.

The <noscript> tag comes next. The content of this tag appears only when a browser lacks scripting support. In this case, the code displays a message and as second button as shown in Figure 1-4. The user clicks No Script Add to submit the information in the Input1 and Input2 textboxes to the server instead of processing the information locally. The server processes this information as part of the script for the Output textbox and sends the information as a new page to the user.

Chapter 2: Creating Your First Scripted Page

In This Chapter

✔ Understanding what scripts do

✔ Working with the Code View toolbar

✔ Writing a simple script

✔ Attaching a function to a button

✔ Adding inputs and outputs to a function

Writing scripts is part science and part art. To write a script, you must meet certain minimum requirements, such as defining the scripting language and providing the required connections between HTML and the code. The order of tasks is often dictated as much by personal preference as by the needs of the script. You also have technique choices to make; some objects and functions overlap in functionality, so you can write code that performs the same task in more than one way.

FrontPage provides some special features that make working with code a lot easier. For example, the Code View toolbar helps you write code faster by providing quick typing features and code-location methods. You also have access to the Dynamic HyperText Markup Language or DHTML Effects toolbar, which contains buttons that allow you to associate specific effects with your code.

Although the helpful features of FrontPage make writing scripts easier, good script design is essential. One way you can improve your scripts is by using input and output arguments efficiently. Careful use of input and output arguments can reduce the total amount of work you have to perform.

Understanding How Scripts Work

JavaScript is an interpreted language. It appears as text in your Web-page file. When the Web page arrives at the client, the client's browser sees the `<script>` tag and passes the information to a local script handler. The local script handler processes the text within the `<script>` tag, performs any required actions, and passes the results back to the browser as needed.

For Windows users, the script handler is the same one you can access using either the CScript (for scripts executed at the command line) or WScript (for scripts executed in Windows) utilities. These two utilities are provided with Windows and reside in the \Windows\System32 folder of your machine — you can use them to execute scripts that you place in script files from your desktop. Because the *context* (the execution environment) is different, the CScript and WScript utilities have access to different objects than the browser, but the basic engine is the same. To see this fact for yourself, open a command window and type **CScript**. Then press Enter and you'll see the name of the scripting host, along with version information. (Windows XP users will likely notice that they're using Windows Script Host Version 5.6.)

After you look at the version information CScript provides, create a new Web page. Type the following code in this Web page, save it, and view it with your browser.

```html
<html>

<head>
    <title>First Script</title>
</head>

<body>

<h1>First Script Example</h1>

<script language="javascript">
    // Create a string to hold the version information.
    var SE = "";

    // Ask the scripting engine about its name and version.
    SE += ScriptEngine() + " Version ";
    SE += ScriptEngineMajorVersion() + ".";
    SE += ScriptEngineMinorVersion() + ".";
    SE += ScriptEngineBuildVersion();

    // Write the result to screen.
    document.write(SE);
</script>

</body>
</html>
```

Congratulations! You've not only proven that the browser script engine is the same one used for everything else in Windows, but you've also written your first script. The example code asks the script engine its name and version information. It may not amaze you too much that the browser reports the same version information as CScript — after all, they use the same engine to do their work. In fact, you can create a text file with a .JS extension (for JavaScript), using the script shown in this section — and use CScript to execute it. The only difference is that you must replace the `document.write(SE);` method with the `WScript.Echo(SE);` method to display the information. A copy of this script appears in the `CScriptVersion.JS` file found in the source code for this chapter on this book's companion Web site.

The idea behind this method of working with scripts is that any application that supports the scripting engine has the same access to the scripting engine features. The browser you use doesn't actually have to process the script because there's already another application to perform the task.

Any updates, patches, or virus fixes you apply to the scripting engine also affect your browser, making it safer to run scripts from sites that you trust.

Using the Code View Toolbar

One of the handiest scripting features of FrontPage is the Code View toolbar shown in Figure 2-1. This toolbar is active only in Code view. To display the toolbar, right-click the toolbar area and choose Code View from the context menu. The next few sections elaborate on the features of this toolbar.

**Book VII
Chapter 2**

Creating Your First
Scripted Page

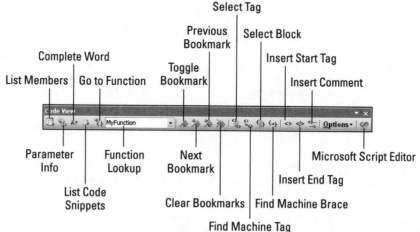

Figure 2-1: Simplify your script coding tasks by making using of this toolbar.

Select Tag

Previous Bookmark | Select Block

Insert Start Tag

Complete Word | Insert Comment

List Members | Go to Function | Toggle Bookmark

Parameter Info | Function Lookup | Next Bookmark | Microsoft Script Editor

Insert End Tag

List Code Snippets | Find Machine Brace

Clear Bookmarks | Find Machine Tag

Working with the Code View toolbar options

The Code View toolbar provides a number of options that make it easier to work with code in FrontPage. For example, the Options drop-down list box contains a list of coding options (such as word wrap and line numbers). Click any option to turn its feature on or off. The following list describes the other features in detail:

✦ **Microsoft Script Editor:** Starts the Microsoft Script Editor when installed on your machine. The Microsoft Script Editor includes a number of features including a debugger that isn't included with FrontPage. Unfortunately, it lacks IntelliSense support, so you need to rely on the included help file to write code. Fortunately, the help file includes detailed JavaScript and VBScript information, including the functions missing from the FrontPage help.

✦ **Insert Comment:** Adds a standard HTML comment to your code, but it isn't a FrontPage comment of the sort that appears in the Design view. You can't add this special type comment by adding a double slash (//) as you would for a scripting comment.

✦ **Insert End Tag:** Creates a starting tag and places the cursor in the middle so you can type the tag type.

✦ **Insert Start Tag:** Creates an ending tag and places the cursor after the slash so you can type the tag type.

✦ **Find Matching Brace:** Locates the *brace* (curly bracket) in your script that matches the one you selected. Using this feature can help you locate statements that have missing braces, or braces that show up in the wrong place.

✦ **Select Block:** Selects the block of code between two braces, using the selected brace as a starting point.

✦ **Find Matching Tag:** Locates the ending tag for a start tag, or vice versa. This feature is helpful when you have a lot of code between tags and want to move between the beginning and end quickly. This feature is especially useful with `<object>` tags because they contain a lot of entries.

✦ **Select Tag:** Selects an entire tag, including all code between the start and end tag.

✦ **Clear Bookmarks:** Removes all bookmarks from a document — important when you finish editing the document and want to deploy it on your Web site.

Because bookmarks reside on your local system, you don't need to worry about whether they'll use additional space on the server.

✦ **Previous Bookmark:** Locates the previous bookmark in the document.

✦ **Next Bookmark:** Locates the next bookmark in the document.

✦ **Toggle Bookmark:** Adds or removes an individual bookmark in the document. The bookmark refers to the entire line and your cursor appears at the beginning of the line when you select the bookmark. When you enable the Line Numbers option, FrontPage also displays a teal square next to any line that has a bookmark . (To enable this feature, choose Line Numbers from the Options drop-down list box.)

✦ **Function Lookup:** Displays the selected function. Simply choose one of the functions in the drop-down list and FrontPage shows it to you. This list includes only functions on the current page.

✦ **Go To Function:** Locates any function referenced within the page. To use this feature, place the cursor on a function call. When the function call appears on the same page, click this button to move to the cursor to the function code.

✦ **List Code Snippets:** Displays a list of standard code snippets — predefined pieces of code — you can use to add code quickly. Simply select a code snippet from the list and FrontPage types the code for you. This feature is explained in more detail in the "Defining code snippets" section later in this chapter.

✦ **Complete Word:** Displays a list of keywords that could complete the current word. For example, when you type the letter *A*, you see all functions, methods, and properties that begin with the letter *A*. The list generally isn't complete — it only contains the keywords that FrontPage tracks directly.

✦ **Parameter Info:** Displays the list of arguments for the current method or function.

✦ **List Members:** Displays a list of properties, methods, and events associated with the current object. When you don't select a specific object, FrontPage takes context into account: You see a list of all members for the window object.

Defining code snippets

Code snippets are small pieces of code you access using the List Code Snippets button shown in Figure 2-1. The list appears at the current cursor position as shown in Figure 2-2. Simply click the code snippet you want to use and FrontPage types the associated code.

Using code snippets saves time because you can create a large amount of code quickly. FrontPage comes with some very common code snippets defined. For example, you can add a document type declaration to your page by using a code snippet (document type declarations tell which set of HTML rules a page uses to define tags).

The code snippets are completely customizable. A good candidate for a code snippet is any piece of code that you use consistently in many of the Web pages you create (such as the `author` meta tag). Double-click Customize List and you see the Code Snippets tab of the Page Options dialog box, shown in Figure 2-3. You can also access this dialog box by choosing the Tools⇨Page Options command.

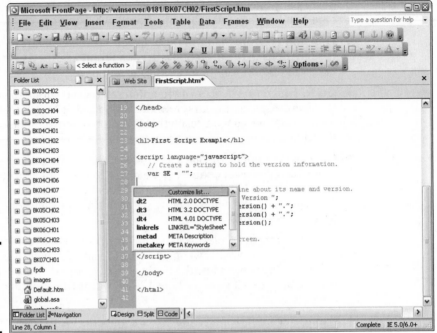

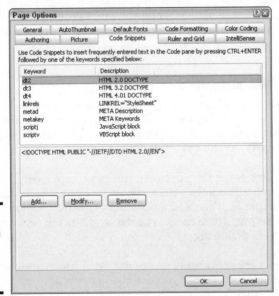

To add a new code snippet, click Add in the Page Options dialog box. You see the Add Code Snippet dialog box. Type a keyword, description, and the code for the snippet. (A *keyword* is a short phrase you can use to identify the code snippet. Make sure you select something that is easy to remember because all you see is the keyword in the code snippet list.) The description should provide enough details about the code snippet that you remember its purpose without having to open the code all the time. However, don't make the description so long that you feel like you're reading a book every time you review it. The code can be anything from a single line of code to a complete function — define whatever you feel is common and consistent enough to make a good code snippet.

The list of code snippets can quickly get too long. You may want to remove some of them to keep your list of code snippets from becoming hard to navigate. To remove an existing code snippet, highlight its entry in the Page Options dialog box and click Remove.

Use this feature with care. FrontPage doesn't ask whether you want to remove the code snippet — it's simply gone.

Sometimes a code snippet won't work as planned, so you need to edit it. To change a code snippet, select its entry on the Page Options dialog box and click Modify.

One of the most common changes is to ensure that the cursor ends up in the right place after FrontPage types the code for you: Simply place the pipe symbol (|) where you think the cursor should go after FrontPage types the code. Remember to remove any existing pipe symbols from the code before you complete the edit.

Creating a Simple Script

One of the most common scripts that developers begin writing is the *inline script* — one that doesn't rely on any special resources to execute. The type of scripts that you're likeliest to write does some simple but vital tasks — such as detecting client settings (so you can compensate for browser-compatibility problems) or otherwise ensuring that your application will run properly. For example, just knowing whether a user has Internet Explorer or Opera is a big help — but you also need to consider specific program versions in some cases. Fortunately, this very common script is also a relatively simple script. Here are some steps to get you started:

1. **Create a new Web page and add all the usual settings to it.**

2. **Select Code view.**

3. Place the cursor beneath any headers you might have created and click List Code Snippets on the Code View toolbar.

You see a list of code snippets.

4. Double-click the `scriptj` **entry.**

FrontPage creates a JavaScript code block for you.

5. Type the following code in the JavaScript code block:

```
// Check for plug-ins. Display a message when there aren't
// any plug-ins to list.
if (window.clientInformation.plugins.length == 0)
    document.writeln("No Plug-ins");

// When plug-ins exist, list each one in turn.
for (Counter = 0;
    Counter < window.clientInformation.plugins.length;
    Counter++)
{
    document.writeln(
        window.clientInformation.plugins[Counter])
}
```

6. Save the document.

7. Look at the document in your browser.

The browser displays either a list of plug-ins or the No Plug-ins message.

The script in this example demonstrates one way to work with objects that can have any number of entries. In this case, a client can have more than one plug-in installed. The plug-in information appears in a *collection*. Think of a collection as a box that contains any number of similar items. All the items are of the same type, but they contain unique content. A baseball card collection consists of baseball cards, but it's unlikely that every card will have information about the same player.

JavaScript looks at collections as arrays. An *array* is a single memory structure grouping many values, where each value can be accessed using the same variable name, but with a number, called an index, singling out that particular value from the group. Arrays work much like apartments in a building. Every apartment has the same address. So, to look for John Smith you begin by looking for the building. After you find the building (the name of the array), you look for John Smith's apartment. The `window.clientInformation.plugins[Counter])` entry performs the same task as locating a particular apartment. It tells JavaScript to look for a particular item in the `plugins` array, which is actually a collection.

Notice how the code also uses the `window.clientInformation.plugins.length` property in two different ways. The first use is to determine whether there are any plug-ins. A length of 0 in a collection means there are no items in the collection, or no plug-ins in this case. The second is to determine how many plug-ins to process as part of the `for` loop.

Associating a Function with a Button

One of the most important scripting tasks is associating a function with an event. You have access to a number of events for just about every object that a browser can access. (I can't think of an object that doesn't include events, but I'm sure there must be one.) Generally, the choice of which event to use is relatively easy to figure out. For example, you use the `onclick` event when you want to track the user's clicks on a particular object and most user interface objects support this event. The first control that developers work with, in most cases, is a pushbutton — and the most common event handled by functions for pushbuttons is `onclick`.

Working with events

Whenever you create a function, it's important to plan thoroughly before you actually write any code. The world is filled with bad code written because someone got very excited about doing something and didn't fully outline what it was they wanted to do. Because many functions replicate tasks you want to do, it pays to write the steps down *as you would do them*. For example, when you want to add two numbers, you follow these steps:

1. **Discover the value of the first number.**

2. **Discover the value of the second number.**

3. **Add the two numbers together.**

4. **Look at the result.**

A function works the same way. You need to obtain two numbers from somewhere — normally a form containing two text boxes. JavaScript adds the two numbers together. It then places the result in a third text box, where the user looks at the result. The process JavaScript uses is the same as the process you use. The only difference is that you don't have to perform the work — you let JavaScript do the work for you.

There's one missing piece: Something has to tell JavaScript to perform the addition. Generally, the developer creates an Add pushbutton and associates the `onclick` event with the function that actually performs the task. The following steps show how to create the required code:

1. **Create a blank Web page and add all the usual settings to it.**

2. **Select Design view.**

3. **Add a form to the Web page. Remove the Submit and Reset buttons. Add three text boxes (**`txtInput1`, `txtInput2`, **and** `txtOutput`**) and one pushbutton (**`btnAdd`**) for the form.**

   Your form should look like the one shown in Figure 2-4. You might want to configure `txtOutput` so that it's read-only. The example also includes default values for `txtInput1` and `txtInput2`.

4. **Select the Add button. Choose the Split view.**

   FrontPage displays the code for `btnAdd` highlighted in the Code view portion of the Split view.

5. **Place the cursor at the end of the highlighted area but before the angle bracket (>), and type the following line:**

   ```
   onclick="btnAdd_Click()"
   ```

   The code you added will execute the `btnAdd_Click()` function when the user clicks Add.

6. **Select Code view.**

7. **Place the cursor on a blank line in the** `<head>` **tag area (but before the** `</head>` **tag) and click List Code Snippets on the Code View toolbar.**

   You see a list of code snippets.

8. **Double-click the** `scriptj` **entry.**

   FrontPage creates a JavaScript code block for you.

9. **Type the following code in the JavaScript code block:**

   ```
   function btnAdd_Click()
   {
       // Get the input values.
       var Input1 = parseInt(AddForm.txtInput1.value);
       var Input2 = parseInt(AddForm.txtInput2.value);

       // Perform the addition.
       var Output = Input1 + Input2;

       // Display the results on-screen.
       AddForm.txtOutput.value = Output;
   }
   ```

10. **Save the document.**

11. **Test the document in your browser.**

    You can add any two numbers together.

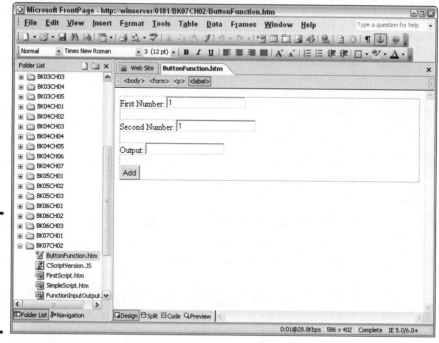

Figure 2-4:
Create the form elements required to add two numbers.

Book VII
Chapter 2

Creating Your First
Scripted Page

Using the DHTML Effects toolbar

Another way to respond to events is to create a special effect for them. The special effect isn't (strictly speaking) productive code; it doesn't actually perform useful work. What special effects do is provide visual cues or other attractive functionality. For example, you can tell FrontPage to display a particular special effect when the user hovers the mouse over a control. The special effect could be a font or other formatting change. Generally, you should avoid such special effects because not all browsers support them and they can cause accessibility problems.

FrontPage makes it easy to add special effects to your Web page using the DHTML Effects toolbar shown in Figure 2-5. This toolbar is only active in Design view. To see this toolbar, right-click the toolbar area and choose DHTML Effects from the context menu.

Figure 2-5:
Add special
effects to
the controls
on a form
for added
interest.

Unlike most toolbars, this toolbar requires you to access its fields in a specific order from left to right when adding a special effect. The following steps discuss how to use the DHTML Effects toolbar to add a special effect:

1. **Select a control you want to add a special effect to in the Design view.**

   FrontPage enables the On field of the DHTML Effects toolbar. The On field lets you select the event that will handle the special effect. The most common event to use to trigger a special effect is mouseover.

2. **Choose one of the events to add a special effect to in the On field.**

   FrontPage enables the Apply field of the DHTML Effects toolbar. This field lets you decide on the kind of special effect to add. The most common special effect is formatting.

3. **Define the kind of special effect you want to add using the Apply field.**

   FrontPage enables the Effect field (the only one without a label in Figure 2-5). The effect setup you choose depends on the content of the Apply field. When working with formatting as the special effect, you can change the font, border, and shading settings.

4. **Select the effect setting you want to change from the Effect field.**

   FrontPage makes the change immediately for simple effects. It displays a dialog box you use to make changes for complex effects. For example, when you choose the Choose Border option, FrontPage displays the Borders and Shading dialog box so you can change the border and shading options.

5. **Make any required changes to the effect settings.**

   FrontPage highlights the field in a special color to show it has a special effect attached to it.

Some people get distracted by the highlighting that FrontPage uses to identify fields with DHTML effects attached. If you want to give them a break, click Highlight Dynamic HTML Effects on the DHTML Effects toolbar to remove the highlighting. This button toggles the highlighting on and off.

To remove DHTML effects from a control, click Remove Effect on the DHTML Effects toolbar. FrontPage removes all DHTML effects for the control, so you should use it with care. Another alternative is to remove the individual webbot and dynamicanimation entries required to implement the DHTML effect.

Providing Inputs to a Function

You can make functions more generic — and reduce the time you spend coding them — by using inputs. Most developers use inputs in various ways to reduce coding chores; if you use them appropriately, you have to look for errors only once, rather than each time you create a new function.

Defining an input is a matter of adding a variable name to the function declaration. You use the variable within the code to identify the caller or any other information you want to pass along. Here's an example of a function with a single input.

```
function General_Click(ClickType)
{
    // Display the button the user clicked.
    alert("You clicked the " + ClickType + " button.");
}
```

You create the function as you normally do using the procedure in the "Working with events" section of the chapter. All this function does is display the pushbutton that the user clicked. Any pushbutton that calls this event handler can count on the same handling — but the information differs by button because you use the ClickType variable to hold the button name.

Providing Outputs from a Function

Event-handler functions normally don't require outputs, but generic functions do. You can place common code that you need for more than one task in a function that is called by other functions. Generic functions further decrease the amount of coding you perform, and reduce the number of potential errors to find. Here's an example of an event handler calling a generic function:

```
function Output_Click(Source)
{
    // Call the external function.
    var TheOutput = TestIt(Source);

    // Display the result.
    alert(TheOutput);
}
```

**Book VII
Chapter 2**

**Creating Your First
Scripted Page**

```
function TestIt(Source)
{
    // Create a string from the input value.
    var ReturnValue =
        "You clicked the " + Source + " button.";

    // Return the new string.
    return ReturnValue;
}
```

You create this setup as you would any other event handler. Adding the generic function is a matter of writing the additional code. Notice that you must declare input arguments as variables within the parentheses of the function declaration — but there's only one output argument, so it doesn't require such a declaration.

To return a value to the caller, use the `return` keyword and supply the value you want to return. A return value can be anything from a string to an object. As with input arguments, JavaScript doesn't place a limit on what you can use as an output argument, so long as it's a legal JavaScript variable.

Chapter 3: Working with Cookies

In This Chapter

✔ Using cookies effectively

✔ Creating cookies

✔ Getting information from a cookie

✔ Ensuring that the cookie expires

*N*o, we're not going to talk about the fresh-from-the-oven variety of cookies in this chapter — cookies also come in browser form. A *cookie* is a piece of information you leave on a user's machine for later use. It can contain any information that you normally place in a variable. In fact, you'll likely use a variable to hold the information until after you store it in the cookie — then, when you retrieve the information from the cookie later, you'll place it in a variable.

Most developers use cookies to store user settings or information that relates to a specific user. For example, if the user likes an orange background and green text when visiting your site, you can store those settings using a cookie. Developers also use cookies for serious reasons. A cookie could keep track of a user's progress on the Web site while shopping. Many shopping-cart applications rely on cookies.

Scripts make cookies easy to create, manage, and remove. In fact, you can set cookies to *expire* so they remove themselves automatically. This lets you use cookies without cluttering the user's machine forever. In addition, you can make sure the information in the cookie isn't too old — if you change the information storage requirements on your site, an old cookie could cause problems.

Using Cookies to Help Users

Some people would have you believe that cookies are inherently evil because they've seen them misused — for example, some companies track their users' movement on the Internet by checking cookie data. In fact, you might know of someone who thinks that cookies are a form of virus — they aren't. Other people see cookies as a panacea for every possible data-storage woe the user might have. Technically, cookies aren't good or evil — they're simply a method of storing data on the user's machine — and whether you use them depends on your storage needs. Keeping storage requirements in mind helps you reduce cookie use to just the essentials — and also helps you build a strong case with the user for allowing them.

Uses for cookies

Cookies are extremely useful. You can store any data you work with on the Web page in a cookie. There aren't any limitations on what you can store so you can even save intermediate or hidden results of calculations. Depending on the user's operating system, browser, system settings, and other variables, however, you have a limit on the amount of data you can store. For example, saving a copy of *War and Peace* is out of the question. Here are a few types of data that Web sites store in cookies:

+ User settings

+ Browser settings

+ Date of last visit

+ Form entries

Understanding cookie issues

There's no doubt that cookies make life easier for developers. Most Web sites try to emphasize the benefits of cookies for users, but the real beneficiary is the developer: Using cookies makes writing scripts a lot easier and safer by providing permanent storage in a location that the developer can't otherwise access. This technique avoids issues of privacy and sidesteps other security issues that many developers are unwilling to cope with. The user can't come back later and say that the developer "stole" information or stored it in an unsafe location because the developer never actually has control over the physical file.

Cookies also benefit companies and service providers. The user's machine stores all the data. Consequently, the company or service provider that owns the Web site doesn't have to allocate additional resources for storing the information.

However, the user does benefit to an extent from cookies — just how much depends on how the developer uses the cookie:

+ **Storing Web-site settings in a cookie:** Most users agree that this use saves time because the user doesn't have to reconfigure the Web site with every visit.

✦ **Storing shopping-cart settings:** Many users will also agree that this use, while not directly helpful to the user, is at least a necessary evil to allow the purchase of goods online.

✦ **Placing a target for ads on the user's machine:** Possible, but don't do it. I don't know of a single user who has any positive thoughts whatsoever about adware that places cookies on their system. Many users go out of their way to delete such cookies, and don't much like whoever places them.

This third type of cookie — the one created by adware — is the reason that many users are so incredibly leery of enabling cookies on their machines. The consensus is that these cookies are used by their developers for less-than-honorable reasons. Every page the adware appears on is also a page where the user is tracked. It doesn't take long for the adware company to discover users' Web-surfing habits and make assumptions about those users. These assumptions become target-marketing data that they in turn sell to someone else — generally marketers of goods that the user doesn't want or need. Such a use of cookies is incredibly tacky (to say the least). If you value your users' goodwill, avoid doing it — or allowing anyone else to do it via your Web site.

Adding a privacy statement

Many users are becoming quite savvy about cookies and their uses. They want to know that you respect their privacy and that you have a privacy policy in place to protect their interests. A *privacy policy* states how you use the information gathered in cookies — and how you intend to protect the user's right to privacy.

Fortunately, adding a privacy policy to your Web page isn't too hard; there are a number of tools you can use to do it. In addition, the privacy policy is standardized in such a way that users can set their browsers to scan the policy and ensure that cookie use is protected.

The most common way to publish and use a privacy policy is by using a standard known as *Platform for Privacy Preferences (P3P)*. The World Wide Web Consortium (W3C) sponsors this technique and you can read about the six easy steps for implementing P3P on your Web site at

`http://www.w3.org/P3P/details.html`

The P3P standard (`http://www.w3.org/TR/P3P/`) also contains a wealth of information you should review.

FrontPage doesn't provide P3P or any other privacy support, so you need a third-party tool to add a privacy policy to your Web site. The example in this section uses the IBM P3P generator, available at

```
http://www.alphaworks.ibm.com/tech/p3peditor
```

The W3C site lists several other generators — I chose this particular generator because it comes with a 90-day free trial. Your code might turn out different from mine if you use another generator for your code.

Your privacy statement will consist of several files, including at least one P3P file that you create by using the P3P generator and an XML reference file. A good generator will also help you create a generic *privacy summary* that you can use as a concise answer to queries from the user, and a *compact policy statement* you can use in the response headers of pages that contain cookies. Where you store privacy information depends on whether you own the server that hosts your Web page:

✦ **If you own the server:** You can place the privacy information in the \w3c folder of your Web site. It's also possible to create linkage between the privacy information and your Web page by using a <link> tag, similar to the one shown here:

```
<link rel="P3Pv1"
        href="http://www.mwt.net/~jmueller/p3p.xml">
```

Adding the compact policy statement is relatively easy if you own the server.

✦ **If you don't own the server:** This is the situation for many people, including small business owners. Internet Explorer 6 has several levels of cookie protection built in. The highest level will likely reject your privacy information because Internet Explorer relies exclusively on the compact policy statement supplied as part of the response headers. (A response header is text that appears at the beginning of a response to a request that tells the requestor about the Web page, such as whether the requestor was able to process the request properly and what data types the sender supports.) Listing 3-1 shows one way you can add a compact policy statement if you don't own the server, plus some test code you can use to verify the results.

Listing 3-1:   Adding a Compact Policy to a Web Page

```
<html>
<head>
<meta http-equiv='P3P'
      content='policyref=" p3p.xml",
      CP="NOI DSP COR NID CURa OUR NOR NAV INT TST"'>
<title>Privacy Demonstration</title>
```

```
<script>
function SetCookie()
{
    var  UserCookie; // Stores the user name.

    // Create the username cookie.
    UserCookie = "UserName=" + escape(InputVal.value);

    // Add the cookie to the document.
    document.cookie = UserCookie;

    // Tell the user the cookie was saved.
    alert("The cookies were saved.");
}

function ReadCookie()
{
    var  ACookie; // Holds the document cookie.
    var  Parsed;  // Holds the split cookies.
    var  Name;    // The user name.

    // Get the cookie.
    ACookie = unescape(document.cookie);

    // Split the cookie elements.
    Parsed = ACookie.split("=");

    // Get the user name.
    Name = Parsed[1];

    // Display the name.
    alert("Your name is: " + Name);
}
... Additional Web Page Code ...
```

Book VII
Chapter 3

Working with
Cookies

The <meta> tag at the beginning of the code is the essential addition to your application. The http-equiv attribute tells the server what kind of response header to add. Some servers don't honor this attribute, so this solution might not work completely in all cases. The content attribute tells the client where to locate the privacy policy for your Web site. Finally, the CP attribute defines the compact policy for your server. Most tools, such as the IBM P3P Policy Editor shown in Figure 3-1, tell you what these codes mean and generate a text file containing them for you.

The test code consists of two functions attached to buttons on the example form. The first creates a cookie and attaches it to the document. The second retrieves the cookie stored in the document and displays the results on-screen. (For more about how these functions work, see the "Creating a Cookie" and "Reading a Cookie" sections of the chapter.)

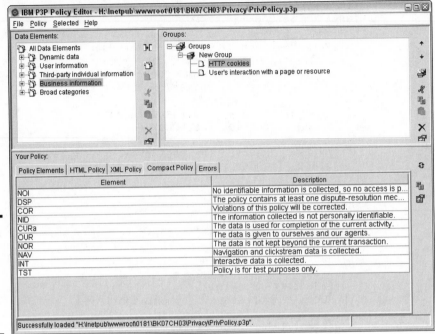

Figure 3-1:
Generate a
compact
policy for
Web pages
that have
cookies.

This is just enough code to create an error with Internet Explorer 6 if the compact policy statement isn't accepted. The reasons a user rejects a compact policy are many. For example, the user can reject a compact policy that includes features such as storing user information. All of the rejection criteria is based on the user's privacy setting. It's a potential problem: If you want users to use the high privacy setting, you must have a compact policy in place and Internet Explorer 6 must accept it. To check your current privacy setting, choose the Tools⇨Internet options command. Select the Privacy tab. You see the Internet Options dialog box shown in Figure 3-2. Notice the explanation of each privacy setting next to the slider.

Even if Internet Explorer 6 decides it won't accept the compact policy, having a privacy policy in place and set up — using the information provided in this section — lets the user rely on the medium-high privacy setting. Although, the medium-high setting isn't quite as comfortable (strict, secure, whatever comfort word you would use) as the high setting, it's much better than the low setting your Web site would require if it didn't have a privacy policy.

The most important consideration for this section is what the privacy policy actually does for the user. The Privacy Report can help you get a line on that:

1. Select View⇨Privacy Report in Internet Explorer.

You see the Privacy Report dialog box.

2. Highlight your Web site URL and click Summary.

You see a Privacy Policy dialog box similar to the one shown in Figure 3-3. This policy contains links where the user can ask additional questions, learn more about your privacy policy, and request a solution for disputes.

The idea is to make using cookies as easy and palatable for the user as possible and to protect the user's rights.

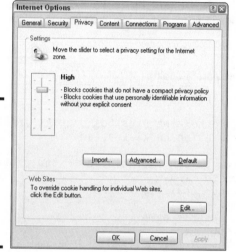

Figure 3-2: Increasing the privacy setting rejects cookies from dubious sources.

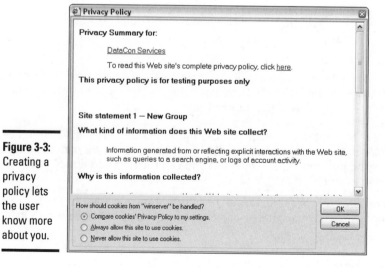

Figure 3-3: Creating a privacy policy lets the user know more about you.

Creating a Cookie

Cookies come in a number of varieties. The type you choose depends on your application needs. As a rule, you want to create a temporary cookie whenever possible. A *temporary cookie* is removed from the user's system when they end their current session, so that none of the data remains on the system. When working with user settings or other data that must survive between sessions, use a permanent cookie. A *permanent cookie* actually appears within a file on the user's system, generally in a central location and it requires expiration data. The "Enforcing Cookie Expiration" section discusses permanent cookies in more detail; Listing 3-2 shows how to create a temporary cookie.

Listing 3-2: Creating a Temporary Cookie

```
function SaveCookie()
{
    // Determine whether the user has cookies enabled.
    if (clientInformation.cookieEnabled)
    {
        // Normally you don't display a message, but it's
        // good for testing.
        alert("Saving Cookie");

        // Save the user's name.
        document.cookie =
            "UserName=" + escape(txtUserName.value) + ";";

        // Save the user's background color preference.
        document.cookie =
            "bgColor=" + escape(document.bgColor);
    }
}
```

A cookie consists (so to speak) of two crumbs: a name and a value. Although both of these are values in the technical sense — each is usually a string of characters — they have different functions:

✦ **Name:** This is the identifier you use for the cookie. Listing 3-2 shows two cookie names: UserName and bgColor. Always choose a name that identifies the purpose of the cookie so you can retrieve and understand its purpose later.

✦ **Value:** Strictly speaking, this is the information you want to save. You can retrieve any variable or object property you want to save as a value.

Unlike many properties, the `document.cookie` property is a collection. Every time you supply a new name-and-value pair, JavaScript creates a new entry for it in the collection. Consequently, when the code assigns the `UserName` value and then the `bgColor` value to the `document.cookie` property, JavaScript actually creates two entries — one for each value.

Reading a Cookie

After you save a cookie, the values it contains are available for use in other functions of your Web page. It doesn't matter what kind of cookie you create, the reading process is the same. The type of cookie only affects how long you can read the values. Listing 3-3 shows typical code for reading a cookie.

Listing 3-3: **Reading a Cookie**

```
function GetCookie()
{
   if (clientInformation.cookieEnabled)
   {
      // When there aren't any cookie values, ask
      // for new entries.
      if (document.cookie.length == 0)
      {
         // Get the user name.
         txtUserName.value =
            prompt("Please type your user name");

         // Get a background color.
         document.bgColor =
            prompt("Type a background color name");
      }
      else
      {

         // Get the cookie values.
         var aCookies = document.cookie.split("; ");

         // Process each of the cookie values.
         for (Counter = 0;
              Counter < aCookies.length;
              Counter++)
         {
            // Divide the cookie into a name and value
            // pair.
            var aCrumb = aCookies[Counter].split("=");

            // Determine the cookie type.
```

(continued)

Listing 3-3 *(continued)*

```
        switch (aCrumb[0])
        {
            case "UserName":
                txtUserName.value = unescape(aCrumb[1]);
                break;
            case "bgColor":
                document.bgColor = unescape(aCrumb[1]);
                break;
        }
    }
}

    // Display a personalized greeting.
    txtGreeting.innerText = "Hello " +
        txtUserName.value + ", glad to see you!";
}
else
{
    // Provide a greeting for users who don't have
    // cookies enabled.
    txtGreeting.innerText =
        "Hello stranger, glad to see you!";
}
}
```

This code considers three possible situations. First, the user has cookie support, but hasn't visited the site before, so there aren't any cookies to read. Second, the user has visited the site before and there are cookies to read. Third, the user's browser doesn't have cookie support.

The first `if` statement checks the `clientInformation.cookieEnabled` property to determine whether the user has cookie support enabled. If not, then the code executes the `else` clause of this `if` statement to display a generic greeting. The code doesn't change the background color because there isn't any way to determine the user's preference.

This feature illustrates an important concept — always provide an alternative for the user who doesn't want to use cookies, even if that alternative is inconvenient for you. Most Web sites either work with cookies or they don't work at all — a poor way to treat the user. Sometimes you can't provide the requested functionality with cookies, but there's usually an alternative, even when using shopping carts. Simply display a message asking the user to call your customer support line to make the order over the telephone. Using this technique can mean you don't lose a sale.

The next step is to determine whether the user has any cookies for your site. When the `document.cookie.length` property is 0, then there aren't any cookies to process and you can assume this is a first-time user. The code prompts for values to store in the cookies, but you can obtain the cookie data using any other technique you want. Notice that the code doesn't store the data in variables, it uses form entries to store the information. This is a common practice because the form entries are global to the entire Web page.

The `else` clause executes when the user has cookie support enabled and there are cookies to process. The code uses the special `split()` method to divide the cookie entries. The `split()` method creates an array that JavaScript stores in `aCookies`. The array contains one entry for each cookie.

Now that the cookies are split, the code uses the `aCookies.length` property to determine how many cookies there are and processes each cookie in turn using a `for` loop. To process a cookie, you must break it into crumbs (a *crumb* is a name-and-value pair). The code uses the `split()` method again to perform this task, placing the resulting name-and-value pair in the `aCrumb` array.

The name crumb always appears in array element 0, so the code can use a `switch` statement to process it. A `switch` is an extended version of the `if` statement. Every `case` entry acts as an `if` statement; thus the code asks whether the name is equal to `UserName` first and `bgColor` second. If the name doesn't match either value, nothing happens.

When the name does match one of the target values, JavaScript follows the code between the `case` entry and the `break` entry. For example, when working with the `UserName` crumb, the code places the value — which always appears in `aCrumb` element 1 — into the `txtUserName.value` property.

You might have noticed the use of the `escape()` and `unescape()` functions in the example. Always *escape* the values you save to a cookie — that is, use the `escape()` function to ensure that any control characters are converted into a form that the text file can accept. Likewise, *unescape* the values when you retrieve them from the cookies, using the `unescape()` function to ensure that control-character data is restored.

Enforcing Cookie Expiration

Temporary cookies work fine for many tasks, in particular those required for shopping-cart applications. However, user settings and other permanent data require the use of a permanent cookie. If the data doesn't last between sessions, there's little use in saving it. Remember, however, that users don't want the data to stay on their machines forever. After all, some users might not visit your site again. To ensure that the data is permanent and yet doesn't remain forever, you create an expiration date. Listing 3-4 shows how to create a cookie with an expiration date.

Listing 3-4:   Saving a Permanent Cookie

```
function btnSave_Click()
{
    var UserCookie;            // Stores the user name.
    var TheDate = new Date();  // Date object.
    var Expire;                // Expiration date.

    // Build an expiration date. Begin by getting the day.
    // of the week.
    switch (TheDate.getUTCDay() + 2)
    {
      case 1:
          Expire = "Sun, ";
          break;
      ... Other Days of the Week ...
      case 7:
          Expire = "Sat, ";
          break;
    }

    // Add the date.
    Expire = Expire + (TheDate.getUTCDate() + 1);

    // Add the month.
    switch (TheDate.getUTCMonth() + 1)
    {
      case 1:
          Expire = Expire + " Jan ";
          break;
      ... Other Months ...
      case 12:
          Expire = Expire + " Dec ";
          break;
    }

    // Add the year.
    Expire = Expire + TheDate.getUTCFullYear() + " ";

    // Add the time.
    Expire = Expire + TheDate.getUTCHours() + ":" +
             TheDate.getUTCMinutes() + ":" +
             TheDate.getUTCSeconds() + " UTC";
```

```
// Create the username cookie.
UserCookie = "UserName=" +
            escape(prompt("Type your name")) +
            "; expires=" + Expire + ";";

// Add the cookie to the document.
document.cookie = UserCookie;

// Tell the user the cookie was saved.
alert("The cookies were saved and will expire on: " +
    Expire + ".");
}
```

The actual cookie-creation process is the same as what happens in Listing 3-2 — defining the date just takes a little more work. You must create a Universal Time Code (UTC) date for your cookie. The date must appear in a very specific format. The code in Listing 3-4 shows how to create such a date, which looks like this in its final form:

```
Sat, 5 Jun 2004 18:44:53 UTC
```

To begin the process, the code creates a `Date` object, `TheDate`. This object provides access to a number of date and time functions, including the UTC functions shown in the code. For example, the `getUTCDay()` function retrieves the day of the week as a number between 0 and 6. Because the date must contain the day as a name, the code uses a `switch` to convert it to text form.

One of the problems with working with time functions is that you can't retrieve the time directly; you must use the method shown. The `getTime()` method returns the number of milliseconds since midnight on January 1, 1970, a really huge number that isn't particularly helpful in this case.

Notice that adding an expiration is simply adding another cookie to the document. The expiration date relies on the keyword `expires`, which you can't use for any other purpose. When JavaScript sees this keyword, it reads the date supplied and acts according to specific rules. When the date is in the past, JavaScript erases the cookies immediately. On the other hand, when the date is in the future, JavaScript creates a file on disk that holds the information. The precise location varies, but when you use Windows 2000 or Windows XP, the cookie appears in the `\Documents and Settings\<Your Login Name>\Cookies` folder. The cookie has your name and the folder in which the associated Web page appears, along with a TXT extension. You can easily open the file and see what it contains by using Notepad.

**Book VII
Chapter 3**

**Working with
Cookies**

Chapter 4: Performing Common Scripted Tasks

In This Chapter

✔ Programming around a user's browser type

✔ Sending users to another page

✔ Getting user feedback

✔ Removing errors from your script

This chapter discusses some of the common tasks you can perform with scripts, but it isn't intended to limit you in any way. You'll see how to discover the user's browser type, send users to another page, provide the user with feedback, and debug your script. While there are limits to what you can do with a script, most developers find that scripts let them perform a vast array of tasks — more than any one book can contain. No, you don't want to write a word processor using a script language, even though such a feat is theoretically possible, but you can provide a better user interface by detecting the user's browser type and accommodating that browser as needed.

Along with providing you with some code to perform common tasks, this chapter also points out the need to build a library of common code (everything from snippets to complete functions). By creating your functions carefully, you can reduce the need to write them again later. The use of input and output arguments tends to isolate the code, which makes it easier to move blocks of code from place to place by using cut-and-paste. The overall goal is to create one source of common code that is ready to use and free of error. Such a library saves an incredible amount of time by reducing development tasks and lets you concentrate on design tasks.

Using Server-Side Includes

You can use a code library in one of two ways. First, you can copy and paste the information you need into your pages. Of course, this means that every time you want to enhance a function you have to open each page that uses it and make the change. Second, you can rely on a Server-Side Include (SSI) to create a connection between the current page and a file that contains all your functions. Using this technique means you only make one change to enhance the usability of your functions — but your server must provide the required support.

To test the SSI method on your server, create a standard HTML file with an SHTM or SHTML extension based on your server. For example, when working with Internet Information Server (IIS), use the SHTM extension because the HTML files on that server normally rely on the HTM extension. The "S" in the extension tells the server that there's a special instruction in the file it needs to address. The server doesn't process the whole file as it would for Active Server Pages (ASP) or other server-side scripts — it just processes the special SSI commands you provide.

After you create the SHTM file, try creating an SSI command in it. For example, here's an SSI command to display the current date:

```
<html>
<head>
```

```
    <title>SSI Example</title>
</head>
<body>
    <h1>Using Server-side
    Includes</h1>
    <p>
        Current Date:
        <!--#config timefmt="%A,
%d %B %Y" -->
        <!--#echo
var="DATE_LOCAL" -->
    </p>
</body>
</html>
```

This simple script displays the local date on-screen. If you see the date when you test this page, your server supports SSI and you can use a very simple technique for including your library of JavaScript functions on any Web page. Simply add the `include` command anywhere in the document (sooner is better) like this:

```
<!--#include file="MyLib.js"
    -->
```

This code places the `MyLib.js` file within the current Web page. You can use all the functions contained within `MyLib.js` even though they don't appear within the Web page. You can find an example of this technique in the `UseSSI.shtm` file located in the source code for this chapter on this book's companion Web site.

Determining the User's Browser Type

Determining the user's browser type can be one of the more important tasks you perform using a script. Most browsers support most standard HTML tags so long as you avoid any odd attributes. In fact, if you're willing to create a completely plain page without any aesthetically pleasing features whatsoever, every browser will work with it just fine — at least most of the time. The compatibility issues for someone who runs a public Web site can be daunting (to say the least) because most developers, companies, and even users aren't satisfied with a plain Web page.

Handling browser compatibility issues

The compatibility issues are many. The fact that no one Web resource discusses them all makes matters more difficult. Given the many versions of browsers that people use, the problem only gets worse. In fact, look at the Webmonkey chart at

```
http://hotwired.lycos.com/webmonkey/reference/browser_chart/index.html
```

to see just how bad things can get — and this chart is only an overview. It also provides links to charts that show the capabilities of Macintosh, Linux, and other browsers. When you start considering specific tags and attributes, the problems become far more significant.

Some Web sites work around the problems of browser compatibility by blocking browsers they don't support and suggesting that the viewer download the correct browser. A less severe solution is to include messages that tell the user the page is "best displayed" using a particular browser and providing a link for downloading that browser. Most users have a negative opinion of these approaches, no matter how well intended, unless you happen to support the browsers they already use (in which case, they won't care).

Instead of avoiding compatibility issues, many Web sites simply ignore them. The Web-page developer uses whatever tool feels comfortable for testing and ignores other potential solutions. When the page works, great; when it doesn't, too bad for the user. Such pages tend to ignore user requests for help.

A few Web pages admirably try to service every potential browser, with mixed results. The code required for such a Web site becomes very complex — the more site features, the harder it is to test. At some point, the pages become a marathon download with dubious results.

The Web sites that seem to get the best results are either private or have a very targeted message. A private Web site is normally controlled by a company that can also tell users to choose from a specific list of browsers, which keeps compatibility issues under control. Targeted message Web sites don't have to control the browser used because the user population is likely to rely on a specific browser. For example, on a public Web site on .NET, programming issues can nearly guarantee that the user has a newer version of Internet Explorer installed — and is likely to have many of its features enabled for use with the programming environment.

The best way to avoid problems when working with a public Web site that has a general message is to avoid gizmos such as scripts that display graphic features depending on the user's cursor position (many buttons use scripts in this way). Here are some other guidelines to follow:

✦ Use accessibility-friendly development techniques.

✦ Rely on Cascading Style Sheets (CSS) to ensure that if a user's browser doesn't understand CSS, it can still display the information. Make sure the CSS file is separate from the Web page so the user can substitute another CSS file as needed.

✦ Use JavaScript as the scripting language whenever possible. Always provide a scripting alternative for browsers that don't have scripting enabled or don't support it.

Using these techniques can reasonably ensure that your Web page will support a range of browsers — Internet Explorer 3.0 and later, Netscape 4.5 and later, Opera 3.6 and later, all versions of Mozilla, and all versions of Firebird.

Make sure you also set the compatibility options on the Authoring tab of the Page Options dialog box in FrontPage so you can avoid special features that work in one version of a browser and not another.

Performing the required detection

Even if you're excessively careful in creating your Web page, users still send reports of compatibility problems. Unfortunately, in most cases, a quick fix for compatibility problems isn't an option after you've spent months putting a complex Web site together. Therefore you need to detect the browser version affected by the problem, and overcome it for that version of that browser. In addition, you have to include code to tell users with excessively old browsers to upgrade.

Handling browsers lacking scripting support

Sometimes the user has scripting disabled, which prevents you from detecting the browser type. In such a situation, the page could work just fine — even without scripting support enabled — unless you use scripting in ways other than detecting the browser. It's still important to give the user who lacks scripting support a way to voice concerns about the compatibility of your Web site. As a minimum, you should provide a <noscript> tag entry similar to the one shown here:

```
<noscript>
    <p>Your browser doesn't support scripting, so I can't
    detect the browser type to ensure my site will work
    properly. Please contact me with any problems at my <a
```

```
href="mailto:JMueller@mwt.net?subject=Browser Problems">
email</a> address. Make sure you include your browser name
and version.</p>
</noscript>
```

Detecting the correct version

One of the problems with browser version reporting is that the browser won't provide an actual version number in many cases. For example, Internet Explorer 6 will tell you that it's actually version 4 unless you know how to parse the version information for the correct number. To see the problem for yourself, try this script code:

```
alert(clientInformation.appName + "\r\n" +
      clientInformation.appVersion + "\r\n" +
      parseInt(clientInformation.appVersion));
```

When you try this code with a product such as Internet Explorer 6, you won't see what you expected. (Figure 4-1 shows the output of this script.) The reason for this "error" is that many Web developers use faulty code for checking version information; they look for a specific version, instead of that version *and newer*. Consequently, vendors began to report the version number that they think the developers expect, rather than the actual version number. Internet Explorer 6 is mostly Internet Explorer-4-compatible, so checking for Internet Explorer 4 is fine in most cases. Of course, when you multiply these oddities by the number of available browser types, the difficulty of verifying the user's browser version becomes obvious — which tells you why some developers simply ignore the problem.

Figure 4-1:
The client's version number isn't always the actual version number.

Using version detection functions

When you want to check for browser versions, you can reduce the complexity of the code you create by incorporating some of the logic into functions. For example, the three functions shown in Listing 4-1 make the resulting check code easier to read.

Listing 4-1: Simple Functions for Detecting Browsers

```
function isBrowser(Name)
{
    // Check for the browser name.
    if (clientInformation.appName.indexOf(Name) != -1)
        return true;
    else
        return false;
}

function isVersion(Version)
{
    // Get the version number.
    var ClientVersion =
        parseInt(clientInformation.appVersion);

    // Perform the comparison.
    if (Version <= ClientVersion)
        return true;
    else
        return false;
}

function isIE6()
{
    // Check for the version information in the
    // appVersion property.
    if (clientInformation.appVersion.indexOf("MSIE 6.0")
        != -1)
        return true;
    else
        return false;
}
```

The first function checks for the existence of a browser name within the appName property. The code uses a technique where it looks for the browser name you supply anywhere within the appName property with the indexOf() method. This method returns the position where a search string appears within the target string. Vendors change the location of the browser name between browser versions, so this is the only way to be sure that you've located the correct information.

Note that there are actually two property collections you can use to retrieve this information. The code shows the clientInformation property collection, but you can also rely on the netscape property collection. Most browsers support both, but the lack of consistency in this area can cause problems.

The second function, isVersion(), returns true when the version number you supply is less than or equal to that of the actual client version. The problem is that you can't check for Internet Explorer 6 directly if you're using this technique; the version number that Microsoft provides is 4. However, this check tells you that the browser is at least above a certain level.

The third function shows how to work around the Internet Explorer 6 version problem. By checking for the code string within the appVersion property, you can detect this specific version. Because various versions of Internet Explorer add new features (such as XML support in Version 5) and lack other features (such as Java support in Version 6), you often need a specific version number to work with this product. Although this function specifically checks for Internet Explorer 6, you can modify it to check for Internet Explorer 5.5 by using MSIE 5.5 — and Internet Explorer 5.0 by checking for MSIE 5.0.

Version bugs and errors

You might think that after you have obtained a product name and version number, your version-detection problems are over. Not quite: Sometimes application bugs can interfere with detection. For example, according to the JavaScript Testing site (at http://segal.org/macjavabugs/enabled/), some versions of the Macintosh report that it lacks Java support even when such support is installed. Supposedly the clientInformation. javaEnabled() method always reports the Java status, but in this case, it doesn't.

Another problem with Java detection is in Internet Explorer 6. The clientInformation.javaEnabled() method always returns true when the user enables Java-applet scripting in the Security Settings dialog box for the current zone. You get a return value of true even when Java isn't installed on the target machine (and there's no hope of running an applet). Consequently, the best you can do is display a message telling the user that applets might not run, using code like this:

```
// Check for Internet Explorer.
if (isBrowser("Explorer"))
{
   // Display the browser type.
   document.write("<p>You're using Internet Explorer</p>");

   // Check for the correct version number.
   if (!isVersion(3))
      document.write(
         "<p>Your browser is too old, please" +
         " upgrade!</p>");
```

```
        // Microsoft shipped IE6 without Java support.
        else if (isIE6())
            if (clientInformation.javaEnabled())
                document.write(
                    "<p>Your browser might not support Java " +
                    "applets.</p>");
            else
                document.write(
                    "<p>Your browser doesn't support Java.</p>");
    }
```

Some prerelease versions of Mozilla are still floating around. These versions read as Netscape because the clientInformation.appName property returns that value. The appVersion property returns a value of 5.0, which means it could easily pass the version -4.5 check required for most compatibility checks. The only way to detect Mozilla, in this case, is to check for the string Navigator in the Netscape check using code like this:

```
// Check for Navigator.
else if (isBrowser("Navigator"))
{
    // Display the browser type.
    document.write("<p>You're using Navigator</p>");

    // Check for the correct version number.
    if (!isVersion(4.5))
        document.write(
            "<p>Your browser is too old, please " +
            "upgrade!</p>");

    if (clientInformation.userAgent.indexOf("Navigator")
        == -1)
        document.write(
            "<p>You're using an older version of Mozilla, " +
            " time to upgrade.</p>");
}
```

In this case, the code uses the indexOf() method to check for the Navigator string in the userAgent property. Lack of this string tells you that your user's browser is Mozilla, not Navigator.

Redirecting Users Based on Need

Redirection is the process of sending a user to another page — whether to a different location on your Web site or to an entirely different Web site. One common use for redirection is to send a user to a new Web site when you change domains; another is to compensate for moved pages.

Some developers also use redirection for statistical checks. For example, you might want to support someone else's site, but also know how many users linked to that site from your site. A redirection lets you capture this information before sending the user on to the new Web site.

You have access to three techniques for redirecting the user. Two of these techniques are automatic and one isn't. Here are the options:

✦ **Scripting:** This is the preferred automatic method when you know the user will have scripting support enabled; it offers the greatest flexibility.

✦ **Meta refresh tag:** This is the preferred automatic method when you don't know whether the user has scripting support enabled. The only problem with this approach is that it's hard to detect whether the user has turned off support for the meta refresh tag.

✦ **Standard link:** You can incorporate the manual method of including a link the user clicks to get to the redirected page. Although it's not nearly as nice, this method always works.

It's actually possible to include all three redirection techniques, just in case one of them fails, in a single page. Listing 4-2 shows an example of how to accomplish this task.

**Book VII
Chapter 4**

**Performing Common
Scripted Tasks**

Listing 4-2:   Redirecting the User

```
<html>
<head>
   <title>Redirection Example</title>
   <META HTTP-EQUIV=Refresh
         CONTENT="10; URL=http://www.mwt.net/~jmueller/">
</head>
<body>
   <noscript>
      <p>
         Click this link to redirect to
         <a href="http://www.mwt.net/~jmueller">
            John's Web Site
         </a>.
      </p>
   </noscript>
   <script language="javascript">
      window.document.location =
         "http://www.mwt.net/~jmueller";
   </script>
</body>
</html>
```

This page can perform the redirection task in any of three ways:

✦ The browser checks for scripting capability. When the browser has scripting capability, JavaScript sends the user to a new page by changing the `window.document.location` property. (Of course, you need to perform any statistical updates *before* you change this property.) The script change happens automatically; on a fast Web site, the user might not even see the intermediate page.

✦ When the browser determines there isn't any scripting support, it displays the manual link in the `<noscript>` tag. The user can choose to click this link and go to the redirected site at any time.

✦ The `meta refresh` tag starts a 10-second timer when the browser loads the page. You adjust the time interval by modifying the number directly after the `CONTENT` attribute. The `URL` portion of the `CONTENT` attribute defines where the user is redirected when the time interval expires.

Providing Form Feedback

You have many options for creating feedback forms using FrontPage. The simplest feedback form doesn't require any code at all. Methods of processing forms without using code can range from using server-side scripts to sending the data in raw form to an e-mail address. It's a technique everyone can use, but it lacks automation — and the user can submit incorrect data even with a well-designed form. Because of this, you should consider the no-scripting option for maximum compatibility whenever possible.

Understanding how FrontPage uses scripting

FrontPage also creates forms with a lot of built-in JavaScript. You don't create the code, FrontPage creates it for you. Such forms have a variety of processing options, everything from using a simple file or e-mail for storage to full-blown database solutions. To use this technique, you create a form and configure it using the Form Properties dialog box shown in Figure 4-2.

After you create a form and tell FrontPage to create code that handles the storage details, you add one or more controls to the form. The Properties dialog box for the control includes a Validation button that you click to display the a validation dialog box, similar to the Text Box Validation box shown in Figure 4-3.

All these configuration entries add JavaScript to your Web page that you won't even see unless you open the page and use the View Source command to display it. It's educational to create a form that has a single field on it so you can control the amount of information you see. Try various configuration settings to see what code FrontPage adds for you. In every case, you add new JavaScript to the page by using simple configuration settings. Figure 4-4 shows what you see when you view the `Feedback.htm` file supplied in the source code for this chapter on this book's companion Web site.

The purpose of this exercise is to discover more about what FrontPage is doing behind the scenes on your behalf. In some cases, you might find that you can perform a check faster or easier using a manual check. When browser compatibility is an issue, you can write variations of the FrontPage provided code to ensure your Web page supports as many browsers as possible.

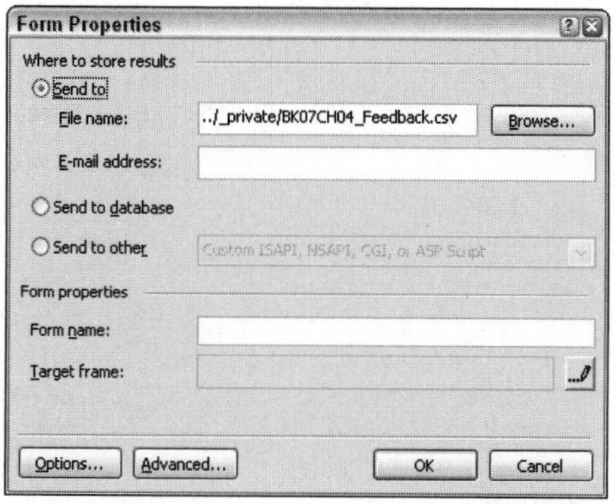

Figure 4-2:
Choose a data storage technique that suits your needs.

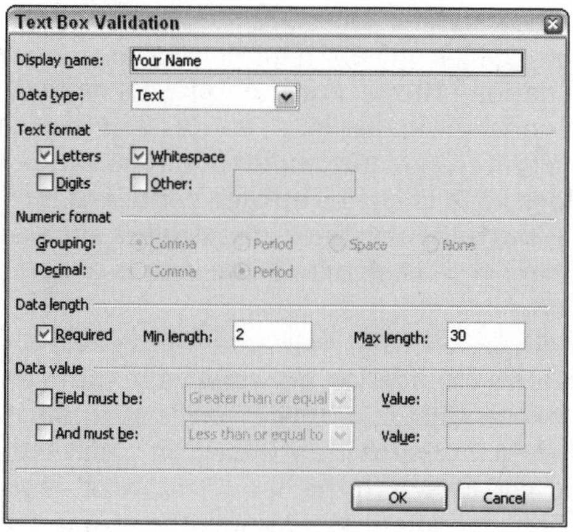

Figure 4-3:
Here you define validation criteria for each control to keep your Web site safe.

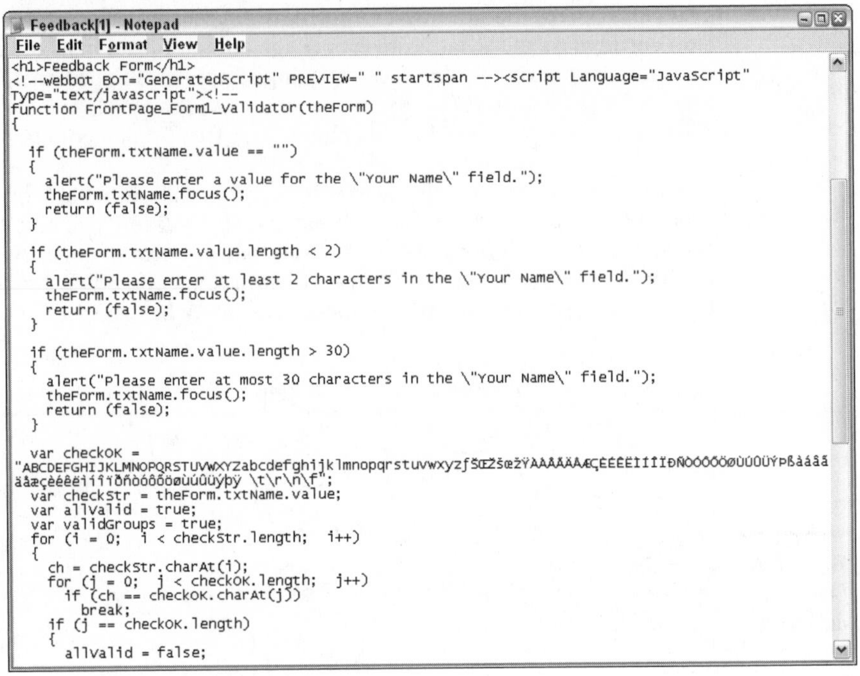

Feedback[1] - Notepad

File Edit Format View Help

```
<h1>Feedback Form</h1>
<!--webbot BOT="GeneratedScript" PREVIEW=" " startspan --><script Language="JavaScript"
Type="text/javascript"><!--
function FrontPage_Form1_Validator(theForm)
{

  if (theForm.txtName.value == "")
  {
    alert("Please enter a value for the \"Your Name\" field.");
    theForm.txtName.focus();
    return (false);
  }

  if (theForm.txtName.value.length < 2)
  {
    alert("Please enter at least 2 characters in the \"Your Name\" field.");
    theForm.txtName.focus();
    return (false);
  }

  if (theForm.txtName.value.length > 30)
  {
    alert("Please enter at most 30 characters in the \"Your Name\" field.");
    theForm.txtName.focus();
    return (false);
  }

  var checkOK =
"ABCDEFGHIJKLMNOPQRSTUVWXYZabcdefghijklmnopqrstuvwxyzƒŠŒŽšœžŸÀÁÂÃÄÅÆÇÈÉÊËÌÍÎÏÐÑÒÓÔÕÖØÙÚÛÜÝÞßàáâã
äåæçèéêëìíîïðñòóôõöøùúûüýþÿ \t\r\n\f";
  var checkStr = theForm.txtName.value;
  var allValid = true;
  var validGroups = true;
  for (i = 0;  i < checkStr.length;  i++)
  {
    ch = checkStr.charAt(i);
    for (j = 0;  j < checkOK.length;  j++)
      if (ch == checkOK.charAt(j))
        break;
    if (j == checkOK.length)
    {
      allValid = false;
```

Figure 4-4: Evaluate the code FrontPage creates for you.

Defining manual code

You can add scripts to forms for various reasons, but one of the most important ones is validation. Look again at the validation criteria you can choose in Figure 4-3 and you'll notice it's all very generic — there's no way to create specific or complex validation criteria. For example, it's impossible to block certain nonexistent ZIP codes from the list of entries a user can make. For example, if you want to create a complex validation, you can't tell FrontPage that when the state field is `California`, the area code field must begin with a number such as `619`. It might be important to conduct such a check to ensure that the information you receive from the user is accurate — but it's not an option in this case.

The natural place to create a connection between your script and the form is to use the `onsubmit` event. Unfortunately, FrontPage automatically overwrites the event entry when it creates code based on your configuration settings. Any event handler you attach to the `onsubmit` event is going to fail because it won't get called. FrontPage has broken the required connection between the Submit button and the event handler.

The best method around this problem is to attach the event handler to another event. For example, to submit the form, the user has to click Submit. You can attach the necessary form-handling code to the Submit button like this:

```
onclick="return CheckSpecialKeyword()"
```

The addition of `return` to the calling syntax means the browser processes the `return` value. When this value is `false`, processing ends and the `onsubmit` event never occurs. Listing 4-3 shows how to construct a simple function for comparing two fields as a unit.

Listing 4-3: Adding Special Form Checking

```
function CheckSpecialKeyword()
{
   // Verify the name.
   if (FrontPage_Form1.txtName.value == "George")

      // When the name is correct, verify the keyword.
      if (FrontPage_Form1.txtKeyword.value == "Special")
      {
         // Display a success message for a correct
         // combination and return true so processing
         // continues.
         alert("The input is correct.");
         return true;
      }
      else
      {
         // Return an error message and stop processing.
         alert("You provided an incorrect keyword");
         return false;
      }
   else
   {
      // Return an error message and stop processing.
      alert("The name " +
            FrontPage_Form1.txtName.value +
            " isn't recognized");
      return false;
   }
}
```

Every possible `return` path must return a Boolean value, as shown in the example code. Only when the two fields match specific values will the function return `true`, so you have control over the content of one field that's based on the content of another.

Debugging Your Script

Debugging is the process of removing errors from your code. A script, like any other code, can contain errors. The two major types of script errors you need to consider are those in the syntax and those in the logic.

Fixing syntax errors

A *syntax error* occurs when you write code incorrectly. For example, you might forget to include a closing parenthesis or brace. Because scripts are interpreted by a local application when you load the Web page and perform tasks with it, you can see syntax errors as they occur. The browser tells you about the error — and where it appears on your Web page — so you can find it easily and fix it. The information commonly includes the precise error and its location, as shown in Figure 4-5. Notice that the Error dialog box tells you what is missing and which line to look on. All you need to do is open FrontPage, go to that line, and locate the missing information. In a few cases, you'll need to look at the lines above and below the error; a single command can extend over several lines.

Figure 4-5:
The browser usually provides specific information about syntax errors.

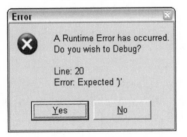

To ensure that you see syntax errors, you must set the browser to display them. For example, when you're working with Internet Explorer, open the Internet Options dialog box (Tools⇨Internet Options) and select the Advanced tab. Then you simply clear the Disable Script Debugging option, put a check next to Display a Notification About Every Script Error, and restart Internet Explorer after making these changes.

Sometimes a syntax error won't show up right away or it might not be obvious. For example, while working on the code for Listing 4-3, I originally used `MyForm.txtName.value` as the method of obtaining the `Name` field value. However, I kept getting a `MyForm Is Undefined` error message from the browser. It wasn't until I looked at the actual browser code on the Web site (using Notepad) that I noticed FrontPage had renamed the form to `FrontPage_Form1`. In this case, my original code was correct from within FrontPage, but was incorrect in reality because FrontPage makes changes when it automatically generates script code. The code in Listing 4-3 is correct because it matches the results FrontPage produces.

Fixing logic errors

A *logic error* occurs when you write the code with correct syntax, but it doesn't produce the correct results. For example, you might write an `if` statement correctly, but fail to provide the correct expression — which gives you the wrong results when the user writes the code. Logic errors require a little more work to fix. To correct a logic error, normally you'd use a debugger (a special program that lets you look at how the code is interpreted by the machine). Unfortunately, FrontPage doesn't come with a debugger, so you have to use the Microsoft Script Editor or another product designed to debug scripts (such as Visual Studio).

When you suspect that you have a logic error, load the Web page in a browser. Perform any setup that reproduces the error. At this point, you have two options: Start the debugger immediately or start it when the browser reaches the first line of executable code. Here's how:

Book VII
Chapter 4

Performing Common Scripted Tasks

✦ To start the debugger immediately, select the View⇨Script Debugger⇨ Open command.

   When your browser lacks this command, it means that an error has occurred and you need to restart it, the system can't run scripts, or you don't have a script debugger installed on your system.

✦ To start the debugger after it reaches the next line of code, select the View⇨Script Debugger⇨Break at Next Statement command.

   With either approach (if you're working with Microsoft Script Editor), you see a debugger display similar to the one shown in Figure 4-6.

The second of these options is generally better unless an error prevents the browser from seeing the code you want to debug.

In Figure 4-6, the display shows the current line of code. You can use commands to display the contents of variables, move one line of code at a time to see results, and perform other coding checks to locate the error. Sometimes just seeing your code execute is enough to find logic errors. Once you get into the Microsoft Script Editor, debugging JavaScript is very much like working with any other code. (There's more about debugging with Microsoft Script Editor in Chapter 5 of Book 8.)

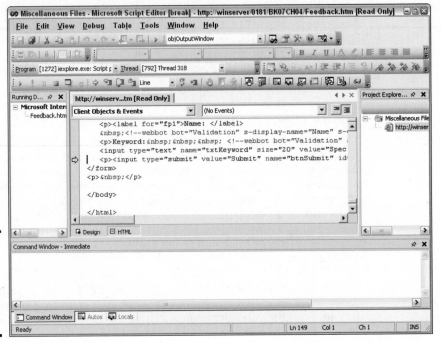

Book VIII

VBA Programming

The 5th Wave   By Rich Tennant

"OK, I think I forgot to mention this, but we now have
a Web management function that automatically alerts
us when there's a broken link on The Aquarium's
Web site."

Contents at a Glance

Chapter 1: Getting to Know VBA

In This Chapter

✔ Using the Visual Basic editor

✔ Working with Project Explorer

✔ Working with the Properties window

✔ Interacting with the Code window

✔ Issuing commands using the Immediate window

✔ Viewing objects using the Object Browser

FrontPage offers more than one programming arena. Developers can create applications within Web pages using various techniques. In addition to Web page programming, you can also create applications that automate FrontPage itself. For example, you can write code that automates the tasks you normally perform to create a new Web page. The code can even make entries, such as the author meta tag, on the Web page for you so that you can concentrate on other issues. The language used to perform FrontPage automation is Visual Basic for Applications (VBA).

VBA is the standard macro language for all Office products. In fact, forms of VBA appear in a number of third-party products such as Corel Draw! and IMSI TurboCAD. However, don't think you can write a macro in FrontPage and simply move it to another product. Although the VBA language is consistent from product to product, the objects you interact with differ. For example, when you're working with Excel, you concentrate on the use of spreadsheet objects. FrontPage has special objects too, such as the `MetaTags` object used to control the meta tags in a document.

You don't actually create the VBA macros for FrontPage by using the FrontPage editor. A special Visual Basic Editor helps you create macro code for speeding up the development process. Consequently, you need to know how to use this editor before you can begin creating your own macros.

Starting the Visual Basic Editor

The first step in creating a VBA macro for FrontPage is starting the Visual Basic Editor. You start the Visual Basic Editor by choosing Tools⇨Macro⇨Visual Basic Editor. When you execute this command, you see the display shown in Figure 1-1.

Some windows might not be open when you initially start the Visual Basic Editor — you can open them using the options on the View menu.

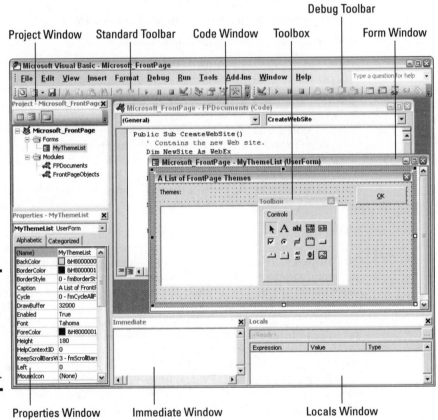

Figure 1-1: The Visual Basic Editor is an editor for writing VBA applications.

Unlike many other Office products, FrontPage lacks a macro security control (the ability to stop macros from running when you don't know the source), which means you can run any macros you create at any time. The security control isn't required from one perspective — you can't tell any FrontPage macro to run automatically like you can in Word, so there isn't a threat of someone inserting a hostile or inappropriate macro into a document and causing damage to your system. However, macros you obtain from other people can contain malevolent code, so you should always exercise care when running macros in FrontPage.

Project Explorer appears in the Project window. You use it to interact with the objects that make up a project. A project is an individual file used to hold your program, or at least pieces of it. The project resides within the FrontPage environment, so when you open FrontPage you also open your project. Project Explorer works much like the left pane of Windows Explorer does. Normally, you see just the top-level objects like the FrontPage objects shown in Figure 1-2.

Figure 1-2:
Use Project
Explorer to
work with
project
objects.

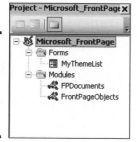

Project Explorer doesn't display any documents, as it would if you were working with other Office products such as Word or Excel. The reason for this difference is that you can't create FrontPage documents that include macros. Aside from that difference, however, you use Project Explorer the same way with any kind of application.

Figure 1-2 does show some of the special objects a project can contain — forms, modules, and class modules. Each type of special object has a distinct purpose:

✦ **Forms:** These contain user interface elements and help you interact with the user.

✦ **Modules:** These contain the nonvisual code for your application. For example, you can use a module to store a special calculation.

✦ **Class modules:** These contain new objects that you want to build. You could use a class module to create a new data type.

To select an object so you can see and change its properties, highlight it in Project Explorer. To open the object so you can modify it, double-click the object.

Right-clicking everything

Project Explorer has a number of hidden talents, which you can find by right-clicking objects to see what you can do with them. For example, right-click the Microsoft_FrontPage entry at the top of Figure 1-2 to see the context menu shown in Figure 1-3.

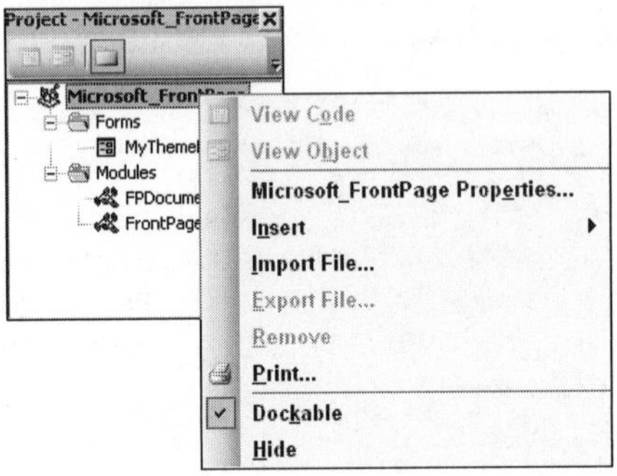

Figure 1-3:
Right-click VBA objects to display contextual menus.

It's amazing to see what's hidden on this menu. Don't worry about using all the menu entries now. Each menu entry appears at least once (and probably more often) in this book. The important thing to remember now is that most objects have a context menu that you can access by right-clicking or by using the Context Menu key (on a Windows keyboard, it's just to the right of the key with the Windows logo).

Working with special entries

Because you can obtain data used in FrontPage from other Office applications, you might need to work with Word or Excel when creating a macro. Nothing prevents you from creating a FrontPage macro that interacts with other applications that support VBA.

Sometimes, when you work with another product, you see a special entry in Project Explorer. For example, when you work with a Word document, you might see a References folder, which contains any references that the Word document makes. Normally the folder lists the templates that the document relies upon for formatting.

In many cases, you can't modify the objects in the special folders. This is the case with the References folder used by Word document objects. The References folder is there for information only. To modify the referenced template, you need to find its object in Project Explorer. In this book, I don't discuss special objects because you normally don't need to work with them.

Using the Properties Window

When you look at an actual object such as an apple, you can see some of its properties — say, whether it's red, green, or yellow (or, for that matter, rotten). Most objects that you click in the Visual Basic Editor have *properties* — sets of specifications that describe the elements of the object. For VBA objects, properties control how they appear on-screen — for example, a button can have a *caption* (the text that users see when they look at the button). The following sections provide details about the Properties window (refer to Figure 1-1).

Understanding property types

A property must describe the object. When you look at an object, you naturally assume something about the information provided by a particular property. For example, when describing the color of an apple, you expect to use *red, yellow,* or *green.* Likewise, VBA object properties have specific types; here are some common examples:

✦ **Text:** This is one of the most common property types. The `Caption` property of a form is one way text is used. The text appears at the top of the form when the user opens it.

✦ **Logical or Boolean values:** This property type determines a logical condition for the object, usually `True` or `False`. For example, if a control has a `Visible` property and this property is set to `True`, the control appears on-screen. Set this property to `False`, and the control won't appear on-screen, even though it still exists as part of the application.

✦ **Numeric values:** Properties that use these specify how or where an object appears on-screen. For example, to describe where to place a control on-screen, set the `Top` and `Left` properties to specific numeric values. These values tell how many pixels are between the top and left corner of the screen and the top-left corner of the control.

✦ **Associated controls:** Sometimes a property can display a drop-down list box from which you can choose the correct value. Other properties display dialog boxes, such as the one for color shown in Figure 1-4.

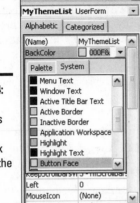

Figure 1-4:
Some
properties
display a
dialog box
to select the
correct
value.

Getting help with properties

Don't expect to memorize every property for every object that VBA applications can create. Not even the gurus can do that. To tell what a particular property will do for your application, just highlight the property, press F1, and VBA displays a Help window similar to the one shown in Figure 1-5 (in most cases).

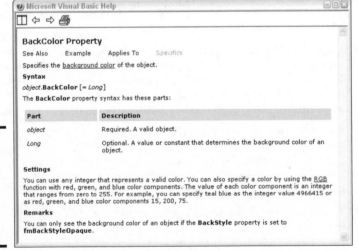

Figure 1-5:
Help
documents
the
properties
that VBA
supports.

Such help screens tell you about the property and how it's used — and they provide you with links for additional information. The additional information is especially important when you start changing the property values in your application code. For example, click the Example link and the help system shows how to write code that uses that property.

Click the See Also link in help screens for more information about a topic — for example, the objects, properties, methods, and events associated with the topic. In some cases, you also get recommended ways to work with an object, property, method, or event.

Using the Code Window

The Code window is where you write your application code. It works like any other editor you've used, except you type in a special language: VBA. Figure 1-6 shows a typical example of a code window, with some code already loaded.

Figure 1-6:
Use the Code window to modify your program.

```
Microsoft_FrontPage - FrontPageObjects (Code)
(General)                    (Declarations)

Option Explicit

Public Sub GetAppStats()
    ' Contains the application information.
    Dim Output As String

    ' Get the application statistics.
    With Application
        Output = Output + .UserName + vbCrLf
        Output = Output + .OrganizationName + vbCrLf
        Output = Output + .Name + vbCrLf
        Output = Output + .Version + vbCrLf + vbCrLf

        ' Get some of the active document information.
        With ActiveDocument
            Output = Output + "Active Document" + vbCrLf
            Output = Output + vbCrLf + .nameProp + vbCrLf
            Output = Output + .DocumentHTML
        End With
    End With

    ' Dispaly the output.
    MsgBox Output, vbInformation, "Application Statistics"
End Sub
```

Opening an existing Code window

Sometimes you won't be able to complete an application in one sitting and have to save it so you can work on it later. When you name and save the file containing your code, it becomes an existing Code window. To open an existing code window, find the module that you want to open in Project Explorer. Then double-click the module entry: The IDE displays the Code window with your code loaded.

The Code window also appears when you perform other tasks. For example, if you double-click one of the controls on a form, the Code window appears so you can add code to the default *event handler* (special code that responds to a specific event). VBA calls the event handler every time the specified event occurs.

Creating a new Code window

When you start a new module within an existing document or template, open a new Code window by using either Insert⇨Module or Insert⇨Class Module. After you save this module or class module, it appears listed in Project Explorer with the other modules and class modules in your project.

Typing text in the Code window

When you type code, VBA checks what you type. If you make a major error (such as typing a word that VBA doesn't understand), you see an error message explaining what went wrong (see Figure 1-7). If the error message seems baffling, click the Help button for additional information.

Figure 1-7: VBA displays an error message when the code isn't correct.

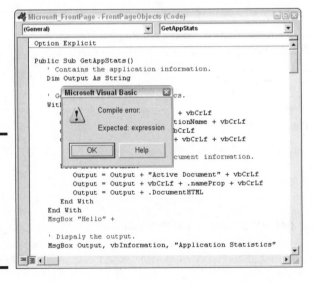

While you type the code for your application, VBA also formats it. For example, if you type a keyword in lowercase letters, VBA changes it so it appears as shown in the help file. Keywords also appear in a different color so you can easily identify them. This book contains examples of the common VBA keywords.

Finding more Code window features

Like other objects in VBA, the Code window has a context menu. When you right-click the Code window, you see a list of optional actions you can perform. For example, you can obtain a list of properties and methods that apply to the object you're currently using in the window.

Getting help with code

Because it's hard to remember precisely how to use every function and method that VBA supports, use the VBA help feature. For any keyword that you type in the Code window, highlight the keyword, press F1, and VBA will look for help on the word you selected.

Make sure that you select the entire keyword, or VBA might not find the information you need. Double-click the keyword to ensure that you highlight the entire word.

Using the Immediate Window

Although you can use the Immediate window for debugging applications, this window can actually help you learn about VBA without writing reams of code. You can execute statements one at a time. Use View⇨Immediate Window to display the Immediate window. This window normally appears at the bottom of the IDE, and it won't contain any information until you type something in it.

Creating a variable in the Immediate window

Most developers spend their days using the Immediate window checking their applications for errors. You can use the Immediate window to ask VBA about the value of a variable, for example. (A variable acts as a storage container for a value such as Hello World.) This feature is always available in the Visual Basic Editor, even if you aren't using VBA for anything at the moment. To try out this feature, type **MyVal = "Hello World"** (don't forget the double quotes) in the Immediate window and then press Enter. Now type **? MyVal** and then press Enter. Figure 1-8 shows the output of this little experiment.

Figure 1-8:
Use the
Immediate
window to
check the
value of a
variable.

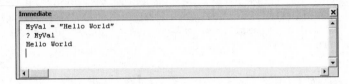

You asked VBA to create a variable named MyVal and assign it a value of
Hello World. The next step is to ask VBA what MyVal contains by using
the ? operator. Figure 1-8 shows that MyVal actually does contain Hello
World.

Creating a one-line program

Experimenting with the Immediate window is one of the fastest ways to learn
how to use VBA because you get instant results. You can also copy successful
experiments from the Immediate window to the Clipboard, and then paste
them into the Code window. Using this method ensures that your code contains fewer errors than if you were to type it directly into the Code window.

If you read the preceding section, "Creating a variable in the Immediate
window" and followed along, then you created a variable named MyVal.
The variable still exists in memory unless you closed the VBA Editor. You
can use this variable for a little experiment — your first program. Type
MsgBox MyVal into the Immediate window and then press Enter. You see
a message box like the one shown in Figure 1-9.

Figure 1-9:
The
MsgBox
function
produces a
message
box like this.

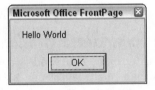

Congratulations! You just completed your first VBA application. The code
you typed asked VBA to use the MsgBox function to display the text in the
MyVal variable. Click OK to clear the message box.

Using Object Browser

VBA provides access to a lot of objects, more than you'll use for any one program. With all the objects that you have at your disposal, you might forget the name of one or more of them at some time. Object Browser helps you find the objects you need. In fact, you can use it to find new objects that could be useful for your next project. Use the View⇔Object Browser command to display Object Browser, as shown in Figure 1-10. Normally, at that point, you need to filter the information in some way.

Figure 1-10: View the objects that VBA makes available via Object Browser.

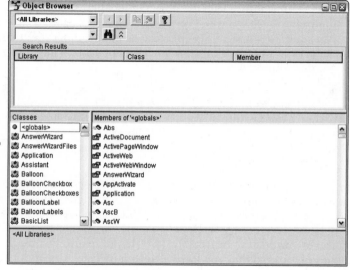

Browsing objects

Object Browser contains a list of the contents of all projects and libraries loaded for the Visual Basic Editor. You can view the list of projects and libraries using the Project/Library drop-down list box. When you start Object Browser, this list box reads <All Libraries>, which means that you're viewing everything that VBA has to offer — usually too much for someone to make sense of it all.

Projects and libraries are different, but you don't usually have to worry about them when you use the objects they contain. A *project* is the VBA code contained in one of the files that you load into the application. In most cases, you use a project to store the code you create. A *library* is external code contained in a Dynamic Link Library (DLL) file. The DLL contains support routines used by the application or VBA. This code is normally written by a developer, using a language such as Visual Basic or Visual C++. You can't easily edit the code in a DLL.

The projects and libraries list might look complicated at first, but you can narrow the list down to a few types of entries. Of course, you always see your project templates. In addition to project templates, you find the following libraries in the list:

✦ **Application:** This library has the name of the application, such as FrontPage or FrontPage Editor, and also includes the features that the application provides for VBA users. For example, the FrontPage library has an `Application` object that contains a list of application-related properties, events, and methods such as the `ActiveDocument` property used to work with the current document.

✦ **Office:** This library lists the objects that Microsoft Office supports. For example, this is where you find the objects used to support Office Assistant. Of course, if you're using an application other than Microsoft Office, you won't see this library. Your application might provide another alternative.

✦ **Stdole:** This library contains some of the Object Linking and Embedding (OLE) features that you use in the application. For example, when you embed a picture into a FrontPage document, this library provides the required support. You can use this library in your VBA applications, too, but the Office- or application-related library usually provides access to objects that are easier and faster to use.

✦ **VBA:** This library contains special utility objects that VBA developers need. For example, it contains the `MsgBox` function (which I demonstrate earlier in this chapter, in the "Using the Immediate window" section).

Whenever you want to browse the libraries for a specific object, limit the amount of material that you have to search by using the options in the Project/Library drop-down list box (*filtering* the content). This technique is also helpful when you perform searches.

Looking for names and features in Object Browser

When you *almost* remember the name of a method or other programming feature that you want to use, the search feature of Object Browser can make your life easier. Simply type the text you want to look for in the Search Text field (the empty box beneath All Libraries) and then click the Search button (the one with a symbol that looks like binoculars) in Object Browser. The Search Results field (shown in Figure 1-11) shows what happens when you look for `MsgBox`.

Whenever you choose (highlight) one of the entries in the Search Results field, the bottom two panes change to show the entry you've chosen. This feature helps you locate specific information about the search result and see it in context with other methods, properties, and events. Notice that the bottom pane tells you more about the selection item. In this case, it tells you how to use the `MsgBox` function.

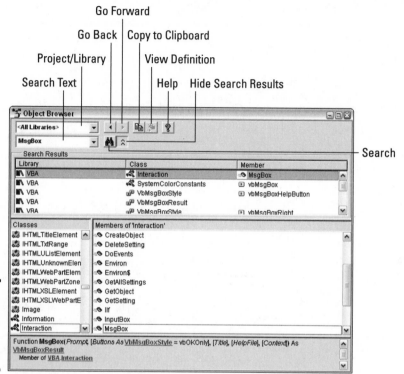

Figure 1-11:
Search for
the method
that you
want to use.

Cutting and pasting in Object Bowser

Whenever you find a method, property, or event that you want to use in Object Browser, you can copy the information to the Clipboard by clicking the Copy to Clipboard button (the one with a symbol that looks like two documents) and then pasting directly into your application code. Using this feature means not only that you type less code, but also that you have fewer errors to consider.

Getting help in Object Browser

Sometimes the information at the bottom of Object Browser display isn't enough to tell you about the element that you're viewing. When this happens, highlight the element you want to know more about, and then press F1: VBA displays the help screen for that element.

Chapter 2: Your First VBA Program

In This Chapter

✔ Developing an application plan

✔ Creating a VBA program

✔ Developing a sub

✔ Developing a function

✔ Deciding the scope of variables

✔ Running your application

✔ Accessing your program from other VBA code

*W*riting code in the Immediate window (as described in Chapter 1) gives you instant feedback, but it's not very permanent — the resulting program lasts only as long as you have the VBA Editor open. This chapter shows you how to move from the Immediate window into the Code window, which is where you create programs of a lasting nature — the kind that you can use to perform the same task more than once. Because of the time required to write the code, it only pays to create an application that you can use more than once. The benefit of writing a program is that you can perform a repetitive task quickly.

Good programs rely on structure to reduce errors, improve reliability, make the code easier to reuse, and enhance your ability to use the code in more than one place. The obvious structuring element is physical. By using physical structure, you can divide your program into small pieces that are easy to write and understand.

Another form of structure includes the concept of privacy. You need to consider who can see your program and how they can use it. *Scope,* which is a set of limits imposed on program access, is important because you want to make some parts of your application completely private (for efficiency) and other parts completely public (for usability).

After you finish your application, you want to run it in FrontPage. Fortunately, FrontPage provides a number of ways to accomplish this task and you can choose the method that suits your needs. Some applications run in the background and don't require much user interaction, while others run in the foreground and interact with the user a lot.

Deciding What to Do

Whenever you decide to create a program, start with a plan. A program is a built thing; just as a builder needs a plan to construct a house, you need a plan to construct your program. You could easily tell whether a builder decided to build a house without using a plan, and it's just as easy to determine when someone writes a program without using a plan. The program's users can see the application isn't well designed because it doesn't work as anticipated. The plan you use doesn't have to be complicated, but you do need to think about these questions:

✦ What will the program do?

✦ How will the program accomplish its task?

✦ When will the program run?

✦ Who will use the program?

✦ Why is the program important?

Professional developers use a number of complex and hair-raising methods to answer these questions. You work on much smaller programs, and you can normally answer the questions quite easily. Don't make this more complicated than necessary. For example, you might answer the first question by saying that the program will count the number of words in a document.

The reason you want to go through this process is to ensure that you've given plenty of thought to the program you want to create. It's easier to answer the functional questions *before* you write any code than it is to fix the code later. Writing down your answers also helps you keep the program on task so it doesn't become something you didn't intend. This is a common problem for everyone; even developers with a lot of experience write programs that quickly grow beyond the original intent.

Steps to Create a VBA Program

Writing a program usually involves four steps. In this section, I tell you about the four steps while you create your first permanent program — one that you can run as often as you like.

Step 1: Design the program

In the "Deciding What to Do" section of the chapter, I tell you how to plan your program as well as what questions you should ask in preparation for writing the program. This step is actually part of the design phase, but most developers make it a separate step. Thinking through your application before you commit something to paper is important.

After you plan your application, you can use any of a number of techniques to design the program. The best way to design most simple applications is to use a method called *pseudo-coding,* a method in which you write down a list of steps in your own words that say what you want VBA to do.

Using pseudo-code is a good way to think about how you want to write the code without getting too concerned about coding issues. This example displays a dialog box. The pseudo-code could be as easy as

```
Display the message box.
See which button the user clicked.
End the program.
```

You can also add pseudo-code as comments to the VBA code that you write. Using your pseudo-code as a basis for comments helps you include the thought process used to design the program in your code. Never write a program that is devoid of comments — situations change, and if you need to modify your code later, having the original idea written down is a valuable starting point.

Step 2: Implement the design

The wording for this step is just a fancy way of saying that you need to write some code. Before you can write some code, you need to open the Visual Basic Editor by using the Tools⇨Macro⇨Visual Basic Editor command.

The first thing to do is create a Code window. To do that, use the Insert⇨ Module command. The Visual Basic editor creates a blank Code window where you can type your program. A blank Code window can be a scary experience, but you don't need to worry because you already have some text (the code snippet created in step 1) to put into it. The Code window includes a container in which to store the code called a Sub (for *sub-procedure*) and the pseudo-code. Add a ' (single-quote) character in front of each pseudo-code statement to ensure that VBA knows that this is pseudo-code. (Single-quote characters designate comments in VBA.)

You could actually run the Sub you've created, but it wouldn't do anything. To make this example do something, add code to it that VBA understands. This means converting the English statements such as *Display the message box.* into VBA. To display a message box, use the MsgBox function that I describe in Chapter 1.

The MsgBox function is capable of doing more than the Chapter 1 example shows. First, it can return a Result that shows which button the user selected. The Result variable holds the selection information so that you can use it in other ways. You can also tell MsgBox which buttons to display and to provide a title. Here's a more advanced version of the MsgBox function from Chapter 1 — type it directly beneath the ' Display the message box. comment.

```
Result = MsgBox("Click a Button", vbYesNoCancel, "A Message")
```

This code tells VBA to display a message box with "Click a Button" as the text and "A Message" on the title bar. The message box includes the Yes, No, and Cancel buttons. After VBA displays the message box, it waits for the user to make a decision. When the user clicks one of the three buttons, VBA stores the choice in the Result variable. (That's a lot for one piece of text to do!)

The pseudo-code says that the code must detect which button the user clicked. You can use another message box to display the information like this:

```
MsgBox Result
```

This is the same technique that I use in Chapter 1. The only difference is that the information contained in Result relies on a user selection. You don't know which button the user will select in advance, but this code works no matter which button the user clicks.

The final piece of pseudo-code says that VBA should end the program. You do this with the End Sub statement. Whenever VBA runs out of instructions to process, it ends the program. Figure 2-1 shows what your code should look like now. Make sure you save the code, at this point, using the File➪Save command.

Figure 2-1:
Writing code is easy when you use pseudo-code to describe it first.

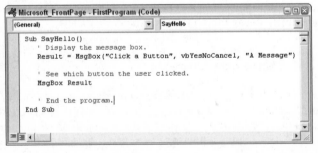

Step 3: Test, test, test

It's time to run the application for the first time. The easiest way to run an application is to click the Run Sub/User Form button on the toolbar (it's the one that looks like the Play button on a VCR). Click the button to see the first message box.

The message box contains the title, message, and buttons that you asked VBA to display in the code. Checking the contents of the message box to verify that it contains everything you thought it would contain is one example of *testing*. If you want to ensure that your program always works the way you originally designed it, you need to test as many of its features as possible.

Click Yes to see the next message box. Look at the code again. Notice that this message box contains the result (the return value) of the MsgBox function. The number 6 in this situation isn't very useful to humans, but it's quite usable for the computer. A program converts this number to something that humans can understand. For now, you know that clicking Yes produces a number 6.

When you click OK, the program ends, and you don't see any other message boxes. This condition verifies that the last step of the pseudo-code is complete.

Don't assume the testing process is over; there are two other buttons on the initial message box. Unless you test those buttons, you won't know that they work. Run the program again, but try the No button the second time and the Cancel button the third time.

The return value displayed in the second message box should change for each button. Clicking No should produce a value of 7, and clicking Cancel should produce a value of 2. If you don't see these values, your program has an error. Professionals call a programming error a *bug*.

Step 4: Swat the bugs

Bugs can appear when you test your program. Planning and writing your code carefully reduces the number of bugs, but everyone makes mistakes (as often as not, these result from misunderstanding how a function works). Testing your programs helps you find the bugs. After you find the bugs, you have to look at your code and discover the coding errors that created the bugs.

Not every bug is even your fault — it could be an error in the documentation for the function. Microsoft is well known for committing mistakes of this sort and then telling everyone that it really meant to do that. (Microsoft is fond of calling this an undocumented feature.) You might find that a bug isn't actually in your program but somewhere in VBA itself. Microsoft might tell you about these errors, but it often leaves them as a surprise for you to discover.

TIP

Microsoft won't knock on your door to tell you that it made a mistake. You have to search for these errors on your own at a central Web site that Microsoft has set up. The Microsoft *Knowledge Base* is a special kind of search engine that helps you find information about problems with VBA and the associated fix. You can find the Microsoft Knowledge Base at http://search.support.microsoft.com/search/default.aspx.

Writing Your First Sub

One of the first tasks that many developers want to perform is to gain access to document statistics. Knowing document statistics can point out common document issues, such as old documents that require editing. The statistics can also help categorize the document by size or the author who last edited the document. Consequently, many developers choose some type of statistical program as their first programming effort, just like the first sub discussed in this section.

FrontPage uses several unique methods to create document statistics. All of these statistics begin with the Application object. You don't actually have to reference the Application object unless you specifically want to work with it because the Application object is the default object. The next level down is the WebWindows object, which contains information about the current Web. Below the WebWindows object is the PageWindows object, which contains specific information about an open document. Next you reference the ActiveDocument — normally the same as the open document, unless you're using frames or other technologies that let you work with multiple documents. Listing 2-1 shows how these various objects work together to let you access document statistics.

Listing 2-1:   Using a Sub to Retrieve Document Information

```
Sub GetSummary()
    ' Create a title based on the Web.
    Title = "File Located At: " + _
        WebWindows(0).Web.RootFolder

    ' The information is located in the active document.
    With WebWindows(0).PageWindows(0).ActiveDocument

        ' Get the document name.
        Results = "Name: " + .nameProp

        ' Get the document title.
        Results = Results + vbCrLf + "Title: " + .Title

        ' Add the last modification date.
        Results = Results + vbCrLf + _
            "Last Modification: " + .fileModifiedDate
    End With

    ' Display the results.
    MsgBox Results, , Title
End Sub
```

The code begins by getting the URL for the Web. To access this information, the code requests information about the first open `WebWindow`. FrontPage could have more than one `WebWindow` open. When this happens, you access each `WebWindow` using its specific number. The first `WebWindow` is `WebWindows(0)`, the second is `WebWindows(1)`, and so on. The number in parentheses lets you access one member of a collection of `WebWindows`. The Web object within the `WebWindow` tells you about that `Web`. In this case, the code accesses the `RootFolder` property, which contains the location of this `Web` on the server, and places that value in the `Title` variable.

Notice the underscore character (_) at the end of the first line of code. Use the underscore to continue the code on the next line when a line of code becomes too long. Failure to include the underscore normally results in an error message because VBA treats each line of code as a separate instruction unless you include the underscore.

The next statement tells VBA that you want to perform a number of tasks using the `WebWindows(0).PageWindows(0).ActiveDocument` object. You know that `WebWindows(0)` is the first `WebWindow`. The `WebWindow` contains a collection of `PageWindows`, which are open documents. As with the `WebWindows` collection, you access an individual `PageWindow` using a number. In this case, the code accesses the first open document or `PageWindow`.

You can also use the document name to access the `PageWindow` object. For example, when the document is named `Temp.htm`, you can access it using `WebWindows(0).PageWindows("Temp.htm")`.

Now that the code has told VBA which object to work with, it places the values of individual properties in the `Results` variable. The first property is `nameProp`, which contains the name of the document without the file extension. This first entry consists of two strings: `"Name:  "` and `.nameProp`. Notice how the code uses the plus sign (+) to add the two strings together. This process is also called *concatenation*.

The next line accesses the document's `Title` property. Notice that the code adds the `vbCrLf` constant to the string this time. The `vbCrLf` constant tells VBA to add a carriage return (place the cursor at the beginning of the line) and a line feed (place the cursor on the next line) to the string. These special characters are called *control characters* because they control some aspect of the output (in this case, the placement of the cursor).

The final line of code displays the results of all the code so far. It uses the `MsgBox` function to display the information. The output includes the string that the code created with document properties, along with the special title it created. In this case, the code doesn't provide a special button setup, so it

**Book VIII
Chapter 2**

**Your First VBA
Program**

simply skips that `MsgBox` argument by leaving it blank. (You still have to add the comma to make the code skip the argument. When VBA sees the blank space, it uses the default value for that argument.) To use this example, you must open a document — any document you can access with FrontPage will do. Figure 2-2 shows typical output from this example.

Figure 2-2:
Use
properties
to discover
information
about
documents.

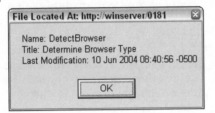

Name: DetectBrowser
Title: Determine Browser Type
Last Modification: 10 Jun 2004 08:40:56 -0500

OK

File Located At: http://winserver/0181

Writing Your First Function

The example in the "Writing Your First Sub" section (Listing 2-1) is nice, but you might want to use more than one piece of information. VBA users commonly rely on *functions* to perform repetitive tasks. That's what the example in this section shows.

Listing 2-2 uses a `Sub` named `GetSummary2` to call the `GetDocProperty` function multiple times. In every case, a special variable stores the result. At the end of the program, `GetSummary2` displays all the information that the program has accumulated. (In this case, I'm assuming you have open four FrontPage-accessible documents of any type.)

Listing 2-2:   Using a Function to Retrieve Document Information

```
Sub GetSummary2()
    ' Create a title based on the Web.
    Title = "Files Located At: " + _
            WebWindows(0).Web.RootFolder

    ' Get the statistics for the first window.
    Output = GetDocProperty(0)

    ' Get the statistics for the second window.
    Output = Output + vbCrLf + vbCrLf + GetDocProperty(1)

    ' Get the statistics for the third window.
```

```
   Output = Output + vbCrLf + vbCrLf + GetDocProperty(2)

   ' Get the statistics for the fourth window.
   Output = Output + vbCrLf + vbCrLf + GetDocProperty(3)

   ' Display the results.
   MsgBox Output, , Title
End Sub

Function GetDocProperty(WinNumber As Integer) As String
   ' The information is located in the active document.
   With WebWindows(0).PageWindows(WinNumber).ActiveDocument

      ' Get the document name.
      Results = "Name: " + .nameProp

      ' Get the document title.
      Results = Results + vbCrLf + "Title: " + .Title

      ' Add the last modification date.
      Results = Results + vbCrLf + _
         "Last Modification: " + .fileModifiedDate
   End With

   ' Return the results.
   GetDocProperty = Results
End Function
```

Listing 2-2 begins with `GetSummary2`. The Sub contains code for tasks that aren't repeated, such as getting the location of the Web and displaying the results on-screen. `GetSummary2()` calls `GetDocProperty()` for each of the tasks that are repeated. In this case, the code calls `GetDocProperty()` once for each open document. Notice that `GetSummary2()` places the result of each call in a variable. It also supplies the number of the window that it's interested in to `GetDocProperty()`.

The `GetDocProperty` function introduces several new ideas. The first idea is a *return value*. Functions can return a value to the caller. The second idea is the use of an argument. An *argument* is input to a `Sub` or `Function`. In this case, `WinNumber` is the input to the `WebWindows(0).PageWindows(WinNumber)` collection.

The actual code within the `GetDocProperty` function looks the same as the example in the "Writing Your First Sub" section; in this case, the code makes the function equal to `Results`. This is how you return a value to the caller. Figure 2-3 shows the output of this example.

Book VIII
Chapter 2

Your First VBA
Program

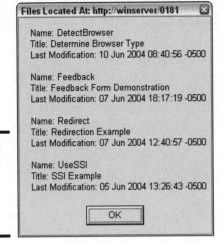

Figure 2-3:
Use
functions
to return
multiple
results.

Getting the Scoop on Scope

You might think the concept of scope is confusing and difficult to understand because it seems complex. Actually, *scope* is simply the range of what a program can see and how much it lets others know. When you look at the MsgBox function, you care about the inputs that you provide and the output that the function produces. These are the *public* (visible) elements of the MsgBox function. As a user, you don't have to care what happens inside the MsgBox function, even though that information is important to the MsgBox function itself. These inner workings — the ones you can't see — are the *private* (invisible) elements of the MsgBox function.

There are two reasons that scope is important to you as a VBA user. First, if every part of a program could see every other part of a program, chaos would result — there would be too much information to track. Second, programs have to protect their data to ensure that it doesn't get damaged in some way. In short, you want to make some parts of your program visible so people can use them, but other parts invisible so they remain protected.

Understanding the purpose of scope

Scope relies on two keywords: Public and Private. You can use them to define the scope of variables or classes. Scope has an effect on just about every kind of programming element you use in this book, so it's important to understand how it works. The heart of the matter is the two keywords:

✦ Public: This keyword tells VBA that it should allow other program elements to see the affected elements.

✦ `Private`: This keyword tells VBA that it should hide the affected element from other programming elements.

Defining the effects of scope

The best way to learn about scope is to begin working with it. You can experiment with simple uses of scope to see how a change in scope affects your programs. The most important rule is that scope only affects everything outside the current block of code. (A block is defined by a sub, function, or other structural element.)

Making a module private by adding `Option Private Module` at the beginning of the module means that everything in that module is invisible to the outside world. Even if the module contains a `Public Sub`, only the other elements inside the module can see it — the `Public Sub` is invisible to everything outside the module. Likewise, when declaring a `Private Sub`, everything within the current module can still see it, but nothing outside the current module can.

Listing 2-3 demonstrates some of the basic elements of scope. Other examples in the book refine this concept, but this is a good starting point.

Listing 2-3:   Using Global Variables

```
' Declare a private global variable.
Private MyGlobalVariable As String

Public Sub GlobalTest()
    ' Set the value of the global variable.
    MyGlobalVariable = "Hello"

    ' Display the value.
    MsgBox MyGlobalVariable

    ' Call the GlobalTest2 Sub
    GlobalTest2

    ' Display the value on return from the call.
    MsgBox MyGlobalVariable
End Sub

Private Sub GlobalTest2()
    ' Show that the global variable is truly global.
    MsgBox MyGlobalVariable

    ' Change the value of the global variable.
    MyGlobalVariable = "Goodbye"
End Sub
```

**Book VIII
Chapter 2**

**Your First VBA
Program**

Notice that `MyGlobalVariable` is private. You can't access this global variable outside the current module. However, both of the sub-procedures in this module can access the global variable.

As another example, `GlobalTest` is a public `Sub`, but `GlobalTest2` is private. You can verify the use of scope, in this case, by opening the Macro dialog box (Tools⇨Macro⇨Macros): You see `GlobalTest` listed, but `GlobalTest2` won't appear in the list.

Type and run the example code in Listing 2-3 to see how the two `Sub` elements affect each other. You should see three dialog boxes:

✦ The first dialog box reads `Hello` because `GlobalTest` sets the value of `MyGlobalVariable`.

✦ The second dialog box also reads `Hello` because `MyGlobalVariable` is truly global. Even though the value of this variable was set in `GlobalTest`, `GlobalTest2` can read it.

✦ The third dialog box reads `Goodbye` because `GlobalTest2` has set `MyGlobalVariable` to another value.

Three Ways to Run Your Program

Running your program from within the Visual Basic Editor is fine when you want to test it. However, the goal is to run it from the application and not have to open the Visual Basic Editor first. You have a lot of choices for running any VBA program — more than most people want to remember. VBA provides three common methods for running applications, but most VBA users never need to think beyond the first method, which is using the Macro dialog box.

Using the Macro dialog box

The Macro dialog box is the most common way to run a VBA program. Every time that you create a new `Sub`, it appears in the list of macros you can run. You don't have to do anything special. You can always access every program you create by using this method, which is why it's the most popular method. Here's a hands-on tour of what this dialog box can do:

1. **Choose Tools⇨Macro⇨Macros.**

   The Macro dialog box appears, as shown in Figure 2-4 (the `SayHello` macro from the "Step 2: Implement the design" section of this chapter).

2. **Run a macro by highlighting it and then clicking the Run button.**

Figure 2-4:
Use the
Macro
dialog box
to access
the
programs
you create.

You should see the same two dialog box sequences that appear during a test of the program (as described earlier in this chapter).

3. Try out this dialog box on other tasks.

- To edit a macro: Highlight the macro name and then click the Edit button; the application opens the Visual Basic editor. The Code window displays the code associated with the program that you highlighted.

- To remove an old macro: Click the Delete button.

- To create a new named macro: In the Macro Name field near the top of the Macro dialog box (shown in Figure 2-4) type a new macro name (such as **SayGoodbye**); the Macro dialog box enables the Create button and disables everything else. This field normally contains the name of whichever macro you've highlighted in the list.

Using the quick launch methods

It isn't always convenient or efficient to open the Macro dialog box to run the programs that you design. If you use the same program several times a day, opening the Macro dialog box every time becomes a waste of time. What you need is a *quick launch method* — a way to start the program that doesn't require you to open the Macro dialog box.

FrontPage lacks some of the amenities that other Office products provide. For example, when you're working with Excel or Word, you can assign a hotkey combination to a macro. It's important to remember this particular option when you run FrontPage macros from other Office products because the hotkey option — accessed using the Options button in the Macro dialog box (not shown in Figure 2-4) — gives you a method of quick activation for products that support it.

**Book VIII
Chapter 2**

**Your First VBA
Program**

Defining a toolbar button

The best method for activating your macro in FrontPage is to add it to a toolbar as a special button. Using this method means that all you have to remember is to look at the toolbar.

Many people place custom buttons on the same toolbars that the application uses for other purposes. This is fine if you don't mind seeing the toolbar grow longer and longer till it disappears off the right side of the screen. It's better to create a custom toolbar so that you can show or hide the buttons associated with your programs when you need them.

To add a VBA program to a toolbar, you can begin by creating a custom toolbar for the task or you can select an existing toolbar. (The "Customizing Toolbars" section found in Chapter 2 of Book 1 discusses the techniques you use to add a custom toolbar to FrontPage and then add buttons to it.) When you're working with macros, you add the button by using the Macros entry in the Categories list found on the Commands tab of the Customize dialog box (shown in Figure 2-5).

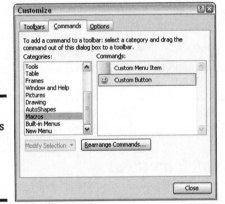

Figure 2-5:
Add macros as toolbar buttons or as menu entries.

After you add the button to the toolbar, assign a macro to it by right-clicking the button and choosing Assign Macro from the context menu. You see the Macro dialog box. Select a macro, click OK, and you're ready to go.

Defining a menu entry

You might use a program often enough to attach it to a regular program element but not often enough to take up space on a toolbar. In this case, you can use a menu to hold the quick-launch option. You use the same set of steps shown in the "Defining a Toolbar Button" section to perform this task. The only difference is that you drag the custom button or custom menu item to the menu you want to use (instead of to a toolbar).

Accessing the program from other VBA code

Never write a piece of code twice when you can write it once and use it many different times. Saving time is one of the reasons to use VBA; saving time writing VBA code is a good way to increase that benefit. The first idea that you have to understand is that you can *call* (tell VBA to execute) any VBA program you created in another program. Here's a simple example that you can add to the Code window:

```
Sub SayHello2()
' Show that we're using the SayHello2 program.
MsgBox "We're in SayHello2!"

' Call SayHello
SayHello
End Sub
```

Notice how this sample uses pseudo-code to describe what happens when you run the program. Remember that pseudo-code is a list of steps the program must perform written in a form that you can understand. The first task is to prove that you executed the SayHello2 program by displaying a message box that contains a message that doesn't appear in SayHello. The second task is to call SayHello. Make sure you save your program at this point.

When you run this program, it displays three message boxes. The first one reads, We're in SayHello2! The second and third message boxes look just like the ones you've seen for the SayHello program used throughout this chapter.

Chapter 3: Storing and Modifying Information

In This Chapter

✔ **Working with variables and constants**

✔ **Understanding data types**

✔ **Using operators**

This chapter refines the concept of a variable by describing VBA variable types and how to modify their content. Understand, however, that computers don't see information the same way we do — ways of representing information that seem obvious to us are invisible to the computer.

As far as the computer is concerned, everything is a series of bits that it has to move around. Data types were invented, sometimes by trial and error, to make the bits easier for humans to understand. For example, when you see the letter *C* on the display, all the computer "sees" is a series of eight bits that form a special number. Interpretation of this number as the letter *C* is for your benefit. Understanding the machine's perspective (that everything is a series of bits) makes this chapter easier to understand.

Understanding Variables and Constants

VBA provides many levels of data interpretation. Some data interpretations help you make your program reliable, others make it run faster, still others provide accuracy, and a few make the data easier to interpret. One of the two big distinctions is between variables and constants. You can modify a *variable* anytime that the program can access it. A *constant*, however, retains the same value all the time.

Making the declaration

You use different methods to mark variables and constants in your program. Variables have a scope and a data type; constants have only a scope. (See the "Defining the Data Types" section later in this chapter for descriptions of data types and how to use them.) You must declare variables, specifying both scope and data type so VBA knows how to work with them. Listing 3-1 shows some examples of variable and constant declarations.

Listing 3-1:   Variable and Constant Declarations with Scope

```
Option Explicit

' This variable is visible to other modules.
Public MyPublicVariable As String
' This variable is visible only to this module.
Private MyPrivateVariable As String
' Using Dim is the same as making the variable private.
Dim MyDimVariable As String

' This constant is visible to other modules.
Public Const MyPublicConstant = "Hello"
' This constant is visible only to this module.
Private Const MyPrivateConstant = "Hello"

Public Sub DataDeclarations()
    ' Only this Sub can see this variable.
    Dim MyDimSubVariable As String

    ' Only this Sub can see this constant.
    Const MySubConstant = "Hello"
End Sub
```

The variable declarations rely on the keywords Public and Private for scope as well as a data type keyword following the variable name to define the data type. In Listing 3-1, all the variables are strings (or text). True, you could use the Dim keyword to make a variable private, but I don't recommend it. Using the word Private is clearer, and clarity is highly useful as a coding habit.

The two kinds of constant declarations also rely on the keywords Public or Private for scope. Notice that you include the keyword Const to mark the value as a constant. The constant has a name and a value assigned to it. However, notice that it doesn't have a data type because you can't assign one to a constant. VBA stores constants as a series of bits, using the type of the information that you provide. Because you can never change the value of a constant, the question of data type isn't important.

Variables or constants defined within a Sub or Function are private to that Sub or Function. Consequently, VBA requires that you use the Dim keyword, instead of the Public, Private, or Const keywords, in this case. Notice that the constant still includes the Const keyword but lacks a Private or Public keyword for the same reason.

Knowing which storage type to use

At first, it might seem like you should always use variables so that you can always access the data and change it. Variables do provide flexibility that constants don't provide, and you can use them more often than not to store your data. However, constants also have distinct advantages including

✦ **Speed:** Using constants can make your application faster. Constants require less memory, and VBA can optimize your program to perform better when you use them.

✦ **Reliability:** Constants have a reliable value. If a constant has a specific value when the program starts, it stays the same until the program ends.

✦ **Ease of reading:** Most VBA users rely on constants to make their programs easier to read. The `vbCrLf` constant (in the examples in Chapter 2) is the same no matter how many programs you create. Every developer who sees this constant knows that using it is like pressing Enter: VBA adds a carriage-return-and-line-feed combination.

There are other ways constants can take the place of variables. For example, the Object Browser makes it easy to work with constants: Highlight a constant in the Object Browser and you see its associated value, as shown in Figure 3-1. An entry at the bottom of the Object Browser tells you that the highlighted entry is a public constant with a value of `"Hello"`.

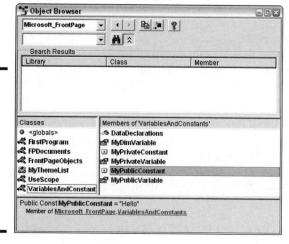

Figure 3-1:
Use constants to provide quick access to standard values in the Object Browser.

Defining the Data Types

A *data type* is a method of defining the data to make it easier to work with in a program. The computer still sees the data as a series of bits, but VBA works with different data types in different ways. The computer can see the binary value, 1000001b, but it doesn't recognize it as anything but a binary value. VBA, on the other hand, can see this binary value as the number 65 or the letter *A* depending on the data type that you assign to the value. The data type is important in understanding the value and working with it. Using a data type also ensures that the program follows certain rules. Otherwise, the data could become corrupted because the program could mishandle it. VBA supports a number of standard data types — including `Byte`, `Boolean`, `Integer`, `Long`, `Currency`, `Decimal`, `Single`, `Double`, `Date`, `String`, `Object`, and `Variant` — which are discussed in greater detail in the next few sections.

Using strings for text

This data type is one that you've already seen in the message box examples: the string. When you create a message box, you use a string as input. The string is the most useful and most-often used data type in VBA.

A string, like the text you're reading now, is a sequence of characters. The characters aren't always printable, but can include control characters that determine how the text appears on-screen. A string can also include special characters, such as punctuation — including relatively specialized marks such as circumflexes, or umlauts. Although a string can contain all these elements, the main content of a string is always text.

Using character codes

Strings can contain a number of elements. In previous examples, I show you strings that contain control character constants such as `vbCrLf`. This constant actually contains two control characters: a carriage return and a line feed. The result of using both control characters together is the same as pressing Enter on the keyboard.

Strings can also use a special function, `Chr()`, to create special characters. You can combine this function with the Character Map utility (normally available on the Start⇨Programs⇨Accessories menu) to produce any character that you need for your program. Figure 3-2 shows a typical Character Map display.

When you hover the mouse pointer over a character, the balloon help displays the Unicode character number in hexadecimal or base 16. A base 16 number uses the numbers 0 through 9 and the letters *A* through *F* to represent values. For example, the number 10 in base 10 (decimal) appears as the letter *A* in hexadecimal. Likewise, the number 16 in decimal is 10h (hexadecimal). (VBA uses h for hexadecimal numbers and b for binary numbers—it's important to know how to use the h and the b suffix when writing programs that require hexadecimal and binary numbers.) Computers use hexadecimal because it works better with the binary values a computer can produce.

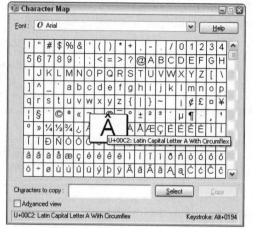

Figure 3-2:
Character
Map
displays all
the printable
characters
available for
a particular
font.

Selecting the character displays the Unicode number in the lower-left corner of the Character Map dialog box and displays the character in a larger size. Listing 3-2 shows Chr() function in use.

Listing 3-2:   Creating Special Characters

```
Public Sub ShowCharacter()
    ' Declare the string.
    Dim MyChar As String

    ' Tell what type of character the code displays.
    MyChar = "Latin Capital Letter A with Circumflex: "

    ' Add the character.
    MyChar = MyChar + Chr(&HC2)

    'Display the result.
    MsgBox MyChar, , "Special Character"
End Sub
```

When run, this program displays a capital letter *A* with a circumflex. Notice how the code uses the Chr() function. The hexadecimal value from Character Map appears as &HC2. The &H denotes a hexadecimal value, and the C2 is the number of the character.

Getting the data you need

Strings can contain more information than you need or contain it in a form that you can't use. You might use a string to provide storage for several pieces of information that you need to send to another location. When the string arrives at its destination, the receiving program unpacks the individual data elements from the string.

All these actions rely on some form of *parsing* — removing and interpreting sub-elements from a storage element such as a string. You can create a single string that contains Hello World and separate it into two pieces, Hello and World, by using parsing. A program could store these separate elements and use them for various purposes.

The three functions that you use to extract information from a string are Left(), Right(), and Mid(). As their names suggest, you use the first to extract the left side of the string, the second to extract the right side, and the third to extract the middle. These three functions require location information and input on where to start and stop extracting information. You use the InStr() and InStrRev() functions to find this information. Listing 3-3 shows some of the techniques that you can use to parse a string.

Listing 3-3: Finding Information in Strings Using Parsing

```
Public Sub ParseString()
    ' Create a string with elements the program can parse.
    Dim MyStr As String

    ' Create an output string.
    Dim Output As String

    ' Fill the input string with data.
    MyStr = "A String To Parse"

    ' Display the whole string.
    Output = "The whole string is: " + MyStr

    ' Obtain the first word.
    Output = Output + vbCrLf + "The First Word: " + _
            Left(MyStr, InStr(1, MyStr, " "))

    ' Obtain the last word.
    Output = Output + vbCrLf + "The Last Word: " + _
            Right(MyStr, Len(MyStr) - InStrRev(MyStr, " "))

    ' Obtain the word String.
    Output = Output + vbCrLf + "The Word String: " + _
            Trim(Mid(MyStr, _
                    InStr(1, MyStr, "String"), _
                    Len(MyStr) - InStr(1, MyStr, "To")))

    ' Output the result.
    MsgBox Output, , "Parsing a String"
End Sub
```

The code begins by creating two variables: one to hold the input data and a second to hold the output data. The input string has a simple phrase that code can parse ("A String to Parse"). The parsing happens as three tasks:

1. The first parsing task is easy — locate the first word in the phrase. To perform this task, the Left function retrieves text starting at the first character and continuing until the first space. The InStr() function returns the position of the first space as a number.

2. The second parsing task is more complicated. The Right function returns the right end of the string. The InStrRev() function returns the number of characters from the beginning of the string to the last space. The Len function returns a value of 17 (the length of the string), and InStrRev() returns 12 (the number of characters from the beginning of the string to the last space). After InStrRev() is subtracted from Len, the result is 5. *Parse* (the last word in the string) contains 5 characters. The Right() function returns Parse.

3. The third parsing task is to look for the word *String* in MyStr. The example code shows that you can perform nesting as needed. The nesting begins with the Trim() function, which removes any extra characters. The Mid() function requires three arguments for this example:

- The string you want to work with.

- The starting position.

    Notice this code also uses the InStr() function, but it searches for *String,* not a space.

- The length of the string.

Subtracting from the length of the string (17) the position of *To* within the string (10) is 7 characters. The 7 characters include the word *String* and the space that follows, which is the reason for using the Trim() function.

Using numbers for calculations

Numbers form the basis for a lot of the information computers store. You use numbers to perform tasks in a spreadsheet, to express quantities in a database, and to show the current page in a document. Programs also use numbers to count loops, to determine the position of characters in a string, and to check the truth value of a statement. And VBA uses numbers to determine which character to display on-screen or how to interact with your code.

Understanding the numeric types

You look at a number as a single entity — a number is simply a number. The computer views numbers in several different ways because the processor actually works with different kinds of numbers in different ways. (In fact, at one time, the math coprocessor used to work with money and numbers with decimal points with separate chips within the computer.) The four basic number types include

+ **Integer:** This is a number without a decimal. An *integer* can hold any whole number, such as 5, but not a number with a decimal, such as 5.0. Although these two numbers are the same, the first is an integer, and the second isn't.

+ **Real:** A *real* number is (for all practical purposes) one that contains a decimal point. The decimal portion doesn't have to contain a value. The number 5.0 is a perfectly acceptable real number. A real number is stored in a completely different format than an integer. (The storage technique only matters to the processor — you don't need to know it to use VBA.)

+ **Currency:** Financial calculations usually require special accuracy. Even a small error can cause problems. The `Currency` numeric type stores numbers with extreme precision, but at an equally large cost in both processing time and memory use.

+ **Decimal:** Computers normally store information by using a base-2 (binary) format. You use a base-10 (decimal) format for working with numbers. Small errors can occur when converting from one numbering system to the other — and these can accumulate into huge errors. The decimal numeric system stores numbers in a simulated base-10 format, which eliminates many computing errors. However, this system requires more memory and processing time than any other numeric type.

Computers also determine a numeric type based on the amount of memory that the data requires. VBA supports three integer types, including `Byte` (1 byte of storage), `Integer` (2 bytes of storage), and `Long` (4 bytes of storage). The extra memory stores larger numbers: 0 to 255 for `Byte`; –32,768 to 32,767 for `Integer`; and –2,147,483,648 to 2,147,483,647 for `Long`. Listing 3-4 demonstrates various data types.

Listing 3-4:   Demonstrating the Differences in Data Type Ranges

```
Public Sub DataRange()
    ' Declare the numeric variables.
    Dim MyInt As Integer
    Dim MySgl As Single
    Dim MyDbl As Double
    Dim MyCur As Currency
    Dim MyDec As Variant
```

```
' Define values for each variable.
MyInt = 30 + 0.00010001000111
MySgl = 30 + 0.00010001000111
MyDbl = 30 + 0.00010001000111
MyCur = 30 + 0.00010001000111
MyDec = CDec(30 + 0.00010001000111)

' Display the actual content.
MsgBox "Integer:" + TwoTab + CStr(MyInt) + _
        vbCrLf + "Single:" + TwoTab + CStr(MySgl) + _
        vbCrLf + "Double:" + TwoTab + CStr(MyDbl) + _
        vbCrLf + "Currency:" + vbTab + CStr(MyCur) + _
        vbCrLf + "Decimal:" + TwoTab + CStr(MyDec), _
        vbOKOnly, _
        "VBA Data Types"
End Sub
```

The first few variable types use standard declarations. However, notice that you can't declare the decimal data type directly — you must declare it as a Variant in VBA. (See the "Working with variant data" section for more information about the Variant type.) The code assigns each variable the same value. Notice that the code must use the CDec function to insert a decimal value into the Variant because VBA doesn't include a decimal data type.

The application output demonstrates something interesting about the numeric data types. Each type silently dropped any decimal data it couldn't hold. This is just one of many reasons to carefully consider the numeric data type you use.

Performing conversions between numbers and strings

Most display features, such as the MsgBox function and forms, require strings, even for numbers. When you work with numeric data, you must convert the data to a string to display it. Listing 3-5 demonstrates some of the essential string-to-number and number-to-string conversion functions.

**Book VIII
Chapter 3**

**Storing and
Modifying
Information**

Listing 3-5: Converting Between Numbers and Strings

```
Public Sub NumberConvert()
    ' Create some variables for use in conversion.
    Dim MyInt As Integer
    Dim MySgl As Single
    Dim MyStr As String

    ' Conversion between Integer and Single is direct
    ' with no data loss.
    MyInt = 30
```

(continued)

Listing 3-5 *(continued)*

```
      MySgl = MyInt
      MsgBox "MyInt = " + CStr(MyInt) +  vbCrLf + "MySgl = " _
             + CStr(MySgl), , "Current Data Values"

      ' Conversion between Single and Integer is also direct
      ' but incurs data loss.
      MySgl = 35.01
      MyInt = MySgl
      MsgBox "MyInt = " + CStr(MyInt) + vbCrLf + "MySgl = " _
             + CStr(MySgl), , "Current Data Values"

      ' Conversion between a String and a Single or an
      ' Integer can rely on use of a special function. The
      ' conversion can also incur data loss.
      MyStr = "40.05"
      MyInt = CInt(MyStr)
      MySgl = CSng(MyStr)
      MsgBox "MyInt = " + CStr(MyInt) + vbCrLf + "MySgl = " _
             + CStr(MySgl), , "Current Data Values"

      ' Conversion between a Single or Integer and a String
      ' can rely on use of a special function when making a
      ' direct conversion. The conversion doesn't incur any
      ' data loss.
      MyInt = 45
      MySgl = 45.05
      MyStr = MyInt
      MsgBox MyStr, , "Current Data Values"

      ' You must use a special function in mixed data
      ' situations.
      MyStr = "MyInt = " + CStr(MyInt) + _
              vbCrLf + "MySgl = " + CStr(MySgl)
      MsgBox MyStr, , "Current Data Values"
End Sub
```

The code begins by declaring an Integer, a Single (a real number), and a String. Although the code relies on these three data types, the principles shown apply to any of the data types. Notice that you can perform direct conversion between numeric types without relying on a function. An integer value can always convert to a real number without data loss. Be careful about going the other way, though — you can run into problems with data loss. The conversion process drops the decimal value but uses proper rounding (any decimal less than 0.5 rounds down), as do the CInt and CLng functions.

Conversion from a string to a numeric value might not require the special functions shown in the code. Use the conversion functions, as shown, (`CInt` for `Integer` conversion and `CSng` for `Single` conversion) to ensure that VBA converts the data correctly. Try changing the source code so that it reads `MyInt = MyStr` — it works as normal, in this case, but this behavior isn't guaranteed.

The code also shows that you can assign a numeric value directly to a string as long as that's the only assignment you make (you don't assign any other values). Always use the correct conversion function when you work with mixed data types.

Using Boolean values to make decisions

The `Boolean` type is the easiest to use and understand; it's like a light switch. This type is used to indicate `yes` or `no`, `true` or `false`, and `on` or `off`. You can use this type to work with any two-state information. Listing 3-6 shows several conversion techniques that you can use with `Boolean` values.

Listing 3-6:   Making Decisions with Boolean Values

```
Public Sub BooleanCheck()
    ' Create a Boolean data type.
    Dim MyBool As Boolean

    ' Set MyBool to True
    MyBool = True

    ' Display the native value.
    MsgBox "MyBool = " + CStr(MyBool), , "Native Value"

    ' Display the numeric value.
    MsgBox "MyBool = " + CStr(CInt(MyBool)), , _
            "Numeric Value"

    ' Make MyBool equal to a number. Only the number
    ' 0 is False; everything else is True.
    MyBool = CBool(0)
    MsgBox "MyBool = " + CStr(MyBool), , _
            "Converted Numeric Value"
End Sub
```

The code begins by declaring a `Boolean` variable and setting its value. As with numeric variables, you can assign a `Boolean` variable directly to a string as long as that's the only thing you do. When working in a mixed data type environment, such as the one shown in the code, you must use the appropriate function (such as `CStr`) to perform the conversion.

The Boolean type isn't numeric — it's logical . . . simply a decision value. You can convert it to a number, as shown in the example code. The value is always -1 for True values and 0 for False values.

VBA also lets you convert a numeric value to a Boolean type by using the CBool function shown in the code. Any value that you store in the Boolean, other than 0, equates to True. Converting the Boolean back to a number still shows -1 for True values and 0 for False.

Using currency values for money calculations

Money usually requires special handling on a computer because rounding can introduce significant errors. Even small incremental errors can result in large errors if they accumulate over time. The Currency data type provides special handling for money calculations but at a slight performance hit because the Currency data type requires additional memory and processing cycles.

Along with the Currency data type, VBA provides a number of special functions for calculating common monetary values. These are the same special functions available to you in your Excel spreadsheet. For example, you still have access to the Pmt() function. When you're working with monetary values in a VBA program, the main concern is to use the Currency data type as needed. Listing 3-7 shows how the Currency data type and the Pmt() function work together.

Listing 3-7:   Working with Monetary Values

```
Public Sub ShowPayment()
    ' Create the required variables. All non-monetary
    ' values use the Double type to ensure accuracy. The
    ' monetary values use the Currency data type.
    Dim Rate As Double
    Dim Periods As Double
    Dim PresentValue As Currency
    Dim FutureValue As Currency

    'Calculate the monthly payment on a mortgage.
    Rate = 0.005              ' 6 Percent divided by 12 Months
    Periods = 60              ' 5 years
    PresentValue = 120000     ' $120,000.00 loan
    MsgBox CStr(Pmt(Rate, Periods, PresentValue)), , _
           "Mortgage Output"

    ' Calculate the monthly payments required to build
    ' a savings account to 120000
    Rate = 0.0025             ' 3 Percent divided by 12 Months
    Periods = 240             ' 20 years
    PresentValue = -5000      ' $5,000 current savings.
    FutureValue = 120000      ' $120,000.00 savings in 20 years
```

```
        MsgBox CStr(Pmt(Rate, Periods, PresentValue, _
                FutureValue)), , "Savings Output"
End Sub
```

The code shows two examples. The first determines the minimum that you would need to pay each month on a 5-year loan of $120,000 compounded at a 6-percent interest rate. The second shows how much you would need to pay into a savings account each month to have saved $120,000 in 20 years if you start with $5,000 in the account, and the bank gives you a 3-percent interest rate. Running the example shows that the mortgage payment is $2,319.94 per month and that the savings rate is $337.79 per month.

Using date and time values

Tracking time and date in your program can be important. Sometimes, it's simply a matter of knowing the last time you updated a Web page with new information, but time and date serve other purposes as well. For example, you could create statistical information about your Web pages by using FrontPage macros and storing them in a local file or even a database for later analysis.

Both date and time variables rely on the Date data type, which contains both date and time information. You can separate the information as needed. You can also assign date and time to the variable independently, by using the Date and Time functions, or together, by using the Now function. Listing 3-8 demonstrates various time functions. Notice that you can control individual elements, making it easy to change just what you need.

Listing 3-8:   Keeping Track of the Time

```
Public Sub ShowTime()
    ' Create a time variable.
    Dim MyTime As Date

    ' Obtain the current time.
    MyTime = Time

    ' Display the hours, minutes, and seconds.
    MsgBox "The current time is: " + _
            vbCrLf + "Hours: " + CStr(Hour(MyTime)) + _
            vbCrLf + "Minutes: " + CStr(Minute(MyTime)) + _
            vbCrLf + "Seconds: " + CStr(Second(MyTime)), , _
            "Current Time"
End Sub
```

VBA provides access to the whole time value by using the Time function. You can also use the Hour, Minute, and Second functions for specific information. Not shown in the example is how you can set the current time by using Time on a line by itself and supplying a time value such as Time =

#1:0:0# (for 1:00 a.m.). In this case, Time acts as a property, rather than a statement, and accepts input in any valid format, such as #1 PM# for 1:00 p.m. (or 1300 in military time). Notice that time and date values always appear within the # symbols rather than the double quotes used for strings.

Working with variant data

The "Understanding the numeric types" section demonstrates one use of the Variant data type. However, a Variant can hold any data type, including objects. A program can use a Variant when VBA doesn't provide direct support for a particular data type (such as the Decimal type), or when the type of information that the user will provide is unknown when you write the program. In short, a Variant is the universal data type for VBA.

Working with Operators

Operators determine how VBA works with two variables and what result the combination produces. The examples in this chapter use operators to add numbers and *concatenate* (add) strings. In both cases, your code uses the + operator to perform the task. However, the result differs. When using numbers, the result is a summation, such as 1 + 2 = 3. When using strings, the result is a concatenation, such as Hello + World = Hello World. VBA groups operators into four areas:

✦ **Arithmetic:** Operators that perform math operations such as addition (+), subtraction (-), division (/), and multiplication (*)

✦ **Comparison:** Operators such as less-than (<), greater-than (>), and equals (=) that compare two values and produce a Boolean result

✦ **Concatenation:** Operators such as & and + used to add two strings together

✦ **Logical:** Operators such as Not, And, Or, and Xor used to perform Boolean operations on two variables

VBA also assigns operators a *precedence,* or order of use. When your code contains the equation MyVal = 1 + 2 * 3, VBA performs the multiplication first and then the addition — resulting in a value of 7 — because multiplication has a higher precedence than addition. However, the equation MyVal = (1 + 2) * 3 has a result of 9 because parentheses have a higher precedence than multiplication. The rules that VBA uses for precedence are the same rules you learned in math class.

Chapter 4: Creating Structured Programs

In This Chapter

✔ **Developing applications using structures**

✔ **Using the** If...Then **statement**

✔ **Using the** Select...Case **statement**

✔ **Using** loop **statements**

✔ **Changing the application flow with** GoTo

*S*tructures help organize your VBA code so it can perform more tasks more efficiently. Special statements can help organize the code so it accomplishes tasks based on decisions or performs the same task multiple times. This chapter shows how to use special statements to make decisions, perform tasks more than once, or redirect control to another area of the program.

These statements also improve program flexibility. A program that uses the right statements can perform a wider variety of tasks and take outside conditions into account, such as the day of the week or the current state of the computer. Statements that control program flow are essential to writing programs that need less input from you and perform more tasks automatically. For example, VBA can help you create FrontPage documents that automatically reflect special events such as a document template change (you might want to include a comment or other feature that a document template change normally doesn't affect).

Exercising Control with Structures

Few programs use all the statements in the program file all the time. You might want the program to perform one task when you click Yes and another task when you click No. The statements for both tasks appear in the code, but the program executes only one set of statements.

To control program execution, the developer adds special statements — such as the If...Then statement — that show the beginning and end of each task and also decide which task to execute. You may think that letting the computer decide which task to execute would cause the developer to lose control of the program. However, the developer hasn't lost control of the program because the decision-making process is predefined as part of the program design.

Most developers refer to the combination of beginning and ending statements for a task as a *control structure* because it adds control to a program. The If...Then statement and its accompanying End If statement combine to form an If...Then control structure.

Because the program contains more than one task, it has more than one path of execution. When you add control structures, the number of execution paths increases exponentially. For example, a program with one control structure has two paths of execution, but a program with two control structures has four paths. As you can imagine, the task of debugging the application becomes harder when you add control structures, so designing your program carefully is important.

You can also *nest* control structures. A program might require multiple decision points to address a specific need. For example, the program might need to decide whether you requested an apple or an orange. When you select an apple, the program then might have to decide between a yellow, green, or red apple. The program can't make the second decision without the first, so the second decision is nested within the first.

Making a Decision with the If...Then Statement

Most programs require decision-making code. When you need to make the same decision every time that you perform a task, and the outcome of the decision is always the same, then making the decision is something you can tell VBA to do for you using the If...Then statement.

All forms of If...Then statements can use any expression that equates to a Boolean value, including a variable of the Boolean data type. The term *expression* refers to any equation or variable that VBA can interpret as a means of determining when it should perform the tasks within the If...Then structure. For example, the expression 2 > 1 is true, so VBA would perform the tasks within the If...Then structure. You can also use variables for these expressions, such as A = B.

Using the If...Then statement

The If...Then statement is the simplest form of decision-making code. This statement tells VBA to perform a task if a condition is true. If the condition isn't true, VBA ignores the statements within the If...Then structure.

The example in this section uses an If...Then statement to check which document is open. When the correct document (in this case, one with a title you specify) is open, it displays a success message. The code in Listing 4-1 shows how a simple If...Then statement works.

Listing 4-1: Using an If...Then Statement for Decisions

```
Public Sub TestIf()
    ' Determine whether the test page is open.
    If ActiveDocument.Title = "Macro Test Page" Then

        ' Display a success message when the page is open.
        MsgBox "The test page is open!", vbInformation, _
               "Page Type Success"
    End If
End Sub
```

The code begins by obtaining the ActiveDocument.Title property value. It compares this value to the "Macro Test Page" string. When the two values compare successfully, the page is correct — and the code displays a success message.

Notice that the MsgBox() function includes the vbInformation constant in this case. This constant differs from other constants such as vbOKOnly because it changes the icon displayed in the message box, rather than affecting the buttons. The icon you choose affects not only the message box display, but also the sound Windows plays when it displays the message box on-screen. The change in sound reflects the display of a specific kind of message box.

Using the If...Then...Else statement

The If...Then...Else statement makes one of two choices. If the expression controlling the statement is true, VBA executes the first set of statements. On the other hand, if the expression is false, VBA executes the second set of statements.

The example in this section uses such a statement to display one message when the user has the correct Web page open and another message when the user has the wrong Web page open. Listing 4-2 shows the code that you need to make these two checks.

Listing 4-2:   Using the If...Then...Else Statement for Comparisons

```
Public Sub TestIfElse()
    ' Determine whether the test page is open.
    If ActiveDocument.Title = "Macro Test Page" Then

        ' Display a success message when the page is open.
        MsgBox "The test page is open!", vbInformation, _
               "Page Type Success"
    Else

        ' Display an error message otherwise.
        MsgBox "Open the test page!", _
               vbExclamation Or vbRetryCancel, _
               "Page Type Error"
    End If
End Sub
```

The code begins by checking for the correct Web page title. If the title matches the "Macro Test Page" string, the code displays the success message. In an production application (one that you would use in a working environment), the code would perform a task based on the content of the page you selected.

When the user opens the wrong page, the code displays an error message. Looking for a particular action on the part of the user and displaying an error message when the action is incorrect is a very common task. In cases where an error message is necessary, a message box that simply displays the OK button is probably not enough. Such a box suggests that either there isn't any other course of action (the failure is bad enough that the application can't recover) or the developer was too lazy to include another course of action.

Generally, it's better to allow the user to retry the action (if appropriate), or to indicate that the user should not try again. Giving the user the opportunity to choose is important because you can't be there to help the user make a choice based on the current situation. The MsgBox() function in this example shows how to change both the icon used to display the message box and the kind of buttons that VBA displays. The user sees the error message, hears the error tone, and has the opportunity to retry the task or simply do something else. Figure 4-1 shows the error-message dialog box created in this case.

Figure 4-1:
Choose
icons and
buttons
consistent
with the
purpose
of the
message
box.

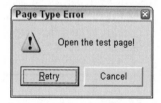

Using the If...Then...ElseIf statement

When making multiple comparisons, you can use the If...Then...ElseIf
statement to make the code easier to read. Using this format can also reduce
the number of decisions that VBA must make, which ensures that your code
runs as quickly as possible. Listing 4-3 shows how to use the
If...Then...ElseIf statement.

Listing 4-3:   Using the If...Then...ElseIf Statement for Comparisons

```
Public Sub CheckGenerator()
    ' Create a variable to check the page generator.
    Dim Generator As String

    ' Fill the variable with input from the Web page.
    Generator = _
        ActivePageWindow.File.MetaTags("Generator")

    ' Check for the latest generator.
    If Generator = "Microsoft FrontPage 6.0" Then

        ' Display a success message.
        MsgBox "The code generator is current."

    ElseIf Generator = "Microsoft FrontPage Express 2.0" Then

        ' Display an update message.
        MsgBox "Time for an update!"
    Else

        ' The generator isn't one we own.
        MsgBox "Unknown generator, check this file!"
    End If
End Sub
```

Creating Structured
Programs

The code begins by creating a variable to hold the name of the *code generator* (a programmer term for the application used to create the Web page) used to create the Web page. Notice the method used to get the information. The `ActivePageWindow.File.MetaTags` collection contains all of the tags for the selected Web page. The `"Generator"` string is an index into the collection — it chooses one of the meta tags from the collection. You can use the same technique to access any meta tag properties you define for a Web page. The index always appears as part of the `name` attribute, as shown here.

```
<meta name="GENERATOR" content="Microsoft FrontPage 6.0">
```

After the code obtains the name of the generator, it uses this value to detect the application name. In this case, the code checks for three values: the name of the current version of FrontPage, one of the older versions of FrontPage, and unknown generators. The fact that `Generator` doesn't match one of the predefined values doesn't mean the code generator is unknown, simply that you haven't checked for that particular code generator.

Making a Choice Using the Select Case Statement

You can use the `If...Then...Else` or `If...Then...ElseIf` statements to meet all decision-making needs. However, using these statements can quickly make your code hard to read if you're telling it to make a lot of decisions in rapid succession. These statements have to be used when you perform complex expression-checking procedures. VBA provides the `Select Case` statement as an easier-to-read choice when you're making a single selection from a list of choices. If you know that a variable contains one of several choices and all you need to check is the choice, using the `Select Case` statement makes sense.

Using the Select Case statement

The `Select Case` structure begins with the `Select Case` statement and ends with an `End Case` statement. You provide a variable that the `Select Case` statement can use for selection. Within the `Select Case` structure are Case *clauses,* or values that the `Select Case` structure uses for comparison. When the value of a clause matches the value of the input variable, the `Select Case` structure performs all tasks required by that clause.

The example in this section is a different version of the `If...Then...ElseIf` statement shown in Listing 4-3. The example shows how the `Select Case` statement makes the code easier to read and reduces the amount of typing you have to do. Listing 4-4 shows the code needed to make the choices.

Listing 4-4: Using a Select Case Statement for Multiple Decisions

```
Public Sub CheckGenerator2()
    ' Determine the generator version.
    Select Case ActivePageWindow.File.MetaTags("Generator")
        Case "Microsoft FrontPage 6.0"
            ' Display a success message.
            MsgBox "The code generator is current."

        Case "Microsoft FrontPage Express 2.0"
            ' Display an update message.
            MsgBox "Time for an update!"
    End Select
End Sub
```

The code checks each kind of code generator without having to review it as part of an If...Then...ElseIf statement. You provide the source of the information only one time and VBA executes only the case that matches the correct code generator. The way the code is written makes it easy to locate a particular case quickly when you need to make changes.

This technique can be more memory efficient and faster too. The code in Listing 4-3 creates a variable to hold the data. The reason for this step is that otherwise VBA would have to waste time reevaluating the ActivePageWindow.File.MetaTags("Generator") property for every code generator. It's faster to place the information in a local variable and let VBA work with it. Unfortunately, the local variable consumes memory and your computer doesn't have an unlimited supply. The Select Case statement eliminates this requirement.

Using the Case Else clause

A Select Case statement should normally contain the optional Case Else clause to ensure you handle all cases, even those you don't expect when you write the program. Adding this clause requires little time and adds an important error-trapping feature to your program. You could easily change the program from the previous section to include a Select Case statement like the one shown in Listing 4-5.

Listing 4-5: Handling Unforeseen Decisions with Case Else

```
Public Sub CheckGenerator2()
    ' Determine the generator version.
    Select Case ActivePageWindow.File.MetaTags("Generator")
        Case "Microsoft FrontPage 6.0"
            ' Display a success message.
```

(continued)

Listing 4-5 *(continued)*

```
          MsgBox "The code generator is current."

     Case "Microsoft FrontPage Express 2.0"
          ' Display an update message.
          MsgBox "Time for an update!"

     Case Else
          ' The generator isn't one we own.
          MsgBox "Unknown generator, check this file!"
  End Select
End Sub
```

The older version of the code could cause problems when the Web page doesn't have one of the required entries. This version provides an error message telling you that the code generator is unrecognized. It exits before the code has a chance to create an error condition.

Performing a Task More than Once Using Loops

Many tasks that you perform require more than one check, change, or data manipulation. You don't change just one table entry in a Web page; you change all the affected entries. Likewise, you normally don't review just one property in the document, you review all of them. You need a method for reading and writing data multiple times in FrontPage.

Loops provide a method for performing tasks more than one time. You can use loops to save code writing time. Simply write the code to perform the repetitive task once and then tell VBA to perform the task multiple times.

When using loops, you decide how the code determines when to stop. You can tell the loop to execute a specific number of times or to continue executing until the program meets a certain condition.

Using the Do While...Loop statement

A Do While...Loop statement keeps performing a task until a certain condition is true. The loop checks the expression first and then executes the code within the structure if the expression is true. You use this loop to perform processing zero or more times. A Do While...Loop works especially well if you can't determine the number of times that the loop should execute when you design your program.

One example of a situation where you won't know how many times to perform a task is a property that contains a collection of items. For example, the `Application.Themes` property contains a `Themes` collection of individual `Theme` objects. Listing 4-6 shows a typical example of using a `Do While...Loop` statement to process this kind of collection.

Listing 4-6: Listing Themes Using a Do While...Loop Statement

```
Public Sub DoWhileDemo()
    Dim Counter As Integer   ' Loop counter.
    Dim Output As String     ' Output data.

    ' Set the initial counter value.
    Counter = 0

    ' Keep processing until all themes as listed.
    Do While Counter < Application.Themes.Count And _
            Counter < 20

        ' Get the theme name.
        Output = Output + _
                Application.Themes(Counter).Name + _
                vbCrLf

        ' Update the counter.
        Counter = Counter + 1
    Loop

    ' Display the results.
    MsgBox Output, , "Themes on This System"
End Sub
```

When it's working with collections, a `Do While...Loop` statement generally relies on a counter to detect the end of the processing cycle. The code begins by setting `Counter` to a known value so the `Do While...Loop` expression can perform an initial comparison. In this case, the expression consists of two clauses:

✦ The first clause tells VBA to keep performing this task until `Counter` is equal to `Application.Themes.Count`. The `Application.Themes.Count` property contains the total number of items in the collection. Consequently, if there are 50 themes installed on the machine, the loop would execute 50 times.

✦ The second clause tells VBA to perform this task a maximum of 20 times. When there really are 50 FrontPage themes installed on the system, this clause tells VBA to process only 20 of them. Of course, if there are only 19 themes installed, you see all 19 of them.

To access an individual Theme object, the code uses a numeric index. You specify an index by providing a counter variable in parentheses behind the collection name like this: Application.Themes(Counter). After the code accesses the individual Theme object, it places the value of the Name property into Output. The technique shown in Listing 4-6 works only with collections that have number indexes — some collections rely on string indexes and require a different kind of processing (see the "Using the For Each...Next statement" section of this chapter).

The code adds the current theme name to a list of previous theme names by concatenating the Name property to the current value of Output, as shown in the code. It adds the vbCrLf constant to the string so that each theme name appears on a separate line in the output.

Notice that the next task the code performs is to add 1 to Counter. When you use a counter in a Do While...Loop expression, you must update it during every cycle or the loop will execute forever. This is called a *continuous loop* or an *endless loop*. VBA won't tell you about this kind of error — you must know that you have to add the update expression to the loop. As far as VBA is concerned, executing the task forever is a perfectly splendid idea.

Fortunately, there's a way out of the continuous loop problem. Simply press Ctrl+Break (using the actual Break key on your keyboard) and VBA will ask whether you want to stop the program. Some developers consider Ctrl+C and Ctrl+Break as equivalent — and they are, in some cases — but not so in this one. Always press Ctrl+Break to stop a VBA program.

The final step in this example is to display the output. You see a list of themes installed on your system. The list varies depending on the custom themes you create and the FrontPage features you install.

Using the Do...Loop While statement

The Do...Loop While statement works the same as the Do While...Loop statement. The difference is that this statement always executes once because the expression that verifies a need to loop appears at the end of the structure. Even if the expression is false, this statement still executes at least one time. You can use this statement when you want to ensure that a task is always completed at least one time.

Using the Do Until...Loop statement

The Do Until...Loop statement continues processing information until the expression is false. You can view the Do While...Loop statement as a loop that continues while a task is incomplete. The Do Until...Loop statement continues until the task is finished. The subtle difference between the two statements points out something interesting — they rely on your perspective of the task to complete. These two statement types are completely interchangeable. The big difference is how you define the expression used to signal the end of the looping sequence.

Using the Do...Loop Until statement

The `Do...Loop Until` statement is the counterpart of the `Do Until...Loop` statement. This statement examines the expression at the end of the loop, so it always executes at least once, even if the expression is `false`.

Using the For...Next statement

The `For...Next` statement is very handy for performing a task a specific number of times. As long as you can determine how many times to do something in advance, this is the best looping option to use because there's less chance of creating an infinite loop. You can create absurdly large loops, but they eventually end.

In many cases, the `For...Next` statement is interchangeable with the `Do While...Loop` statement when working with FrontPage. Listing 4-7 illustrates this versatility.

Listing 4-7:   Listing Themes Using a For...Next Statement

```
Public Sub ForNextDemo()
    Dim Counter As Integer  ' Loop counter.
    Dim Output As String    ' Output data.

    ' Keep processing until all themes as listed.
    For Counter = 0 To Application.Themes.Count - 1

        ' Get the theme name.
        Output = Output + _
                Application.Themes(Counter).Name + _
                vbCrLf

        ' Check for 20 themes.
        If Counter = 19 Then

            ' If there are 20 themes, then exit.
            Exit For
        End If

    Next

    ' Display the results.
    MsgBox Output, , "Themes on This System"
End Sub
```

This example performs the same task as Listing 4-6. The difference is in how it performs the task. To begin, notice that the code doesn't have to set the initial value of Counter because the For...Next expression performs that task. The For...Next expression also ensures that Counter is updated so you don't have to worry about updating Counter manually. However, the essential task of updating Output is still the same as in Listing 4-6.

The Do While...Loop statement allows you to define two clauses for the expression, but this isn't possible using a For...Next statement. To overcome this problem, you use an If...Then statement to check for the second condition.

Remember that Counter starts with 0, so when you want to check for 20 items, you actually need to look for a Counter value of 19 to compensate for item 0.

The code uses the special Exit For statement to exit the For...Next statement early. You can use this particular feature in any loop when you think you might need to end the loop early. Always place the Exit For statement within a conditional statement, as shown, or the loop will exit before the first loop is completed. Whenever VBA executes a Exit For statement, the loop ends immediately.

Using the For Each...Next statement

The For Each...Next statement is similar to the For...Next statement in operation. However, this statement doesn't rely on an external counter. It uses an object index as a counter. The advantage of using this statement is that you don't have to figure out how many times to perform the loop — the object provides this information. The disadvantage of using this statement is that you lose a little control over how the loop executes because the counter is no longer under your control.

Unlike many other Office products, FrontPage relies heavily on a wealth of collections that require use of the For Each...Next statement because they use string, rather than numeric, indexes. Because of the emphasis on string indexes, the For Each...Next statement is the most useful looping tool for FrontPage users. Listing 4-8 shows a typical example of how to use it.

Listing 4-8:   Processing Collections that Use String Indexes

```
Public Sub CheckAllTags()
    Dim AllTags As MetaTags ' Holds all the tags.
    Dim ThisTag As Variant  ' Holds just one tag.
    Dim Output As String    ' Contains the output.

    ' Get all of the meta tags.
```

```
   Set AllTags = ActivePageWindow.File.MetaTags

   ' Use a for each loop to process them.
   For Each ThisTag In AllTags
       Output = Output + ThisTag
       Output = Output + vbTab + AllTags(ThisTag) + vbCrLf
   Next

   ' Display the results.
   MsgBox Output, , "Meta Tags in Current Page"
End Sub
```

The code begins by obtaining a copy of all the meta tags from the
`ActivePageWindow.File.MetaTags` property. The main reason to perform this extra step is to enhance application performance — so VBA
doesn't have to go get a copy of the tags every time you create a local
copy of a processing loop.

Notice that the code has no loop counter; it doesn't even show an index
because the index is implied. The `For Each...Next` expression places a
single meta tag into `ThisTag` during each loop. It processes every meta tag
one and only one time. The result, in this case, is a string that contains the
meta tag name — not its value, which is added to the output.

To obtain the meta tag value, the code uses an index with `AllTags`. The index
works because it's the name of the meta tag you want, not a numeric value.
The final step is to display a dialog box containing the list of meta tag names
and their associated values. Make sure you have a Web page that contains
meta tags open when you run this example or you'll receive an error message.

Redirecting the Flow Using GoTo

You might run into situations where the existing program flow won't work,
and you have to disrupt it to move somewhere else in the code. The `GoTo`
statement provides a means of redirecting program flow. Used carefully, the
`GoTo` statement can help you overcome specific programming problems.

Unfortunately, the `GoTo` statement has caused more problems (such as creating hard-to-understand code and hiding programming errors) than any other
programming statement because it has a great potential for misuse. Novice
programmers find it easier to use the `GoTo` statement to overcome programming errors rather than to fix these problems. Always use the `GoTo` statement
with extreme care. Designing your code to flow well before you write it — and
fixing errors as you find them — are both easier than reading code with misused `GoTo` statements.

Using the GoTo statement correctly

The GoTo statement does provide an essential service: It helps you redirect program flow. Before you use the GoTo statement, however, ask yourself whether there's some other way to perform the redirection, such as using a loop. Listing 4-9 shows an example of correct GoTo usage.

Listing 4-9:   Using the GoTo Statement

```
Public Sub CorrectingErrors()

    Dim TheInput As String  ' User input value.

' Restart point after an error.
Restart:

    ' Include error handling.
    On Error GoTo HandleError

    ' Get a number from the user.
    TheInput = InputBox("Type a number between 0 and 9", _
                    "Numeric Input", "0")

    ' Determine whether the test page is open.
    If CInt(TheInput) >= 0 And CInt(TheInput) <= 9 Then

        ' Display a success message when the page is open.
        MsgBox "You Entered: " + TheInput, vbInformation, _
            "Success!"
    Else

        ' Display an error message otherwise.
        If MsgBox("Incorrect Number, Use 0 Through 9", _
            vbExclamation Or vbRetryCancel, _
            "Error") = vbRetry Then

            ' Try the operation again.
            GoTo Restart
        End If
    End If

    ' Exit the Sub when successful.
    Exit Sub

' Take care of any errors.
HandleError:

    ' Reset the error.
    Err.Clear
```

```
    ' Display an error message.
    If MsgBox("Incorrect Non-Numeric Input!", _
            vbExclamation Or vbRetryCancel, _
            "Error") = vbRetry Then

        ' Try the operation again.
        GoTo Restart
    End If
End Sub
```

This example shows several new techniques, including two techniques for trapping errors. Notice that the code begins by creating a *label*. A label is a word followed by a colon. The GoTo statement relies on labels to know where to restart the application code.

The InputBox() function displays a dialog box with a space where the user can type information. In this case, TheInput receives the value the user typed in the dialog box. Of course, there isn't any way to know whether the user typed the correct value at this point. The InputBox() function merely provides a way for the user to enter a value.

The code begins this check by converting TheInput to an integer using the CInt() function. When the user enters a number between 0 and 9, the code displays a success message. However, when the user enters a number outside that range, the code displays an error message, saying the number is incorrect. When the user clicks Retry, the code uses a GoTo statement to redirect program flow to the Restart label to give the user another chance to type the correct value.

This first error check assumes the user typed a number, just the wrong number. When the user types something unexpected, VBA raises a type mismatch error when it comes to the CInt() function. For example, the string value "Hello World" is perfectly acceptable to the InputBox() function, but doesn't work with the CInt() function because the data type is wrong. The On Error Goto statement (another form of GoTo statement) handles this problem by redirecting the user to the HandleError label. The user is informed that non-numeric input is unacceptable. When the user clicks Retry, the code again redirects the user to the Restart label. The goal of this code is to keep working with the user to obtain the correct information.

The code also contains an Exit Sub statement before the HandleError label. This statement tells VBA to exit without executing the error-handling code when the user provides the correct input.

Avoiding misuse of the GoTo statement

Many programmers misused the GoTo statement so severely in the past that most books tell you not to use it at all. Misuse of the GoTo statement leads to buggy code that is hard to read. In addition, GoTo statements can hide poor program design. However, the GoTo statement can also accomplish useful work, so the goal is to avoid misuse of the GoTo statement and concentrate on useful tasks. Here are some ways to avoid misusing the GoTo statement:

✦ **Loops:** Never use a GoTo statement as a loop replacement. The statements used for loops signal others about your intent. In addition, standard loop statements contain features that keep bugs, such as endless loops, to a minimum.

✦ **Exits:** Avoid using a GoTo statement as a means of exiting a program. You can always use the End statement for that task.

✦ **Program-flow problems:** If you detect problems with the flow of your program, check your pseudo-code and design documents again. Make sure you implement the design correctly. The design might require change as well. Don't assume that the design is always correct, especially if this is a first attempt.

Chapter 5: Trapping Errors and Squashing Bugs

In This Chapter

✔ Understanding the various types of bugs

✔ Figuring out how to track down bugs

✔ Getting to know the Locals window

✔ Getting to know the Watch window

*E*ven the best programmer in the world makes mistakes. It's part of the human condition. Don't be surprised when a bug creeps into your well-designed and -implemented VBA program. Bugs are the gremlins of the computer industry — they're insidious and evil.

Fortunately, you can hunt down bugs and squash them. You can also prevent bugs from occurring in the first place by coding your VBA program carefully. The goal of this chapter is to help you understand what you can do to prevent bugs in your VBA program and what to do when they get in anyway.

You won't figure out how to write perfect programs because no one does. As a result, you use *error trapping* to detect bugs and do something about them before they can cause problems. In the cases where you can't detect the bug, you use *error handling* to fix the problem the bug causes and help your VBA program recover. This chapter covers the fine points of dealing with bugs. Debugging scripts is covered in Book VII, Chapter 4.

Knowing the Enemy

Users look at bugs as nonentities devoid of any characteristics. All a user knows is that a bug causes the program to crash and lose data. You can't afford to have that perspective. Bugs have personalities, in that they vary by

✦ Type

✦ Cause

+ Effect

+ Severity

+ Other factors that you include in your personal classification system

Locating a bug means knowing about its personality so that you can find it quickly. It helps to classify the bug by type. Each bug type has a different prevention and troubleshooting method. You can classify bugs into the following four types:

+ Syntax

+ Compile

+ Run-time

+ Semantic

The best way to find bugs is to know your coding style. Keeping notes helps you understand patterns in your programming so that you can correct techniques that lead to bugs. More importantly, understanding your personal style helps you develop techniques for finding bugs based on past mistakes. Knowing what you did in the past helps you locate and squash bugs today.

Understanding syntax errors

Syntax errors are the easiest errors to avoid but are also some of the hardest errors to find. A *syntax error* can include a spelling mistake, misuse of punctuation, or a misuse of a language element. When you forget to include an `End If` for an `If...Then` statement, it's a syntax error.

Typos are a common syntax error. They're especially hard to find when you make them in variable names. For example, VBA views `MySpecialVariable` and `MySpecialVaraible` as two different variables, but you might miss the typing error. Adding `Option Explicit` to the beginning of every module, form, and class module that you create eases this problem. You can rely on VBA to find most variable typos when you add this simple statement to your code. In fact, this statement should become a standard part of every program you create. (See the "Understanding compile errors" section for details on using `Option Explicit`.)

You can easily miss some of the subtle aids to locating syntax errors if you don't view carefully enough tasks that the Integrated Development Environment (IDE) performs. The balloon help shown in Figure 5-1 for the `MsgBox` function provides a cue that you could miss. VBA displays the balloon help shown in the figure only when it recognizes the function name that you type. When you don't see the balloon help, it's a cue that VBA doesn't recognize the function name, and you need to look at your code. Unfortunately, this feature works only where VBA normally displays balloon help — it doesn't work when you type property names.

Figure 5-1:
Balloon help helps locate syntax errors in your code.

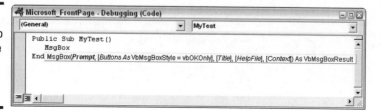

No matter what you do, a few syntax errors can slip by and cause bugs in your program. You can look at the errors for hours and not actually see them because you've worked with the code for so long. Asking someone else to look at your code often helps, but make sure that you ask someone with the same or better programming skills that you have to ensure that they understand your code.

Syntax errors also include errors in *logic* (the construction of expressions in your program). You can create a loop that processes the loop structure statements once too often or not often enough. An If...Then statement can use an expression that works most of the time but isn't quite right, so it doesn't produce the correct result all of the time. Code with logic errors runs because VBA doesn't know that the expression is incorrect. The only way to find this kind of syntax error is to debug the program. See the "Time for a Bug Hunt" section for details.

Understanding compile errors

The VBA *compiler* is actually a syntax checker. Unlike compilers used by other languages, the VBA compiler doesn't turn your code into a free-standing module that you can execute outside the Office environment. Instead, VBA uses the compiler to look for errors that prevent the program from running properly. You might create an If...Then statement and not include the corresponding End If statement. The compiler runs constantly, so VBA finds some mistakes almost immediately after you make them.

VBA uses the compiler to find many of the syntax errors that you make and displays error messages similar to the one shown in Figure 5-2. You can try this feature in the following way. Open a new project, create a Sub (the name isn't important), and type **MsgBox()**. Then press Enter. VBA displays the message box shown in Figure 5-2. When you use parentheses after MsgBox, VBA expects that you want to include a result variable to hold the result, such as MyResult = MsgBox("My Prompt"). You should also notice that the errant line of code appears in a highlight color, which is normally red.

Figure 5-2:
VBA finds some syntax errors.

Missing elements are another type of syntax error that VBA finds with relative ease. When you fail to include an End If for an If...Then statement, VBA always finds it and displays an error message similar to the one shown in Figure 5-2. However, VBA won't find this error, in most cases, until you try to run the program. In addition, it doesn't show the errant If...Then statement — VBA normally highlights the End Sub or End Function statement instead, thus making this error a little harder to find.

The compiler also finds many of the punctuation errors that you can make in your code. When a line of code becomes too long, and you try to move to the next line without adding a continuation character, the compiler notices the error and tells you about it. The complier also notes missing periods between elements of a statement or missing parentheses from function calls (when needed).

When you add Option Explicit to your code (see Listing 5-1), the compiler checks variables for a number of problems such as correct declaration. If you try to, say, assign a string value to an integer, VBA initially allows you to make this error when you type the code. However, when you try to run the code, the compiler sees the type mismatch and tells you about it. The compiler can detect many variable errors that would go unnoticed otherwise, making your code less likely to contain errors.

Understanding run-time errors

Run-time errors happen when something outside your program is incorrect. A disk access request can fail, or you can type the wrong information. Your VBA code is correct, but the program still fails because of this external error. Run-time errors are the reason why many large companies such as Microsoft run *beta programs*. (A beta program is a vendor-sponsored version of a program distributed before the developers have finished it for the purpose of testing and evaluation.) Sending beta programs to a large base of users can help you find run-time errors that depend on a particular machine configuration or a specific kind of user entry technique.

You can trap run-time errors or change the program flow to ensure that they don't happen. Refer to Chapter 4 for two essential techniques for changing program flow to avoid run-time errors using the GoTo statement. Error trapping helps your program overcome errors that you can't predict when you write a program.

Understanding semantic errors

A particularly difficult error to find and understand is the *semantic error*, which is an error that happens when the VBA code and logic are correct, but the meaning behind the code isn't what you intended. For example, you could use a Do...Until loop in place of a Do...While loop. Even if the code is correct and you use the correct logic, the code won't produce the result that you expected because the meaning of a Do...Until loop is different from a Do...While loop.

The meaning that you assign to your code has to match the words that you use to write the code. Just like a good book uses precise terms, a good program relies on precise statements to ensure that VBA understands what you want to do. The best way to avoid semantic errors is to plan your application carefully, use pseudo-code to pre-write the design, and then convert the pseudo-code to VBA code. When you skip steps in the process, you can introduce semantic errors because you won't communicate your ideas well to VBA.

Introducing semantic errors in subtle ways is easy. Writing an equation the wrong way can result in output errors. When you use the wrong equation to determine the next step in a loop, the problem becomes worse because the error looks like a syntax or runtime error. The steps between loops or the expression used to make a decision are very important. The most common error is leaving the parentheses out of an equation. VBA interprets $1 + 2 * 3$ as 7, but $(1 + 2) * 3$ as 9. The missing parentheses are easy to miss when you frantically search for an error.

Time for a Bug Hunt

Because the VBA IDE provides a special tool called a *debugger*, you never have to hunt bugs alone. The debugger is a built-in feature that you access

**Book VIII
Chapter 5**

Trapping Errors and
Squashing Bugs

by using a special Debug toolbar. Figure 5-3 shows the Debug toolbar. Add it to your IDE by right-clicking the toolbar area and then choosing Debug from the list of available toolbars.

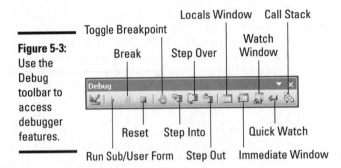

Figure 5-3:
Use the Debug toolbar to access debugger features.

Executing a break

Whenever you open your program in the VBA IDE and execute it from there, the program is in debug mode. Using debug mode lets you stop the program and see what it's doing at any particular moment. Not only can stopping the program help you find bugs, but it can also help you discover more about VBA and how to use it. You could use this feature to view other people's code to see how they perform programming tasks.

Before you can stop execution of your program, you need to tell VBA where to stop. A stop within a VBA program is a *breakpoint*. To add a breakpoint to your code, highlight the stopping point and then click the Toggle Breakpoint button on the Debug toolbar. When you click the Run Sub/User Form button, VBA automatically stops at the point that you selected.

When your program has a natural stop, such as in a form or at an InputBox statement, you can also click the Break button on the Debug toolbar to stop the program and view it in the debugger. The Break button differs from the Reset button because the Break button only pauses execution. Clicking the Reset button always completely stops the program, and to start it again, you have to restart it from the beginning.

Another way to execute a break is to use the Debug.Assert method. You can use any Boolean expression with this method. If the expression is true, program execution continues as normal. However, if the expression is false, the program breaks so that you can examine the value. This form of break is helpful when you know that a program should have variables with a certain range of values.

Whenever you execute a break, the program is temporarily stopped. Click the Run Sub/User Form button to start the program from the current stopping point. As far as the program is concerned, it never stopped.

Taking individual steps

Whenever you execute a break in a running program, the debugger enables the Step Into, Step Over, and Step Out buttons. You use these three buttons to take individual steps within the program — to execute one line of code at a time. The reason why you want to do this is to see the effect of each statement on the program data. When you think that a statement changes a string in a certain way, you can prove it to yourself by viewing the effect of that particular statement.

You use the Step Over button, in most cases, because you want to see the effects of statements in the current Sub or Function. Clicking the Step Over button moves from line to line in the current code. The code still executes in any Function or Sub called from the current Function or Sub, but you don't see it. The code executes in the background.

When you suspect that the called Function or Sub has an error, use the Step Into button to go into that Function or Sub from the current location. The IDE moves the cursor from the current position to the called Function or Sub so that you can see the code while it executes. You still view one line at a time when using this button. The difference is that you see the called code in addition to the Function or Sub of interest.

When you debug a called Function or Sub, you might decide that there really isn't an error in that section of the code. Instead of stepping through one statement at a time until you return to the calling code, you can use the Step Out button to return immediately. VBA still executes all the code in the called function — it just happens in real time rather than one line at a time.

Viewing the data tips

When you execute a program break, you can view the current value of variables in several ways. The easiest way is to use the data tips feature shown in Figure 5-4. (See the "Using the Locals Window" and "Using the Watch Window" sections for other techniques.) To see this view, simply hover the mouse pointer over any variable — and that includes objects.

Figure 5-4:
Rely on
data tips
whenever
possible to
see the
value of a
variable.

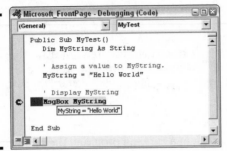

Using the Immediate window to your advantage

The Immediate window is a valuable debugging tool. You can display the
Immediate window by clicking the Immediate Window button on the Debug
toolbar (refer to Figure 5-3). Chapter 1 shows that you can actually create a
mini-program by using it. The Immediate window can perform simple assignments, and you can use it to determine the value of a variable.

The Immediate window can also act as an output screen. The most common
way to do so is by using the `Debug.Print` method. Listing 5-1 contains some
code that shows how to use this valuable debugging method.

Listing 5-1:   Using the Debug Object

```
' Ensure all variables are defined properly.
Option Explicit

Public Sub UseDebug()
    ' The variable that receives the input.
    Dim InNumber As Byte

    ' Ask the user for some input.
    InNumber = InputBox("Type a number between 1 and " + _
                    "10.", "Numberic Input", "1")

    ' Print the value of InNumber to the Immediate window.
    Debug.Print "InNumber = " + CStr(InNumber)

    ' Stop program execution if InNumber is not in the
    ' correct range.
    Debug.Assert (InNumber >= 1) And (InNumber <= 10)

    ' Display the result.
    MsgBox "The Number You Typed: " + CStr(InNumber), _
            vbOKOnly Or vbInformation, _
            "Successful Input"
End Sub
```

Notice how this sample uses the Debug.Print and the Debug.Assert methods in combination. The Debug.Print method outputs the current values to the Immediate window, and the Debug.Assert method checks for a specific input range. When the range is incorrect, the program breaks, and you can see the errant value in the Immediate window.

Using the Locals Window

The Locals window shows all the variables that the current code segment can see. This means you can see variables defined within the current Sub or Function as well as global variables. You display the Locals window by clicking the Locals Window button on the toolbar. Figure 5-5 shows a typical example of the Locals window.

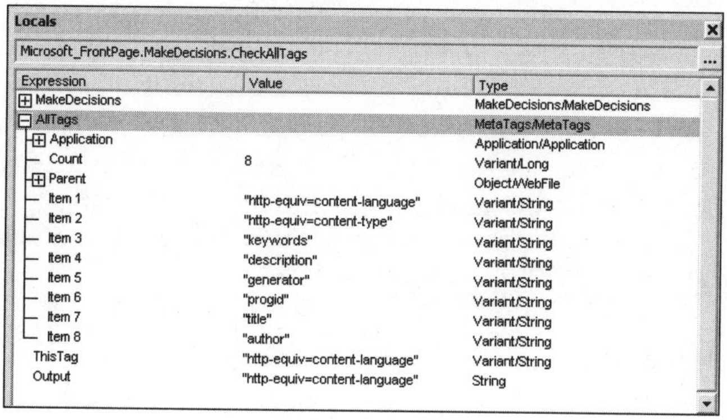

Figure 5-5:
Use the
Locals
window to
see visible
variables.

Locals			×
Microsoft_FrontPage.MakeDecisions.CheckAllTags			...
Expression	**Value**	**Type**	
⊞ MakeDecisions		MakeDecisions/MakeDecisions	
⊟ AllTags		MetaTags/MetaTags	
⊞ Application		Application/Application	
— Count	8	Variant/Long	
⊞ Parent		Object/WebFile	
— Item 1	"http-equiv=content-language"	Variant/String	
— Item 2	"http-equiv=content-type"	Variant/String	
— Item 3	"keywords"	Variant/String	
— Item 4	"description"	Variant/String	
— Item 5	"generator"	Variant/String	
— Item 6	"progid"	Variant/String	
— Item 7	"title"	Variant/String	
└ Item 8	"author"	Variant/String	
ThisTag	"http-equiv=content-language"	Variant/String	
Output	"http-equiv=content-language"	String	

The Locals window displays three kinds of information: variable name, value, and data type. The display begins with MakeDecisions, which is the name of the module in this case. This entry contains all the global variables that the current code can see.

The next entry is AllTags, which is an object of type MetaTags. The Locals window helps you see all of the properties for this object. For example, the Count property has a value of 8.

TIP

You can use property values to determine whether the object is behaving as you anticipated.

You can also see local variables here. The first entry is ThisTag, which is of type Variant/String. Even though the data type declared in the code is Variant, the actual data type is String. The code also includes a variable declared as type String, Output.

Using the Watch Window

The Watch window works similarly to the Locals window, but it has a different purpose: The Locals window shows variables in their raw format, and only the variables you can see locally. You might want to see other variables, or you can use a function to change a variable before you view it. The Watch window helps you perform tasks like these, but it requires a little more work to use. You can display the Watch window by clicking the Watch Window button on the toolbar. Figure 5-6 shows a typical example of the Watch window.

Figure 5-6:
The Watch window tracks variables and expressions.

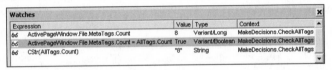

Notice that this window adds a `Context` field. This field tells you where a variable is defined. Because you can use variables from any location, knowing where they come from is important.

Adding a new watch expression

The easiest way to add a watch expression is to highlight the expression in your code and then drag it to the Watch window. VBA automatically enters all the correct information for you — you don't need to do anything else but look at the value. You can also highlight the expression and click the Quick Watch button on the toolbar. When you use this method, you see a Quick Watch dialog box that tells you about the new watch expression. Click Add to add the new watch or Cancel to change your mind.

Using the Add Watch window

A watch expression might be more complex than a single variable or even an expression in your code. Look at the second expression in Figure 5-6. This expression doesn't come from the code — I created it by using the Add Watch window. The Add Watch dialog box (see Figure 5-7) gives you full control over the expression. To display the Add Watch dialog box, highlight any expression in your code, right-click the highlight, and then choose Add Watch from the context menu that appears.

Figure 5-7:
Use the Add
Watch
dialog box
to modify
expressions
or create
new ones.

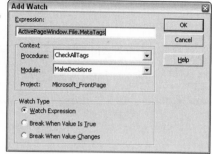

You can modify an expression by changing the content of the Expression field. For example, in Figure 5-6, I highlighted the `AllTags.Count` entry in the code and added the `CStr` part of the expression. You can also use this dialog box to change the context of a `watch` expression. It might help to have access to global variables in every procedure, not just the current procedure. A common local variable could also appear in more than one `Sub` or `Function`.

Notice the three options in the Watch Type group. VBA assumes you want to create a `watch` expression. That's what you get when you create a quick `watch` or use the drag-and-drop method. You can also set a `watch` to cause the program to break when the value is `true` or when it changes. Creating a `break` condition is one of various handy ways to use the Watch window.

Chapter 6: Working with Classes, Arrays, and Collections

In This Chapter

✔ Understanding how classes work

✔ Using arrays within a program

✔ Using collections within a program

*B*efore you can perform any complex tasks with VBA, it's important to get a handle on classes, arrays, and collections. *Classes* act as blueprints for creating objects. An *object* contains a combination of code and data that defines a particular kind of application feature. For example, forms — and all the controls they contain — are objects. The Clipboard also requires use of an object. In short, objects are an essential part of working with VBA because they reduce the amount of code you have to write. In many cases, FrontPage creates the required objects for you; in other cases, you have to tell VBA to create an object (such as a pushbutton) by using a particular class to define what you want.

Arrays and collections are also useful. Many variables you create store a single data element. When you create an integer, it holds a single number. Placing a new number within the integer removes the old value. However, the real world doesn't work this way (for example, a computer can have more than one disk drive; installing a new drive doesn't turn the old one into something else). Your contact database contains more than one name, just as a mailbox can contain more than one piece of mail. You need a method of storing more than one piece of information in a single variable so you can model the real world in your programs. VBA provides two ways to do so: arrays and collections.

Arrays provide a way for your programs to store more than one item in a single container. Think of the array as a large box with a bunch of small boxes inside. Each small box can store a single value. You decide how many small boxes the array can hold when you create the array. Use arrays when you need to store a number of related items of the same data type.

Collections, on the other hand, always relate to objects. In most cases, a main object contains one or more sub-objects. For example, a FrontPage `Application` object contains a `Themes` collection, which is made up of individual `Theme` objects. The `Application` can contain one or more `Themes`. FrontPage is packed with object collections that you can access from VBA.

Coding Considerations for Classes

A *class* is a description of an object: It's the blueprint that VBA uses to build a particular type of object when you request one. The class isn't the object; it's merely the building instructions for the object. This is important to remember because many information sources confuse objects and classes. To better understand how objects work, first you have to keep them separate.

You might want to think of a class as a substitute for a `Function` or a `Sub`, but classes are separate. A `Function` or `Sub` always describes a procedure — a list of steps. A class describes a thing. You can visualize a file because it's a thing. That's why VBA uses classes to describe the file system and objects to work with individual file system elements such as a drive. Although you might read that objects are substitutes for procedures, the two kinds of programming have definite places in your programmer's toolbox. Make sure that you work with both as needed.

You can also create your own classes, but this is outside the scope of this book. For more information on creating classes, check out *VBA For Dummies*, 4th edition, by John Mueller (published by Wiley).

Working with classes

To build an object, you tell VBA to *instantiate* (create an instance of) the object. All the code required to build the object appears in the class. Here's a simple example of the two-step process used to instantiate an object.

```
' Create a reference to the file system.
Dim MyFileSystem As Object

' Create a reference for the target drive.
Dim MyDrive As Object

' Fill these two objects with data so they show the
' available space on drive C.
Set MyFileSystem = CreateObject("Scripting.FileSystemObject")
Set MyDrive = MyFileSystem.GetDrive("C")
```

VBA creates the `MyFileSystem` object, based on the blueprint provided by the `FileSystemObject` class. Likewise VBA creates the `MyDrive` object, based on the `Drive` class.

Telling VBA that you want to create these two objects by using the Dim state-ment is not the same as instantiating them. The Set statement instantiates the object. You Set an object equal to the blueprint contained within a class.

You can instantiate objects by using a number of techniques — the example shows two of them. In the first case, the CreateObject() function instanti-ates the object based on a string you provide that contains the class name. In the second case, MyDrive is instantiated based on an existing class descrip-tion contained within the MyFileSystem object. The GetDrive method tells VBA which Drive object to use within the MyFileSystem object.

A third method (not shown in the example) is to use the New keyword and the name of the class. To use this third technique, you must provide a refer-ence to the file that contains the class code. For example, to add a reference for the FileSystemObject class, choose the Tools⇨References command. You see the References dialog box shown in Figure 6-1. Check the Microsoft Scripting Runtime entry, as shown in the dialog box and click OK.

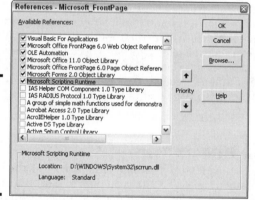

Figure 6-1:
Add references as needed to access classes within VBA.

After you add a new reference, you can view the classes it contains by using the Object Browser. You can now use the New keyword to instantiate the FileSystemObject class, as shown here:

Book VIII Chapter 6

Working with Classes, Arrays, and Collections

```
' Create a reference to the file system.
Dim MyFileSystem As FileSystemObject

' Create a reference for the target drive.
Dim MyDrive As Drive

' Fill these two objects with data so they show the
' available space on drive C.
Set MyFileSystem = New FileSystemObject
Set MyDrive = MyFileSystem.GetDrive("C")
```

Notice that you can now use specific object names when you create the variables; you don't have to know the actual name of the class. Using a reference also makes your application substantially easier to debug. The downside of using a reference is that VBA tends to load the entire Dynamic Link Library (DLL) that contains the class code for the object you want to create.

Loading the entire DLL can use up additional memory and resources, so you need to weigh the relative benefits: Which is more important — code that's easier to read and debug, or a higher demand placed on system resources?

Understanding the class types

Classes come in two varieties: components and controls. A *component* is a class that describes an object without a user interface. The FileSystemObject class is a component. It shows VBA how to create an object that lacks a user interface. You usually create components with VBA. (All the examples in this chapter show how to create components.)

A *control* is a class that describes an object that includes a user interface or affects the user interface. The CommandButton class is a control because it includes a user interface. Don't assume that every control provides a viewable piece of the user interface. When you use the Timer class, it's still a control (even if it doesn't have a user interface) because it interacts with the user and affects the user interface. It's very hard to create controls with VBA. You should use another language, such as Visual Basic (not VBA), Visual C++, or Visual C#, when you want to create special controls for your VBA program.

Using the With statement

VBA provides an interesting feature that makes it easier to write code for an object. The With statement tells VBA that you plan to perform a number of tasks by using the same object. After referencing an object with the With statement, every dotted statement within the structure applies to that object. Using this technique reduces the amount of code you have to type — and it can reduce the chance of typos. Listing 6-1 shows an example of the With statement in use.

Listing 6-1:   Using the With Statement

```
Public Sub UsingWith()
    ' Create a reference to the file system.
    Dim MyFileSystem As FileSystemObject

    ' Create a reference for the target drive.
    Dim MyDrive As Drive

    ' Output string.
```

```
Dim Output As String

' Fill these two objects with data so they show the
' available space on drive C.
Set MyFileSystem = New FileSystemObject
Set MyDrive = MyFileSystem.GetDrive("C")

With MyDrive

    ' Get the drive statistics.
    Output = "Space: " + CStr(.AvailableSpace) + _
        vbCrLf + "Drive Letter: " + .DriveLetter + _
        vbCrLf + "Drive Type: " + CStr(.DriveType) + + _
        vbCrLf "File System: " + .FileSystem + vbCrLf + _
        "Free Space: " + CStr(.FreeSpace) + vbCrLf + _
        "Is Ready: " + IIf(.IsReady, "Yes", "No") + _
        vbCrLf + "Path: " + .Path + vbCrLf + _
        "Serial Number: " + CStr(.SerialNumber) + vbCrLf + _
        "Share Name: " + .ShareName + vbCrLf + _
        "Total Size: " + CStr(.TotalSize) + vbCrLf + _
        "Volume Name: " + .VolumeName + vbCrLf

    ' You can next With statements.
    With .RootFolder

        ' Get the Root Folder statistics
        Output = Output + _
            vbCrLf + "Root Folder Statistics" _
            + vbCrLf + "Name: " + .Name + vbCrLf + _
            "Size:" + CStr(.Size)
    End With
End With

    ' Display the results.
    MsgBox Output, , "Drive C Statistics"
End Sub
```

This code shows many, but not all, the statistics you can obtain from a Drive object. The With statement makes the code shorter. (Imagine typing Drive that many times without using the With statement.)

Notice that many of these statistics are numbers, so you have to convert them to a string before displaying them. The DriveType property is actually an enumeration, which converts to a number. To convert this number to human-readable text, you create a switch statement.

The IsReady property is a Boolean value. The IIf() function is a special method of creating an If...Then...Else statement inline with the rest of the code. In this case, the code converts the IsReady property from a Boolean value to one of two strings, Yes or No, depending on whether IsReady is True or False.

**Book VIII
Chapter 6**

**Working with
Classes, Arrays,
and Collections**

The example also demonstrates that you can *nest* With statements (place one With statement within another With statement). The MyDrive object contains a RootFolder property with additional properties. To access these properties, you normally type MyDrive.RootFolder first. By using a With statement, all you need to type is the name of the property you want to access.

Using Arrays for Structured Storage

An *array* is a list of items. When you write a list of tasks to perform for the day, for example, you create an array. The piece of paper is a single container that holds a number of strings, each of which is a task that you have to perform. Likewise, you can create a similar "piece of paper" in your VBA program — an array — and use that array to hold multiple items.

Understanding array usage

You can define arrays by using several techniques. However, all these techniques use the same basic approach. Listing 6-2 contains an example that demonstrates the essential array usage process.

Listing 6-2:   Creating and Using an Array for String Data

```
' Tell VBA to start all arrays at 0.
Option Base 0

Public Sub SingleDimension()
    ' Define an output string.
    Dim Output As String

    ' Define a variant to hold individual strings.
    Dim IndividualString As Variant

    ' Define the array of strings.
    Dim StringArray(5) As String

    ' Fill each array element with information.
    StringArray(0) = "This"
    StringArray(1) = "Is"
    StringArray(2) = "An"
    StringArray(3) = "Array"
    StringArray(4) = "Of"
    StringArray(5) = "Strings"

    ' Use the For Each...Next statement to get each array
    ' element and place it in a string.
    For Each IndividualString In StringArray
```

```
            ' Create a single output string with the array
            ' array elements.
            Output = Output + IndividualString + " "
        Next

        ' Display the result.
        MsgBox Trim(Output), _
                vbInformation Or vbOKOnly, _
                "Array Content"
    End Sub
```

Notice that the code begins with an Option Base 0 statement. This statement tells VBA whether you want to start counting array elements at 0 or 1. The default setting is 0. Most programming languages use 0 as the starting point, which is why Microsoft made 0 the default for VBA. However, older versions of Visual Basic (including VBA) use 1 as the starting point. When you want to ensure that your program works in every environment, include the Option Base 0 statement.

The code for SingleDimension begins with some variable declarations. Notice the StringArray declaration. When you want to create an array, you follow the variable name with a pair of parentheses that contains the number of elements. You can also create an empty array by leaving the number out, but then you need to use the ReDim statement to set the number of elements later. See the upcoming "Understanding the array types" section for details.

Because the array begins at 0 and not at 1, you can actually store *six* items in an array defined as having five elements. The number you include in the declaration is always the top element number of the array, not the actual number of elements.

The code that follows fills each of these elements with a string. Notice the use of numbers in the statement. This number is an *index*. The statement StringArray(1) = "Is" places the word Is in the second array element by using an index of 1. You can always access an individual element by using its index.

This example shows how to use a For Each...Next statement to access each array element in turn. Notice that you don't need to use an index in this situation because the For Each...Next statement keeps track of the index for you. The IndividualString variable is a Variant — the only acceptable type when using a For Each...Next statement. You don't have to convert IndividualString when you add it to Output because VBA tracks it as a Variant/String. Check out this statement in the Debugger and you can see how it works.

The final statement displays a message box containing the value of Output. This message box presents the list of the strings originally added to the array as a single string.

Understanding the array types

You can classify arrays in several ways. The first method is by the kind of data that the array holds. A String array is different from an Integer array. An array always keeps the array data type unique. Using a Variant data type lets you mix data types within an array. You should use this technique carefully because it can (all too easily) lead to bugs that are difficult to debug.

A second method is to define the number of array dimensions. A *dimension* is the number of directions in which the array holds information. A simple list such as the one in the earlier "Understanding array usage" section is a single-dimensional array. A table that consists of rows and columns is a two-dimensional array. You can create arrays with any number of dimensions. Listing 6-3 shows an example of a two-dimensional array that holds the result of a calculation.

Listing 6-3: Creating and Using a Two-dimensional Array

```
Public Sub TwoDimension()
    ' Create variables to hold the array dimensions.
    Dim Input1Value As Integer
    Dim Input2Value As Integer

    ' Create an array to hold the calculation results.
    Dim CalcResult() As Integer

    ' Create some loop variables for the calculation.
    Dim Loop1 As Integer
    Dim Loop2 As Integer

    ' Create an output string for the display.
    Dim Output As String

    ' Obtain the array dimensions.
    Input1Value = InputBox("Type the first array dimension.")
    Input2Value = InputBox("Type the second array dimension.")

    ' Redimension the array.
    ReDim CalcResult(Input1Value, Input2Value)

    ' Perform the calculation.
    For Loop1 = 1 To Input1Value
        For Loop2 = 1 To Input2Value
            CalcResult(Loop1, Loop2) = Loop1 * Loop2
```

```
        Next
    Next

    ' Create a heading.
    Output = "Calculation Results" + vbCrLf + _
        "In Tabular Format" + vbCrLf + vbCrLf

    ' Define the column heading values.
    For Loop1 = 1 To Input2Value
        Output = Output + vbTab + CStr(Loop1)
    Next

    ' Define the rows.
    For Loop1 = 1 To Input1Value
        Output = Output + vbCrLf + CStr(Loop1)
        For Loop2 = 1 To Input2Value
            Output = Output + vbTab + _
                CStr(CalcResult(Loop1, Loop2))
        Next
    Next

    ' Create a message box to show the result.
    MsgBox Output, vbInformation Or vbOKOnly, "Results"
End Sub
```

The `TwoDimension` sub-procedure begins by declaring some variables. Notice that it doesn't define the number of elements in `CalcResult` — the code tells VBA only that it's an array.

The code displays two input dialog boxes using the `InputBox()` function. Each input dialog box collects an array dimension. Normally the code would include some type of error check to ensure that the user types a correct value, but the code is left out, in this case, for the sake of clarity. The results of the user input are places in `Input1Value` and `Input2Value`.

At this point, the code has the information needed to dimension the array (make it a certain size), so it uses the `ReDim` statement to change the `CalcResult` dimensions. Changing the dimensions erases the content of the array unless you include the `Preserve` keyword. A double loop serves to address the two dimensions of the `CalcResult` array. (The calculation is a simple multiplication, but you can perform any task in the loop.)

After the array is filled with data, it's time to create an output string. The code uses simple assignment to create a heading, generates the row heading using a single loop, and then uses a double loop to create the output information. The final statement displays an output message box that contains a table of the information.

**Book VIII
Chapter 6**

**Working with
Classes, Arrays,
and Collections**

Using Collections to Create Data Sets

You can view a collection as an advanced form of an array. Like an array, a collection maintains a list of items in one package. Because these items are related in more than a superficial way (for example, a group of worksheets in the same workbook), many people refer to the list of items as a *data set*. Using a collection is different from an array, however, and you might find that you like using them better than arrays. A collection has some advantages — such as not requiring the ReDim statement — but it's a little more complicated to use. This section explains these differences in detail and shows how to use collections in a program.

Understanding collection usage

The easiest way to understand a collection is to create one of your own. You can create collections and add them to a class that you create, or use them by themselves. VBA doesn't place restrictions on how you use collections. Listing 6-4 creates a simple collection and then provides a means of adding, removing, and listing elements in the collection.

Listing 6-4:   Creating and Using a Simple Collection

```
Public Sub SimpleCollection()

    Dim UserChoice As String        ' Collection change.
    Dim ChoiceStr As String         ' Modification choices.
    Dim MyCollection As Collection  ' Create a collection.
    Dim Item As String              ' Collection item.
    Dim Element As Variant          ' A single item.
    Dim Output As String            ' A list of items.

    ' Define the modification choices.
    ChoiceStr = "Select an option: " + vbCrLf + _
        "1. Add an Item" + vbCrLf + _
        "2. Delete an Item" + vbCrLf + _
        "3. Exit the Program"

    ' Create the collection.
    Set MyCollection = New Collection

    ' Continue the loop until the user exits.
    Do While Not UserChoice = "3"

        ' Display a dialog box containing the collection
        ' options.
        UserChoice = InputBox(ChoiceStr, "Collection Choices")
```

```
    ' Use a select statement to process the input.
    Select Case UserChoice

        ' Add an element.
        Case "1"
            Item = InputBox("Type a new item:", "New Item")
            MyCollection.Add Item

        ' Remove an element.
        Case "2"
            Item = InputBox("Type the item number", _
                            "Remove Item")
            MyCollection.Remove CInt(Item)
    End Select

    ' Get a list of the items.
    Output = ""
    For Each Element In MyCollection
        Output = Output + Element + vbCrLf
    Next

    ' Display the list.
    MsgBox Output, , "Collection Content"
    Loop
End Sub
```

The example begins by creating a list of modification choices that let you work with the collection. It also instantiates the collection. At this point, the collection is ready to use, so the example defines a loop to continue processing user choices until the user selects option 3, Exit the Program.

The application relies on simple input dialog boxes to obtain user input. You could also create a custom form for the task, but using the InputBox() function works fine, in most cases, and reduces the application complexity. The first input dialog box asks the user to specify a task to perform: (1) add an item to the collection, (2) remove an item from the collection, or (3) exit the program.

The Select Case statement looks for a particular string. Using this technique means that even if the user enters the incorrect value, nothing terrible will happen. The application simply asks the user for the input again. This is an example of coding the application so it's naturally fault-tolerant. Of course, a buffer overflow or other Microsoft-induced error could still derail your application.

When the user selects option 1, the code displays an input dialog box that the user can use to enter a new item. In this case, the new item can be any string. The application treats numeric input as a string. The MyCollection.Add() method adds the new item to the list.

**Book VIII
Chapter 6**

**Working with
Classes, Arrays,
and Collections**

When the user selects option 2, the code displays an Input dialog box that requests the number of an item to remove. (This code should include error trapping, but the example leaves it out for the sake of clarity.) The user must provide a number within the range of collection item values. For example, when the collection contains four items, the user can type a number between 1 and 4. The MyCollection.Remove() method removes the item from the list.

The code lists the items once per loop. Building the output string is a matter of using a For Each...Next statement to concatenate the collection items into a string. Notice that you don't need to know anything about the collection to use this technique as long as the individual elements are strings. Notice the code sets Output to a blank string before it rebuilds the string. Because the application doesn't exit between listings, Output will contain the results of every loop if you don't clear it before you rebuild the string. A simple MsgBox() function displays the results.

Creating collections that use keys

You can normally create collections without keys (identifiers for each collection item), and they work fine. A collection that relies on user input is an exception. It's easier to get string input from users than to ask them to count down a row of entries and provide a number. Database collections also provide an opportunity to use keyed entries. In fact, many predefined collections use keyed entries to make it easier to develop programs with them. Listing 6-5 shows an updated version of Listing 6-4. In this case, the collection relies on keys for removing items.

Listing 6-5:   Using Keyed Data with a Collection

```
Public Sub KeyedCollection()

    Dim UserChoice As String        ' Collection modification
       choice.
    Dim ChoiceStr As String         ' Modification choices.
    Dim MyCollection As Collection  ' Create a collection.
    Dim Item As String              ' Selected collection
       item.
    Dim Element As Variant          ' A single item.
    Dim Output As String            ' A list of items.

    ' Define the modification choices.
    ChoiceStr = "Select an option: " + vbCrLf + _
       "1. Add an Item" + vbCrLf + _
       "2. Delete an Item" + vbCrLf + _
       "3. Exit the Program"

    ' Create the collection.
    Set MyCollection = New Collection
```

```
     ' Continue the loop until the user exits.
     Do While Not UserChoice = "3"

        ' Display a dialog box containing the collection
              options.
        UserChoice = InputBox(ChoiceStr, "Collection Choices")

        ' Use a select statement to process the input.
        Select Case UserChoice

           ' Add an element.
           Case "1"
              Item = InputBox("Type a new item:", "New Item")
              MyCollection.Add Item, Item

           ' Remove an element.
           Case "2"
              Item = InputBox("Type item name", _
                              "Remove Item")

              ' Check for a number or string.
              If Val(Item) >= 1 And _
                 Val(Item) <= MyCollection.Count Then
                 MyCollection.Remove CInt(Item)
              Else
                 MyCollection.Remove Item
              End If
        End Select

        ' Get a list of the items.
        Output = ""
        For Each Element In MyCollection
           Output = Output + Element + vbCrLf
        Next

        ' Display the list.
        MsgBox Output, , "Collection Content"
     Loop
  End Sub
```

You might wonder where the difference is in the two examples. Look at the `MyCollection.Add()` method entry. Notice that it includes `Item` as both the value for the collection entry as well as the key. Adding this second argument lets you access the collection using either a number or a string. Because the code is so small, it's almost always better to use keys when you're working with the user.

However, you don't get the added flexibility free. The collection now consumes twice as much memory for each entry as it did before. The item value and its key require separate memory locations. In addition, there's a small

Book VIII
Chapter 6

Working with Classes, Arrays, and Collections

performance penalty for using this approach. Consequently, even though this method is optimal for working with users, you should use a numeric index when you're creating collections for the application's internal use.

Now that the collection is keyed, you can use either a number or a string to remove a collection item. Look at code for option 2: The user still sees an Input dialog box. However, the code now checks the value of Item using the Val() function. The Val() function won't cause an error when the user inputs a string instead of a number. The Val() function outputs a 0 when the user inputs a string. Because the index values are between 1 and the number of collection elements, a value of 0 usually indicates a string key value. You still have to use the CInt() function to convert the input value because Val() outputs a Double, not an Integer.

Accessing collection items

VBA uses collections quite often. For example, the Drives collection contains multiple Drive objects. You should notice something interesting about the relationship between collections and objects. Microsoft usually uses an s at the end of the name to denote a collection (such as the Drives collection).

The balloon help that you see when you type an object name normally contains methods and properties for that object. It can also contain other objects and collections. When you look through the list of items, anything plural is normally a collection.

You see another clue when you double-click a property and then press F1 to display help. VBA help not only tells you that the item is a collection, but usually it also displays a hierarchical chart to show where the collection fits within the object hierarchy — and what types of items the collection can contain.

The Debugger can also help you ferret out collections. The Watch window shown in Figure 6-2 shows how the MyFileSystem object holds the Drives collection, which contains multiple Drive objects (the first Drive object is highlighted in the figure). You can click the plus signs next to each item to see each drive and its current content. Look especially in the Type column where you can see the data type used for each item in the collection.

Another place to acquaint yourself with collections is the Object Browser. The Help file is useful only when you know what you're looking for. The Debugger is also problematic because you have to build something before you can see what it contains. The Object Browser is different. When you know what you need but not what to call it, you can select the library in question and browse.

Figure 6-3 shows the Scripting library used for the example in Listing 6-1. This figure shows three collections and the objects that they contain: `Drives`, `Files`, and `Folders`. When you find something interesting, highlight it, and then press F1. When you know what you're looking for, help can be useful.

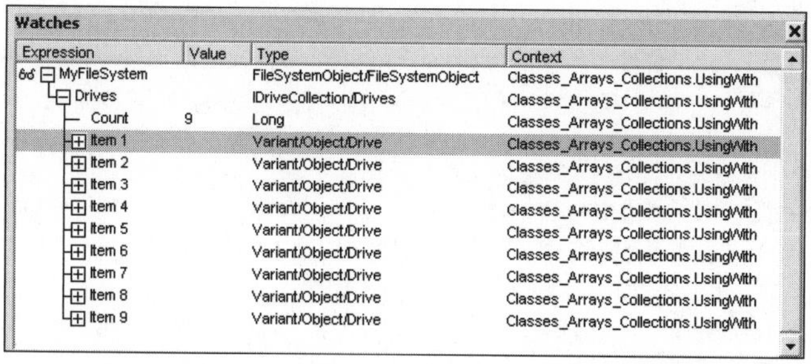

Figure 6-2: Use the Debugger to see predefined collections.

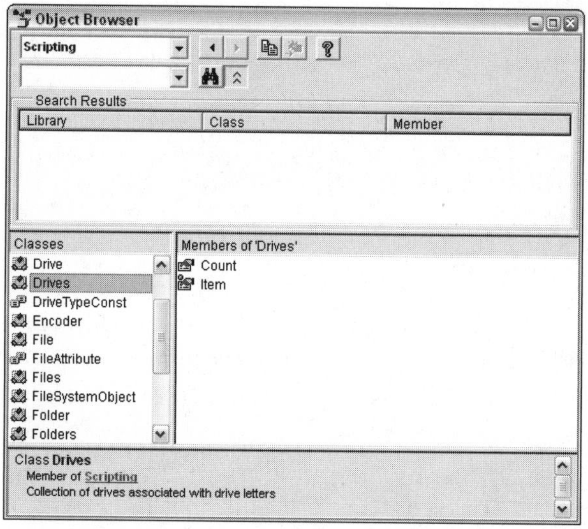

Figure 6-3: Browse for the collections you need to use in your program.

**Book VIII
Chapter 6**

Working with Classes, Arrays, and Collections

Chapter 7: Working with FrontPage Objects

In This Chapter

☞ Working with FrontPage-related objects

☞ Creating FrontPage documents

☞ Developing FrontPage templates with automation

☞ Using the FrontPageEditor objects

☞ Working with the Webs collection

The VBA programs you create for FrontPage are part of the application, rather than the document. Consequently, all of the main FrontPage objects are available to you any time you create a program, even when you don't have a document open. Although some objects (such as `FPHTMLBody`) require a document connection, you can begin writing an application immediately in FrontPage.

This chapter describes the various FrontPage-related objects that are available from VBA. You use these objects to create new document types, as well as add to existing documents. You can also use VBA to enhance templates and provide specialized formatting in your FrontPage documents.

Understanding FrontPage Objects

FrontPage provides a number of objects you can use to interact with the program and documents. You can perform any task from creating new documents to listing the templates installed in the current machine using these objects. However, because FrontPage doesn't associate your program with any particular document, you must provide additional code to check for specific documents (such as checking the Web page title or verifying the file is a Web page and not a CSS page) or write the code to work with any document (such as a macro that inserts generic tags).

FrontPage works with several libraries. In addition to the standard Office, VBA, and StdOLE (standard object linking and embedding) libraries, a minimal FrontPage setup also includes the `FrontPage`, `FrontPageEditor`, and

Microsoft_FrontPage libraries. Each of these libraries works with major FrontPage object groups. Microsoft groups the FrontPage objects into two major categories: Page and FrontPage.

The Page objects affect individual documents directly. These objects appear in the FrontPageEditor library. The Microsoft documentation says that these objects work with Internet Explorer 4.0 or above, but you can make the objects work with other browser by employing careful testing. You can find a detailed list of these objects at

http://msdn.microsoft.com/library/en-us/vbafpd10/html/fphowExplorePOM.asp

The FrontPage objects affect the application, the application environment, and the user. For example, this is where you find the CommandBars collection used to change the application toolbars. You can find a hierarchical chart of these objects at

http://msdn.microsoft.com/library/en-us/vbafpw10/html/
    fptocObjectModelApplication.asp

Using the Application object

You use the Application object to access most application features (such as product name and version). This object also contains information about the user such as the user name and organization. Finally, you use this object to access information about the current document, including formatting and content. Listing 7-1 shows some of the ways you can use the Application object.

Listing 7-1: Using the Application Object

```
Public Sub GetAppStats()
    ' Contains the application information.
    Dim Output As String

    ' Get the application statistics.
    With Application
        Output = Output + .UserName + vbCrLf
        Output = Output + .OrganizationName + vbCrLf
        Output = Output + .Name + vbCrLf
        Output = Output + .Version + vbCrLf + vbCrLf

        ' Get some of the active document information.
        With ActiveDocument
            Output = Output + "Active Document" + vbCrLf
            Output = Output + vbCrLf + .nameProp + vbCrLf
            Output = Output + .DocumentHTML
        End With
```

```
End With

' Display the output.
MsgBox Output, vbInformation, "Application Statistics"
End Sub
```

The code in this example begins by working with the `Application` object properties. You can get the user's name and organization to verify identity, or at least configuration. This information is suspect because it depends on the user entering the correct information during installation. In addition, someone else may actually use the software to log in under the registered user's name. Bottom line: It's one check you can perform, but it probably shouldn't be the only one.

The `Name` and `Version` properties identify the product you're using to create the document (such as FrontPage 2.0, Word 2003, or FrontPage 2003). This information is always correct because the product generates it for you. You can also get product specific information such as the product code.

The `ActiveDocument` object contains a number of interesting properties and methods, many of which appear in the remaining examples in this chapter. The `nameProp` property tells the active document name, while the `DocumentHTML` property contains the complete HTML for the document. Figure 7-1 shows the output for this program.

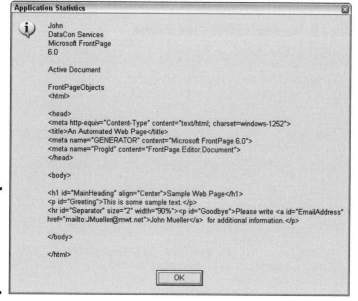

Figure 7-1: Listing application, user, and document information.

**Book VIII
Chapter 7**

**Working with
FrontPage Objects**

Using the FrontPageEditor (Page) objects

The `FrontPageEditor` objects or `Page` objects (Microsoft uses both terms to refer to the same object class) are the most useful FrontPage elements: You use these objects to create Web pages. Any element you can add to a Web page is also accessible as a `Page` object.

Unfortunately, the documentation for this set of objects is a little skimpy, even if you look online at

```
http://msdn.microsoft.com/library/en-us/vbafpd10/html/fphowFPSpecMethods.asp
```

The secret is to look at the associated Internet Explorer interface elements at

```
http://msdn.microsoft.com/workshop/browser/mshtml/reference/ifaces/interface.asp
```

For example, if you want information about the `FPHTMLHeaderElement`, look at the `IHTMLHeaderElement` documentation instead. You can also use the `IHTMLHeaderElement` object directly. All of the FP*XXXX* objects have I*XXXX* twins, so you shouldn't have problems with the documentation.

Ultimately, you can build any kind of Web page you want. The Web page can use straight HTML tags or incorporate cascading style sheets (CSS). CSS is a technique for separating the formatting information from the actual content on Web pages; doing so makes them easier to use and more accessible to users with special needs. Listing 7-2 shows one way to use these objects.

Listing 7-2: Automating Web-Page Creation

```
Public Sub ChangePage()

    ' Create the Web page elements.
    With Application.ActiveDocument

        ' Create a heading.
        Dim Heading As FPHTMLHeaderElement
        Set Heading = .createElement("H1")
        With Heading
            .Id = "MainHeading"
            .innerText = "Sample Web Page"
            .Align = "Center"
        End With

        ' Create some text.
        Dim Greeting As FPHTMLParaElement
        Set Greeting = .createElement("P")
        With Greeting
            .Id = "Greeting"
            .innerText = "This is some sample text."
```

```
      End With

      ' Create a horizonal line.
      Dim Separator As FPHTMLHRElement
      Set Separator = .createElement("HR")
      With Separator
         .Id = "Separator"
         .Size = "2"
         .Width = "90%"
      End With

      ' Create a combined element.
      Dim Contact As FPHTMLParaElement
      Dim EmailAddr As FPHTMLAnchorElement
      Set Contact = .createElement("P")
      Set EmailAddr = .createElement("a")
      With EmailAddr
         .Id = "EmailAddress"
         .href = "mailto:JMueller@mwt.net"
         .innerText = "John Mueller"
      End With
      With Contact
         .Id = "Goodbye"
         .insertAdjacentHTML "afterBegin", _
         "Please write " + EmailAddr.outerHTML + _
            " for additional information."
      End With

      ' Change the Web page title.
      .Title = "An Automated Web Page"

      ' Design the Web page content.
      .body.insertAdjacentHTML "afterBegin", _
         Heading.outerHTML + Greeting.outerHTML + _
         Separator.outerHTML + Contact.outerHTML
   End With
End Sub
```

To use this macro, create a new Web page. Give it any name you want —
the example uses FrontPageObjects.htm. To show just what the macro
changes, the example purposely doesn't include any formatting, setting
changes, or any other modifications you would normally make after creating
a new Web page. Open the new Web page and run the macro: It creates content for you automatically.

All objects in this section follow the same general steps in their creation:

1. The code defines the object.

Make sure you use the correct object type; otherwise your code will fail.

2. **The code calls the** `createElement` **method.**

Here the string you provide is critical. For example, make sure you supply `H1` as input when you want to create a level-1 header.

3. **After the code creates the element, it defines the necessary properties.**

Make sure you include an `Id` property value at this point; this value gives your object a reference name, making it easier to work with later.

Notice that you can combine elements. The `Contact` object contains text and the `EmailAddr` object. You combine elements using the `insertAdjacentHTML` method, which requires a location and the text value as input. The code uses the `EmailAddr.outerHTML` property because it contains the full HTML tag for the object.

As with all HTML documents, you can access the `<head>`, `<title>`, and `<body>` tags from VBA. These essential tags give the HTML document structure. The example shows how to modify the `<title>` and `<body>` tag content. You set the `Title` property directly. The `body` property requires use of the `insertAdjacentHTML` method. Only after the code sets the `body` property does the content you've created appear in the FrontPage editor (as shown in Figure 7-2).

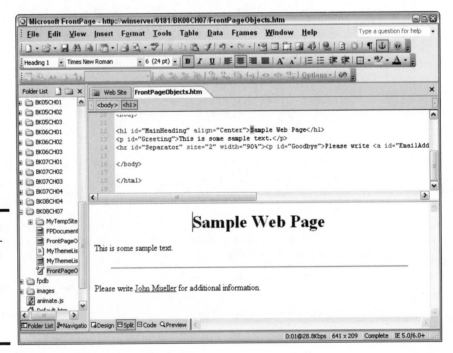

Figure 7-2:
Automatic-
ally create
standard
Web page
content
using a
script.

Figure 7-2 shows that the output of this program is *well formed* (complies with all of the required Web standards) and *complete* (no missing tag elements). This technique can help you automate some of the more repetitive page-creation tasks — and it's especially helpful when each Web page follows the same basic format but can contain variable elements. Although VBA is a more flexible way to create variable content than using templates, you can get the best of both worlds by combining VBA and templates. For example, a combination of VBA and a template could create a Web page based on the person logged into the machine that includes special features such as adding the person's name as the author.

Understanding the Themes collection

FrontPage comes with a wealth of themes. Because you could have so many themes to track, it's important to know how to list them. Listing 7-3 shows one way to perform this task, using the Themes collection. You'll find a second method of displaying the theme information as ThemeLister2() as part of the source code for this chapter on this book's companion Web site.

Listing 7-3:   Accessing FrontPage Theme Information

```
Public Sub ThemeLister()
   ' Holds an individual theme.
   Dim ThisTheme As Theme

   ' Holds the theme list.
   Dim Output As String
   Output = ""

   ' Display only 20 themes at a time.
   Dim Counter As Integer
   Counter = 1

   ' Get the theme list.
   For Each ThisTheme In Application.Themes
      Output = Output + "Label: " + ThisTheme.Label
      Output = Output + "  Name: " + ThisTheme.Name
      Output = Output + "  Format: " + ThisTheme.Format + _
            vbCrLf

      ' Stop after 20 items and display the list.
      If Counter = 20 Then

         ' Reset the counter.
         Counter = 1

         ' Display the theme information.
```

(continued)

Listing 7-3 *(continued)*

```
        MsgBox Output, , "Themes Listing"

        ' Reset the output string.
        Output = ""
    Else

        ' Increment the counter.
        Counter = Counter + 1
    End If
Next

' Display the last few themes when necessary.
If Counter > 1 Then
    MsgBox Output, , "Final Themes Listing"
End If
End Sub
```

This example begins by creating a single Theme object used to hold an individual theme. The code places the output from Theme into Output, a string used for displaying the information in a message box. Because there isn't any way to know how many themes a computer holds, the code also relies on a counter to display 20 themes at a time.

After the code creates the essential objects, it builds a list of themes. You might wonder why I didn't use a For...Next loop, rather than the For Each...Next loop shown. Attempting to use an index to access the individual Theme objects in the Themes collection causes FrontPage to crash in some cases. The method shown always works.

Notice that the code gets the Label, Name, and Format properties from the ThisTheme object. You might also want to view the Version or other properties, but these three properties are all you need in most cases.

The Format property contains the version of the theme, not the version of FrontPage. Most recent themes use version 2.0. When you download a FrontPage 98 theme, the version number is usually 0.0 or 1.0. Older themes might not have the same functionality as newer themes provide. Make sure you use version 2.0 or newer themes to ensure maximum browser and FrontPage compatibility.

The Label and Name properties provide essentially the same information. The Label property contains the friendly version of the name. Use the Label property when you want to create lists for users and the Name property when you want to create lists for selecting a specific theme for a Web page. Combine both fields (keeping the Name field hidden) when you need to ask the user which theme to select and then use that information to add the theme to the current Web page.

The code uses an If...Then statement to check the value of Counter. When Counter is less than 20, the code simply increments (adds one to) Counter. However, when Counter reaches 20, it's time to display the partial list of themes. To perform this task, the code must perform three steps: reset Counter (so it counts up to 20 again), display the partial list on-screen using the MsgBox() function, and reset Output so it doesn't contain the partial list of themes any longer.

It's possible that the themes list won't be divisible by 20, so there's a remainder when the loop exits. The final piece of code displays the final message box containing the remaining themes when Counter is greater than 1. When Counter equals 1, the application has just executed the code to display the partial theme list and clear Output, so there's nothing to display. Figure 7-3 shows typical output from this application.

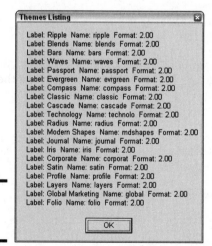

Figure 7-3:
Listing
themes.

Understanding the Webs collection

The Webs collection provides you with access to your Web site. The Web site can be a remote location or a local hard drive. Any time you open a site in FrontPage, you create a new WebEx object that FrontPage places in the Web collection. However — as with any other collection you might use — you can also add new Web sites to your FrontPage setup programmatically by creating a new `WebEx` object (using the `Webs.Add` method). Listing 7-4 shows how you can create a new `WebEx` object and then garner statistics and information from it.

Listing 7-4: Working with the Webs Collection

```
Public Sub DisplayWebs()
    ' Holds an individual Web object.
    Dim AWeb As WebEx

    ' Holds an individual folder.
    Dim AFolder As WebFolder

    ' Contains the output information.
    Dim Output As String

    ' Define a Web object.
    Application.Webs.Add "D:\My Web Site"
    Application.Webs.Open "D:\OnlineSite"

    ' Display some statistics.
    For Each AWeb In Application.Webs

        ' Get the site name.
        Output = AWeb.Title + vbCrLf + vbCrLf

        ' Parse the folder list.
        For Each AFolder In AWeb.AllFolders
            Output = Output + AFolder.Name + vbCrLf
        Next

        ' Display the results.
        MsgBox Output, vbInformation, "Web Statistics"
    Next
End Sub
```

This example begins with FrontPage as you initially open it. There are no Web sites open, so the code begins by opening two Web sites. Notice that one call uses the `Add` method, while the other uses the `Open` method. You can use either method when you're working with an existing Web. However, if you're converting a folder to a Web or establishing a new Web, your best bet is to use the `Add` method. Note that you'll need to change the locations shown in the example code to match Web sites on your local system (unless you add these folders to your machine).

After the code has opened some Web sites to work with, it uses the `Webs` collection to access individual `WebEx` objects. In this case, the individual object has a slightly different name from that of the collection it supports. Each

WebEx object contains information about the individual Web site, including a list of files and folders. You can also apply themes and templates, search for files or folders, and set viewing options (such as hiding specific files and folders).The code uses the AllFolders collection to get a list of all the folders the Web site contains. Each WebFolder object contains information about a single folder and any files (and other folders) it contains. You can also use the RootFolder object or Folders collection to access folders level by level (rather than all at once). In this case, the code records just the folder name.

You can also open a remote site by using the Add or Open methods of the Webs collection, using a statement such as

```
Application.Webs.Open "ftp://ftp.mysite.net/" ', "myname", "mypassword"
```

A Web site would use just the URL. For example, you might use Application.Webs.Open "http://winserver/0181" to access a Web site.

Some earlier versions of FrontPage seem to ignore Add or Open method calls that contain remote locations. Interestingly enough, all of the Microsoft examples show local drives as the location. In these earlier versions, FrontPage considers a remote location as a combination of a local and a remote Web site. Consequently, every time you open a remote location, you add two WebEx objects to the Webs collection. The DisplayWebsNoOpen sub-procedure supplied with the example code lets you test a remote Web site using display code similar to the code shown in Listing 7-4.

Understanding the WebWindows collection

The WebWindows collection contains one WebWindowEx object entry for every FrontPage window you have open. FrontPage associates every window with a single Web site. Look again at Listing 7-4 and you'll notice that the code opens two Web sites, which means that FrontPage opened two WebWindowEx objects. Every time you open a file located in the current Web site or create a new file, FrontPage also creates a PageWindowEx object that it places in the PageWindows collection. All these entries help you track the status of the open Web sites FrontPage is managing.

Understanding the relationships among these various objects is essential because you have to move from one to the next in a logical order. Listing 7-5 demonstrates how the various collections and objects interact. Because you can use index values with the collections, you can access a particular object quickly.

Listing 7-5: Working with the Webs Collection

```
Public Sub ListWebWindows()
    ' Holds an individual Web window.
    Dim AWindow As WebWindowEx

    ' Holds an individual Page window.
    Dim APage As PageWindowEx

    ' Contains the output information.
    Dim Output As String

    ' View each of the windows in turn.
    For Each AWindow In Application.WebWindows

        ' Get the window information.
        Output = Output + AWindow.Caption + vbCrLf

        ' Display the Web site associated with this window.
        Output = Output + vbTab + AWindow.Web.Title + vbCrLf

        ' View each of the pages in turn.
        For Each APage In AWindow.PageWindows
            Output = Output + vbTab + APage.Caption + vbCrLf
        Next
    Next

    ' Display the results.
    MsgBox Output, vbInformation, "Web Window Statistics"
End Sub
```

The code begins by creating the various objects needed for this example. Notice that the names don't precisely correspond to the usual naming conventions for collections and associated objects.

The first level of access is the `WebWindows` collection. The code uses this collection to get a single `WebWindowEx` object. A `WebWindowEx` object contains all of the content for a single window.

After the code gets the `WebWindowEx` object, it uses the `Web` object to determine the name of the Web site associated with the window. You have full access to all Web site information through the `Web` object and can follow this object down to locate both folders and files.

The `WebWindowEx` object also contains the `PageWindows` collection. Every open file tab in a window appears within this collection as a `PageWindowsEx` object. The code uses the `Caption` property to get the name of the file. The final step is to output this information. Figure 7-4 shows the results.

Figure 7-4:
The
relationship
between
Web
windows,
pages, and
sites.

Figure 7-4 shows that I have two windows open, both of which have an open Web site. Each of the windows also has two files open. The filenames for the local drive include the `file:///` `protocol` indicator to show that they're files, not some other type of object. The filenames for the remote site include the HTTP protocol to show they're located on a Web site.

It's also important to know that the `WebWindows` collection deals only with the local copy of a file when you work with remote sites that rely on a Remote Web Site setup. Unlike the `Webs` collection, which includes entries for both the local and remote `WebEx` object, the `WebWindows` collection contains only the local `Web` object. Consequently, when you list the Web site (including two open files), you see the output shown in Figure 7-5. The local copy of the Web site is listed — the remote Web site isn't.

Figure 7-5:
Remote site
connections
only include
the local
file store.

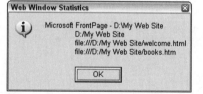

Working with FrontPage Documents

Documents are at the center of FrontPage operation, just as they are for any other application you use. The purpose of using an application is to manipulate data in some way. Even utilities, such as a server monitor or a network-security application, work with data. Consequently, getting the data-manipulation capability (in the form of document control) from your applications is important.

FrontPage documents are easier to work with than many documents because they're pure text: You can see any changes quickly and you don't have to worry about hidden elements. On the other hand, the FrontPage document environment is more complicated than many other environments because you have the concept of a complete Web site to consider. The Web site contains multiple folders, files, and resources such as graphics and templates. The following sections show how to automate Web site creation while keeping the complexities of FrontPage usage in mind.

Automating Web-site creation

Preparing a new Web site for use is a time-consuming undertaking if you do it regularly. Fortunately, in FrontPage this process is easy to automate so you can perform the task in seconds, without missing a single setting, and with extreme consistency. Listing 7-6 shows one technique for creating a Web site automatically (and some of the settings you might want to change).

Listing 7-6:   Creating a Web Site

```
Public Sub CreateWebSite()
    ' Contains the new Web site.
    Dim NewSite As WebEx

    ' Contains the default Web page.
    Dim WelcomePage As WebFile

    ' Create the new site.
    Set NewSite = Application.Webs.Add("C:\MyTempSite")

    ' Configure the new site.
    With NewSite

        ' Define the navigation key values.
        .Properties("vti_navbuttonprevlabel") = "Previous"
        .Properties("vti_navbuttonhomelabel") = "Go Home"
        .Properties("vti_navbuttonnextlabel") = "Next"
        .Properties("vti_navbuttonuplabel") = "Up a Level"

        ' Set the language and character set.
        .Properties("vti_defaultlanguage") = "en-us"
        .Properties("vti_defaultcharset") = "windows-1252"
        .Properties("vti_encoding") = "utf8-nl"

        ' Apply the changes.
        .Properties.ApplyChanges

        ' Refresh the site to match the new properties.
```

```
      .Refresh

      ' Define a theme for the site.
      .ApplyTheme ("Spring")

      ' Add basic folders to the new site.
      .RootFolder.Folders.Add "Graphics"
      .RootFolder.Folders.Add "Products"
      .RootFolder.Folders.Add "Contact Us"

      ' Add an initial Web page.
      Set WelcomePage = .RootFolder.Files.Add("Index.HTM")
      WelcomePage.Open
   End With
End Sub
```

The code begins by creating several objects. It uses the `Application.
Webs.Add` method to create the `NewSite` object. This is a local object that
you can publish later, using the `NewSite.Publish` method. For now, it's
easier to work with the Web site locally so data-transfer times don't become
a problem — and so you can maintain some level of security over the new
site.

Setting up a new Web site means modifying properties. You can see these settings by right-clicking anywhere in the FrontPage Web Site tab and selecting
Site Properties from the context menu. Modifying the properties in code is a
little more difficult because you have to discover the names that Microsoft
uses for the standard property entries. The example shows some standard
properties you can modify.

Microsoft doesn't tell you much about the 32 properties that a Web site supports. The help file for the `Properties` property tells you about only one
property — and it isn't even a default property. You can use the debugger to
learn the names of any default property supported by any FrontPage object.
In most cases, the vti properties are FrontPage Server Extension meta keys
(special words that identify FrontPage features). You can find a complete list
of these meta keys at the SharePoint Products and Technologies site:

```
http://msdn.microsoft.com/nhp/Default.asp?contentid=28001891
```

Look in the following folder, and you'll see the vti values in alphabetical
order, as shown in Figure 7-6:

```
SharePoint Team Services SDK\RPC Protocol\FrontPage Server Extensions RPC
   Methods\Meta Keys
```

Figure 7-6:
The hidden location of the vti values.

After the code changes the properties, it uses the `Properties.ApplyChanges` method to make the changes permanent. It then calls the `Refresh` method to synchronize the information between the program and the FrontPage application. You must perform both steps to ensure you can see the changes your program makes later.

Generally, you want the same theme used for an entire Web site so the pages all look consistent. The `ApplyTheme` method lets you apply a theme to a Web site before you create any pages for it. This step ensures that your Web site has a consistent appearance from the start.

When you know you need to create certain folders for every Web site, it pays to make them part of the setup routine. The code does so, using the `RootFolder.Folders.Add` method to add the three standard folders to this Web site.

Every Web site also needs an *index* — a default page. The code adds this page using the `RootFolder.Files.Add` method. Because you'll normally start working on this page immediately, it pays to have the code open it for you using the `Open` method. As a further refinement, you can automate the process of creating this initial page by adding code to write some of the page automatically. Listing 7-2 shows some techniques you can use to perform this task; Figure 7-7 shows the state of the Web site at this point.

Notice that the Web page includes the character set and the theme requested in Listing 7-6. These two additions will appear on every Web page, along with any other defaults that you include. A seemingly small change when you create your Web site can save you a lot of time as you develop the content.

Designing a basic template application

Templates can greatly reduce the work required to generate new Web pages because they take care of the common coding for you. All you need to worry about is the unique content of the page. Using templates also makes it easier to maintain a consistent page appearance because every page starts with the same content, layout, and functionality. Chapter 5 of Book 2 tells you all about templates, so use that chapter to create a template for this example.

When you have a template ready to use, it's time to make it work for you. Listing 7-8 shows how to use VBA to automate template usage in FrontPage.

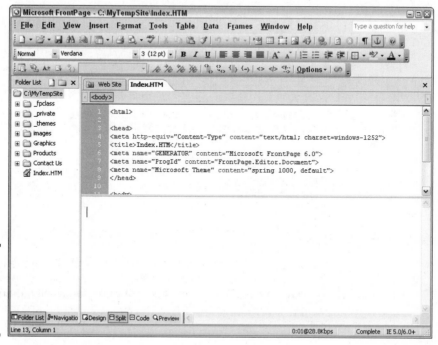

Figure 7-7:
The results of automatic site creation.

Book VIII
Chapter 7

Working with
FrontPage Objects

Listing 7-8: Adding Template Functionality

```
Public Sub MakeStandardPage()
    ' Contains the target Web site.
    Dim TheSite As WebEx

    ' Get the site.
    If (Application.Webs.Count > 0) Then
        If (Application.Webs(0).Title = "C:/MyTempSite") Then
            Set TheSite = Application.Webs(0)
        Else
            Set TheSite = Application.Webs.Add("C:\MyTempSite")
        End If
    Else
        Set TheSite = Application.Webs.Open("C:\MyTempSite")
    End If

    ' Set the Web site to use a template.
    TheSite.ApplyTemplate TheSite.Title + _
        "\Templates\Standard.tem", True

    ' Contains the target folder.
    Dim Target As WebFolder

    ' Get the target folder.
    Set Target = TheSite.RootFolder.Folders("Products")

    ' Contains the Web page template.
    Dim StdPage As WebFile

    ' Create the new page.
    Set StdPage = TheSite.RootFolder.Files("Standard.HTM")
    StdPage.Copy Target.Url + "\NewFile.HTM", True, True

    ' Contains the new Web Page.
    Dim NewPage As WebFile

    ' Open the page for editing.
    Set NewPage = Target.Files("NewFile.HTM")
    NewPage.Open
End Sub
```

The code begins by determining the status of the Web site. If the Web site isn't open, the code opens it; otherwise the code uses the existing copy. This code is a little crude, but it gets the job done. Your programs will require similar code to ensure they detect the FrontPage status and react accordingly.

Next, the code applies the new template to the Web site, using the `ApplyTemplate` method. This method enables you to replace templates as needed; it ensures that you can switch between document types. (For example, you might use one template for product information and another for contacts.)

You normally need to provide a location for the new file. The code assumes a standard location, but you could select a location in code if you use a form. The idea is to make the program flexible so you can use it for more than just one file.

At this point, the code has to make a copy of the template file and place it in the target location. The `TheSite.RootFolder.Files("Standard.HTM")` property contains the location of the template. The code uses the `StdPage.Copy` method to create a copy in the target location. (Notice that the code renames the file to `NewFile.HTM` as part of the copying process.)

Finally the code assigns the new file to a `WebFile` object and uses the `Open` method to open it for editing. You can add code here that helps customize the object automatically — for example, you can ask the user a series of questions that helps format the new file and add some content to it.

Book IX

Advanced Programming

The 5th Wave   By Rich Tennant

"Well, it's not quite done. I've animated the gurgling spit sink and the rotating Novocaine syringe, but I still have to add the high-speed whining drill audio track."

Contents at a Glance

Chapter 1: Using Active Server Pages

In This Chapter

↳ Working with ASP

↳ Developing with ASP

↳ Creating pages that use variables

Active Server Pages (ASP) is the name of a server-side scripting language developed by Microsoft for use with Internet Information Server (IIS). Microsoft originally designed ASP to replace Dynamic Link Libraries (DLL); the idea was to make updates to an application faster and easier. IIS still runs many applications as DLL, but ASP has proven immensely popular because it's easy to learn, fast, and relatively simple to update.

To use ASP, you create a file with an ASP extension on the server. As with all scripting, ASP relies on special keywords. You mix the HTML you want the viewer to see with these special keywords (which the server interprets) to create a cohesive package. ASP can make decisions to match the client, the server, the environment, or other conditions. The code also has access to server variables so you can (for example) display the time at the server as part of your Web page.

Understanding How ASP Works

ASP is a simple scripting language that mixes HTML code and script. The server replaces the script with an interpretation in the form of HTML. For example, when you include a request for the time, the output includes the time as text, and does not include the original request you typed in the code. You can discover more about ASP in *Active Server Pages 2.0 For Dummies* by Bill Hatfield. Microsoft has also created a special form of ASP for the managed code environment provided by the .NET Framework called ASP.NET. You can see how ASP.NET differs in *ASP.NET For Dummies* by Bill Hatfield.

Advantages and Disadvantages of Server-Side Scripting

Like all other scripting languages, ASP is interpreted when you request the page from the server. You write text with special code words that the server interprets and then sends as HTML to your browser. Unlike a client-side script, a server-side script doesn't require any special support from the browser, so you gain a significant advantage because there are fewer compatibility issues to consider.

ASP also lets you access the server directly. The simplest form of access is through server variables that describe the server and provide access to basic services such as the time. However, you also can create complex scripts that perform other kinds of access, such as working with databases or interacting with other servers. A server-side script can provide powerful access to your company and its data that isn't easily available using a client-side script.

Security is another advantage of using ASP. Unlike client-side scripts, server-side scripts are fully under your control. It's easier to create a secure environment using ASP than it would be using other technologies, so long as you follow basic guidelines such as checking inputs for data type and length.

The main disadvantage of all this processing power is that the script runs on the server — which means the server has to dedicate processing cycles and resources to the script. Thus using ASP incurs a performance penalty; you can handle fewer users with the server. In addition, running the code on your server could create reliability problems because the code can cause the server to crash. In short, you don't get server-side functionality free — you pay a price in performance and reliability.

ASP provides a lot of functionality — too much to describe fully in a single chapter. The following sections get you started and provide everything you need to write simple scripts. It's also important to know a scripting language such as JavaScript (which I discuss in Book 7). You can find a complete ASP reference at

```
http://msdn.microsoft.com/library/en-us/iissdk/iis/iis_web_pages.asp
```

Adding directives

You can create an ASP file that consists entirely of HTML and IIS will display it without complaint. In fact, you generally start an ASP file by creating a blank HTML file and adding any common HTML elements to it because the output ASP provides is HTML. (However, an ASP page that doesn't include any script isn't very useful.) Before you add any script to a page, you must add a directive that defines the script language you want to use. Directives tell IIS how to react to the ASP file. Here's an example of the language directive:

```
<%@Language = "JavaScript" %>
```

All such standard directives begin with the @ (at) symbol to set them apart from other types of instructions. The @ symbol is followed by a keyword, which is `Language` in this case. The keyword is followed by an = (equals sign) and the value you use want to use, which is `"JavaScript"` for this example. Always include the language direction in your ASP file, even though the value isn't absolutely required, to ensure that IIS always knows which language the page uses. Otherwise IIS uses the default language the Administrator sets up, which might not be correct for your page.

Defining script elements

All ASP script appears within a set of <% %> delimiters. The <% delimiter begins the script area and the %> ends the script area. IIS assumes that every piece of information outside the <% %> delimiters is HTML and displays this information directly in the user's browser. Always make sure your script appears within the delimiters. Listing 1-1 shows an example of an ASP file that contains a mix of HTML and script.

Listing 1-1:   Mixing HTML and Script

```
<%@Language = "JavaScript" %>
<html>
<head>
   <title>First ASP</title>
</head>
<body>
   <h1>First ASP Page</h1>
   <p>Time:
   <%
      // Create a date object.
      var Now = new Date();

      // Months have to be handles specially.
      var ThisMonth = Now.getMonth() + 1;

      // Display the date.
      Response.Write(ThisMonth + "/" +
                     Now.getDate() + "/" +
                     Now.getYear());
   %>
   </p>
</body>
</html>
```

This page contains all the HTML you would expect. In fact, if it didn't begin with the language directive, you could easily dismiss it as an ordinary HTML page containing a few odd characters and a script. All of the required tags are in place.

The script outputs the server date, not the client date. Consequently, the script points out an important difference between using JavaScript on the client versus on the server: You can create scripts that output dates for both client *and* server, as shown in Listing 1-2.

Listing 1-2:   Client Versus Server Scripting

```
<%@Language = "JavaScript" %>
<html>
<head>
   <title>First ASP</title>
</head>
<body>
   <h1>First ASP Page</h1>
   <p>Server Date:
   <%
      // Create a date object.
      var Now = new Date();

      // Months have to be handles specially.
      var ThisMonth = Now.getMonth() + 1;

      // Display the date.
      Response.Write(ThisMonth + "/" +
                     Now.getDate() + "/" +
                     Now.getYear());
   %>
   </p>
   <p>Client Date:
   <script>
      // Create a date object.
      var Now = new Date();

      // Months have to be handles specially.
      var ThisMonth = Now.getMonth() + 1;

      // Display the date.
      document.write(ThisMonth + "/" +
                     Now.getDate() + "/" +
                     Now.getYear());
   </script>
   </p>
</body>
</html>
```

The client-side script appears in a <script> tag, not within the <% %> delimiters. You need two machines (a server and a client) to see this setup in action. Set the client machine to a different date than the server. Display the page and you'll see that the server date matches the date on the server and the client date matches the date on the client. The date you see depends on where the script code is processed.

Also notice that except for the method used — `Response.Write()` versus `document.write()` — the code is the same for the client as for the server. Sometimes it's possible to write blocks of client code and server code that are practically interchangeable.

Creating a Simple ASP Page

One of the best ways to build your skill at working with ASP is to create pages and try out various techniques. You can build a whole series of pages that display text (for example), and save them as example code later. The easiest ASP page is the one that you build one step at a time, using the information you know in ways that do something new. The sections that follow take information you know about FrontPage and use it to build a simple ASP page.

Defining a simple display

Most developers create ASP pages according to how many HTML pages they want to automate in some way. For example, the developer might want to display the current date or perform calculations based on user input. Starting with an HTML page that already contains a lot of the information you need to present reduces the time spent coding and makes the development process easier. To create a simple ASP page, right-click the folder you want to use for storage and choose New⇨Blank Page from the context menu. FrontPage creates a new HTML page as usual. The only change from your usual routine is to give this page an ASP, rather than an HTM, extension.

Use the usual tools to create a display in Design view. The example uses a simple header, a label, and a text box, but you can use any tools you choose to create the HTML element of your display. Leave blank areas for the script generated information. For example, when you want to display the information in a textbox, create the textbox, but leave the content blank.

After you create the HTML, you write the script in Code view. Most scripts that you can create on the client also work fine on the server. The only time you can't move processing from the client to the server is when the processing involves client specific information such as the client date.

There are no particular limits on where you can place a script when you're using ASP, as long as the script appears within the <% %> delimiters. For example, you can place output from a script directly within a tag, as shown in Listing 1-3. In this case, the script outputs a simple piece of text that appears on-screen within the textbox.

Listing 1-3:   Writing Scripts Within a Tag

```
<%@Language = "JavaScript" %>
<html>
<head>
    <title>Simple Information Display Within Tag</title>
</head>
<body>
    <h1>Script Display Within a Tag</h1>
    <form method="POST" action="--WEBBOT-SELF--">
        <!--webbot bot="SaveResults"
                U-File="../_private/form_results.csv"
                S-Format="TEXT/CSV" S-Label-Fields="TRUE" --
        >
        <p>
            <label for="txtMessage">Message </label>
            <input type="text" name="txtMessage" value="
            <%
                Response.Write("Hello World");
            %>
            " size="20" id="txtMessage" readonly>
        </p>
    </form>
    <p> </p>
</body>
</html>
```

The HTML you create must follow the rules. Notice that this script appears as part of the value attribute of the <input> tag. The HTML ends with the first double quote, followed by the script, and begins again with the second double quote. When you view this page from the client, the text output from the script appears within the double quotes as it should.

The script itself uses the Response.Write() method to output the text Hello World to the user. Use the Request object whenever you want to view data coming into the server (or part of the server input mechanism) and the Response object whenever you want to output information from the server. For example, the server status information and the client request information are both part of the Request object, while the output stream is part of the Response object.

Processing GET input information

When you display a form on a Web page, you need to provide some means for getting that information from the user's machine to your server or you won't see the information the user provided. The two common techniques of performing this task are called the GET method and the POST method. The GET method requires the server to get the input data as part of the query string the user provides while the POST method places this information in the request header (text that tells the server what the user wants). To use the GET method of input processing, you tell the browser to build a query string. For example, a form might pass the string:

```
http://www.myform.com/GetMethod.asp?txtMessage=John&B1=Submit
```

In this case, the query string consists of two name-and-value pairs. The first name is txtMessage and its associated value is John. The second name is B1 and its associated value is Submit. Your code can process this query string and do something interesting with it.

> **TIP**
>
> Generally, GET processing of data is less secure than using the POST method because the GET method exposes the data through the query string. The POST method doesn't use a query string, so the data is less susceptible to damage or intentional modification. However, the GET method is more useful when you want someone to save the settings for the Web page as an Internet Explorer shortcut. That's because a shortcut won't save the hidden POST method settings.

Performing a GET or POST input setup

Before you begin writing any code, it's important to perform a little extra setup with the form you create. The following steps tell how to set up a form so you can process incoming information using ASP:

1. **Right-click the form you want to use to submit the data and choose Form Properties from the context menu.**

   You see the Form Properties dialog box.

2. **Choose the Send to Other option and select Custom ISAPI, NSAPI, CGI, or ASP Script from the drop-down list associated with the Send to Other option.**

3. **Click Options.**

   You see the Options for Custom Form Handler dialog box shown in Figure 1-1.

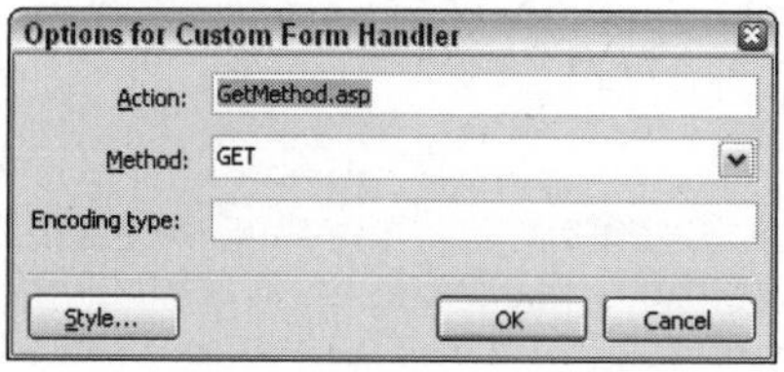

Figure 1-1:
Set the form submission options.

4. Type the name of the Web page used to handle the GET or POST input in the Action field.

5. Choose GET or POST in the Method field, click OK, and click OK again to close the Form Properties dialog box.

FrontPage changes the form options to allow for custom processing by an ASP script.

Writing the GET script

After you configure the form to rely on custom processing and design the page to contain all of the controls you want to use, it's time to add some script. One common task that developers use a script to perform is to accept input as a query string that configures the entries on a form. Listing 1-4 shows how to perform this task.

Listing 1-4:   Configuring a Form Using Script and the GET Method

```
<form method="GET" action="GetMethod.asp" name="MyForm">
    <p>
        <label for="txtMessage">Message </label>
        <input type="text" name="txtMessage" value=
            <%
                // Determine whether there is input to
                // process.
                if (Request.QueryString("txtMessage").Count == 0)

                    // If not, write a default string.
                    Response.Write("\"Hello World\"");
                else

                    // If so, write the supplied string.
                    Response.Write("\"" +
                        Request.QueryString("txtMessage") +
                        "\"");
            %>
            size="20" id="txtMessage">
    </p>
    <p>
        <input type="submit" value="Submit" name="B1">
        <input type="reset" value="Reset" name="B2">
    </p>
</form>
```

This example has two modes of operation, depending on whether the user provides a query string:

✦ When a user calls this page without providing a query string, the `Request.QueryString("txtMessage").Count` property contains 0 and the code displays a default value.

Notice that this example streamlines the code so the entry doesn't have a lot of extra spaces in it. You output a double quote to the Web page by using the `\"` escape code. The backslash tells JavaScript to interpret the double quote literally, rather than as a string delimiter.

✦ When the user does provide a query string (such as after clicking Submit), the `Request.QueryString("txtMessage").Count` property contains a value greater than 0. The value is 1 for every query-string entry that matches the index value you provide.

The code uses the `Request.QueryString()` method to obtain the query string value supplied by the user and display it on-screen in place of the normal default value. Saving the query-string values from a previous session allows a user to return to a form with the previous values in place. This technique saves valuable user time on many Web sites.

Processing POST input information

Using the `POST` method doesn't display any of the data the user is sending as a query string, so it's more secure than using the `GET` method. Someone using special equipment could still see and modify the information, but the casual user can't modify it. However, the fact that the `POST` method doesn't rely on a query string also means you can't use the same techniques as you'd use with the `GET` method to access the form's data.

After you configure the form using the technique found in the "Performing a `GET` or `POST` input setup" section of this chapter, you can begin adding code. Listing 1-5 shows the `<form>` portion of the code. This example performs precisely the same task as the `GET` method in Listing 1-4. Comparing the two listings will provide insights on how the `GET` and `POST` method differ.

Listing 1-5: Configuring a Form Using Script and the POST Method

```
<form method="POST" action="PostMethod.asp" name="MyForm">
    <p>
        <label for="txtMessage">Message </label>
        <input type="text" name="txtMessage" value=
            <%
                // Determine whether there is input to process.
                if (Request.Form("txtMessage").Count == 0)
```

(continued)

Listing 1-5 *(continued)*

```
                    // If not, write a default string.
                    Response.Write("\"Hello World\"");
                else

                    // If so, write the supplied string.
                    Response.Write("\"" +
                        Request.Form("txtMessage") +
                        "\"");
            %>
            size="20" id="txtMessage">
    </p>
    <p>
        <input type="submit" value="Submit" name="B1">
        <input type="reset" value="Reset" name="B2">
    </p>
</form>
```

The first difference you notice when looking at Listing 1-5 is that the `method` attribute of the `<form>` tag is set to `POST`, rather than `GET`. This simple change affects how your browser sends the data to the server.

This example uses the `Request.Form()` method to obtain data using "txtMessage" as the index. When the `Request.Form("txtMessage").Count` property for this entry contains 0, the code provides a default value as input to the textbox. Otherwise, it uses the `Request.Form("txtMessage")` method to access the form value and display it on-screen.

Working with session data

Session data is information that you don't display to the user but need to perform tasks with ASP. For example, the timeout value, the time the server will keep a connection open, is session data. ASP provides access to two kinds of session data:

✦ Permanent values that IIS defines for you.

✦ Special values you define as part of the session.

Session variables are permanent for the entire session, so you can use them to share information between pages. As a user moves from one location to another, you can track their session variables and ensure that whatever environment the user wants remains intact. One of two events will clear the session variables:

✦ The user closes the browser window.

✦ The session times out because the client hasn't sent a request within the required timeframe. This timeframe varies based on the Web server and the users that visit it — the Webmaster normally tunes the Web server to meet specific user needs.

You access all session data using the Session object. The Session object uses predefined properties for permanent values and the Collection property for values you define. Listing 1-6 shows how to use both session data types. The listing contains only the essential code — you can find the complete listing in the folder for this chapter in this book's companion Web site.

Listing 1-6:   Using Session Variables

```
<h1>Using Session Variables</h1>
<h2>
    <% Response.Write("Session: " + Session.SessionID); %>
</h2>
<h2>
    <%
        if (Session.Contents("PrevValue") == null)
            Response.Write("Previous Value: 0");
        else
            Response.Write("Previous Value: " +
                Session.Contents("PrevValue"));
    %>
</h2>
<form method="POST" action="Sessions.asp" name="MyForm">
    <p>
    </p>
    <p>
        <label for="txtValue1">Value 1: </label>
        <input type="text" name="txtValue1" value=
            <%
                // Determine whether to process input.
                if (Request.Form("txtValue1").Count == 0)

                    // If not, write a default string.
                    Response.Write("\"1\"");
                else

                    // If so, write the supplied string.
                    Response.Write("\"" +
                        Request.Form("txtValue1") +
                        "\"");
            %>
            size="20" id="txtValue1">
```

(continued)

Listing 1-6 *(continued)*

```
</p>
... Other input and output controls. ...
<p>
    <label for="txtOutput">Output: </label>
    <input type="text" name="txtOutput" value=
        <%
            // Determine whether to process input.
            if ((Request.Form("txtValue1").Count > 0) &&
                (Request.Form("txtValue2").Count > 0))
            {
                // Obtain the first value.
                var Value1 =
                    parseInt(Request.Form("txtValue1"));

                // Obtain the second value.
                var Value2 =
                    parseInt(Request.Form("txtValue2"));

                // Create the result.
                var Output = Value1 + Value2;

                // Display the result.
                Response.Write("\"" +
                    Output +
                    "\"");

                // Save the result as a session variable.
                Session.Contents("PrevValue") = Output;
            }
            else
                Response.Write("\"0\"");
        %>
        size="20" id="txtOutput" readonly>
```

The code begins by displaying the *session identifier,* which is a unique number for each session. When the client makes its first request, IIS creates a session identifier for that client — and the client keeps that number throughout the session. You can use the session identifier provided by the Session.SessionID property as a means for identifying a specific user.

The next task is to display the previous value of the calculation for this form. Because this is a custom value, the code accesses it using the Session.Contents("PrevValue") property. The PrevValue index identifies the custom session variable — you can use any name desired, but the name must be unique for the entire session or one value will overwrite values with like names. When this value is absent, IIS returns null (or nothing), so the code displays a default value of 0. Otherwise, it displays the actual session variable value.

You can mix data-storage techniques in a single session. The example also relies on the techniques used to access data saved using the POST method. This data is only accessible to this form, not every form on the Web site as session data is.

The txtOutput textbox performs a calculation rather than rely on user input for the data. The code uses the parseInt() function to convert the text data on the form into an integer value. It then adds these two values and places them in Output. Next, the code displays Output on-screen. Finally, the code saves the value as a session variable. Notice the technique used to assign the value to the session variable using:

```
Session.Contents("PrevValue") = Output;
```

Using Server Variables

Server variables tell you about the server and the information the server receives. For example, you can discover the server name by requesting the SERVER_NAME variable. The ALL_HTTP server variable tells you what information the client sent as part of its request.

You request a server variable using the Request.ServerVariables() method. Provide the name of the server variable you want to access within quotes as a method argument. Microsoft is constantly adding new server variables, so you should check the list at http://msdn.microsoft.com/library/en-us/iissdk/iis/servervariables.asp when you want to discover new server variables. Listing 1-8 shows several of the common server variables you use when processing user input.

Listing 1-8: Obtaining Server Variables

```
<body>
    <h1>Server Variable List</h1>
    <h2>ALL_HTTP</h2>
    <p>
    <%
        Response.Write(Request.ServerVariables("ALL_HTTP"));
    %>
    </p>
    <h2>ALL_RAW</h2>
    <p>
    <%
        Response.Write(Request.ServerVariables("ALL_RAW"));
    %>
```

(continued)

Listing 1-8 *(continued)*

```
    </p>
    <h2>SERVER_NAME</h2>
    <p>
    <%
        Response.Write(Request.ServerVariables("SERVER_NAME"));
    %>
    </p>
</body>
```

Some server variables appear to repeat each other when you read about them on the Microsoft Web site. For example, the descriptions of ALL_HTTP and ALL_RAW sound similar, but they're quite different. Although the client information you receive from either is the same, Figure 1-2 shows that each is formatted differently. The ALL_HTTP server variable returns the names of the server variables and their associated information, while ALL_RAW returns just the information.

The ALL_HTTP and ALL_RAW server variables return multiple pieces of information, but this output is the exception rather than the rule. Most server variables return just one piece of information (such as the SERVER_NAME server variable that returns just the name of the server, as shown in Figure 1-2).

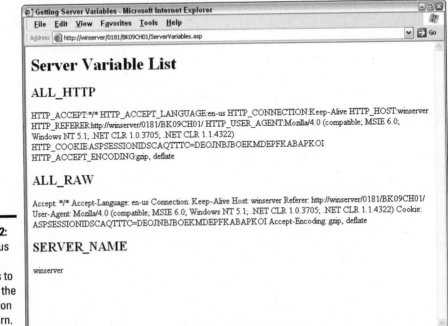

Figure 1-2:
Try various server variables to discover the information they return.

Chapter 2: Using PHP

*P*HP stands for PHP Hypertext Processor. This is what's known as a *recursive acronym,* one that uses the acronym itself as part of the definition for the acronym. Confused? Don't be. The name may be hard to understand, but the language isn't.

PHP is an open-source scripting language that's similar to Active Server Pages (ASP); it fulfills the same purpose for the Apache Web server, and for many other Web-server products. This chapter uses PHP with Internet Information Server (IIS) and discusses techniques for making it work in that environment. When you use PHP with a Web server, PHP provides server-side processing (working like ASP in that respect), not client-side processing (as JavaScript does). Make sure you also check out *PHP 5 For Dummies* by Janet Valade for detailed information about PHP.

Unlike ASP, PHP also works at the command line. You can create PHP applications that run at the command line, just as a JavaScript or VBScript application does. However, unlike JavaScript, which is truly a generic scripting language, the PHP focus is on Web pages. Even so, you can perform an amazing number of tasks with PHP at the command line.

Understanding PHP

PHP is an interpreter that accepts a mix of HTML and script. You create a text file with a PHP extension that the Web server passes to the PHP interpreter. The interpreter passes a resulting HTML page back to the server, which the server sends to the client. PHP is free — one reason it's so popular — but there are many other reasons, including these:

✦ **Multiple platform support:** PHP provides support for a number of platforms — and for a number of Web servers on each platform. When you write an application using PHP, you aren't tied to a specific machine, which means your application is a lot more flexible. You can write a PHP application on a Windows machine with IIS installed and run it on Linux with Apache installed — as long as you don't use platform-specific features (of which there are only a few).

✦ **Extensibility:** A number of third parties have written extensions to PHP, so it supports a wealth of interfaces. For example, you have complete access to components and controls on your system through extensions.

✦ **Fast productivity:** PHP is designed to make you productive very quickly. Knowing another programming language (such as JavaScript) definitely helps, but you can still write basic scripts without investing years of study.

✦ **Specialized text and document handling:** Unlike a lot of languages, PHP provides great support for a number of document formats. For example, PHP supplies a number of functions for working with Portable Document Format (PDF) files. It also provides great eXtensible Markup Language (XML) support. There are even functions for working with Shockwave Flash files.

✦ **Broad database support:** It's possible to interact with a number of Database Management Systems (DBMS) using PHP. A single application can include support for both SQL Server and MySQL (a free DBMS you can use on any Windows system).

One of the goals of PHP is to get as much community support as possible. When you look at any of the documentation online, you notice that people comment on it, augment it, and even provide sample code for the function, method, property, event, or object in question. This continual refinement process makes it easier for everyone to participate in the development of PHP and everyone can have a voice in creating new features. Contrast this kind of development with languages that are strictly controlled by a vendor — unless you're a big customer, vendors seldom listen to requests for individual additions.

Getting Set Up with PHP

The examples in this chapter show how to create PHP applications using FrontPage. However, FrontPage doesn't come with PHP support installed. In fact, Microsoft doesn't provide any instructions for working with PHP at all, so this chapter is really a step beyond the "normal" uses for FrontPage. To ensure that you can use PHP to its full potential with FrontPage, the following sections provide setup tips and hints you can use to create a good PHP installation — one that works well with IIS.

Downloading PHP

Before you begin working with PHP, you download it from the PHP Web site at `http://www.php.net/downloads.php`. Make sure you download the Windows binaries and not the source code. The binaries are already compiled (made executable) and ready to use. To use the source code, you must compile it first using any programming language product that the source code file supports — if you download C source, for example, then you need a C programming language product. You have two binary download choices:

+ **ZIP File:** This is a 6.7 MB download that contains all the binaries for the Windows platform. When you download this package, you have everything that PHP has to offer for Windows; you won't have to look for other PHP elements in the future. (However, you might still have to download support for particular extensions when you want to do something special. The PHP manual and online resources tell you when you need to perform such a download and usually provide the URL for the download site.)

+ **Installer:** This 1 MB download includes only the Windows installer for the Common Gateway Interface (CGI). The benefit of using this option is that it does reduce the overall download time, (especially for dial-up connections) and you don't have to waste as much space on your hard drive installing the full package. However, you pay a performance penalty by using CGI rather than Internet Server Application Programming Interface (ISAPI), which is a new kind of interpreter available for PHP 4. In addition, although this option performs some server setup for you, it doesn't install file-extension support, so you end up performing some manual configuration.

The PHP binary installation files don't include a manual. The best way to work with PHP is to use the online manual at

`http://www.php.net/manual/en/index.php`

Using the online manual ensures that you always have the latest PHP information, which improves the code you write and reduces errors (older documentation might have flaws). The links at the top of the page also provide access to newsgroups and other PHP sites. A special link lets you report bugs in PHP. As an alternative to using the online documentation, you can download the manual at

`http://www.php.net/docs.php`

Installing PHP

The installation procedure depends on which version of PHP you use and what platform you want to use. The PHP developers want to ensure you have the best possible installation instructions, so they provide a list of them at

http://www.php.net/manual/en/installation.php

Make sure you use the correct instructions for your platform and the binary file you downloaded.

IIS users run into a few problems that the installation instructions don't highlight very well (or at all). Generally, you'll get a better installation when you download the ZIP file and unpack it into a folder on your hard drive (such as C:\PHP4). Here are a few other things to watch out for:

✦ Always copy one of the INI (initialization) files from the PHP folder to the Windows folder. Name this file PHP.INI or the settings will fail.

✦ Use the ZIP-file approach when you're working with IIS 6.0 (the one found in Windows 2003). The Windows Installer approach doesn't work; IIS 6.0 has stronger security that the Windows Installer approach doesn't consider.

✦ Set the doc_root INI file setting, as described in the installation instructions, when you choose to use the CGI approach, but leave it blank when using ISAPI.

✦ Always leave the asp_tags setting in the INI file set to off. Otherwise your ASP scripts might not work properly.

Creating an IIS setup for PHP

The installation instructions don't really help much with IIS configuration. You can find additional IIS specific instructions at

http://www.php.net/manual/en/install.iis.php

However, these instructions are a little generic and you can get a better installation by taking a few detours. The following steps provide a quick and simple technique for configuring IIS to use PHP.

1. **Open the Internet Information Services console (Control Panel➪Administrative Tools➪Internet Information Services).**

You see a list of Web servers, Web sites, folders, and files for your machine and any remote machines you can access.

2. **Right-click the Default Web Site or other Web site you want to use and choose Properties from the context menu.**

   You see the Default Web Site Properties dialog box.

3. **Select the Home Directory tab and click Configuration.**

   You see the Application Configuration dialog box. This dialog box helps you configure IIS to use other file extensions so that you can display information from other sources, such as PHP. The PHP setup actually offers a number of options, but using the ISAPI setup offers the highest performance.

4. **Select the App Mappings tab and click Add.**

   You see the Add/Edit Application Extension Mapping dialog box. This dialog box tells IIS to run a particular application when a client requests a file with a certain file extension. PHP files normally use a PHP file extension, so IIS should run the PHP ISAPI Dynamic Link Library (DLL) to fulfill a PHP file request.

5. **Click Browse.**

   You see an Open dialog box.

6. **Select Dynamic Linked Library in the Files of Type field.**

7. **Highlight the** `PHP4ISAPI.DLL` **file (normally in the** `C:\PHP\SAPI` **folder) and click Open.**

   Windows adds `PHP4ISAPI.DLL` to the Executable field of the Add/Edit Application Extension Mapping dialog box.

8. **Type PHP in the Extension field. Click OK.**

   Windows adds the PHP file extension to the App Mappings tab of the Application Configuration dialog box.

9. **Click OK twice to make the change permanent. Close the Internet Information Services console.**

10. **Copy the** `PHP4TS.DLL` **and** `PHP4TS.LIB` **files located in the** `\PHP` **folder to the Windows system folder.**

    On newer systems, the path to the system folder is `\Windows\System32`.

    PHP is ready to use on your server.

Creating a Simple PHP Page

PHP is a very flexible language. You can perform an amazing number of tasks with it, both at the command line and within a browser. Creating simple PHP pages for experimentation purposes helps you understand PHP better and still do useful work.

Displaying a hello message

Remember that PHP works at the command line. One of the first tasks you might want to perform is displaying a simple hello message at the command line. This first example serves as a check to ensure PHP itself is working before you try it with IIS. Here's the simple hello-message code:

```
<?php
print("Hello World");
?>
```

The code begins with the special identifier for PHP script. Every PHP script starts with `<?php` and ends with `?>`.

Between this starting and ending point is an application statement. The `print()` function accepts a string as input. The string is *delimited* (set apart) with double quotes to show that it's a string, and to indicate where the string begins and ends. Every PHP statement ends with a semicolon.

You test this example at the command prompt. Simply type the code into a text editor such as Notepad and save it to your PHP folder with a PHP extension such as `FirstScript.php`. Open a command-line prompt and type **PHP FirstScript.php**. Then press Enter. Figure 2-1 shows an example of the output you might see.

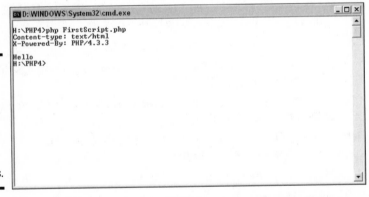

Figure 2-1: Use PHP at the command prompt as well as in Web site applications.

The code tells PHP what to do — display a hello message. However, that's not all the information that PHP supplies. The command prompt in Figure 2-1 shows three pieces of information:

✦ The type of content that PHP has processed — in this case, either text or HTML.

✦ The version of PHP used to process the file.

✦ The results of the command.

Getting the PHP status information

After you know that PHP is working, you can test it with IIS. The easiest way to work with PHP in FrontPage is to begin with a Web page. Create a blank Web page and add all the HTML elements you need to it. Don't worry about filling in any information that PHP provides immediately. All you want to do at first is create the HTML code.

The next step is to save the file, close it, and change the file extension to PHP. Now you're ready to add the PHP code. Remember that PHP is simply text, as with any other scripting language. Unfortunately, you won't get IntelliSense help when writing PHP code in FrontPage, but you can see it as plain text, which is fine for most simple applications.

The example in this section shows a special feature of PHP — one that you need to know about to troubleshoot problems. Listing 2-1 shows a special function you can use on a Web page.

Listing 2-1:   Diagnosing Problems by Checking PHP Status

```
<html>
<head>
   <title>A Simple PHP Script</title>
</head>
<body>

   <?php
   print(phpinfo());
   ?>

</body>
</html>
```

The code in Listing 2-1 might not look like much, but the `phpinfo()` function is very powerful. It tells you the status of your PHP installation — and probably provides more information than you'll ever need. Figure 2-2 shows typical output from the code shown in Listing 2-1.

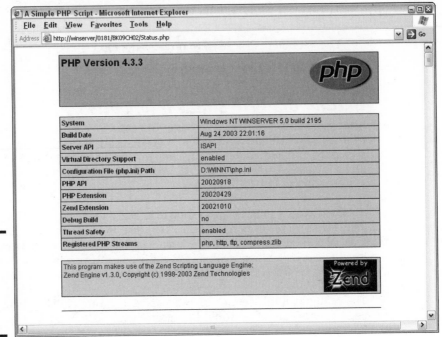

This page goes on for quite a while. It tells you about the version of PHP running on your system, the PHP settings, and provides a list of any extensions you have installed, along with the extension settings. You'll find this overview of PHP very helpful when you experience problems getting a particular feature to work.

One of the more important reasons to create this page, however, is to ensure your IIS setup is working. When you run the code in the "Displaying a hello message" section, you know that PHP is working, but this check ensures that IIS can connect to PHP to process pages. When you experience an error displaying this Web page, verify that you have created the correct file extension entries and that the PHP4TS.DLL and PHP4TS.LIB files are in the Windows system folder.

Using general programming techniques

PHP works like many scripting languages. Knowing a scripting language such as JavaScript (demonstrated in Book 7) is a good start because everything you know transfers directly to PHP. Listing 2-2 provides a sample of the various PHP control structures at your disposal.

Listing 2-2: Using PHP Control Structures

```
<html>
<head>
   <title>
      Basic Control Structures and Scripting Techniques
   </title>
</head>
<body>

<h1>Making Decisions Using If</h1>
<?php
   // Create a variable to hold the date.
   $Today = getdate();

   // Display the date information.
   print("The date information:<br/>");
   print_r($Today);

   // Use the date to make a decision.
   if ($Today[weekday] == "Tuesday")
      print("<p>It's Tuesday meeting time!</p>");
   else
      print("<p>It isn't Tuesday; back to work.</p>");
?>

<h1>Using a While Loop</h1>
<?php
   // Track the current count.
   $Counter = 1;

   // Perform this task five times.
   while ($Counter <= 5)
   {
      // Perform a task based on the value of $Counter.
      switch ($Counter)
      {
         case 1:
            // Print a random number between 1 and 10.
            print("The first number is: ".rand(1, 10));
            print("<br/>");
            break;
         case 2:
            // Print a random number between 1 and 10.
            print("The second number is: ".rand(1, 10);
            print("<br/>");
            break;
         case 3:
            // Print a random number between 1 and 10.
```

(continued)

Listing 2-2 *(continued)*

```php
            print("The third number is: ".rand(1, 10));
            print("<br/>");
            break;
        case 4:
            // Print a random number between 1 and 10.
            print("The fourth number is: ".rand(1, 10));
            print("<br/>");
            break;
        case 5:
            // Print a random number between 1 and 10.
            print("The fifth number is: ".rand(1, 10));
            print("<br/>");
            break;
        }

        // Increment the counter.
        $Counter++;
    }
?>

<h1>Using a Do...While Loop</h1>
<?php
    // Create a counter.
    $Counter = 0;

    // Perform a task at least once.
    do
    {
        // Display the counter value.
        echo("Counter equals $Counter");

    // Check the continuation expression.
    } while ($Counter > 0);
?>

<h1>Using a For Loop</h1>
<p>
<?php
    // Create an array of words based on a string.
    $StringArray = split(" ", "This is a split string.");

    // Process the array one word at a time.
    for ($Counter = 0;
        $Counter < count($StringArray); $Counter++)
        print($StringArray[$Counter]."<br/>");
?>
</p>
```

```
<h1>Using a Foreach Loop</h1>
<p>
<?php
    // Create an array of words based on a string.
    $StringArray = split(" ", "This is a split string.");

    // Process the array one word at a time.
    foreach ($StringArray as $Value)
        print($Value."<br/>");
?>
</p>

</body>
</html>
```

The example demonstrates a number of PHP coding techniques. The first task is to make a decision based on the day of the week. When you create a date variable using the `getdate()` function, PHP actually creates an array of date information. This array contains separate elements for the date, year, month, and other date elements, as shown in Figure 2-3. Variable names always begin with a $ (dollar sign) by convention.

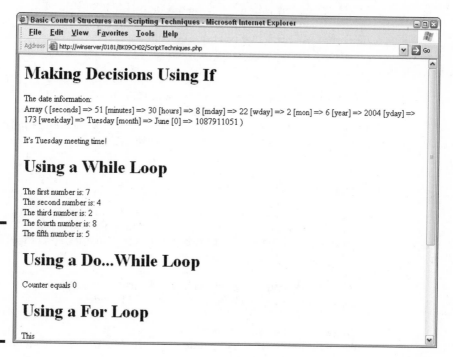

Figure 2-3: Use PHP control structures to change application data flow.

Notice that the code uses the `print()` function to display the string, but relies on the `print_r()` function to print the `$Today` array. The `print()` function displays general text, while the `print_r()` function is a special way to print complex variables. When you use the `print()` function to show an array, it displays the word `array`, but not the array content. The code also adds HTML tags to the output. Generally, you'll see better application performance when you display the HTML directly, but sometimes it's easier to place some HTML tags within your code.

Figure 2-3 shows keys next to each array value. You use these keys to access individual array values. For example, to access the day of the week, you use the `weekday` key like this:

```
$Today[weekday]
```

The code compares this value to `"Tuesday"`. When the values match, the code displays a message saying it's time for a meeting. On all other days, the message tells the user to get to work.

The next task in the list is to display five random strings and to identify each number with a unique string. To perform the task, the code combines a `while` statement with a `switch` statement. Each iteration of the `while` loop updates the value of `$Counter` until the output is greater than 5 and the loop ends. As the value of `$Counter` changes, the `switch` statement matches different cases and outputs the appropriate strings.

The `print()` function within the `switch` statement displays the random number produced with the `rand()` function. The `rand()` function accepts two input values, the minimum random number and the maximum random number that you want to see. PHP uses a unique concatenation (combining two strings) technique. Simply place a dot (`.`) between the two values, as shown here:

```
print("The first number is: ".rand(1, 10));
```

What actually happens, in this case, is that PHP converts the output of the `rand()` function to a string first. It then combines the string provided with the random-number string to produce a single string that is input to the `print()` function and displayed on-screen.

The next task is to demonstrate the operation of the `do...while` statement, which always executes at least one time. In this case, the code purposely sets `$Counter` to a value that is going to be false. When using a `while` statement, the code wouldn't execute even one time. However, the `do...while` statement does execute the code once; the expression is evaluated after the code executes.

Notice that this example shows a new way to output information to the display. The echo() function works like the print() function. However, you can use it to output multiple strings instead of the single string that print() supports. This example also shows another way to display the content of variables. PHP sees the $Counter in the string as a variable, not as a string, as shown in Figure 2-3. The output is Counter equals 0, rather that Counter equals $Counter as you might expect. PHP lets you place variables directly within strings for display on-screen.

PHP provides a wealth of string-handling functions. The next task is to split a string into individual words and display each word on-screen. The code actually shows two methods for performing this task. The first relies on a for loop, while the second uses a foreach loop. As shown in Listing 2-2, using a foreach loop can save coding time because you don't need to provide a loop counter variable.

The code relies on the split() function to display the string into separate words. You provide two inputs to the split() function. The first input is the character that divides the string elements you want to separate, which is a space in this case. You can use other characters (such as a slash to split date elements) as needed. The second input is the string that you want to split. The output from the split() function is an array of string elements (words in this case).

Notice how the code sets up the for loop. You use the count() function to determine the number of elements in an array. The code compares this value to $Counter and ends the loop when all the array elements are processed.

Working with Forms

If you need complex forms that respond to a variety of user needs, PHP makes them easy to create. As with other PHP applications, it's important to create the form first and then add the PHP code. Start by using an HTM file extension for the file so that you gain access to the full form creation features of FrontPage. After you create all the HTML elements — including all form elements — you save and close the file, change the file extension to .PHP, and reopen the file to add your PHP code.

Avoiding potential problems

FrontPage tends to add a lot of webbots and other special features to a form that PHP won't understand. This lack of FrontPage feature support is one of the issues you'll need to consider when deciding whether to use PHP for your next project. When you use PHP for a project, a good general rule is to avoid some of the FrontPage gizmos that could cause problems later. For example, don't count on using the Navigation view to set up a structure that will appear in your automatic page links — this feature won't work. You can still set up a structure (for planning purposes) in Navigation view, but you can't use that view to automate some tasks.

Another problem when using PHP is that you can't rely on the automatic form-processing capability that FrontPage provides. Use the following steps to set up a form for use with PHP.

1. **Right-click the form and choose Form Properties from the context menu.**

   You see the Form Properties dialog box.

2. **Select Send to Other and choose the ISAPI, NSAPI, CGI, or ASP Script option.**

3. **Click Options.**

   You see the Options for Custom Form Handler dialog box.

4. **In the Action field, type the location and name of the page containing the script that will process the form.**

5. **Select GET or POST in the Method field.**

6. **Click OK twice.**

   FrontPage sets up the form for use with PHP.

Processing a request

Form processing means accepting input from the user, doing something with the input, and then sending some type of response. PHP offers functionality similar to ASP in this case. You have full access to everything the client sends and can act upon it as you see fit. Listing 2-3 shows a typical form processing example.

Listing 2-3: Processing Form Data

```php
<?php
    // Process the request data.
    // Get the txtName value.
    if ($_REQUEST["txtName"] == null)
        $UserName = "Type Your Name";
    else
        $UserName = $_REQUEST["txtName"];
?>
```

```
<html>
<head>
   <title>PHP Form Processing</title>
</head>
<body>

<h1>Simple PHP Form Processing</h1>
<form method="GET" action="AForm.htm">
   <p>
      <label for="txtName">Type Your Name: </label>
      <input type="text" name="txtName" size="20" value=
         <?php
            print('"'.$UserName.'"');
         ?>
      id="txtName">
   </p>
   <p>
      <label for="txtReversed">Your Name Reversed: </label>
      <input type="text" name="txtReversed" size="20" value=
         <?php
            if ($UserName <> "Type Your Name")
               print('"'.strrev($UserName).'"');
            else
               print('""');
         ?>
      id="txtReversed" readonly>
   </p>
   <p>
      <input type="submit" value="Submit" name="B1">
      <input type="reset" value="Reset" name="B2">
   </p>
</form>

</body>
</html>
```

The form contains two textboxes and two pushbuttons. The `txtName` textbox lets the user input a name. The `txtReversed` textbox shows the name reversed after the user submits the form. The two standard pushbuttons submit and reset the form as needed.

The code begins with a PHP script that appears outside the Web page. As with ASP, a PHP script can appear anywhere in the file. In this case, the PHP script checks for a query string named `txtName`. When this value is `null`, it means the user hasn't submitted the form yet, so the code assigns a default value to the variable. Otherwise, the user has submitted the form previously and the code retrieves this value from the query string. The `$_REQEST` variable is an array that PHP creates for you by default; it includes any and all query string variables.

You can insert PHP code within an HTML tag. The second piece of code changes the `value` attribute of the `txtName` `<input>` tag. Because `$UserName` always contains a value due to the earlier processing, the code simply prints it. Notice how the code concatenates double quotes to each side of the value to ensure that it displays properly. PHP lets you use either the single quote or the double quote — interchangeably — for a delimiter, so the output can include one or the other as needed.

The `txtReversed` `<input>` tag also has its `value` attribute changed. This time the code changes the value based on the content of `$UserName`. When `$UserName` contains the default value, the code simply displays a blank on-screen. This action displays the form with a blank reversed name value until such time as the user enters a name.

When the user does enter a name, the code uses the `strrev()` function to reverse the character order. It then displays the text on-screen after concatenating the required double quotes.

Chapter 3: Working with Web Services

In This Chapter

✔ Working with Web services

✔ Using SOAP for communication

✔ Creating Amazon applications

✔ Creating Google applications

✔ Finding other Web services

*W*eb services provide a means of sharing code between two applications, even when the parties involved don't know each other. The Web service is the part of the application that offers something to a client application. For example, a Web service could help you search for information on the Internet, or create an insurance quote after your application provides the required input. The one element that all Web services share is use of the eXtensible Markup Language (XML) to exchange information. Book VI tells you more about XML.

XML is a great technology, but it doesn't provide quite enough structure to fulfill all Web-service requirements. A special form of XML is the Simple Object Access Protocol (SOAP). This technology specifies a message format that Web services can use and makes it easier to send and receive information.

Currently, there are three major public Web services that are hosted by Internet vendors: Amazon Web Services, Google Web Services, and eBay Web Services. Each Web service performs a specific task associated with that vendor. For example, you can buy and sell goods using eBay Web Services, look for information using Google Web Services, and purchase new or used books using Amazon Web Services. A number of other public Web services exist as well — more than many developers realize. This chapter discusses two of the most popular solutions: Amazon Web Services and Google Web Services.

Understanding Web Services

Most Web services rely on a request-and-response strategy. The *request* defines the kind of information you want to know and how detailed that information will be. The Web service returns the information you request (when it's available) in a standardized format — the *response* — specified by their database schema. A *schema* defines the organization of information in a database. The Web service vendor tells you about the request format and database schema as part of the documentation you receive when you request access to the Web service.

Many vendors also allow your application to request the database schema using a special format called Web Services Description Language (WSDL) described in the "Using WSDL to request data" section of this chapter. The use of WSDL is completely optional — the development environment normally uses WSDL to automate tasks, but FrontPage doesn't provide this kind of automation. Consequently, you almost never need to use WSDL with FrontPage. WSDL is useful for verifying the database schema when you suspect it has changed from the documented form and also helpful when working with development environments that access WSDL directly.

A Web service also performs some type of useful work. The useful work might be something as simple as interpreting your request, calculating the answer, and sending the result back. In many cases, the Web service accepts your request (normally some search criteria), interacts with the database through a search engine to obtain the information you requested, and sends the information back to you. You can also perform other tasks using Web services — for example, make a purchase or sell goods to others.

The final consideration for a Web service (at least from the Web-service user's perspective) is that it executes on the remote machine, not on your machine. In short, you're using resources on that other machine with the permission of the machine's owner. The remote machine can set requirements for using the Web service, as well as require you to perform specific setup and security checks as part of your request. In most cases, you need to obtain this permission by requesting it, usually as part of the Web service's documentation-download process.

Working with SOAP

SOAP is simply a specialized form of XML that creates a messaging system between a requestor (client) and a Web service (server). This section assumes that you already understand XML. To understand SOAP, you need to consider the features that make up a SOAP message. A SOAP message includes the following elements:

✦ SOAP message

✦ XML envelope

✦ HyperText Transfer Protocol (HTTP) or Simple Mail Transfer Protocol (SMTP) transport

Think about this system in the same way that you do a letter — with SOAP providing the letter content, XML as the envelope to hold the letter, and HTTP or SMTP as the mail carrier to deliver the letter. The most common transport protocol in use today is HTTP, so that's the technique described in this section. Keep in mind, however, that theoretically SOAP can use any of a number of transport protocols — and probably will in the future.

Understanding the SOAP package

A simple SOAP message consists of a package that contains both a header and a body (sort of the same arrangement used by an HTML page). The package is the root node required by all XML messages, so in that sense SOAP messages aren't any different from other XML messages. The package normally contains these two elements (the header is optional):

✦ **Header:** Contains information that isn't associated with the data itself. For example, the header commonly contains a transaction ID when the application needs one to identify a particular SOAP message.

✦ **Body:** Contains the data in XML format. When an error occurs, the body contains fault information, rather than data. See the "Considering SOAP message fault tolerance" section of this chapter for details on fault messages.

SOAP is essentially a one-way data transfer protocol. While SOAP messages often follow a request/response pattern, the messages themselves are individual entities — this means they don't rely on the immediate presence of a server, nor do they expect a response when a request message contains all of the required information. For example, some types of data entry may not require a response because the user is inputting information and may not care about a response.

The package in which a SOAP message travels, however, may provide more than just a one-way transfer path. For example, when a developer encases a SOAP message within an XML envelope, the request and response both use the same HTTP transport connection between client and server. HTTP creates and maintains the connection, not SOAP. Consequently, the connection follows the HTTP way of performing data transfer — using the same techniques as a browser uses to request Web pages for display.

Understanding the XML envelope

All SOAP messages use XML encoding. SOAP follows the XML specification and you can consider it a true superset of XML. In other words, it adds to the functionality already in place within XML. Anyone familiar with XML will feel comfortable with SOAP at the outset — all you really need to know is the SOAP nuances. Although the examples in the SOAP specification don't show an XML connection (other than the formatting of the SOAP message), every SOAP message contains an XML header.

Understanding the HTTP transport

The HTTP portion of a SOAP message looks much the same as any other HTTP header — in fact, if you don't look carefully, you might pass it by without paying any attention. As with any HTTP transmission, there are two types of headers — one for requests and another for responses.

An overview of the request header

As with any request header, the HTTP portion of a SOAP message will contain an action (POST, in many cases), the HTTP version, a host name, and some content length information. The Post action portion of the header will contain the path for the SOAP listener. Also located within a request header is a Content-Type entry of text/xml (meaning the message consists of a combination of text and XML) and a charset entry (generally utf-8). A *charset* (or *character set*) defines the way characters are encoded — how many bits are used to represent each character. The utf-8 entry is important right now because many SOAP toolkits don't support utf-16 or other character sets.

You'll also find the unique SOAPAction entry in the HTTP request header. It contains the Uniform Resource Identifier (URI) of the component used to parse the SOAP request. If the SOAPAction entry is "", then the server will use the HTTP Request-URI entry to locate a listener instead. This is the only SOAP-specific entry in the HTTP header — everything else could appear in any HTTP-formatted message.

An overview of the response header

The response header portion of the HTTP wrapper for a SOAP message contains all of the essentials as well. You'll find the HTTP version, status, and content length as usual. There are two common status indicators for a response header: 200 OK or 500 Internal Server Error. The SOAP specification allows use of any value in the 200 series for a positive response, but a server must return a status value of 500 for SOAP errors to indicate a server error.

Whenever a SOAP response header contains an error status, the SOAP message must include a SOAP fault section. The "Considering SOAP message fault tolerance" section of this chapter describes the fault portion of the message. All you need to know now is that the HTTP header provides the first indication of a SOAP fault that will require additional processing.

Considering SOAP message fault tolerance

Sometimes a SOAP request generates a fault message instead of the anticipated reply. Common sources of fault messages include these:

+ The server may not have the means to answer your request.

+ The request your application generated may be incomplete.

+ Bad communication may prevent your message from arriving in the same state as you sent it.

+ Messages that the client produces that the server can't process (the documentation you receive might be incorrect).

+ Errors on the server such as a missing application.

+ SOAP version mismatches.

When a server returns a fault message, it doesn't return any data. The message contains only fault information. With this in mind, the client-side applications you create must be prepared to parse SOAP fault messages and return the information in such a way that the user understands the meaning of the fault.

The fault message resides within the body of the SOAP message. A fault envelope will generally contain a `faultcode` and `faultstring` element that tells you which error occurred. All of the other SOAP fault-message elements are optional. The following list tells you how they're used:

+ `faultcode`: The `faultcode` contains the name of the error that occurred. It can use a dot syntax to define a more precise error code. The `faultcode` always begins with a classification — for example, a `SOAP-ENV` error code followed by a `MustUnderstand` subcode, which tells you that the server couldn't understand the client request. Because it's possible to create a standard SOAP `faultcode` list for a particular Web service, you can use these codes directly for processing purposes.

+ `faultstring`: This is a human-readable form of the error specified by the `faultcode` entry. This string should follow the same format as HTTP error strings. You can see the HTTP error-string format in the HTTP specification at `http://www.normos.org/ietf/rfc/rfc2616.txt`. A good general rule to follow is to make the `faultstring` entry short and easy to understand.

✦ `faultactor`: This element points to the source of a fault in a SOAP transaction. It contains a Uniform Resource Identifier (URI) similar to the one used for determining the destination of the header entry. According to the specification, you must include this element if the application that generates the fault message isn't the ultimate destination for the SOAP message.

✦ `detail`: You'll use this element to hold detailed information about a fault when available. For example, this is the element used to hold server-side component return values. This element is SOAP message body-specific, which means you can't use it to detail errors that occur in other areas like the SOAP message header. A `detail` entry acts as an envelope for storing detail sub-elements, each of which includes a tag containing namespace information and a string containing error-message information.

Using WSDL to request data

WSDL (Web Services Description Language) is another kind of XML file that provides a means for describing a Web service in detail. It tells you which methods a Web service supports and the kind of data (arguments) to provide as input. The WSDL file also describes the output of each function and some of the calling details, such as the URL to use for the SOAP message.

Most vendors supply WSDL so that the Integrated Development Environment (IDE) you use can create the method and argument definitions needed. In many cases, you can also view the WSDL file to fine tune and troubleshoot the applications you write manually. Some WSDL files become quite complex, however, so you should always rely on the documentation as your first source of information. Use the WSDL to find problems such as changes in the Web service that don't appear in the documentation (for example, changes in the arguments you provide when you call a method).

Some developers originally found WSDL less than helpful — and it doesn't work with every SOAP toolkit you can download. The SOAP samples help developers who must create messages manually get the format correct. However, when you use a product such as Visual Studio .NET, the IDE downloads the WSDL from the Web service site — and you won't actually have to worry about the construction of the SOAP message. Visual Studio .NET is still using SOAP to communicate, but WSDL removes all of the SOAP details from view.

You can find a wealth of resources about WSDL on the Internet. For starters . . .

✦ One of the more interesting offerings includes the ZVON reference at

`http://www.zvon.org/xxl/WSDL1.1/Output/index.html`

✦ The W3C has a tutorial at `http://www.w3schools.com/wsdl/default.` `asp`. Originally, Microsoft and IBM promoted WSDL on their Web sites, but you can now find the specification on the W3C site at `http://www.w3.` `org/TR/wsdl`. You can find the IBM view of Web Services at either of these sites:

```
http://www-106.ibm.com/developerworks/webservices/
http://www.alphaworks.ibm.com/tech/webservicestoolkit
```

✦ A WSDL search engine (where you can find services that rely on both SOAP and WSDL) appears at

```
http://www.salcentral.com/salnet/webserviceswsdl.asp
```

✦ Both major Web services described in this chapter provide WSDL access to their products. Google and Amazon have had this support from the beginning. eBay recently added such support to their Web service. Figure 3-1 shows a typical example of a WSDL file. This particular Amazon Web Services WSDL file, designed for American and Japanese users, resides at

```
http://soap.amazon.com/schemas3/AmazonWebServices.wsdl
```

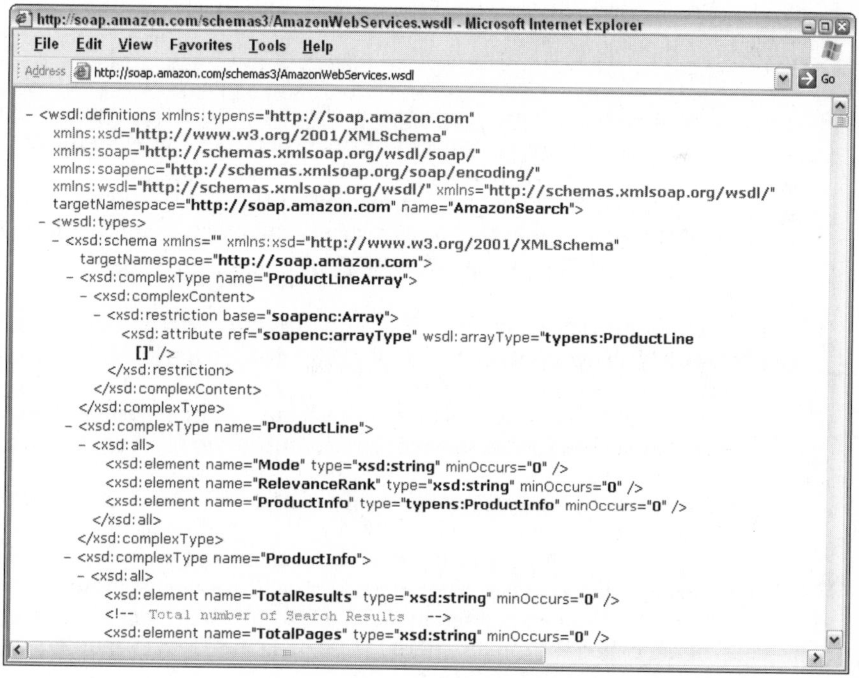

Figure 3-1: Check the WSDL file when in doubt about Web service documentation.

Figure 3-1 shows that a WSDL file really is just another form of XML. In this case, the XML file begins with some WSDL-specific definitions. The next section describes the database schema, including all the complex data types that the database relies on. When you scroll down a little farther, you find all the method definitions — the information you can request from Amazon. For example, Figure 3-2 shows the `AuthorRequest()` method definition used for the examples in the "Creating a Connection to Amazon.com" section of this chapter.

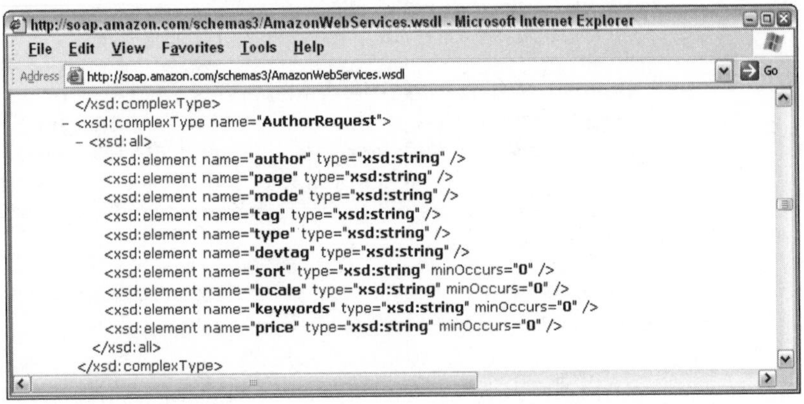

Figure 3-2:
Look for
method
declarations
to
understand
what the
vendor
needs as
input.

The method declaration tells you the name of an argument, such as `author`, and its data type, which is `string` in this case. Knowing these two pieces of information helps you create the right kind of input values. Look at the `price` argument entry. The presence of the `minOccurs="0"` attribute and value tells you that this particular argument isn't required for a successful call, but you can include it when desired.

Creating a Connection to Amazon.com

Amazon Web Services is one of the easiest public Web services to use. To obtain access to this service, you must sign up for it at

```
http://www.amazon.com/gp/aws/landing.html/ref=sd_str_as_ws/
```

After you sign up for Amazon Web Services and download the Amazon Web Services Kit, you can begin making direct queries from Amazon using nothing more than a browser. In fact, Amazon Web Services uses a special technique called REpresentational State Transfer (REST) that lets you make the query using a specially formatted URL.

Using a URL to contact Amazon

FrontPage developers can experiment with Amazon Web Services using nothing more than a browser and a specially formatted URL. The domain you contact using the URL actually connects to the Web service. The Web service reads the query string you provide, makes the appropriate request, and sends an appropriate response. Here's a typical Amazon Web Service request that you can simply plug into the Address field of your browser after you download and install the Amazon Web Services Kit (even though the URL appears on several lines in the book, you type it as a single line in your browser).

```
http://xml.amazon.com/onca/xml3?t=webservices-20&dev-t=Your-Developer-
    Token&AuthorSearch=John%20Mueller&mode=books&type=lite&page=1&f=xml
```

This URL may look complicated, but it's relatively easy once you know what the individual entries mean. The following list describes each entry in detail:

✦ `http://xml.amazon.com/onca/xml3`: This is the actual Web service URL for XML queries — SOAP queries use a different URL. All of the arguments — the description of the query — appear after the URL. You separate each argument with an ampersand (&). The list of arguments is separated from the URL by a question mark (?).

✦ `t=webservices-20`: This entry contains the associate number. You apply to Amazon to become an associate. When you sell goods for Amazon, Amazon gives you a percentage of the sale as an incentive. When you don't have an associate number, use the `webservices-20` value shown.

✦ `dev-t=Your-Developer-Token`: This entry contains the *developer token* of the requestor. Amazon issues this token to you when you sign up for the Amazon Web Services kit. This token is your permission to use the Web service; every request must include a developer token or the Web service won't honor it.

✦ `AuthorSearch=John%20Mueller`: This entry contains the kind of search, in this case an author search, and the author's name. Amazon supports a number of request types, but the `AuthorSearch` is one of the most common. Notice the query replaces the space in my name with a %20. You can't use spaces in queries, so you use this special character combination instead. The %20 represents an escaped character. You can use any of a number of techniques to convert a regular string to an escaped string. The example in the "Relying on XSLT to transform Amazon data" section, later in this chapter, shows one of the easiest and most reliable ways to perform this task.

✦ `mode=books`: This entry tells the Web service to look for books. You can also look for other product types such as CDs.

✦ `type=lite`: This entry tells the Web service to provide only an overview of the information. You can also tell it to provide the details by specifying a heavy search.

✦ `page=1`: This entry tells the Web service to return the first page of search results. If you want the second page, then you type page=2 instead. Amazon Web Services won't return any information when you request a page that doesn't exist.

✦ `f=xml`: This entry defines the query format. In this case, we're using XML. The Amazon Web Services supports other formats. In some cases, you can provide an eXtensible Style Language Transformation (XSLT) filename on your Web site in place of this entry. However, the XSLT file must be in a public place that Amazon Web Services can locate easily.

When you feel a bit more familiar with that long URL, try using it. Figure 3-3 shows typical results from this request. (Note that I replaced my developer token with `"Your-Developer-Token"` wherever it appears in the figure.)

Figure 3-3:
Use your
browser to
test Amazon
Web
Service
queries.

```
http://xml.amazon.com/onca/xml3?t=webservices-20&dev-t=Your-Developer-Token&AuthorSearch=John M - Mic...

File   Edit   View   Favorites   Tools   Help

Address   http://xml.amazon.com/onca/xml3?t=webservices-20&dev-t=Your-Developer-Token&AuthorSearch=John%20Mueller&mode=books!     Go

<?xml version="1.0" encoding="UTF-8" ?>
- <ProductInfo xmlns:xsi="http://www.w3.org/2001/XMLSchema-instance"
    xsi:noNamespaceSchemaLocation="http://xml.amazon.com/schemas3/dev-lite.xsd">
  - <Request>
    - <Args>
        <Arg value="Mozilla/4.0 (compatible; MSIE 6.0; Windows NT 5.1; .NET CLR 1.0.3705; .NET
          CLR 1.1.4322)" name="UserAgent" />
        <Arg value="1AQ02SF6NGHYG2YANQNV" name="RequestID" />
        <Arg value="us" name="locale" />
        <Arg value="John Mueller" name="AuthorSearch" />
        <Arg value="1" name="page" />
        <Arg value="Your-Developer-Token" name="dev-t" />
        <Arg value="webservices-20" name="t" />
        <Arg value="xml" name="f" />
        <Arg value="books" name="mode" />
        <Arg value="lite" name="type" />
      </Args>
    </Request>
    <TotalResults>94</TotalResults>
    <TotalPages>10</TotalPages>
  - <Details url="http://www.amazon.com/exec/obidos/ASIN/0672322919/webservices-20?dev-
      t=Your-Developer-Token%26camp=2025%26link_code=xm2">
      <Asin>0672322919</Asin>
      <ProductName>Peter Norton's Complete Guide to Windows XP</ProductName>
      <Catalog>Book</Catalog>
    - <Authors>
        <Author>Peter Norton</Author>
        <Author>John Paul Mueller</Author>
        <Author>John Mueller</Author>
```

Look at the top of the results and you'll see all the arguments used to make the query. You'll also find the total number of results returned by the search (94) and the number of pages required to display those results (10). After the general information, you'll find a list of book entries. These entries include information like the title, authors, publisher, release date, and price.

You can easily make mistakes in formatting your query string. The most common mistake is not including enough arguments to perform the search. In this case, you receive an error message such as, `Your request has one or more parameters missing. Please check and retry`. The most common missing argument is the developer token, but you should check all required arguments.

Another common error is not making the search specific enough. It may seem that you included enough information, but Amazon still returns an error message: `There are no exact matches for the search`. When this happens, make sure you specify a `mode` argument. Figure 3-4 shows a typical error message, this one with a missing `mode` argument. In this case; Amazon won't point out the missing `mode` argument — , but the list of arguments can help you spot specific problems in your request.

```
http://xml.amazon.com/onca/xml3?t=webservices-20&dev-t=Your-Developer-Token&AuthorSearch=John M - Mic...
 File   Edit   View   Favorites   Tools   Help
 Address   http://xml.amazon.com/onca/xml3?t=webservices-20&dev-t=Your-Developer-Token&AuthorSearch=John%20Mueller&type=lite&pa       Go

 <?xml version="1.0" encoding="UTF-8" ?>
 - <ProductInfo>
   - <Request>
     - <Args>
         <Arg value="Mozilla/4.0 (compatible; MSIE 6.0; Windows NT 5.1; .NET CLR 1.0.3705; .NET
           CLR 1.1.4322)" name="UserAgent" />
         <Arg value="15YTTKMQYBZ6E88KS8YM" name="RequestID" />
         <Arg value="us" name="locale" />
         <Arg value="John Mueller" name="AuthorSearch" />
         <Arg value="1" name="page" />
         <Arg value="Your-Developer-Token" name="dev-t" />
         <Arg value="webservices-20" name="t" />
         <Arg value="xml" name="f" />
         <Arg value="lite" name="type" />
       </Args>
     </Request>
     <ErrorMsg>There are no exact matches for the search.</ErrorMsg>
 </ProductInfo>
```

Figure 3-4:
Check for
missing
arguments
after
receiving
an error
message.

Creating a Web page to interact with Amazon

Normally, you need some means of transforming the data shown in Figure 3-1 to human-readable form. When working with FrontPage, using XSLT provides the best solution because it doesn't require a lot of coding. However, Amazon doesn't know how you want to present the date they provide, so the XML you receive doesn't include any form of XSLT declaration. The XSLT declaration normally takes the following form:

```
<?xml-stylesheet type="text/xsl"
                 href="amazon-seller-search-popup.xsl"?>
```

in the XML file. The `href` attribute tells where to find the XSLT file. Without this information, the browser will never display anything but XML on-screen. The situation isn't hopeless — you have other options, such as writing a script that performs the transformation process by using another technique.

The example in Listing 3-1 shows how you can download a response from Amazon, store the information locally, and use XSLT to translate it. The result is the same as you'd get by modifying the XML file to include the required linkage information — but the process is far more automatic.

Listing 3-1:   Translating Amazon Data Using XSLT and JavaScript

```
function GetData(XslFile)
{
    // Convert the author name to use %20 instead of spaces.
    var AuthName = SubmissionForm.AuthorSearch.value;
    AuthName = escape(AuthName);

    // Build a string that will hold the complete URL.
    var XmlFile = "http://xml.amazon.com/onca/xml3?" +
                  "t=" + SubmissionForm.t.value + "&" +
                  "dev-t=" + SubmissionForm.devt.value + "&" +
                  "AuthorSearch=" + AuthName + "&" +
                  "mode=" + SubmissionForm.mode.value + "&" +
                  "type=" + SubmissionForm.type.value + "&" +
                  "page=" + SubmissionForm.page.value + "&" +
                  "f=" + SubmissionForm.f.value;

    // Create an XML document object and load the data from
    // the Amazon Web Service into it.
    var XMLData = new ActiveXObject("Msxml2.DOMDocument.5.0");
    XMLData.async=false;
    XMLData.load(XmlFile);
```

```
    // Create an XSLT document and load the transform into it.
    var XSLTDat = new ActiveXObject("Msxml2.DOMDocument.5.0");
    XSLTDat.async = false;
    XSLTDat.load(XslFile);

    // Display the output on screen.
    document.write(XMLData.transformNode(XSLTDat));
}
```

The script relies on named text boxes on the Web page for input. The first
task the code performs is to URL-encode the AuthName value, using the
escape() function. You URL-encode values to ensure that they contain no
spaces or other special characters that could confuse the Web server. The
escape() function replaces such values with character combinations (such
as %20 for a space) that the Web server can understand. The code then combines the various values with the XML site's URL to create a request URL
(similar to the one described in the "Using a URL to contact Amazon"
section).

The next step is a little tricky and definitely Windows-specific. The code creates an instance of the Microsoft XML component. The ActiveXObject()
function performs this task. The Msxml2.DOMDocument.5.0 string identifies
the component. You might have to use Msxml2.DOMDocument.4.0 on older
machines — the last part of the string identifies the component version
number. Setting the async property to false is important because you don't
want the call to load the XML to return until the browser actually receives
this file. Finally, the XMLData.load() function loads the response from
the Amazon Web Service. The code now has a local copy of the data from
Amazon.

At this point, the code has data to work with, but no XSLT file. The next step
loads the XSLT file defined by the XslFile variable. The coupling between
the XML response and the XSLT occurs in the XMLData.transformNode()
function call. This call produces output that the document.write() function then sends to the current page. The result is that you see the transformed XML on-screen, as shown in Figure 3-5. The URL doesn't change,
even though the content differs; you're still theoretically on the same Web
page.

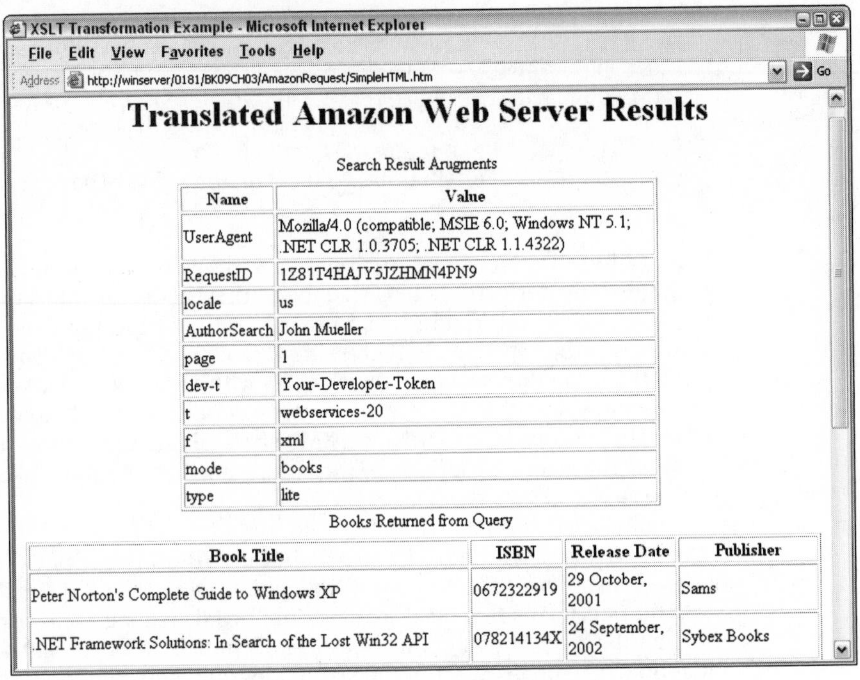

Figure 3-5:
Use XSLT to
create a
Web page
containing
transformed
XML data.

Relying on XSLT to transform Amazon data

The XSLT file used to transform the Amazon data creates two tables: One shows all parameters used to make the request (which normally you wouldn't include in a production system); the other shows the results of the search. Amazon provides an amazing amount of information about the books; the example shows only a few essentials to get you started. Listing 3-2 shows the XSLT file for this example.

Listing 3-2:   Creating a Transformed View of Amazon Data

```
<?xml version="1.0" encoding="UTF-8"?>
<xsl:stylesheet version="1.0"
 xmlns:xsl="http://www.w3.org/1999/XSL/Transform"
 xmlns:fo="http://www.w3.org/1999/XSL/Format">
<xsl:template match="/">
<html>
<head>
   <title>XSLT Transformation Example</title>
</head>
<body>
   <!-- Display a heading. -->
```

```
<h1>Translated Amazon Web Server Results</h1>

<!-- Displays the arguments used_u102 ?or the call. -->
<table align="center" border="1" width="60%">
    <caption>Search Result Arugments</caption>
    <tbody>
        <tr>
            <th>Name</th>
            <th>Value</th>
        </tr>
        <xsl:for-each select="ProductInfo/Request/Args/Arg">
            <tr>
                <td><xsl:value-of select="@name"/></td>
                <td><xsl:value-of select="@value"/></td>
            </tr>
        </xsl:for-each>
    </tbody>
</table>

<!-- Display the search result values. -->
<table align="center" border="1" width="100%">
    <caption>Books Returned from Query</caption>
    <tbody>
        <tr>
            <th>Book Title</th>
            <th>ISBN</th>
            <th>Release Date</th>
            <th>Publisher</th>
        </tr>
        <xsl:for-each select="ProductInfo/Details">
            <tr>
                <td><xsl:value-of select="ProductName"/></td>
                <td><xsl:value-of select="Asin"/></td>
                <td><xsl:value-of select="ReleaseDate"/></td>
                <td><xsl:value-of select="Manufacturer"/></td>
            </tr>
        </xsl:for-each>
    </tbody>
</table>

</body>
</html>
</xsl:template>
</xsl:stylesheet>
```

The code begins with the usual declarations. It then outputs the heading. Notice that this is pure HTML and that the code isn't doing anything but outputting this text. The code moves on to the body where it outputs a heading.

The XSLT-specific code begins when the code starts creating a table. Notice the head of the table is standard HTML, but that the next selection is an `<xsl:for-each>` element. This statement tells the parser to look at all the child elements of the `ProductInfo/Request/Args/` node of the Amazon response data. The system will process each `<Arg>` element in turn. The next step is to use the `<xsl:value-of>` element to retrieve the name and value attributes of each `<Arg>` element. Notice how the code uses the `attribute` axis to ensure the parser retrieves the attribute values and not the element values.

After the code processes all arguments, it moves on to the `<Details>` element of the Amazon response data. The code uses the `<xsl:for-each>` element again to select each of the books in turn. It uses the `<xsl:value-of>` element to select each element value in turn. Notice that in this case, the code doesn't rely on an axis; it uses the selected element directly. The code ends by completing the HTML page, and then completing both the template and the stylesheet.

Creating a Connection to Google

Google is a little more complex to use than Amazon Web Services because it relies on SOAP, rather than REST, to perform its work. Like Amazon, you have to sign up for Google before you can use their Web service. Amazon and Google Web Services represent the two most common alternatives to providing your own Web-service capabilities. Some custom Web-service-access solutions are in use, but these are generally giving way to pure SOAP or pure REST techniques. For example, eBay started as a custom solution, but has recently added full SOAP support, similar to that of Google Web Services.

Even though Google Web Services uses a different access technique from Amazon Web Services, the actual process is quite similar. In both cases, you perform three tasks:

✦ Create code to access the Web service.

✦ Provide a means of translating the data so you can see it on-screen.

✦ Create an XSLT file to perform the transformation.

As with Amazon Web Services, you must download the Google Web Services Kit to use Google Web Services. As part of the download process, you fill out forms that tell Google that you'll abide by their rules. After the request process is complete, you receive a developer key for using Google Web Service in your e-mail. You can download the kit at

`http://www.google.com/apis/`

Making the call

The first task is to call Google to obtain the data you need. In this case, you create objects that let you perform a SOAP request. The code in Listing 3-3 is Microsoft-platform-specific, but the essential steps apply to any platform. You must create some type of SOAP object, fill it with request data, and send it to Google. In this case, the call performs an advanced Google search.

Listing 3-3: Using SOAP to Call Google

```
function CallGoogle()
{
   // Create the SOAP client.
   var SoapClient = new ActiveXObject("MSSOAP.SoapClient30");

   // Initialize the SOAP client so it can access Google
   // Web Services.
   SoapClient.MSSoapInit(
      "http://api.google.com/GoogleSearch.wsdl",
      "GoogleSearchService",
      "GoogleSearchPort");

   // Make a search request.
   var ThisResult =
      SoapClient.doGoogleSearch(
         "Your-License-Key",
         SubmissionForm.SearchStr.value,
         1,
         10,
         false,
         "",
         false,
         "",
         "",
         "");

   // Return the results.
   return ThisResult;
}
```

The code begins by creating a SOAP client. When the client communicates with the server, it ensures that the message traffic flows as anticipated and that the request is formed correctly. The `SoapClient.MSSoapInit()` function creates a connection to the server. This step isn't the same as sending data to the server — all it does is create the connection. Make special note of these tasks that the `SoapClient.MSSoapInit()` function performs:

✦ Downloads the most current copy of the Google WSDL file from the Web site and uses it as a basis for making calls.

✦ Creates a specific name for the task that the Web service call will perform in the form of a Web service name.

✦ Specifies the port, the point of connection, to the Web service.

At this point, the code can make a request of Google Web Services. It performs this task by sending all of the required arguments as part of the SoapClient.doGoogleSearch(*key*, *q*, *start*, *maxResults*, *filter*, *restrict*, *safeSearch*, *lr*, *Ie*, *oe*) function call. Here's a list of the arguments and their meanings:

✦ *key:* Every request you make requires the license key you obtained from Google. When you make a request without the license key or using the key found in the Google examples, you'll receive an invalid authorization key message.

The examples in this chapter use "Your-License-Key" as the sample key. You must replace the sample key with a real key.

✦ *q:* This string argument contains the search request. Google accepts a string of any length, but uses only up to ten arguments to perform the search.

✦ *start:* This numeric argument contains the 0-based starting point for the search. You must couple this starting point with the number of results you request, with 10 results being the maximum. Consequently, if you want to view the third set of results and you request 10 results for each set, you would set this argument to 30.

✦ *maxResults:* Google lets you request a maximum of 10 results.

✦ *filter:* The documentation doesn't make this particular argument very clear. You provide true or false as the input values — not the values described in the Automatic Filtering section of the Google Web API Reference. Turning filtering on means that Google looks for results that have the same title and snippet. The Web service returns only the first result with a particular title and eliminates the others. In addition, Google returns only the first two results from a particular Web host.

✦ *restrict:* This argument restricts the results you receive to a particular country of origin. Don't confuse this argument with a language restriction. For example, when you select the United States as the country of origin, you could still receive pages written in Spanish or German. However, you won't receive results from either Spain or Germany. The Restricts section of the Google Web API Reference contains a chart of country codes you must use for this argument.

✦ *safeSearch:* Generally, you can use this argument to ensure you don't receive any results with pornographic or other objectionable content.

✦ *lr:* Sometimes you need a result in a specific language. This argument doesn't restrict the country that you get a result from, but it does restrict the language of the result. For example, you could tell Google that you want results written only in Japanese. The Restricts section of the Google Web API Reference contains a chart of country codes you must use for this argument. As with most restrictions, this argument will create holes in the result set and affect the start argument value.

✦ *Ie* **and** *oe:* These arguments are ignored. You still need to provide them as part of the SOAP message, but leave the content blank (an empty string).

On return from the call, `ThisResult` contains the return data from Google in the form of a SOAP message. This object isn't an XML document. You must retrieve the XML document by using the technique shown in Listing 3-4.

Translating the request

It's important to remember that Google uses SOAP, not straight XML, to respond to a request. Consequently, you can't load the information directly into an XML document to process it. Listing 3-4 shows how the code retrieves just the body of the SOAP message — the part containing the XML data — which it can then process using XSLT.

Listing 3-4: Translating Google Data Using XSLT and JavaScript

```
function GetData(XslFile)
{
   // Get the search data.
   var TheResult = CallGoogle();

   // Place the resulting information in an XML document.
   var ProcDoc = new ActiveXObject("Msxml2.DOMDocument.4.0");
   ProcDoc.async = false;
   ProcDoc.loadXML(TheResult.context.xml);

   // Create an XSLT document and load the transform into it.
   var XSLTData = new
         ActiveXObject("Msxml2.DOMDocument.4.0");
   XSLTData.async = false;
   XSLTData.load(XslFile);

   // Display the output on screen.
   document.write(ProcDoc.transformNode(XSLTData));
}
```

Before the script can do anything, it must obtain the search results from Google. When using Google Web Services, you must rely on SOAP to perform this task. SOAP is extremely flexible, so you can use a number of techniques to make a request with it. The "Making the call" section of the chapter shows one such technique.

The next step is a little tricky and definitely Windows-specific: The code creates an instance of the Microsoft XML component. The `ActiveXObject()`

function performs this task. The `Msxml2.DOMDocument.4.0` string identifies the component. You might have to use `Msxml2.DOMDocument.5.0` on newer machines with Microsoft Office 2003 or another new product loaded — the last part of the string identifies the component version number. Setting the `async` property to `false` is important because you don't want the call to load the XML to return until the browser actually receives this file. Finally, the `ProcDoc.loadXML()` function loads the response from Google Web Services. Notice that the code uses the `loadXML()` function to load text formatted as XML, rather than XML from a file.

The code now has a local copy of the data from Google. This local copy will disappear as soon as the function ends, so you don't have to worry about update requirements, but it's important to understand that the copy resides in memory on your machine somewhere.

At this point, the code has data to work with, but no XSLT file. The next step loads the XSLT file defined by the `XslFile` variable. Notice that the code uses the `XSLTData.load()` function because the XML appears in a file that the application must load into memory. The coupling between the XML response and the XSLT occurs in the `XMLData.transformNode()` function call. This call produces output that the `document.write()` function then sends to the current page. The result is that you see the transformed XML on-screen, as shown in Figure 3-6. Notice that the URL doesn't change, even though the content differs; you're still (theoretically) on the same Web page.

Figure 3-6:
Use XSLT to transform the Google data.

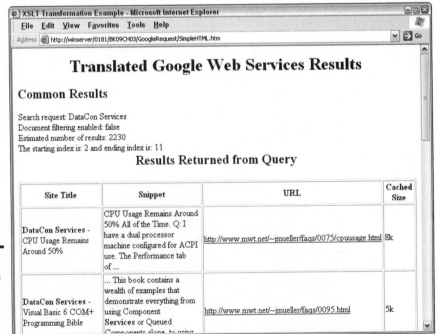

Displaying the data on-screen

Google Web Services can provide a lot of information about each site that you obtain as part of a search request. Generally, all you need is the title, description, link, and optionally the download size of the site to make a decision about it. Listing 3-5 shows how to display these various pieces of information so they appear as shown in Figure 3-6.

Listing 3-5:   Creating a Transformed View of Google Data

```
<?xml version="1.0" encoding="UTF-8"?>
<xsl:stylesheet version="1.0"
   xmlns:xsl="http://www.w3.org/1999/XSL/Transform"
   xmlns:fo="http://www.w3.org/1999/XSL/Format">
<xsl:output method="xml" indent="yes"/>
<xsl:template match="/return">
<html>
<head>
   <title>XSLT Transformation Example</title>
</head>
<body>
   <!-- Display a heading. -->
   <h1 align="center">Translated Google Web Services
         Results</h1>

   <!-- Display some common information. -->
   <h2>Common Results</h2>
   <label>
      Search request:
      <xsl:value-of select="searchQuery"/>
   </label><br/>
   ... Other Common Results ...

   <!-- Display the search result values. -->
   <table align="center" border="1" width="100%">
      <caption><h2>Results Returned from Query</h2></caption>
      <tbody>
         <tr>
            <th>Site Title</th>
            <th>Snippet</th>
            <th>URL</th>
            <th>Cached Size</th>
         </tr>
         <xsl:for-each select="resultElements/item">
            <tr>
               <td>
                  <xsl:value-of select="title"
                     disable-output-escaping="yes"/>
               </td>
```

(continued)

Listing 3-5 *(continued)*

```
                    <td>
                       <xsl:value-of select="snippet"
                          disable-output-escaping="yes"/>
                    </td>
                    <td>
                       <xsl:text disable-output-escaping="yes">
                          &lt;a href='
                       </xsl:text>
                       <xsl:value-of select="URL"/>
                       <xsl:text disable-output-escaping="yes">
                          '&gt;
                       </xsl:text>
                       <xsl:value-of select="URL"/>
                       <xsl:text disable-output-escaping="yes">
                          &lt;/a&gt;
                       </xsl:text>
                    </td>
                    <td><xsl:value-of select="cachedSize"/></td>
                 </tr>
              </xsl:for-each>
           </tbody>
        </table>

   </body>
   </html>
   </xsl:template>
   </xsl:stylesheet>
```

The code begins with the usual declarations. The `<xsl:output method= "xml" indent="yes"/>` tag is important because it determines the kind of output the parser creates. You can also choose `text` as the output method or tell the parser that you don't want the output indented. Notice that the code also matches the `return` element, using the `<xsl:template match= "/return">` tag. All the data appears within this element; you may as well match the root node of the XML document.

The code then outputs the heading. Notice that this is pure HTML and that the code isn't doing anything but outputting this text. The code moves on to the body where it outputs a heading.

The XSLT-specific code begins when the code outputs some of the common information returned by Google. None of this information requires special handling, so the code uses a simple `<xsl:value-of select="searchQuery"/>` tag to retrieve and display the information. The information is surrounded by descriptive text and enclosed within a `<label>` to make it easier to see.

Each return value requires special handling, so the code relies on a table. Notice the head of the table is standard HTML, but that the next selection is an `<xsl:for-each>` element. This statement tells the parser to look at all of the children of the `resultElements/item` node. The system will process each `<item>` element in turn. The next step is to use the `<xsl:value-of>` element to retrieve the name and value attributes of each `<item>` element. Because some of these entries contain the text version of the HTML tags — such as `&gt;` for the greater-than (>) symbol — you must include `disable-output-escaping="yes"` attribute with the `<xsl:value-of>` element. Otherwise the code displays the > symbol but doesn't create a tag. The code ends by completing the HTML page, and then completing both the template and the stylesheet.

Locating Other Web Services

You may find the Web services described in this chapter indispensable and want to try Web services from other vendors. Public Web services are popping up in unexpected places; in time, standards organizations will set up directories to make access easier. For now, here are some Web-service sites to try:

✦ **Microsoft MapPoint Web Service:** `http://www.microsoft.com/mappoint/net/`

✦ **Web Services Finder:** `http://www.15seconds.com/WebService/`

✦ **The Flash-DB Web Services Directory:** `http://www.flash-db.com/services/`

The Web Services Finder is simply a search engine that helps you locate Web services. Type in a task you want done and the search engine looks for a Web service to perform the task.

The Flash-DB Web Services Directory is especially nice; many of these Web services perform essential tasks and are exceptionally easy to use. For example, you can provide a UPC symbol as input to one Web service and receive produce information as a response. Another Web service lets you provide a ZIP code as input and provides a location as output.

Chapter 4: Enhancing FrontPage with Visual Studio .NET

In This Chapter

✔ Understanding FrontPage extensions

✔ Writing a FrontPage extension

✔ Using the new FrontPage extension

*Y*ou might never need a chapter that shows how to create FrontPage extensions (added programs that make FrontPage more useful) using Visual Studio .NET (Microsoft's premier programming language product). Given all the capabilities that FrontPage possesses, you can already create Web applications that contain both simple and complex scripts. Using FrontPage, you can process user data on the client or the server; using VBA, you can automate tasks and even add features to FrontPage. In fact, careful VBA programming even lets you interact with other Office applications. Even so, you might eventually need another solution for reasons like these:

✦ VBA runs too slow

✦ You want to perform a task that VBA doesn't support

✦ You want to protect your valuable source code from prying eyes

✦ Developers in your organization already know a .NET language

If that's the case, one alternative solution is to enhance the capabilities of FrontPage by adding extensions. This chapter assumes that you know how to use Visual Studio .NET fairly well — that you've already created several applications with it.

Creating FrontPage Extensions

The purpose of building a FrontPage extension is to do something that you can't do using standard techniques such as VBA or scripting. The following list describes a few of the common issues you must consider for any FrontPage extension:

✦ **Easy interface:** FrontPage provides an exceptionally easy interface when working with Visual Studio .NET. For one thing, you really don't worry too much about individual documents — a FrontPage extension can work with documents generically. FrontPage is so easy to use because you don't have to consider which document is loaded unless you really *want* to work with a specific document.

✦ **Generic extensions:** When you're working with some Office products, you find that an extension becomes document-specific by default because you attach the extension to the document through the Properties dialog box. With Word, for example, you add two entries on the Custom tab: The first defines the location of the DLL containing the extension; the second contains the DLL name. These two entries load the extension DLL for that document, but not for any other document you might have loaded. In addition, you're limited to just one extension per document, so the code will have to cover all needs for that document.

✦ **Document- and context-checking code is required:** Not everything about working with FrontPage makes life easier. For one thing, the generic nature of extensions can backfire on you unless you perform a lot of checking within the extension code. A user could (for example) load an XML file and try to run an extension that you created for HTM files. The result could be somewhat humorous or downright terrible, depending on the features provided by your FrontPage extension.

✦ **Extensive project setup is required:** A FrontPage extension is different from a Word or Excel extension; while creating it, you don't attach the extension to a document. Instead of using (for example) the Class Library project — which is relatively simple to set up — you must use the Shared Add-in project, which requires more effort. Consequently, although FrontPage extensions are exceptionally easy to code, they also require more time because the project requires more detailed definition.

Creating a FrontPage Extension

In addition to requiring more attention to detail, FrontPage extensions also require specific .NET support on both the server and the client:

✦ You must have a copy of Visual Studio .NET — preferably Visual Studio .NET 2003 — to work with the example in this section. Make sure you have the .NET Framework 1.1 installed on your development system.

Although you don't absolutely have to have all this support installed (an older version of Visual Studio .NET or the .NET Framework will do), using the latest version of all the required software provides a better chance of success.

✦ The user must also have the .NET Framework 1.1 installed. In fact, the user must have the same version of the .NET Framework you do, to ensure maximum compatibility. Users can download the .NET Framework at

```
http://msdn.microsoft.com/library/default.asp?url=/downloads/list/
    netdevframework.asp.
```

Creating the project

This example relies on the Shared Add-in project that appears in the Extensibility Projects folder of the Visual Studio .NET New Projects dialog box. This dialog box appears automatically when you open Visual Studio .NET or you can display it using the File➪New➪Project command. The following steps tell you how to set up and configure a Shared Add-in project:

1. **Type a name for the new extension in the Name field of the New Project dialog box.**

2. **Select a location for the extension using the Location field. Click OK.**

   Visual Studio .NET displays the Welcome to the Extension Wizard page of the Extensibility Wizard dialog box.

3. **Click Next.**

   You see the Select a Programming Language page. This page offers you the choice of using Visual Basic .NET, C#, or Visual C++ as the programming language for the extension. (The example uses C# as the programming language. However, the same principles demonstrated in this chapter for C# work for the other languages as well.)

4. **Choose a programming language. Click Next.**

   You see the Select an Application Host page shown in Figure 4-1. Notice that you can create extensions for any of a number of applications or create a generic extension that works with all of them.

Figure 4-1:
Choose which applications to support with your extension.

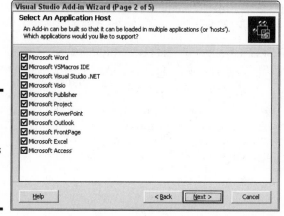

5. **Check just the Microsoft FrontPage entry and clear all of the other entries. Click Next.**

   You see the Enter a Name and Description page. This is where you define the name that FrontPage displays after you load the extension. It isn't the name of the file. The example uses `"Unique User ID Creator"` as the name and `"This extension creates a unique ID based on a user's first name, last name, and a random number."` for the description.

6. **Type a name for the extension in the field labeled, "What is the name of your Extension?" Then type a description in the field labeled, "What is the description for your Extension?" Click Next.**

   You see the Choose Extension Options page.

7. **Select the option that fits the needs of your extension:**

   • **I would like my Extension to load when the host application loads:** Choose this option when you want the extension to load immediately — especially if the extension provides a feature the user is likely to need often.

   • **My Extension should be available to all users of the computer it was installed on, not just the person who installs it:** Choose this option when you want the extension to affect all FrontPage users. Always check this option when creating a generic extension that everyone can use. Clear this option when you create an extension that provides an administrator or advanced user feature that not everyone needs. The example has both options checked.

8. **Click Next.**

   You see the Summary page. This is the time to check all of the settings to ensure the extension will have the features you want.

9. **Click Finish.**

   Visual Studio .NET creates the new extension for you based on the settings you selected.

The resulting project actually contains two applications, as shown in Figure 4-2. The `UniqueID` application contains the extension code required to make your extension operational. This is the application you modify to create the extension. The `UniqueIDSetup` application contains setup code that will install the extension on other machines. Normally you won't need to modify this application; it already contains everything needed to install the extension.

Figure 4-2:
The Visual
Studio
Extension
Wizard
creates two
applications
for you.

Writing the code

Visual Studio .NET creates a lot of the code you need. For example, it creates
a reference to the application that loads the extension you create, along with
the application instance (in case there's more than one instance of the application loaded on the user's machine). You can find the object declarations
for the variables at the end of the `Connect.cs` file.

The generated code doesn't include custom features needed to activate your
extension (such as a button or menu entry the user can select). You have to
define these objects yourself. The example defines one `CommandBarButton`
at the end of the coding area in the `Connect.cs` file, like this:

```
// Define a button to activate the add-on.
CommandBarButton  ccbCreateID;
```

After you create a means of accessing the extension, you must create three
kinds of code for the extension. The required additions (outlined in the
upcoming subsections) are

+ Startup routine

+ Shutdown routine

+ Event handlers that perform useful work

Developing a startup routine

The startup routine ensures your extension has all the required access to
the target application, and it places the button for your extension within the

target application menu. You don't necessarily place the extension entry on the Tools menu (as shown here) — any menu is acceptable, so long as the extension task works with that menu. For example, an extension that performs formatting should appear on the Format menu, not the Tools menu. Listing 4-1 shows the code required to perform this task.

Listing 4-1:   Starting the Extension

```
public void OnStartupComplete(ref System.Array custom)
{
    CommandBars AllCB;        // All the command bars.
    CommandBar  ThisCB;       // A single command bar.
    Object      MissingItem;  // A missing item.

    // Obtain the list of command bars.
    AllCB =
        (CommandBars)applicationObject.GetType().InvokeMember(
            "CommandBars", BindingFlags.GetProperty, null,
            applicationObject, null);

    // Get the Tools command bar.
    ThisCB = AllCB["Tools"];

    // Determine whether the custom command already exists.
    try
    {
        // If the button exists, reuse it.
        ccbCreateID =
            (CommandBarButton)
                ThisCB.Controls["Create Unique User ID"];
    }
    catch
    {
        // The button doesn't exist, so create it. Begin by
        // getting the missing item.
        MissingItem = Missing.Value ;

        // Create a new button. Assign a value to the caption
        // and set the button to display only the caption.
        ccbCreateID =
            (CommandBarButton)
                ThisCB.Controls.Add(1, MissingItem, MissingItem,
                                    MissingItem, MissingItem);
        ccbCreateID.Caption = "Create Unique User ID";
        ccbCreateID.Style = MsoButtonStyle.msoButtonCaption;
    }

    // Define a tag for the button to make it easier to find.
    ccbCreateID.Tag = "Create Unique User ID";

    // Assign an action to the button. This step ensures that
```

```
// FrontPage will load the extension DLL if it isn't
// already loaded. Otherwise, clicking the button could
// fail. Use the program ID found in the GuidAttribute
// entry associated with this class.
ccbCreateID.OnAction = "!<UniqueID.Connect>";

// Make the button visible.
ccbCreateID.Visible = true;

// Assign an event handler to the button.
ccbCreateID.Click +=
    new _CommandBarButtonEvents_ClickEventHandler(
        this.ccbCreateID_Click);

// You must release the COM objects used in the extension.
AllCB = null;
ThisCB = null;
}
```

The application begins by obtaining the list of command bars from the target application. The very convoluted code is the result of working with COM in this case. Taking the code apart makes it easier to understand:

✦ The `AllCB` object requires a data-type coercion of `CommandBars` since the `InvokeMember()` returns a simple object.

✦ Visual Studio .NET provides `applicationObject` — a simple object — making it possible to work with any number of applications using a single extension.

✦ The `GetType()` method requests the type of `applicationObject`, which is FrontPage in this case.

✦ The `InvokeMember()` method makes a request of FrontPage as defined by the arguments that follow. The request type is `BindingFlags.GetProperty` or a property value.

✦ The call specifically requests the `CommandBars` property and defines the source of that property as `applicationObject`.

✦ Because `AllCB` is typed, you don't have to jump through too many hoops to use it. All you need to provide is an index to the menu you want to use to hold the `CommandBarButton` object, `ccbCreateID`. This is a generic utility, so the code places it on the FrontPage Tools menu.

The startup routine is called every time a copy of FrontPage starts. During the first invocation (the first copy of FrontPage is started), the special button for this utility doesn't exist. However, during subsequent invocations, the button does exist — so the code reuses the button, rather than creating a new one. The code still requires a connection to that button, so it creates another reference to it.

When the button doesn't exist, FrontPage returns an error, but instead of displaying an error message, the code creates the missing button. The secret, in this case, is the `System.Reflection.Missing.Value` property. This value represents the missing item and tells FrontPage that the code will supply it. The code begins by adding a new control using the `ThisCB.Controls.Add()` method (adding the button to the Tools menu). The code supplies the `MissingItem` object as input for all of the values the `Add()` method needs. Once the button is created, the code adds a `Caption` property value and tells FrontPage how to display it (as just a caption). You can also create buttons with icons or that use only icons.

The `ccbCreateID.Tag` is legitimately optional, but you'll find that it's easier to locate the button later when you add it. Your code might need to add other settings or disable the button when the user loads specific files. The `Tag` property provides a handy way to locate the button as needed to perform these tasks.

Always assign an action to any button you create. Otherwise, FrontPage won't load the DLL when the user clicks the button. FrontPage won't tell you when it unloads your DLL and there isn't any way to find out. In addition, the user won't receive the same response every time. Selecting a menu option once might display an error message or crash FrontPage, but it might not do anything at all the next time. Notice how the code assigns the program ID for this DLL to the `ccbCreateID.OnAction` property so FrontPage can locate it later in the Registry.

The next two lines of code let the user access the extension. First, the code must make the extension visible by setting the `ccbCreateID.Visible`. Second, the code assigns an event handler to the `ccbCreateID.Click` event. The event handler must appear within the current class.

The final step is to release all COM objects you use to start up the extension. In this case, the code has used both `AllCB` and `ThisCB` to access FrontPage command bars, so it sets them to `null`. The reason you can't wait for the garbage collector to perform this task is that the garbage collector doesn't know these objects exist.

Developing a shutdown routine

Shutting an extension down is a lot easier than starting one up. For one thing, you know that the menu item exists. Listing 4-2 shows the shutdown code for this example.

Listing 4-2: Shutting the Extension Down

```
public void OnBeginShutdown(ref System.Array custom)
{
   Object   MissingItem;   // A missing item.

   // Create the missing item.
   MissingItem = Missing.Value;

   // Delete the command button created earlier.
   ccbCreateID.Delete(MissingItem);

   // Make sure you release the COM object before leaving the
   // program.
   ccbCreateID = null;
}
```

The code uses the System.Reflection.Missing.Value property again to create the MissingItem object. This object represents anything that FrontPage might be missing to complete the ccbCreateID.Delete() method. The MissingItem object doesn't actually represent anything — it's a placeholder.

After the code deletes the menu item the extension created in FrontPage, it needs to release any COM objects still in use. In this case, the only COM object still in use is ccbCreateID.

Make sure you perform this vital step or your extension could produce memory leaks (nasty side effects that rob the machine of useful memory).

Performing a useful task

The code, to this point, has affected the extension. You also need the code to initialize the extension — and to make FrontPage aware of it. The code in this section is different because it interacts with the user. Listing 4-3 shows the task-related code for this example.

Listing 4-3: Displaying a Dialog Box and Producing Output

```
private void ccbCreateID_Click(CommandBarButton
   cmdBarbutton,ref bool cancel)
{
   FrmUserID   ThisID;   // Dialog box for user information.
   String      Output;   // The output value.
```

(continued)

Listing 4-3 *(continued)*

```
// Initialize the dialog box.
ThisID = new FrmUserID();

// If the user clicks OK, process the information.
if (ThisID.ShowDialog() == DialogResult.OK)
{
    // Define an output value.
    Output = ThisID.txtLastName.Text.Substring(0, 1) +
             ThisID.txtFirstName.Text +
             DateTime.Now.Second.ToString();

    // Display it as a message box.
    MessageBox.Show(Output);
}
}
```

I added a simple form to the example. It contains an OK and Cancel button, along with two fields where the user can enter data. The type of this form is FrmUserID. The code creates an instance of this form and displays it to the user.

When the user enters data and clicks OK, the code continues processing. Otherwise it exits without producing a result. Because this is an anticipated action, the code doesn't need to do anything else.

The code processes the public textbox information from the form the user just filled out, and adds the current seconds to it. The result is a string that contains the first initial of the user's last name, followed by the user's first name, and finishing with a random number. The code uses the MessageBox.Show() method to display this information.

Configuring and Using the Extension

When you have a FrontPage extension created and ready to use, it's time to install and test it. Even though the Microsoft documentation says (in several places) that you should be able to work with the extension immediately after compiling it, in practice the extension doesn't appear to work that way — an installation is required.

Before you make any changes to your FrontPage extension, make sure you *uninstall* it. Otherwise, you won't see any of your changes when you test the extension again. Always install, test, and then uninstall during the debugging process. Even though this seems like a lot of extra work, the technique saves time in the long run.

Installing the extension

After you create and compile the code, it's time to test it in FrontPage. First you have to install the extension, just as the user does. The following steps describe how to perform this task:

1. **Double-click the installation program,** Setup.exe, **in one of the following folders:**

    \UniqueID\UniqueIDSetup\Debug

    \UniqueID\UniqueIDSetup\Release

You see the initial Welcome dialog box that includes the name of the application.

2. **Click Next.**

You see the Select Installation Folder dialog box shown in Figure 4-3. Notice that the dialog box lets the user choose an installation folder, but defaults to an installation folder that includes your company name (when you add one to Visual Studio .NET).

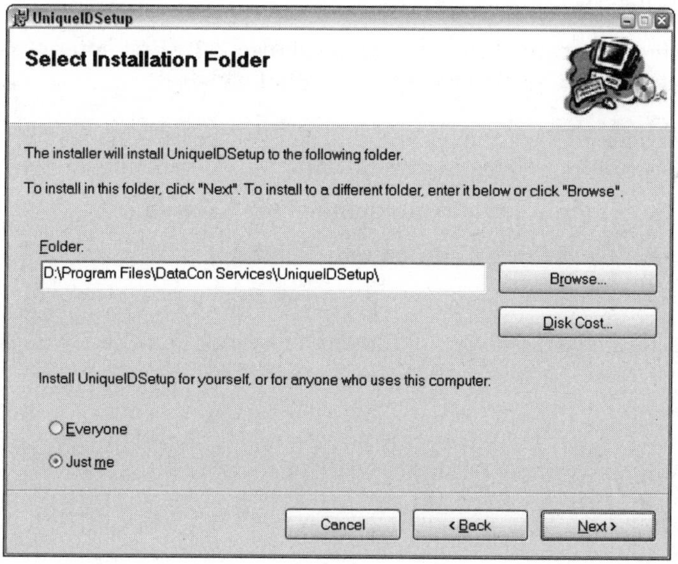

Figure 4-3:
Visual
Studio .NET
personalizes
the
installation
program
for you.

3. **Click Next twice.**

Setup creates the installation folder. It then installs and registers the components you created.

4. Click Close.

The dialog box closes and you're ready to use the extension.

Testing the extension

Testing the extension requires several steps. Some of them are quite simple, while others require some level of observation. Here are the testing steps to try for this example:

1. Open FrontPage, look at the Tools menu.

You should see the Create Unique User ID entry that the extension provides. When you don't see this entry, make sure you installed the extension by looking for its entry in the Add/Remove Programs applet of the Control Panel. A missing entry could also mean a coding error (for example, the `Visible` property wasn't set to `true`).

2. Select the Tools⇨Create Unique User ID option.

You see the Enter User Information dialog box.

3. Type values in the User's First Name and User's Last Name fields. Click OK.

FrontPage displays a dialog box showing the first letter of the user's last name, the first name, and a random number.

4. Click OK.

The output dialog box disappears.

5. Select the Tools⇨Create Unique User ID option.

You see the Enter User Information dialog box.

6. Click Cancel.

Nothing happens. Congratulations — your FrontPage extension works!

Index

Symbols and Numerics

& (ampersand), concatenation
operator, 596
<!--...--> (angle bracket...)
control comments, 66
XML comment delimiter, 438
<%...%> (angle bracket...), script
element delimiters, 665
<%...%> (angle bracket...), script
statement delimiters, 342–345, 665
<...> (angle bracket...), XML elements,
434–435
<?...?> (angle bracket...), XML
processing instructions, 433–434
* (asterisk), arithmetic multiplication
operator, 596
@ (at sign), ASP directives, 665
= (equal sign), comparison operator, 596
> greater-than operator, 596
< less-than operator, 596
- (minus sign), arithmetic subtraction
operator, 596
+ (plus sign)
arithmetic addition operator, 596
concatenation operator, 573, 596
/ (slash), arithmetic division
operator, 596
_ (underscore), continuation
character, 573
3D bevel, clip art, 282

A

<a>, anchor tag, 55
<abbr>, abbreviation tag, 55
Access
copying and pasting, 321–322
dragging and dropping, 321

interactive Web pages
ANSI SQL support, 398
ASP versus ASP.NET, 390–391
buffer size, specifying, 399
connection strategy, 390–391
connections, advanced properties,
397–400
connections, custom, 395–397
connections, Database Results
Wizard, 391–400
connections, new, 391–400
connections, selecting, 400–401
data source links, defining, 393–395
data views, 402–404
ExtendedAnsiSql parameter, 398
file links, defining, 392–393
MaxBufferSize parameter, 399
MaxScanRows parameter, 399
PageTimeout parameter, 399
PivotTable views, 407–409
read-only database access, 399
ReadOnly parameter, 399
relational data views, 406–409
row scans, limiting, 399
safe transaction environment, 399
SafeTransactions parameter, 399
search forms, 405–406
thread number, specifying, 399
Threads parameter, 399
timeout, specifying, 399
report views, 320–322
accessibility
CSS (Cascading Style Sheets), 265
forms, 90–91
frames, 118–119
tables, 98–99
accessing special objects, 487
<acronym>, acronym tag, 55
acronyms, tagging, 54–55
Active Server Pages (ASP). *See* ASP
(Active Server Pages).

B

C

M

S

T

U

Notes

BUSINESS, CAREERS & PERSONAL FINANCE

0-7645-5307-0

0-7645-5331-3 *†

Also available:
- Accounting For Dummies †
0-7645-5314-3
- Business Plans Kit For Dummies †
0-7645-5365-8
- Cover Letters For Dummies
0-7645-5224-4
- Frugal Living For Dummies
0-7645-5403-4
- Leadership For Dummies
0-7645-5176-0
- Managing For Dummies
0-7645-1771-6

- Marketing For Dummies
0-7645-5600-2
- Personal Finance For Dummies *
0-7645-2590-5
- Project Management For Dummies
0-7645-5283-X
- Resumes For Dummies †
0-7645-5471-9
- Selling For Dummies
0-7645-5363-1
- Small Business Kit For Dummies *†
0-7645-5093-4

HOME & BUSINESS COMPUTER BASICS

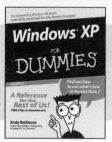

0-7645-4074-2

0-7645-3758-X

Also available:
- ACT! 6 For Dummies
0-7645-2645-6
- iLife '04 All-in-One Desk Reference
For Dummies
0-7645-7347-0
- iPAQ For Dummies
0-7645-6769-1
- Mac OS X Panther Timesaving
Techniques For Dummies
0-7645-5812-9
- Macs For Dummies
0-7645-5656-8

- Microsoft Money 2004 For Dummies
0-7645-4195-1
- Office 2003 All-in-One Desk Reference
For Dummies
0-7645-3883-7
- Outlook 2003 For Dummies
0-7645-3759-8
- PCs For Dummies
0-7645-4074-2
- TiVo For Dummies
0-7645-6923-6
- Upgrading and Fixing PCs For Dummies
0-7645-1665-5
- Windows XP Timesaving Techniques
For Dummies
0-7645-3748-2

FOOD, HOME, GARDEN, HOBBIES, MUSIC & PETS

0-7645-5295-3

0-7645-5232-5

Also available:
- Bass Guitar For Dummies
0-7645-2487-9
- Diabetes Cookbook For Dummies
0-7645-5230-9
- Gardening For Dummies *
0-7645-5130-2
- Guitar For Dummies
0-7645-5106-X
- Holiday Decorating For Dummies
0-7645-2570-0
- Home Improvement All-in-One
For Dummies
0-7645-5680-0

- Knitting For Dummies
0-7645-5395-X
- Piano For Dummies
0-7645-5105-1
- Puppies For Dummies
0-7645-5255-4
- Scrapbooking For Dummies
0-7645-7208-3
- Senior Dogs For Dummies
0-7645-5818-8
- Singing For Dummies
0-7645-2475-5
- 30-Minute Meals For Dummies
0-7645-2589-1

INTERNET & DIGITAL MEDIA

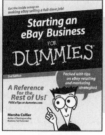

0-7645-1664-7

0-7645-6924-4

Also available:
- 2005 Online Shopping Directory
For Dummies
0-7645-7495-7
- CD & DVD Recording For Dummies
0-7645-5956-7
- eBay For Dummies
0-7645-5654-1
- Fighting Spam For Dummies
0-7645-5965-6
- Genealogy Online For Dummies
0-7645-5964-8
- Google For Dummies
0-7645-4420-9

- Home Recording For Musicians
For Dummies
0-7645-1634-5
- The Internet For Dummies
0-7645-4173-0
- iPod & iTunes For Dummies
0-7645-7772-7
- Preventing Identity Theft For Dummies
0-7645-7336-5
- Pro Tools All-in-One Desk Reference
For Dummies
0-7645-5714-9
- Roxio Easy Media Creator For Dummies
0-7645-7131-1

* Separate Canadian edition also available
† Separate U.K. edition also available

SPORTS, FITNESS, PARENTING, RELIGION & SPIRITUALITY

0-7645-5146-9

0-7645-5418-2

Also available:

Adoption For Dummies
0-7645-5488-3

Basketball For Dummies
0-7645-5248-1

The Bible For Dummies
0-7645-5296-1

Buddhism For Dummies
0-7645-5359-3

Catholicism For Dummies
0-7645-5391-7

Hockey For Dummies
0-7645-5228-7

Judaism For Dummies
0-7645-5299-6

Martial Arts For Dummies
0-7645-5358-5

Pilates For Dummies
0-7645-5397-6

Religion For Dummies
0-7645-5264-3

Teaching Kids to Read For Dummies
0-7645-4043-2

Weight Training For Dummies
0-7645-5168-X

Yoga For Dummies
0-7645-5117-5

TRAVEL

0-7645-5438-7

0-7645-5453-0

Also available:

Alaska For Dummies
0-7645-1761-9

Arizona For Dummies
0-7645-6938-4

Cancún and the Yucatán For Dummies
0-7645-2437-2

Cruise Vacations For Dummies
0-7645-6941-4

Europe For Dummies
0-7645-5456-5

Ireland For Dummies
0-7645-5455-7

Las Vegas For Dummies
0-7645-5448-4

London For Dummies
0-7645-4277-X

New York City For Dummies
0-7645-6945-7

Paris For Dummies
0-7645-5494-8

RV Vacations For Dummies
0-7645-5443-3

Walt Disney World & Orlando For Dummies
0-7645-6943-0

GRAPHICS, DESIGN & WEB DEVELOPMENT

0-7645-4345-8

0-7645-5589-8

Also available:

Adobe Acrobat 6 PDF For Dummies
0-7645-3760-1

Building a Web Site For Dummies
0-7645-7144-3

Dreamweaver MX 2004 For Dummies
0-7645-4342-3

FrontPage 2003 For Dummies
0-7645-3882-9

HTML 4 For Dummies
0-7645-1995-6

Illustrator CS For Dummies
0-7645-4084-X

Macromedia Flash MX 2004 For Dummies
0-7645-4358-X

Photoshop 7 All-in-One Desk Reference For Dummies
0-7645-1667-1

Photoshop CS Timesaving Techniques For Dummies
0-7645-6782-9

PHP 5 For Dummies
0-7645-4166-8

PowerPoint 2003 For Dummies
0-7645-3908-6

QuarkXPress 6 For Dummies
0-7645-2593-X

NETWORKING, SECURITY, PROGRAMMING & DATABASES

0-7645-6852-3

0-7645-5784-X

Also available:

A+ Certification For Dummies
0-7645-4187-0

Access 2003 All-in-One Desk Reference For Dummies
0-7645-3988-4

Beginning Programming For Dummies
0-7645-4997-9

C For Dummies
0-7645-7068-4

Firewalls For Dummies
0-7645-4048-3

Home Networking For Dummies
0-7645-42796

Network Security For Dummies
0-7645-1679-5

Networking For Dummies
0-7645-1677-9

TCP/IP For Dummies
0-7645-1760-0

VBA For Dummies
0-7645-3989-2

Wireless All In-One Desk Reference For Dummies
0-7645-7496-5

Wireless Home Networking For Dummies
0-7645-3910-8

HEALTH & SELF-HELP

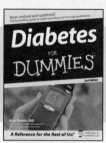

0-7645-6820-5 *†

0-7645-2566-2

Also available:

- Alzheimer's For Dummies
  0-7645-3899-3
- Asthma For Dummies
  0-7645-4233-8
- Controlling Cholesterol For Dummies
  0-7645-5440-9
- Depression For Dummies
  0-7645-3900-0
- Dieting For Dummies
  0-7645-4149-8
- Fertility For Dummies
  0-7645-2549-2

- Fibromyalgia For Dummies
  0-7645-5441-7
- Improving Your Memory For Dummies
  0-7645-5435-2
- Pregnancy For Dummies †
  0-7645-4483-7
- Quitting Smoking For Dummies
  0-7645-2629-4
- Relationships For Dummies
  0-7645-5384-4
- Thyroid For Dummies
  0-7645-5385-2

EDUCATION, HISTORY, REFERENCE & TEST PREPARATION

0-7645-5194-9

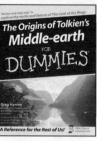

0-7645-4186-2

Also available:

- Algebra For Dummies
  0-7645-5325-9
- British History For Dummies
  0-7645-7021-8
- Calculus For Dummies
  0-7645-2498-4
- English Grammar For Dummies
  0-7645-5322-4
- Forensics For Dummies
  0-7645-5580-4
- The GMAT for Dummies
  0-7645-5251-1
- Inglés Para Dummies
  0-7645-5427-1

- Italian For Dummies
  0-7645-5196-5
- Latin For Dummies
  0-7645-5431-X
- Lewis & Clark For Dummies
  0-7645-2545-X
- Research Papers For Dummies
  0-7645-5426-3
- The SAT I For Dummies
  0-7645-7193-1
- Science Fair Projects For Dummies
  0-7645-5460-3
- U.S. History For Dummies
  0-7645-5249-X

Get smart @ dummies.com®

- **Find a full list of Dummies titles**
- **Look into loads of FREE on-site articles**
- **Sign up for FREE eTips e-mailed to you weekly**
- **See what other products carry the Dummies name**
- **Shop directly from the Dummies bookstore**
- **Enter to win new prizes every month!**

* Separate Canadian edition also available
† Separate U.K. edition also available

Available wherever books are sold. For more information or to order direct: U.S. customers visit www.dummies.com or call 1-877-762-2974.
U.K. customers visit www.wileyeurope.com or call 0800 243407. Canadian customers visit www.wiley.ca or call 1-800-567-4797.